GOVERNING HIBERNIA

Governing Hibernia

British Politicians and Ireland 1800–1921

K. THEODORE HOPPEN

OXFORD
UNIVERSITY PRESS

OXFORD

UNIVERSITY PRESS

Great Clarendon Street, Oxford, OX2 6DP,
United Kingdom

Oxford University Press is a department of the University of Oxford.
It furthers the University's objective of excellence in research, scholarship,
and education by publishing worldwide. Oxford is a registered trade mark of
Oxford University Press in the UK and in certain other countries

Published in the United States of America by Oxford University Press
198 Madison Avenue, New York, NY 10016, United States of America

British Library Cataloguing in Publication Data
Data available

Library of Congress Control Number: 2015959951

ISBN 978–0–19–820743–6

Printed in Great Britain by
Clays Ltd, St Ives plc

For

Victoria

Matthew

Oliver

Louis

Daniel

&

Tessa

Preface

This book is a study in British and Irish history. It attempts to examine and to explain the outcome of the Anglo-Irish Act of Union between its enactment in 1800 and its effective demise in 1921. The main emphasis is upon the approach adopted by the politicians in charge of the new United Kingdom towards the overall government of the smaller island—how this changed and shifted over time—without neglecting Irish dimensions or the effects of the resulting policies upon Ireland itself.

Over the years I have greatly benefited from invaluable comments made by those who attended the seminars and lectures in England, Scotland, and Ireland in which I attempted to lay out my initial and evolving intentions. Four scholars have given generous help on particularly knotty problems: Nicholas Canny, Howell Lloyd, Philip Morgan, and Christopher Woods. To Roy Foster and Bernard Porter my debt is incalculable. They read the whole text to my very great benefit. It will be all too obvious that I have sometimes been too stubborn or too imperceptive to take the advice I so often sought and so generously received. The Leverhulme Trust gave a handsome grant that enabled me to get the project under way.

Without the love and support of Alison at the beginning of my work and of Anne towards its conclusion this book would never have appeared. I owe to both of them a gratitude that goes beyond what mere words can express. The Dedication to my six grandchildren is a small recognition of the light and delight that they have all brought into my life.

I am grateful to those in charge of the various archives, libraries, and record offices in which I have worked for their kindness and cooperation. Particular thanks regarding papers in their possession are due to Her Majesty Queen Elizabeth II, the Duke of Bedford, the Duke of Devonshire, the Duke of Northumberland, the Marquess of Normanby, the Marquess of Salisbury, the Earl of Bessborough, and the Honourable Simon Howard. The staff at the Brynmor Jones Library at the University of Hull deserve a special word of thanks.

It has been my good fortune to have been able to devote much of my life to studying the history of Ireland, a country of which I shall always be proud and to which I shall always be grateful for having, in April 1947, given shelter to a homeless 5-year-old refugee.

K.T.H.

Contents

Contents

Abbreviations

AC	Alnwick Castle, Northumberland
BI	Borthwick Institute, York
BL	British Library, London
Bodl.	Bodleian Library, Oxford
BU	Birmingham University
CCC	Churchill College Cambridge
CH	Castle Howard, Yorkshire
ChH	Chatsworth House, Derbyshire
CKS	Centre for Kentish Studies, Maidstone
CUL	Cambridge University Library
DIB	*Dictionary of Irish Biography*, ed. J. McGuire and J. Quinn, 9 vols (Cambridge, 2009)
DRO	Devon Record Office, Exeter
DU	Durham University
DuRO	Durham Record Office, Durham
GRO	Gloucestershire Record Office, Gloucester
HC	House of Commons Paper
HH	Hatfield House, Hertfordshire
HMC	Historical Manuscripts Commission
HO	Home Office
HRO	Hampshire Record Office, Winchester
IWM	Imperial War Museum, London
LRO	Liverpool Record Office
MC	Mulgrave Castle, Yorkshire
NAI	National Archives of Ireland, Dublin
NLI	National Library of Ireland, Dublin
NLS	National Library of Scotland, Edinburgh
NU	Newcastle University
ODNB	*Oxford Dictionary of National Biography*, ed. H. C. G. Matthew and B. Harrison, 60 vols (Oxford, 2004)
PA	Parliamentary Archives, Westminster
Parl. Deb.	Parliamentary Debates: Series 1 1803–20; Series 2 1820–30; Series 3 1831–91; Series 4 1892–1909; Series 5 1909–81 (Lords and Commons in separate volumes in Series 5). For period before Series 1 referred to as [Cobbett's] *Parliamentary History*

PRONI	Public Record Office of Northern Ireland, Belfast
RA	Royal Archives, Windsor
RIA	Royal Irish Academy, Dublin
RU	Reading University
ScRO	Scottish Record Office, Edinburgh
SHC	Surrey History Centre, Woking
ShU	Sheffield University
SoRO	Somerset Record Office, Taunton
SRO	Staffordshire Record Office, Stafford
SU	Southampton University
SuRO	Suffolk Record Office, Ipswich
TCC	Trinity College Cambridge
TCD	Trinity College Dublin
TNA	The National Archives, Kew
WA	Woburn Abbey, Bedfordshire
WRO	Wiltshire and Swindon Record Office, Chippenham
WSRO	West Sussex Record Office, Chichester

Non ego nec Teucris Italos parere jubebo,
Nec nova regna peto; paribus se legibus ambae
Invictae gentes aeterna in foedera mittant.
[I shall never command Italians to obey Trojans, nor do
I seek any new royalty; Let two nations,
Each still unsubjected, enter into an everlasting compact
Under equal terms.]

(Pitt slightly adapting a passage from Virgil's *Aeneid*, book 12,
in the Commons debate on the Union, 31 January 1799)

If we intend to lay the foundation of better things it is we ... who must govern the Irish for their own good and not according to their bad pleasure.

(Lord Clarendon to Lord John Russell, 13 August 1848,
Bodleian Library, Clarendon Papers, Irish Letter-Book III)

Governing Paddy has never been a hopeful or pleasant task, but it is a duty which Englishmen must perform as best they can.

(Lord Wodehouse to Lord John Russell, 27 October 1865,
Bodleian Library, Kimberley Papers, MS 4035)

It is a curious reflection to inquire why Ireland should bulk so largely in our lives. How is it that the great English parties are shaken to their foundations, and even shattered, almost every generation, by contact with Irish affairs? ... Ireland is not a daughter State. She is a parent nation. The Irish are an ancient race. 'We too are', said their plenipotentiaries, 'a far-flung nation'.

(Winston Churchill in the Commons debate
on the Treaty, 15 December 1921)

In moments of crisis, political leaders fall back on unspoken assumptions, and their intentions can often only be judged in the light of what we can discover about those assumptions.

(James Joll, *1914: The Unspoken Assumptions:
An Inaugural Lecture* (London, 1968))

Introduction

This book is a study of the attitudes and intentions that informed the ways in which those in charge of the new constitutional entity created by the Act of Union of 1800—the United Kingdom of Great Britain and Ireland— approached and conducted the government of the smaller western island for which they had now acquired a more direct and immediate responsibility. But, while its perspective is generally one that looks out from the British core towards what might be called—and was often at the time regarded as— an Irish periphery, its very title can, with equal grammatical validity, be read as suggesting that, from time to time, it was Hibernia that did the 'governing', not least by shaping and moulding British political life in deep and lasting ways.

As has often been pointed out, not least by Union-period politicians, the Anglo-Irish relationship possessed a long, complicated, and sometimes intensely remembered history.[1] Ever since the Normans arrived in Ireland in the late twelfth century, arguments have taken place over how best to describe and understand the interactions between the two islands. Inevitably these have often reflected the very different outlooks and prejudices of those involved. What for one party was exploitation, was, for the other, civilization. Historians too have found it difficult to agree about the central concepts that might best be deployed in laying bare the complications—cultural, economic, political— that have characterized contacts between Britain and Ireland. Often pressed into service have been the notions of colonialism and (more recently) post-colonialism. Whatever their undoubted merits, it can hardly be denied that, over time, these have become so capaciously vague as to lose much in the way of analytical bite and that, in the hands of imaginative votaries, they have, despite recent injections of 'complexity and nuance', sometimes begun to

---

[1] A history remembered and deployed not only by the Irish. In a letter of August 1921 Lloyd George did not hesitate to lecture de Valera (of all people) on matters historical—with references to Grattan, O'Connell, Davis, Parnell, and even the Duke of Wellington—when insisting that 'the British Government have [now] offered Ireland all that O'Connell and Thomas Davis asked, and more' (Lloyd George to de Valera, 26 August 1921, *Further Correspondence relating to the Proposals of His Majesty's Government for an Irish Settlement*, H[ouse of] C[ommons Paper] 1921 [Cmd 1529], xxix. 417–19).

resemble helium-filled balloons ascending so high into the heavens of abstraction that the conclusions generated have tended to rest more in the clouds of solipsism than upon the terra firma of mundane comprehension.[2]

Although, therefore, the 'colonial turn', if one may so call it, has certainly generated helpful insights with regard to Britain's involvement with Ireland, it is here suggested that a closer concentration upon one particular aspect of the control exercised by London administrations under the Union might perhaps also have its uses. Central to this approach is an examination of the manner in which ministers and cabinets, when attempting to establish the (from their point of view) most effective ways of governing Ireland, tended to move along a spectrum ranging from, at the one extreme, policies of differentiation—of seeing Ireland as so different that *sui generis* and often distinctly non-British rules and methods could best keep things from falling apart—to, at the other extreme, policies deliberately conceived to assimilate Ireland into the norms and behaviour patterns of a larger metropolitan (that is, British) centre. This second alternative, though no less strongly based on the idea that Ireland was different, sought to remedy this obvious 'defect', not by the deployment of specifically Hibernian solutions, but by attempting to transform the country into something that might eventually become a kind of duplicate Britain of the West.

These shifting and dichotomous procedures were, of course, nothing new. Indeed, they had shaped many of the lenses through which Ireland had been perceived by British monarchs, ministers, and politicians for centuries before 1800. Already in the Middle Ages London had worried about the ease with which the Anglo-Norman element in Ireland was drifting away from its origins and becoming absorbed into the cultural and political values of an alien Gaelic society. By the sixteenth and seventeenth centuries, when the Reformation had introduced new and powerful points of differentiation, consistent attempts were being made to bind Ireland more closely to the British core by deliberate policies of what one historian has called 'Making Ireland British' and another 'Making Ireland English', a difference in terminology characteristic of discussions of this kind.[3] And, while the aim of incorporating Ireland more closely into a wider British polity experienced some

---

[2] See the useful contributions in K. Kenny (ed.), *Ireland and the British Empire* (Oxford, 2004), especially those by Kevin Kenny, Alvin Jackson, and Stephen Howe; also Howe's *Ireland and Empire: Colonial Legacies in Irish History and Culture* (Oxford, 2000) and 'Colonized and Colonizing: Ireland in the British Empire', in A. Jackson (ed.), *The Oxford Handbook of Modern Irish History* (Oxford, 2014), 65–82; and D. Fitzpatrick, 'Ireland and Empire', in A. Porter (ed.), *The Oxford History of the British Empire: The Nineteenth Century* (Oxford, 1999), 494–521.

[3] N. Canny, *Making Ireland British 1580–1650* (Oxford, 2001); J. Ohlmeyer, *Making Ireland English: The Irish Aristocracy in the Seventeenth Century* (New Haven, 2012). See also A. Grant and K. J. Stringer (eds), *Uniting the Kingdom? The Making of British History* (London, 1995) and, for a contemporary view, Sir William Herbert's *Croftus Sive de Hibernia Liber* of the 1590s in the edition of A. Keaveney and J. A. Madden (Dublin, 1992), xiii. 97, 107.

notable setbacks, the general notion of greater integration (and Cromwell in particular laid down something of a model with his parliamentary union of the 1650s when Irish MPs briefly sat at Westminster) eventually became a ghostlike—and sometimes more than a ghostlike—presence within the corridors of power at Whitehall.

What the Act of Union did was to present the issue of Ireland more directly to ministers in London than had been the case when Irish government had—and especially in the early and middle parts of the eighteenth century—been largely subcontracted to a collection of local Protestant notables. But, if the hope was that henceforth Ireland could be controlled more easily and efficiently, this soon disintegrated amid the immediate pressures of war with France and then, over the next century or so, in response to uncertain lurches between coercion and conciliation and to shifts (sometimes ideological, sometimes pragmatic) between policies designed, in one mode, to recognize Ireland's distinctiveness, and, in another, to eliminate distinctions in the cause of fuller United Kingdom coherence and integration. Ireland's experience under the Union, whatever else it involved, certainly did not involve much in the way of long-term consistency on the part of those in charge of the state.

By contrast, Scotland, having experienced the final defeat of the Jacobites in 1746, did indeed become more closely integrated into the Great Britain established by the Anglo-Scottish Union of 1707. And, even if feelings of difference capable of bursting into brief efflorescence did not disappear, they never amounted to anything that might convincingly be seen as 'political nationalism'.[4] Wales (which maintained no separate legal existence after the Laws in Wales Acts of 1535 and 1542) like Scotland sustained integrationist enthusiasms incongruously buoyed up by notions of romantic nationhood typified by the enthusiastic adoption in 1856 of a new 'national' anthem: *Hen wlad fy nhadau* ('Land of our Fathers'), in which ancient Wales was praised for having been, above all, a land of warriors, singers, and bards. However, a more accurate reflection of the true state of things was revealed when, after initial dismay over the so-called Treason of the Blue Books of 1847 (caused by government commissioners criticizing Welsh 'backwardness'), it became generally accepted that 'something had to be done' and especially so in the way of anglicizing reform. Indeed, by 1863 one of the MPs for Swansea was telling a

---

[4] C. Kidd, 'Sentiment and Revival: Scottish Identities in the Aftermath of Enlightenment', in L. Brockliss and D. Eastwood (eds), *A Union of Multiple Identities: The British Isles c.1750–c.1850* (Manchester, 1997), 110–26. Special arrangements in 1707 for Scots Law and Scottish religious sensibilities, while acknowledging 'difference', ultimately helped to solidify feelings of Caledonian integration, even though Scotland's political trajectory rarely lacked complications. See N. Lloyd-Jones, 'Liberalism, Scottish Nationalism and the Home Rule Crisis, c.1886–93', *English Historical Review*, 129 (2014), 862–87.

local Eisteddfod audience: 'Remember that you are all Englishmen, though
you are Welsh ... Depend upon it, we most consider ourselves Englishmen.'[5]

While these were not sentiments that the Union rulers of Ireland were
ever very likely to evoke, this did not in itself lead to the universal triumph
of inward-looking attitudes divorced from developments in Britain or, for
that matter, the British Empire overseas. Indeed, geographical closeness to
and constitutional involvement with Britain gave Ireland a unique position
within the imperial universe, and this in turn enabled aspiring Irishmen and
women—Catholic as well as Protestant—to find rewarding openings for their
talents in Asia, Africa, and elsewhere, opportunities that made it possible to
sustain a congenial combination of Irishness, on the one hand, and, on the
other, attachment to an empire encompassing a fifth, perhaps even a quarter,
of all the human beings on earth.[6] Small wonder then that, under the Union,
the resonances between what the government was doing in Ireland and what it
was doing overseas became increasingly noticeable and reciprocal as to both
deployment and effect.[7]

But, while the London government's post-Union shifts between policies of
differentiation and assimilation were not uncommon within the Empire as a
whole, powerful analogies can also be found in continental Europe, analogies
of which at least some British politicians, notably Gladstone, were by no
means unaware and especially so in connection with the Home Rule controversies of the 1880s.[8] Gladstone had in fact experienced a kind of foreshadowing of his later Irish involvement when acting in 1858–9 as Special
Commissioner to the Ionian Islands off the west coast of Greece and since
1815 a British protectorate. As such he had been obliged to deal with the
Risospast (union with Greece) movement and also with a great many rather
difficult Orthodox bishops,[9] an experience that reinforced what was already a

---

[5] P. Morgan, 'Early Victorian Wales and its Crisis of Identity', in Brockliss and Eastwood
(eds), *A Union of Multiple Identities*, 93–109. Official reports were published in blue covers. On
Gladstone's general views on Wales, Scotland, and Ireland, see J. Vincent, 'Gladstone and
Ireland', *Proceedings of the British Academy*, 63 (1977), 193–238.

[6] C. A. Bayly, *Imperial Meridian: The British Empire and the World 1780–1830* (London,
1989), 3.

[7] S. B. Cook, *Imperial Affinities: Nineteenth-Century Analogies and Exchanges between India
and Ireland* (New Delhi, 1993); J. Ridden, 'Britishness as an Imperial and Diasporic Identity:
Irish Elite Perspectives, c.1820–1870s', in P. Gray (ed.), *Victoria's Ireland? Irishness and British-
ness, 1837–1901* (Dublin, 2004), 88–105. For a rather different approach to such matters, see
S. Belmessous, *Assimilation and Empire: Uniformity in French and British Colonies, 1541–1954*
(Oxford, 2013).

[8] Already in 1869–70 Gladstone had used the diplomatic service to collect continental
evidence about tenurial matters in connection with his planned Irish Land Act of 1870. See
*Parts I and II: Reports from Her Majesty's Representatives respecting the Tenure of Land in the
several Countries of Europe*, HC [C.66 and C.75] lxvii. 1–548, 549–930.

[9] B. Knox, 'British Policy and the Ionian Islands, 1847–1864: Nationalism and Imperial
Administration', *English Historical Review*, 99 (1984), 503–29. The islands were peacefully
transferred to Greece in 1864.

well-developed interest in the European dimensions of British policy generally. In particular, he became much given to talking about Ireland, not only in
terms of its place within the United Kingdom, but as a phenomenon with
reverberations of a broader European kind.

In 1885 Gladstone lectured a resistant Lord Hartington about the relevance
for the Irish case of 'the prolonged experience of Norway (I might perhaps
mention Finland) and the altogether new experience of Austria-Hungary'. He
asked cabinet colleagues to 'inform' themselves 'thoroughly on certain historical cases' and did the same when speaking of Home Rule in the Commons in
April 1886. Norway had, he pointed out, been forcibly united with Sweden in
1814, but clear constitutional distinctions had ensured that all eventually
became sweetness and light. Again, the Austro-Hungarian *Ausgleich* of 1867
had, he argued, brought about a peaceful 'duality of power'. Surely, the United
Kingdom was in every way capable of matching, indeed of improving upon, the
excellence and success of arrangements such as these.[10] Gladstone's Liberal
colleague, Henry Labouchere, pointed to Russia as having two 'Irelands':
Poland and Finland. The former was ruled with a rod of iron and was
convulsed by troubles; the latter had been granted local autonomy (Home
Rule) and was peaceful and content.[11] Another Liberal MP, James Bryce (who
later served as chief secretary for Ireland), had the nerve to offer his party leader
a series of lecture-letters containing pan-European analyses of the Irish question. While again mentioning Norway, Finland, and Austro-Hungary, Bryce
also threw in references to Portugal—where 'Philip II's attempt to bring about
an incorporating union [with Spain] ended in failure'—and the rather more
relevant case of the evolving relationship between Denmark and Iceland, which
he had visited in 1872 and which, though larger than Ireland, had far fewer
inhabitants.[12]

Curiously absent from Gladstone's Home Rule encomiums were references to Italy. He had hailed Italian unification (Rome only excluded) in
1859–60 but remained blind to Piedmont's insensitive expansionisms, even
though these had been foreshadowed in Cavour's earlier condemnations of
Irish devolution as 'a project at once odious and criminal'.[13] And it may even

---

[10] Gladstone to Hartington, 8 and 11 September 1885 and Hartington to Gladstone, 10 and 12
September 1885, B[ritish] L[ibrary] Gladstone Papers Add. MS 44148; Parl[iamentary] Deb[ates]
3: ccciv. 1046–52 (8 April 1886); also Gladstone's *Special Aspects of the Irish Question* (London,
1892), 343–72. In fact the Swedish–Norwegian Union was essentially a personal union under a
single king (of Sweden), though Norway was initially presided over by a viceroy (Swedish at first
and from 1829 Norwegian). The Austro-Hungarian *Ausgleich* of 1867 established a dual monarchy
under a single ruler but left all the other nationalities of the Hapsburg Empire out in the cold.

[11] Parl. Deb. 3: cccv. 1334 (18 May 1886).

[12] Bryce to Gladstone, 1 December 1885, 29 May and 29 November 1886, 20 April 1893,
Bodl[eian] L[ibrary] Bryce Papers MSS 11 and 12.

[13] R. Shannon, *Gladstone 1809–1865* (London, 1982), 426, 434, 438; C. di Cavour, *Considerations on the Present State and Future Prospects of Ireland* (London, 1845), 132; also

have been that Gladstone's eventual adoption of Home Rule was, in certain respects at least, the outcome of a growing realization that the events of 1859–60 marked, not so much a move towards Italian 'unification', as one towards the aggrandisement of Piedmont.[14] In May 1865 the then viceroy of Ireland, Lord Wodehouse, recorded in his diary a meeting in London with 'Baron Donnafugate, Italian Commissioner (for Sicily)', who 'gave a bad account of affairs in Sicily. He says the Sicilians sigh for English Government & he fears a counter revolution. They want autonomy under our protection. The very thing the Ionians have just cast away as oppressive.'[15]

In his espousal of devolution for Ireland, Gladstone could, however, look northwards for more positive cases where assimilation was giving way to something closer to and even beyond his own Home Rule approach, though movement in that respect, whether in Ireland or elsewhere, was seldom entirely one way. Finland, which had come under Russian rule in 1809, was, like Ireland, generating strong narratives about history, landscape, and people that together helped to transform abstract concepts of the nation into concrete visual, textual, and polemical articulations of national consciousness. Tsarist Russia, though at first supportive of Finnish cultural and linguistic particularism as furnishing a wedge between the Finns and their former Swedish overlords, shifted to a policy of coercive Russification towards the end of the nineteenth century. Although this lasted for only a few years, the situation was not resolved until, with the Russian Revolution, Finland obtained complete independence in 1917, though the subsequent civil war, if shorter than that which followed the Anglo-Irish Treaty of 1921, yielded nothing to it in the way of savagery.

Norway, however, after experiencing early attempts by Sweden to tighten central control, began to outrun Finland in the matter of autonomy before achieving full independence in 1905, in part at least because Sweden was

---

N. Mansergh, *The Irish Question 1840–1921*, new edn (London, 1965), 68–75. In 1859 Gladstone called on Cavour, who had, it seems, never travelled south of Florence and confessed to knowing more about England than about Sicily, whose inhabitants he claimed spoke 'Arabic' (D. Mack Smith, *Cavour* (London, 1985), 216, 210, 58).

[14] L. Riall, *Sicily and the Unification of Italy: Liberal Policy and Local Power, 1859–1866* (Oxford, 1998), 88–91, 118, 126–7, 136, 176–7; Riall, *Risorgimento: The History of Italy from Napoleon to Nation State* (Basingstoke, 2009), 35, 144, 147–9; Riall, *Under the Volcano: Revolution in a Sicilian Town* (Oxford, 2013), which concerns the estate granted to Nelson's family and the sort of land war that broke out there, something with close Irish parallels.

[15] *The Journal of John Wodehouse, First Earl of Kimberley for 1862–1902*, ed. A. Hawkins and J. Powell, Royal Historical Society Camden Fifth Series, ix (1997), 163. The baron's title was doubtless derived from the small place in south-eastern Sicily, the name of which was appropriated by Giuseppe di Lampedusa in his great novel *Il Gattopardo* (1958), set in the second half of the nineteenth century, in the first chapter of which the Prince of Salina's nephew, Tancredi, makes the now-famous remark 'If you want things to stay as they are, things will have to change', a sentiment not without echoes so far as Ireland is concerned.

simply a much weaker power than Russia.[16] The broadly analogous case of Denmark and Iceland—inevitably shaped by the enormous distances involved—also witnessed movement from assimilationism in the early nineteenth century to greater autonomy as time went on, culminating, first in the so-called Act of Union of 1918, which divided the Danish realm into a dual monarchy of two sovereign states, and then in the total independence of 1944.[17] Nor did Iceland's progress go unnoticed among supporters of Irish nationalism, some of whom rather optimistically looked to its successes as providing Ireland with encouragement and Britain with a pattern to follow.[18]

While the very nature of the relationship between dominant political cores and weaker peripheries made it impossible for those in charge of the former to avoid occasional reconsiderations of what they were about—and especially so in times of turbulence—such reconsiderations (though not without certain similarities) were never identical, shaped as they inevitably were by unique contingencies, changing ideologies, and different histories. A common feature can, however, be found in the fact that ideas of assimilation and differentiation underlay much of the thinking involved. What distinguished the Anglo-Irish connection was not that it seems to have functioned very differently from those to be found elsewhere in Europe, but that it possessed a very long historical pedigree, longer by far than the relationships between Russia and Finland and Sweden and Norway and longer even than that between Denmark and Iceland. If such Nordic cases cast revealing light upon the governmental situation created by the Irish Act of Union of 1800, developments elsewhere in Europe—in Austro-Hungary, in Italy, in Spain, in Switzerland, in the creation of an independent Belgium, in the unification of Germany and the construction of an increasingly centralized French state—also possess undoubted relevance, though it would require a scholar of superhuman linguistic abilities to do justice to them all.[19]

But, because the inhabitants of that 'other country'—the past—rarely, if ever, behave in the way that tidy-minded historians would have liked them to

---

[16] K. Nurmi, 'Imagining the Nation in Irish and Finnish Popular Culture in the Nineteenth and Early Twentieth Centuries', in B. Heffernan (ed.), *Life on the Fringe? Ireland and Europe, 1800–1922* (Dublin, 2012), 39–61; B. Kissane, 'Nineteenth-Century Nationalism in Finland and Ireland: A Comparative Analysis', *Nationalism and Ethnic Politics*, 6 (2000), 25–42; H. A. Barton, 'Finland and Norway, 1808–1917', *Scandinavian Journal of History*, 31 (2006), 221–36; D. Kirby, *A Concise History of Finland* (Cambridge, 2006), 129–49.

[17] G. Hálfdanarson, 'Severing the Ties—Iceland's Journey from a Union with Denmark to a Nation State', *Scandinavian Journal of History*, 31 (2006), 237–54; G. Karlsson, *The History of Iceland* (London, 2000), 200–23.

[18] A. McGill, *The Independence of Iceland: A Parallel for Ireland* (Glasgow, 1921); D. L. Sigurdsson, '"A Parallel Much Closer": The 1918 Act of Union between Iceland and Denmark and Ireland's Relations with Britain', *Irish Historical Studies*, 34 (2004), 79–92.

[19] See the essays by divers hands in H.-H. Nolte (ed.), *Europäische Peripherien im 20. Jahrhundert* (Stuttgart, 1997).

behave, it should be emphasized that the interpretation put forward in this book is not proposed in any spirit of universal or exclusive enlightenment. Many important things do not fit neatly into its generalizations. It does not address or seek to explain everything that is to be explained. There are other ways of looking at the same evidence, and there is other evidence that has not, either deliberately or accidentally, been examined here. What *is* claimed is that it puts forward arguments that do no violence to such evidence and that it provides an authentic and credible way of looking at the governmental relationship between Britain and Ireland during the years between 1800 and 1921. In any case, no mere historian can even begin to toy with the idea of applying to a work of history Gustav Mahler's famous comment about his music—that it should 'be like the world. It must embrace everything.'[20] Nonetheless, the hope remains that what follows may shed some new light upon aspects of the Anglo-Irish relationship and do so in a manner that is interesting to those who read it.

[20] D. Mitchell, *Gustav Mahler: The Wunderhorn Years* (London, 1975), 286.

Part I

A Faraway Country, *c.*1800–*c.*1830

1

Bringing Ireland into the Fold:
A Kind of Theory

The Anglo-Irish Union of 1800 was about security, imperial ambition, and keeping Ireland (tolerably) quiet and the French at bay. All the rest was hot air, though sometimes hot air of a distinctly revealing kind. What was less clear was how such things might best be achieved. The very word 'union' suggested a closer relationship, but closeness could take many forms: from calm and comprehensive uniformity to intrusive and coercive control. And, while the former approach was most often deployed by those favouring union during the propaganda wars of 1799–1800, the latter proved nearest to reality in the three decades immediately thereafter.

The background to all this had been laid down not long after the defeat of the Catholic James II at the Battle of the Boyne (1690), when the government in London had effectively subcontracted the administration of Ireland to local magnates, who, having 'undertaken' the task, soon became known as 'undertakers' (a term they heartily disliked). Given that London's chief representative in Ireland, the lord lieutenant, resided in Dublin for only six months in every twenty-four when the generally weak and obedient Irish parliament was in session, this proved a satisfactory arrangement for all the parties concerned. London set firm limits to what the undertakers and the parliament could do. In return, the former, now rich in patronage and official jobs, knew precisely how far they could go. Rather like newspaper editors under communism, their own self-censorship made cruder measures unnecessary. However, by the late 1760s the system was breaking down, not least because of the strains produced by the Seven Years War (1756–63). On the one hand, a so-called (Protestant) Patriot party was making its discontents increasingly obvious. On the other, the undertakers themselves were neither as united nor as effective as they had once been. As a result, lords lieutenant (or viceroys, as they were also known) began to take up more or less permanent residence in order to seek direct control of the Irish parliament. By the early 1780s a new crisis had broken out, again in part the result of overseas war, in this case Britain's defeat in America. And in 1782 the Irish parliament was accorded significantly greater powers at the beginning of what (not altogether accurately) has become known as a period of 'legislative independence'.

During all these years the idea of a union between Britain (itself a creation of the Anglo-Scottish union of 1707) and Ireland had attracted some flickering interest as a possible 'solution' to the problems posed by Irish government. But this had been intermittent, unfocused, and easily ignored. However, the outbreak of war with revolutionary France in 1793 gave the matter of Irish security greater prominence, though it also placed such strains upon leading ministers that coherent thinking about Ireland became ever more difficult to sustain. William Pitt, prime minister since 1783, though consistently finding Ireland a bore, was nonetheless increasingly attached to the idea that union might simultaneously provide a way out of military danger and 'solve' an urgent problem that had never much engaged his interest.

Already in 1784 the lord lieutenant, the Duke of Rutland—shortly before receiving the famous apophthegm from C. T. Grenville that 'Ireland is too great to be unconnected with us, and too near to be dependent on a foreign state, and too little to be independent'—had urged Pitt that 'a fixed and systematic plan should be determined in cabinet for the future government of Ireland'.[1] With many British politicians unhappy about the granting of 'legislative independence' in 1782, with even more resenting the collapse of the 'commercial propositions' of 1783 (denounced by Henry Grattan as 'a creeping union: a virtual union'[2]) and the disintegrative implications of the Irish parliament's behaviour during the Regency Crisis of 1788, the question of the Anglo-Irish relationship was being given a more prominent place on the political agenda of the time.

Initially, however, the idea of union was batted about in the expectation more of its possibility than of its probability. In 1792 Pitt admitted that it had 'long been' in his mind. Two years later Burke thought it might well prove 'a bold experimental remedy, justified, perhaps called for, in some really desperate crisis'.[3] Yet, as late as 1796, Pitt's characteristically fitful course was still in evidence in his confession to Camden, then lord lieutenant, that Ireland continued to occupy little of his thoughts.[4]

---

[1] Grenville to Rutland, 3 December 1784, H[istorical] M[anuscripts] C[ommission], *Fourteenth Report, Part I The Manuscripts of His Grace the Duke of Rutland, K.G. Preserved at Belvoir Castle*, iii (1894), 155; Rutland to Pitt, 15 August 1784, *Correspondence between the Right Honble William Pitt and Charles Duke of Rutland, Lord Lieutenant of Ireland 1781–1787*, ed. P. Stanhope (Edinburgh, 1890), 36.

[2] T. Bartlett, *Ireland: A History* (Cambridge, 2010), 197.

[3] Pitt to Westmorland (viceroy), 25 June 1792, N[ational] A[rchives of] I[reland] Westmorland Papers 1/57; Burke to Fitzwilliam, *c.*26 September 1794, *The Correspondence of Edmund Burke*, ed. T. W. Copeland et al., 10 vols (Cambridge, 1958–78), viii. 20–1; also R. Hobart (Chief Secretary) to Westmorland, 25 June 1792, NAI Westmorland Papers 1/57; Buckingham to W. W. Grenville, 14 October 1792, HMC, *Thirteenth Report, Appendix Part III: The Manuscripts of J. B. Fortescue, Esq. Preserved at Dropmore*, ii (1894), 322.

[4] Camden to Pitt, 7 May 1796, T[he] N[ational] A[rchives] Pitt Papers PRO 30/8/326.

However, the outbreak of rebellion in Ireland in 1798 turbo-charged what had hitherto proved a dilatory political machine. The day after getting the news Pitt wrote to Camden with the (by now rhetorical) query 'Cannot crushing the rebellion be followed by an act ... for an union?'[5] And in less than a month a first detailed plan had been drawn up.[6] By August Pitt was feeling 'very impatient', anxious to develop 'some new ideas on the subject', and writing to Cornwallis (Camden's successor) 'urging the necessity of bringing forward the great work of union, which can never be so well accomplished as now'.[7]

Cornwallis had been appointed because a soldier was needed to deal with the security implications of the uprising. Already a species of panic had begun to generate demands in ascendancy Ireland that extreme and condign punishment be visited upon the rebels, demands that Cornwallis did his best to restrain, convinced as he was that the existing Irish elite was so 'blinded by their passions and prejudices' as to be quite unfitted to pursue the more nuanced and subtle policies now required.[8] But, even if Pitt could now be seen to be 'thinking on the subject of Ireland', the great misfortune remained, as one member of that elite pointed out, that 'for many years' ministers had 'never thought of her, except when she became extremely troublesome'[9]—a complaint that was to echo (and convincingly so) throughout the next 120 years.

And thus Pitt and his colleagues decided on a union partly because of long-standing irritations about the consequences of the constitutional settlement of 1782, partly because of the critical state of the war with France, and, most immediately, because of the rebellion in Ireland. But, even as the details were being worked out, one observer had already identified a problem that, although superficially only one of nomenclature, was to prove continuously subversive of the enterprise as a whole. Whereas the Anglo-Scottish Union of 1707 had produced a 'Great Britain', inhabited by Britons, the union with Ireland was to generate a United Kingdom, the inhabitants of which

[5] Pitt to Camden, 28 May 1798, C[entre for] K[entish] S[tudies] Camden Papers U840/0190A/6.
[6] Pitt to Auckland, 4 June [1798], [W. Eden] Bishop of Bath and Wells, *Journal and Correspondence of William, Lord Auckland*, 4 vols (London, 1861–2), iv. 2; Pitt to Camden, 11 June 1798, CKS Camden Papers U840/0190A/7; J. H. Rose, *Pitt and Napoleon: Essays and Letters* (London, 1912), 338–41.
[7] Pitt to Lord Grenville, 5 and 6 August 1798, HMC, *Manuscripts of J. B. Fortescue*, iv (1905), 273–5; also Sylvester Douglas to Pelham, 3 August 1798, B[ritish] L[ibrary] Pelham Papers Add. MS 33106.
[8] Camden to Portland, 31 May 1798 and 5 June [1798], TNA [Home Office, Ireland Series] HO 100/76 and 77; Camden to Pelham, 6 and 11 June 1798, BL Pelham Papers Add. MS 33105; Cornwallis to Portland, 16 September 1798 and 1 December 1800, TNA HO 100/78 and 94.
[9] Beresford to Auckland, 9 August 1798, *The Correspondence of the Right Hon. John Beresford Illustrative of the Last Thirty Years of the Irish Parliament*, ed. W. Beresford, 2 vols (London, 1854), ii. 169.

were never to enjoy any generally accepted semantic appellation.[10] How, indeed, could a people become or feel 'united' if they did not even share a common name?

Initially, however, union was billed by its supporters as the great cement that would bind all together, a notion that continued to be saluted well after it had become clear that implicit promises about emancipation for Catholics (specifically their right to sit in parliament) had been removed from the menu. The injunction of the undersecretary, Edward Cooke, in October 1798 that the idea of union 'must be written up, spoken up, intrigued up, drunk up, sung up, and bribed up'[11] is, therefore, primarily to be understood as part of a noisy campaign for emollient Anglo-Irish togetherness mounted in the hope that an optimistic and protean volley of words might help to disguise the underlying tyranny of hard facts and home truths. The result, initially at least, was that the Union could be discussed, explained, and defended, not for what it actually seemed to be, but for what its defenders insisted it might well become.

Those who argued for union in the 1790s and went on to laud its benefits in the decades that followed invariably cried up the advantages Ireland would gain from a closer and more direct connection with and exposure to Britain's greater wealth, freedoms, efficiency, and strength. A limited kitty of hurray words was deployed to demonstrate that Ireland would cease to be a separate, diminished, poverty-stricken entity, and that, instead, Britain and Ireland together would become, as Sylvester Douglas (a former chief secretary) put it in April 1799, 'aliquot parts of one incorporated realm'.[12] And in the slipstream of incorporation would come a cornucopia of delicacies: unspecified but 'complete and reciprocal benefits', the rendering of 'England and Ireland one country in effect', 'settled habits of morality and true religion', with the credit and capital now pent up within Great Britain descending 'like water to a level' across the whole of the new and now synchronized partnership.[13]

Predictably, language of this sort—shaped as it was by panicky reactions to the risings of 1798—veered erratically between intimations of mutual Anglo-Irish respect and unvarnished suggestions that Celtic primitives could hardly avoid enrichment from the superior dynamism of the larger island. This latter

---

[10] Lord Radnor to Addington, 25 January 1799, D[evon] R[ecord] O[ffice] Sidmouth (Addington) Papers 152M/C1799/OI/8 and 10.

[11] A. Jackson, *The Two Unions: Ireland, Scotland, and the Survival of the United Kingdom 1707–2007* (Oxford, 2012), 7.

[12] [Cobbett's] *Parliamentary History of England from the Earliest Period to the Year 1803*, xxxiv. 850 (22 April 1799).

[13] Bayham (Camden) to Stewart (Castlereagh), 4 February 1793, P[ublic] R[ecord] O[ffice of] N[orthern] I[reland] Castlereagh Papers D3030/42; J. Ehrman, *The Younger Pitt: The Continuing Struggle* (London, 1996), 171; [Cobbett's] *Parliamentary History*, xxxiv. 885 (22 April 1799: Douglas) and 727 (11 April 1799: Auckland).

version of the unionist doctrine could create pronounced disjunctions between Pitt's soothing parliamentary deployment of Virgil to demonstrate that two nations, each unsubjected, were entering an everlasting compact on equal terms[14] and patronizing lectures from many pro-unionists (not excluding Pitt) about a peerless Britain graciously extending its bounty to a childlike and benighted neighbour. There was, indeed, much talk of 'superior civilization', 'the first of nations', 'the true envy of Europe', the promise that Ireland was about to enter the Elysian fields, perhaps even, in time, become 'another England'.[15] Concurrently, therefore, with repeated anticipations of an Ireland moving from monochrome provincialism into the glorious technicolour of imperial integration by means of 'an incorporation assimilating all the interests of the two countries' now to 'become one and the same', there were frank admissions that such things were possible only because one partner was so superior that, by some undoubted but opaque process of osmosis, its 'industrious habits and pursuits' would inevitably, perhaps even 'speedily', be 'communicated to the other'.[16]

It is difficult to know whether such panglossian arguments for union had much of a foothold in either reality or sincerity. Did George Johnstone MP really believe that 'the distinction of English and Irish' was now abolished, or Lord Hawkesbury (the future second Earl of Liverpool and prime minister) that there would now 'be no parties, but the parties of the British empire', with union bestowing 'integrity and harmony' on all privileged to live under its beneficent shade? Did Lord Darnley really anticipate that Ireland's interests would henceforth be no less 'impartially considered in the united parliament than those of Scotland, Wales [or] Devonshire' (though putting Ireland on a level with Devon was a nice touch)? Were Portland's afflations about 'this great work' being 'the most glorious, and I trust the most beneficial event that has yet taken place in the course of His Majesty's auspicious reign or that of any of his royal predecessors' more than simple relief that the deed had actually been done?[17] But, while it is certainly tempting to interpret such language as mere cynicism, a political capacity to believe a dozen impossible things before breakfast should also perhaps be kept firmly in mind.

---

[14] See [Cobbett's] *Parliamentary History*, xxxiv. 285 (31 January 1799) for the quotation from *The Aeneid* (book 12).

[15] J. Smyth, 'The Act of Union and "Public Opinion"', in Smyth (ed.), *Counter-Revolution and Union: Ireland in the 1790s* (Cambridge, 2000), 150.

[16] *Proceedings of the Irish House of Lords 1771–1800*, ed. J. Kelly, 3 vols (Dublin, 2008), iii. 470, 341, 479 (10 February 1800 and 22 January 1799); *Report of the Debate in the House of Commons of Ireland on Friday the 14th of February 1800* (Dublin, 1800), 72; *Speech of Patrick Duigenan, LL.D. in the Irish House of Commons, Wednesday Feb. 5 1800* (Dublin, 1800), 24.

[17] [Cobbett's] *Parliamentary History*, xxxv. 78 (21 April 1800), 114 (25 April 1800), 190 (8 May 1800); Portland to Cornwallis, 9 August 1800, TNA HO 100/94.

Pitt's particular contribution to the debate did not lie primarily in his spasmodic taste for tranquillizing emollience. 'Blending' was a favourite word, and there was much talk of 'equality of laws', of communicating to 'the sister kingdom the skill, capital, and the industry which have raised this country to such a pitch of opulence' and of 'an incorporation by a thorough intercourse of traffic and manners'.[18] Rather more revealing were the violent denunciations of Hibernian malice and wickedness that even the keenest Irish supporters of union can hardly have relished.[19] The Irish, declared Pitt, were, without exception, notorious for 'the ignorance and want of civilization' that marked their 'country more than almost any in Europe' and by a 'malignity' that had produced 'that distressed state which we now deplore'.[20] The all-encompassing brutality of such remarks—which were to be echoed again and again in the decades that followed—meant that those in Ireland who had ears to hear cannot ever have found it entirely straightforward to buy into more benign, if still patronizing, references to imminent manifestations of British capital and British manners, hand-in-hand, many suspected, with their near-cousin, British self-congratulation all round.[21]

Unsurprisingly, one of the most percipient of those involved, Castlereagh, sustained more subtle and realistic thoughts. As early as January 1799 he had told Pitt that any removal of 'the traits of distinctiveness' between Britain and Ireland could be achieved only at some remote period. And, while proud of his work in passing the Union and in consequence feeling 'less an Irishman and more an Englishman than hitherto', he was also worried (as was Cornwallis) at what was likely to ensue from any post-union refusal to grant Catholic emancipation and from any smooth continuation of the policy of governing Ireland 'upon a garrison principle'.[22]

---

[18] 'Extracts from Speeches made in the Parliaments of Great Britain and Ireland previously to the Act of Union', in *Royal Commission on the Financial Relations between Great Britain and Ireland, First Report ... Appendices*, H[ouse of] C[ommons Paper] 1895 [C. 7720-I], xxxvi. 490–1; [Cobbett's] *Parliamentary History*, xxxiv. 39–40 (21 April 1800); K. T. Hoppen, 'An Incorporating Union? British Politicians and Ireland 1800–1830', *English Historical Review*, 123 (2008), 330.

[19] Even the heroically 'realistic' Irish Lord Chancellor, Lord Clare—never slow to denounce his fellow countrymen for their 'squalid misery and profound ignorance'—confined his strictures to 'the *mass* of the Irish people'. Pitt made no exceptions. See *Proceedings of the Irish House of Lords*, ed. Kelly, iii. 445 (10 February 1800).

[20] [Cobbett's] *Parliamentary History*, xxxiv. 270 (23 January 1799). *The Times* similarly hoped the Union would make it possible 'to humanize the barbarous Irish' and 'render Ireland worth the possession' (12 April 1799 and 5 December 1798).

[21] [Cobbett's] *Parliamentary History*, xxxiv. 459 (12 February 1799: Addington), 379 (7 February 1799: Windham), 480–1 (14 February 1799: Peel the Elder), 727 (11 April 1799: Auckland).

[22] Castlereagh to Pitt, 17 January 1799, TNA Pitt Papers PRO 30/8/327; Memorandum to Cabinet (*c.* September 1800), in *Memoirs and Correspondence of Viscount Castlereagh, Second Marquess of Londonderry*, ed. Charles Vane [3rd] Marquess of Londonderry, 12 vols (London,

What was, however, perhaps more remarkable was that some of the most prominent Irish opponents of union based their own arguments, not on the undesirability of assimilation or incorporation, but upon what they perceived to be the Union's incapacity to engineer the future delivery of precisely such aspirations and promises. While this was not a universal view—others talked of the 'independence of Ireland' being 'written in the immovable records of heaven'[23]—much was made of the expectation that, as George Ponsonby put it, 'all the fine words, identification and consolidation, will not have a very magical effect', that, indeed, these were no more than 'pretended' objects.[24] And the whole thrust of the most dramatic (though hardly the most able) speech in the Irish House of Commons against the Union, that by Henry Grattan in February 1800, was based, not upon any fundamental opposition to assimilation as such, but upon a denial that this was ever going to be achieved. There was to be no 'identification of Establishments', no 'identification of commerce', in short, 'no identification of interests', still less 'of feeling and sympathy'.[25]

Despite such criticisms, the Acts of Union passed by the two parliaments entered the statute book garnished with the ringing words 'consolidate', 'united', and 'incorporated', even though they actually provided considerably more detail about mighty matters such as the excise duty to be levied by Britain on 'Irish mead or metheglin' (a half-pence per gallon of 'English measure' as it happens).[26] Indeed, the allocation of space within the final texts casts a curious light upon some of the priorities involved: endless clauses about 'beer, glass, leather, stained paper, paper, silk, spirits, refined sugar, sweets [and] tobacco', nothing at all about how Ireland was henceforth to be governed. And what this meant, as soon became obvious, was that all the fine talk about assimilation had been nothing more than that, fine talk.

Ministers seem, almost casually, to have assumed that 'evidently and of necessity' the existing arrangements of a lord lieutenant, with a chief secretary, undersecretaries, and a cabal of local advisors should 'be continued', it being 'conceived' that, as this was 'a matter relating solely to the crown', it need not 'be inserted in the Act of Union'.[27] In public, however, little was said about all

---

1848–53), iv. 392–400; Cornwallis to Portland, 1 December 1800, *The Correspondence of Charles, First Marquis Cornwallis*, ed. C. Ross, 3 vols (London, 1859), iii. 306–7.

[23] Sir John Parnell in *A Report of the Debate in the House of Commons in Ireland, on Wednesday and Thursday the 5th and 6th of February 1800* (Dublin, 1800), 180.

[24] Ibid. 165 (Ponsonby), also 195 (Burrowes).

[25] Ibid. 228; for similar views, see *A Report of the Debate in the House of Commons of Ireland on Tuesday and Wednesday the 22nd and 23rd of January, 1799* (Dublin, 1799), 71 (Ball); *Report of the Debate in the House of Commons of Ireland on Friday the 14th of February 1800*, 41 and 62 (Foster and Burrowes); [Cobbett's] *Parliamentary History*, xxxiv. 337 (7 February 1799: Grey) and xxxv. 57–72 (21 April 1800: Grey).

[26] The Act passed by the British Parliament is 39 & 40 George III c. 67; that by the Irish Parliament 40 George III c. 38 (Irish).

[27] Portland to Cornwallis, 12 November 1798, TNA HO 100/79.

of this during the long debates at Westminster and College Green,[28] a silence
that created considerable confusion among those entrusted with the Act's
practical implementation. Indeed, as late as October 1800, with Cornwallis
contemplating imminent departure, it was still unclear whether the office of
lord lieutenant 'would be continued after he relinquished it'.[29] As a result,
there was at first a good deal of uncertain clutching at straws, with the prime
minister (Addington) instructing subordinates to act 'on union principles' and
Lord Hardwicke, the first post-Union viceroy, cloudily declaring his intention
to behave in full 'conformity to the true principles of the Union'.[30] His
predecessor, Cornwallis, had famously insisted that there must be 'a union
with the Irish nation' not merely 'with a party in Ireland' and less famously
that it could succeed only if the Catholics 'were incorporated with the British
government'—a concept more forceful than clear.[31] Nor did the key buzzword
of 'incorporation' vanish once post-Union practice had so clearly rendered it
redundant. Addington happily used it when prime minister and so did
publicists like Francis Plowden.[32]

Two episodes in the months immediately after the Union reveal the tran-
sient nature of its supposed agenda. The first revolved around the sudden (if
rather tardy) realization that, amid the complexities of passing the Union into
law, a good deal had been overlooked. The minister chiefly concerned with
such second thoughts was Thomas Pelham, an erstwhile Foxite who had
moved into Portland's coalitionist ambit and had in July 1801 (as Lord
Pelham) succeeded Portland as Home Secretary. It was Pelham's sudden,
intense, and unsuccessful campaign to 'incorporate', not only the two parliaments, but the two executives, that highlights the very incomplete nature of
the Union as a practical measure. He mounted his efforts from an important
redoubt, for the Home Secretary had gradually come to assume a general, if ill-
defined, superintendence of Irish affairs. He also knew Ireland, having served
as chief secretary (1783–4 and 1795–8) and chaired the important secret
committee on Irish disaffection that reported in the spring of 1801. But,

---

[28] A rare exception was the glancing claim by John Foster, the anti-union speaker of the Irish
Commons, that uniting the parliaments but keeping a lord lieutenant in Dublin would render
Ireland 'a colony on the worst of terms' (*Speech of the Honourable John Foster ... 17th Day of
February 1800* (Dublin, 1800), 39).

[29] G. C. Bolton, *The Passing of the Irish Act of Union: A Study in Parliamentary Politics*
(Oxford, 1966), 207.

[30] E. Littlehales (reporting Addington) to Abbot, 16 September 1801, BL Hardwicke Papers
Add. MS 35720; Hardwicke's 'Counter Statement in Answer to the Paper of Considerations',
ibid., Add. MS 35772.

[31] Cornwallis to Portland, 8 October 1798, TNA HO 100/79; to Pitt, 8 October 1798, TNA
Pitt Papers PRO 30/8/327; to Ross, 30 September 1798, *Correspondence of Charles, First Marquis
Cornwallis*, ed. Ross, ii. 414–15.

[32] J. Kelly, 'The Historiography of the Act of Union', in *The Irish Act of Union*, ed. M. Brown,
P. M. Geoghegan, and J. Kelly (Dublin, 2003), 8–9.

although a significant, well-liked, and sometimes effective politician, Pelham entirely lacked any kind of killer instinct, owing, in part at least, to 'bouts of depression and self-loathing'.[33]

The problem as perceived by Pelham and some others was put most clearly by the talented but manic Lord Redesdale, whose promising career fell apart during his time as Lord Chancellor of Ireland between March 1802 and March 1806. 'Those who contrived the Union', he wrote in January 1806,

> seem to have thought only of carrying that measure without considering how the machine was to work afterwards. Indeed, they seem to have fancied that such would be the wonderful effect of the Union, that after its accomplishment, the machine of government in Ireland would move of itself ... The consequence is that, in many parts, the machine cannot work at all ... This country will not be governed until governed by English minds.[34]

While Redesdale believed that the superior insights of English minds (like his own) were most effectively injected into Ireland by the local presence of active viceroys and chief secretaries who would keep the Irish party clans in check—'the King of Spain might as well think to govern Mexico without a Viceroy'[35]—Pelham held that such arrangements necessarily involved a weakening of the influence of the metropolitical centre.

Pelham fired his dramatic missile in September 1801 under the bland title 'Considerations upon the Situation of the Lord Lieutenant and his Chief Secretary'.[36] The main aim of this intentionally savage intervention, rendered, however, less effective by Pelham's growing reputation for ministerial idleness,[37] was to clothe the union emperor in more than merely rhetorical assimilationist apparel. 'If', Pelham argued, 'the chief object professed in proposing the Union was to identify the interests of both countries which had before been considered distinct, it follows I think that even the appearance, as well as the reality, of separate councils directing the Government of each ought carefully to be avoided.' The extinction of the Irish parliament had rendered the post of viceroy not only redundant but objectionable as constituting an obstacle to efficient rule. All should now be done by the Home Secretary (that is, Pelham), the small Irish Office set up in London by

---

[33] D. R. Fisher in *ODNB*.

[34] Redesdale to Wickham, 30 January 1806, HMC, *Manuscripts of J. B. Fortescue*, iii (1899), 25.

[35] Redesdale to Addington, 16 January 1803, DRO Sidmouth Papers 152M/C1803/OZ/383, and 30 July 1803, ibid., C1803/OZ/68; also to Perceval (his brother-in-law), 20 October 1803, G[loucestershire] R[ecord] O[ffice] Mitford (Redesdale) Papers D2002/3/1/20 and BL Perceval Papers Add. MS 49188.

[36] Numerous copies exist—e.g. TNA Abbot Papers PRO 30/9/136; TNA HO 100/180; H[ampshire] R[ecord] O[ffice] Wickham Papers 38M/49/5/176/4; BL Hardwicke Papers Add. MS 35771; BL Pelham Papers Add. MS 33119.

[37] P. Polden, 'The Domestic Policies of the Addington Administration, 1801–4', University of Reading Ph.D. Thesis (1975), 195–6.

Castlereagh as a clearing house for information between the two capitals should be closed down, and Ireland brought under what, in modern terms, might be called unmediated 'direct rule'.[38]

The reactions to this saw so many energetic political felines enter the fray that Pelham's solitary parrot was soon rendered very dead indeed. Hardwicke, not only viceroy but half-brother to Charles Yorke, who succeeded Pelham at the Home Office in August 1803, immediately despatched representatives to London to put forward the ingenious, counter-intuitive, and self-interested argument that Pelham's proposals involved the very opposite of assimilation. By ruling directly from London, the government would, in Hardwicke's view, simply be allowing corrupt, dubious, and bigoted Irish political mice to play to their hearts content unsupervised by the immediate presence of those 'English minds' alone talented enough to transform Irish into British (for which read 'morally and practically superior') ways of doing things.[39] Addington, as prime minister, first wobbled by making sympathetic noises to Pelham, but then came down decisively on the other side.[40] Once Pelham, notorious also for failing to respond to correspondence from Ireland, had been worsted, Hardwicke allowed himself the smug satisfaction of declaring: 'It is unlucky to have any man for an enemy; but if one must have an enemy, it is better that he should be a fool.'[41] Yet, even some of those who thought Pelham's views extreme, were, nonetheless, appalled at the complete lack of post-Union administrative innovation. Edward Cooke admitted that he should 'have known better' than to expect a 'new system', Lord Clare despaired that 'a rational system of government' would ever be introduced, while Charles Long, on becoming chief secretary in September 1805, was mystified that so little thought had been given 'to the changes (if any) which have taken place in consequence of the Union in the offices of chief secretary, chancellor of the [Irish] exchequer, commander-in-chief, or even in that of the lord lieutenant himself'.[42]

---

[38] Pelham's 'Observations on Lord Hardwick's Instructions to Colonel Littlehales' (1801), TNA Abbot Papers PRO 30/9/124. There is some evidence that Pitt and Camden had in August–September 1799 considered abolishing the viceroyship: Duke of York to Prince of Wales, 15 September 1799, *The Correspondence of George, Prince of Wales 1770–1812*, ed. A. Aspinall, 8 vols (London, 1963–71), iv. 79; A. P. W. Malcomson, *John Foster (1740–1828): The Politics of Improvement and Prosperity* (Dublin, 2011), 179.

[39] Hardwicke to Addington, 26 August and 24 October 1801, BL Hardwicke Papers Add. MS 35771 and DRO Sidmouth Papers 152M/C1801/OI/9; to Abbot, 15 July 1801, TNA Abbot Papers PRO 30/9/113; Hardwicke's Memorandum of 1 September 1801, BL Hardwicke Papers Add. MS 35771; Hardwicke's 'Observations on Pelham's Considerations', 24 October 1801, TNA HO 100/180.

[40] Addington to Pelham, 2 August 1801, BL Pelham Papers Add. MS 33107; Littlehales to Hardwicke, 22 September 1801, BL Hardwicke Papers Add. MS 35720; Littlehales to Abbot, 24 September 1801, TNA Abbot Papers PRO 30/9/124.

[41] Hardwicke to Littlehales, 28 April 1803, HRO Wickham Papers 38M/49/8/70/83.

[42] Cooke to Auckland, 8 October 1801, *Eighteenth-Century Irish Official Papers in Great Britain: Private Collections Volume Two*, ed. A. P. W. Malcomson (Belfast, 1990), 311–12; Clare

A second, related, post-Union episode sheds further light on the complexity of the issues and personalities involved. Two months after Hardwicke's appointment in March 1801, a new chief secretary was sent over to Dublin. This was Charles Abbot, who was related, through his mother's second marriage, to Jeremy Bentham and who shared some of Bentham's administrative and reforming instincts. Unusually for a new chief secretary, he already knew something of Ireland, having undertaken an extensive tour in 1792.[43] But, while he arrived in Dublin full of assimilationist zeal for efficiency and the exposure of corruption, he combined this with support, not for Pelham's incorporation plans, but for their clear contrary—namely, approval of the viceregal role in general and of Hardwicke in particular.[44]

Abbot's earlier visit to Ireland had convinced him of that country's financially mendicant status, akin to the behaviour of a 'rich but indebted merchant … refusing to be liable for the prime cost, debts, or future losses of the joint concern', a state of things that could simply not 'be endured'.[45] Having been a leading light on the Finance Committee that had recently investigated the public offices in London, he saw his role as chief secretary to be that of a high-toned cleanser of the far dirtier Augean administrative stables to be found in Dublin. Specifically told that 'the eradication of Irish abuses' was to be his primary duty, Abbot began with a flurry of circulars demanding up-to-date financial information from Irish officials unaccustomed to such fervour, speed, and efficiency. Only by such means could, he believed, a 'real union … imparting to Ireland the blessings of a British government' be achieved.[46]

The notion that Ireland exhibited pathological extremes of 'corruption' was widespread among British politicians themselves deeply involved in pushing through the Union by means that, even by contemporary standards, gave forth a distinctly rancid smell. Cornwallis thought Ireland 'the most corrupt country' and its political class 'the most corrupt people under heaven'. In response, Castlereagh (himself of course Irish) found it convenient to sail under the banner later inscribed by the historian Lecky with the slogan 'Corrupting to

---

to Auckland, 22 October [1801], *'A Volley of Execrations': The Letters and Papers of John FitzGibbon, Earl of Clare 1772-1802*, ed. D. A. Fleming and A. P. W. Malcomson (Dublin, 2005), 452–3; Long to Redesdale, 25 September [1805], GRO Mitford Papers D2002/3/1/21.

[43] See his diary of this tour in TNA Abbot Papers PRO 30/9/23. This also contains interesting reflections on Irish political and constitutional matters. I am grateful to Christopher Woods for help in this connection.

[44] Abbot to Addington, 27 September 1801, TNA Abbot Papers PRO 30/9/123, also 'Instructions to Littlehales' PRO 30/9/124; Abbot to Addington, 27 October 1801, DRO Sidmouth Papers 152M/C1801/OI/15 and HRO Wickham Papers 38M/49/5/176/7.

[45] Abbot's Journal TNA PRO 30/9/23, 212.

[46] Yorke to Abbot, 12 October 1801, TNA Abbot Papers PRO 30/9/120; *The Diary and Correspondence of Charles Abbot, Lord Colchester, Speaker of the House of Commons 1802-1817*, ed. Charles, Lord Colchester, 3 vols (London, 1861), i. 280, 286–300; Abbot to Addington, 13 February 1801, ibid. i. 236.

Purify'. Pitt, in effect, did much the same.[47] Nor, indeed, did this prudish nose-in-the-air stance fade with the Union's enactment; quite the reverse. As so often, Redesdale put it most colourfully: 'There is no nation in India where the minds of men have been more corrupted ... where sordid selfishness is more the general characteristic ... The Union has ... done little for Ireland.'[48] To such patronizing execrations (which were regularly repeated throughout the union period) Irish observers might well have retorted 'Physician Heal Thyself', for there can be little doubt, especially in these early years, that, objectively measured, Irish jobbery had nothing to learn from its vigorous and entrenched British equivalent.[49]

Abbot combined moralism about finance with another approach that could be, and often was, deployed by commentators on both sides of the Irish Sea: the recourse historical. If later British politicians often moaned about their Irish counterparts' weakness for plucking arguments from the bran tub of olden times, their own predecessors were far from guiltless in this respect. Abbot mollifyingly pointed to William Molyneux's support for union and more fiercely to the prosperity that had, he claimed, characterized Ireland 'under Lord Strafford's vigorous and prudent administration'.[50] This soon became a standard trope, with other British politicians talking about the still vital and usually injurious effects of the disorders of the thirteenth century (Redesdale), 'ancient feuds and ancient jealousies' (Westmorland), 'remote and almost forgotten periods' (Canning), 'early misgovernment' after Ireland's Norman Conquest (Goulburn), the whole period from 'Strongbow to Lord Wellesley' (Darnley), and some even making comparisons between the blessings provided by the Union and those ushered in when the Sabines united with Rome (Cooke).[51]

Unsurprisingly Abbot's pugnacious zeal evoked hostility, especially among those who had supported the Union but never suspected that reforming versions of 'assimilation' might actually have any purchase upon Hibernian

---

[47] Cornwallis to Pitt, 7 December 1798, TNA Pitt Papers PRO 30/8/327; to Ross, 8 June 1799, *Correspondence of Charles, First Marquis Cornwallis*, ed. Ross, iii. 102; W. E. H. Lecky, *A History of Ireland in the Eighteenth Century*, new edn, 5 vols (London, 1892), v. 343; [Cobbett's] *Parliamentary History*, xxxiv. 248 (23 January 1799).

[48] Redesdale to Addington, 24 January 1806, DRO Sidmouth Papers 152M/C1806/OI/1; also Fox to Bedford, 16 June 1806, *Memorials and Correspondence of Charles James Fox*, ed. Lord John Russell, 4 vols (London, 1853–7), iv. 143; A. Wellesley (Chief Secretary) to ?, 25 December 1807, M. Roberts, *The Whig Party 1807–1812*, 2nd edn (London, 1975), 38; Peel to Liverpool, 20 October 1813, BL Peel Papers Add. MS 40285.

[49] Malcomson, *John Foster (1740–1828)*, 260–2.

[50] Abbot's Journal TNA PRO 30/9/23, 210; Abbot to Addington, 13 February 1801, *Diary and Correspondence of Charles Abbot*, ed. Charles, Lord Colchester, i. 236.

[51] Parl[iamentary] Deb[ates] 1: xxxiii. 823 (2 April 1816: Redesdale), xxi. 456 (31 January 1812: Westmorland), xxi. 523 (3 February 1812: Canning); Parl. Deb. 2: vi. 1482 (22 April 1822: Goulburn) and xi. 238 (8 April 1824: Darnley); [E. Cooke], *Arguments for and against an Union* (Dublin, 1799), 3.

realities. Lord Clare denounced Abbot as 'the most arrogant, presumptuous, empty prig I have ever met with'; John Beresford, preferring moderation, merely dismissed him as 'a vain, silly man'.[52] Soon Abbot was hopelessly entangled, not knowing to whom in London he should write, rapidly losing the prime minister's support, anxious only to return to England as soon as he possibly could.[53] In February 1802 he was elected Speaker of the House of Commons, his eight-month stint as chief secretary marking the start of a turnover so rapid that no less than five individuals held the office over the next four years. His immediate successor, William Wickham, quickly found that Abbot's reform project had run entirely into the sands. And, when it was (partially) revived, this was at the hands of a leading Irish politician (John Foster) rather than at those of any British master of the assimilating mode.[54]

Only in the more easily manipulated world of words did the (in itself contradictory) Pelham–Abbot assimilationist programme achieve even the mildest form of traction, with sporadic but increasingly formulaic salutes woven into the official instructions given to viceroys on appointment or deployed when officials and politicians wanted to present themselves as forward-looking, aspirational, and intent on something more than main-chance support for the status quo.[55] By 1808 the then chief secretary, Sir Arthur Wellesley (the future Duke of Wellington), had simply given up on the whole idea:

> The misfortune of Ireland is that the existing evils are so great and so obvious that everybody sees them and it is easy to find out how things ought to be by adverting to England. The difficulty is to bring them from the state in which they are in this country to that in which they are in England and I have not yet seen any practical solution for this difficulty.[56]

And so the great enterprise of post-Union assimilation—always more impressive in the realm of oratory than in that of reality—was laid to rest, though, as with Dracula, its vital spirits continued an underground and undead existence, ready for revival when circumstances changed and the times once more became receptive to the heartbeats of its aspirations and promises.

---

[52] Clare to Auckland, 19 September [1801], PRONI Sneyd Papers T3229/1/38; Beresford to Auckland, 5 September 1801, ibid., T3229/2/63.
[53] Abbot to Addington, [1801], BL Hardwicke Papers Add. MS 35707; Littlehales to Abbot, 16 September1801, TNA Abbot Papers PRO 30/9/124.
[54] Wickham to Abbot, 9 September 1802, TNA Abbot Papers PRO 30/9/173; Bartlett, *Ireland*, 240–2; Malcomson, *John Foster (1740–1828)*, 263–6.
[55] See, e.g., Bedford's 'Instructions' of 1806, W[oburn] A[bbey] Bedford Papers Irish Box 2; Bedford to Fox, [February 1806], ibid.; Grenville to Bedford, 12 December [1806], ibid.; Hardwicke to Redesdale, 4 April 1803, BL Hardwicke Papers Add. MS 35772; Parl. Deb. 1, xxi. 509 (3 February 1812).
[56] Wellesley to Manners, 14 January 1808, S[outhampton] U[niversity] Wellington Papers WP1/189/74; also Wellesley to R. S. Tighe, 25 December 1807, ibid., WP1/181/42.

2

Keeping Ireland at Arm's Length: A Kind of Reality

I

What had taken place immediately after the Union presented a curiously paradoxical air. Superficially the Irish Protestant ascendancy was no longer in business on its own account but had been taken over by a larger international corporation, which, though itself 'Protestant', possessed different and more complex priorities. Yet, the deeper condition of things had hardly changed at all. Not only were Irish ascendancy anti-unionists like John Foster rapidly resurrected into favour, but the demands of war with France, unrest in Ireland, disturbances in England itself, together with a host of long-held attitudes (prejudices, if you prefer) combined to keep the smaller island firmly incarcerated within the box of foreign exoticism that it had long inhabited.

What, however, the Union had done was to unleash flocks of British author–travellers upon Ireland anxious to 'discover' this new part of the United Kingdom. But such discovery took time, and, while these visitors often proved physically and culturally adventurous, few contemporary British politicians followed their lead, something reinforced rather than impaired by reports from official investigations undertaken in these years into Irish social and economic conditions, for these too spent a good deal of their energy in asserting the country's peculiarity 'or at least its difference from Britain'. What all were agreed upon was that Ireland was and remained 'anomalous' (a favourite word), with writers interpreting this in terms of optimistic hope, politicians in terms of pessimistic unease.[1] If, therefore, the outburst of post-Union

---

[1] See G. Hooper (ed.), *The Tourist's Gaze: Travellers in Ireland 1800–2000* (Cork, 2001), pp. xx–xxi; Hooper, *Travel Writing and Ireland, 1760–1860: Culture, History, Politics* (Basingstoke, 2005), 4–6, 64, 106–7; C. J. Woods, *Travellers' Accounts as Source-Material for Irish Historians* (Dublin, 2009), *passim*; N. Ó Ciosáin, *Ireland in Official Print Culture, 1800–1850: A New Reading of the Poor Inquiry* (Oxford, 2014), 17.

travel writing on Ireland had any effect upon political opinion in Britain, this was probably shallow and certainly anything but immediate.

Generally speaking, British politicians continued to see Ireland and its inhabitants as primitive, barbaric, corrupt, violent, unreliable, dangerous, and badly in need of Anglo-Saxon discipline. And the Union did little to change such attitudes, which were promiscuously held by those with direct experience of Ireland and those with none. As it happens, the members of Addington's administration of 1801–4 were unusually strong in direct experience of Ireland—Portland, Westmorland, Hobart, Pelham, Castlereagh—though some prominent men almost gloried in their disinclination to cross the Irish Sea, insisting that only ignorance could generate high-minded impartiality. 'Why should Canning go to Ireland?' Peel suspiciously asked, as if such a visit by a politician not holding Irish office must automatically be considered a suspect act.[2]

If the Union inevitably increased certain kinds of direct confrontation, this generally led to neither understanding nor sympathy. The hundred Irish MPs now at Westminster were denounced as 'wild Irish ... Paddies'. Nor were the twenty-eight Irish peers in the upper house designated any differently: they too were simply 'the Paddies'.[3] Ireland's 'lack of civilization', as Pitt called it in his union speech of January 1799, was constantly referred to rather than (as he had promised) urgently addressed in the decades that followed. Eldon and Peel were agreed that any news emanating from Ireland must automatically be distrusted as almost certainly mendacious, self-interested, and false.[4] Small wonder, then, that those who were not entirely ignorant (a comparatively select group) were perfectly prepared to join those who were so in expressing views that ranged from contempt at worst to at best a sort of weary caricature. Men ransacked the globe to find countries and territories of equivalent psychological remoteness, while uneasily aware that the distance between Holyhead and Dublin was less than 70 miles. Those who so frequently talked of the world's most distant regions when discussing the strange otherness of Ireland were, it would seem, simultaneously emphasizing and justifying what sometimes struck even them as a species of invincible ignorance. Siberia in general made numerous appearances, as did more specific references to the distant peninsula of Kamchatka, surrogate, perhaps, for a place so remote as to

---

[2] Peel to Goulburn, 19 September 1824, S[urrey] H[istory] C[entre] Goulburn Papers 340/35; G. C. Bolton, *The Passing of the Irish Act of Union: A Study in Parliamentary Politics* (Oxford, 1966), 44–6; L. Mitchell, *Holland House* (London, 1980), 105; Parl[iamentary] Deb[ates] 1: xi. 261 (8 April 1824).

[3] Lord Sheffield cited in Bolton, *The Passing of the Irish Act of Union*, 86; Richmond (viceroy) to Liverpool, 19 January 1811, N[ational] L[ibrary of] I[reland] Richmond Papers MS 61.

[4] Eldon to Redesdale, [24] August 1803, G[loucestershire] R[ecord] O[ffice] Mitford Papers D2002/3/1/23; Peel to Anglesey, 7 April 1828, P[ublic] R[ecord] O[ffice of] N[orthern] I[reland] Anglesey Papers D619/26B/13.

be virtually incomprehensible.[5] Some talked of Tibet, others of China; some of Africa, others of Japan; some of 'Indian Negroes' when discussing Irish savages, others of 'the Cingalese, the Candyans, the Malabars of Ceylon'.[6] Lord Talbot, when viceroy, abandoned human analysis altogether and thought the Irish 'as mischievous and full of tricks as monkeys, and as little to be depended upon', an analysis previously essayed by Lord Auckland, who, at the time of the Union, had felt 'somewhat *triste*' about the extent to which 'our new countrymen can be humanized'. Palmerston, who had large estates in County Sligo and was a tolerable landlord, was trying hard in 1826 'to civilize some thousands of natives ... I do not despair of persuading them in the course of time to wear clothes'.[7]

Deploying the language of an amiable (or not so amiable) anthropologist surveying 'primitive' peoples proved irresistible for those governing Ireland in these years. Visiting Roscommon when chief secretary in 1814, Peel was 'highly amused' by the fact that 'every hour produces some absurd application ... A woman applied to me to know the result of a suit in Chancery, as she thought I must have "brought tidings into these parts". I am quite confirmed in the opinion ... that the common people believe that "the Government" is a large animal that lives in the Castle.' And fifteen years later, when, as Home Secretary, Peel had special Irish responsibilities, he still thought it useful to express the opinion that a country at such low levels of civilization required distinctly medieval forms of handling by politicians of all parties and dispositions.[8]

While, therefore, post-Union travel writers exploring Ireland quickly persuaded themselves that the best way to sell their wares was to be seen as

---

[5] Anon., 'English Theories and Irish Facts', *Dublin University Magazine*, 6 (1835), 682; Peel to Whitworth, 29 February 1816, C[entre for] K[entish] S[tudies] Whitworth Papers U269/0225/18; Redesdale to Abbot, 21 July 1804, *The Diary and Correspondence of Charles Abbot, Lord Colchester, Speaker of the House of Commons*, ed. Charles, Lord Colchester, 3 vols (London, 1861), i. 523.

[6] Redesdale to Perceval, 23 October 1803, GRO Mitford Papers D2002/3/1/20; [Cobbett's] *Parliamentary History*, xxxiv. 689 (19 March 1799); Redesdale to Addington, 21 January 1806, D[evon] R[ecord] O[ffice] Sidmouth Papers 152M/C1806/OI/1; Attorney-General Joy to Archdeacon Singleton (Secretary to Viceroy Northumberland), 2 April 1829, B[ritish] L[ibrary] Peel Papers Add. MS 40327; *A Report of the Debate in the House of Commons of Ireland Held on Tuesday and Wednesday the 22nd and 23rd of January 1799* (Dublin, 1799), 42; P. Bew, *Ireland: The Politics of Enmity 1789–2006* (Oxford, 2007), 82.

[7] B. Jenkins, *Era of Emancipation: British Government of Ireland, 1812–1830* (Kingston and Montreal, 1988), 134; Auckland to Beresford, 20 January 1800, *The Correspondence of the Right Hon. John Beresford Illustrative of the Last Years of the Irish Parliament*, ed. W. Beresford, 2 vols (London, 1854), ii. 240; Palmerston to Mrs Arbuthnot, 15 October 1826, *The Correspondence of Charles Arbuthnot*, ed. A. Aspinall, Royal Historical Society Camden Third Series, xxxv (1941), 84.

[8] Peel to Whitworth, 28 August 1814, CKS Whitworth Papers U269/0225/9; to Leveson-Gower, 19 November 1829, *Sir Robert Peel from his Private Papers*, ed. C. S. Parker, 3 vols (London, 1891–9), ii. 136.

translators of a hidden, strange, and hitherto unknowable Ireland into the 'plain' language of British conversation, so did those charged with the governance of Ireland perceive themselves to be either immediately or indirectly in charge of a neighbouring island of distinct, almost shocking, peculiarity. What rendered all of this stranger still was that very similar vibrations were being created within Ireland itself, especially among the notable tribe of post-Union novelists such as Morgan, Edgeworth, Maturin, the Banims, Lover, and Lever, who so insistently portrayed both their characters and the surroundings they inhabited as wild, distinct, and picturesque that one eminent critic has convincingly described the predominant stance of their fiction as one of 'auto-exoticism' or the looking for one's own identity in the 'unusual, the extraordinary, the exotic aspects of experience, to conflate the notions of one's distinctness and one's distinctiveness'. Even so the 1820s undoubtedly mark a watershed between a fiction attempting 'to reconcile a celebration of cultural' difference 'with the possibilities of reconciliatory union' and later Irish novels of a distinctly 'more complex and disillusioned' character'.[9] Overall, however, there seems to have existed in the early nineteenth century a species of unrealized conspiracy between two very different groups—one in Ireland and one in Britain—both equally determined to present, to explain, and if possible to understand Ireland in terms that emphasized that, whatever else Ireland was, it was not England.

And from these emphases on primitiveness there flowed the unsurprising political view that what, above all, Ireland needed was regular applications of a stern British prefectorial cane. Obeisances were, admittedly, occasionally made to what might be called the 'benign' (if no less patronizing) view that certain Hibernian characteristics—impulsiveness, generosity, reckless courage—also deserved a passing salute, but in these years this maintained at best a fleeting grip on contemporary political minds.[10] Peel, the second-longest-serving chief secretary in the whole post-Union period and a man who made unusually serious efforts to learn about Ireland, never managed to rid himself of fiercely critical opinions about the country in his care. There was 'less moral courage in Ireland than in any country on the face of the earth'; outsiders could have no idea of its 'moral depravation' and 'almost total annihilation of the agency of conscience'.[11] As prime minister, Liverpool combined a vaunted lack of interest in Ireland and its government with a

---

[9] J. Leerssen, *Remembrance and Imagination: Patterns in the Historical and Literary Representation of Ireland in the Nineteenth Century* (Cork, 1996), 37–8, 43, 225; R. F. Foster, *Words Alone: Yeats and his Inheritances* (Oxford, 2011), 40.

[10] Goulburn to Peel, 26 November 1824, BL Peel Papers Add. MS 40330; Parl. Deb. 1: vi. 1514 (22 April 1822).

[11] Jenkins, *Era of Emancipation*, 286; Peel to Whitworth, 24 January 1816, BL Peel Papers Add. MS 40290; to Abbot, 25 December 1816, *Sir Robert Peel from his Private Papers*, ed. Parker, i. 236–7.

readiness to blame all of its problems upon 'the customs and disposition of the people'.[12] Those directly given the task of undertaking Irish affairs quickly fell into a kind of gallows jocularity generated by feelings of besieged colonial entitlement. Peel made jokes about the fact that he occasionally found himself speaking 'as an Irishman'. Palmerston amused correspondents by picturing himself as 'a bit of an Irishman'. Richmond, when viceroy, teased his chief secretary Wellesley Pole (Wellington's brother) by referring to the native Irish as Wellesley Pole's 'fellow countrymen', which indeed they were.[13] A third brother, Marquess Wellesley (lord lieutenant 1821–8 and 1833–4), while occasionally talking rather grandly of Ireland as 'my unhappy country', humorously reported to London that all was as well 'as any country can be under the auspices of poverty, discord, and disease'.[14] Peel, in more ironic mode, delivered himself of the unforgettable maxim: 'I never yet saw an Irishman that had not something Irish about him.'[15]

What, of course, this amounted to was the construction of a truth universally acknowledged to the effect that the Irish, like tigers, could never change their spots. At the same time there was no shortage of Irishmen anxious to wash away their Hibernian dirt by so loudly declaring a detestation of their own countrymen and women that they began to seem ridiculous even to critical English eyes. Lord Clare's attacks on 'the profound ignorance, and barbarous manners, and brutish ferocity of the mass of the Irish people' and his admission to being 'sickened with this rant of Irish dignity and independence' rendered him not one whit less profoundly Irish in the minds of those in government.[16] Lesser men of similar stamp like Patrick Duigenan, who sat in both the Dublin and London parliaments, were seen in England as little more than 'useful idiots' on the extreme Protestant side of things.[17] The less frantic, but no less Irish, John Wilson Croker, who acted as Peel's spin doctor, still found it useful (perhaps even necessary) to make clear his belief that the Irish

---

[12] Liverpool to Peel, 4 October 1813, BL Peel Papers Add. MS 40181; Parl. Deb. 1: xxviii. 862 (26 July 1814). For similarly confident judgements, see Redesdale to Addington, 30 July 1803, DRO Sidmouth Papers 152M/C1803/OZ/68; Parl. Deb. 1: xxxiii. 836 (2 April 1816: Sidmouth).

[13] Peel to Liverpool, 14 September 1812, BL Peel Papers Add. MS 40280; Palmerston to Anglesey, 6 January 1829, S[outhampton] U[niversity] Palmerston Papers GC/AN/20; Richmond to Wellesley Pole, 8 February 1812, N[ational] L[ibrary of] I[reland] Richmond Papers MS 67.

[14] Wellesley to Littleton, 2 September 1833, S[taffordshire] R[ecord] O[ffice] Hatherton Papers D260/M/01/7; Wellesley to Wellington, 15 August 1826, SU Wellington Papers WP1/860/14.

[15] Peel to Goulburn, 29 September 1826, SHC Goulburn Papers 304/37.

[16] *Proceedings of the Irish House of Lords 1771–1800*, ed. J. Kelly, 3 vols (Dublin, 2008), iii. 445; also *'A Volley of Execrations': The Letters and Papers of John FitzGibbon, Earl of Clare 1772–1802*, ed. D. A. Fleming and A. P. W. Malcomson (Dublin, 2005), *passim*.

[17] *Speech of Patrick Duigenan, LL.D. in the Irish House of Commons, Wednesday, Feb. 5, 1800* (London, 1800); P. M. Geoghegan in *DIB*; T. Bartlett, *The Fall and Rise of the Irish Nation: The Catholic Question 1690–1830* (Dublin, 1992), 284–5, 290.

were at best 'restless, yet indolent ... impetuous, impatient, and improvident'. 'Who will call this people civilized?' he demanded. 'No wonder that they are turbulent.'[18] Admittedly it was not always easy to avoid this kind of national self-loathing if one wanted, especially from modest beginnings, to make a successful metropolitan political career. Superfine talent and money obviously helped, though even Castlereagh's early successes depended notably on his supporters' strong insistence that, though Irish, he was 'so very unlike an Irishman'.[19] The Wellesley brothers (or at least four of the five) managed to integrate themselves fully into the post-Union polity by sheer talent, though the future Duke of Wellington, when asked in 1805 whether he was 'an Englishman or an Irishman', thought the question certainly required a carefully calibrated response. 'I acknowledge that I rather prefer England because my friends and relations reside there,' he replied, though at bottom 'all countries are alike to me, who have been so much abroad and who have had as unsettled life as I have'.[20] Those of lesser ability could not, however, afford so balanced a frame of mind. Indeed, Castlereagh's half-brother, when looking for diplomatic preferment from the prime minister in 1822, was held by the latter to be 'very much mistaken if he supposes that he can ever make himself a man of much consequence in this country. He is not sufficient an Englishman *even for the Continent* ... and still less for Great Britain.'[21]

Although many (though by no means all) members of the ascendancy in Ireland were aware of their betwixt-and-between status—not really English, not really Irish—all of them would have been dismayed by the critical manner in which they were perceived by the British political class, for, when Ireland featured in the correspondence of early nineteenth-century politicians in London, little effort was made to distinguish between different groups. Pretty well the only thing that could be said in their favour was that they were not Catholics. But, while this was indeed a big thing, it was far from enough to blot out all the other Hibernian faults they shared with their popish countrymen. Why, British politicians and especially those directly in charge of the sister isle asked themselves was Ireland so poor, so disturbed, so primitive, so unlike England? First, because of the taint of idolatrous popery, but, second (and by no means less important), because of the laziness, greed, harshness, and

[18] Croker's *Sketch of the State of Ireland* (1808) in *The Croker Papers: The Correspondence and Diaries of the late Right Honourable John Wilson Croker*, ed. L. J. Jennings, 2nd edn, 3 vols (London, 1885), i. 448–9.

[19] Cornwallis to Portland, 20 November 1798, *The Correspondence of Charles, First Marquis Cornwallis*, ed. C. Ross, 3 vols (London, 1859), ii. 439.

[20] To Lady Olivia Sparrow, 8 November 1805, J. Wilson, *A Soldier's Life: Wellington's Marriage* (London, 1987), 73. See J. Severn, *Architects of Empire: The Duke of Wellington and his Brothers* (Norman, OK, 2007).

[21] Liverpool to C. Arbuthnot, 21 October 1822, *Correspondence of Charles Arbuthnot*, ed. Aspinall, 35.

corruption of the Irish landed and professional classes. Above all, the gentry—or so it seemed in England—were too often absentees seen in London, Cheltenham, or Bath spending the rents of estates they did little to improve. Protestant professional men also got it in the neck, as when one exasperated chief secretary, after much aggravation, declared himself 'really sick of the freaks on the Irish Bench' whose judgments struck him as not only bizarre but often inconsistent as well.[22]

The main critical thrust was, however, reserved for landlords, not only as owners of estates but when acting (or failing to act) as magistrates. 'The disinterested administration of local justice is the forte of English gentlemen. It is not that of their Irish brothers, and do what you will with the magistracy of Ireland, you will never mould it into a resemblance of the magistracy of this country.'[23] What was especially hurtful here was not only the element of truth, but the even larger element of (by no means entirely justified) English self-congratulation. This view of Peel's, if not universal, was, however, very general indeed. Some British politicians simply lumped all Irishmen and women together as unregenerate primitives. Wickham, when chief secretary, told the prime minister in 1802 'to be without ceasing' on his 'guard against everybody and everything that is Irish ... The system ... of supplanting and calumniating each other is so deeply rooted in *them all.*' Two decades later another chief secretary, Goulburn, felt the same, believing as he did that all parties and groups in Ireland were simply knee-deep in 'absurdity'.[24] But the fiercest anger was reserved for those who should have known better and who, by their grasping avarice and avoidance of responsibility, were bringing all government into disrepute. Independent Tories like Hardwicke (viceroy 1801–5) and strong Tories such as Wellington (chief secretary 1807–9, prime minister 1828–30) and Sidmouth (prime minister 1801–4, Home Secretary 1812–22) were all agreed on this.[25] So were enthusiastic Whigs like Bedford, who served as viceroy in the Ministry of All the Talents of 1806–7. So were eccentric Whigs like the second Marquess of Lansdowne, who did, however, admit that Catholics were even worse: 'servile, timid, false, mistrustful, and vindictive', with Protestants merely 'Mamelukes to the Catholic Egyptians'.[26] Canningites

[22] Leveson-Gower to Peel, 24 August 1829, N[ational] A[rchives of] I[reland] Leveson-Gower Letter-Book MS 737.

[23] Peel to J. L. Foster, 22 December 1821, R[oyal] I[rish] A[cademy] J. L. Foster Papers 23G.39/3.

[24] Wickham to Addington, 8 December 1802, H[ampshire] R[ecord] O[ffice] Wickham Papers 38M49/5/10/35; Goulburn to Peel, 22 December 1824, BL Peel Papers Add. MS 40330.

[25] Hardwicke to Pelham, 16 January 1802, T[he] N[ational] A[rchives] [Home Office Irish Series] HO100/109; Wellington to Clancarty, 16 July 1829, SU Wellington Papers WP1/1035/38; and to Northumberland, 7 July 1830, WP1/1130/21; Sidmouth to Whitworth, 21 April 1816, CKS Whitworth Papers U269/0218/3.

[26] Bedford to Spencer, 23 October 1806, TNA HO 100/136; to Elliot, 27 September 1806, N[ational] L[ibrary of] S[cotland] Elliot of Wells Papers MS 12915; Wycombe [from 1805 2nd

like William Lamb (chief secretary 1827–8, prime minister 1834 and 1835–41), Charles Grant (chief secretary 1818–21), and Lord Francis Leveson-Gower (chief secretary 1828–30) unanimously felt that, as a class, the Irish gentry were a sorry crew, interested only in money and electoral influence, in return for which they were content to 'surround themselves with paupers'.[27] Years after ceasing to be chief secretary, Charles Abbot (then Speaker of the House of Commons) was still arguing that nothing good would ever come out of Ireland until its gentry roused themselves into the kind of action that was 'beyond all legislative reach'.[28] But how little the Union nostrums of greater intercourse with other parts of the United Kingdom (still Abbot's sovereign remedy in 1814) had achieved in raising the tone of the Irish gentry is made plain in some tart responses from Wellington to an Irish proprietor who protested against the constant denigration of his class and by denunciations from the Duke of Northumberland when viceroy in 1829 of Irish landlords (who were, of course, a good deal poorer than his Croesus-like self) as, quite simply, 'heartless'.[29] Indeed, so disillusioned did British ministers become with the Irish Protestant community that they began to make private jokes about them, as when Peel, driven to distraction by the endless demands for a peerage from the wealthy Tipperary MP and flour miller John Bagwell, recalled how he and a previous viceroy had often laughed over Bagwell's ineligibility on the grounds that he already enjoyed the distinguished titles of 'Old Bags' and 'Marshal Sacks'.[30]

Closer examination suggests that such critical comments were as much alibis for confusion as the products of a considered framework of ideas. In truth, post-Union governments in general and cabinets in particular could rarely be bothered to focus consistently upon Irish questions at all. Indeed, the long opposition to and neglect of the whole issue of allowing Catholics to sit in parliament seems sometimes to have owed as much to casual evasion as to visceral opposition and contempt. A belief that, if only one looked smartly away, the Hibernian ogre would disappear seems to have informed most administrators until, that is, the question of Catholic emancipation caused so much panic that, quite unprecedentedly, the cabinet met no less than thirty-two times in the fifty-seven days after 17 January 1829 to consider an

---

Marquess of Lansdowne] to Grey, 15 January 1804, D[urham] U[niversity] Grey Papers GRE/B38/11/2.

[27] Parl. Deb. 2: vi. 179 (8 February 1822: Lamb) and ii. 100 (28 June 1820: Grant); Leveson-Gower to Peel, 2 July 1829, NAI Leveson-Gower Letter-Book MS 736.

[28] Abbot to Peel, 17 October 1814, *Sir Robert Peel from his Private Papers*, ed. Parker, i. 157.

[29] Wellington to Clancarty, 6 June 1822, *Despatches, Correspondence, and Memoranda of Field Marshal Arthur Duke of Wellington*, ed. [2nd] Duke of Wellington, 8 vols (London, 1867–80), i. 241–2; Northumberland to Peel, 4 May 1829, A[lnwick] C[astle] Northumberland Papers DNP/71.

[30] Peel to Whitworth, 19 May 1814, CKS Whitworth Papers U269/O225/5.

essentially Irish concern.[31] And, while parliament did, indeed, discuss Irish affairs with somewhat greater assiduity and more persistent energy than ministers, its level of attention was substantially less intense than the famous—and now exploded—myth about the busy activities of no less than '114 commissions and 60 committees' dealing with Ireland between 1800 and 1833 once tended to suggest.[32]

II

The parliamentary and legislative attention given to Ireland—and certainly Ireland sporadically pushed itself up the political agenda with explosive force—was usually the outcome of desperate efforts by viceroys and chief secretaries to extract some sort of decision—almost, on occasion, any sort of decision—from a cabinet understandably obsessed with foreign wars until 1815 but no less disinclined to consider Irish matters in the decade or so thereafter. The largest single class of official correspondence from Ireland to be found in the archives of leading ministers in London unsurprisingly concerned that mighty staple of the contemporary political world, patronage. But the second largest was made up of an endless stream of letters from lords lieutenant, chief secretaries, and their subordinates complaining of neglect, inattention, sometimes of a failure to generate any kind of response at all. Pitt had often ignored Ireland before the Union, as indeed had many of his colleagues.[33] By 1805 an ailing prime minister never thought 'of Ireland except when he is pressed for votes in parliament' and was unwilling to give even ten minutes of his time to 'the multitude of points of a more or less public nature which it is absolutely necessary ... to refer to him'.[34] A representative sent by Hardwicke to London found ministers both inattentive and ill-informed. Indeed, Hardwicke thought that 'the affairs of Ireland are seldom considered in England, except when some point presses, and then everything is done in a hurry'. His letters were ignored, sometimes for more than three months, and the quick turnover of chief secretaries meant that 'this country does not receive that portion of

[31] Memorandum by Lord Ellenborough in SU Wellington Papers WP1/1004/19.

[32] N. Ó Ciosáin, '"114 Commissions and 60 Committees": Phantom Figures from a Surveillance State', *Proceedings of the Royal Irish Academy*, 109C (2009), 367–81.

[33] Westmorland to Pitt, 12 October 1790, C[ambridge] U[niversity] L[ibrary] Pitt (Pretyman) Papers Add. MS 6958/856; Auckland to Beresford, 28 August 1799, BL Auckland Papers Add. MS 34455; Cooke to Auckland, 29 January 1799, [W. Eden] Bishop of Bath and Wells, *Journal and Correspondence of William, Lord Auckland*, 4 vols (London, 1861–2), iv. 82; Cornwallis to Ross, 11 July 1800, *Correspondence of Charles, First Marquis Cornwallis*, ed. Ross, iii. 276–8.

[34] Hardwicke to Yorke, 24 August 1805, A. P. W. Malcomson, *John Foster (1740–1828): The Politics of Improvement and Prosperity* (Dublin, 2011), 202; Vansittart to Redesdale, 22 June 1805, GRO Mitford Papers D2002/3/1/38.

attention to which it is entitled'.[35] In 1806 William Elliot, one of the by-now rapidly rotating chief secretaries, found it difficult to get any kind of hearing when attending parliament in London. Five years later his successor again thought 'Irish affairs ... to be almost forgotten'. Peel always found the cabinet too busy and was once reduced to waving a miniature pike at the Home Secretary in a desperate attempt to catch his attention. Liverpool's motto concerning Ireland might best, Peel felt, be summed up as 'Quieta non Movere'.[36] As a result, Irish legislation was sometimes so badly drafted and based on so partial an understanding as to be entirely ineffective.[37]

Within parliament itself Irish law-making enjoyed the unusual, even contradictory, distinction of bulking relatively large while occupying less time than this might suggest. It is also clear that, *pace* promises of assimilating laws on a United Kingdom basis, the proportion of specifically Irish bills enacted was higher in the years up to 1830 than in the following decades. More generally, given the widespread, sometimes implied sometimes explicit, promise that the Union would 'set in train a process of assimilating English and Irish law, parliament's early achievements in this regard do not greatly impress'.[38] Nor were the, admittedly fitful, attempts (notably by Redesdale) to align the legal systems of England and Ireland any more successful.[39] Indeed, even after certain undoubted quasi-legal alignments had been brought about by the Union (as when the fifth article laid down that 'the Churches of England and Ireland, as now by law established, be united into one Protestant Episcopal Church, to be called the United Church of England and Ireland'), the resulting reality often fell well short of expectations. Thus in 1807 Bishop O'Beirne of Meath was getting hot under the collar about all the talk from supposedly 'informed persons' about 'the Church of Ireland as if it were still something separate and distinct', though he was no less disturbed to find that the bad old habit of appointing Englishmen to Irish dioceses was still in full

---

[35] Littlehales to Hardwicke, 22 September 1801, BL Hardwicke Papers Add. MS 35720; Hardwicke to Yorke, 15 November 1804, ibid., Add. MS 35706; to Pitt, 14 November 1804 and 12 January 1805, TNA Pitt Papers PRO 30/8/328; to Pitt, 3 February 1805, BL Hardwicke Papers Add. MS 35710.

[36] Elliot to Trail, 8 October 1806, NLS Elliot of Wells Papers MS 12913; Wellesley Pole to Richmond, 15 March 1811, NLI Richmond Papers MS 65; Peel to Whitworth, 6 November and 6 December 1813, 11 April 1814, CKS Whitworth Papers U269/0225/2, 3, 4.

[37] Peel to Flint, 1 September 1814, *Sir Robert Peel from his Private Papers*, ed. Parker, i. 96; K. T. Hoppen, 'An Incorporating Union? British Politicians and Ireland 1800–1830', *English Historical Review*, 123 (2008), 343–4; Hoppen, *Elections, Politics, and Society in Ireland 1832–1885* (Oxford, 1984), 1–33.

[38] T. A. Spalding, *Federation and Empire: A Study in Politics* (London, 1896), 49, 73; J. Innes, 'Legislating for Three Kingdoms: How the Westminster Parliament Legislated for England, Scotland and Ireland, 1707–1830', in J. Hoppit (ed.), *Parliaments, Nations and Identities in Britain and Ireland, 1660–1850* (Manchester, 2003), 37.

[39] Abbot to Hardwicke, 1 and 4 February 1802, GRO Mitford Papers D2002/3/2/7; J. Pollock to A. Wellesley, 30 June 1807, SU Wellington Papers WP1/170/73.

swing.[40] As regards the latter point, he found himself whistling in the wind, for it remained the common view among English politicians that the Irish church was sclerotic and ineffective, its supine dependence on 'the strong arm of government' making the presence of superior English ecclesiastics unavoidable if laxities and corruptions were ever to be overcome. Nor was O'Beirne's case rendered any the stronger by the fact that his (Irish) episcopal colleagues included too many feeble performers, not least Bishop Jocelyn of Clogher, who was deprived of his see for having been discovered in a London public house in what a contemporary newspaper delicately described as 'a situation with a private in the Foot Guards, to which we will not more minutely allude'.[41]

What is so striking about all of this is that British politicians in general, not excluding even the responsible cabinet ministers, seem almost to have gloried in their lack of interest in and knowledge of Irish affairs. Certainly their insouciance is remarkable, for, as Richard Brinsley Sheridan pointed out in 1807, being 'unacquainted with the affairs of Ireland' before the Union was one thing, 'but after the event, such a declaration was as ridiculous as to say they knew nothing about Middlesex or Yorkshire'. Ridiculousness did not, however, prove any barrier to almost deliberate ignorance. Spencer Perceval, for example, claimed to believe that the building of more Anglican churches would alone solve all Hibernian problems.[42] Addington, throughout his career, seems to have possessed the attention span of a gnat when it came to Ireland, declaring blandly in 1812 that, alas, he 'had not of late attended with any great minuteness to what was going on in Ireland' and in 1818 choosing to be at the seaside in Weymouth rather than briefing a new chief secretary about to leave for Dublin. By 1822 he had given up entirely on 'that noble but unhappy country', convinced that no amount of application could produce any change in its 'temper, disposition, and condition'. Wellington felt the same in 1826, as did Pelham when Home Secretary in 1803. And, when Portland held the same office, he made no bones about the fact that he 'always found Ireland a dinner bell at the cabinet'. Liverpool, prime minister for almost fifteen years, seems to have sustained a state of invincible ignorance and needed careful coaching in discussions of Irish legislation.[43]

---

[40] O'Beirne's Memorandum, [c.6 November 1807], SU Wellington Papers WP1/177/23/2.

[41] Redesdale to Addington, 17 September 1802, DRO Sidmouth Papers 152M/C1802/OI/53; Hawkesbury to A. Wellesley, 6 May 1807, SU Wellington Papers WP1/166/83; K. T. Hoppen, *Ireland since 1800: Conflict and Conformity*, 2nd edn (London, 1999), 78.

[42] Parl. Deb. 1: ix. 1093–4 (7 August 1807); D. Gray, *Spencer Perceval: The Evangelical Prime Minister 1762–1812* (Manchester, 1963), 146.

[43] Wickham to Hardwicke, 8 April 1802, BL Hardwicke Papers Add. MS 35713; Parl. Deb. 1: xxi. 425 (31 January 1812); Sidmouth to Grant, 21 August 1818, TNA HO 100/195; to Wellesley, 24 December 1822, BL Wellesley Papers Add. MS 37300; *The Journal of Mrs Arbuthnot*, ed. F. Bamford and Duke of Wellington, 2 vols (London, 1950), i. 134 (5 January 1822); Hardwicke to Pelham, 24 May 1803, DRO Sidmouth Papers 152M/C1803/OZ/297; Redesdale to Sidmouth, 24 September 1813, TNA HO 100/172; B. Jenkins, *Henry Goulburn 1784–1856: A Political Biography* (Liverpool, 1996), 149.

And so, in a moment, in the twinkling of an eye, all ideas of planned, as opposed to emergency, assimilation sank beneath the post-Union waves, as politicians repeatedly emphasized that the vast differences between Britain and Ireland must, at least for the time being, mean that all the fine promises of 1799–1800 remain exactly that, fine promises. After all, even in the 1790s key figures such as Grenville, Portland, Camden, and Cooke had already spent a good deal of time denying that 'what is right and expedient to be done here will be expedient to be done in Ireland under circumstances so extremely different'.[44] And, then, the same people that had privately held such sentiments but had publicly orated about incorporation all round, suddenly woke up on 1 January 1801 to find that their private thoughts had been right all along. Yes, Ireland was totally different, they once again started telling themselves and the world at large. 'Whoever looks at Ireland with English eyes', announced the angriest of all the English exiles in Dublin (Lord Chancellor Redesdale) in May 1802, 'and thinks of Ireland with English opinions only, will fall into many errors'. Indeed, he himself, as he now admitted, had been obliged to pursue legal stratagems of a brutality that would have been quite 'improper in England' but was 'unquestionably necessary here'. And why? Because 'the people of Ireland are not yet fitted to receive all the benefits of the English constitution'.[45] That great waverer and minister in the All the Talents administration, William Windham, saw Ireland in 1807, not only as different, but so much so as to be considered no more than a distant 'out-post' of the metropolitan centre. Liverpool found Ireland so aberrant and baffling that he concluded it 'a political phenomenon not influenced by the same feelings as appear to affect mankind in other countries'.[46] And in this judgement the prime minister proved an apt pupil of his able and opinionated chief secretary Robert Peel, whose long period in that office (1812–18) might most accurately be understood as having operated under the banner 'Hibernia Sui Generis'. The importance of telling MPs that 'Ireland was not England' and was 'not to be governed as England is' may have seemed universally recognized, but Peel felt that it needed very frequent saying all the same. 'It is really fit that they should know a little better than they do the difference between England and Ireland.' Assimilation, he believed, could be no more than a remote prospect,

---

[44] Grenville to Westmorland, 24 March 1791, G. O'Brien, *Anglo-Irish Politics in the Age of Grattan and Pitt* (Dublin, 1987), 161; Portland to Camden, 13 October 1795 and 29 August 1796, T[rinity] C[ollege] D[ublin] Camden Papers MSS 1762 and 1763; Camden to Portland, 3 April 1797, ibid., MS 1763; Cooke to Castlereagh, 13 November 1799, CUL Pitt (Pretyman) Papers Add. MS 6958/2544; [Cobbett's] *Parliamentary History*, xxxiv. 689 (19 March 1799).

[45] Redesdale to Eldon, 29 May 1802, H. Twiss, *The Public and Private Life of Lord Chancellor Eldon, with Selections from his Correspondence*, 3 vols (London, 1844), i. 431; to Sidmouth, 19 April 1806, DRO Sidmouth Papers 152M/C1806/OI/8; also to Addington, 21 and 30 July 1803 and 24 January 1806, ibid., C1803/OZ/109, C1803/OZ/68, C1806/OI/1.

[46] Parl. Deb. 1: ix. 1210 (13 August 1807); Liverpool to Peel, 28 January 1816, BL Peel Papers Add. MS 40181.

profoundly to be wished for perhaps, but for the present wholly impossible.[47] Peel's close friend and successor as chief secretary, Henry Goulburn, thought MPs still needed reminding that Ireland's peculiarities forbade assimilation. The members of the Select Committee on the Employment of the Poor in Ireland found that country in 1822 an 'exception to the general rule'. Seven years later Wellington took precisely the same view.[48] By then the concrete existence of deep Anglo-Irish differences had, indeed, become a cliché of the day,[49] though rarely one that was analysed much beyond references to Catholicism, Irish primitivism, or innate Anglo-Saxon superiority.

Nor could isolated flamboyant gestures of an integrative kind do much to disguise such attitudes, certainly not the visit of George IV in 1821, an event more remarkable for its air of Ruritanian farce than for anything more substantial. Much has been made of the king's visit to Scotland orchestrated by Sir Walter Scott into a feast of highlandolatory, but he came to Ireland first (and then to Hanover) before heading north. At least Dublin was spared the kilt and the flesh-coloured tights, though George did sport 'a rosette, composed of Shamrock of more than twice the size of a military cockade'.[50] Accompanied by Castlereagh and Sidmouth, he was predictably greeted by raucous enthusiasm. He announced that his heart had always been Irish, received Catholic bishops wearing their full canonicals, and made his visit tolerable by being drunk much of the time. But, while Scotland may well have registered some integrative results, all that happened in Ireland was that the port of Dunleary, from which the king departed, was renamed Kingstown.

III

Given that this was so, it should perhaps have occasioned small surprise that the Union did not usher in the nirvana some had talked about during its progress through the two parliaments. Practice diverged sharply from promise. Those who had always hoped it might mean something substantial in the way of psychological change and denominational adjustment—Cornwallis

---

[47] Parl. Deb. 1: xxxii. 922 (27 February 1816); Peel to Whitworth, 28 February 1816, *Sir Robert Peel from his Private Papers*, ed. Parker, i. 210; to Liverpool, 20 October 1813, BL Liverpool Papers Add. MS 38195.

[48] Parl. Deb. 2: ix. 1283–4 (26 June 1823); Jenkins, *Era of Emancipation*, 208; Wellington to Northumberland, 16 July 1829, AC Northumberland Papers DNP/72.

[49] T. C. Croker, *Researches in the South of Ireland* (London, 1824), 2.

[50] S. J. Connolly, 'Union Government, 1812–23', in W. E. Vaughan (ed.), *A New History of Ireland V: Ireland under the Union I, 1801–70* (Oxford, 1989), 67–9; J. H. Murphy, *Abject Loyalty: Nationalism and Monarchy in Ireland during the Reign of Queen Victoria* (Cork, 2001), 7–9.

notably, but also Castlereagh—could hardly have been surprised, though they might well have been disappointed. Those who simply went on pointing to Ireland's continuing and probably incorrigible peculiarities were joined by others—many of whom might well be described as 'the usual suspects'—who pointed just as readily to the Union's failure to inaugurate the much-vaunted process of assimilation. In 1812 Henry Grattan asked: 'Where is the consolidation? Where is the common interest? Where is the heart that should animate the whole?' Ireland had, according to Lord Grenville, unreflectingly been denied all the promises of integrated consideration made in 1799–1800.[51] There was, indeed, no lack of men eager to demonstrate that the assimilationist emperor seemed to be very naked indeed, though few went so far as the politically eccentric Lord Byron, who bid 'Adieu to the Union so-called as "Lucus a non lucendo", an union from never uniting ... [an] union of the shark with his prey, the spoiler swallows up his victim, and thus they become one and indivisible'.[52] In similar vein Charles Grant saw the Union as having rendered almost everything in Ireland 'dark'. Other parliamentarians emphasized that Ireland was 'still in feeling and in fact a country foreign to England', that it could not be treated like Sussex or Devon, that its legal framework remained different and strange, and that, therefore, it was rightly and necessarily being governed exactly 'as our slave colonies'. Or, as Gladstone put it many years later, 'the maintenance of the Union between 1800 and 1829 was really a maintenance not by moral agency, but through the agency of force'.[53]

Views of this sort (echoed in Edward Wakefield's important two-volume *Account of Ireland* of 1812, where much was made of the fact that the country was still being ruled as 'a distant province' under a Union that was at best 'half effected'[54]), and the realities upon which they were based, were at once the cause and the result of a wider political and administrative disconnection. Irish MPs and peers proved remarkably reluctant to attend parliament in London at all, put off by the expense, the need to nurse their constituencies, and a distinctly lethargic frame of mind regarding the new constitutional dispensation.[55] In the administrative sphere Abbot's early attempts at assimilation proved a complete failure, not least because of their peremptorily Anglo-Saxon

---

[51] Parl. Deb. 1: xxii. 733 (23 April 1812) and xxxiii. 832 (2 April 1816).

[52] Ibid. xxii. 651 (21 April 1812). See J. Beckett, 'Politician or Poet? The 6th Lord Byron in the House of Lords, 1809-13', *Parliamentary History*, 34 (2015), 201–17.

[53] Parl. Deb. 1: xvii. 132 (13 May 1813: Grant); Parl. Deb. 2: ix. 1181–2 (24 June 1823), xii. 230 (10 February 1825: Parnell), xi. 276 (8 April 1824: Lansdowne), vi. 210 (10 February 1822: Buckingham), ix. 1219 (25 October 1823: Hume); Parl. Deb. 4: x. 1600 (6 April 1893: Gladstone).

[54] E. Wakefield, *An Account of Ireland, Statistical and Political*, 2 vols (London, 1812), ii. 326. See also G. C. Lewis, *On Local Disturbances in Ireland; and on the Irish Church Question* (London, 1836), 31.

[55] P. Jupp, *The First Duke of Wellington in an Irish Context* (Southampton, 1997), 12; Jupp, 'Irish MPs at Westminster in the Early-Nineteenth Century', in J. C. Beckett (ed.), *Historical Studies: Papers Read before the Irish Conference of Historians*, vii (1969), 80.

character and the bitter opposition of both pro- and anti-unionists in Ireland. As a result, the Dublin Castle machinery simply trundled along in its old grooves or got lost in so complex a web of confusion that no one, least of all a succession of bemused chief secretaries (Peel alone partially excepted), had any clear idea of what was going on or what indeed he himself was supposed to be doing.[56]

Even in those areas that sometimes generated contemporary and later claims that some kind of alignment was taking place, all was not as it at first seemed. Military assimilation looked superficially impressive but turned out to be largely window dressing undertaken to please the king and the Duke of York. It amounted to this: the viceroy lost much (but not all) of his military patronage, and the post of commander-in-chief in Ireland was replaced by that of commander of the forces. But while, as a result, a 'uniformity of system' was now assumed to exist, with Ireland becoming a mere military 'district', in practice much remained the same. As Hardwicke pointed out in January 1803, 'though the army in Ireland is part of the British army, yet the situation of the two countries is totally different; and after the rebellion [of 1798] from which Ireland escaped, it cannot be expected to subside at once into the same state of tranquillity and confidence which is happily enjoyed in England'.[57] And, although the Union had been aimed at avoiding the dangers of divided authority, in military matters it soon became apparent that theoretical assimilation was no cure for the divergent imperatives presented by Britain, on the one hand, and Ireland, on the other.[58]

While economics in general and finance in particular constituted the jewels in the distinctly pinchbeck incorporative crown, they did so, not so much because of deliberate intent, but largely because sudden emergencies precluded the leisurely inaction that had marked the years immediately before the Union. Even so, in 1801 London complained that it was actually receiving less information about Irish revenue and expenditure than had been the case in the 1790s. Nor by 1803 had any real efforts been made to prevent Ireland from following idiosyncratic policies with regard to the taxation of exports in general and corn exports in particular.[59] Seven years after the Union the

---

[56] 'A *Volley of Execrations*', ed. Fleming and Malcomson, 429–41, 445; D. Kanter, *The Making of British Unionism, 1740–1848: Politics, Government and the Anglo-Irish Constitutional Relationship* (Dublin, 2009), 123; Eldon to Redesdale, [*c.* August 1802], GRO Mitford Papers D2002/3/1/23; Long to Redesdale, 15 September [1805], ibid., D2002/3/1/21; K. Whelan, 'The Other Within: Ireland, Britain and the Act of Union', in D. Keogh and K. Whelan (eds), *Acts of Union: The Causes, Contexts and Consequences of the Act of Union* (Dublin, 2001), 30.

[57] Hardwicke to Addington, 11 January 1803, BL Hardwicke Papers Add. MS 35702; Yorke to Hardwicke, 18 June 1801, ibid., Add. MS 35701; Sir H. Taylor to Canning, 21 June 1827, SU Wellington Papers WP1/908/13.

[58] A. Blackstock, 'The Union and the Military, 1801–c.1830', *Transactions of the Royal Historical Society*, 6th series, x (2000), 333–41.

[59] Vansittart to Abbot, 10 September [1801], TNA Abbot Papers PRO 30/9/120; Pelham to Hardwicke, 31 January 1803, BL Hardwicke Papers Add. MS 35770.

Irish Board of Excise as an organization still differed fundamentally from its British counterpart, the chief secretary (Arthur Wellesley) arguing that Ireland required the continuation of a tax regime at once distinct and distinctly more moderate in its impositions. So much for Pitt's original view of April 1799 (supported by Cornwallis) that the income tax should promptly be extended to Ireland once the Union had become law.[60]

What eventually and rather suddenly produced a shift in gear was the fact that the expectations of Castlereagh and Pitt (here relying on projections made by Cooke) as to the respective 'burdens' to be carried in war and peace by Britain and Ireland respectively proved very wide of the mark. The Irish debt increased far more quickly than the British because Britain found unexpected capacities for sustaining high levels of taxation, with the result that the unavoidable financial amalgamation that took place in 1817 did so at a time and in a manner that none had foreseen: although Irish taxation had doubled since 1801, the Irish debt had quadrupled.[61] Quite simply, the French wars had wrecked the financial provisions of the Union. Already in 1812 the annual interest on the Irish debt exceeded Ireland's net permanent revenue, so that by 1816 the Irish Exchequer was virtually bankrupt. Yet, despite all this, even after the merging of the exchequers in 1817, Ireland still retained a kind of separate mini-budget with respect to the costs of civil administration and grants for a range of charities and other entities inherited from pre-Union days.[62]

Some further consequential amalgamations necessarily followed with regard to customs and excise (1823), stamps (1827), and the Post Office (1831), yet very substantial fiscal differences remained. Attempts to extend to Ireland 'English' imposts such as the property tax and the window tax failed. Indeed, although Irish tax levels were ramped up in a desperate attempt to meet wartime expenses, Ireland was never subjected to the important land tax, while its version of the so-called assessed taxes levied on luxuries of various kinds remained lower and markedly different from the British equivalent.

---

[60] Wellesley to Hawkesbury, 13 November 1807, SU Wellington Papers WP1/178/42; to Foster, 23 December 1807, ibid., WP1/181/24; to Wellesley Pole, 5 September 1810, *Supplementary Despatches and Memoranda of Field Marshal Arthur Duke of Wellington*, ed. [2nd] Duke of Wellington, 15 vols (London, 1858–72), vi. 587–8; Pitt to Castlereagh, 7 April 1799, *Memoirs and Correspondence of Viscount Castlereagh, Second Marquess of Londonderry*, ed. Charles Vane [3rd] Marquess of Londonderry, 12 vols (London, 1848–53), ii. 250; Castlereagh to Pitt, 14 April 1799, ibid. ii. 271.

[61] Malcomson, *John Foster (1740–1828)*, 159, 175–6, 244–6.

[62] Kanter, *The Making of British Unionism*, 151–3; D. S. Johnson and L. Kennedy, 'Nationalist Historiography and the Decline of the Irish Economy: George O'Brien Revisited', in S. Hutton and P. Stewart (eds), *Ireland's Histories: Aspects of State, Society and Ideology* (London, 1991), 18–19; P. Jupp, *British Politics on the Eve of Reform: The Duke of Wellington's Administration 1828–30* (London, 1998), 156. Currency amalgamation in 1826 proved a notably damp squib involving little more than an alteration in the unit of account. See G. L. Barrow, *The Emergence of the Irish Banking System 1820–1845* (Dublin, 1975), 29.

At no point in the French wars was the income tax extended to Ireland; indeed, even after its British reimposition in 1842, Ireland was exempted for a further eleven years.[63] The Irish looked at their debts and complained; the British at their tax levels and did likewise. Wellington when prime minister slapped down an aristocratic protest from Ireland by pointing out that 'Irish gentlemen must not suppose that the immense advantages enjoyed by Ireland are not calculated and that Ireland can long be exempt from bearing her part of the burthen'.[64] As ever, perspectives altered cases.

While, therefore, the failed Abbot reforms experienced a sort of low-key afterlife through the absorption of certain (mostly 'financial') Irish departments into their cross-channel equivalents and sporadic doses of fashionable 'economical reform' all round, this was never part of any distinctly integrationist drive. Indeed, the whole business coexisted comfortably with its direct opposite, especially in the fields of welfare, education, policing, and economic development, where a recognition of peculiarly Irish circumstances generated very un-British administrative activities. Hence the creation of various boards of commissioners under the authority of the lord lieutenant, no less than ten being established in the thirty years after the Union (though not all survived until 1830). With responsibility for such matters as navigation, employment, public health, education, and charitable bequests, these constituted a distinctly Hibernian *démarche*. If this was assimilation as proclaimed in 1799–1800, then ordinary words had lost their meaning.

What helped to underpin this direction of travel in the immediate post-Union period was the continued existence of separate administrations and administrative machines in London and Dublin, a state of things that was both a generator and a beneficiary of Anglo-Irish distinctiveness—as Pelham had predicted in 1801. The phrase 'the Irish government' marches through the political discourse of the time, while its near cousins 'the Irish cabinet' and 'Irish ministers' remained in common use to identify the viceroy, chief secretary, undersecretary, and a coterie of legal and other advisors at Dublin Castle.[65] In 1821 the lord lieutenant, Talbot, talked about 'his government'

---

[63] See D. Kanter's important 'The Politics of Irish Taxation, 1842–53', *English Historical Review*, 127 (2012), 1121–55; also *Report from the Select Committee on Taxation of Ireland*, H[ouse of] C[ommons Paper] 1865 (330), xii. 8; M. Daunton, *Trusting Leviathan: The Politics of Taxation in Britain, 1799–1914* (Cambridge, 2001), 44; S. Dowell, *A History of Taxation and Taxes in England*, 2nd edn, 4 vols (London, 1888, repr. 1965), ii. 274–5, iii. 158–9.

[64] Wellington to Downshire, 1 June 1830, SU Wellington Papers WP1/1122/3; also Clancarty to Wellington, 16 July 1824, ibid., WP1/796/8.

[65] See, e.g., Redesdale to Addington, 16 January 1803, DRO Sidmouth Papers 152M/C1803/OZ/383; to Yorke, 18 August 1803, BL Hardwicke Papers Add. MS 45037; Auckland to Beresford, 4 October 1804, *Correspondence of the Right Hon. John Beresford*, ed. Beresford, ii. 298; Wellesley Pole in Parl. Deb. 1: xvii. 203* (30 May 1810); Sidmouth to Richmond, 6 October 1812, NLI Richmond Papers MS 63; Peel to Whitworth, 18 May 1814, CKS Whitworth Papers U269/0225/5; Sidmouth to Grant, 21 August 1818, TNA HO 100/195; Peel to Goulburn,

as opposed to 'the British government'. Indeed, for the Home Secretary too, Talbot was 'the head ... of the Irish government', just as Liverpool was the 'head of the British'.[66] Of course, London's was the ultimate and superior authority, as Spencer Perceval (then Chancellor of the Exchequer) forcefully pointed out in 1808, though Dublin was by no means unwilling to strike out in directions of which London either did not approve or was never told.[67] And, far from any anticipated incorporation reducing the size of the administrative apparatus in Dublin, the very opposite occurred, as the number of civil servants in Ireland grew by more than 40 per cent in the years between 1797 and 1829 to a size that one authority has judged 'more appropriate to a separate kingdom' than to an integral part of a larger polity.[68]

Contemporaries quickly realized that, in some respects, the Union had in truth passed almost unnoticed over the deep structures of Irish administrative and political life. In 1812 the idiosyncratic but influential MP C. W. Wynn complained to the Commons that, while the 'main recommendation' for the Union had been that 'henceforward there should be one state, one parliament, and one cabinet', the chief secretary 'was constantly imagining that Ireland was a separate kingdom, of which the Duke of Richmond was king, and himself prime minister'.[69] Much later, in the 1870s, when very different political melodies were being played, Tory commentators were equally quick to blame the very incompleteness of the Union for existing Hibernian discontents: no real incorporation had taken place, a mere 'mockery of royalty was maintained', and Ireland was being left to hang, as it were, between proper union and colonial dependency.[70]

Even the precise form of government so casually allocated in 1800 proved at best difficult to operate, at worst a rickety and half-hearted continuation of what had existed previously. With Irish MPs now sitting in London, the Dublin administration gave forth a Janus-like air, looking now across the Irish Sea, now restlessly examining its own navel. Ireland's 'remoteness' had been wheeled out as a reason (when, that is, reasons had been provided at all) for retaining the viceroy, chief secretary, and their appendages. And, indeed, Anglo-Irish travelling in the early nineteenth century was not for the

2 February 1822, SHC Goulburn Papers 304/36; Wellington to Peel, 14 July 1829, SU Wellington Papers WP1/1035/32.

[66] Talbot to Sidmouth, 6 November 1821, SRO Talbot Papers D649/9/3; Sidmouth to Talbot, 10 September 1819, TNA HO 100/197.

[67] Perceval to Foster, 9 April 1808, Malcomson, *John Foster (1740–1828)*, 239; Gray, *Spencer Perceval*, 416; Bartlett, *The Fall and Rise of the Irish Nation*, 321.

[68] Jupp, *British Politics on the Eve of Reform*, 113–14, 155.

[69] Parl. Deb. 1: xxi. 613–14 (3 February 1812); also Sir H. Parnell in Parl. Deb. 2: ix. 1182 (24 June 1823).

[70] Anon., 'The Home Rule Agitation', *Dublin University Magazine*, 73/496 (1874), 478; H. L. Jephson, 'Irish Statute Law Reform', *Journal of the Statistical and Social Inquiry Society of Ireland*, 7 (1878–9), 376.

faint-hearted, though mental distance proved at least as important as its geographical counterpart. In rough weather sea crossings could take an age. Redesdale was on board for twenty-two hours in May 1805, kept sentient by large doses of brandy and wine. In August 1815 even Peel's *summer* passage from Holyhead took a heroic thirty-three hours, during which 'the men were all sick, and the women and children thought they were going to the bottom'. But the pressure for travelling was unremitting, and Peel undertook no less than nine such journeys during his first two years as chief secretary.[71]

When added to the other perceived drawbacks of service in Ireland—dealing with endless petitions, with violent unrest, with 'corruption', with broken promises, with inefficiency, with bad weather, with ingratitude, in short, dealing with the Irish generally—travelling helped to make the task of governing Hibernia all too much like an unrelieved bed of nails. Feeling 'demob. happy' soon became the default stance of those contemplating the end of their terms. Hardwicke looked forward to departure 'as a man who is tired of the toils and labours of the world' and yearns 'for relief from his misery'. Peel could not wait in 1818 to be once again 'free as air ... from the ten thousand engagements which I cannot fulfil ... from the perpetual converse about the Harbour of Howth and Dublin Bay haddock'. Eight years later Goulburn bleakly described himself as holding 'the most disagreeable office under Government'.[72] Nor were things rendered any easier by the manner in which London ministries made no real effort to define the powers and responsibilities of the senior posts in the Dublin administration. Even the relationship between viceroys and chief secretaries remained vague, with prime ministers like Liverpool blandly declining to offer guidance of any kind on a matter they found distant and uninteresting.[73]

The Home Office in London, the department supposedly 'in charge' of Irish affairs, proved both inconsistent and intermittent in its attentions. With a total staff of only twenty-two as late as 1829, this is perhaps unsurprising, though successive Home Secretaries insisted upon their authority with regard to Ireland while doing little to make it a reality.[74] Newly-appointed Irish ministers were rarely given useful briefings beyond the vapid and formulaic memoranda issued to viceroys, which could, in Northumberland's case, take

[71] Redesdale to Vansittart, 24 May 1805, BL Vansittart Papers Add. MS 31229; Peel to Croker, 8 August 1815, *The Croker Papers*, ed. Jennings, i. 75.

[72] Hardwicke to Yorke, 13 March [1806], BL Hardwicke Papers Add. MS 35706; Peel to Croker, [c. June 1818], *The Croker Papers*, ed. Jennings, i. 116; Jenkins, *Henry Goulburn*, 174.

[73] Peel to Liverpool, 31 October 1816, BL Peel Papers Add. MS 40292; Liverpool to Peel, 4 October 1813, ibid., Add. MS 40181.

[74] Jupp, *The Governing of Britain 1688–1848: The Executive, Parliament and the People* (London, 2006), 138; F. and W. Wickwire, *Cornwallis: The Imperial Years* (Chapel Hill, NC, 1980), 233; Hardwicke to Yorke, 20 August 1801, BL Hardwicke Papers Add. MS 35771; Wickham to Redesdale, 4 May 1802, HRO Wickham Papers 38M49/5/6; Bathurst to Richmond, 15 February 1812, NLI Richmond Papers MS 70.

twenty-four elegantly penned pages to say precisely nothing at all. Sometimes they were not even told with which London office they should communicate.[75] At times, indeed, useful communication between London and Dublin collapsed completely, with bitter recriminations and grim jokes traded back and forth, one viceroy being described by Wellington when prime minister as having 'gone mad. He is bit by a mad Papist.'[76] Individuals within the Irish administration fell out among themselves with equal vigour. Marquess Wellesley, when viceroy, thought the chief secretary (Goulburn) 'a most narrow minded silly dilly'. Wellesley himself (widely considered the sad wreck of a once dynamic politico) moaned self-pityingly about being obliged to 'submit to the kicks of the ass and the dirt of the donkey … degraded, vilified, an object of scorn and detestation, without protection or even care'.[77] Richmond, who impressed even local topers by his habitual drunkenness, was at daggers drawn with his chief secretary Wellesley-Pole. The curious policy of appointing viceroys and chief secretaries with diametrically opposed views on leading issues of the day—examples are Talbot (backwoods Tory) and Grant (inefficient 'liberal') 1818–21 and Wellesley (erratic 'progressive') and Goulburn (flinty Peel clone) 1821–7—sacrificed efficiency to platonic aspirations for political 'balance'. As a result, rather than being required to enforce a considered policy, ministers in Ireland were allowed to drift off along idiosyncratic paths of their own choosing. Some proved hyperactive like Abbot, others aloof and lackadaisical like his successor Elliot, who combined the office (1806–7) with a debilitating unwillingness to have any 'intercourse with Irishmen'. Grant (1818–21) seems on occasion to have taken more than three months to reply to important letters from the Home Office. Lamb, the future Melbourne, coasted along (1827–8), but was at least considered to be 'inactive with style', while Wellington, when chief secretary (1807–9), was so busy pursuing a military career abroad that his impact was at best fitful, at worst non-existent.[78]

[75] N. Gash, *Mr Secretary Peel: The Life of Sir Robert Peel to 1830* (London, 1961), 378; Talbot to Sidmouth, 7 September 1819, TNA HO 100/197; Sidmouth to Talbot, 10 September 1819, ibid.; for viceroys' 'Instructions', see Richmond's of 1807 in NLI Richmond Papers MS 60 and Northumberland's of 1829 in AC Northumberland Papers DNP/70.

[76] Palmerston's Journal for Autumn 1828, in E. Ashley, *The Life and Correspondence of Henry John Temple, Viscount Palmerston*, 2 vols (London, 1879), i. 182; Wellington to Anglesey, 19 November 1828, PRONI Anglesey Papers D619/26A/41; [7th] Marquess of Anglesey, *One-Leg: The Life and Letters of Henry William Paget, First Marquess of Anglesey K.G. 1768–1854* (London, 1961), 210.

[77] Wellesley to Wellington, 25 August 1826, SU Wellington Papers WP1/860/22; to Plunket, 19 March 1824, D. Plunket, *The Life, Letters, and Speeches of Lord Plunket*, 2 vols (London, 1867), ii. 145–6.

[78] *Henry Richard [Fox], Lord Holland, Memoirs of the Whig Party during my Time*, ed. Henry Edward [Fox], Lord Holland, 2 vols (London, 1852), ii. 164; Grant to Sidmouth, 3 November 1818, TNA HO 100/195; P. Ziegler, *Melbourne: A Biography of William Lamb, 2nd Viscount Melbourne* (London, 1976), 92. For Arthur Wellesley's military peregrinations, see Long to Wellesley, 12 May 1807, SU Wellington Papers WP1/166/115; Castlereagh to Wellesley, 7 June 1807,

Nor did the London government go out of its way to render service in Ireland either personally or politically attractive. Sometimes, indeed, it treated viceroys with almost casual contempt. The worthy if dull Talbot was sacked in 1821 with, as he put it, 'less time than I would deem it right to turn a servant away', while Anglesey, who admittedly proved irritatingly independent, was widely and semi-publicly ridiculed by ministers and indeed the king.[79] Small wonder that able operators were difficult to find. Few men took the office in order to get rich. While the remuneration was high, the expenses were higher still. Between 1784 and 1812 the salary was £20,000 a year Irish or about £18,500 British; then it rose to £30,000 before falling back to £20,000 British in 1831. A shifting and opaque sum was also provided as a *contribution* towards expenses, as much as £6,232 in 1841.[80] And these sums were very considerable. Hardwicke in 1802 tried to convince Dubliners 'that the Union has produced no alteration [i.e. reduction] in the style of living at the Castle'. It was argued that only a 'regal display' could invest 'the metropolis of Ireland with something of a charm' and make 'the Irish still think they were an independent people'.[81] And, whatever the truth of such dubious claims, successive lords lieutenant threw themselves into the task with, on the whole, remarkable degrees of enthusiasm and expense. Hardwicke devoted many days to entertaining 'in a very laudable Hibernian style'. Talbot, though complaining of being 'dragged to an ordinary dinner and ball, without a single soul there beyond a damn corporation member', put on no less than 88 dinners for peers and 196 for commoners at Dublin Castle in 1818 alone, with yet more free food laid on at the viceregal lodge in Phoenix Park.[82] And, although Marquess Wellesley was so indebted that he spent most of his first viceroyalty 'alone up at the Park, dining with his natural son, Mr [Edward] Johnston, and seeing no creature', Anglesey kicked off by spending £6,000 on viceregal wines and liqueurs and in a single fortnight mounted fourteen dinners, attended another three, and held two drawing-rooms and four

ibid., WP1/170/32; R. Muir, *Wellington: The Path to Victory, 1769–1814* (New Haven, 2013), 189–207, 221–33.

[79] Talbot to Gregory, 10 January 1822, *Mr Gregory's Letter-Box 1813–1835*, ed. Lady Gregory (first published 1898; rev. edn, Gerrards Cross, 1981), 108; George IV to Wellington, 20 November 1828, SU Wellington Papers WP1/967/6; Anglesey to Wellington, 14 November 1828, ibid., WP1/966/13; Wellington to Bathurst, 24 November 1828, Marquess of Anglesey, *One-Leg*, 210.

[80] K. T. Hoppen, 'A Question None could Answer: "What was the Viceroyalty For?" 1800–1921', in P. Gray and O. Purdue (eds), *The Irish Lord Lieutenant c.1541–1922* (Dublin, 2012), 137.

[81] Hardwicke to Addington, 22 July 1802, TNA Pitt Papers PRO 30/8/328; to Hawkesbury, 30 December 1805, TNA HO 100/128; Parl. Deb. 3: iv. 944–6 (7 July 1831).

[82] Corry to Abbot, 10 October 1802, TNA Abbot Papers PRO 30/9/140; Talbot to Gregory, 22 July 1819, PRONI Talbot Papers D4100/1/1; Talbot's entertainment books, SRO Talbot Papers D649/9/7.

balls.[83] It was, indeed, reckoned by those in the know that viceroys spent much more than their nominal salaries, with both Bedford and Richmond each laying out 'upwards of £38,000 per annum'.[84] Others, like the Lord Chancellor of Ireland (on £10,000 a year) and on occasion the chief secretary (on about £4,000 plus travelling expenses), stressed their high-mindedness in accepting offices the incomes of which matched neither anticipated costs nor indeed self-evaluations of their own talents.[85]

Thus did negative pecuniary perceptions compound men's reluctance to cross the Irish Sea. At almost every vacancy there formed a long queue of refusniks until eventually some willing or semi-willing victim agreed to accept. In 1801 Hardwicke was approached after three others had declined. Six years later Richmond emerged only after the Dukes of Beaufort and Rutland had refused. In 1827 the undersecretary noted that 'so many Protestant noblemen have refused the viceroyalty that I fear the king will find it difficult to nominate one'. Nor were chief secretaries any easier to find: hence the rapid turnover, especially in the period 1801–9.[86] Serving viceroys were rarely consulted when chief secretaries were appointed, nor were chief secretaries when new viceroys were being sought.[87] This could produce confusion, even internecine warfare, within the administrative machine, as Charles Long discovered on arriving as chief secretary in October 1805.[88] The result was a tendency (especially in the case of viceroys) to appoint colourful untalented individuals so long as they were rich and willing to sprinkle their wealth generously across the Irish political scene. The bluff military Richmond (later famous for his Brussels ball on the eve of Waterloo) and Bedford, a worshipper at the shrine of Charles James Fox ('that great and good and virtuous man'),[89] were notable examples of the breed. But the grandest, showiest, and most credulous was Hugh Percy, the fabulously wealthy third Duke of Northumberland, viceroy from February

[83] *The Journal of Mrs Arbuthnot*, ed. Bamford and Wellington, i. 157–8; Marquess of Anglesey, *One-Leg*, 185, 371.

[84] Parl. Deb. 1: xvii. 528–9 (7 June 1810); Perceval to Richmond, 28 September 1810, NLI Richmond Papers MS 66; to George III, [30 May 1810], *The Later Correspondence of George III*, ed. A. Aspinall, 5 vols (Cambridge, 1962–70), v. 600.

[85] Mitford (Redesdale) to Addington, 3 February 1802, *The Later Correspondence of George III*, ed. Aspinall, iv. 8–9; Abbot to Addington, 11 March 1801, *Diary and Correspondence of Charles Abbot*, ed. Charles, Lord Colchester, i. 255.

[86] Polden, 'The Domestic Policies of the Addington Administration', 379, 386, 388; Duke of Montrose to Addington, 10 February 1801, DRO Sidmouth Papers 152M/C1801/OZ/37; Elliot to Bedford, 6 April 1807, W[oburn] A[bbey] Bedford Papers Irish Box 1; Gregory to Talbot, 15 June 1827, PRONI Talbot Papers D4100/9/2; *A Political Diary 1828–1830 by Edward Law, Lord Ellenborough*, ed. Lord Colchester, 2 vols (London, 1881), i. 130–3.

[87] Hardwicke to Vansittart, 9 April 1805, BL Vansittart Papers Add. MS 31229; to Pitt, 14 November 1804, TNA Pitt Papers PRO 30/8/328; *Mr Gregory's Letter-Box*, ed. Lady Gregory, 164.

[88] Long to Pitt, [October] 1805, TNA Pitt Papers PRO 30/8/328.

[89] Bedford to H. Grattan, 23 September 1806, WA Bedford Papers Letter-Book B (Irish).

1829 to November 1830, but never to hold public office again. Welcomed sarcastically by a chief secretary (who had been kept in ignorance about his appointment) as one 'who can drive straight into the Castle with his open purse and if it be possible ... [with] a pretty daughter', Northumberland arrived with £90,000-worth of plate and wearing 'all his splendid outfit as ambassador at Paris'.[90] Some thought his appointment verging on the ridiculous, 'for he is a stupid posing man ... as rich as Croesus, fond of magnificence, his wife ... covered with diamonds ... a poor creature, vain, ostentatious and null'. Others simply dismissed him as 'a bore beyond all bores',[91] so feeble that no one, it was said, noticed when he took to his bed for eight days, Northumberland brought the first three post-Union decades to an inglorious end. Unless British standards and norms are somehow to be perceived in his response to a deputation of distressed weavers—an order for a new waistcoat—these no longer possessed even the low levels of traction that had (just possibly) once been the case.[92] The fact that Peel, nonetheless, considered him 'the best chief Governor' who ever held office[93]—because unthinking stolidity and an unquestioning faith in Wellington constituted all that was required—says as much about the cynicism of leading men as about Ireland's place in the contemporary political firmament.

IV

One highly visible phenomenon did, however, claim for Ireland a prominent, if fitful, niche in the political preoccupations of the time: its reputation, often real, sometimes imagined, for violence and unrest of all kinds. While other developments (notably O'Connell's campaigns for Catholic emancipation and repeal of the Union, which until the mid-1840s provided a constant backdrop to ministerial decision-making[94]) changed and oscillated in their power to attract governmental attention, violence, because of its dramatic immediacy but also because of the ready-formed perceptual lenses through which it was scrutinized, was impossible to ignore. Yet, while undoubtedly there was a good deal of it about in post-Union Ireland, levels of violence in parts of contemporary England were far from negligible. But neither the Luddite

[90] *Mr Gregory's Letter-Box*, ed. Lady Gregory, 124; F. M. L. Thompson in *ODNB*; *A Political Diary 1828–1830 by Edward Law*, ed. Lord Colchester, i. 310.
[91] *The Journal of Mrs Arbuthnot*, ed. Bamford and Wellington, ii. 231–2; *The Letters of the Third Viscount Palmerston to Laurence and Elizabeth Sulivan 1804–1863*, ed. K. Bourne, Royal Historical Society Camden Fourth Series, xxiii (1979), 227.
[92] Spring Rice to Lansdowne, 1 September 1829, BL [3rd Marquess of] Lansdowne Papers B95 (provisional reference); *Mr Gregory's Letter-Box*, ed. Lady Gregory, 165.
[93] Gash, *Mr Secretary Peel*, 654.   [94] On O'Connell, see especially Chapters 3 and 4.

machine-breaking of 1811–16 in the English Midlands and North nor the rural disorders in East Anglia in 1822 nor the Swing rioting of 1830, though they produced concern in government circles, ever really generated the iron-fisted panic with which Irish unrest was almost invariably treated.[95] Admittedly Habeas Corpus was suspended in February 1817 for eleven months in England, having been greatly broadened in scope the previous year. It was, however, not suspended there again until 1866 and then only in response to the leakage of Fenian unrest from Ireland.[96] And, while the Six Acts passed after Peterloo in 1819 significantly cut back on civil liberties, governments were usually prepared to react with greater sang-froid when it came to English disturbances than when dealing with those in Ireland. Not only that, but in England parliament and Whitehall were more (though not invariably) willing to delegate the power to control collective protests to local bodies and officials acting within the normal confines of the law.[97] As Sidmouth informed Talbot in October 1821: 'Some risque must be incurred in England for the purpose of putting down an actual and most formidable danger in Ireland; and I am convinced that this can only be done by an overwhelming military force, instantly assembled and instantly deployed.'[98]

When, therefore, ministers looked to Ireland in the post-Union decades, they perceived a country considerably more turbulent than an England itself not consistently notable for quietude, their judgement rendered objectively sharper by the impact of rebellions and agrarian disorder, and subjectively so by ingrained attitudes that injected Irish violence with additional and worrying doses of political anxiety. Thus, if early nineteenth-century Irish crime (not, of course, a direct surrogate for 'disorder') could be said—on a population basis—to have been twice as severe as that in England,[99] contemporary analysts immediately transformed this from an arithmetical to a geometrical

---

[95] P. Horn, *The Rural World 1780–1850: Social Change in the English Countryside* (London, 1980), 167–78; E. J. Hobsbawm and G. Rudé, *Captain Swing* (London, 1969), 253–63; M. I. Thomis, *The Luddites: Machine-Breaking in Regency England* (Newton Abbot, 1970), 145–53; M. Escott, 'Tumult, Riot, and Disturbance: Perspectives on Central and Local Government's Roles in the Management of the 1830 "Captain Swing Riots" in Berkshire', *Southern History*, 32 (2010), 139–58; C. J. Griffin, *The Rural War: Captain Swing and the Politics of Protest* (Manchester, 2012), *passim*.

[96] S. H. Palmer, *Police and Protest in England and Ireland 1780–1850* (Cambridge, 1988), 184–5, 528.

[97] C. Tilly, *Popular Contention in Great Britain 1758–1834* (Cambridge, MA, 1995), 212; Thomis, *The Luddites*, 145.

[98] Sidmouth to Talbot, 23 October 1821, TNA HO 100/201 cited in Palmer, *Police and Protest in England and Ireland*, 224.

[99] As is contended in Palmer, *Police and Protest in England and Ireland*, 45. By the 1860s and 1870s, when data had become a little more reliable, Irish crime levels on a population basis—as measured by indictable offences of all kinds—were lower (but also different in character) from those of England and Wales: see K. T. Hoppen, 'Grammars of Electoral Violence in Nineteenth-Century England and Ireland', *English Historical Review*, 109 (1994), 601–2.

progression and turned 'twice' into 'four times' as severe. What always puzzled and troubled British observers was the nature, if any, of the connection between rural disorder in Ireland—the activities of agrarian secret societies and so forth—and movements of a more directly political nature. With memories of 1798 still fresh, this was indeed a problem to tax the finest minds, though even the finest rarely succeeded in formulating a tolerably convincing or practically applicable analysis.

What cannot be denied is that the post-Union decades experienced a lively continuation of the Whiteboy outbreaks that had commenced in the 1760s and had established many of the patterns of behaviour later to become commonplace: oath-bound secret societies, intimidation of those perceived to have offended against some kind of popular social and economic code, above all, an obsession with 'property' or at least 'occupation' rights, mainly, but not exclusively, in land. By the time of the Union two versions of disorder predominated: primarily agrarian movements in Munster and parts of Leinster and more distinctly (though by no means exclusively) sectarian ones especially in the Ulster borderlands. Yet, cutting across such distinctions, the major outbreaks of the early nineteenth century were shaped, not only by an established rhetoric and methodology of protest, but also by the changing imperatives of different locations and different times. From the perspective of London, it was, above all, the frequency of unrest that gave cause for concern: the Threshers in north-east Connacht in 1806–7, the Shanavests and Caravats in Munster in 1809–11, the east-Leinster Carders in 1813–16, the so-called Ribbon protests in Clare and Westmeath in 1819–20, the Munster Rockites of 1819–23, the Leinster Whitefeet of 1830–4, and the Clare Terry Alts of 1831–2.[100] While such outbreaks were worrying in themselves, when they were viewed within the perspective and memory of the rebellions of 1798 and 1803 the greater worry was that agrarian violence might more and more closely become harnessed to overtly political ends.

What this generated was legislation far more repressive than in Britain: in 1800 suspension of Habeas Corpus and an act for suppressing rebellion, continued into 1801, revived in 1803, continued into 1804; in 1807 an Insurrection Act, continued into 1810, revived in 1814, continued into 1817, revived in 1822, and continued into 1825, in which year came another Act for suppressing dangerous associations valid until 1828, with further enactments planned for 1829.[101] Indeed, in the matter of violence, the purportedly assimilationist agenda of the Union seems to have possessed no purchase at all, with ministerial opinion and practice experiencing little development or

---

[100] Hoppen, *Ireland since 1800: Conflict and Conformity*, 49–50.

[101] Gash, *Mr Secretary Peel*, 572. See also *A New History of Ireland VIII: A Chronology*, ed. T. W. Moody, F. X. Martin, and F. J. Byrne (Oxford, 1982), 295–310; Hoppen, 'An Incorporating Union?', 349; R. B. O'Brien, *Dublin Castle and the Irish People*, 2nd edn (London, 1912), 59.

change during the thirty years or so after the rebellion of 1798. Instead, the notion that Ireland's continuing violence demanded special solutions of a distinctly un-English kind became an all-pervasive commonplace of political discourse and communication. So often was it explicitly stated that its implicit embedment within the belief system of Britain's political class became very deep indeed. That it needed stating—both privately and publicly—so often was not, therefore, because repetition alone could render it a truth universally acknowledged, but because, in the absence of any alternative analysis or policy, repression had become the only administrative technique seen to be capable of handling the central dilemma of Irish government.

An emphasis upon Irish violence was, therefore, the outward and visible manifestation of those attitudes of distance, ignorance, and prejudice that have already been discussed. That its roots, of course, long predated the Union gave it, if anything, additional vigour and force. What, nonetheless, needs saying is that the Union seems to have had virtually no early impact upon its striking intensities. With the 1798 rebellion fresh in men's thoughts, this was not perhaps surprising. But what is crucial to keep in mind is that, with few exceptions, the view of the British political class was that *all* the inhabitants of Ireland were somehow to blame for, at best tolerating, at worst encouraging, 'instances of savage ferocity ... which, God be thanked, are repugnant to the very nature of Englishmen'. Nor was Pitt himself in any way reluctant to demand 'the most vigorous' exertions when it came to Hibernian disorder.[102] The Irish 'malcontents', one and all, were simply 'madmen, and they ought to be treated as such', what with their rebellions, their horrible savagery of 'torture, half-hanging', all of it alien 'to the principles of civilized [that is, British] life'.[103] The Irish, it was being implicitly argued, were, by their own native ferocities, virtually forcing the government to treat them with matching vigour. Who in the world could blame ministers driven to distraction for resorting to the nearest pacificatory instruments to hand (for example, Orangemen), even if these were themselves known to indulge in activities hateful to the finer and more advanced mores of the Anglo-Saxons? Noses simply had to be held while one's repugnant Irish enemies were being kept in check by one's almost equally repugnant Irish 'friends'.

Hence the reliance on the largely Orange yeomanry, especially in the face of possible invasion or widespread insurgency. Hardwicke followed this path from his appointment in 1801 onwards, with the enthusiastic support of Redesdale, who outbid the viceroy in sheer intellectual, linguistic, and sectarian brio by insisting that Ireland could be kept in order only by an exclusively

---

[102] Grenville to Portland, 12 January 1799, H[istorical] M[anuscripts] C[ommission] *Manuscripts of J. B. Fortescue*, iv (1905), 439; Malcomson, *John Foster (1740–1828)*, 125.
[103] [Cobbett's] *Parliamentary History*, xxxv. 1241 (23 March 1801: Townshend) and 1031 (12 March 1801: Whitebread).

'Protestant garrison' commanded, if any such could be found, by 'a Cromwell ... not subject to the control of a cabinet in England'.[104] As viceroy, Richmond scattered appointments among a line of 'strong' and 'red-hot' Protestants, even making Patrick Duigenan, the reddest and hottest of them all, a privy councillor in 1808. Six years later Peel worked hard to keep Protestants and Catholics 'disunited', while Whitworth found solace in the belief that the former could always be persuaded to remain loyal because the latter seemed so keen to annihilate them, a policy of 'differential sectarianism' that lost none of its vigour during the decade or so that followed.[105]

If 1798 provided powerful underpinning for such an approach, Emmet's practically modest but (in the event) rhetorically resonant rising in July 1803 gave it ministerial wings by means of repeated utterances of the powerful phrase 'I told you so'. Hardwicke, who had not anticipated the outbreak, immediately went into martial mode, combining demands for more troops, coercive legislation, and fiercer dispositions all round with spine-chilling warnings that future risings would inevitably be followed by foreign invasion.[106] Not only did the Home Secretary respond enthusiastically, especially regarding coercion, but it is significant that two of the chief secretaries in these years—Wickham and Nepean—were men with 'security' backgrounds.[107] The combination of 1798 and 1803, however different the two events, provided strong support for those already disposed to see the wielding of the sword as the sovereign, perhaps the only, remedy for Ireland's endless discontents.[108]

Talk of 1798 and 1803, however, merely reinforced existing dispositions to see extreme violence as the most obvious manifestation of a distinctiveness created by the primitive and inferior character of Ireland's inhabitants. Politicians and administrators (usually one and the same) conducted a conversation of mutual ghoulishness, constantly pointing to worse and worse

[104] H. Senior, *Orangeism in Ireland and Britain 1795–1836* (London, 1966), 144–5; Redesdale to Abbot, 15 August 1802, *Diary and Correspondence of Charles Abbot*, ed. Charles, Lord Colchester, i. 106–8; to Colchester (as Abbot had become), 30 October 1823, ibid. iii. 303; also T. Bartlett, *Ireland: A History* (Cambridge, 2010), 242–5.

[105] Bartlett, *The Fall and Rise of the Irish Nation*, 290; Peel to Whitworth, 16 June 1814, CKS Whitworth Papers U269/0225/8; R. W. Davis, 'Wellington and the "Open Question": The Issue of Catholic Emancipation 1821–1829', *Albion*, 29 (1997), 43.

[106] Hardwicke to Yorke, 11 April, 28 and 30 July, 17 September, 18 Ocober 1803, BL Hardwicke Papers BL Add. MS 35702 and TNA HO 100/113 and 114; to Hawkesbury, 11 July 1804 and 11 January 1806, BL Hardwicke Papers Add. MSS 35709 and 35710; to Addington, 28 July 1803, ibid., Add. MS 35708; to Pelham, 17 July 1803, TNA HO 100/112.

[107] Hawkesbury to Hardwicke, 2 February 1805, BL Hardwicke Papers Add. MS 35710; M. Durey, 'William Wickham, the Christ Church Connection and the Rise and Fall of the Security Service in Britain, 1793–1801', *English Historical Review*, 121 (2006), 717, 727–8, 737.

[108] Wellesley Pole to Ryder, 23 July 1810, *Eighteenth-Century Irish Official Papers in Great Britain: Private Collections Volume Two*, ed. A. P. W. Malcomson (Belfast, 1990), 103; Peel to Whitworth, 7 July 1814, CKS Whitworth Papers U269/0225/8; Peel to Liverpool, 24 January 1816, *Sir Robert Peel from his Private Papers*, ed. Parker, i. 206–7.

instances of Hibernian depravity. It is striking that even the Foxite Duke of Bedford, who, in some respects, positively oozed goodwill as viceroy (1806–7), nonetheless thought it imperative to lose not a moment in 'preparing repressive legislation as forceful as any enacted by previous administrations'.[109] And why was there so much violent unrest? Well, it was not, in the main, because of poverty and the like but simply because—as Liverpool put it—of 'the customs and disposition' of the Irish people generally. Whitworth, demanding martial law, detected 'a rancorous hatred of Government and such an open defiance of law, as will require all its vigilance and exertion to counteract'.[110] Richmond talked of hanging all and sundry, declared himself 'perfectly ready to meet violence with the utmost exertions', and denounced every concession as simply feeding a tiger that would and could never be satisfied.[111]

V

The most able and eloquent exponent of harsh measures was Peel, who served as chief secretary for an unprecedentedly long term and possessed qualities of application and analysis that impressed his older and more experienced superiors. And certainly, in one respect, his approach differed significantly from that of the other chief secretaries and viceroys of the time. Uniquely Peel made serious attempts to understand and inform himself about the country whose affairs he was charged to manage and control. On appointment he was shocked to find that Dublin Castle possessed no working library that would assist new ministers in reading their way into both the contemporary and the historical aspects of their responsibilities.[112] He immediately set about putting one together and in due course collected well over 1,000 items—pamphlets, books, and periodicals—as the basis of a fund of printed information and wisdom relevant to the task of Irish government. He also asked the Irish topographer and statistician William Shaw Mason to augment this, with the result that a so-called Select Irish Library was put together, consisting of some 300 composite volumes 'uniformly bound in green Morocco', with shamrocks

---

[109] Senior, *Orangeism in Ireland and Britain*, 179; Bedford to Howick, 25 October 1806, DU Grey Papers GRE/B6/17/2; Howick to Bedford, 15 January 1807, ibid., GRE/B6/17/9; Grenville to Bedford, 14 December 1806, WA Bedford Papers Irish Box 1.

[110] Parl. Deb. 1: xxviii. 862 (26 July 1814); Whitworth to Sidmouth, 13 December 1813 and 5 May 1814, CKS Whitworth Papers U269/0218/4 and TNA HO 100/178; also Whitworth to Peel, 11 April 1814, Whitworth Papers U269/0218/5; Whitworth to Sidmouth, 16 June 1814, HO 100/178.

[111] Gray, *Spencer Perceval*, 416; Richmond to Hawkesbury, 7 August 1807, TNA HO 100/142; to Sidmouth, 29 June 1812, HO 100/167.

[112] R. A. Gaunt, *Sir Robert Peel: The Life and Legacy* (London, 2010), 19.

stamped on the spines. Mason even published a catalogue of part of the collection dealing with the writings of authors 'brought down to the year 1820', divided into publications dealing with antiquities, history, biography, topography, statistics, 'tourists', and finance. It was an impressive achievement, and the whole of the resulting enterprise is still kept together in its green bindings in the library of the House of Lords.[113] From it Peel was able to derive information from an extensive range of writers including James Ware, Mervyn Archdall, Richard Stanihurst, John Davies, Charles Vallancey, Roderick O'Flaherty, Charles O'Conor, William Molyneux, William Petty, and Arthur Young, as well as from productions by recent travellers to Ireland, sixteen of them published since the Union.

But, while this was indeed an impressive enterprise and would have left the dedicated reader (and Peel can certainly be awarded high marks for application) with staggeringly detailed insights into Irish mentalités, it seems to have left no great practical impression upon Peel's attitudes and approaches to governing Hibernia. Within months he was—in a striking example of how being cerebral and possessing scholarly resources can sometimes provide more an excuse for prejudice than a tool for enlightenment—delivering himself of exactly the same views and 'insights' as those that had by then become the common Irish coin of British politicians generally.

Thus, for the young Peel, as for so many others, Ireland was best seen simply as a wild and woolly place inhabited by people who had turned the pursuit of mayhem into a virtual art form.[114] After eighteen months he claimed to have become 'so familiarized to murder and robbery ... that I shall never be reconciled to a ... state of tranquillity', and by 1816 he was of the firm opinion that 'an honest despotic Government would be the fittest government for Ireland'.[115] He bore down on the Irish press with unparalleled and effective ferocity, reporting gleefully that he had been 'very sparing in the extension of mercy', and was delighted when the prime minister too demanded actions 'as cannot fail to strike terror'. One minute he declared that coercion had proved effective; the next he was again predicting rebellion and outrage in every county.[116] And, indeed, this kind of 'now you see it, now you don't' depiction

---

[113] See the fifty-one-page *Bibliotheca Hibernica Or a Brief Descriptive Catalogue of a Select Irish Library, Collected for the Right Hon. Robert Peel* (Dublin, 1823; facsimile repr., Shannon, 1970). The complete collection was acquired by the House of Lords Library in 1897 from the executors of the third baronet. See House of Lords Library Catalogues, *Peel Tracts*, 2 vols (January 2006).

[114] Peel to Liverpool, 15 October 1813, BL Peel Papers Add. MS 40285; to Abbot, 15 December 1816, *Sir Robert Peel from his Private Papers*, ed. Parker, i. 236–7; Parl. Deb. 1: xxviii. 163–72 (23 June 1814).

[115] Peel to Goulburn, 9 February 1814, SHC Goulburn Papers 304/35; Peel to Gregory, 15 March 1816, BL Peel Papers Add. MS 40290.

[116] B. Inglis, *The Freedom of the Press in Ireland 1784–1841* (London, 1954), 144, 149–50; Peel to Liverpool, 14 January 1816, C. D. Yonge, *The Life and Administration of Robert Banks, Second*

of Irish violence and the government's success or otherwise in suppressing it remained a regular feature of administrative analysis, not only in the years between 1800 and 1830 but throughout the Union period as a whole.[117]

Peel's arguments, notable, therefore, more for their lucid combativeness than for their originality, were welcomed by a governing elite already deeply inclined to what might be christened the 'coercive turn'. Talbot proved especially receptive, not least to demands from Irish aristocrats for more in the way of 'imprisonment and whipping'.[118] His more 'liberal' successor, Marquess Wellesley, defended coercion as the only route to Ireland's eventually becoming capable of 'receiving any benefit of good government'.[119] Just as Irish ministers in the immediate post-Union decade had—and not always inaccurately—detected 'great agitation' on all sides, so in the 1820s 'associations of a secret nature' were, it was claimed, 'in constant correspondence throughout the country' with a 'general and simultaneous rising of the Roman Catholic population ... expected in every part of Ireland'.[120] Redesdale, in retirement, was still stirring the pot with strident Peel-style demands for an Irish 'government of a dictator, firm and well judging, assisted by a great armed force ... [and, once again!] a Cromwell'. The far-from-retired Wellington, made even more afraid by the overt power of O'Connell's Catholic Association than by the hidden power of agrarian banditti, was doing much the same, with excited predictions of imminent civil war and demands 'for the prosecution of everybody that can be prosecuted'.[121]

This kind of thinking seems, in turn, to have helped create an overall disposition at Dublin Castle made up equally of colonial siege mentality and a kind of in-joking flippancy designed to render fear tolerable. Colourful imaginations could so effectively embroider (a doubtless worrying) reality

Earl of Liverpool, 3 vols (London, 1868), ii. 250; Liverpool to Peel, 20 January 1816, ibid. ii. 251–2; also Peel to Liverpool, 14 September 1812 and 5 October 1813, BL Peel Papers Add. MSS 40280 and 40285; to Gregory, 17 April 1813, ibid., Add. MS 40282; to Whitworth, 7 July 1814, ibid., Add. MS 40287; to Sidmouth, 17 August 1816, TNA HO 100/190.

[117] Hoppen, 'A Question None could Answer', 133–4.

[118] Talbot to Gregory, 7 December 1819, *Mr Gregory's Letter-Box*, ed. Lady Gregory, 89; Gregory to Talbot, 21 November 1821, PRONI Talbot Papers D4100/3/17.

[119] Wellesley to Peel, 30 January 1825, *Sir Robert Peel from his Private Papers*, ed. Parker, i. 502–4; also to Goulburn, 16 February and 6 June 1823, SHC Goulburn Papers 304/44 and 71. His judgement was, however, inconsistent and unreliable: see Wellesley to Canning, 25 December 1824, 30 August 1825, 9 August 1826, BL Canning Papers 86 (provisional reference).

[120] Elliot to Spencer, 24 November, 5 and 23 December 1806, NLS Elliot of Wells Papers MS 12911; Wellesley to Peel, 31 January and 22 May 1822, 22 June 1823, NLI Wellesley Papers MS 322; Talbot to Sidmouth, 2 December 1821, SRO Talbot Papers D649/9/3.

[121] Redesdale to Colchester, 30 October 1823, *Diary and Correspondence of Charles Abbot*, ed. Charles, Lord Colchester, iii. 303; Wellington to Goulburn, 3 November 1824, SHC Goulburn Papers 304/35; to Peel, 3 November 1824, *Sir Robert Peel from his Private Papers*, ed. Parker, i. 348; to George IV, 1 August 1828, SU Wellington Papers WP1/950/1; to Peel, 14 and 27 October 1828, ibid., WP1/963/39 and 964/18.

that in the minds of those in power Ireland became a sort of wild west in which a beleaguered garrison was obliged to draw up its wagons against encircling bands of barbarous savages. Lord Clare's prediction of February 1800 that the Union would end the need to rule 'under the ban of military government' proved singularly mistaken.[122] Only a year later Abbot thought 'safety' could be secured only by the building of 'two or three great fortresses', a view endorsed by Portland's administration of 1807–9.[123] Redesdale viewed the whole of Ireland as simply 'a garrisoned country, in which obedience is to be obtained only by the awe inspired by force', while Arthur Wellesley's term as chief secretary was marked by an unambiguously military approach to all aspects of government. For Wellesley the Union had 'no strength here but our army', and 'Ireland, in a view to military operations, must be considered as an enemy country', which is why he fretted about leaving his wife in a land (or 'camp' as he called it) remarkable for instability and unrest.[124] Ireland would, he believed, respond best to 'general officers and bayonets', and, even when commanding in the Peninsular campaign, he still worried about the land of his birth, insisting that the only way with the Irish was 'to keep them down by main force'.[125] Throughout the initial post-Union decades British visitors to Ireland were, indeed, taken aback by the overwhelmingly martial atmosphere they encountered: soldiers everywhere, a sense of 'military preparedness and unease', the entrance to Dublin 'fortified with palisades and cannon', the appearance at times of something close to 'a state of siege', with chief secretaries looking to local commanders as they would to 'a deputy governor of a province'.[126]

A sense of fear and isolation almost inevitably encouraged the kind of gallows humour that often seems to tempt 'colonial' administrators placed over lesser breeds without the law. 'Going native' in post-Union Ireland was, however, not the option it had, to a modest extent, been in the later medieval period and to some small degree still was in contemporary India, the one remoter in time, the other in distance. Nonchalance became a kind of whistling to keep one's spirits up, a common enough reaction among individuals

[122] *Proceedings of the Irish House of Lords*, ed. Kelly, iii. 441 (10 February 1800).

[123] Abbot to Addington, 5 October 1801, TNA Abbot Papers PRO 30/9/115; R. B. McDowell, *Public Opinion and Government Policy in Ireland, 1801–1846* (London, 1952), 69.

[124] Redesdale to Abbot, 15 August 1802, TNA Abbot Papers PRO 30/9/119; Wellesley to Hawkesbury, 7 May 1807, SU Wellington Papers WP1/167/45; Wilson, *A Soldier's Wife: Wellington's Marriage*, 73.

[125] E. B. Mitford, *Life of Lord Redesdale* (London, 1939), 208; *The Private Journal of Judge-Advocate Larpent, Attached to the Head-Quarters of Lord Wellington during the Peninsular War*, ed. G. Larpent, 3rd edn (London, 1854), 75 (16 March 1813).

[126] Palmerston to E. Sulivan, 12 September 1808, *The Letters of … Palmerston to Laurence and Elizabeth Sulivan*, ed. Bourne, 104; Hooper, *Travel Writing in Ireland, 1760–1860*, 88; *The Letters of King George IV, 1812–30*, ed. A. Aspinall, 3 vols (Cambridge, 1938), iii. 301; V. Crossman, *Politics, Law and Order in Nineteenth-Century Ireland* (Dublin, 1996), 16.

placed, as were viceroys, chief secretaries, and the other civil and military administrators of post-Union Ireland, amid an 'alien' population. Black jokes and heightened language—the word 'murder' was batted about with exaggerated and casual frequency—became sovereign cures for depression and marked one out as belonging to a select, pioneering, even valorous group. Richmond talked of 'a little fighting' being of no consequence, of losing 'a few valuable lives' and hanging 'a good many that richly deserve it'. His successor, Whitworth, thought a decent rebellion with much loss of life would clear the air and ultimately 'be favourable to the tranquillity of the country'. 'Everything is going on smoothly here,' he reported in May 1815, 'barring murder, rape, and robbery'.[127] Peel, rarely reluctant to descend from the restful plateau of high-mindedness, concluded that it was better to have 'a massacre in Ireland' than a 'conflict in parliament' and sent Goulburn 'an affecting account of two or three burnings [and] cardings', sufficient, he felt, 'to carry the Insurrection Act'. And Goulburn himself, when chief secretary, enthusiastically welcomed violent rustic outbreaks of 'family feuds' or faction fighting as providing 'pretty sure indications of returning peace'.[128] Even the early optimism of travel writers about Ireland's post-Union potential had faded into a depressed realization that nothing much had changed.[129]

What, of course, all this was designed to emphasize was that only very un-British measures would have any success in bringing Ireland to heel. England and Ireland were totally different societies, and while, as Fox admitted in 1805, the former was not innocent of unrest, yet Irish repression must needs be 'very different from that which belongs to the people of this country'.[130] Coercive laws that were required in Ireland—where 'liberties' were less important than the defence of property—'would not be borne with in England'.[131] Thus, while in England magistrates were honourable and efficient, in Ireland paid stipendiaries were needed to put backbone into magistrates who combined bigotry with lackadaisical uselessness, as Peel forcefully pointed out in 1814. Viceroys believed themselves faced with 'deep-seated' conspiracies and delighted in being able to report that regular convictions and executions were yielding

[127] Richmond to Peel, 3 March 1813, *Sir Robert Peel from his Private Papers*, ed. Parker, i. 75; Whitworth to Peel, 18 November 1813 and 24 May 1815, G. Broeker, *Rural Disorder and Police Reform in Ireland, 1812–36* (London. 1970), 6, and CKS Whitworth Papers U269/0218/7.

[128] Peel to Whitworth, 13 July 1814, CKS Whitworth Papers U269/0225/8; to Goulburn, 24 January 1814, SHC Goulburn Papers 304/35; Goulburn to Sidmouth, 2 January 1822, TNA HO 100/203. For 'carding', see n. 143.

[129] W. H. A. Williams, 'The Irish Tour, 1800–50', in B. Colbert (ed.), *Travel Writing and Tourism in Britain and Ireland* (Basingstoke, 2012), 109.

[130] Parl. Deb. 1: i. 1762 (12 December 1803: Hawkesbury) and 1649 (5 December 1803: Hely-Hutchinson), iii. 325 (8 February 1805: Fox).

[131] Hawkesbury to Richmond, 1 October 1807, NLI Richmond Papers MS 70; Parl. Deb. 1: ix. 1086–7 (7 August 1807: Milton).

excellent results.[132] In 1822 one former soldier, now a Whig MP with leanings towards Canning, recalled a visit to Ireland when he had seen a 'man tied to the scaffold, hung up by the back, another part of his person tied to the calves of his legs, his back excoriated with flogging, and salted, until the whole presented a shocking and undistinguishable mass of bleeding flesh'. Upon remonstrating, he was told: 'You know nothing of the Irish. They can be governed only by cats-o'-nine-tails and halters.'[133]

What was to be done? For Peel the solution was simple. Ireland needed 'a very strong government, that is a government that dare do and sustain strong acts and thus create an impression of its vigour and firmness', the kind of thing exemplified by Dublin Castle lecturing Tipperary magistrates to cease their feeble laxity, toughen up, and feel free to call on full military support.[134] Peel, however, differed from men like Talbot for whom fierceness could always do duty for impact, by wanting not only repression but effective repression. And here some small-scale precedents existed that he was able to build upon and allow to blossom into a state apparatus alien to anything that Britain had experienced, or indeed is yet to experience—namely, a national police force famously reorganized in 1836 but in almost every essential a characteristic product of the immediate post-Union period. The Dublin Police Act of 1808— passed during Arthur Wellesley's chief secretaryship—expanded numbers, extended the area covered, enforced central control, and ensured that Dublin was far more intensively policed than London. It was also directed as much to suppressing rebellion as to reducing 'normal' crime.[135] And some years later the endless demands for more troops to be sent to Ireland persuaded Peel that a more extensive and regular police force might help to free at least some soldiers for more obviously military duties elsewhere.[136]

The first embodiment of Peel's ideas was the Peace Preservation Force set up in 1814, the revolutionary legislation for which passed almost uncontested through parliament. The PPF was designed to be a highly mobile agency free from control by local magistrates and acting as 'outrage specialists' capable of

---

[132] Parl. Deb. 1: xxviii. 172 (23 June 1814: Peel); Talbot to Sidmouth, 1 December 1821, BL Wellesley Papers Add. MS 37298; Wellesley to Sidmouth, 3 January 1822, ibid.; Goulburn to Peel, 30 January 1822, BL Peel Papers Add. MS 40328.

[133] Parl. Deb. 2: vii. 1531 (8 July 1822: Wilson).

[134] James Traill (undersecretary) to the Tipperary magistrates, 4 July 1807, SU Wellington Papers WP1/173/29/4. Not only did Thomas Drummond, when undersecretary, famously adopt a very different approach to the Tipperary bench in 1838, but already in 1829 the Tory chief secretary, Lord Francis Leveson-Gower, was proving far more critical than Traill in 1807. See Chapter 3, Section I.

[135] Palmer, *Police and Protest in England and Ireland*, 150–7; K. T. Hoppen, *The Mid-Victorian Generation 1846–1886* (Oxford, 1998), 114–16.

[136] Hardwicke to Pelham, 18 August 1803, TNA HO 100/112; to Yorke, 17 September and 18 October 1803, HO 100/113; Peel to Sidmouth, 18 May 1814, HO 100/178; Whitworth to Sidmouth, 30 November 1815, HO 100/187; Palmer, *Police and Protest in England and Ireland*, 211.

being sent to particularly 'disturbed' areas. By 1822 it comprised 2,300 men patrolling half the counties of Ireland.[137] And, although numbers declined thereafter, this was only because the establishment (also in 1822) of an entirely new body operating throughout the whole country marked an even more decisive move towards specifically Hibernian forms of law enforcement. Within two years this new Constabulary had recruited 4,792 men, the bulk of whom were initially located in the central and western counties. By 1828 numbers had increased to 5,541, by 1830 to 5,940 working out of a total of 1,143 stations scattered every few miles across the countryside with half-a-dozen or so men in each post.[138]

None of the politicians involved in this dramatic turn in Irish policy— notably Peel and Goulburn—made any bones about the fact that they were treating Ireland in a distinctly unusual, unprecedented, and quite un-English manner. Indeed, they almost gloried in having introduced into Ireland something akin to those gendarmeries of continental Europe so generally and fiercely condemned as inimical to the rights of free-born Englishmen. Irishmen, being 'essentially different' and inhabiting an essentially different country, merited, they felt, altogether sterner treatment.[139] In 1814 Whitworth (a former diplomat who knew France) forcefully demanded that the Irish, having a character 'blind and infuriated as that of the French', must be treated to French methods of policing.[140] And, even if some found the term 'gendarmerie' a little strong, Peel was unabashed about introducing the full continental system, though 'called by some less startling name'.[141] And that the new undertaking was proving itself visibly successful was evident to, among many others, Sir Walter Scott when he visited Ireland in 1825. The police there reminded him of 'the Gendarmerie of France', being 'in fact soldiers on foot and horse ... This would seem a violent and unconstitutional proceeding in Britain but in Ireland it works well.'[142]

What Union, therefore, had achieved was not any significant degree of assimilation, but, in many respects, the complete opposite. Without the Irish

---

[137] Broeker, *Rural Disorder and Police Reform in Ireland*, 55–70; M. Beames, *Peasants and Power: The Whiteboy Movements and their Control in Pre-Famine Ireland* (Brighton, 1983), 158; Palmer, *Police and Protest in England and Ireland*, 224–5.

[138] Palmer, *Police and Protest in England and Ireland*, 267.

[139] Parl. Deb. 1: xxviii. 163–74 (23 June 1814: Peel).

[140] Whitworth to Sidmouth, 16 June 1814, TNA HO 100/178.

[141] Peel to Wellesley, 12 April 1822, BL Wellesley Papers Add. MS 37299; to J. L. Foster, 22 December 1821, RIA J. L. Foster Papers 23G.39/3; to Wellington, 27 July 1829, SU Wellington Papers WP1/1034/2; to Leveson-Gower, 14 August 1829, BL Peel Papers Add. MS 40337; Goulburn to Wellesley, 29 March 1822, BL Wellesley Papers Add. MS 37298; Parl. Deb. 2: vii. 863–4 (7 June 1822: Grant); Lord W. Russell to Lord J. Russell, 25 August 1827, *Early Correspondence of Lord John Russell 1805–40*, ed. R. Russell, 2 vols (London, 1913), i. 260.

[142] Scott to Laidlaw, [10 August 1825] and to Morritt, 25 August [1825], *The Letters of Sir Walter Scott 1787–1832*, ed. H. J. C. Grierson, 12 vols (London, 1932–7), ix. 200, 210.

parliament acting as a buffer, British politicians were now directly confronted by Irish realities they found difficult to understand or influence. 'I have a tale to unfold that will freeze your very soul' began one of Lord Bathurst's Irish correspondents in 1817, while Peel gave so graphic an account in 1814 of the vicious 'carding' used by Irish secret societies to punish backsliders that MPs could hardly believe what they were hearing.[143] Indeed, all the harmonizing talk of 1799–1800 about togetherness had turned out, at best, to constitute a set of conceptual Potemkin villages, at worst, to be something close to a political fraud in which white was not white, black not black, nor even grey grey. All the excited denunciations of supine Irish magistrates—wherever 'Field Marshal Funck commands ... the Enemy is certain of appearing formidable'[144]—achieved nothing beyond relieving the feelings of frustrated administrators. All the special provisions, the specifically Hibernian shifts and expedients, had done no more than leave Ireland in much the same state as before. Both Irish crime conviction rates and Irish murder rates remained stubbornly high. The new Constabulary both caused and suffered from worrying levels of death and injury,[145] while O'Connell's campaign for Catholic emancipation seemed to have become unstoppable.

The result was that even Peel, as chief secretary the hardest of the hard, eventually began to think that perhaps a few of the golden promises of the union debates might be dusted down and allowed some kind of modest outing in the racing calendar of Anglo-Irish political expectations. By 1828 and 1829 he was talking about moving away from always treating Ireland as some kind of special case, possibly even reducing its administrative distinctiveness, about preferring slow-acting long-term 'ordinary law' solutions, about establishing 'a system of measures for the permanent civilization of Ireland' instead of always looking for instant obedience, about the undoubted fact that repeated doses of coercive legislation had 'worked no permanent good'. None of this meant that all was now sweetness and light; far from it. What it did mean was that the time had come to make Ireland pay for its own turbulence: 'We relieve her from taxes to which other parts of the United Kingdom are subject; we support our own poor and hers also.'[146] But it did also suggest that new directions were being considered, that realizations of failure had begun to gnaw at men's minds, that the wind was beginning to shift, that, in no straightforward or complete manner, some of the Union's more explicitly

---

[143] Bartlett, *The Fall and Rise of the Irish Nation*, 345. Carding involved scraping a nail-studded board violently down the victim's back.

[144] William Gregory, undersecretary, writing in 1813: Jenkins, *Era of Emancipation*, 99.

[145] Palmer, *Police and Protest in England and Ireland*, 196–7; Broeker, *Rural Disorder and Police Reform in Ireland*, 195.

[146] Peel to Leveson-Gower, 26 December 1828, BL Peel Papers Add. MS 40336; to Leveson-Gower, 30 July and 19 November 1829, ibid., Add. MS 40337.

positive and integrationist agenda might perhaps at least be permitted to achieve a delayed and safely partial implementation.

Separation, distancing, alienation, allowing Ireland to float, as it were, further and further out into a psychological Atlantic had not, by any account, proved much of a success. Perhaps assimilation had not been such a bad idea after all. Perhaps now it might, for good or ill, even be given a trial.

Part II

Menus of Assimilation, *c.*1830–*c.*1868

3

A Changing Climate

I

In the late 1820s both the ideological and the pragmatically inclined weather began to change. Even some of the fiercest proponents of the view that an Ireland rendered remote and incomprehensible by its idiosyncratic peculiarities deserved nothing but the stick began to realize that post-Union government had not, by any standards, proved much of a success, possibly no sort of success at all. With regard to the smaller island, the new United Kingdom seemed to be making little progress of any kind. Indeed, in many respects, its situation, viewed from a London perspective, had regressed from merely unintelligible disorder into the far more troubling challenges of O'Connell's campaign for Catholic emancipation, because, while the scatter-gun violence of agrarian secret societies had long caused panic and fear, it had not, unlike the Catholic Association, sought to undermine the foundations of the new state. The granting of emancipation in 1829 by Wellington's administration and the coming into power (after decades in the wilderness) of the Whigs in November 1830 were, therefore, events of profound importance, not only for governance in general, but for the future character of the Anglo-Irish relationship in particular.

Yet, the changes and adjustments in political, administrative, and, indeed, cultural attitudes towards Ireland that gathered pace in the 1830s grew out of more than immediate and specific circumstances. Important too was the manner in which utilitarian universalism—the belief that, at bottom, all human beings are best understood as behaving according to the same passions and desires—had begun to infect important elements in the higher political world. This was palpably the case with the so-called Bowood set, who looked to the leadership of the Whig third Marquess of Lansdowne[1] (whose enormous Irish estates provided a large part of his income and demanded a

---

[1] See Lansdowne to Downshire, 1 November 1829, P[ublic] R[ecord] O[ffice of] N[orthern] I[reland] Downshire Papers D671/C/12/414 about the contemporary tendency 'to assimilate the population of the two countries'.

significant amount of his attention), but also significantly, if less powerfully so, with respect to those whose political outlooks were less directly connected to philosophical perceptions of any kind. But, while such developments hinted that the Irish ogre could now be granted some very careful release from its Tory cage, they did not involve instant invitations to enter British political drawing rooms, even if carefully supervised visits to the servants' quarters might now be allowed, possibly even encouraged. And, while the advent of a broadly Whig administration was certainly significant, the notable shifts that began to occur in governmental approaches to Ireland were not confined to one party, if only because contemporary divisions between those who adopted a social market, non-interventionist, individualist, and mechanical view of society, on the one hand, and those with a more paternalist and organic view, on the other, took place as much within as between the formal political groupings of the time.[2]

II

Signs that something close to an unravelling of the accepted wisdoms of the post-Union period was about to take place can be seen towards the end of 1829, not least in the activities of Wellington's Tory administration (1828–30), initially so severe towards Ireland, in truth a harbinger of things to come. Goderich's immediately previous 'coalition' ministry had already in August 1827 put forward plans of a distinctly reformist character designed to bring into being an Ireland less backward, less sectarian, and less dramatically isolated from Anglo-Saxon norms.[3] And Wellington's chief secretary, the former Canningite Lord Francis Leveson-Gower, had produced a memorandum urging a 'community of feeling and interest between the two countries' and delivered himself of a (private) pronouncement that, though generated from a very different party standpoint, strikingly anticipated Thomas Drummond's famous public reminder of May 1838 to the magistrates of Tipperary that 'property had its duties as well as it rights': 'I make every allowance for the fears and feelings of men residing in Tipperary, but the constant introduction of politics and party spirit into every subject is irritating to the last degree.'[4]

[2] P. Mandler, *Aristocratic Government in the Age of Reform: Whigs and Liberals 1830–1852* (Oxford, 1990), *passim*; B. Hilton, *The Age of Atonement: The Influence of Evangelicalism on Social and Economic Thought, 1785–1865*, new edn (Oxford, 1991), especially 203–51; Hilton, 'Comments', in A. Morrison (ed.), *Free Trade and its Reception 1815–1960*, 3 vols (London, 1998), i. 82–5.

[3] B. Jenkins, *Era of Emancipation: British Government of Ireland, 1812–1830* (Kingston and Montreal, 1988), 254.

[4] R. B. O'Brien, *Thomas Drummond Under-Secretary in Ireland, 1835–40* (London, 1889), 284; Leveson-Gower to Peel, 29 October 1829, N[ational] A[rchives of] I[reland] Leveson-Gower

In May 1830 the Lansdowne Whig Thomas Spring Rice sensed that leading Tories were already involving themselves in 'the present tendency to assimilate the two countries',[5] something that all those with eyes to see could hardly have helped noticing. As Home Secretary under Wellington, Peel in particular saw Catholic emancipation, not as some pragmatic defusion of Hibernian violence, but as a deliberate act of yielding to 'a moral necessity' that demanded that Britain, in its relations with Ireland, must 'run the hazards of change'.[6] But, if in certain respects this shift in Peel's thinking might well be regarded as simply 'liberal', it actually interwove dispositions towards peremptory Hibernian chastisement with the distinctly novel conviction that Ireland's only salvation now lay in embracing (or being forced to embrace) an English-style market economy in which a predominantly Catholic population might be persuaded to adopt the values and comforts of middle-class capitalism.[7]

The Irish policies of Wellington's administration were, in truth, markedly more assimilationist than those of its post-Union predecessors. The prime minister happily corresponded with those eager 'to assimilate the laws and manners of the two countries'. His Irish ministers produced plans for administrative reforms that would 'bring about that community of feeling and interest between the two countries so much in the interest of both to encourage'. In July 1829 he himself submitted to the cabinet proposals of a broadly ameliorative nature involving the appointment of a committee to investigate Irish poverty, one of the few contemporary examples of forward cabinet planning so far as Ireland was concerned, though in the end little was done.[8] And it was perhaps such initiatives, despite, perhaps even because of, their largely theoretical nature, that persuaded the Benthamite Lansdowne (now lord president of the council) to canvass the otherwise bizarre idea that Wellington himself be appointed viceroy of Ireland by the new government of November 1830.[9]

While, therefore, the young John Stuart Mill famously remarked in March 1829 that the granting of emancipation had 'given a shake to men's minds

Letter-Book MS 737. For the very different comments of James Traill, undersecretary in 1807, see Chapter 2, Section V.

[5] Parl[iamentary] Deb[ates] 2: xxiv. 566 (11 May 1830).

[6] Ibid. xx. 730 (5 March 1829).

[7] *Memoirs of the Right Honourable Sir Robert Peel*, ed. Earl Stanhope and E. Cardwell, 2 vols (London, 1856–7), i. 10; B. Hilton, 'The Ripening of Robert Peel', in M. Bentley (ed.), *Public and Private Doctrine: Essays in British History Presented to Maurice Cowling* (Cambridge, 1993), 63–84.

[8] Memorandum by Leveson-Gower, [late 1828], S[outhampton] U[niversity] Wellington Papers WP1/979/10; also WP1/999/13; P. Jupp, *British Politics on the Eve of Reform: The Duke of Wellington's Administration 1828–30* (London, 1998), 101–2; Jupp, *The First Duke of Wellington in an Irish Context* (Southampton, 1997), 15–17.

[9] Lansdowne to Grey, 26 December [1830], D[urham] U[niversity] Grey Papers GRE/B38/10, because he could not believe that Wellington's 'real views would differ much from ours'.

which has loosened all old prejudices'[10] and the coming-to-power of the Whigs undoubtedly marked a new departure in all sorts of respects, in the short term there was rather more continuity than was then, or has subsequently, often been allowed. Even so, an increasingly public unveiling of certain feelings among Whigs who had spent an eternity in opposition helped to encourage the manifestation of distinct shifts with regard to official policy towards Ireland. It certainly suited many Whigs to talk loudly about the three wasted decades that had followed the Union, during which, they felt: 'No effort had been made ... to conciliate the people of that country or to endeavour to unite them under one system of government. Thirty years had been allowed to elapse ... down to the accession of Lord Grey's administration, during which the Irish people had reaped no benefit whatsoever from the Union.'[11] Indeed, one prominent Whig, who served as lord lieutenant between 1839 and 1841, pointedly contrasted Pitt's promises of 'equal laws, equal rights, and equal participation in all the blessings and advantages of the English constitution' with the wholesale failure of Tory governments to implement anything of the kind.[12]

Lord Grey's coalition administration of 1830–4 is, with regard to the governance of Ireland, best seen as transitional and especially so in its cautious replacement of distant and coercive certainties with an approach characterized by policies of integration, of 'solving' the Irish 'problem' by bringing about, through direct administrative action, social, economic, and cultural adjustments designed to generate a nearer (it was hoped eventually a total) equivalence between the two islands. That a shift was underway was obvious to all. Benthamites such as Lansdowne and Spring Rice followed their mentor (a man O'Connell also greatly admired) in having 'little sense of racial or gender differences', indeed, 'little sense of any kind of difference'.[13] The so-called Liberal Anglicans—men such as Russell, Duncannon (later Bessborough), Morpeth (later Carlisle), and Mulgrave (later Normanby)—many of whom worshipped at the shrine of Charles James Fox, though they approached Ireland by a different route, came in the main to similar and sometimes stronger and more novel conclusions. For them the goal was a comprehensive, Christian, and non-sectarian United Kingdom 'nation' to be forged out of 'the apparently antagonistic elements of Protestant and Catholic, Anglican and Nonconformist, Irish and English' underpinned by 'national unity, social

---

[10] Mill to D'Eichthal, 11 March 1829, *Collected Works of John Stuart Mill*, ed. J. M. Robson and Others, 33 vols (Toronto, 1963–91), xii. 28.

[11] Lord Hatherton (chief secretary 1833–4), Parl. Deb. 3: xxiii. 722 (9 May 1836).

[12] Viscount Ebrington, ibid. xxxiv. 340 (10 June 1836).

[13] K. T. Hoppen, 'Riding a Tiger: Daniel O'Connell, Reform, and Popular Politics in Ireland, 1800–1847', in T. C. W. Blanning and P. Wende (eds), *Reform in Great Britain and Germany 1750–1850: Proceedings of the British Academy* (Oxford, 1999), 134–5; B. Hilton, *A Mad, Bad, and Dangerous People? England 1783–1846* (Oxford, 2006), 330.

order, and moral progress' all round.[14] More 'secular' figures like Holland (the arch-Foxite) and Palmerston, though they stood apart from such pieties, nonetheless shared a similar appreciation of the direction towards which the Anglo-Irish future should henceforth be steered. The man who stood most clearly at a tangent was Grey himself, and it was this that was largely, though not exclusively, responsible for the transitionary character of his administration with regard to the place that Ireland should occupy within the changing polity of post-Union affairs.

What, in general, lay behind these shifting attitudes was not so much any sophisticated understanding of Irish realities as an ethnocentric conviction that Irish problems were similar to English problems, 'albeit more difficult politically', and that therefore they demanded similar, perhaps even identical, solutions,[15] an approach given turbo-charged acceleration by the widespread feeling that it was time to try something new, in particular that the waving of olive branches might not be without effect. Even Stanley, the new chief secretary and possibly the least sympathetic minister in the government, agreed that serious 'remedial measures' were now required, though, he quickly added, not ones too rapidly introduced upon 'ill-digested' notions.[16] Melbourne, as Home Secretary under Grey and therefore nominally 'in charge' of Ireland, at first took a similarly cautious line, talking vaguely of 'the manifestation of a spirit of conciliation to all', while Anglesey, appointed viceroy again in December 1830, noted that the new Whig policies of 'strict impartiality', though necessary in the long term, were also likely to antagonize those many political partisans of all stripes with which Ireland was more than ordinarily endowed.[17]

Of course the issuing of emollient pronouncements did not of itself indicate any intense desire for assimilation between Britain and Ireland. Yet their flurried appearance and a repeated tendency to propose a goal of equivalence between the two islands certainly implied a very different policy from that which had gone before. Thus the establishment of an Irish Board of Works in

---

[14] R. Brent, *Liberal Anglican Politics: Whiggery, Religion, and Reform 1830–1841* (Oxford, 1987), 18; B. Hilton, 'Whiggery, Religion and Social Reform: The Case of Lord Morpeth', *Historical Journal*, 37 (1994), 830; Mandler, *Aristocratic Government*, 276–7. Lansdowne, Spring Rice, Russell, Duncannon, and Mulgrave all served in the Whig cabinets of 1830–4 and (together with Morpeth) in those of 1835–41.

[15] I. Newbould, *Whiggery and Reform, 1830–41: The Politics of Government* (London, 1990), 284.

[16] Stanley to Melbourne, 4 January 1831, L[iverpool] R[ecord] O[ffice] Derby Papers 167/1.

[17] Melbourne's 'Instructions' on Anglesey's reappointment in late 1830, R[oyal] A[rchives] Melbourne Papers [on microfilm in Bodleian Library] MP93; Melbourne to Anglesey, 26 February 1831, ibid., MP93; Anglesey to Melbourne, 18 June 1832, ibid., MP94. Anglesey had served as viceroy under Wellington but had effectively been dismissed in early 1829 because of his insufficiently orthodox Toryism. He then served again under Grey from November 1830 to September 1833.

1831 was largely seen as bringing Ireland up to Anglo-Saxon standards with regard to communications and economic infrastructure in general. It also involved a distinct transfer of authority from Dublin to London and the centralization of what had previously been a series of uncoordinated bodies of a peculiarly Irish character.[18] Initial thoughts about reforming (in effect reducing) the institutional structures of the Church of Ireland turned much on how best to deal with a body very obviously different from the Church of England (to which the Union had joined it 'for ever') but whose treatment had undoubted implications for the ecclesiastical policy of the United Kingdom as a whole.[19] And the resulting legislation, the Irish Church Temporalities Act of 1833, which reduced the number of bishops and involved substantial changes in the allocation of revenues, was designed to preserve the church as a viable institution on fundamentally English lines while foreshadowing important developments in England itself regarding the establishment of an ecclesiastical commission and the tenure of church lands.[20]

III

While Stanley still thought Ireland should 'be kept in order by actual force' and Grey wanted reform but on 'truly conservative principles',[21] the opposite pole among Whigs was represented by Lord John Russell, who in 1831 produced a strikingly emotional poem extolling the 1798 aristocratic revolutionary (the adjective probably impressed Russell rather more than the noun) Lord Edward Fitzgerald: 'Erect and firm Lord Edward stood | His glorious aim his country's good'.[22] Two years later, while staying with Marquess Wellesley at the viceregal lodge in Dublin, Russell drew up a memorandum that, after insisting that law and order be even-handedly maintained, proposed wide-ranging changes regarding landlord–tenant relations (including the state purchase of 'distressed' estates), official payment of Catholic priests, and further serious reforms of the established church.[23] And, precisely because

---

[18] Parl. Deb. 3: vi. 63–8 (15 August 1831); *Report from the Select Committee of the House of Lords Appointed to Inquire into the Operation of the Acts Relating to the Drainage of Lands in Ireland*, H[ouse of] C[ommons Paper] 1852–3 (10), xxvi. 78; R. B. McDowell, *The Irish Administration 1801–1914* (London, 1964), 203–14.

[19] Grey to Anglesey, 24 October 1832, DU Grey Papers GRE/B3/315; Duncannon to Grey, 4 January 1833, ibid., GRE/B7/7/55.

[20] O. Brose, 'The Irish Precedent for English Church Reform: The Church Temporalities Act of 1833', *Journal of Ecclesiastical History*, 7 (1956), 205–11.

[21] Stanley to Anglesey, 1 January 1832, PRONI Anglesey Papers D619/31D; Grey to Anglesey, 25 October and 14 December 1832, ibid., D619/28A.

[22] *Early Correspondence of Lord John Russell*, ed. R. Russell, 2 vols (London, 1913), i. 53.

[23] Memorandum of 18 October 1833, in ibid. ii. 42–4.

Russell, like most Whigs, was convinced that it was 'upon law and government that the prosperity and morals, the power and the intelligence, of every nation depend', he was desperately anxious to translate a desire to exhibit 'due, kind, paternal attention' and 'fellow-feeling ... with the great mass of the [Irish] people' into a reality in which Ireland would be more closely aligned to the glories of English political perfection.[24] He saw the Whig administration ushering in a new dawn for Ireland and reminded Stanley's successor as chief secretary that the Irish government should stop looking at the country 'through a police telescope ... with Orange glasses'. In June 1832 the diarist Charles Greville met Russell (then in cabinet as paymaster general) and was told that, as regards Ireland, a completely new policy was required, that the old structures must be pulled down and new ones built.[25]

For Whigs the real problem was how to stop trying to run Ireland exclusively through an extreme Protestant party, while still giving no more than limited countenance to O'Connellite 'extremism' and achieving this balance even though enlightened Irish Whigs—that is, men like themselves, 'moderate, unprejudiced, and really attached to the government'—were a 'body lamentably small'.[26] But, while this would certainly be difficult, it was not a state of things without its appeal to characteristically complacent Whig sensibilities, involving as these did ambitions to hold the ring in Ireland between less intelligent and more visceral groups of various kinds, or, as Grey put it, sustaining 'an observation of the *juste milieu* as the French have it'.[27] 'It will', Anglesey told Melbourne in January 1831, 'be my peculiar anxiety to inculcate in the minds of both Protestants and Catholics of the higher classes, that the very existence of the state and preservation of their respective properties depend upon their cordial cooperation and good understanding'.[28] Matching the deed to the word, he descended upon County Clare three months later to sort out the extreme Protestant party—'a nest of hornets'— and lecture their O'Connellite opponents on how the country now 'had a patriot king, a reforming and independent and a benevolent government and a chief governor with no other object but to promote the prosperity of Ireland'.[29] Admittedly, the new ministry's initial and understandable obsession with parliamentary reform meant that Irish policy often tended to be made up

[24] Parl. Deb. 3: iv. 345–6 (24 June 1831).
[25] Russell to Littleton, 28 October [1833], S[taffordshire] R[ecord] O[ffice] Hatherton Papers D260/M/01/8; *The Greville Memoirs 1814–1860*, ed. L. Strachey and R. Fulford, 8 vols (London, 1938), ii. 310 (15 July 1832), also iii. 379–80 (25 June 1837).
[26] Holland to Grey, 2 January 1831, DU Grey Papers GRE/B34/66; Russell to Grey, 8 October 1833, ibid., GRE/B50A/6/40.
[27] Grey to Anglesey, 11 June 1832, DU Grey Papers GRE/B3/290.
[28] Anglesey to Melbourne, 2 January 1831, RA Melbourne Papers MP93.
[29] Anglesey to Stanley, 7 April 1831, B[ritish] L[ibrary] 3rd Marquess of Lansdowne Papers B121 (provisional reference).

on the hoof, with Melbourne, without much thought or analysis, casually tossing a colourful medley of significant and marginal odds and ends into the Hibernian pot: reforming grand juries, education, and corporations, repealing the Sub-Letting Act, providing for the poor, and doing something about vestries.[30]

Gestures, it was assumed, could sometimes have an impact more speedy and direct than concrete proposals, however genuine. And here the ministry's determination to sack the ultra-Tory William Gregory from the post of undersecretary, which he had held since 1812 and in which he had acted as local enforcer for a succession of Tory chief secretaries (notably Peel), undoubtedly created waves of considerable force. Peel's parliamentary defence of his friend—'a man of greater integrity and honour … he had never met with'—was briskly swatted away by the government's contention that 'the existence of public partiality … was precisely the reason why the removal had taken place'.[31] And, when seen within the context of Duncannon's insistence in 1832 that ministers should proceed 'by doing that in Ireland which you do in England' and Wellesley's in 1834 that Ireland should be governed only by the 'ordinary' law of England,[32] such actions were not without their effect upon those in Ireland who believed that a new era was in process of being brought to birth.

However, the administration of 1830–4 did not consist only of Whigs, but also included liberal Tories and various classes of moderates united only by agreement over parliamentary reform. This, and the leadership of Grey, meant that its approach to Ireland was often ambiguous, sometimes even contradictory. Grey, in particular, while moaning about being obliged to think of nothing but Ireland,[33] was at once bored and irritated by what he saw as Hibernian inclinations to combine disorder with frivolity. His main political cause had always been Catholic emancipation, and its concession by Wellington's administration meant that, as G. M. Trevelyan put it, 'his Irish clock had stopped in 1829'.[34] Distinctly worried about Irish unrest, he looked, in this regard, especially to Stanley, with the result that some strongly coercive legislation was passed, notably the Suppression of Disturbances (Ireland) Act of 1833, actions that Littleton as chief secretary and Wellesley as viceroy

---

[30] Melbourne to Stanley, 2 January 1831, A. D. Kriegel, 'The Irish Policy of Lord Grey's Government', *English Historical Review*, 86 (1971), 27; idem, 'The Whig Government and Ireland, 1830–1835', Duke University Ph.D. Thesis (1964), 97.

[31] Parl. Deb. 3: i. 1369–70 (20 December 1830).

[32] Duncannon to Grey, 10 September 1832, DU Grey Papers GRE/B7/7/55; Wellesley to Littleton, 7 August 1834, SRO Hatherton Papers D260/M/01/13.

[33] A. Hawkins, *The Forgotten Prime Minister: The 14th Earl of Derby*, 2 vols (Oxford, 2007–8), i. 72.

[34] G. M. Trevelyan, *Lord Grey of the Reform Bill: The Life of Charles, Second Earl Grey* (London, 1920), 292.

(1833–4) thought counterproductive and unnecessary.[35] Grey was also much exercised by what he considered to be rank Irish ingratitude for all the bounty offered by his government. 'What a people,' he exclaimed in 1832; 'they seem to be irreclaimable by kindness and an impartial administration'. Indeed, he saw himself as heading a ministry that was doing 'much more than any former government has ever done … to remove the evils of which they complain'.[36] And there can be little doubt that, notwithstanding Stanley's influence or some exasperated explosions from Viscount Althorp at the Exchequer and from the unpredictably radical Earl of Durham as privy seal to the effect that Ireland might well be helped by a dictatorship,[37] Grey's administration was much more troubled about imposing coercion than its Tory predecessors had ever been. Not only did Grey insist that one should never 'enforce the law without legislation to abate the grievance—one measure was to be accompanied by the other', but he was equally convinced that, should ordinary laws prove insufficient, only 'the least unconstitutional addition to them' should ever be introduced and then 'for the shortest possible time'. And, in Dublin, Anglesey felt the same, expressing a deep distrust of 'laws which are not of a strictly constitutional character' and of 'every species of coercive measure which necessity does not imperatively call for'. Indeed, utterly convinced that a new age must now be ushered into being, he frankly told Grey that, 'in this era of the world, the bayonet must not be *always* depended upon'.[38] And in truth the strong coercion measure of 1833, passed just as Stanley was departing the Irish Office, was sparingly used by his successors, replaced in 1835 by milder legislation that was never put into operation at all, and completely repealed in 1840. Thus, while Habeas Corpus had been suspended in Ireland for eight of the thirty years between 1801 and 1830, during the thirty-eight years that followed it was suspended for only four.[39]

[35] Stanley to Grey, 20 April 1831, LRO Derby Papers 167/1; Stanley to Melbourne, 28 December 1830, ibid. 167/1; Stanley to Anglesey, 1 January 1832, ibid. 168; Parl. Deb. 3: xi. 140 (13 March 1832); *Memoir and Correspondence Relating to Political Occurrences in June and July 1834 by the Right Hon. Edward John Littleton First Lord Hatherton*, ed. H. Reeve (London, 1872), 54, 110; E. A. Smith, *Lord Grey 1764–1845* (Oxford, 1990), 290.

[36] Grey to Anglesey, 11 December 1832, DU Grey Papers GRE/B3/320 and 28 July 1832 PRONI Anglesey Papers D619/28A.

[37] E. A. Wasson, *Whig Renaissance: Lord Althorp and the Whig Party 1782–1845* (New York, 1987), 272, 307; S. J. Reid, *Life and Letters of the First Earl of Durham*, 2 vols (London, 1906), i. 316–17.

[38] Lord Ellenborough's diary for 15 March 1832 in *Three Early Nineteenth Century Diaries*, ed. A. Aspinall (London, 1952), 195; Grey to Anglesey, 16 March 1831, PRONI Anglesey Papers D619/28A; Anglesey to Melbourne, 18 April 1831, LRO Derby Papers 117/7; Anglesey to Grey, 1 August 1832, SRO Hatherton Papers D260/M/01/1; Grey to William IV, 30 December 1830, *The Reform Act, 1832: Correspondence of the Late Earl Grey with His Majesty King William IV*, ed. Henry, Earl Grey, 2 vols (London, 1867), i. 39.

[39] V. Crossman, 'Emergency Legislation and Agrarian Disorder in Ireland, 1821–41', *Irish Historical Studies*, 27 (1991), 220–3; Printed Cabinet Paper of 25 January 1870 'Of Exceptional Legislation Relating to Ireland': Bodl[eian Library] Clarendon Papers Irish 65.

But, even when Grey and Stanley (who in June 1831 became the first chief secretary to join the cabinet) pursued a harsh line in favour of coercion, neither took notable issue with the necessity of otherwise attempting to assimilate Ireland more closely to the state of things pertaining in Britain generally and in England particularly. Stanley's intellectual curiosity regarding Irish history had, for example, persuaded him that—in Angus Hawkins's words—'the establishment of English legal institutions had to supersede atavistic native notions of land ownership' and that it was 'upon the foundation of English principles of property that proper commercial policies and common, widely sanctioned moral values ... should be upheld'.[40] This striking anticipation of views that achieved dominance only some decades later, together with an insistence that, so far as Ireland was concerned, Grey's was 'the best government that ever existed', positioned Stanley, despite his coercive tendencies, with at least one foot firmly in the reformist camp.[41]

At the same time Stanley's resignation from the government in May 1834 and the subsequent emergence of a more unambiguously Whig cabinet undoubtedly provided 'reformers' such as Russell and the liberal Anglicans generally with greater room for manœuvre. Melbourne as prime minister, though a less enthusiastic innovator, was, nonetheless, mostly to be found on the side of assimilation. Nor were such opinions confined to the higher echelons of power. Rising men like Sir George Grey (Earl Grey's nephew) told the Commons in March 1833 that 'he did not regard Ireland as a province, but as an integral part of the empire'. The intellectual banker George Grote spoke dramatically about himself feeling now 'as much an Irishman as an Englishman', quoting Louis XIV's analogous comment to the effect 'that the Pyrenees no longer exist'.[42] Self-congratulation was, as usual, never far away, with Sir Daniel Sandford gilding his nine-month spell in parliament with an assimilationist war cry that was to be heard, variously expressed, over the years to come: 'Every approach they [the Irish] had made to civilization and happiness had been the produce of their approximation to the character and institutions of this country.'[43] His reform-minded colleague Thomas Bish, daringly, but unavailingly, suggested that parliament should occasionally sit in Dublin in order to create so 'complete, binding and real [a] union' that, by a 'blending of the two people ... Ireland would then be like a county of England—like Kent and Gloucester'—a form of words soon so comprehensively embraced that it became almost a cliché of Anglo-Irish discourse and debate.[44]

---

[40] Hawkins, *Forgotten Prime Minister*, i. 76.   [41] Parl. Deb. 3: xi. 140 (13 March 1832).
[42] Russell to Melbourne, 9 September 1837, TNA Russell Papers PRO 30/22/2F; Parl. Deb. 3: xvi. 35 (1 March 1833: Grey) and xv. 1242 (27 February 1833: Grote).
[43] Ibid. xxiii. 12 (25 April 1834).
[44] Ibid. xxiv. 400–1 (12 June 1834). Thomas Talfourd was another Liberal MP who insisted that the Union could be sustained only 'by a moulding and blending of the nations into one' (ibid. xxvi. 550–1 (1 April 1835)).

Nor were these new political breezes confined to the Whigs or to those who were now beginning to call themselves 'Liberals'. While Peel's moves over emancipation (whatever their precise motivation) certainly removed an important obstacle, they were accompanied by a new and increasing dissatisfaction with the endless doses of coercion that his own policies had once so frequently generated.[45] During Grey's administration, Peel, anxious to stop the government from lurching too far in a radical direction, kept Tory ultras 'relatively quiet' in order to allow 'himself the freedom to support the principles of Whig moderation with which he could find little fault'. Indeed, Morpeth went so far as to claim in 1835 that 'Peel and J. Russell completely fraternise'.[46] Certainly Peel's integrationist credentials were being regularly buffed up, as when in April 1834 he denied that Ireland was 'so differently circumstanced from England ... that she requires a system of legislation adapted to these peculiar circumstances'.[47] His was at this stage, however, a rather modified version of the creed. Yes, Ireland must be integrated more fully into a formal United Kingdom polity so that a complete equivalence might eventually be achieved; but No, this did not mean that such processes could be supported only by 'the formal and nominal adopting of similar institutions'—a line of argument that never entirely lost its appeal both inside and outside the Tory party.[48]

IV

The main, though by no means the only, reason for Melbourne's assimilationist acceleration was the Whig failure to obtain a clear majority at the general election of January 1835 and the consequent need of support from radicals and from O'Connell's Irish Party, which had returned thirty-four members to parliament. There had even been some pre-election contacts with O'Connell, though the ultimately successful discussions began in February and were greatly moved forward by Melbourne's brother-in-law, Viscount Duncannon, a member of the cabinet since 1830, a large landowner in County Kilkenny, unusually prepared to refer to the Irish as 'my countrymen', and unique among leading Whigs in being happy to entertain O'Connell at his London residence.[49] The result was the so-called Lichfield House Compact, for

---

[45] Peel to Leveson-Gower, 9 October 1829, DU Grey Papers GRE/B36/3/4; Peel to Northumberland, 2 November 1829, ibid.
[46] Newbould, *Whiggery and Reform*, 85, 187, 104, 181; also Peel to Goulburn, 26 April 1833, *Sir Robert Peel from his Private Papers*, ed. C. S. Parker, 3 vols (London, 1891–9), ii. 220.
[47] Parl. Deb. 3: xxiii. 87 (25 April 1834).   [48] Ibid. xxxiv. 778–9 (10 June 1836).
[49] A. H. Graham, 'The Lichfield House Compact, 1835', *Irish Historical Studies*, 12 (1961), 209–25; D. Howell-Thomas, *Duncannon: Reformer and Reconciler 1781–1847* (Norwich, 1992), 118; K. T. Hoppen, *Elections, Politics, and Society in Ireland 1832–1885* (Oxford, 1984), 259. See

its creators 'an alliance on honourable terms of mutual co-operation', and in the view of Angus Macintyre 'one of the most decisive events in British political history between 1832 and 1847'.[50]

There was a certain piquancy in this development, because it depended, not only upon Whig willingness to contemplate reforms designed to render Ireland less foreign, peculiar, and *sui generis*, but also upon a matching O'Connellite programme with the same ends in view. Indeed, if anyone can at this time be identified as an arch-assimilationist, it is O'Connell himself. Not only was he always a highly pragmatic operator, but he carried almost no baggage as an apostle of Irish (or Gaelic) national separateness. Indeed, no other contemporary politician operated in a more truly United Kingdom mode. While those British ministers given direct responsibility for governing Ireland (many of whom undoubtedly adhered to a broadly assimilationist agenda) almost invariably did so as 'superior' persons stooping downwards in order to help a damaged relative, O'Connell energetically involved himself in a whole series of programmes, which, though not unconnected with his Irish priorities, resonated with equal force throughout the two islands as a whole. He enthusiastically adopted the cause of parliamentary (and general) reform, the emancipation of slaves, the rights of Jews, the separation of church and state, and individual liberty of conscience. If, on the issue of franchise extension, he did not agree with the Chartists in every particular, he agreed with them on most things. Whatever their precise character, his policies tended to respond to the rhythms of the new United Kingdom rather than to exclusively Irish drumbeats. As Gladstone put it in 1889, O'Connell, 'having adopted the political creed of Liberalism ... was as thorough an English Liberal, as if he had had no Ireland to think of'.[51]

Small wonder, then, that O'Connell saw the Lichfield House Compact as a mechanism for bringing about a closer alignment as to rights and privileges between Britain and Ireland. He began to speak of a readiness to consent to the Union if steps were taken to produce 'an identity of laws, an identity of institutions, and an identity of liberties'. He looked, in a geographical usage that was to become ubiquitous among British politicians, to a new state in which 'there would be no distinction between Yorkshire and Carlow, between Waterford and Cumberland'. What, he asked in 1841, 'is union without identification? If we have union, why should we not have assimilation?'[52]

the contemporary print 'A Family Group' by John Doyle (in F. Cullen and R. F. Foster, *'Conquering England': Ireland in Victorian London* (London, 2005), 40) of a smiling O'Connell flanked by Ebrington and Duncannon.

[50] A. Macintyre, *The Liberator: Daniel O'Connell and the Irish Party 1830–1847* (London, 1965), 144.

[51] Hoppen, 'Riding a Tiger: Daniel O'Connell, Reform, and Popular Politics in Ireland', 121–43; W. E. Gladstone, 'Daniel O'Connell', *Nineteenth Century*, 25 (1889), 156.

[52] Parl. Deb. 3: xlii. 1320 (15 May 1838) and lvi. 1083 (25 February 1841).

Indeed, such declarations produced almost a kind of love fest between O'Connell and the Whigs in the 1830s. 'It is a pleasure', Russell wrote to him in May 1839, 'to acknowledge the constant and disinterested support which you have given to the ministry in which I hold the department [the Home Office] closely connected with the affairs of Ireland.'[53] And much the same integrationist enthusiasms motivated those non-aristocratic Irish Liberals standing outside the O'Connellite camp. They too sought 'the closest possible assimilation of the laws and institutions of both countries to the end that, by complete incorporation, the system of imperial legislation may be rendered permanently beneficial to the interests of the United Kingdom'.[54]

Again and again O'Connell insisted that union must, indeed should, imply closer integration. In 1839 he demanded equality of franchise on the grounds that, if the 'Union had any principle to support it, it was the identity of interests between the two countries. If there was not that identity between them, then it was the union of master and slave.' Union meant, in O'Connell's view, that Ireland should 'share the advantages of the British institutions'.[55] He thanked Melbourne for heading the first administration trying 'to make Ireland an efficient and useful portion of the Empire' and pledged that his own movement would support amalgamation in return for a 'perfect equality of rights, law and liberties'.[56]

Like many contemporary (and especially Irish) politicians, O'Connell was particularly given to arguments in the historical mode, so much so that his opponents sometimes had little difficulty in responding with the retort satirical. He could wax eloquent about the wickedness of Henry II, the fact that many excellent Irish institutions predated the Norman Conquest, how Irish boroughs received legitimacy from their origins among the 'free Danes', how— in language that almost prefigured the 1916 Declaration of Independence— Ireland had repeatedly asserted its 'rights' in 1172, 1200, 1236, and many times thereafter, claims that unsurprisingly led a non-O'Connellite reformer to 'wonder that the honourable member did not throw in by way of prologue something concerning the age of St Patrick'.[57] Nonetheless, even politicians like Richard Lalor Sheil who were moving away from O'Connell's political orbit found it useful to adopt similar positions concerning the Anglo-Irish

---

[53] Russell to O'Connell, 9 May 1839, T[he] N[ational] A[rchives] Russell Papers PRO 30/22/2C.

[54] The declared object of the Ulster Constitutional Association founded in June 1840: B. A. Kennedy, 'Sharman Crawford's Federal Scheme for Ireland', in H. A. Cronne et al. (eds), *Essays in British and Irish History in Honour of James Eadie Todd* (London, 1949), 243.

[55] Parl. Deb. 3: xlv. 990 (28 February 1839), xlix. 346 (15 July 1839), xxix. 1315 (31 July 1835).

[56] O'Connell to Melbourne, 10 May 1838, *The Correspondence of Daniel O'Connell*, ed. M. R. O'Connell, 8 vols (Dublin, 1972–80), vi. 160; O. MacDonagh, *The Emancipist: Daniel O'Connell 1830–47* (London, 1989), 137.

[57] B. D. Crowe, 'The Parliamentary Experience of the Irish Members of the House of Commons, 1833–41', Queen's University Belfast Ph.D. Thesis (1995), 215.

relationship. 'By the same policy both countries must be governed ... Do you think that we will, or that we ought, to acquiesce in any measure short of complete equality with England?' What was needed was for Britain to 'place us on a noble level, and establish a glorious parity between us', so that we could 'fill our hearts with the glorious consciousness of British citizenship'.[58]

Irish MPs in the 1830s—and especially those of an O'Connellite/Liberal persuasion—spent a good deal of time insisting that their country formed an integral part of a greater political entity. The government must, they argued, 'consider the Irish people as British subjects'; they were 'subjects of the same realm ... and consequently entitled to and heirs to the same rights, privileges, and protection'.[59] Sheil himself, in a debate of February 1833, had dramatically cried out 'Englishmen! We are your countrymen', while Spring Rice (an incompetent Chancellor of the Exchequer from 1835 to 1839), in an interminable speech of 23 April 1834 involving much talk of Henry VII, Poynings' Law, and the 1790s, announced that, just as North Britain was an excellent name for Scotland, so he profoundly hoped all would henceforth 'prefer the name West Britain to that of Ireland'.[60]

Melbourne's administration responded to all this with a controlled enthusiasm, which, though doubtless more noticeable in demeanour and language than in actions, certainly marked a distinct change from what had gone before. In part this sprang from the parliamentary realities that had led to the Lichfield House Compact. But no less important was the fact that Ireland— as a political and social problem in the years 1835–41—was allocated to the attentions of sympathetic elements within the capacious family of Whiggery, those that looked especially to the inspiration of Charles James Fox. Most prominent among them were Russell at the Home Office (1835–9), Duncannon as privy seal (1835–40), and—directly in charge of Ireland—Mulgrave as lord lieutenant (1835–9 and then Russell's successor at the Home Office in 1839–41), Ebrington as the next lord lieutenant (1839–41), and Morpeth as chief secretary (1835–41) and patron of the innovative and influential undersecretary Thomas Drummond. This, indeed, was one of the few periods during which Ireland under the Union was controlled by men of similar, often closely similar, views and dispositions. They were also an unusually talented group, in marked contrast to plodding Tory predecessors such as Talbot, Northumberland, and Haddington, the last accurately described by a contemporary as 'destitute not only of shining but of plausible qualities'.[61]

At their head Melbourne offered broadly sympathetic, if somewhat indolent, support. His declaration that, while Catholicism displayed 'enormous

---

[58] Parl. Deb. 3: xxxi. 1100 (29 February 1836).
[59] Parl. Deb. 3: xxxvii. 947 (10 April 1837: Browne) and xlvii. 252 (18 April 1839: Roche).
[60] Ibid. xv. 270 (6 February 1833: Sheil) and xxii. 1193–4 (23 April 1834: Spring Rice).
[61] *Greville Memoirs*, ed. Strachey and Fulford, iv. 416.

errors ... the main opinions of that church' were essentially 'the same as those of our own' and that it was therefore 'not fitting to treat the Roman Catholics ... as if they were worshippers of Juggernaut'[62] was welcomed by and found echoes among the Foxites. The implication that, as far as the fundamental truths of Christianity were concerned, there was no unbridgeable difference between Protestants and Catholics, while deeply resented in some quarters, played directly, for example, to the sensibilities of the devout Morpeth, who publicly talked of 'that union which I hope includes us all—the worship of a common creator, the doctrines of a common gospel, and the faith of a common cross'.[63]

Although Melbourne's relaxed insouciance could sometimes grate, he left no doubts as to his steady adherence to the view that, as he put it in May 1840, 'with respect to rights, privileges, and immunities, it was of the last importance that they [the Irish] should be placed upon the same footing with this country'.[64] Mulgrave was specifically told that he must now carry 'the Roman Catholic Relief Bill into actual practical effect' and face down the violent opposition of the high Protestants—a distinctly more forceful approach than the one Melbourne himself had adopted when chief secretary in 1828.[65] And Mulgrave (created Marquess of Normanby in 1838) threw himself into what he saw as the connected tasks of conciliation and assimilation with all the theatrical bravado typical of one who had published no fewer than four romantic novels before arriving in Ireland. His formal entry into Dublin in May 1835 involved bands playing 'national airs', while the viceroy remained uncovered in spite of heavy rain, which rather inconsiderately washed away pro-Mulgrave inscriptions on the banners waved by the crowd to reveal less flattering messages beneath. At once taking himself to a tailor, he ordered a new fancy green uniform, and by the next year the whole viceregal family was to be seen parading similarly attired to celebrate St Patrick's Day.[66] O'Connell, not himself disdainful of public display, was so impressed that Morpeth could report that 'Dan says you give great satisfaction—dignified, impartial etc.', while adding, somewhat deflatingly, that 'you are to take this just as you choose'. Mulgrave toured Ireland with unusual enthusiasm, replying to numerous addresses with repeated mantras to the effect that his duty

---

[62] Parl. Deb. 3: xxx. 727 (20 August 1835).

[63] *The Viceregal Speeches and Addresses, Lectures and Poems of the Late Earl of Carlisle*, ed. J. J. Gaskin (Dublin, 1866), 249; Brent, *Liberal Anglican Politics*, 66.

[64] Parl. Deb. 3: liii. 1163 (4 May 1840).

[65] Melbourne to Mulgrave, 7 February 1837, M[ulgrave] C[astle] Mulgrave Papers MM/145; Lamb (i.e. Melbourne) to Anglesey, 11 May 1828, RA Melbourne Papers MP93.

[66] P. Gray, 'A "People's Viceroyalty?" Popularity, Theatre and Executive Politics 1835–47', in Gray and O. Purdue (eds), *The Irish Lord Lieutenancy c.1541–1922* (Dublin, 2012), 158–78; J. Prest, *Lord John Russell* (London, 1972), 97.

was 'to see that in every respect Ireland is treated as an integral part of the British Empire'.[67]

Of course, much of this could be classified as the kind of superficial bromides that had not been entirely lacking, even in the very different decades immediately following the Union. But constant repetition, together with the kind of actions that *had* been lacking before 1829/30, undoubtedly indicated the arrival of a changing political environment. Mulgrave made what were, for a serving viceroy, unusual appearances in the House of Lords to inform peers that his mission was 'to treat the English and the Irish as one nation'. He followed instructions from London to reduce the militarization of tithe collection, to give 'effect to the Catholic Relief Bill', and to destroy 'extreme parties' of all kinds. In return, he was told that the Dublin administration constituted one of the government's bright spots.[68] 'The attempt', Russell wrote, 'to govern Ireland fairly is a noble one and the next thing to success in such an endeavour is a failure from too honest and straightforward a conduct.'[69]

A species of mutual backslapping took hold of Melbourne's Irish administration, all of it uplifting, little of it entirely unmerited. Not that those concerned were unaware of the difficulties and problems involved. Indeed, Normanby (as he had then become) stressed the importance of raising Ireland economically to English levels 'if the countries are to continue united' and likened his viceroyalty to 'the sending of an expedition into a previously hostile territory'.[70] His Whig successor, Lord Ebrington (from 1841 Earl Fortescue), though less showy, went even more 'native' in his opinions, regarding O'Connell's later campaigns to repeal the Union as perfectly proper forms of agitation, not least because, with 'loyalty to the queen and attachment to the monarchy ... [forming] the general profession of repealers, all appeals to physical force are disclaimed', and, he added in a remarkable conclusion, because the Union itself had been 'passed at no remote period and *by no justifiable means*.[71] 'I am', he told O'Connell, 'and ever have been most anxious to obtain for the Irish people a full and equal share of all the privileges of the British constitution.' And so commonplace had opinions of this kind

---

[67] Morpeth to Mulgrave, 18 May 1835, MC Mulgrave Papers M/439; *Addresses Presented to His Excellency the Earl of Mulgrave from the Different Parts of Ireland during the Years 1835 and 1836* (Dublin, 1836), 102, 259, 333.

[68] Parl. Deb. 3: xxxix. 249 (27 November 1837); Russell to Mulgrave, 25 May 1835, TNA Russell Papers 30/22/1E, 27 May 1835, MC Mulgrave Papers M/777, 5 August 1836, ibid., M/864.

[69] Russell to Mulgrave, 6 January 1836, MC Mulgrave Papers M/818, and 9 December 1837, ibid., M/890.

[70] Normanby to Spring Rice, 14 November 1836, MC Mulgrave Papers M/662; *The Morpeth Roll: Ireland Identified in 1841*, ed. C. Ridgway (Dublin, 2013), 36.

[71] Ebrington to Normanby, 8 September 1840, D[evon] R[ecord] O[ffice] Fortescue Papers 1262M/L1/160; emphasis added.

become in government circles that, shortly before the fall of Melbourne's ministry, Ebrington received a letter from a future Whig Chancellor of the Exchequer to the effect that 'it is always a good argument, at any rate in parliament, that you are doing in Ireland as in England', a form of words that might have been lifted directly from the recipient's own correspondence of six months before: 'We must deal with Ireland as with England.'[72] Morpeth, who served as chief secretary with both Mulgrave and Ebrington, took precisely the same line when condemning those who opposed assimilation and reform for, in effect, announcing 'as one country to its sister and co-ordinate country: you are a conquered nation and my religion shall be yours'.[73]

It was, indeed, Morpeth who reaped the most public and dramatic Hibernian 'reward' for his political activities in Ireland, the so-called Morpeth Roll presented to him on the government's electoral defeat and resignation in the summer of 1841. This enormous and unique document proclaimed that during his 'official career in Ireland' Morpeth's 'happy destiny' had been 'to assist in those good measures of policy whose object has been to raise Ireland to a first equality with other parts of the empire'. Although O'Connell's political machine had been instrumental in the roll's production, the fact that a quarter of a million or so individuals subscribed to or signed it is evidence of a genuine regard that went well beyond the world of formal public politics. Now consisting of 652 pieces of paper stuck together to make a production that, if fully extended, would be as tall as the Empire State Building, it is still stored in a box at Castle Howard in Yorkshire, Morpeth's equally impressive country seat. That it contains the signatures, not only of O'Connell himself, but also of Thomas Davis and Charles Gavan Duffy, hints at the unexpectedly lengthy survival of a unified prelapsarian version of Irish nationalism.[74]

Similar views as to the manner in which the Anglo-Irish connection might be rendered more intimate achieved almost totemic popularity in the 1830s. Viscount Howick from within the cabinet told the Commons in July 1835 that Ireland must be rendered 'a part of ourselves ... I desire that the two countries should be united, not merely in name, but in fact, that Ireland should be bound to us by the closest and most indissoluble ties.' This wish for alignment and coordination even led to the suggestion that Catholicism become the established religion in Ireland (something Melbourne favoured at least in theory), because 'the establishments in each of the three divisions of the United Kingdom could then be supported on the irresistible grounds of

---

[72] Ebrington to O'Connell, 9 December 1838, DRO Fortescue Papers 1262M/FC/94; C. Wood to Ebrington, 25 March 1841, ibid. 1262M/LI/190; Ebrington to Normanby, 8 September 1840, ibid. 1262M/LI/160.

[73] Parl. Deb. 3: xlii. 1260 (14 May 1838).

[74] *Morpeth Roll*, ed. Ridgway, 10, 18–23, 83, 87, 99.

their practical utility'. In the 1840s Russell supported 'the establishment of the Catholic religion [in Ireland] provided the Protestant was preserved'. Earl Fitzwilliam thought the establishment of Presbyterianism in Scotland meant that it was 'wrong' and an 'injustice' that the majority faith in Ireland was not treated in the same way. And Macaulay too declared support for 'any well-digested plan for establishing the Catholic Church in Ireland'.[75]

In practice, Ireland's denominational arrangements presented real difficulties for all governments, not only in the 1830s, but throughout the whole of the Union period, with the peculiar situation of the Church of Ireland—established yet catering for a small minority—proving especially perplexing. Virtually all Whigs agreed, not only that something had to be done, but that, in an ideal world, no government should have been faced with what had actually come to pass. As prime minister Grey could never quite decide upon the best course to follow and unhappily presided over endless debates between those, like Russell, who wanted root-and-branch reform of the Church of Ireland involving the 'appropriation' of parts of its revenues for essentially secular purposes, and those, like Stanley, to whom such ideas were anathema. What made matters peculiarly difficult and eventually led to the (compromise) Church Temporalities Act of 1833 were precisely the dilemmas created by the Union's latching together the Churches of England and Ireland into a quasi-legal if—in many respects—theoretical entity.[76] Even after the legislation of 1833, Grey remained perplexed by the circumstances of the Anglican communion in Ireland, its character 'so anomalous that nothing like ... [it] was ever before known in the history of the world'.[77] What of course rendered all of this almost impossibly difficult were the inevitable reverberations between the English and Irish parts of the new post-Union 'United Church'. Tampering with one had such obvious implications for the other that Grey was obliged to remind his Irish viceroy to 'remember that it is not for Ireland alone or in an Irish parliament that we are to legislate' with regard to institutions that were now 'one in principle and by law', however different their characters and contexts undoubtedly remained. In turn, Anglesey argued that the only way in which a Protestant establishment could be safely sustained in Ireland was to align it more directly with English modes of behaviour, commitment, and appeal.[78]

[75] *Greville Memoirs*, ed. Strachey and Fulford, v. 166–7 (9 March 1844); Parl. Deb. 3: lxxxiv. 1407 (23 March 1846: Fitzwilliam); Macaulay to Sir J. Gibson, 29 November 1843, *The Letters of Thomas Babington Macaulay*, ed. T. Pinney, 6 vols (Cambridge, 1974–8), iv. 161.

[76] Hawkins, *Forgotten Prime Minister*, i. 116–21, 131–45; N. Gash, *Sir Robert Peel: The Life of Sir Robert Peel after 1830* (London, 1972), 48–53, Macintyre, *The Liberator*, 39–42, 131–6.

[77] Parl. Deb. 3: xxiv. 254 (6 October 1834).

[78] Grey to Anglesey, 25 October 1832, PRONI Anglesey Papers D619/28A; [7th] Marquess of Anglesey, *One-Leg: The Life and Letters of Henry William Paget, First Marquess of Anglesey* (London, 1961), 262; Anglesey to Stanley, 21 March 1832, PRONI Anglesey Papers D619/31H.

V

Of course, one way to achieve such goals, though by paths rather different from those Anglesey had in mind, was to attempt the wholesale Protestant-ization (or more precisely the wholesale Anglicanization) of Ireland. This approach had long roots, but achieved particular thrust during the first half of the nineteenth century. Almost immediately after the Union Ireland's energetic cold-war warrior, Lord Redesdale, not only emphasized the import-ance of mass conversions but optimistically insisted that the 'Irish might be Protestantized if due pains were taken for the purpose. Given good bishops and good judges, and twenty years will do much.' The first post-Union chief secretary agreed, as did the prime minister, Henry Addington, who told Redesdale that 'no impression can be more deeply rooted in my mind than that of the importance of rendering Ireland a Protestant Country'.[79]

The big push in this respect did not, however, manifest itself until the 1820s as part of what was soon to become a strongly assimilationist impulse at virtually every level, religious, social, and political. English evangelicals turned their attention to Ireland as mission territory capable of being rendered more congruent with British practices and precedents. Irish bishops of similar disposition began to be appointed and promoted, notably William Magee, translated from Raphoe to Dublin in 1822 and within five months publicly calling his (not always enthusiastic) clergy to spiritual battle against Popery with the help of new proselytizing societies and the distribution of apocalyptic literature. In 1825 Magee told a parliamentary committee looking into the 'state of Ireland' that, with respect to that country, the reformation might, strictly speaking, be said 'only now to have begun'.[80] Other local enthusiasts, such as Revd T. D. Gregg, populist leader of the Dublin Protestant Operative Association and Reformation Society, similarly proclaimed that Ireland was now 'a missionary country' ripe for conversion to that species of Christianity that had made England and the Empire at once the godliest and the mightiest imperial power in the history of the world.[81]

The harvest actually reaped by the time the missionary campaigns had subsided in the 1850s was meagre to say the least: a few priests abandoned

[79] Redesdale to Perceval, 23 May 1805, BL Perceval Papers Add. MS 49188; Abbot to Redes-dale, 16 December 1802, G[loucestershire] R[ecord] O[ffice] Mitford Papers D2002/3/1/19; Addington to Redesdale, 7 January 1803, ibid., D2002/3/1/17; also Redesdale to Abbot, 19 November 1802, TNA Abbot Papers 30/9/119; Redesdale to Addington, 27 December 1802, DRO Sidmouth Papers 152M/C1802/OI/49.
[80] D. Bowen, *The Protestant Crusade in Ireland, 1800–70: A Study of Protestant–Catholic Relations between the Act of Union and Disestablishment* (Dublin, 1978), p. ix and *passim*; *Minutes of Evidence Taken before the Select Committee of the House of Lords Appointed to Inquire into the State of Ireland*, H.C. 1825 (521), ix. 138.
[81] Hoppen, *Elections, Politics, and Society in Ireland*, 312.

Rome, some 'Protestant refuges' were set up for small bands of lay converts, much ill-will was generated during the Famine by attempts to entice the starving in return for food and shelter. But the failure of the enterprise should not disguise the fact that behind the rhetoric there had lain a determined attempt at a kind of Anglo-Irish assimilation on the basis of common religious beliefs and values. In the view of one leading protagonist, the enterprise had always at heart been one, not simply of rescuing souls, but of transforming the Irish into 'Englishmen', of encouraging them 'to blend England with all their dearest, their holiest, their most ennobling recollections, to trace thither the pedigree of their blessings, to make it in heart and spirit, the country of their earthly affections'.[82] Indeed, given that Protestantism was perceived (however inaccurately) as a binding force in the Union, it is little wonder that the 'challenge of integrating the Catholic Irish' was seen in terms of, among other things, a moral transformation in which Protestant principles would bolster respect for the constitution and inject existing British social and political attitudes into recalcitrant Hibernian veins.[83]

While all of this was primarily a campaign undertaken in Ireland itself and while it was characterized by a very different set of attitudes from that found among the Foxite Whigs given charge of Ireland in the 1830s, it also articulated assimilationist aims and sought to move in the same direction of travel. If, therefore, it can hardly have been completely congenial to Russell, it shared (though from a very different perspective) some of the gut Protestantism that underpinned his own essentially Erastian political and religious views. And it was such views, especially when in tension with the less 'advanced' opinions of Stanley, that helped shape the background to the religious policies of the Grey and Melbourne administrations. The result was a compromise, not only over reforming the Church of Ireland, but also regarding legislative reactions to the intense popular agitation for changes in the tithe system that underpinned its finances, both of them issues leading to policies theoretically designed to prop up the established church but in practice striking out in very new directions indeed. Eventually a kind of settlement was reached and the so-called Tithe War subsided in response to various measures passed between 1832 and 1838 providing for modest reductions in the amounts to be paid, exemption for yearly tenants and tenants-at-will, and Treasury cash to pay the bulk of arrears accumulated since 1830.[84] In many respects this 'solution' was little more than

---

[82] Hoppen, *Elections, Politics and Society in Ireland.* 196; D. Bowen, *Souperism: Myth or Reality: A Study in Souperism* (Cork, 1970), 110; S. J. Brown, 'The New Reformation Movement in the Church of Ireland', in Brown and D. W. Miller (eds), *Piety and Power in Ireland 1760–1960: Essays in Honour of Emmet Larkin* (Belfast, 2000), 191–2.

[83] I. Whelan, *The Bible War in Ireland: The 'Second Reformation' and the Polarization of Protestant–Catholic Relations, 1800–1840* (Madison, WI, 2005), 267; D. H. Akenson, *The Church of Ireland: Ecclesiastical Reform and Revolution, 1800–1885* (New Haven, 1971), 132–4.

[84] The best account of this complicated matter is Macintyre, *The Liberator*, 167–200; also Akenson, *Church of Ireland*, 148–59, 180–94.

a smoke-and-mirrors affair, for, while the (admittedly reduced) burden now shifted from small tenants to landlords, this had an inevitable impact upon the level of rents. But, with agitation declining and tithe fatigue infecting politicians of all stripes, not excluding O'Connell, matters reached a sort of tired (if temporary) condition of stasis.[85]

Russell and others were also keen to develop strategies designed to inculcate loyalty to the state on the part of the Catholic clergy by paying them government stipends and thus aligning them more closely to the pecuniary situation of their established counterparts. This had, of course, long been in the minds of those responsible for the government of Ireland. It had informed Pitt's union aspirations and also the so-called Veto Controversy of 1808 when the Catholic hierarchy had eventually rejected proposals that the appointment of bishops should (as in most continental countries) become subject to ministerial veto in return for state salaries and other inducements. Even so, Whig ministers kept dreaming Erastian dreams about handing out cash in return for clerical obedience. In 1832 Grey was casting about for a good plan to put flesh on Anglesey's arguments that, 'until the priest is paid by the Government, no Government can depend upon either priest or people', believing £250,000, possibly only £150,000, would do the trick. Stanley too, though he foresaw difficulties, felt that the good effects of any payment scheme would be 'incalculable'.[86] Plans to stuff priests' mouths with gold soon became the fall-back argument of ministers anxious to create a peaceful Ireland more closely aligned to English models of politico-ecclesiastical practice. Russell clearly saw it as a way of consolidating Irish Catholics into the new union polity, as did Mulgrave, Lansdowne, Palmerston, Duncannon, Grey, Melbourne, and many other leading figures.[87] At a cabinet in October 1848 (attended by the lord lieutenant who had come over especially from Dublin) Russell was still so effectively pushing the matter forwards that ministers provisionally agreed to find £340,000 for the purpose.[88] But, while additional impetus came from cross-party support for what became known as

[85] Mulgrave writing to Russell (11 May 1838, TNA Russell Papers PRO 30/22/2B) declared himself 'heartily tired of the question'.

[86] Grey to Anglesey, 15 January 1832, PRONI Anglesey Papers D619/28A; Anglesey, *One-Leg*, 251; Anglesey to Grey, 10 January 1831, DU Grey Papers GRE/B3/39; Stanley to Grey, 3 January 1832, LRO Derby Papers 167/2.

[87] Russell to Mulgrave, 9 and 27 December 1837, MC Mulgrave Papers M/890 and 893 and to Clarendon, 18 November 1849, Bodl. Clarendon Papers Irish 26; Mulgrave to Russell, 11 December 1837, TNA Russell Papers PRO 30/22/2F; Lansdowne to Grey, 26 December [1832], DU Grey Papers GRE/B38/10; Lansdowne's Memorandum of March 1848, TNA Russell Papers PRO 30/22/7B; Palmerston to his brother William, 25 December 1843, E. Ashley, *The Life and Correspondence of Henry John Temple, Viscount Palmerston*, 2 vols (London, 1879), i. 463; Palmerston's Memorandum of 31 March 1848, TNA Russell Papers PRO 30/22/7B; Russell to Duncannon, 17 September 1843, W[est] S[ussex] R[ecord] O[ffice] Bessborough Papers 250; Grey to William IV, 19 December 1831, *The Reform Act, 1832*, ed. Grey, ii. 45–6.

[88] Prest, *Lord John Russell*, 291–2.

'endowment'—about £100 to £150 annually per priest was suggested by a Tory chief secretary in 1844[89]—the theoretically wonderful notion of thus pushing Ireland towards peaceful assimilation fizzled out in the face of increasingly determined opposition from the intended recipients and their ecclesiastical superiors. Yet hope never quite died in ministerial breasts. Interminable talk continued throughout the 1840s and, for some true believers, into the late 1860s, by which time even Russell felt moved to signal its utter impracticability in the face of continued resistance from the Catholic hierarchy in Ireland.[90]

Throughout the 1830s, Russell, while accepting that the Irish were a distinct (indeed difficult) people, was entirely in agreement with those who argued that the aim of official policy must be to ensure that, by whatever means, they would ultimately cease to be 'distinguishable from the people of England and Scotland'.[91] Indeed, he was strongly of the opinion that it was precisely because so much attention had been given to the notion of difference that many good things showered upon the English and Scots were withheld from the Irish. His famous remark of 1837 (later much referred to by Gladstone), that 'whereas Scotland is inhabited by Scotchmen and England by Englishmen, yet, because Ireland is inhabited by Irishmen you will refuse them the same measure of relief',[92] must therefore be seen as a more or less exact reflection of his own complex outlook on the matter: differences should ultimately be diminished, even undone, and, in the meantime, smoothed over by integrationist and liberal reforms. It was, indeed, Russell, a permanent member of Whig cabinets after 1831 and Home Secretary from 1835 to 1839, who proved both ideologically and practically the ringmaster of the assimilationist thrust. And, while he provided the strategic Foxite fuel in London, supportive viceroys and chief secretaries manipulated the tactical machinery in Ireland itself. In public at least this machinery was especially devoted to generating theatrical gestures designed to add colour to legislative innovation, with Mulgrave (or O'Mulgrave as choleric Tories called him) their most extravagant viceregal enthusiast and Ebrington and Bessborough playing strong supporting parts. This involved grand processions, green uniforms, dramatic celebrations of St Patrick's Day, paid-for puffs in newspapers,

---

[89] Graham to Eliot, 20 October 1843, BL Graham Papers Ir/6; Eliot to Graham, 8 and 14 January 1844, ibid., Ir/13. The Graham Papers were consulted on microfilm prior to their move from the Cumbria Record Office to the British Library, now BL Add. MSS 79591–79755. The original references are given throughout, not least because the microfilm version includes items subsequently lost.

[90] D. A. Kerr, *'A Nation of Beggars'? Priests, People, and Politics in Famine Ireland, 1846–1852* (Oxford, 1994), 172–6; Parl. Deb. 3: clxxxi. 1063–76 (26 February 1866).

[91] Parl. Deb. 3: xxxvi. 289 (7 February 1837: Roebuck).

[92] Ibid. 207 (7 February 1837).

afflations about the value of public opinion, tours of the countryside, emollient speeches without end, and much much more.[93]

What practical effect all of this had is difficult to assess, though O'Connell and his followers certainly responded with distinct enthusiasm. For Russell it constituted a necessary, but not of course a sufficient, aspect of the new Whig manner of ruling Ireland, though privately he saw such public initiatives in a less flamboyant light than Mulgrave's theatricalities were designed to evoke. That, nonetheless, a substantial change from former methods and approaches must now be undertaken and must also be seen to be in train was something about which he had no more than tactical reservations, as he told the king's secretary in 1835. And that this *was* an entirely new 'system' was something about which neither Russell nor his Whig colleagues had any doubts.[94] As he reminded Melbourne in 1837:

> The attempt to govern on Orange maxims broke down in 1829. The attempt to govern by a neutrality between different parties broke down in 1834. Neither of these plans can be permanently re-established … I remember you were the first person in 1829 by whom I heard it said that Ireland would henceforth claim to be treated according to its importance as a branch of the United Kingdom. It has done so, and will do so, and has a right to do so.[95]

Nor were such sentiments restricted to private letters. In fact, eirenic publicity was exactly what Russell sought as an effective assimilationist poultice for Irish discontents, as when he told the Commons in May 1838 that, 'if you will stand together with Ireland, if you will make Ireland strength of your strength, a part of your united body, then, indeed, with respect to any convulsions that may take place … you have the power to defeat and overcome them'.[96] Russell's whole approach became increasingly based on the principle, the overriding necessity, of equivalence between the kingdoms, a sentiment that was to provide the chief theme of his speeches on Ireland in these years. Indeed, he was still and no less forcefully repeating the mantras of the 1830s when on the threshold of becoming prime minister himself in 1846: Irishmen should be the equals of Englishmen, offices should be given to Catholics, Irish landlords must be compelled to act more fairly to their tenants as was done by their counterparts in England.[97]

---

[93] Gray, 'A "People's Viceroyalty?"', 158–78. Nor was this kind of thing neglected by Peel's viceroys in the 1840s: see C. Read, 'Peel, De Grey and Irish Policy, 1841–1844', *History*, 99 (2014), 1–18.

[94] Russell to Sir H. Taylor, 21 October 1835, TNA Russell Papers PRO 30/22/1E; Spencer to Russell, 12 April 1837, ibid., PRO 30/22/2E.

[95] Russell to Melbourne, 9 September 1837, ibid., PRO 30/22/2F. Melbourne expressed his agreement with this in a reply of 12 September 1837, ibid., PRO 30/22/2F.

[96] Parl. Deb. 3: xlii. 1202 (14 May 1838).

[97] Prest, *Lord John Russell*, 99; Russell to Duncannon, 11 April 1846, TNA Russell Papers PRO 30/22/5A.

Lesser politicians too were bowled along by the excitement of it all. Spring Rice told the king in 1837 that everything was now for the best in the best of all Hibernian worlds: agriculture was improving, the linen industry was prospering, education expanding, with only sectarianism still to be dealt with.[98] A more acute, though by no means unprejudiced, observer, George Cornewall Lewis (a future Chancellor of the Exchequer and Home Secretary and active in the 1830s on commissions enquiring into Irish poverty and education), having become convinced that it was circumstances rather than character that created the 'problems' of Ireland, had also now come to believe that overall improvement was best achieved through integration and levelling-up to English standards. With Ireland now 'clay under the potter's hand', it was essential (as he believed Whig ministers realized) that in Ireland 'improvement and civilization must ... descend from above', because it could never at present 'rise spontaneously from the inward workings of the community'.[99] Two well-informed observers, looking back from the 1850s to the Lichfield House period, agreed that this had indeed been a time when government had used assimilationist reforms to refashion the Irish 'clay' into shapes that might eventually come to resemble those that Britannia had long enjoyed. Sir Alexander MacDonnell, who had been Morpeth's private secretary and had then joined the Board of National Education, saw it as a period of growing reformist administration, though he added with the benefit of hindsight that at the time 'we were far from sanguine'. Sir Thomas Larcom, who served as undersecretary for Ireland, was even more convinced that the 1830s had been a decade when London had 'by the direct action of the executive' discovered a method for taking the government of Ireland into its own hands.[100]

None of this, however, meant that suddenly sweetness and light had begun to shine throughout the land or that all old prejudices had been magicked into oblivion. Perhaps the most notable and publicized trip down old-style memory lanes was the famous complaint of May 1836 by Lord Lyndhurst, a former Tory Lord Chancellor of England, to the effect that high-minded Anglo-Saxon politicians were being constantly and tediously obliged to 'contend with a population alien to Englishmen, speaking, many of them, a different language, professing a different religion, regarding the English as invaders, and ready to expel them at the first opportunity'.[101] And, while such sentiments certainly

---

[98] Spring Rice to William IV, 13 January 1837, N[ational] L[ibrary of] I[reland] Monteagle Papers MS 545.

[99] Lewis to E. W. Head, *Letters of the Right Hon. Sir George Cornewall Lewis, Bart. to Various Friends*, ed. G. F. Lewis (London, 1870), 49–50; G. C. Lewis, *On Local Disturbances in Ireland; and on the Irish Church Question* (London, 1836), 1.

[100] MacDonnell to Carlisle, 12 March 1855, C[astle] H[oward] Carlisle Papers J19/1/56; Larcom's Memorandum of July 1857, NLI Larcom Papers MS 7504.

[101] Parl. Deb. 3: xxiii. 734–5 (9 May 1836).

involved very distinct denials of contemporary Whig truths about Ireland, their linguistic turn had so long been established in metropolitan minds that, at some level or other, they never thereafter entirely ceased to prove instinctual, comfortingly tribal, and difficult to discard.

Even on the Whig side Grey continued to find the Irish in general and O'Connell in particular incomprehensible and unappealing, given their 'Jesuitical' arguments and eagerness to bite the hands that fed them.[102] Melbourne too never managed to overcome the feeling that the Irish as a whole were 'a very violent and very noisy people to deal with, but not a very courageous people, particularly not morally courageous'. And he did little to hide a general bafflement, which, when combined with a naturally indolent frame of mind, resulted in a sort of nonchalant indifference: 'There have been so many [tithe] bills that I hardly recollect one from the other and have no very distinct remembrance of that of last year.'[103] Russell, who saw himself— and not without reason—as especially sympathetic to many (not all) Irish aspirations, could still casually write to Mulgrave about the latter's governance of 'Paddy Land', while senior colleagues had no difficulty in combining their new Hibernian *démarche* with thinking the Irish untruthful (Wood), steeped in 'moral cowardice' (Clarendon), their constant whining creating what might best be described as the 'Bogtrotter Question' (Palmerston).[104] Indeed, it is far from clear whether lasting or firm convictions as to Irish 'improvability' ever obtained any real grip upon ministerial minds. As viceroy during the Famine, Clarendon, having previously served as British minister in Spain, could now only 'shrug my shoulders ... and say "Cosas de Irlanda" just as I used to account for every devilment by "Cosas de España"'. Still, his views remained unambiguously assimilationist. We 'must govern the Irish for their own good' and according to the values and methods that had made Britain great.[105]

VI

While, therefore, there can be no doubt that the atmosphere of British political life in relation to Ireland had begun to change in the fourth decade of the

[102] Grey to Anglesey, 16 August 1831 and 14 December 1832, PRONI Anglesey Papers D619/28A.
[103] Melbourne to Anglesey, 30 January 1832, RA Melbourne Papers MP94; to Wellesley, 22 October 1833, BL Wellesley Papers Add. MS 37306; to Russell, 11 March 1838, SU Melbourne Papers MEL/RU/465.
[104] Russell to Mulgrave, [c.1836], MC Mulgrave Papers M/807; Wood to Russell, 7 October 1846, TNA Russell Papers PRO 30/22/5D; Clarendon to Carew, 15 October 1850, T[rinity] C[ollege] D[ublin] Carew Papers MS 4021; Palmerston to Graham, 20 June 1861, BL Palmerston Papers Add. MS 48582.
[105] Clarendon to G. C. Lewis, 18 September 1847, Bodl. Clarendon Papers Irish Letter-Book I; to Russell, 13 August 1848, ibid. III.

century, this functioned more at the level of conscious judgement than of instinctual response and implied no sudden vaporization of traditionally hostile attitudes. And such attitudes continued to be applied—much to the bewildered puzzlement of Irish gentlemen and landowners—to pretty well everyone in Ireland, not merely to peasants, small farmers, Catholics, and the other usual suspects. Chief secretaries declared themselves 'nearly sick of the freaks on the Irish Bench'. Ministers wondered whether the Irish would ever be really fit for free government, given that most were 'half or rather whole Barbarians'.[106] Irish MPs, with very few exceptions (Littleton in 1833 thought at most 6 of the 105), were a hopeless collection of negative complainers: 'St Patrick's Day', noted one parliamentarian, 'Irish MPs mostly drunk'. The new intake after emancipation was an especially dubious lot, exhibiting 'coarse manners, fierce deportment', one of them, allegedly, known to have robbed mail coaches.[107] Indeed, at all levels the Irish were at best seen as incompetents to be patronized and improved, Disraeli's declaration that 'these men are discontented because they are not amused' being pretty well par for the course.[108]

While idiosyncratic radicals like Roebuck declared that 'a sort of mendicant whine' underpinned the 'misery of Ireland', sainted radicals like Cobden could be equally fierce: the Irish were 'first cousins if not elder brothers to the Hindoos ... the poor ryots are more hopeful clients'. O'Connell, who enthusiastically supported so many of Cobden's favourite causes, fared no better. He 'always treated me with friendly attention, but I never shook hands with him or faced his smile without a feeling of insecurity; and as for trusting him on any public question where his vanity or passions might interfere, I should have as soon thought of an alliance with an Ashantee chief'.[109] And, in the broader community, assimilationism could sometimes be completely undermined by behaviour of a strikingly old-world kind, as when in the 1830s an absentee landlord from England was to be found visiting tenants armed with 'parcels full of beads, little mirrors, broaches, and other gew-gaws'. Villages on Achill reminded one visitor of 'a cluster of Hottentot kraals'. Eminent scientists who thought 'the negro race decidedly inferior to the white' were no less convinced

---

[106] Leveson-Gower to Peel, 24 August 1829, NAI Leveson-Gower Letter-Book MS 737; Newbould, *Whiggery and Reform*, 136–7.

[107] Littleton to Anglesey, 2 July 1833, SRO Hatherton Papers D260/M/O1/2; *Disraeli, Derby and the Conservative Party: Journal and Memoirs of Edward Henry, Lord Stanley 1849–1869*, ed. J. Vincent (Hassocks, 1978), 123; *Three Early Nineteenth Century Diaries*, ed. Aspinall, 295, 314.

[108] W. F. Monypenny and G. E. Buckle, *The Life of Benjamin Disraeli, Earl of Beaconsfield*, 6 vols (London, 1910–20), v. 91.

[109] Parl. Deb. 3: clxxvii. 751, 757 (27 February 1865) and clxxxi. 696–7 (17 February 1866: both Roebuck); Cobden to Bright, 18 October 1850, *The Letters of Richard Cobden*, ed. A. Howe, 4 vols (Oxford, 2007–15), ii. 242 (also i. 60; ii. 65, 72); to G. Combe, 4 October 1848, J. Morley, *The Life of Richard Cobden*, 2 vols (London, 1881), ii. 27.

that the Celt was inferior to the Teuton.[110] John Walter, proprietor of *The Times* and Liberal member for Nottingham, had no hesitation in telling the Commons that the Irish 'were about as fit for self-legislation as the blacks. The House may not be aware, but it is nevertheless a fact that the blacks have a proverb that "If nigger were not nigger, Irishman would be nigger".' Others simply threw up their hands and hoped that the ocean would 'roll for twenty-four hours over the Emerald Isle'.[111]

An especially fertile locus for distrust continued to be the widespread belief that the Irish were dishonest and corrupt, particularly regarding official appointments, a curious conviction in the light of the no less intense pursuit of jobs and honours in contemporary Britain. Mulgrave regarded Irishmen hunting for patronage as 'egregious rats and [he was happy to say mostly] disappointed jobbers'.[112] As chief secretary Littleton reported one Irish MP writing to him 'asking for one living, an assistant barristership, and four chief constableships of police, and intimated that he had a much higher object for himself', while another had burst into his room at the Castle demanding a post for his brother and announcing grandly that 'the Frenches have represented their county [Roscommon] seven hundred years. They do not write letters: they demand audiences.'[113] Wearily Graham told the Tory viceroy, De Grey, that 'the chain which binds Ireland to England must be composed of gold and steel, but it is not safe to omit the use of the nobler metal'. As prime minister, Peel, doubtless recalling his own time in Dublin, warned De Grey that he would in time become 'very familiar ... with the expression "My father over and over again refused a peerage"'. And Eliot, De Grey's more liberal chief secretary, rapidly came to the same conclusion: '*Nimium ne crede colori*, be it green or be it orange, it would seem that there is no man in Ireland of any sort or party who is above doing a job.'[114] Whig viceroys like Clarendon, being of the same opinion, employed the same linguistic turn. 'Irishmen are natural jobbers', so much so that, 'when a man catches a cold here or is not seen for a few days, he is voted dead or as good as by a crowd of applicants who ask for his place'.[115] Some of the Englishmen appointed chief secretary could not refrain from criticizing Irishmen who had previously held the post for 'gross

[110] H. Inglis, *A Journey throughout Ireland during the Spring, Summer, and Autumn of 1834*, 5th edn (London, 1838), 36; *Letters from Ireland: Harriet Martineau*, ed. G. Hooper (Dublin, 2001), 139; *Extracts from Journals Kept by George Howard, Earl of Carlisle*, ed. Lady C. Lascelles (For Private Circulation, [1873]), 356, reporting the words of Thomas Huxley when visiting the viceregal lodge on 27 March 1862.

[111] Parl. Deb. 3: xcv. 792 (7 December 1847) and xiv. 691 (24 July 1832).

[112] Mulgrave to Melbourne, 26 January 1837, CH Carlisle Papers J19/11/2.

[113] Littleton's Journal for 27 July 1833, SRO Hatherton Papers D260/M/F/5/26/9.

[114] Graham to De Grey, 29 June 1843, BL Graham Papers Ir/4; Peel to De Grey, 23 November 1841, BL Peel Papers Add. MS 40477; Eliot to Peel, 4 August 1844, ibid., Add. MS 40480.

[115] Clarendon to Wood, 31 March 1850, B[orthwick] I[nstitute] Hickleton Papers A4/57; to Normanby, 2 August 1847, Bodl. Clarendon Papers Irish Letter-Book I.

abuses of patronage' or from giving lectures to Irish ministers and officials in Dublin. 'Patronage', Edward Horsman loftily told the Irish attorney-general, 'is no longer a property but a trust—and it is the recognized duty of every public man to serve the public first and his own relatives last.' This, he declared, was the guiding principle of any true Briton, but 'you will forgive me for saying that I have not thought it was sufficiently yours ... I have had to check nepotism in several departments, a very disagreeable duty'.[116] All of this is, however, rendered fantastical in the light of Horsman's undoubted ignorance of Ireland, his peculiar practice of conducting business with his wife prominently ensconced in a corner of the room, and the notoriously relaxed attitude towards patronage on the part of his own superior, Lord Carlisle, which, when brought to the prime minister's attention by Horsman's successor (the Irishman, H. A. Herbert), was breezily waved aside by Palmerston with the quip that 'a lord lieutenant ought to be able to do a job now and then'.[117]

Such attitudes grew out of antipathy, but also out of ignorance, though this seems, among British politicians, to have been less pronounced than it had been in the decades immediately after the Union. Irish observers, however, remained to be convinced that Westminster knew what it was about when discussing Irish affairs in general and Irish legislation in particular. 'Unhappily', noted Archbishop Laurence of Cashel in 1833, 'Irish Acts are almost always slow in progress, and when they pass the legislature are seldom remarkably intelligible. Englishmen know little of this country, and Irishmen, when consulted' prove too intemperate for their opinions to be of use. English chief secretaries often arrived in Dublin entirely unacquainted with Ireland and then, without taking breath, expressed outrage that in England 'no one seems to know that Ireland exists'.[118] Clarendon urged those in England who spouted strong views to come and actually visit the country before again opening their mouths, while Horsman moaned that London civil servants (especially those at the Treasury) never took any notice of his suggestions or requests.[119]

On the other hand, there can be no doubt that an increasing proportion of those more or less directly responsible for Irish affairs now came—for good or

[116] Horsman to Carlisle, 7 December 1855, CH Carlisle Papers J19/1/62 criticizing Sir William Somerville, Sir John Young, and Sir Thomas Redington (all of them Irish, the first two chief secretaries, the last undersecretary); also Horsman to Fitzgerald, 17 May 1856, ibid., J19/1/65.

[117] Hoppen, *Elections, Politics, and Society in Ireland*, 260; *Disraeli, Derby and the Conservative Party*, ed. Vincent, 169.

[118] Laurence to Littleton, 17 June 1833, SRO Hatherton Papers D260/M/01/6; Cardwell to Carlisle, 14 November 1860, CH Carlisle Papers J19/1/91.

[119] Clarendon to H. Reeve, 11 June 1849, H. E. Maxwell, *The Life and Letters of George William Frederick, Fourth Earl of Clarendon*, 2 vols (London, 1913), i. 293; Horsman to Carlisle, 18 June 1856, CH Carlisle Papers J19/1/65.

ill—to the job with some previous knowledge of Ireland itself. Stanley's first house as a married man had been on the Derby estate in Tipperary and he continued to own this until the late 1860s. Several chief secretaries were themselves Irish: Somerville, Naas, Young, Herbert, and Fortescue, as was the viceroy Lord Bessborough. Littleton was married to a daughter of Marquess Wellesley and Hardinge to Castlereagh's half-sister, while De Grey's wife was Irish. Indeed, the leading assimilationist politicians of the mid-century decades (Russell, Stanley, Peel) all had direct knowledge of Ireland, either because they had spent their early careers there or because they or their families owned substantial Irish estates, as did Palmerston (a frequent visitor to his Sligo property) and lesser figures such as Fitzwilliam and Devonshire. Clarendon had served as a commissioner of customs in Ireland in the late 1820s, two decades before becoming lord lieutenant in 1847. Cobden, Bright, and Macaulay all came to Ireland, while later ministers such as Spencer Walpole, W. E. Forster, W. H. Smith, H. A. Bruce, and Robert Lowe undertook extensive visits before taking office, while Wodehouse (who married a daughter of the third Earl of Clare) was busily collecting information on the country well before coming over as viceroy in 1864.[120]

To what extent such foreknowledge and direct contact proved enlightening is by no means clear. Certainly some men—Cobden and Lowe, for example—returned with all their previous opinions strengthened and confirmed. But though many came to mock, repeated immersions could sometimes lead to increased understanding if not always to sympathy, as can be seen in the cases of Derby and Palmerston. Indeed, broadly sympathetic insights could at times emerge from unexpected sources. The much vilified Charles Trevelyan, whose conduct of famine relief while at the Treasury has attracted both contemporary and subsequent condemnation, gloried in his own Celtic background, which he saw as furnishing particular fellow-feelings for the Irish—an attitude at once unusual and almost dangerously idiosyncratic. 'However superior the German race may be in some points, I would not have Ireland Anglo-Saxon if I could; and it has always appeared to me, that in the infinitely varied distribution of the rich gifts of Providence, the Celtic race has no reason to complain of its share.' Yet, even so, and perhaps precisely because of such thoughts, Trevelyan could not resile from projects designed to, in his words, produce a 'moral and physical regeneration' in Ireland along superior English lines. Although not desiring Ireland Anglo-Saxon, he nonetheless wanted

[120] Letters of Thomas Babington Macaulay, ed. Pinney, v. 64–70; Prest, Lord John Russell, 60, 134, 290, 427; Eglinton to Derby, 23 and 26 September 1858, LRO Derby Papers 148/3 (Walpole); Hawkins, Forgotten Prime Minister, i. 332; J. L. Sturgis, John Bright and the Empire (London, 1969), 118; Letters of the Rt Hon. Henry Austin Bruce GCB Lord Aberdare of Duffryn, 2 vols (Oxford, 1902), i. 138, 173, 222–3; Letters of Richard Cobden, ed. Howe, i. 18–19, 60; Morley, Life of Cobden, ii. 27; Ashley, Life and Correspondence of Henry John Temple, Viscount Palmerston, i. 47–8, 100–2, 117, 182, 438; J. Winter, Robert Lowe (Toronto, 1976), 64.

somehow to inject English values into a country still culturally and psycho-
logically distinct.[121] Cornewall Lewis (who knew much more about Ireland
than Trevelyan), while also adopting a broadly racial analysis, came to what
were surprisingly counter-intuitive conclusions. On the one hand, he pointed
out that the most violent and disturbed parts of Ireland often tended to be
inhabited by people with comparatively little 'Celtic blood'—he indicated
Kilkenny and Tipperary, whose inhabitants were 'large-limbed and fair-
haired'—while strongly 'Celtic' Kerry and west Galway were, by comparison,
generally quiet and subdued. On the other, he suggested that what he called
'circumstances' were largely to blame for Ireland's problems, something that
made him doubt 'whether a people of German race would have turned out
much better'—indeed, a 'peasantry of Protestant Germans might, if properly
oppressed and brutalised, be made as bad as the Irish. You remember the
German *Bauernkrieg*.'[122] This was, of course, a double-edged argument, for,
while it exonerated the Irish in certain respects, it also suggested that only men
of English origins possessed the fizz and gumption to react courageously to
oppression and exploitation.

Nor was Lewis's analysis without either later supporters or an interesting
afterlife. In 1851 the land agent W. S. Trench attributed Tipperary's violence
to the peasantry's 'Cromwellian' blood, while a poor law inspector blamed 'an
infusion of Teutonic blood. They will not lie down under the handicap
endured by my Donegal neighbours.' Thirty years later an American professor
thought a 'mixture of English blood' made peasants 'more obstinate'. Unsurprisingly, not everyone agreed, least of all W. N. Hancock, effectively the
government's chief statistician, who in 1870 informed Gladstone that Tipper-
arymen were genetic heirs to 'the bravest races of Celtic Irishmen', that
Westmeath and Longford were stocked with people of the ancient 'ruling
Irish race', and that King's County had always resisted 'Anglo-Saxon government'.[123] What of course gave such contradictory arguments an especially
potent charge was the way in which they intersected with continuing mid-
century debates about Ireland's backwardness and the importance of aligning
the country more and more closely with the enlightened and economically
effective values and mores developed by the English 'race' (and perhaps even
by the Scots).

---

[121] Trevelyan to T. S. Spring Rice, 10 November 1846, N[ewcastle] U[niversity] Trevelyan
Papers CET18/9/144–7.
[122] Lewis to E. W. Head, 9 April 1836, *Letters of the Right Hon. Sir George Cornewall Lewis*, ed.
Lewis, 49–50.
[123] Hoppen, *Elections, Politics, and Society in Ireland*, 375.

4

Direct and Scenic Routes

I

If the increasing rhetoric after 1830 about assimilation reflected a shift in thinking about the nature of the Anglo-Irish relationship and in turn generated discussions concerning the character of Irish government, the implementation of integrative measures and programmes furnished physical manifestations of the new departure. These programmes and measures took many forms, but can usefully be divided into two main categories: those that were unambiguously assimilationist and those that genuflected to perceptions of Irish distinctiveness by adopting what might be called Hibernian means to deliver ultimately 'English' goals. The former took the direct route, the latter more meandering byways. Both, however, were driven by the conviction that the Union's central advantage lay in the fact that 'by its common sense' it could mightily help to 'modify and regulate the magnificent and flowing ideas of Irishmen'.[1]

A broad context for all this emerges from the fact that, while the proportion of time devoted by parliament to Irish affairs rose after 1830 (a reflection in part of the presence of O'Connellite MPs), the proportion of legislation devoted to *specifically* Irish matters fell significantly, with even the Famine years, though they witnessed a spike, failing to match levels achieved throughout the three decades immediately following the Union.[2] It would seem, therefore, that, while parliament was prepared to devote an increasing amount of time to considerations of Ireland and its problems, governments were less and less willing to address these problems by mean of special and exclusively Hibernian legislation.

Also noticeable was a change in the nature and intensity of coercive laws of a specifically Irish character. These had been both highly visible and aggressive

---

[1] Parl[iamentary] Deb[ates] 3: lxxxv. 563 (3 April 1846: Seymour).
[2] P. Jupp, 'Government, Parliament and Politics in Ireland, 1801–41', in J. Hoppit (ed.), *Parliaments, Nations and Identities in Britain and Ireland, 1660–1850* (Manchester, 2003), 154; T. A. Spalding, *Federalism and Empire: A Study in Politics* (London, 1896), 49, 70.

in the years after 1798, when they had reflected the London government's view of Ireland as, above all, a violent and dangerous place requiring repression of an unusually severe kind. After an outburst of strongly coercive measures under Grey's administration of 1830-4—much of it demanded by Stanley as chief secretary—the decades that followed were marked by either the virtual absence of draconian coercion or the introduction of purely reactive laws in response to political disturbances such as the rebellion of 1848 or the Fenian threat in the mid-1860s. Indeed, the coercive menu was more or less completely blank between 1835 and 1843, with Morpeth, on becoming chief secretary in the former year, announcing a distinctly softer approach to issues of law and order and especially so with regard to military support for the enforced collection of tithes. Russell too was in no doubt that the government's policy could now best be summed up by the phrase 'conciliation and not coercion for Ireland', an approach that Ebrington consciously saw himself implementing when viceroy in the years that followed.[3] More notable still were the altered views of Tories such as Peel and Graham when in office between 1841 and 1846. As prime minister, Peel lectured his first viceroy (De Grey) about avoiding 'laws of a very repressive and coercive character', while Graham at the Home Office had become even more convinced 'that measures of simple repression and coercion will not avail'.[4] By the mid-1850s viceroys and chief secretaries were talking of the 'tranquillity' now there was 'such an element of prosperity in Ireland' and of how the whole island was 'almost entirely without crime'.[5]

Ministers went out of their way to emphasize their enthusiasm for the new dispensation. Horsman, when chief secretary, told the Commons in June 1856 that the bill he was putting forward was entirely 'precautionary' and 'nominal'. Indeed, 'he did not believe the majority of Irish country gentlemen, at the present moment, could tell him whether their counties were proclaimed or not'.[6] And it is in this context that the frequent renewal of the 1847 Crime and Outrage Act should be seen, for renewal was simpler than drawing up new bills and anything of a more permanent character would have offended

---

[3] Parl. Deb. 3: xxix. 1326 (31 July 1835: Russell); D. D. Olien, *Morpeth: A Victorian Public Career* (Washington, 1983), 134-5; Russell to Duncannon, 7 December 1843, W[est] S[ussex] R[ecord] O[ffice] Bessborough Papers 250; Ebrington to Charleville, 8 February 1841, D[evon] R[ecord] O[ffice] Fortescue Papers 1262M/LI/178. See V. Crossman, *Politics, Law and Order in Nineteenth-Century Ireland* (Dublin, 1996), 199-228, for a list of the relevant legislation 1776-1920.

[4] Peel to De Grey, 12 June 1843, B[ritish] L[ibrary] Peel Papers Add. MS 40478; Graham to Heytesbury, 23 May 1845, BL Graham Papers Ir/21. The Graham Papers were consulted on microfilm prior to their move from the Cumbria Record Office to the British Library, now BL Add. MSS 79591-79755. The original references are given throughout, not least because the microfilm version includes items subsequently lost.

[5] Horsman to Carlisle, 17 March 1855, C[astle] H[oward] Carlisle Papers J19/1/56; Carlisle's Diary for 1 January 1856, ibid., J19/8/34.

[6] Parl. Deb. 3: cxlii. 1391 (12 June 1856).

contemporary notions of individual rights. It was, in any case, as one modern authority has suggested, the existence in Ireland of the English provision of Habeas Corpus, rather than its occasional suspension, that would most 'have impressed continental policemen'.[7] Overall, therefore, the thirty-five years after 1830 marked a period of generally mild law-and-order legislation, which gradually came to be seen as so 'normal' that as late as December 1865 the then viceroy (Wodehouse), though certainly worried about Fenianism's 'deep roots', could still convince himself that, sooner rather than later, 'the whole organisation would dissolve in inextinguishable laughter'.[8]

II

All in all an assimilationist thrust was becoming widely evident. Already in 1830 ministers had come to the conclusion that the Irish system of county 'governors' should be replaced by the typically English system of county lords lieutenant, in the hope that this would inject a much-needed sense of paternalistic responsibility into a landed class notorious for feckless extravagance and a disposition to exploit the poor.[9] Perhaps the area in which the most persistent (though not always the most successful) efforts at assimilation were mounted was that of the law and legal affairs in general. As early as 1829 the chief secretary was making arrangements to assimilate the provisions regarding insolvent debtors. In the mid-1840s English legislation concerning the control and management of banks was more or less fully transplanted to Ireland in very rapid order indeed.[10] And at about the same time Graham was urging the viceroy to ensure that the provisions of the recent English marriage act were speedily extended to Ireland. From the back benches Sir Robert Shafto Adair addressed the Commons, not 'as an English or as an Irish, but as a British subject', while Richard Monckton Milnes argued that 'there should be no difference in the character of their legislation for Ireland and for Yorkshire'.

---

[7] W. E. Vaughan, 'Ireland *c.*1870', in Vaughan (ed.), *A New History of Ireland V: Ireland under the Union I 1801–70* (Oxford, 1989), 762–3.

[8] Wodehouse to Russell, 28 December 1865, T[he] N[ational] A[rchives] Russell Papers PRO 30/22/15H.

[9] Melbourne to Anglesey, 28 December 1830, R[oyal] A[rchives] Melbourne Papers MP93; Grey to Anglesey, 29 December 1830, P[ublic] R[ecord] O[ffice of] N[orthern] I[reland] Anglesey Papers D619/28A; Stanley to Anglesey, 4 August 1831, L[iverpool] R[ecord] O[ffice] Derby Papers 168.

[10] Leveson-Gower to Peel, 18 August 1829, N[ational] A[rchives of] I[reland] Leveson-Gower Letter-Book MS 737; G. L. Barrow, *The Emergence of the Irish Banking System 1820–1845* (Dublin, 1975), 175, 188; *Sir Robert Peel from his Private Papers*, ed. C. S. Parker, 3 vols (London, 1891–9), iii. 134–9; R. D. Collison Black, *Economic Thought and the Irish Question 1817–1870* (Cambridge, 1960), 150–1.

From the front bench Lord Clanricarde insisted that 'the laws of England and Ireland' should be 'assimilated and, as far as practicable, rendered identical', as did Henry Labouchere when accepting office as chief secretary with a seat in the cabinet in June 1846 and pledging that his policy would be to manage 'a fusion of system between the different parts of the United Kingdom'. And early in 1852 the Tory viceroy Lord Eglinton thought that 'an assimilation of the jury system' would greatly help to keep the lid on Irish discontents.[11]

As time went on the moves towards legal fusion became more and more pronounced. In 1850 Joseph Napier (eight years before becoming Lord Chancellor of Ireland) could simultaneously oppose the abolition of the lord lieutenancy on the grounds that some 'national peculiarities' demanded recognition and urgently insist that the 'great object' of parliament must 'be to identify Ireland as much as possible with England' and see to it that 'one uniform system [of law] should be adopted for both countries'.[12] Sometimes the application of English legal reforms to Ireland was swift, sometimes less so, occasionally nonexistent, as with the divorce reforms of 1857 over which the government got distinctly cold feet in the face of strident objections from all sides in Ireland against the imposition of alien godlessness.[13] The 1831 English transfer of bankruptcy jurisdiction to a chief judge in bankruptcy took twenty-six years to cross the Irish Sea, but cross it it did, as, more speedily, did the 1842 transfer of the equity jurisdiction of the court of exchequer to the chancery court (Ireland 1850) and the 1851 establishment of a court of appeal in chancery (Ireland 1856). In some cases there was hardly any delay at all, as when the English Common Law Procedure Act of 1854 was extended to Ireland less than two years later, its proposer in the Commons automatically assuming that, if 'the principle of these reforms had been accomplished in England, there was no reason why they should not be extended to Ireland'. Indeed, by then it had quite simply become accepted wisdom that, in the great majority of cases, 'the laws and institutions of Ireland should be assimilated to those of England'.[14]

[11] Parl. Deb. 3: civ. 117 (30 March 1849: Adair) and lxxxvii. 387 (8 June 1846: Monckton Milnes); Clanricarde's Memorandum of April 1848, TNA Russell Papers PRO 30/22/5A; Labouchere to Russell, 21 June 1846, ibid.; Eglinton to Walpole, 13 March 1852, Sc[ottish] R[ecord] O[ffice] Eglinton Papers GD3/5/1355.

[12] A. C. Ewald, *The Life and Letters of the Right Honble Sir Joseph Napier*, new edn (London, 1892), 61; Parl. Deb. 3: cx. 1346–7 (10 May 1850).

[13] D. Fitzpatrick, 'Divorce and Separation in Modern Irish History', *Past & Present*, 114 (1987), 172–96; D. Urquhart, 'Ireland and the Divorce and Matrimonial Causes Act of 1857', *Journal of Family History*, 38 (2013), 301–20; also Parl. Deb. 3: cxlv. 511–13 (19 May 1857), cxlvi. 325–6 (25 June 1857), cxlvii. 754–6 (30 July 1857), 1062 (4 August 1857) and 1990 (21 August 1857), cxlix. 1923–5 (29 April 1858). Ireland therefore retained the older system by which an act of parliament was required for each divorce.

[14] J. C. Brady, 'Legal Developments, 1801–79', in Vaughan (ed.), *A New History of Ireland V: Ireland under the Union I, 1801–70*, 470–1; Parl. Deb. 3: cxxxviii. 76 (3 May 1855: Whiteside); R. More O'Ferrall to Russell, 17 March 1846, TNA Russell Papers PRO 30/22/5A; also Sir R. Peel to Palmerston, 30 January 1862, S[outhampton] U[niversity] Palmerston Papers GC/PE/21.

The same was true of other areas of government. Thus the English and Irish pension lists were substantially amalgamated. The official policy regarding vaccination was coordinated. Irish convict prisons were modelled on those in England (though some deviation occurred later).[15] Stamp duties on the press were equalized in 1836. The government inspectorates that were such a feature of the period, notably those for factories and mines and emigration, though they had 'local' staff, ran on centralized London-controlled lines according to which Ireland was treated in the same way as Yorkshire or Essex, treated, in other words, exactly as Pitt had promised in 1800.[16] Russell's overheated response to the re-establishment of a Catholic hierarchy in England and Wales—the Ecclesiastical Titles Act of 1851—was drafted as a piece of United Kingdom legislation, a case of logic leading to a classic shot into one's own foot.[17]

Many aspects of Irish administration were increasingly coming under the control of civil servants with non-Irish backgrounds, usually gifted authoritarians determined to drag what they saw as a backward island into the modern practices of a greater and more advanced nation, men such as Thomas Drummond, undersecretary, George Nicholls, poor law commissioner, James Shaw Kennedy and Duncan McGregor, inspectors-general of constabulary, and William Brereton, chief inspector of the revenue police. As time went on government departments in London came more and more to assume an almost direct supervision of Irish affairs, sometimes to the annoyance of ministers in Dublin.[18] Few aspects of administrative concern remained untouched or at least unconsidered. The militia was to be controlled from London, not Dublin. On the foundation in London of the Department of Science and Art in 1853 a determined effort was made to bring the relevant Irish bodies under its direct command, with the responsible minister declaring himself quite 'unwilling to admit that there are circumstances in the condition of Ireland so exceptional' as to require special treatment.[19] Similarly, the new civil service entrance examination system set up in the wake of the Northcote–Trevelyan Report of 1853, though at first less dramatic than has sometimes been supposed, was certainly unambiguous in one respect: it was to operate

---

[15] Stanley to Grey, 25 August 1832, LRO Derby Papers 169; Parl. Deb. 3: clxix. 1791–2 (23 March 1863); *Convict Prisons, etc. (Ireland) Copies of Correspondence*, H[ouse of] C[ommons Paper] 1854 (344), lviii. 167–90, also P. Carroll-Burke, *Colonial Discipline: The Making of the Irish Convict System* (Dublin, 2000), 95–103, 179 ff.

[16] B. Inglis, *The Freedom of the Press in Ireland 1784–1841* (London, 1954), 211; O. MacDonagh, *Early Victorian Government* (London, 1977), 180.

[17] G. I. T. Machin, *Politics and the Churches in Great Britain 1832 to 1868* (Oxford, 1977), 225.

[18] Horsman to Carlisle, 25 February 1855, CH Carlisle Papers J19/1/63.

[19] Palmerston to Sir J. Young, 9 December 1854, SU Palmerston Papers GC/YO/5; R. A. Jarrell, 'The Department of Science and Art and the Control of Irish Science, 1853–1905', *Irish Historical Studies*, 23 (1983), 333–9.

(as Gladstone insisted in 1857) uniformly throughout the United Kingdom and to be controlled by a central commissioner in London.[20]

Especially striking was the way in which Russell's administration treated those who had led the Young Ireland rebellion of 1848. Although the law under which they were convicted certainly had specifically Irish elements, ministers almost fell over themselves in trying to prevent Smith O'Brien and his associates from becoming martyrs by treating them as 'normally' as possible. In fact the viceroy at the time, Clarendon, complained that his superiors in London were proving themselves quite insufficiently bloodthirsty when they insisted that British constitutional norms must continue to be applied to those 'who are as fit for them as Esquimeaux'.[21] Clarendon calmed down, and the prime minister, in both assimilationist and sensible modes, pointed out 'that executions for political offences, however justifiable, are seldom politic—a martyr transported is not nearly so interesting as a martyr hanged'[22]—a sentiment that those in power during the admittedly more difficult circumstances of the Easter Rising of 1916 might have done well to recall. Indeed, so wedded had ministers become to the concept of trying to handle law and order issues identically throughout the United Kingdom that, by the early 1860s, influential voices were even being raised in favour of abolishing the post of paid professional resident magistrate in Ireland and instead relying, as in England, upon local amateurs.[23]

III

One long-standing campaign provides both a revealing compendium of assimilationist pressures and confirmation of their eventual deflation and failure: that for the abolition of the lord lieutenancy and the consequent removal of the administrative grit from the post-Union relationship that Pelham's failed proposals of 1801 for closer integration had sought to achieve. Additional support for abolition was supplied by the endless difficulties ministers encountered when trying to persuade some reluctant victim to accept the posts of viceroy or chief secretary.[24] In 1833 Littleton was the fourth man

---

[20] Parl. Deb. 3: cxliv. 1274–5 (24 February 1857); K. T. Hoppen, *The Mid-Victorian Generation 1846–1886* (Oxford, 1998), 111–12.

[21] Clarendon to Bedford, 7 August and 17 September 1848, Bodl[eian Library] Clarendon Papers Irish 80 and 81.

[22] Crossman, *Politics, Law and Order in Nineteenth-Century Ireland*, 87–8.

[23] P. Bonsall, *The Irish RMs: The Resident Magistrates in the British Administration of Ireland* (Dublin, [1997]), 17.

[24] For this and much of what follows, see K. T. Hoppen, 'A Question None could Answer: "What was the Irish Viceroyalty for?"', in P. Gray and O. Purdue (eds), *The Irish Lord Lieutenancy, c.1541–1922* (Dublin, 2012), 132–57.

approached for the latter post. In 1834 the lord lieutenancy was 'hawked over all England and rejected'; 'it has now', reported well-informed sources, 'travelled to Scotland, and the Dukes of Gordon and Buccleuch are mentioned' (neither accepted). Five individuals declined before Heytesbury was eventually appointed in 1844.[25] On entering office in 1847 Clarendon boasted of his 'patriotic, uncompensated sacrifice'; on leaving in 1852 he marvelled at his having consented 'to be an exile from England in order to stand in the pillory here'. In 1855 Carlisle, then desperate for any kind of job, accepted what had, he sadly admitted, become one of the government's 'comparatively insignificant offices'.[26]

In the eyes of many, abolition of the viceroy's post would, therefore, kill two plump birds with one stone: the difficulty of finding persons prepared to take it on and the problem its continuation posed for the task of moulding Britain and Ireland into one amalgamated whole. And, while the idea itself went back at least to the time of the Union, it only now began to take wing, at first as a 'radical' proposal (something that militated against early take-off) in the shape of a Commons motion put forward in June 1823 by Joseph Hume, long notorious for inducing extreme boredom in all condemned to hear him speak.[27] For Hume and for some of his supporters the initial impetus for abolition was provided by a desire for financial prudence and administrative efficiency as much as by ideas of assimilation, his motion of 1823 being (silently) seconded by the eminent economist David Ricardo. Nonetheless, the ensuing debate laid down many of the points that were to be repeatedly rehearsed over the decades thereafter. Hume questioned whether the 'parts' of the United Kingdom were as yet 'united in spirit' and whether the Irish 'participated in those blessings of the British constitution' promised in 1800. Predictably he answered this carefully crafted enquiry by asserting that, far from Ireland having 'become the same as a county of England', it was in practice still governed 'as our slave colonies'. Predictably, too, he proved less precise as to what should replace the viceroy and chief secretary, talking vaguely about lords lieutenant of counties, as if Ireland *as a whole* could be put on the same basis as, for example, Rutland. But it was still early days in this—as it proved—lengthy argument, and Peel's retort that Ireland's still

[25] Grey to Anglesey, 9 May [1833], D[urham] U[niversity] Grey Papers GRE/B3/377; Wellesley to Littleton, 20 December 1834, S[taffordshire] R[ecord] O[ffice] Hatherton Papers D260/M/01/15; A. B. Erickson, *The Public Career of Sir James Graham* (Oxford, 1952), 280.

[26] Clarendon to Lewis, May 1847, H. E. Maxwell, *Life and Letters of George William Frederick, Fourth Earl of Clarendon*, 2 vols (London, 1913), i. 276; Clarendon to Carew, 28 February 1852, T[rinity] C[ollege] D[ublin] Carew Papers MS 4021; Carlisle to Palmerston, 16 February 1855, SU Palmerston Papers GC/CA/447.

[27] D. R. Fisher (ed.), *The History of Parliament: The House of Commons 1820–1832*, 7 vols (Cambridge, 2009), v. 753. On the abolition issue in general, see P. Gray, '"Ireland's Last Fetter Struck off": The Lord-Lieutenancy Debate 1800–67', in T. McDonough (ed.), *Was Ireland a Colony? Economics, Politics and Culture in Nineteenth-Century Ireland* (Dublin, 2005), 87–101.

primitive conditions required the presence of a 'local executive' as a 'necessary check upon a country so remote, which was an ancient kingdom', ensured that Hume's motion was rejected without a division.[28]

Because, however, the issue provided so useful a proxy for debates concerning the nature of the Union, it continued to attract attention out of all proportion to the intrinsic merits of the offices concerned. And, although of course the lord lieutenancy continued until 1922, this had more to do with the difficulty of finding a viable alternative than with any Tarzan-like attachment either to the post itself or to the merits of those who held it. It is, however, not without significance that the period during which the greatest desire for change was evident coincided more or less precisely with that during which assimilationist debates were at their most intense.

Within four years of Hume's first motion, even a viceroy (Wellesley) had caught the bug and was trying to persuade his chief secretary (the future prime minister Melbourne) that only abolition could ensure that 'local powers would be moved by the common united principle of action from the mainspring of England'.[29] Indeed, Hume obviously felt sufficiently encouraged to have another try in May 1830. The intention of the Union had been, he now declared, 'not only to unite the two countries in name, but to blend them into one complete whole'. Spring Rice, soon to become a senior member of both the Grey and Melbourne administrations, made the key point that, whereas the immediate post-Union 'tendency had been to localize everything in Ireland ... the present tendency was to assimilate the two countries'. Althorp too backed Hume, because he could see 'no more reason for supporting a separate local government in Ireland than in one of the northern counties of England'. And, while Leveson-Gower, the chief secretary, indulged in vacuities to the effect that 'assimilation' was not inimical to the retention of specifically Irish institutions, O'Connell turned out to be the only really eloquent defender of the lord lieutenancy, in his view a symbol of Irish distinctiveness. This time there was a division, and Hume lost by 229 votes to 115.[30]

Leveson-Gower's successor, Stanley, proved unable to come to any consistent view of the matter. Now he wanted to keep the office, now he wanted it abolished, a wobbling attitude in part dictated by a desire to join the cabinet while keeping the viceroy, Anglesey (of whom he thought little), firmly shut out.[31] More importantly, Wellington emerged in 1831 as the lord lieutenancy's strongest and most influential defender: 'It was necessary that Government should be on the spot ... to be ever present and ever active to put down that

---

[28] Parl. Deb. 2: ix. 1212–41 (25 June 1823: Hume) and 1233–4 (Peel).
[29] Wellesley to Lamb, 5 June 1827, RA Melbourne Papers MP98.
[30] Parl. Deb. 2: xxiv. 555–80 (11 May 1830).
[31] Stanley to Grey, 10 March 1831, DU Grey Papers GRE/B11/8/6, and 24 September 1832, LRO Derby Papers 169.

bane of the country, the acts and power of Demagogues.' By contrast, Grey proved pragmatically lukewarm, while several Irish MPs not attached to O'Connell supported abolition.[32] Abolitionism seems, indeed, to have become something of a political vogue. In 1838 Brougham, now no longer Lord Chancellor, told the Lords that the existence of the viceroyalty stood in the way of consolidating 'the two countries in all respects' and of ensuring that there should be 'no more difference between Yorkshire and Ireland than between Scotland and Yorkshire'.[33] Of greater significance was Russell's move against the office, even though at first he felt constrained by the fact that abolition 'would be dreadfully galling to the Irish in general' because of its seeming denial of Irish distinctiveness. Melbourne had come to the same opinion but on the narrower grounds that, because the whole administrative apparatus in Dublin was so corrupt and ineffective—'the Augean stables were more easily cleaned'—only a complete clear-out could generate any real improvement.[34]

The result was that the ever-optimistic Hume was encouraged to think it worth mounting a third parliamentary attempt in 1844. The fact that a Tory government was then in office in no way cooled his ardour, the issue having become, in his view, one that transcended the narrow imperatives of party difference. Thus the banner of 'perfect assimilation' was raised once again, as Hume quoted Pitt's union speech of 2 April 1800. One MP said the viceroyalty had become a joke; Russell hoped for complete abolition; Peel preferred gradual disappearance because, as he proclaimed, the whole of the United Kingdom 'should be governed the same way', though perhaps not just yet. His doubts brought about a temporary halt, and Hume withdrew his motion, as he had done in 1823.[35]

But with the arrival of a Whig administration in June 1846 Hume's ideas achieved a significant boost, largely because Russell was now prime minister and determined to pursue a general policy of amalgamation as far as Ireland was concerned. Within a year of coming into office, and with the Famine well under way (for which, see Chapter 5), he was telling a fellow cabinet member that the viceroyalty caused 'separation rather than union' and that a London-based secretary of state for Ireland would do the job more effectively and in a truly integrationist mode.[36] The immediate impulse behind so strong a view was the illness of the existing viceroy, Lord Bessborough, whose death on 16 May 1847 was announced to the cabinet the following day by a weeping

---

[32] Parl. Deb. 3: iv. 645–6 (4 July 1831) and vi. 31–2 (15 August 1831).

[33] Parl. Deb. 3: xliv. 22–3 (9 July 1838).

[34] Russell to Normanby, 28 October 1838, M[ulgrave] C[astle] Mulgrave Papers M/920; Melbourne to Normanby, ibid., MM/192.

[35] Parl. Deb. 3: lxxiv. 834–61 (9 May 1844); Peel to Eliot, 9 May 1844, BL Peel Papers Add. MS 40480.

[36] Russell to Lansdowne, 4 May 1847, BL 3rd Marquess of Lansdowne Papers B102 (provisional reference).

Russell, together with the news that Clarendon would be both the next and the last viceroy, with all of those present (and also, it seems, the queen) expressing their agreement that this must now mean the comparatively imminent and total 'abolition of the office'.[37]

If, however, the abolitionist train had suffered temporary diversion down a branch line, it had certainly not been derailed. By September 1849 Russell was telling Clarendon that the existence of a lord lieutenant meant that all the proposals emanating from Dublin Castle were invariably regarded by ministers as 'exclusively Irish' and therefore not to be trusted. He lamented that Pitt's short-sightedness had meant that, unlike Scotland, Ireland had retained a distinct administrative apparatus, and that abolishing the viceroyalty would correct this mistake and ensure that 'Englishmen [would] take the same interest in a question from Galway as in a question from Gloucester'[38]—an assertion that, given the government's actions three months earlier over the so-called rate-in-aid to help Irish poor law unions bankrupted by the costs of famine relief, might well have raised a hollow laugh in Ireland itself.[39]

Nothing deterred, Russell in 1850 took firm personal hold of the assimilationist baton. In January he informed the queen that the cabinet now fully expected Clarendon to resign and the viceroyalty to be abolished on 1 June 1851 and that 'all approved of the object'.[40] Endorsement came from every side. Cornewall Lewis, looking to Smith O'Brien's failed rising of 1848, believed abolition would 'do a good deal for incorporating Ireland into the general system of the United Kingdom'—as Pitt had, of course, promised half a century before. Peel and Graham, having broken with the Tory Party over free trade, wanted complete amalgamation under the Home Secretary and opposed even the appointment of a London-based secretary of state.[41] However, while, with one important exception, leading politicians all seemed to be singing from the abolitionist hymn sheet about 'centralization' and ceasing to 'govern Ireland like a colony', there was little agreement as to the precise nature any new dispensation might take.[42] Russell's Commons motion of 17 May 1850 was, as usual, strong on generalities but weak on specifics. 'I think', the prime minister grandly announced, 'no one will deny that, upon general principles, the two countries, being united, there ought to be one single administration', a truth now almost

---

[37] Diary of John Cam Hobhouse for 17 May 1847, BL Broughton Papers Add. MS 43750; Maxwell, *Life and Letters of George William Frederick, Fourth Earl of Clarendon*, i. 277.

[38] Russell to Clarendon, 13 September 1849, Bodl. Clarendon Papers Irish 26.

[39] For the rate-in-aid question, see Chapter 5, Section III.

[40] Russell to Queen Victoria, 21 January 1850, R[oyal] A[rchives] A/20/116.

[41] Lewis to Clarendon, 18 March and 4 June 1850 (reporting the views of Peel and Graham), Bodl. Clarendon Papers C.530.

[42] Clarendon to Russell, 11 September 1849, Bodl. Clarendon Papers Irish Letter-Book IV; to C. Villiers, 14 June 1850, ibid., Letter-Book V; Maxwell, *Life and Letters of George William Frederick, Fourth Earl of Clarendon*, i. 305–6; Clare to Lansdowne, 25 January 1850, BL 3rd Marquess of Lansdowne Papers B86 (provisional reference).

universally acknowledged by, among others, Peel, Lansdowne (who actually referred to Pelham's proposals of 1801), Hume, Roebuck, Sir George Grey, Lord Naas, and Earl Grey.[43] Eventually Russell's motion was passed by 295 votes to 70, an enormous majority of 225. Many Irish members had, however, voted against, and the strongest speeches had come from the minority side. At one political extreme the Irish Tory Sir Joseph Napier, though keenest of the keen as a proponent of a 'decidedly' Protestant Union, would have nothing to do with removing 'national peculiarities' or 'destroying the distinguishing lineaments which had been stereotyped by the hand of God'. At the other was the Irish 'advanced Liberal' William Torrens McCullagh, whose brilliantly heretical speech denounced the whole business as no more than 'a pleasing rhetorical mode of expression ... no better than a solemn trifling'. But what in the end killed Russell's proposal stone dead was the opposition of the Duke of Wellington (now so revered a figure that none dared stand against him on issues of this kind), who flatly declared that military necessity demanded the presence *in Dublin* of a viceroy who could put down rebellion and disorder. Only Wellington could have successfully handed down a judgement so much in the spirit of *Roma locuta est, causa finita*. And with it Russell's massive majority became no more than a whisper in the wind.

While this defeat could, in retrospect, be seen as a hint that the assimilationist enterprise might eventually grind to a halt, enough steam remained in the boiler to ensure that efforts to abolish the viceroyalty maintained a real, if, in the end, limited afterlife. In 1857 and 1858 the freewheeling radical J. A. Roebuck inaugurated the last sustained debates on the matter. One side again aired the slogans 'Cork ought to be like York' and 'Ireland should become part of England', the other that the Irish possessed 'strong feelings of nationality' (a Tory) and that it was mere 'maudlin sentimentality' to 'weep over the abolition of the lord lieutenancy' when 'no tears' were shed 'for the lost liberties' of Ireland as a whole (a member of the Independent Opposition).[44] In both years Roebuck's motion was soundly defeated.

A few administrative memoranda on the precise roles of the various members of the Irish government followed, most of them projecting bafflement as much as clarity.[45] Though the Liberal viceroy, Carlisle, long continued to weary men

---

[43] See the debates in Parl. Deb. 3: cxi. 171–234 (17 May 1850), 1008–30 (10 June 1850), 1405–67 (17 June 1850); cxii. 458–77 (27 June 1850).

[44] Parl. Deb. 3: cxlvi. 1048–110 (7 July 1857) and cxlix. 149, 712–81 (25 March 1858). The continuing complexity of such things was nicely caught in Somerville and Ross's story 'Philippa's Fox-Hunt' in *Some Experiences of an Irish RM* (1899): 'You know the story they tell of her? She was coming home from London, and when she was getting her ticket the man asked if she had said a ticket to York. "No thank God, Cork!" says Mrs Knox.'

[45] Memoranda by Larcom (undersecretary) July 1857, March 1858, June 1858, October 1860, in N[ational] L[ibrary of] I[reland] Larcom Papers MS 7504; by Cardwell (chief secretary) September 1860, ibid.; by Carlisle (viceroy) October 1860, ibid.; by Deasy (Irish attorney-general) October 1860, CH Carlisle Papers J19/11/13.

with his abolitionist views, the whole matter soon became little more than an ever-rolling argument whose prospective goal remained eternally and frustratingly out of reach. Aberdeen in 1853 and Derby in 1855 dismissed abolition as an imminent proposition. Palmerston declared it a splendid idea in theory, but impossible to implement. Wodehouse, on taking office as viceroy in 1864, felt that Britain was simply stuck with the office: 'I put on a grave face, but it is a hard matter not to laugh.'[46] After the late 1860s the only leading politician who still took either the office or its abolition with any great seriousness was (revealingly) Gladstone, who hoped to replace the lord lieutenant with a member of the royal family resident in Ireland, who, he optimistically hoped, would, just like Home Rule, help to underpin and support the Union as a whole.

IV

While legal and administrative matters exercised mid-century governments and did so, with regard to Ireland, in a distinctly integrationist manner, they were not in themselves areas about which the public at large was invariably much exercised. However, a broadly similar approach also underpinned actions of a more politically and socially visible character. Sometimes these too took the 'direct', sometimes the 'scenic', route, sometimes they yielded an outcome, sometimes they ran into the sands of party arguments and disputes. When, in 1835, bills to reform local government in Britain (more specifically municipal corporations) were passed, the Whigs turned their attention to Ireland and did so with unambiguously assimilationist intentions: Britain had received a beneficial reform, therefore Ireland should do so too. Indeed, during the parliamentary debates on the issue, one peer actually insisted that it was Pitt's famous quotation from Virgil of 1799 to the effect that the nations were being united into an everlasting compact on equal terms that must constitute the guiding principle behind any extension of municipal reform across the Irish Sea.[47] And all the official reasons given for reforming corporations in Ireland boiled down to the importance, indeed necessity, of following the English model of 1835. Melbourne dismissed Anglo-Irish distinctions

---

[46] Carlisle to Palmerston, 26 June 1857, SU Palmerston Papers GC/CA/496; Parl. Deb. 3: cxxiv. 170–6 (17 February 1853: Aberdeen); *Benjamin Disraeli Letters*, ed. J. A. Gunn et al., 10 vols to date (Toronto, 1982–), vi. 558; Palmerston to Sir G. Grey, 22 and 28 August 1864, SU Palmerston Papers Letter-Book I, and to Wodehouse, 25 September 1864, ibid., GC/WO/11; Wodehouse to Palmerston, 27 September 1864, ibid., GC/WO/2, and to De Grey, 7 December 1864, BL Ripon Papers Add. MS 43522.

[47] [Cobbett's] *Parliamentary History*, xxxiv. 285 (31 January 1799); Parl. Deb. 3: xxxiii. 244 (26 April 1836). On the question of Irish municipal reform, see A. Macintyre, *The Liberator: Daniel O'Connell and the Irish Party 1830–1847* (London, 1965), 227–61.

regarding temperament, degrees of 'civilization', and propensity to violence as 'not differences worthy of any great consideration', the potential 'points of resemblance' being 'of far greater weight'.[48] His ministers queued up to sing the same song. Lansdowne demanded 'strict parity', Russell an Irish bill 'similar' to that enacted for England and drawn up in close 'conformity' to it.[49] In the King's Speech of February 1836 the government announced a bill entirely 'upon the same principles as those of the acts which have already passed for England and Scotland', a plan welcomed enthusiastically by the viceroy in Dublin.[50] Spring Rice felt that any policy designed to incorporate the 'popular party ... with English interests and to identify them with English feelings' demanded exactly this kind of approach. Brougham went further still, declaring that it would be 'a most partial, unfair, and unsafe view of their legislative duties, to adopt one rule for Ireland after having adopted another rule for England'.[51]

However, in the end, the proposals for Irish municipal reform were severely watered down by opposition from a Tory party fearful of a complete transfer of power from themselves (virtually all corporations had been in their hands) to O'Connell and his followers. But even though such fears encouraged a wrecking operation that meant that the eventual legislation of 1840 proved a distinctly mouse-like affair, Peel himself still felt it important to insist that this did not imply any fundamental breach in assimilationist principles. Equality, he declared, remained crucial, but could sometimes be best achieved by means other than 'the formal and nominal adopting of similar institutions'. Indeed, he fully accepted that British 'rights and political privileges' should be extended throughout all parts of the United Kingdom.[52] Stanley and Graham put forward equally now-you-see-it-now-you-don't arguments, talking mysteriously about 'the promptings of sagacity', 'anomalous states', and 'political experience'.[53] What, in the end, all of this really reveals is not any deepseated divergence from the integrative mode so much as embarrassed persiflage designed to disguise party advantage beneath a conservative distaste for theories and universal remedies. With Peel driven to denunciations of 'the speculative perfection of theory' and to musing about 'truths which lie too deep for argument', it was evident that, here at least, reason had lost out to

[48] Parl. Deb. 3: xxxii. 1127–8 (18 April 1836).

[49] Ibid. xxxii. 1150–1 (18 April 1836: Lansdowne) and xxix. 1313–14 (31 July 1835: Russell); Russell to Mulgrave, 2 January 1836, MC Mulgrave Papers M/817; to Melbourne, 20 January 1836, RA Melbourne Papers MP13.

[50] Parl. Deb. 3: xxxi. 4 (4 February 1836); Mulgrave to Russell, 17 January 1836, TNA Russell Papers PRO 30/22/2A.

[51] Spring Rice to Newport, 19 August 1835, NLI Monteagle Papers MS 551; Parl. Deb. 3: xliv. 706–8 (27 July 1838: Brougham).

[52] Parl. Deb. 3: xxxiv. 778–9 (10 June 1836), xxxvi. 397 (8 February 1837), xliii. 459 (29 May 1838).

[53] Ibid. xxxii. 49 and 86 (8 March 1836).

prejudice.[54] In any case, already two years before the eventual Corporations Act of 1840 the cause of local government reform in Ireland had been more substantially addressed by means of the Irish Poor Relief Act of 1838, which, quite apart from its primary effects upon the management of poverty, introduced franchise and electoral changes that were to prove very important indeed.[55]

London politicians were, in any case, not infrequently convinced that long-term assimilation could best be achieved by pioneering methods tailored to meet the still 'primitive' nature of mid-nineteenth-century Irish society. These alone, they believed, could bring Ireland up to Victorian speed and, having once worked their magic, could then be gradually merged into practices and institutions of a more civilized and Anglo-Saxon character. While, therefore, the police reforms introduced by Peel and Goulburn in 1814 and 1822 had been unvarnished reactions to Irish violence and perceptions of Irish violence, the manner in which they were subsequently extended and refined had everything to do with hopes that Irish social behaviour could by such means be encouraged (perhaps 'forced' might be a better term) to adopt the more benign modes of conduct not always entirely accurately thought to pertain in Scotland and England. Police reform might, for example, help to turn the Irish magistracy into a less visceral and more 'English' body of men.[56] And, indeed, Peel saw such things as, above all, part of a shift away from a policy of subcontracting the government of Ireland to a small Protestant elite, a move that the granting of Catholic Emancipation in 1829 had, in his mind, made completely unavoidable. As one official put it a quarter of a century later, both Peel and the Whigs had effectively been looking for ways by which they might 'govern a million people who [had long] governed the other millions' and do so by 'the direct action of the executive'.[57] After 1829 Peel desperately wanted something different for Ireland in place of insurrection acts and the like. Already in 1830 the chief secretary had produced a memorandum accepted by the Tory cabinet proposing an increase in police numbers and closer and more direct control by the lord lieutenant, in effect a foreshadowing of the Whig Constabulary Act of 1836.[58] And it was, indeed, precisely the police

[54] Parl. Deb. 3: xxxi. 1059–60 (29 February 1836) and xxii. 69 (25 April 1834). Had he been reading the last line of Wordsworth's Immortality Ode (1807): 'Thoughts that do often lie too deep for tears'?

[55] Graham to Eliot, 23 November 1843, BL Graham Papers Ir/11, and 24 December 1844, *The Life and Letters of Sir James Graham*, ed. C. S. Parker, 2 vols (London, 1907), i. 424; Bessborough to Russell, 11 September [1846], TNA Russell Papers PRO 30/22/5C.

[56] Leveson-Gower to Peel, 29 October 1829, NAI Leveson-Gower Letter-Book MS 737.

[57] Memorandum by Thomas Larcom (undersecretary), July 1857, NLI Larcom Papers MS 7504; also Leveson-Gower to Peel, 29 October 1829, NAI Leveson-Gower Letter-Book MS 737; Peel to Leveson-Gower, 30 July 1829, *Sir Robert Peel from his Private Papers*, ed. Parker, ii. 122–4.

[58] N. Gash, *Mr Secretary Peel: Sir Robert Peel to 1830* (London, 1961), 625.

force's 'advanced development' that persuaded the government to inject the final doses of centralization brought forward in the latter year. Melbourne acknowledged that this was the case and that henceforth the constabulary must be seen as helping to transform Ireland into a peaceful and (it was hoped) broadly non-sectarian equivalent of England. Not only that, but the creation in 1829 of London's metropolitan police had given greater legitimacy to centralizing concepts. If power there could descend from the Home Secretary directly to commissioners, why could it not do so in Ireland from the viceroy to the inspector-general of constabulary?[59] In short, a kind of reciprocity of influences had been established between England and Ireland in which initiatives in the latter fed into and received inputs from the former. Above all, the Act of 1836 was seen as a means of pacifying Ireland by less militaristic and (it was implied more 'English') means than had previously been the case. In many respects, therefore, the constabulary finally established in 1836, though distinctly 'Irish', was largely the product of assimilationist thinking in London by administrations now more interested in encouraging Anglo-Saxon tranquillity in Ireland than in maintaining the position of minority and sectarian groups.[60] As time went on, and certainly until the emergence of the Fenian threat, the thrust of official policy was designed—in the words of a former inspector-general in Ireland—'to assimilate the Constabulary of Ireland to that of England' and to 'give the establishment as much of the constitutional character of a police, and as little of that of a military force'.[61]

V

A similar trajectory can be detected in the development of the Irish electoral franchise in the 1830s and 1840s. The Irish Reform Bill of 1832 (and until the 1880s England, Scotland, and Ireland were always treated individually as to electoral law) was drawn up in the knowledge that much of the heavy lifting in

[59] S. H. Palmer, *Police and Protest in England and Ireland 1780–1850* (Cambridge, 1988), 353, 359–60; Parl. Deb. 3: xxxiii. 483–4 (2 May 1836: Melbourne). The 1836 Act effected no immediate increase in the size of the Irish constabulary, something that did not occur until the mid-1840s: Palmer, *Police and Protest*, 330, 361; G. Broeker, *Rural Disorder and Police Reform in Ireland, 1812–36* (London, 1970), 238.

[60] R. Hawkins, 'The "Irish Model" and the Empire: A Case for Reassessment', in D. M. Anderson and D. Killingray (eds), *Policing the Empire: Government, Authority and Control, 1830–1940* (Manchester, 1991), 25.

[61] *Constabulary Ireland. Report of Commissioners*, HC 1866 [3658], xxxiv. 188–9—a view endorsed by Richard Mayne, the long-serving Metropolitan Police commissioner and signatory of the report. See also Lord de Ros's Memorandum on Constabulary of February 1857 in NLI Larcom Papers MS 7617.

this area had already been performed in 1800 and 1829 and amid heroic ignorance regarding technical details on the part of the ministers concerned. While Stanley, as chief secretary, complained that he could never persuade the cabinet to give sustained attention to the Irish franchise, he himself proved at once ill-informed and confused.[62] Not that this prevented him from regularly announcing his and the ministry's main aim to be that of aligning Irish electoral law and practices more closely to the way things were done in Britain by establishing a similar system 'throughout the three kingdoms'[63] (itself a revealing phrase considering that English and Scottish electoral law and practices long remained very different indeed). Melbourne too claimed that there should be a single central theme running through the government's reform legislation, as did O'Connell, who, on this as on a carefully selected list of other issues, was all for assimilation and for insisting that the Irish should 'be identical with the English [Reform] Bill'.[64]

In the event Stanley—and not only Stanley—completely failed to grasp the (admittedly complex) mysteries of Irish franchise law, not least when it came to the identification of potential voters, Ireland having had a system of registration since 1727 whereas England's was newly minted in 1832. O'Connell's claim that the cabinet was 'working without sufficient knowledge of the state of things in Ireland' was fully borne out by events. Nor was this especially unusual at a time when 'responsible' British politicians, while announcing and regularly pursuing an assimilationist agenda, found it all too easy to adopt the tones of lordly indifference assumed by a former chief secretary in 1836, who, upon being corrected for declaring that two towns in Kerry more than 40 miles apart were 'adjoining', blandly responded by telling the Commons that, 'at all events, the two places were in the same county'.[65] Given such flashes of seemingly invincible ignorance among those charged with Irish affairs, it is perhaps not surprising to find that many of the contemporary claims that notions of assimilation lay behind the Irish Reform Act of 1832 turned out to have little or no purchase upon electoral realities of any kind. Thus, whereas in England and Wales about 1 in 17 borough dwellers now had the vote, in Ireland the proportion was 1 in 26, while in county constituencies (which had different franchise rules and where the bulk of the Irish people lived) the difference was enormous: 1 in 24 in England and Wales as against 1 in 116 in Ireland.[66]

[62] Stanley to Grey, 23 October 1831, DU Grey Papers GRE/B11/8/13.

[63] Parl. Deb. 3: iii. 862 (24 March 1831), ix. 595–6 (19 January 1832), xiii. 119 (25 May 1832), xiv. 529 (18 July 1832).

[64] Ibid. xiv. 624 (23 July 1832); O'Connell's 'First Public Letter on the Irish Reform Bill' (25 May 1831), cited in a Memorandum on the Franchise (*c.*1840) in LRO Derby Papers 20/5.

[65] K. T. Hoppen, 'Politics, the Law, and the Nature of the Irish Electorate 1832–1850', *English Historical Review*, 92 (1977), 747.

[66] K. T. Hoppen, 'The Franchise and Electoral Politics in England and Ireland 1832–1885', *History*, 70 (1985), 204.

When these dramatic disparities began to sink into the consciousness of politicians now increasingly motivated by aspirations of equivalence, a universal cry of 'something must be done' was immediately raised. No more than a year after the Irish Reform Act the chief secretary was already drawing up proposals designed to produce the kind of coordination the legislation of 1832 had failed to deliver. His successor admitted a 'great disproportion between the franchise in England and that in Ireland' and promised that 'those who act with him were already engaged' in trying to remedy the situation.[67] Rather late in the day it was realized that major obstacles to such an alignment were posed by the existence of very different legal procedures laid down for the identification of those eligible to be on the electoral rolls. In England a more or less complete registration took place every year, whereas in Ireland voters could be granted so-called certificates, which entitled them to vote for eight years without further investigation and, in practice, regardless of whether they retained the property or occupation qualifications without which it was then generally impossible to become an elector.[68] Not only did the Irish system prove especially open to abuse; it made it extremely difficult to obtain accurate statistics concerning the numbers legally entitled to vote. Already in 1836 demands were being made for its reformation along English lines.[69] And early in 1840 Stanley, from the opposition benches, introduced a bill to achieve just this, as did Morpeth on behalf of the government in 1841. However, these attempts failed, considerations of party advantage and simple ignorance about the intricacies of registration law combining to torpedo both simplification and alignment.[70]

To no considerable extent, however, did any of this diminish demands that the Irish franchise in general be brought closer to that of England. O'Connell, whose knowledge of the technical aspects seems to have been no greater than that of ministers, was all in favour and introduced an assimilationist bill in 1839 because, as he put it, without an 'identity' between the two countries, the Union was merely one of 'master and slave'.[71] In 1842 the Tory government tried to achieve what O'Connell had proposed—namely, 'identity' as to registration—with ministers once again batting the magic word 'assimilation' about in their correspondence on the matter.[72] Joseph Hume, the veteran

---

[67] Littleton to Althorp, 14 January 1834, SRO Hatherton Papers D260/M/01/2; Parl. Deb. 3: xlv. 1001 (28 February 1838).

[68] See K. T. Hoppen, *Elections, Politics, and Society in Ireland 1832–1885* (Oxford, 1984), 5–9.

[69] J. D. Jackson to Peel, 31 August 1836 and 28 September 1837, BL Peel Papers Add. MS 40424.

[70] Hoppen, 'Politics, the Law, and the Nature of the Irish Electorate', 765–6. See also various memoranda and printed papers on the matter in LRO Derby Papers 20/9.

[71] Parl. Deb. 3: xlv. 990–1 (28 February 1839).

[72] Graham to Eliot, 26 September, 4 November, 12 December 1842, BL Graham Papers Ir/1, also 20 October 1843, ibid., Ir/6.

opponent of the viceroyalty, and Sir Charles Grey, a Whig backbencher, also demanded 'perfect equality between England and Ireland' so that 'at no very distant day ... the English and the Irish franchises should be made identically the same'.[73] A former minister and future Chancellor of the Exchequer (Charles Wood) advised the viceroy that 'it is always a good argument, at any rate in parliament, that you do in Ireland as in England'.[74] And so it continued, with politicians of all stripes demanding 'substantial and bona fide equality' (Peel), 'equal laws' to induce the Irish to 'feel towards us as brothers' (Macaulay, who accompanied this with yet another reference to Pitt's Virgil quotation of 1799), and 'equal rights' for Ireland on the franchise (Russell), and asserting that 'the more strictly the machine is copied [from England] the better' (Clarendon).[75]

Amid all of this rhetoric the actual situation on the ground was, in fact, moving in the opposite direction. In particular, the Famine reduced the number of Irish voters so severely—from about 90,000 in 1833 to 45,000 in 1849[76]—that the disparities grew rather than diminished. Everyone realized that something drastic had to be done. Equally, everyone agreed that any solution must ensure that the size of the electorate in Ireland should (proportionately) be brought closer to that of England. And this guiding principle lay behind what amounted to emergency legislation in the shape of the Irish Franchise Act of 1850. Given the context of famine, there was no time for delicate fine-tuning and most contemporaries accepted that the only speedy way of achieving the desired goal was to strike out in an entirely new direction. Clarendon acknowledged that desperate situations required desperate remedies: 'The Irish constituencies ... are dwindling away and ... if a general election were to come, the paucity of electors would be disgraceful.'[77] And Russell, introducing the bill, pointed out that, because 29 per cent of adult males had the vote in English but only 2 per cent in Irish counties, it must be 'wisdom to unite the people of Ireland with the people of Great Britain, in showing, by equal treatment of both and giving them equal franchise, you have full confidence in the manner in which they will use that equality and that franchise; and that they may have all the freedom that exists in any other part of the United Kingdom'. Lord Aberdeen, soon to succeed Russell as prime minister, and, after the Tory split over the Corn Laws, now a Peelite peer,

---

[73] Parl. Deb. 3: liv. 398 (20 May 1840: Hume) and 409 (20 May 1840: Grey).

[74] Wood to Ebrington, 25 March 1841, DRO Fortescue Papers 1262M/LI/190.

[75] Peel's Cabinet Memorandum of February 1844, BL Peel Papers Add. MS 40540; Parl. Deb. 3: liv. 1357 (19 June 1840: Macaulay); Russell to Lansdowne, 31 October 1843, BL 3rd Marquess of Lansdowne Papers B102 (provisional reference); also Russell to Bessborough, 11 April 1846, TNA Russell Papers PRO 30/22/5A; Clarendon to Russell, 14 January 1848, Bodl. Clarendon Papers Irish Letter-Book II.

[76] Hoppen, 'The Franchise and Electoral Politics in England and Ireland', 207–8.

[77] Clarendon to Russell, 9 January 1850, Bodl. Clarendon Papers Irish Letter-Book V.

Order ID: 204-0379709-5181968

Thank you for buying from tourmaline books and music on Amazon Marketplace.

Delivery address:
Mr Innes J Grant
114 OLDFIELD ROAD
HAMPTON
Middlesex
TW12 2HR
United Kingdom

	Order Date:	12 Dec 2017
	Delivery Service:	Standard
	Buyer Name:	Stephen C Garfit
	Seller Name:	tourmaline books and music

Quantity	Product Details	Price	Total
1	**Governing Hibernia: British Politicians and Ireland 1800-1921 [Hardcover] [2016] Hoppen, K. Theodore** **SKU:** WTY-ZT1-KHE **ASIN:** 0198207433 **Listing ID:** 0728S12YR64 **Order Item ID:** 51150676419315 **Condition:** New	£23.89	£23.89
		Subtotal:	£23.89
		Shipping:	£2.80
		Total:	£26.69
		ORDER TOTAL: £26.69	

Thanks for buying on Amazon Marketplace. To provide feedback for the seller please visit www.amazon.co.uk/feedback. To contact the seller, go to Your Orders in Your Account. Click the seller's name under the appropriate product. Then, in the "Further Information" section, click "Contact the Seller."

found it easy to agree, because, as he pointed out, the 1841–6 ministry had already been aiming its Irish legislation in precisely this direction.[78] And, indeed, the 1850 Act, which placed most Irish voting qualifications upon the novel basis of poor law valuations, had, by adopting *sui generis* provisions, begun to move Irish franchise levels fully into line with those of Scotland and much closer to those of England and Wales than had previously been the case, a trend that Edward Cardwell, when chief secretary, was intent on reinforcing yet further in 1860 when proposals for additional reforms were being considered.[79]

VI

An even more dramatic and unambiguous policy of inventing specifically Hibernian means to render Irish practices and mentalities more like those of the kingdom's predominant entity is to be found in the field of education. On the one hand, the Irish national school system established in 1831 was quite unlike anything then existing in Britain. On the other, the aim of its founders was to nail Ireland more firmly into the United Kingdom by reducing both sectarianism and Irish cultural particularism. Initially this can be seen as part of that programme of liberal Anglicanism (espoused by many contemporary Whigs) aimed at educating religiously diverse groups together in order to encourage the creation of a unified sense of identity.[80] As it was put by one chief secretary when writing to a Catholic bishop in 1831, the state was, above all, intent on 'uniting the children of the different religious persuasions in the same schools'.[81] And, while the overall project was—as to structure and extent—specifically Irish, the Whigs saw it as providing a template for a similarly organized schools system in England, a kind of assimilation in reverse. Already in February 1839 tentative announcements were being made for the establishment of a national system in England based on non-sectarian schools. Although these proposals (chiefly the work of Russell) came to nothing, the Tory government in 1842 was still talking about the importance of further

[78] Parl. Deb. 3: cx. 1368 (10 May 1850); M. E. Chamberlain, *Lord Aberdeen: A Political Biography* (London, 1983), 420.
[79] Hoppen, 'The Franchise and Electoral Politics in England and Ireland', 210; Cardwell to Carlisle, 22 January 1860 and [late January 1860], CH Carlisle Papers J19/1/86. For the 1850 Act, see Hoppen, *Elections, Politics, and Society in Ireland*, 17–31.
[80] R. Brent, *Liberal Anglican Politics: Whiggery, Religion and Reform 1830–1841* (Oxford, 1987), 222, 228–9; also M. Daly, 'The Development of the National School System, 1831-40', in A. Cosgrove and D. McCartney (eds), *Studies in Irish History presented to R. Dudley Edwards* (Dublin, 1979), 150–63.
[81] Stanley to Bishop Doyle of Kildare and Leighlin, 13 January 1831, LRO Derby Papers 167/1.

extending 'the principle of united education' in Ireland.[82] However, bitter and sustained opposition, especially from clergy of all kinds and above all from the established Church of Ireland, so undermined what had originally been a central aspect of the national system that by 1854 very few schools were still being jointly run by Catholic and Protestant patrons or managers, the rest having, in effect, become exclusively sectarian. The denominationally 'mixed' education policy had, therefore, clearly failed, and its chief Anglican proponent, Archbishop Whately of Dublin (here at extreme odds with his episcopal colleagues), resigned from the National Commission over this and other related discontents.[83]

One important aspect of Whately's influence—and that of successive commissioners and administrators—did, however, long remain a key part of the programme upon which the national system operated—namely, cultural integration. Crucially, national teachers worked more or less entirely through the medium of the English language. And, while it would be wrong to see the system as a deliberate attempt to undermine the use of Irish, it can hardly have been without some impact in this respect. Irish was almost certainly already declining, though by the start of the Famine it may well have been the case that two out of every five people still used the language regularly. However, the Famine certainly accelerated the decline, with the census of 1851 recording Irish speakers as 23.3 per cent of the total population concentrated especially in the west of the country, a proportion that had fallen to 15.1 per cent by 1871.[84] While, therefore, the national system had a dramatic effect upon the people's ability to read and write, it was reading and writing in English. The proportion of those aged 5 and over able to read rose from 47.3 per cent in 1841 to 61.3 in 1861 in line with a continuing growth in the numbers attending national schools. While this certainly encouraged a form of assimilation with England, it simultaneously encouraged the growth of stronger and more forceful forms of nationalism able and willing to compete on a single linguistic playing field with its antagonists in England and elsewhere.[85]

Another important aspect of Whately's influence (and that of successive commissioners and administrators) long remained a key part of the programme by which the national system operated—namely, a strong emphasis

---

[82] Brent, *Liberal Anglican Politics*, 227–9; Peel to Eliot, 13 November 1842, BL Peel Papers Add. MS 40480.

[83] *Report from the Select Committee of the House of Lords appointed to Inquire into the Practical Working of the System of National Education in Ireland*, HC 1854 (525), xv, pt i, 34; D. H. Akenson, *The Irish Education Experiment: The National System of Education in the Nineteenth Century* (London, 1970), 273.

[84] O. MacDonagh, 'The Age of O'Connell, 1830–45', and D. H. Akenson, 'Pre-University Education, 1782–1870', in Vaughan (ed.), *A New History of Ireland V: Ireland under the Union, I, 1801–70*, 166 and 537.

[85] Hoppen, *Elections, Politics, and Society in Ireland*, 457.

in its schoolbooks, not upon any separate identity that Ireland might possess, but upon its integrated role as an ancillary element within an economically advanced world power. From the start the commissioners produced large numbers of textbooks designed to infuse children with practical skills and compliant attitudes, compliant, above all, to the norms of the entity established by the Union of 1800. These textbooks were, indeed, so highly regarded that about half of all those published were sold outside Ireland in Britain and other parts of the Empire. Their contents were designed to fashion a bond of allegiance 'between the allegedly fractious Irish and the imperial motherland' and to help create a worldwide imperial family with similar, even identical, values, outlooks, and aspirations. One aspect of this endeavour was that most of the white peoples of the Empire—including the Irish—were rarely depicted in either racialist or stereotypical terms. Indeed, the Irish made unusually positive and benign appearances, as, for example, 'a clever, loving people ... now [1861] ... one of the soberest nations of Europe'.[86] However, the converse side of this particular coin was that Ireland more or less disappeared from national schoolbooks as anything other than a geographical entity. Whately, in particular, expunged references from other writers to pretty well anything that could raise a national (let alone a nationalist) cheer: harps, shamrocks, 'the green banks of the Shannon', even the travails of what might be considered Ireland substitutes, such as Poland. A notorious example of such negations was the quotation from a poem by Jane Taylor first printed in a textbook of 1835 and regularly continued thereafter.

> I thank the goodness and the grace
> That on my birth have smiled,
> And made me in these Christian days,
> A happy *English* child.[87]

Official textbooks at all levels drove the message home: 'Great Britain and Ireland form the single most powerful kingdom in the world', 'On the east coast of Ireland is England where the queen lives. Many people who live in Ireland were born in England, and we speak the same language and are called one nation.'[88] Apart, however, from such generalities, the commissioners' textbooks had almost nothing to say about the practical circumstances of Irish life. Even the 'history' of the world 1500–1800 in six pages managed to avoid dangerous topics like the Reformation, while the nine pages devoted to

---

[86] J. Coulahan, 'The Irish and Others in Irish Nineteenth-Century Textbooks', in J. A. Mangan (ed.), *The Imperial Curriculum: Racial Images and Education in the British Colonial Experience* (London, 1993), 54–61.

[87] A. McManus, *The Irish Hedge School and its Books, 1695–1831* (Dublin, 2002), 230, emphasis added. Jane Taylor (1783–1824) is best known as the author of 'Twinkle, Twinkle little Star'.

[88] Coulahan, 'The Irish and Others', 55; R. V. Comerford, *Ireland* (London, 2003), 36.

subsequent years steered well clear of Ireland in favour of raising cheers for the abolition of the slave trade. Nor was the Irish language given much thought, an approach that, as one scholar has noted, almost certainly received 'the tacit approval of the great majority of Irishmen'.[89] Instead, a policy of inculcating young Irish minds with the governing ideas of English society lay so much at the centre of the project that, in the examinations for potential teachers started in 1848, the crucial questions asked concerned the importance of property and property relationships: 'Passages from the New Testament are often quoted to prove that the security of property was not recognized by the Apostles; show that this opinion is exactly the reverse of the fact.'[90] A Catholic bishop who appeared as a witness before the Powis Commission on Irish primary education in 1868 recalled:

> There is scarce anything in their books about the history of Ireland. There was in the 'Third Book' a description of the Lakes of Killarney and the Giant's Causeway, but (I don't know for what reason unless, perhaps, that it was too 'national') these extracts have been expunged from the last edition, and in their place has been inserted a description of some lakes in Hindostan.

Despite, he went on, a few feeble attempts in recent years to 'make the children acquainted with something like the history of their own country', less attention continued to be given to Irish history and geography than to detailed information concerning 'Britain's overseas colonies and their picturesque people'.[91] If, therefore, a modest slowing-down of the assimilationist thrust in education was beginning to take place in the late 1860s to match more dramatic diminutions elsewhere, the national commissioners long remained faithful to the integrationist convictions within which their schools had first been imagined and then developed.

VII

While, overall, there can be little doubt that the most enthusiastic mid-century apostles of the benefits to be derived from Anglo-Irish homogeneity were to be found in the Whig camp, there can be equally little doubt that important figures in the Conservative fold held similar views. The history of Peel's

---

[89] Akenson, *Irish Education Experiment*, 383–4.

[90] T. A. Boylan and T. P. Foley, *Political Economy and Colonial Ireland: The Propagation and Ideological Function of Economic Discourse in the Nineteenth Century* (London, 1992), 97–8.

[91] *Royal Commission of Inquiry into Primary Education (Ireland)*, HC 1870 [C. 6 II], pt iii, 679 (Q. 15572); D. Fitzpatrick, 'Ireland and the Empire', in A. Porter (ed.), *The Oxford History of the British Empire: The Nineteenth Century* (Oxford, 1999), 503.

administration of 1841–6 makes this clear. Peel had certainly changed his view of Ireland and how it should be governed since the time of his chief secretaryship, and especially so in the 1830s. Above all, he now sought the 'rapid assimilation of the Irish and British markets and economies',[92] a policy best realized, he believed, not only by conciliating majority opinion in Ireland, but by administering the country in ways that owed more to British models than to notions of Irish exceptionalism. Both Peel and Graham were even prepared, both in public and in private, to put on sackcloth and ashes as a deliberate signal that new leaves were being energetically turned. Peel admitted in 1844 that the previous 'garrison principle' had been 'unjust ... dangerous, but above all ... utterly impracticable', while Graham publicly ate dirt when telling the Commons how 'deeply [he] regretted' earlier statements about Irish affairs and now hoped—'from the bottom of my heart'—that more recent 'actions towards Ireland have been better than my words'.[93] What these actions now chiefly consisted of was the setting-up of the Devon Commission to enquire into agrarian matters in 1843, the Charitable Bequests Act of 1844 (to enable Catholic bodies to accept appropriate legacies), an increased grant for the Catholic seminary at Maynooth, and the establishment of the Queen's Colleges to augment the university provision provided by the Anglican Trinity College in Dublin—not all of them greeted with the enthusiasm their authors had hoped for. The overall intention, however, was clear enough: that Ireland should no longer be treated merely as, in Graham's words, a 'rebellious colony', but be 'reconciled to Great Britain on terms which will command the hearts and affections of her people' by the implantation of British, that is, 'free institutions'.[94] Ireland must, as Peel told the Commons in February 1844, be governed by 'ordinary rules', something that would allow the 'entertaining [of] bright hopes' for a 'future' in which, 'by the wonderful applications of science, we are, I trust, still further to shorten' the existing sense of 'distance' between the two islands.[95] Peel, like Graham, had convinced himself that 'mere force' could no longer be pressed into service as 'a permanent remedy' for Ireland's 'social evils' and that a new approach was urgently required.[96] Given that, as the viceroy (Heytesbury) put it, 'the instruments for the administration of the law are the same in Ireland as in England', it was becoming more and more necessary to abandon coercive legislation and

---

[92] P. Gray, *Famine, Land and Politics: British Government and Irish Society 1843–1850* (Dublin, 1999), 37–8.

[93] Peel to Heytesbury, 8 August 1844, BL Peel Papers Add. MS 40479; Parl. Deb. 3: lxxix. 921 (17 April 1845: Graham).

[94] Kerr, *Peel, Priests and Politics*, 110–351; MacDonagh, *The Emancipist*, 259–63; Macintyre, *The Liberator*, 180–4; Graham to Peel, 20 October 1843, BL Peel Papers Add. MS 40449.

[95] Parl. Deb. 3: lxxiii. 254 (23 February 1844).

[96] Peel to Graham, 19 October 1843, BL Peel Papers Add. MS 40449.

116 *Governing Hibernia*

thus make 'the amalgamation of the two nations' possible, even, it was hoped, likely.[97]

Because the Tory leadership viewed this new departure through rosy-tinted spectacles, it entirely failed to grasp how repeated and vague statements about high-minded goodness all round lacked the power to elicit much in the way of an enthusiastic response. In large part this was because conciliatory rhetoric rapidly lost force when translated into negligible action, when, that is, any kind of concrete translation was attempted at all. Simply to hope that the best was being done to mitigate 'the disease which consumes the vitals of that unhappy country' or to lament that mighty projects were constantly being brought low by the 'anomalous circumstances of Ireland' amounted to excuses rather than action.[98] Indeed, emollient persiflage consistently outran delivery. To talk of adopting 'kind and indulgent legislation for Ireland' or to remind people that Catholics were Christians 'professing a faith identical with ours in all the great truths'[99] was all very well, but, when practical outcomes proved modest, political harvests proved modest too. And, because ambivalence tended to mark Peel's Irish measures and effusions, there was no lack of critics queuing up to condemn his propensity for deploying arguments of a distinctly *esprit de l'escalier* character. From his own side Disraeli accused Peel of habitually bringing 'forward as his own ... these very schemes and proposals to which, when in opposition, he always avowed himself a bitter and determined opponent' (a notable case of a pot saluting a fellow-travelling kettle), while, for the Whigs, Macaulay was fiercer still: 'Did you think, when session after session you went on attacking those whom you knew to be in the right and flattering the prejudices of those whom you knew to be in the wrong, that the day of reckoning would never come? That day has come, and now ... you are doing penance for the disingenuousness of years.'[100] But, however accurately Macaulay aimed his arrows, it was becoming clearer with every passing day that the Irish policies of Peel's government were differing less and less from those of the Whigs.[101] Indeed, while Whigs like Russell and Normanby continued, throughout the early and mid-1840s, to talk as they had done in the 1830s, they now (not always to their delight) began to find that comments about dealing 'with Ireland as we deal with England', 'perfect equality between

[97] Heytesbury to Peel, 11 August 1844, BL Peel Papers Add. MS 40479; Graham to De Grey, 1 March 1844, *Life and Letters of Sir James Graham*, ed. Parker, i. 404–5; Graham to Peel, 3 October 1845, *Sir Robert Peel from his Private Papers*, ed. Parker, iii. 190–1.

[98] Graham to Heytesbury, 21 December 1844, BL Graham Papers Ir/19 and 21 October 1844, ibid., Ir/17.

[99] Peel's Memorandum of February 1844, BL Peel Papers Add. MS 40540; Peel to Lady De Grey, 29 February 1844, ibid.; also Parl. Deb. 3: lxxix. 1040 (18 April 1845: Peel).

[100] Parl. Deb. 3: lxxix. 563–4 (11 April 1845: Disraeli) and 657 (14 April 1845: Macaulay).

[101] D. Kanter, *The Making of British Unionism, 1740–1848: Politics, Government, and the Anglo-Irish Constitutional Relationship* (Dublin, 2009), 264, 276.

the two countries', or about how 'blending' meant that Ireland had not 'lost but incorporated its independence', were being no less enthusiastically mouthed on the government front bench. Graham now claimed to want completely 'to amalgamate the two nations', and even when out of office in 1849 continued to argue the case for making Ireland 'really united to us ... beginning with the church, not omitting the elective franchise and trial by jury, and ending with the abolition of the lord lieutenancy'.[102]

By the mid-1840s assimilation had quite simply become the dominant concept when Ireland was discussed. Leading peers noted how the drift of legislation had been 'to assimilate the laws of that country to those of Britain' and that, 'if they meant to preserve tranquillity, to support the Union, they must persevere steadily in that course'. Backbenchers hailed Peel's integrating endeavours to make Ireland 'the attached sister of England'. Palmerston acknowledged a 'great change, and a great mitigation of party feeling on Ireland'. Even commentators who deplored the trend recognized its power.[103] Nor was Peel alone in the conviction that any enterprise attempting to 'break up' the 'formidable confederacy' in Ireland against the 'British connexion' could be successful only if it adopted a policy of creating overall uniformity between the two islands, and that crucial to any such endeavour must be the transformation of Ireland's complex and opaque agrarian system along modern, capitalist, and English lines.[104]

---

[102] Parl. Deb. 3: lxx. 1004 (7 July 1843: Russell) and lxxii. 612–13 (13 February 1844: Normanby); Graham to De Grey, 1 March 1844, *Life and Letters of Sir James Graham*, ed. Parker, i. 404–5; Graham to Eliot, 24 December 1844, ibid. i. 424; Graham to Lewis, 7 January 1849, ibid. ii. 76.

[103] Parl. Deb. 3: lxxxi. 1123 (24 June 1845: Clanricarde), lxxx. 546 (19 May 1845: McGeachy), lxv. 304 (18 July 1842: Palmerston); D. O. Madden, *Ireland and its Rulers; since 1829*, 3 vols (London, 1843–4), i. 127–8.

[104] Parl. Deb. 3: lxxix. 1040 (18 April 1845); Peel to Heytesbury, 1 August 1844 and 17 October [1844], BL Peel Papers Add. MS 40479; Memorandum on Ireland of 11 February 1844, LRO Derby Papers 36.

5

Poverty, Famine, Land

I

Amid the broad move towards an acceptance that the best means of governing Hibernia was to encourage an overall assimilation between Ireland and Britain, two items stood at the head of the agenda: Irish poverty and Irish land. And, because these emerged with special prominence just before and during the Great Famine, each came to constitute a totemic key for assimilationism generally and for social and economic assimilationism in particular, with the result that tendencies that had begun to move the political weather in the 1830s now took on the all-consuming urgency of absolute and immediate necessity.

On the whole, the period before 1830 or thereabouts had witnessed only fitful signs that Irish social and economic redemption would soon come to be identified with doing as England had done and was more and more dramatically doing. In 1804 a parliamentary committee had firmly concluded that 'the adoption of a general system of provision for the poor of Ireland, by way of parish rate, as in England, or in any similar manner, would be highly injurious to both countries, and would not produce any real or permanent advantage, even to the lower classes of people'. Twenty-five years later, an Irish viceroy was still making the same point, not least because of an innate opposition to poor laws of any kind.[1] That this was, however, no longer the universal view is clear from the report in 1830 of a successor committee on Irish poverty, which, while rejecting the decisive certainties of 1804, found itself unable to come to any conclusion as to whether or not Ireland should be aligned to English practices in its treatment of the poor.[2]

---

[1] *Report from the Committee Respecting the Poor of Ireland*, H[ouse of] C[ommons Paper] 1803–4 (109), v. 771; B. Jenkins, *Era of Emancipation: British Government of Ireland, 1812–1830* (Kingston and Montreal, 1988), 281.

[2] *Report of the Select Committee on the State of the Poor in Ireland; Being a Summary of The First, Second and Third Reports*, HC 1830 (667), vii. 55.

Two related realities lay behind such discussions: first, that England already had an antique poor law system no longer, many thought, fit for purpose, while Ireland had none at all; second, that Irish poverty seemed to grow directly out of Ireland's complicated and *sui generis* system of land tenure and agrarian relationships. Attention to this last point inevitably led to considerations of the first and, above all, to the manner in which Ireland's problems were generated by the small size of agricultural holdings and the exploitative dynamic created by the cascade of tenurial bonds between large landlords at the narrow apex of society and exploited cottiers and conacre labourers at the broad pauperized base. Already in 1826 the Sub-Letting Act had been designed to restrain the further division of holdings, but it had achieved little apart from extracting laissez-faire pronouncements from O'Connell about the wickedness of seeking to make it 'impossible for a labourer to become a farmer' or for a farmer to become a 'gentleman'.[3]

And, though the Wellington administration had fleetingly considered further legislation, nothing more was done, with the result that, as the Devon Commission found in the mid-1840s, the 1826 Act had entirely failed to retard the miniaturization of holdings, improve the efficiency of agriculture, or affect the manner in which, as one witness put it, 'every class in this country oppresses the class below it, until you come to the most wretched class ... There is no exaction practised by their superiors that they do not practise upon those below them.'[4] While, then, an increasing awareness was developing that something should be done to reform the pattern of Ireland's agrarian 'system', it took time for this awareness to generate action. One of Ricardo's correspondents had argued strongly in 1822 that no improvement could be looked for until 'all small farms and small tenants are got rid of. These are the curse of Ireland.'[5] The Select Committee on the Employment of the Poor in Ireland reporting in 1823 had identified the issue that was to become central to a growing critique of Irish agrarianism, the fact that those at the bottom of the heap were not (as in England) paid in cash wages, but were instead allowed to occupy (without any security) tiny parcels of potato ground in return for their labour, something widely thought to be 'a less clear and intelligible mode' of judging their worth.[6] It was an opinion that Wellington himself endorsed in

---

[3] Jenkins, *Era of Emancipation*, 258.

[4] P. Jupp, *British Politics on the Eve of Reform: The Duke of Wellington's Administration 1828–30* (London, 1998), 163–4; *Index to Minutes of Evidence Taken before Her Majesty's Commissioners of Inquiry into the State of the Law and Practice in Respect to the Occupation of Land in Ireland*, HC 1845 [673], xxii. 621–30; *Evidence taken before Her Majesty's Commissioners*, pt i, HC 1845 [606], xix, Witness 62 Q. 24.

[5] H. Trower to Ricardo, 10 January 1822, *The Works and Correspondence of David Ricardo*, ed. P. Sraffa, 11 vols (Cambridge, 1951–73), ix. 145.

[6] *Report from the Select Committee on the Employment of the Poor in Ireland*, HC 1823 (561), vi. 8. See C. Ó Danachair, 'Cottier and Landlord in Pre-Famine Ireland', *Béaloideas: The Journal of the Folklore Society of Ireland*, 48–9 (1980–1), 154–65.

1830 (and again in 1838), as did his viceroy in Dublin, who hoped that the abolition in 1829 of the Irish forty-shilling freehold franchise would result in substantial evictions (to be tempered, he hoped, by the extension of poor laws to Ireland) and a consequent consolidation of agricultural holdings.[7]

By the early 1830s the whole question of the relationship between poverty and agrarian structures in Ireland was moving up the political agenda, not least because the enormous and growing number of rural poor was threatening to overwhelm the stability of Irish society as a whole. Even with the rate of population increase slowing down (something not immediately apparent at the time), the sheer number of people (some 8,175,000 by 1841) and the fact that less than a quarter of rural inhabitants could be defined as enjoying any kind of economic well-being,[8] meant that those with eyes to see were coming to believe that dramatic economic reconstructions combined with new social mechanisms designed to handle their inevitable consequences were now unavoidable.

The crucial decisions about how to proceed were taken when the reports of the Royal Commission on the State of the Poor in Ireland (chaired by Archbishop Whately) failed to find official favour in 1836. The Commission had rejected the idea of an Irish poor law on the grounds that poverty in Ireland was so extensive that no system of relief modelled on England's new poor law of 1834 could possibly cope, but had put forward alternative recommendations so complicated that ministers found it easy to reject them as impossibly visionary and impractical.[9] By stressing the complete 'otherness' of Irish society, its virtual impenetrability to outside understanding and comprehension, and by adopting remarkably populist and local methods of evidence-gathering ('a type of exoticization of scrutiny'), the Commission seems almost to have gone out of its way to fall back into the tropes of the immediate post-Union period and thus render its conclusions unpalatable to the intellectual and political elites that had come to prominence in the mid-1830s.[10]

---

[7] Wellington to Northumberland, 7 July 1830, A[lnwick] C[astle] Northumberland Papers DNP/75; Northumberland to Peel, 4 May 1829, ibid., DNP/71; R. B. McDowell, 'Wellington and Ireland', *Irish Sword*, 1 (1949–53), 217. See K. T. Hoppen, 'Politics, the Law, and the Nature of the Irish Electorate 1832–1850', *English Historical Review*, 92 (1977), 746–76. Such expectations regarding the effects of the abolition of the forty-shilling freehold franchise proved very wide of the mark.

[8] K. T. Hoppen, *Ireland since 1800: Conflict and Conformity*, 2nd edn (Harlow, 1999), 41.

[9] P. Gray, *The Making of the Irish Poor Law, 1815–43* (Manchester, 2009), 122. This excellent book is by far the best account of the matter, and, while I fully accept its author's emphasis upon the existence of certain differences between the eventual Irish Poor Law of 1838 and the English Poor Law of 1834, there can be little doubt as to the overall contemporary context of agreement concerning the assimilation of Irish and English models and practices.

[10] N. Ó Ciosáin, *Ireland in Official Print Culture, 1800–1850: A New Reading of the Poor Inquiry* (Oxford, 2014), 25, 52, 57, 61, 73, 85, 89, 122.

Having speedily rejected the Commission's cumbersome and detail-driven recommendations, ministers opted instead for an altogether brisker and more 'modern' approach, which, despite occasional genuflections to peculiarly Irish circumstances, was clearly and unambiguously based upon the notion that the best of all possible worlds could be achieved only by seeing to it that, in the treatment of the poor as in so much else, doing what England did could alone mark out the route to eventual economic and social salvation. Whately's behemoth was replaced by a one-man inquiry designed to produce the 'correct' recommendations in no time at all. The task was given to George Nicholls, a banker and English poor-law official with previous form as an enthusiast for the so-called less eligibility test (designed to make workhouse conditions less tolerable than those that could be provided by the worst possible job) and as an opponent to granting what was called 'outdoor' relief at any location outside workhouses themselves.

Already George Cornewall Lewis, who had actually acted as an assistant to the Whately Commission and was the author of an interesting book on rural society in contemporary Ireland, had been active in undermining the Commission's proposals. Lewis favoured the importation of the English system made harsher still by being shorn of its (in his eyes, unfortunate) weaknesses towards the occasional granting of outdoor relief. He wanted gender segregation and compulsory labour. Above all, he looked to legislation that would help to weed out the poorest occupiers of land (the 'redundant population') and thus reduce agrarian violence and once again make landlords, as in England, 'the masters of their own property'. For Lewis the workhouse system was just as applicable to one country as to another. Ireland's existing social structure was too complicated for economic progress. The peasants' 'hold upon the land' must be loosened. Any 'dissimilarity between the laws of different parts of the same kingdom is an evil in itself, and ought, if possible, to be avoided'. In short, the Whately Commission had, quite simply, displayed an 'utter misconception of the entire subject'.[11]

If Nicholls was less of an intellectual heavyweight than Lewis, he was certainly quick on his feet, undertaking a brisk tour of Ireland in the autumn of 1836 in response to 'instructions' from the Home Secretary (Lord John Russell) to 'consider whether such relief [as recommended by the Royal Commission] may not have the effect of promoting imposture, without destroying mendicity'—as loaded an agenda as could possibly have been drawn up. Nicholls's recommendations were unambiguous: with certain adjustments (and even these were played down) 'the Poor Law of Ireland should

---

[11] *Remarks on the Third Report of the Irish Poor Inquiry Commissioners ... by George Cornewall Lewis*, HC 1837 [91], li. 253–90, especially 264–6, 273, 282; Lewis to E. W. Head, 15 July 1836, *Letters of the Right Hon. Sir George Cornewall Lewis Bart. to Various Friends*, ed. G. F. Lewis (London, 1870), 54.

assimilate in all respects as nearly as possible to the Poor Law system now established in England', so that there would, before long, be perfect 'equality of England and Ireland'.[12] It had taken Nicholls only a few weeks to decide what should be done. As he rushed round the country, he had quickly concluded that 'the applicability of our English system' was clear, and that, as he told Russell, 'Ireland stands in need of a system of poor laws based upon' the principles already operating in 'England itself'.[13]

While Nicholls was careful not to present his recommendations 'as a panacea or to rule out auxiliary measures',[14] he believed their implementation to be absolutely necessary if Ireland was to attach itself to the economically successful Anglo-Saxon universe of the time. Both he and the politicians who were to implement his programme were convinced that they were acting in conformity with the universal principles of contemporary society and providing the only means that would enable a backward country to survive that period of painful transition from the primitive to the modern without which it would for ever remain anchored in the poverty-stricken fatalities of the past. He talked of the existence of 'governing' principles, which meant that 'mankind is essentially the same, in every clime and under every variety of circumstances'. Like Lewis he believed that a 'transition period' could not be avoided,

> that season of change from the system of small holdings, allotments, and the subdivision of land, which now prevails in Ireland, to the better practice of day labour for wages, and to the dependence on daily labour for support, which is the present condition of the English peasantry. This transition period is, I believe, generally beset with difficulty and suffering. It was so in England; and it is, and for a time will probably continue to be so, in Ireland.[15]

What, however, Nicholls very clearly did not believe was that the introduction of a poor law could possibly enable Ireland to cope with the devastations that anything approaching widespread famine might—at some future date—impose.[16]

It would, of course, have been extraordinary if absolutely everyone had agreed with Nicholls and Lewis or if all had reached their conclusions by means of identical reasoning. Dissent, certainly strong dissent, was, however, rare and comparatively muted. Whately, naturally enough, was displeased: 'So,

---

[12] *Report of George Nicholls Esq. to His Majesty's Principal Secretary of State for the Home Department, on Poor Laws, Ireland*, HC 1837 [69], li. 203–4, 220, 237.

[13] Nicholls to Morpeth, Clonmel, 23 September [1836], T[he] N[ational] A[rchives] Russell Papers PRO 30/22/2C; to Russell, Dublin, 17 October 1836, ibid.; also to Morpeth, 21 September 1836, C[astle] H[oward] Carlisle Papers J19/11/2.

[14] Gray, *Making of the Irish Poor Law*, 165.

[15] *Report of George Nicholls*, HC 1837 [69], li. 210–11; Nicholls's Memorandum of 21 January 1836, cited Gray, *Making of the Irish Poor Law*, 133; also *Remarks on the Third Report ... by George Cornewall Lewis*, HC 1837 [91], li. 278.

[16] *Report of George Nicholls*, HC 1837 [69], li. 223.

Mr Nicholls is sent here to get one bottle of water out of the Liffey, and one out of the Shannon, and then persuade the ... people that he can give them a better Poor Law than we who have been 3 years considering it.'[17] Whately's objections about the enormous differences between rural society in England and in Ireland (where 'in whole districts, scarcely one of that class of substantial capitalist farmers so universal in England, can be found') were simply overwhelmed, as he later acknowledged, by the 'great desire among many persons in England to assimilate the two countries'.[18] In England, Lansdowne's Bowood set objected to the notion of giving any relief to able-bodied men, while heterodox economic thinkers with an unusual tenderness to peasant societies, such as the MP George Poulett Scrope, while wanting a poor law in Ireland (and ultimately accepting it), would have preferred something more like the old pre-1834 English system to that which actually emerged in 1838.[19] Again, the rhetoric with which Foxites such as Russell and Morpeth embraced Nicholls's proposals certainly exhaled a more populist, indeed anti-landlord, air than did the language of administrators such as Lewis or Nicholls himself. Russell declared that he did not seek to 'please either the Irish landlords, or farmers, but to do good in Ireland', while Morpeth saw their proposals as defending the rights of the inarticulate because too often 'the cry of him who was ready to perish did not find its way to their table'.[20] But most of this was little more than (perhaps unconscious) camouflage. The weight of effective opinion was in favour, not only of an Irish poor law, but of an Irish poor law as fully in accordance with the English precedent of 1834 as possible.

Russell adopted a bracingly universalist approach à la Nicholls. 'Surely', he told Morpeth, 'a man who understands physic is as well qualified to prescribe to an Irishman, as a man who knows Irishmen, but does not know physic.'[21] He denounced the Royal Commission for having failed to understand the laws governing 'the general progress of the community' in favour of an ad hoc ragbag of odds and ends, 'public works in one place, or drain a bog in another, or to start a company in a third'. Nor did he 'see anything so peculiar in the

[17] As reported in Morpeth to Russell, 5 October 1836, TNA Russell Papers PRO 30/22/2C.
[18] *First Report from His Majesty's Commissioners for Inquiring into the Condition of the Poorer Classes in Ireland*, HC 1835 (369), xxxii. 6; E. J. Whately, *Life and Correspondence of Richard Whately, DD Late Archbishop of Dublin*, 2 vols (London, 1866), i. 169.
[19] D. D. Olien, *Morpeth: A Victorian Public Career* (Washington, 1983), 171–2; P. Mandler, *Aristocratic Government in the Age of Reform: Whigs and Liberals 1830–1852* (Oxford, 1990), 174–5; Parl[iamentary] Deb[ates] 3: xlii. 538 (9 April 1838: Scrope). However, by 1846 Scrope was arguing for greater assimilation regarding outdoor relief: to Russell, 23 June 1846, TNA Russell Papers PRO 30/22/5A; also Bessborough to Russell, 3 November 1846, ibid., PRO 30/22/5E.
[20] Gray, *Famine, Land and Politics: British Government and Irish Society 1843–1850* (Dublin, 1999), 33; see also Howick (*not* a Foxite) to N. W. Senior, 5 January 1836, and to Lansdowne, 8 January 1836, N[ational] L[ibrary of] I[reland] Howick Letters MS 21,286(2).
[21] Russell to Morpeth, 10 February [1838], CH Carlisle Papers J19/1/17. See G. Nicholls, *A History of the Irish Poor Law, in Connexion with the Condition of the People* (London, 1856), pp. v–vi.

state of Ireland to prevent the application of ... general [English, i.e. universal] principles to that country'.[22] All in all, Russell declared himself so very pleased with Nicholls that he decided to adopt his plan with only a few 'essential limitations'.[23] As chief secretary, Morpeth was equally delighted, finding that Nicholls's views coincided 'with those which I have ventured to form'. Morpeth's colleague in the Irish administration, the viceroy Lord Mulgrave, felt that the proposed poor law was 'the next step without which nothing can be done towards removing the sort of hopeless poverty in which they [the Irish "lower orders"] are at present inclosed'.[24] Other Whigs from the prime minister downwards saw the matter in the same optimistic light. Even the king, reported Russell gleefully, wanted what his government wanted, in the hope that it would somehow unite all Irishmen, 'the gentry, the farmers, and the poor'. Of at least equal importance was the fact that, even before the bill had been drafted, ministers received assurances that the Tory front bench would give broad support to their unambiguously assimilationist proposals.[25]

II

Notable too was the reaction within Irish political society, where there was much less public opposition or even debate in 1836–8 than there had been in England when the Elizabethan system was being overhauled some years before.[26] Indeed, many of the modish arguments batted about in contemporary analyses of poverty—notably that which made clear distinctions between the 'deserving' and the 'undeserving' poor and opposed giving relief to the latter—were quite as alive in Ireland (and especially among the Catholic clergy) as in England and, being so, constituted a species of cultural assimilationism (or at least mutual identification) largely independent of official influence.[27] Not only that, but O'Connell's own position on the question

---

[22] Parl. Deb. 3: xxxix. 483 (1 December 1837) and xxxviii. 706 (8 May 1837).

[23] Russell to Mulgrave, 30 October 1836, M[ulgrave] C[astle] Mulgrave Papers M/844; to Melbourne, Dublin, 23 September 1838, S[outhampton] U[niversity] Melbourne Papers MEL/RU/59.

[24] Morpeth to Russell, 27 September [1836], TNA Russell Papers PRO 30/22/2C; Mulgrave to Melbourne, 29 April [1837], R[oyal] A[rchives] Melbourne Papers MP100.

[25] Russell to Morpeth, 8 October 1836, CH Carlisle Papers J19/11/2; Parl. Deb. 3: xliii. 5 (21 May 1838: Melbourne); Duncannon's Memorandum of December 1836, TNA Russell Papers PRO 30/22/2D; Stanley to Russell, 18 December 1836, ibid.; Gray, *Making of the Irish Poor Law*, 183; P. Jupp, *The First Duke of Wellington in an Irish Context* (Southampton, 1997), 17.

[26] V. Crossman, *Politics, Pauperism and Power in Late Nineteenth-Century Ireland* (Manchester, 2006), 11.

[27] N. Ó Ciosáin, 'Boccoughs and God's Poor: Deserving and Undeserving Poor in Irish Popular Culture', in T. Foley and S. Ryder (eds), *Ideology and Ireland in the Nineteenth Century* (Dublin, 1998), 93–9.

wavered between outright opposition to providing relief to the able-bodied and vaporous insistences that Ireland was simply too poverty-stricken to attempt an organized relief system of any kind. Always a keen devotee of laissez-faire, O'Connell was also conscious of the fact that pretty well any expression of pretty well any view on the matter might all too easily split his following and fracture the rather complex and ideologically contradictory bases of his support.[28]

Debates over the introduction of an Irish poor law coincided with increased concern about the general nature of agrarian society in a country where, in 1841, over 86 per cent of the population lived outside towns of even 2,000 inhabitants and some 78 per cent of these were engaged in farming of one sort or another. The contrast with England and Wales was dramatic. There less than 53 per cent lived outside towns of 2,500 and above and of these not much over half worked in agriculture.[29] Not only that, but the 'efficiency' of Irish agricultural practices was widely (if not always accurately) held to be primitive and backward when compared with those of England—the result, it was generally claimed, of the over-complex social and economic structures of the Irish countryside, the smallness of holdings, and—a common prejudice— Celtic laziness. Though contemporary wisdom liked to think that improvements in all these areas might be generated by the new poor law, it became increasingly accepted that wider structural changes would also be necessary— changes designed to transform the Irish agricultural world so that it would ultimately resemble that of England. Only a few brawny heretics argued that the English model was inappropriate and that, for example, 'peasant' systems operated with perfect success in continental countries such as Belgium. In the 1830s only Scrope—an essentially untheoretical populist—made any kind of impact here, though by the mid-1840s the more closely argued (though less forceful) analyses of W. T. Thornton and J. S. Mill also began to achieve a modest measure of visibility.[30]

Far more prominent and sweeping were the views of those who advocated assimilation in virtually all aspects of agrarian life. In 1833 the new chief secretary (Edward Littleton) wanted the Irish tithe system adjusted to match that of England, because 'the application of the same principle ... in each country ... would greatly facilitate the arrangement in both', while a former Tory cabinet minister was already convinced that Ireland would never prosper

---

[28] A. Macintyre, *The Liberator: Daniel O'Connell and the Irish Party 1830–1847* (London, 1965), 217–18; see Parl. Deb. 3: xl. 947–65 (9 February 1838) for a fine example of O'Connell's mastery of meaningless waffle.

[29] *Irish Historical Statistics: Population, 1821–1971*, ed. W. E. Vaughan and A. J. Fitzpatrick (Dublin, 1978), 27; K. T. Hoppen, *Elections, Politics, and Society in Ireland 1832–1885* (Oxford, 1984), 103–4; Hoppen, *The Mid-Victorian Generation 1846–1886* (Oxford, 1998), 12.

[30] Gray, *Famine, Land and Politics*, 13–14; Macintyre, *The Liberator*, 206–7.

without 'a gradual enlargement of farms'.[31] In 1835 a parliamentary committee recommended government help for drainage schemes in Ireland on the
grounds that this would lead to a growth in the size of farms and that the
resulting 'increased demand for labour would induce a large number to
abandon their cottier holdings, preferring to work for hire, with a reasonable
certainty of continuous employment, rather than be subject to rent', an
unequivocally Anglo-Saxon solution for what was perceived to be a peculiarly
Hibernian problem.[32] Still more significant were the reports of the Irish
Railway Commissioners, who included the undersecretary Thomas Drummond and who in 1838 produced an extensive survey of Irish socio-economic
conditions together with strongly assimilationist recommendations for improvement. Existing agricultural arrangements meant that, in their opinion,
no 'rational' (a significant word) hope could 'be entertained of the general
introduction of an improved system of husbandry, or the employment of the
labouring poor'. Farming badly needed to become larger in scale, and, while
this should best be achieved humanely, difficulties would inevitably arise
during the transition years, when 'a considerable portion of the Irish peasantry'
must, 'for the general good ... pass ... from the state of pauper tenants to that
of independent labourers, maintained, as the same class are in England, by their
daily labour'. Poor laws would, they concluded, help in a process that 'cannot
much longer be delayed with safety', as also would government grants for
drainage, emigration, and railway construction. Ireland and Britain were now
'inseparably interwoven', and it was in Britain's interests 'that Ireland should
be raised'.[33]

Cornewall Lewis had said much the same in his 1836 book *On Local
Disturbances in Ireland*, and Nicholls too had emphasized the necessity and
dangers of the transition that poor laws would both help to bring about and,
he hoped, enable cottiers and conacre holders to 'endure'.[34] Indeed, the
whole question of agricultural consolidation *à l'anglaise* became closely
intertwined with discussions of poverty and poor relief, though opinions
differed as to whether the necessary process of transition had as yet shown

---

[31] Littleton (chief secretary) to Althorp, 10 November 1833, S[taffordshire] R[ecord] O[ffice]
Hatherton Papers D260/M/01/2; *Three Early Nineteenth Century Diaries*, ed. A. Aspinall (London, 1952), 305.

[32] *First and Second Reports from the Select Committee Appointed to Inquire into the Amount
of Advances Made by the Commissioners of Public Works in Ireland*, HC 1835 (573), xx. 162.

[33] *Second Report of the Commissioners Appointed to Consider and Recommend a General
System of Railways for Ireland*, HC 1837–8 [145], xxxv. 533–9. The report, dated 13 July 1838,
was largely written by Drummond: see H. Wrottesley, *Life and Correspondence of Field Marshal
Sir John Burgoyne Bart.*, 2 vols (London, 1873), i. 408.

[34] G. C. Lewis, *On Local Disturbances in Ireland; and on the Irish Church Question* (London,
1836), 319; *Report of George Nicholls*, HC 1837 [69], li. 211.

any signs of getting under way. Evidence given to the Whately Commission in the 1830s and to the Devon Commission in the 1840s presents a mixed picture: some consolidation, especially in Munster and Connacht, but slow progress and sometimes none at all.[35] Certainly the Devon Commissioners were in 1845 still convinced that 'the smallness of farms, as they are usually let' rendered the 'introduction of the English system ... extremely difficult'.[36] Nicholls did his best for anglicization by publishing a *Farmer's Guide, Compiled for the Use of the Small Farmers and Cotter [sic] Tenantry of Ireland* (Dublin, 1841) in pocket format for the encouragement of 'industrial habits', savings, the avoidance of 'early and improvident marriages', and capitalistic probity all round. But those in political power realized that there was still a long way to go. In 1843 Peel identified one great obstacle to be the 'bankrupt condition of the landlords' in Ireland, and several (unsuccessful) attempts were made during the next three years to introduce legislation to address the problem of insolvent proprietors unable—often of course simply unwilling—to push forward the improvement of their estates and the consolidation of tenant holdings.[37] The following year two memoranda were drawn up for Peel's cabinet proposing further measures designed to anglicize Irish tenurial relations by unravelling their opaque peculiarities in favour of something closer to a capitalist system in which labourers worked for wages, substantial tenants paid rents, and improving landlords beneficently kept everything ticking over with eirenic efficiency. Unless, it was argued, all of Ireland's 'customary practices' were done away with, the country would languish for ever in its existing state of backwardness, 'social disorder, and national inconvenience'.[38] And from the Bowood Whigs came matching arguments in the same year, with their in-house economist Nassau Senior's 'Ireland in 1843', published in the *Edinburgh Review* for January 1844, proposing that English-style agrarian capitalism and its connected social arrangements provided the sovereign, indeed the only, way out of Ireland's deep-seated economic and cultural ills.[39]

---

[35] J. Mokyr, *Why Ireland Starved: A Quantitative and Analytical History of the Irish Economy, 1800–1850*, revised impression (London, 1985), 130–1.

[36] *Report from Her Majesty's Commissioners of Inquiry into the State of the Law and Practice in Respect to the Occupation of Land in Ireland*, HC 1845 [605], xix. 16.

[37] *Sir Robert Peel from his Private Papers*, ed. C. S. Parker, 3 vols (London, 1891–9), iii. 63; P. G. Lane, 'The Encumbered Estates Court, 1848–1849', *Economic and Social Review*, iii (1972), 421–6; R. D. Collison Black, *Economic Thought and the Irish Question 1817–1870* (Cambridge, 1960), 35.

[38] See the 18pp and 48pp Memoranda in L[iverpool] R[ecord] O[ffice] Derby Papers 36.

[39] Gray, *Famine, Land and Politics*, 62–4. 'Ireland in 1843', which its author—correctly—hoped would appeal also to many Tories, is reprinted in N. W. Senior, *Journals, Conversations and Essays Relating to Ireland*, 2nd edn, 2 vols (London, 1868), i. 17–133.

III

That within less than twenty-four months Ireland and its people would begin
to traverse the *via dolorosa* of the Great Famine gives lacerating point to such
ideas and proposals.[40] The chronology of the potato blight (*phytophthora
infestans*) can be briefly stated. The fungus, for which there was then no
cure, first struck in September 1845, and that season's crop (upon which a
very large proportion of the people depended) was about one-third short,
though some parts of the country escaped altogether. In 1846 three-quarters
were lost. Yields were better in 1847, but little had been planted by despairing
people who had eaten their seed potatoes. In 1848 yields were again only two-
thirds of normal. Although thereafter things improved, it was not until 1850
that it became possible to regard the worst as being over, and even then
agricultural dislocation and large-scale emigration (which reached its peak
in 1851) continued for some years more. The best estimates suggest that the
number of so-called excess deaths resulting from hunger and disease (that is,
deaths that would not otherwise have occurred) numbered about 1.1 million
or possibly more in the years 1846–51. Not only that, but during the decade
after 1845 some 2.1 million people emigrated, a process that continued at
substantial levels well into the 1850s. And, while some of these would have left
Ireland even if no famine had occurred, many departed because of it.[41] Of
course, other European countries also experienced the blight, but extensive
industrialization and (in certain cases) more effective action by governments
largely enabled them 'to save their labouring poor from the fate of the Irish'.[42]

During the course of the Famine the approach of ministers shifted and
changed, sometimes dramatically so. Food shortages (usually localized) had
been a common feature of early nineteenth-century Ireland, and, given the
comparatively modest sums required to alleviate them, previous governments
had sometimes proved tolerably generous. In 1830, for example, both Wellington and Peel had agreed that 'the intensity of actual suffering may be so

---

[40] On the Famine and its horrors, see (within an extensive literature) Mokyr, *Why Ireland
Starved*; M. E. Daly, *The Famine in Ireland* (Dundalk, 1986); C. Ó Gráda, *The Great Irish Famine*
(London, 1989); C. Kinealy, *This Great Calamity: The Irish Famine 1845–62* (Dublin, 1994);
Gray, *Famine, Land and Politics*; L. Kennedy et al., *Mapping the Great Irish Famine* (Dublin,
1999); C. Ó Gráda, *Black '47 and Beyond: The Great Irish Famine in History, Economy, and
Memory* (Princeton, 1999); J. S. Donnelly Jr, *The Great Irish Potato Famine* (Stroud, 2001);
C. Ó Murchadha, *The Great Famine: Ireland's Agony 1845–1852* (London, 2011); E. Delaney, *The
Curse of Reason: The Great Irish Famine* (Dublin, 2012); J. Crowley et al., *Atlas of the Great Irish
Famine, 1845–52* (Cork, 2012).

[41] Donnelly, *Great Irish Potato Famine*, 169–86.

[42] C. Ó Gráda, *Ireland before and after the Famine: Explorations in Economic History,
1800–1925*, 2nd edn (Manchester, 1993), 125–33; Delaney, *Curse of Reason*, 123–5; C. Ó
Gráda et al. (eds), *When the Potato Failed: Causes and Effects of the 'Last' European Subsistence
Crisis 1845–1850* (Turnhout, 2007), especially 15–40, 95–107, 123–48.

great that every ordinary consideration must be overlooked and ... the government must not, through adherence to strict principle, close its eyes to such tremendous evils as famine must entail'.[43] But the enormity of the Famine of the 1840s and the resulting costs concentrated ministerial minds into narrower channels and showed that in certain circumstances the assimilationist king could be trumped by the financial ace, a process given additional force by developments in economic thinking, by certain theological doctrines concerning the role of providence, and by less cerebral dissatisfactions about what had long been perceived as the endless difficulties created by bungling Irish improvidence.

The relevant cabinets were by no means agreed as to how to deal with the crisis. But, as time went on and as cherished principles (such as opposition to outdoor relief and to the direct provision of food) were temporarily ditched in the face of overwhelming necessity, widespread anger at the expense of it all gained a steadily stronger purchase on ministerial minds. The chief proponent of keeping costs down was Charles Wood, the Chancellor of the Exchequer in Russell's Whig government of June 1846 to February 1852 and in office for all but the Famine's first ten months. Wood's views were made up of a mixture of long-standing convictions about Irish extravagance, adherence to popular versions of political economy, religious ideas about the workings of divine providence, and a belief that what Ireland needed—and what the Famine now made possible—were social and economic changes of a fundamental kind. Given, however, that the necessary assimilations could not take place overnight, short-term priorities urgently required that expenditure be kept under very tight control indeed.

Within weeks of coming into office Wood was running the great banner of cheeseparing up the Exchequer flagpole, a banner displaying associated heraldic devices concerning the importance of Hibernian self-reliance. 'All that could reasonably be expected from Government has been done,' he announced in early September 1846; 'it seems to me to be the misfortune of Ireland that every man looks to the government for everything ... You must depend upon yourselves, to help yourselves.'[44] And so Wood continued with increasing linguistic and emotional fervour throughout the next years, though he did not always get the cabinet to follow him in every detail. The Irish complained too much, they exaggerated the extent of their troubles, 'England' was far too generous, 'so much was never done for any country, by another, in

---

[43] Peel to Northumberland, 26 June 1830, A[lnwick] C[astle] Northumberland Papers DNP/74; Wellington to Northumberland, 7 July 1830, ibid., DNP/75.

[44] Wood to Bessborough (viceroy), 9 September 1846, TNA Russell Papers PRO 30/22/5C; to Monteagle, September 1846, D. Howell-Thomas, *Duncannon: Reformer and Reconciler 1781–1847* (Norwich, 1992), 294; to Russell, 2 December 1846, TNA Russell Papers PRO 30/22/5F.

the history of the world'.[45] The only consolation was that, the deeper the calamity became, the more likely that Ireland would be so purged by distress that something like a new and more vigorous country would emerge. The logic resembled that of mid-Victorian obstetricians who opposed the use of chloroform in childbirth because only female pain could ensure a safe delivery.[46]

Although Wood's views were unusually fierce, he was typical enough in his striking ability to sustain two virtually contradictory opinions at the same time—namely, that the Irish should be given as little help as possible but be constantly reminded of 'the substantial benefits which during the last eighteen months they have derived from the Union with this country'.[47] The powerful permanent head of the Treasury, Sir Charles Trevelyan, the man ultimately in charge of famine relief, found it no less possible to keep simultaneously in play concepts of penny-pinching economy, Irish self-reliance, and a belief that, at the end of the day, he was supervising a system based on the principle that '*coute qu'il coute* [come what may] the people must not, under any circumstances, be allowed to starve'.[48] Like Wood, he believed that the Irish as a whole, and not least 'the poorest and most ignorant … peasant', could hardly fail to be 'sensible of the advantage … of forming part of a powerful community like that of the United Kingdom, the establishments and pecuniary resources of which are at all times ready to be employed for his benefit'. At times, indeed, his endless wordiness replicates the sanctimonious abasements of Uriah Heep, as when an Irish correspondent was reminded of the extent to which Trevelyan personally rejoiced in the fact that, because of the Union, it had 'fallen to my lot to take an active, altho' a humble, part in assisting' Ireland 'in the hour of her need'.[49] Trevelyan's famous article in the *Edinburgh Review* of January 1848, while acknowledging the Famine's 'deplorable consequences' for 'the empire at large', insisted that, because 'the disease was strictly local … the cure was to be obtained only by the application of local remedies' and that 'the economical administration of the relief could only be provided for by making it, in part at least, a local charge'.[50]

---

[45] Wood to Russell, 9 April 1848, B[orthwick] I[nstitute] Hickleton Papers A4/56; to Russell, 1 September 1847, TNA Russell Papers PRO 30/22/6F; also Goulburn to Peel, 24 November 1846, *Sir Robert Peel from his Private Papers*, ed. Parker, iii. 468–9; J. Young to Peel, 14 January 1847, ibid. iii. 481.

[46] *The Greville Memoirs 1814–1860*, ed. L. Strachey and R. Fulford, 8 vols (London, 1938), vi. 156–7 (9 February 1849); A. J. Youngson, *The Scientific Revolution in Victorian Medicine* (London, 1979), 55, 122.

[47] Parl. Deb. 3: xciv. 50 (8 July 1847).

[48] Trevelyan to Routh, 29 April 1846, N[ewcastle] U[niversity] Trevelyan Papers CET18/6, Trevelyan's underlining; also R. Haines, *Charles Trevelyan and the Great Famine* (Dublin, 2004), 139.

[49] Trevelyan to Spring Rice, 2 September and 10 November 1846, NU Trevelyan Papers CET18/7 and CET18/9.

[50] 'The Irish Crisis', *Edinburgh Review*, 87/194 (1848), 229–319, especially 278.

Ministers with direct responsibility for Ireland and, in the case of the lord lieutenant and to a lesser degree the chief secretary, actually required to spend long periods in the country did, however, tend to take the 'we are all in this together' argument more seriously than their colleagues in London. Bessborough, viceroy during the first eleven months of the Whig government and himself an Irish proprietor, regularly pleaded with the prime minister for more money to meet a destitution 'quite fearful and ... scarcity of provisions so great that it is useless to talk of enabling the people to earn sufficient wages'. 'I wish you could see the real state of the country,' he wrote shortly after coming into office, for it is one that makes it 'useless to think of ordinary means'.[51] And even Bessborough's successor, the wilier and less emotional Clarendon, never ceased to urge that more money be made available. Being in Ireland and having eyes in his head, he lost no time in telling Wood that, while abhorring needless expenditure, it was his duty to reflect the reality of things 'for difficulties don't grow less by shutting one's eyes or by running away from them'. He lectured London about the dangers and the inhumanity of rationing relief, how Irish bitterness would come to haunt British rule, how tired he was of being told that his requests were 'unprecedented and contrary to economic principles', for, while it was perfectly in order to 'apply abstract principles which in time will work in Connaught as among the Esquimaux or New Zealanders ... they won't before midsummer next ... feed starving multitudes'.[52]

Clarendon, indeed, resembled a man who, against all his preconceived views and fully aware that these continued to be the views of his colleagues, could simply not prevent himself from letting facts on the ground induce—at least in the short term—distinct if reluctant changes in perception and understanding. Yes, he too 'would not give relief until the last moment'. Yes, he too realized that 'the financial difficulties' were 'great'. But Trevelyan's notions about 'the natural process which is now doing all that can be desired', or 'Wood's ignorance' and propensity to 'kick and scream' when asked for money, could no longer be borne in the face of 'helpless starvation'.[53]

As prime minister, Russell wavered uneasily between hardliners like Wood and his allies (Earl Grey at the Colonial Office and Sir George Grey the Home Secretary)—the so-called moralists—and Clarendon, the agitated man on the

[51] Bessborough to Russell, 14 January 1847 and 19 September 1846, TNA Russell Papers PRO 30/22/6A and 30/22/5C; also to Russell, 30 September 1846, ibid., PRO 30/22/5C and 1 and 6 October 1846, ibid., PRO 30/22/5D.

[52] Clarendon to Wood, 7 September 1847, BI Hickleton Papers A4/57; to Wood, 30 March 1848, Bodl[eian Library] Clarendon Papers Irish Letter-Book II; to G. Grey, 22 March 1848, ibid., Letter-Book II; to Russell, 23 April 1848, ibid., Letter-Book II; to Russell, 30 January 1849, ibid., Letter-Book III.

[53] Clarendon to Lansdowne, 26 October 1847, 15 and 28 November 1848 B[ritish] L[ibrary] 3rd Marquess of Lansdowne Papers B84 and B85 (provisional references).

spot.[54] In the early months, when the Tories were still in power, he had grandly declared adhesion to full-blown union and assimilation principles.

> I consider this House, as representing the United Kingdom, is bound to consider every part of that kingdom; and if one part is more distressed, at any particular period, than another, it is the bounden duty of this House to attend to it, and there is no call upon the particular part to feel grateful to any other particular part.[55]

A month later, in March 1846, Graham (then Tory Home Secretary) took exactly the same line. 'It is not', he declared, 'a dole given by England to Ireland; it is from the resources of the United Kingdom, of which she is an integral part ... It is not aid from England, it is not generosity; I deny that altogether.'[56]

But, as time went on and costs mounted, Russell (now in office) began to wobble. Conceding that some might still argue that 'the burden be borne by the consolidated fund ... by the imperial Treasury and Exchequer', he now thought it important (and perhaps expedient) to remind his listeners that 'these are sums derived from payments by the people of this country [Britain]; from the taxes which they pay on their soap, their sugar, their tea, their coffee'.[57] In other words, the 'we are all in this together' mantra was being abandoned, and not slowly but all at once. Russell had, indeed, already made it clear to Bessborough that 'it must be thoroughly understood that we cannot feed the people ... We can at best keep prices down where there is no regular market', a view that he and the government were, however, obliged to abandon early in 1847, partly out of necessity and partly because the previous policy of officially sponsored relief works had turned out to be a practical failure and a financial disaster. Even so, Wood still felt it necessary to point out that 'no exertions of a Government, or, I will add, of private charity, can supply a complete remedy for the existing calamity. It is a national visitation, sent by Providence.'[58] As Russell put it, the Irish should really begin to realize that their 'common delusion that God can convert a period of scarcity into a period of abundance is one of the most mischievous that can be entertained'.[59] God, as it were, had spoken; the case was closed. By November 1847 Russell had started to talk, not only in harsher terms but in terms of denigration and anger brought on by the enormity of the crisis and the costs (and inadequacies) of

---

[54] Gray, *Famine, Land and Politics*, 24–6 and *passim*; J. Prest, *Lord John Russell* (London, 1972), 234–54, 265–75, 289–302.

[55] Parl. Deb. 3: lxxxiii. 1085 (17 February 1846).

[56] Ibid. lxxxiv. 1185 (18 March 1846).

[57] Ibid. lxxxix. 437–8 (25 January 1847).

[58] Russell to Bessborough, 11 October 1846, TNA Russell Papers PRO 30/22/5D; Gray, *Famine, Land and Politics*, 262–8; Parl. Deb. 3: lxxxix. 689–90 (1 February 1847: Wood).

[59] Russell to Lansdowne, 11 October 1846, BL 3rd Marquess of Lansdowne Papers B102 (provisional reference).

acceptable 'remedies'. Thus, to those who proposed some measure of tenant compensation, he bleakly replied that 'you might as well propose that a landlord should compensate the rabbits for the burrows they had made on his land'[60]—Irish rabbits, British burrows.

What gave something approaching respectability to such views was the fact (as Russell himself pointed out) that the people of Britain paid taxes—notably income tax and the so-called assessed taxes—that the Irish did not pay, Peel having in 1842 (for largely technical reasons to do with collection) exempted Ireland from his renewal of the income tax, though he had (as was soon forgotten in Britain) increased the Irish spirits and stamp duties in compensation. And when, during the famine, all other economical arguments had been exhausted, the taxation argument was wheeled out with the deadpan smoothness of a conjurer easing an ace out of his sleeve. Already in 1845 parliamentary critics of Ireland's exemptions were increasing in number, and this, in turn, 'generated significant resistance to expenditure by central government on ... famine relief'.[61] By 1847 backbenchers, especially radical Liberals, were making it plain that they objected to giving what they saw as handouts to a nation of tax avoiders. Sir Benjamin Hall (later a minister in both the Aberdeen and Palmerston administrations) pointed out in May 1847 that 'this country'—he mentioned 'England' but probably meant Britain—paid £10,417,000 annually in taxes from which the Irish were exempt, and that therefore assistance could be given only once the oft-repeated wishes of Irish parliamentarians 'that their country be put on the same footing as England' had been fully acceded to.[62] A few weeks later the self-styled 'ultra Radical' John (later Sir John) Salusbury-Trelawny, referring to Ireland's tax status, insisted that 'the burdens of Ireland, instead of being ... too heavy, were far too light. He therefore hoped that the Government would not be induced by the constant howl of the Irish members, by their continued dunning and boring for money', to go on paying for famine relief. Indeed 'howl' was becoming a term not infrequently deployed with respect to Irish requests for help, whether these came from those anxious to relieve the starving or from landlords on the brink of ruin.[63] Nor were staunch Tories any less fierce: 'The House should recollect that the people of Ireland paid no assessed taxes. They had no income tax; while in some districts of England the poor rates were heavier than they were in the most distressed parts of Ireland ... The people of Ireland should in future be compelled to support their own poor.'[64]

---

[60] Russell to Clarendon, 10 November 1847, TNA Russell Papers PRO 30/22/6G.

[61] D. Kanter, 'The Politics of Irish Taxation, 1842-53', *English Historical Review*, 127 (2012), 1128, 1123.

[62] Parl. Deb. 3: xcii. 1326 (31 May 1847).

[63] Ibid. xcv. 775 (7 December 1847: Trelawny) and lxxxix. 955 (5 February 1847: Hastie).

[64] Ibid. cii. 392–3 (7 February 1849: Christopher).

Russell, when trying to ward off viceregal demands from Dublin for more expenditure, was always conscious of such views and, indeed, lectured Bessborough that all 'this money is raised from the taxes' the Irish did not pay.[65] Small wonder, then, that this oft-repeated 'truth'—that the Irish were no more than tax dodgers—provided a species of justification for a decision in early 1849 that blatantly undermined, not just the arguments mounted in favour of assimilating Britain and Ireland, but the basic principles of the Union itself. This was the introduction in February 1849 of the so-called rate-in-aid, imposed on Irish (but not British) poor law unions to raise funds to assist twenty-three bankrupt unions, all but one of them in Munster or Connacht. Unions in Ulster (where the famine had generally been less severe) immediately raised loud complaints and demanded to know why the burden was not being shared with England, Scotland, and Wales, given that all four nations were now supposed to be parts of a single united political entity.[66] Russell once again talked of Ireland's lesser tax burdens and would himself have liked to extend the income tax to Ireland, but the cabinet thought the rate-in-aid simpler, quicker, and possibly productive of more revenue.[67] The Home Secretary, having pointed to the fact that the whole of Ireland (but not Britain) had 'great immunities from taxation', made the wondrous observation that 'Ulster formed part of Ireland and not of England', while a despondent Clarendon—convinced that 'nobody can defend the rate-in-aid on principle. It can only be justified by necessity'—believed that Russell was, as usual, being outflanked by Wood (and Trevelyan) and that, if any parts of England had experienced famine, a very different policy would have taken the stage.[68] And, indeed, Clarendon kept pressing unavailingly for something more, in language that can rarely have come from a senior minister: 'Surely this is a state of things to justify you in asking the House of Commons for an advance, for I don't think there is another legislature in Europe that would disregard such sufferings as now exist in the west of Ireland or coldly persist in a policy of extermination.'[69]

Of course, the whole of Ireland was soon in a rage about the decision, which, as Clarendon told the Duke of Bedford, had fallen 'upon the country and bursts like a shell among the people'. Lansdowne's Kerry agent pertinently

---

[65] Russell to Bessborough, 4 October 1846, TNA Russell Papers PRO 30/22/5D.
[66] Gray, *Famine, Land and Politics*, 311–17; J. Grant, 'The Great Famine and the Poor Law in Ulster: The Rate-in-Aid Issue of 1849', *Irish Historical Studies*, 27 (1990), 30–47.
[67] Parl. Deb. 3: cii. 615 (12 February 1849) and ciii. 109–10 (2 March 1849); Russell to Clarendon, 11 and 13 February 1849, Bodl. Clarendon Papers Irish 26; Kanter, 'Politics of Irish Taxation', 1136–7.
[68] G. Grey to Clarendon, 8 February 1849, Bodl. Clarendon Papers Irish 13; Parl. Deb. 3: ciii. 223–4 (5 March 1849: G. Grey); Clarendon to Bedford, [early 1849] and 9 March 1849, Bodl. Clarendon Papers Irish 80; Clarendon to Russell, 9 and 12 February 1849, ibid., Letter-Book III.
[69] Clarendon to Russell, 28 April 1849, ibid., Letter-Book IV.

asked whether, 'if Ireland were attacked by the French, would you keep an account against us of all the expense that was incurred in repelling the invader, and require us to raise rates to repay it?'[70] One sympathetic English observer visiting Ireland in the summer of 1849 noted sarcastically that he had 'yet to learn that Ireland is not an integral part of Great Britain [*sic*]; I have yet to learn, that doings so disgraceful can exist in Ireland, and not be a shame and disgrace to England'.[71] The chief secretary rather desperately suggested that only the rate-in-aid had saved Ireland from the income tax,[72] an argument that soon became the fig leaf of choice for London politicians unable to square a circle made up of union principles, on the one hand, and irritation at the costs of famine relief, on the other. Disraeli, now beginning to ascend the greasy pole, supported the rate-in-aid because taxes had not yet been equalized throughout the United Kingdom, while Russell, admitting that there was 'much that is just and fair' in the argument against the rate-in-aid, produced figures purporting to show that Britain paid direct and indirect taxes amounting to £12.15 million a year from which Ireland was exempt.[73] Interestingly, the Irish Federalist and land reformer Sharman Crawford supported the extension of the income tax to Ireland precisely on the grounds that, 'if the Union was to be maintained, the principle of united responsibilities must be its basis'. Indeed, the whole rate-in-aid controversy reveals a temporary and highly pragmatic reversal of entrenched attitudes: British politicians undermining the basic tenets of the Union, Irish nationalists (loosely defined) insisting their country profit from the overall strength of the political entity established in 1801.[74]

One of the few to emerge from the rate-in-aid episode with credit (and indeed consistency) was the Englishman Edward Twisleton, the Chief Poor Law Commissioner, who resigned office on 10 March 1849 and subsequently gave his reasons to a parliamentary enquiry.

> I think it extremely undesirable to do anything which tends to make the inhabitants of Ireland regard the mere island of Ireland as an area of taxation. What I think is desirable as a matter of policy is, that they should have just the same feeling towards this country as if there was no sea between us, as if they were locally joined to Devonshire or Cornwall.

---

[70] Clarendon to Bedford, 9 March 1849, ibid. 80; Lansdowne's agent as reported by Senior, *Journals, Conversations and Essays Relating to Ireland*, ii. 4.
[71] S. G. Osborne, *Gleanings in the West of Ireland* (London, 1850), 79.
[72] Parl. Deb. 3: ciii. 1324 (26 March 1849: Somerville).
[73] Ibid. ciii. 68 (1 March 1849: Disraeli) and 109–10 (2 March 1849: Russell).
[74] Ibid. ciii. 49 (1 March 1849: Crawford). See D. P. Nally, *Human Encumbrances: Political Violence and the Great Famine* (Notre Dame, IN, 2011), 151–3, 216–17, 279; Haines, *Charles Trevelyan*, 522.

Not only that, but Twisleton (for whom imperial rather than specifically Irish considerations lay at the heart of the matter) believed, contrary to those who thought 'things' should be allowed to 'take their natural course', that 'it is part of the system of nature that we should have feelings of compassion for those people' and repugnant to suggest that 'their brothers in the rest of the empire are to look on and let them die'.[75]

That, already by the end of 1847, Russell had calculated Treasury expenditure on famine relief at £8 million helps to explain the sense of donor fatigue that increasingly hardened the government's heart. However, the total sum for the whole of the period 1845–50 was estimated by the Treasury itself as little more than Russell's figure for the period up to 1847—namely, £8.1 million—of which less than half consisted of grants.[76] This is less than was raised in Ireland itself, and also has often been contrasted with the £69.3 million or more spent on the Crimean War of 1854–6 and—perhaps more relevantly—with the £20 million provided in 1834 to compensate West Indian and other plantation owners for the emancipation of their slaves—a larger financial operation than any previously undertaken by the state.[77]

But, while such comparisons are certainly pertinent, two other points need to be made. In the first place, there can be little doubt that, however common local food shortages had previously been, the Great Famine was, in the words of Peter Solar, 'no ordinary subsistence crisis', but unprecedented in both recent Irish and European terms. Quite simply, the crop failures caused by the blight 'were extraordinarily severe by nineteenth-century standards', producing, in effect, 'seventeenth-century mortality levels'. In other words, the problem was not merely one of maladministering essentially adequate supplies of food, but 'an absolute shortfall' of supplies, so that an (admittedly inexpert and unsympathetic) government found itself faced with, not only a catastrophe it was not prepared for, but one it could not have been expected to have been prepared for.[78] In the second place, one should perhaps at least direct some attention towards the once-fashionable area of the counterfactual. Given the class interests involved in mid-nineteenth-century Ireland, one wonders

---

[75] *Fifth Report from the Select Committee on Poor Laws (Ireland)*, HC 1849 (148), xv, pt i, 330; *Fourth Report*, HC 1849 (170), xv, pt i, 299.

[76] Russell to Clarendon, 23 September 1848, Bodl. Clarendon Papers Irish 43; Donnelly, *Great Irish Potato Famine*, 118–19. For a somewhat higher estimate, see Ó Gráda, *Black '47 and Beyond*, 77.

[77] Gray, *Famine, Land and Politics*, 333; Donnelly, *Great Irish Potato Famine*, 119; Mokyr, *Why Ireland Starved*, 292; N. Draper, *The Price of Emancipation: Slave-Ownership, Compensation and British Society at the End of Slavery* (Cambridge, 2010), 2, 179, 181, 270, 280–93, 318–19.

[78] P. Solar, 'The Great Famine was no Ordinary Subsistence Crisis', in E. M. Crawford (ed.), *Famine: The Irish Experience 900–1900: Subsistence Crises and Famines in Ireland* (Edinburgh, 1989), 112–31; T. P. O'Neill, 'Food Problems during the Great Irish Famine', *Journal of the Royal Society of Antiquaries of Ireland*, 82 (1952), 99–108.

whether an O'Connellite Repeal administration would have done much better or whether, as David Johnson and Liam Kennedy have speculated, 'an independent parliament, probably dominated by landlords and commercial farmers, would have responded very differently'.[79]

IV

In one respect, however, the reactions of the government and of public opinion in Britain translated frustration over the cost of relief into a channel that had both a long pedigree and distinctly assimilationist overtones—namely, a bitter and growing antipathy to Irish landlords increasingly seen, whether rightly or wrongly, as especially responsible for Irish poverty, distress, and discontent because of their long-standing greed, failures of sympathy, and unwillingness to match the much-lauded generosity of their British counterparts. While, of course, many of the largest landlords were primarily British proprietors who also happened to own substantial Irish estates, critics, much given (and not always correctly) to seeing agrarian conditions in England as little short of paradisiacal, tended to lump all Irish landowners into a single unappetizing bloc. Thus, while there is a good deal of evidence that the larger owners (whether holding land exclusively in Ireland or not) *tended* to be less exploitative, when contemporaries were seeking to identify those responsible for Irish poverty and discontent, it was proprietors as a whole that they had in their sights. Indeed, the almost constant and often intense unpopularity in Britain of Irish landowners throughout the whole of the Union period tends to be obscured by ministerial criticisms of the Irish in general and especially by later official programmes designed to facilitate the redistribution of land by paying its owners large sums to sell their estates, in truth little more than a kick in the groin made bearable by money in the bank.[80]

If much had begun to change in the 1830s with respect to Anglo-Irish political relationships, British attacks on Irish landlords continued unabated, this being a pursuit all could enjoy, furnishing as it did a plausible tool for

[79] D. S. Johnson and L. Kennedy, 'Nationalist Historiography and the Decline of the Irish Economy: George O'Brien Revisited', in S. Hutton and P. Stewart (eds), *Ireland's Histories: Aspects of State, Society and Ideology* (London, 1991). 31; P. Gray, 'The European Crisis and the Relief of Irish Famine, 1845–50', in Ó Gráda et al. (eds), *When the Potato Failed*, 99–100; Ó Gráda, *Black '47 and Beyond*, 83; Hoppen, *Ireland since 1800*, 64.

[80] On this generally, see Hoppen, *Elections, Politics and Society in Ireland*, 89–170; Hoppen, 'Landlords, Society and Electoral Politics in Mid-Nineteenth-Century Ireland', *Past & Present*, 75 (1977), 62–93; Hoppen, 'Landownership and Power in Nineteenth-Century Ireland: The Decline of an Elite', in R. Gibson and M. Blinkhorn (eds), *Landownership and Power in Modern Europe* (London, 1991), 164–80; Hoppen, 'Gladstone, Salisbury and the End of Irish Assimilationism', in M. E. Daly and K. T. Hoppen (eds), *Gladstone: Ireland and Beyond* (Dublin, 2011), 45–63.

analysing Irish discontents as well as warm feelings of self-congratulation and moral, as well as social and economic, superiority. The virtually constant sneers maintained by the Wellington administration were seamlessly adopted by its Whig successor. Peel in 1829 positively salivated at the prospect of getting Irish landlords to pay the bulk of the costs of Irish government egged on by a chief secretary (Leveson-Gower) who blamed Irish 'poverty', above all, upon 'a bad resident gentry', while his successor (Hardinge) asked whether, given such a gentry, it could be a 'matter of wonder that young men ... should become Ribbonmen and outlaws?'[81] Nor did the arrival of Grey's administration produce any change in London's low view of Irish proprietors; quite the reverse. Anglesey, sacked as viceroy by Wellington in 1829 and reappointed by Grey in November 1830, seems to have devoted remarkably large sections of his official and private correspondence to irritated outbursts on the matter: 'The Mischief of Ireland is not in the people. It lies with the absentees and with the demoralized gentry'; 'The lower orders are ... vilely oppressed'; the County Clare was virtually devoid of resident gentlemen; if Irish peasants 'were not the most enduring people on earth, they would not bear the hardships as they do'; 'The landowners are harsh and unkind to the people. They treat them scornfully', in part, he admitted, because so many owners were themselves in debt, mortgaged to the hilt and, all in all, the most financially irresponsible of beings.[82] And the prime minister responded in the same vein: the behaviour of the Clare magistrates was simply 'abominable'; Irish landlords as a whole sat on their hands and completely failed to understand that Ireland's troubles were largely caused by 'their own fears and other remissions'.[83]

And so it went on, with criticisms descending like hailstones from politicians of all parties and observers of all kinds. The Englishman Richard Whately, finding, shortly after his appointment as Archbishop of Dublin, that Irish landowners were no 'better' than the Irish in general, raised a point about the mysteries of the Celtic mind that was often to be repeated by others—namely, that 'a Roman Catholic and an Orangeman ... are much more like each other than either of them to an Englishman'.[84] A Scottish Whig visiting Ireland found resident Tipperary landlords interested in little other than 'shooting, hunting, fishing etc.', while in 1836 the viceroy reported in

---

[81] Peel to Leveson-Gower, 30 July 1829, *Sir Robert Peel from his Private Papers*, ed. Parker, ii. 122–4; Leveson-Gower to Peel, 5 August 1829, N[ational] A[rchives of] I[reland] Leveson-Gower Letter-Book MS 737; Hardinge to Peel, 13 October 1830, McGill University, Montreal, Hardinge Papers.

[82] Anglesey to Holland, 20 April and 12 August 1831, P[ublic] R[ecord] O[ffice of] N[orthern] I[reland] Anglesey Papers D619/27B; to Grey, 15 January and 15 April 1831, ibid., D619/28C.

[83] Grey to Anglesey, 16 and 31 March 1831, ibid., D619/28A.

[84] Whately to Bishop Coppleston of Llandaff, 19 January 1832, Whately, *Life and Correspondence of Richard Whately*, i. 127.

deadpan fashion to Russell at the Home Office that 'the difficulty seems to be to get the landlords to act as if they had any interest in their properties'.[85] George Nicholls, after touring Ireland to assess its suitability for workhouses, was especially delighted by the thought that the cost of these would at last oblige landlords and 'the higher classes generally' to dig into their own pockets to pay for poor relief[86]—just as Peel in 1829 had rejoiced in forcing such men to contribute towards the costs of the police.

The famous letter of May 1838 addressed by the undersecretary Thomas Drummond to Tipperary magistrates about property having its duties as well as its rights and declaring that 'to the neglect of those duties in times past is mainly to be ascribed that diseased state of society in which … crimes have their rise' stands out because of its public nature rather than its sentiments.[87] In 1843 Cornewall Lewis thought that all but Irish landlords 'would suppose it impossible to shave them [tenants] closer than they already are', while Tory ministers in office were usually of the same view. As viceroy in the early 1840s the Tory Earl de Grey kept trying to persuade proprietors 'to do their duty to their poorer neighbours', while Graham at the Home Office not only told De Grey's successor that if only landlords would 'do their duty, much more good would be effected by them than all the pressure for coercion bills', but repeated the same sentiments on the very eve of the Famine: 'The malady is deep-seated in the social system, and time alone and better conduct on the part of the landlords can eradicate it.'[88]

The onset of famine gave jet-propelled charge to these long maturing denunciations of Irish landlordism as harsh, exploitative, inefficient, and (above all) un-English, and this despite the fact that the cabinets of the period (especially the Whig cabinet of 1846–52) were not lacking in ministers with large Irish estates: Lansdowne, Palmerston, and Clanricarde were very substantial owners of Irish land, while Cottenham held significant Irish mortgages.[89] Under Peel's government (which fell in June 1846) Graham continued to fire salvoes from the Home Office, salvoes with which the viceroy in Dublin entirely agreed. 'I have', he rather unnecessarily announced, 'the greatest respect for the rights of property and am earnest in my desire to uphold them, but British feelings are outraged by these sweeping ejectments' of tenants 'cast out by hundreds into

---

[85] *A Scottish Whig in Ireland 1835–38: The Irish Journals of Robert Graham of Redgorton*, ed. H. Heaney (Dublin, 1999), 101; Mulgrave to Russell, 13 September 1836, TNA Russell Papers PRO 30/22/2C.

[86] *Report of George Nicholls*, HC 1837 [69], li. 210.

[87] *A Copy of Correspondence which has Recently Taken Place between Her Majesty's Government and the Magistrates of the County of Tipperary*, HC 1837–8 (735), xlvi. 571–6.

[88] Lewis to G. Grote, Dublin, 11 January 1843, *Letters of the Right Hon. Sir George Cornewall Lewis*, ed. Lewis, 129; C. Read, 'Peel, De Grey and Irish Policy, 1841–1844', *History*, 99 (2014), 1–18; Graham to Heytesbury, 30 March and 28 June 1845, BL Graham Papers Ir/21 and Ir/22.

[89] Prest, *Lord John Russell*, 237.

the highways and hedges without shelter and without pity'.[90] Organizing relief, Trevelyan too lost no time in aiming critical barbs at Irish landlords: Catholic priests did their duty and sometimes heroically so, but landlords 'tried to throw the whole burden upon the Government and urge upon the lord lieutenant schemes for improving their estates and relieving themselves from their difficulties out of the Consolidated Fund'.[91]

Russell too had little hesitation in taking a populist line as far as landlords were concerned. With him, as with most other critics, the core of the matter lay in the argument that Irish proprietors were simply behaving in an un-English way and that the sooner they were forced to adopt Anglo-Saxon patterns of conduct the better. If a choice had to be made, he argued in July 1847, between 'rent and sustenance', then landlords would have to yield on the matter of rent, however much this 'terrible ... solution' spat in the face of economic orthodoxy.[92] Of course, he agreed that English proprietors would also not wish 'to be shot like hares and partridges' by their tenants, but then no landlord in England would 'turn out fifty peasants at once and burn their houses over their heads'. Backbenchers fell over themselves to denounce Irish proprietors for reckless extravagance in the past and ruthless inhumanity at present, for, as one put it, behaving 'very much like slaveholders with white slaves'.[93] Even wealthy absentees like the cabinet minister Lord Lansdowne, who owned over 120,000 acres in Ireland (most of them in poverty-stricken Kerry), condemned peasants and proprietors equally for their inefficient backwardness: both would have to mend their ways, the one as much as the other. In fact, so unpopular had Irish landlords become that even the Tory leadership felt disinclined to push their interests with any enthusiasm during the debates on the Poor Law Amendment Bill passed into law in June 1847.[94]

V

For British politicians the Famine rapidly came to be seen as a species of divine judgement, not only upon the improvidence of all those engaged in Irish

[90] Graham to Heytesbury, 3 April 1846, BL Graham Papers Ir/29; Heytesbury to Graham, 28 April 1846, *The Life and Letters of Sir James Graham*, ed. C. S. Parker, 2 vols (London, 1907), ii. 36.
[91] Trevelyan to Routh, 20, 21 September and 2 October 1846, NU Trevelyan Papers CET18/8; to Monteagle, 9 October 1846, ibid.; also Haines, *Sir Charles Trevelyan*, 5, 248–9.
[92] Russell's Cabinet Memorandum of July 1847 'State of Ireland', TNA Russell Papers PRO 30/22/6D.
[93] Russell to Clarendon, 15 November 1847 and 20 December 1848, Bodl. Clarendon Papers Irish 43; Parl. Deb. 3: xc. 1030 (8 March 1847), also lxxxix. 646 (1 February 1847), cv. 393 (14 May 1849: Roebuck), lxxxix. 955 (5 February 1847: Hastie), lxxxix. 985 (8 February 1847: Napier).
[94] Parl. Deb. 3: xcii. 65–7 (29 April 1847: Lansdowne); Donnelly, *Great Irish Potato Famine*, 97.

agriculture, but also upon themselves for having permitted such a state of things to continue for so long that some kind of disaster had become almost inevitable.[95] The lesson to be learned was that the opportunity for deep-rooted change by radically aligning Irish and British economic practices must not now be missed. From such a perspective the Famine was, therefore, perceived, not only as a terrible disaster, but as furnishing unique and wonderful circumstances making it possible to push forward that programme of assimilationist adjustment that had been given a significant, though still only a preliminary, heave with the introduction of the poor law in 1838.

The aim was unambiguous: to simplify and clarify the complex social and economic structures of rural Ireland—with their landlords, middlemen, large and small tenants, cottiers, conacre holders, landless labourers—and encourage the creation of a capitalist system along 'progressive' English lines, in which landowners owned, (often substantial) tenants rented, and labourers worked for cash wages on land in which they themselves possessed no 'interest' of any kind. Demands that this should, indeed must, happen, and that the catastrophe of hunger would allow it to happen more quickly, became a kind of ideological and political rolling bass underscoring the ways in which politicians viewed the Famine in general and the means by which it might best be ameliorated and understood.

Already by 1846 ministers were encouraging one another to think along these lines. Tories like Graham saw the Famine as, above all, turning the whole of Ireland into a *tabula rasa* 'softened in all its parts by this sudden calamity, and [now] capable of receiving new permanent impressions, if a master hand can be found to direct them'. 'All the social elements of Ireland are now in an unsettled state,' wrote Cornewall Lewis (now an MP) two years later; 'they are all moving in a great seething cauldron of impurities'.[96] Soon after becoming viceroy in July 1846, Bessborough reiterated the orthodoxy now universally acknowledged: that the Famine was the result, not simply of an aberrant agrarian system, but of the ways in which that system offended in every sense against the laws of nature itself. Labourers must henceforth work solely for money wages, many landowners must 'be annihilated and many of those who now call themselves farmers must fall into their *natural position*, that of labourers'. This 'transition' would, he admitted, 'not be rapid, and until improved cultivation compels the farmers to employ more labourers, numbers will be without employment' and without the means to survive.[97]

---

[95] Russell, in his letter to Clarendon, 21 Apri 1848, Bodl. Clarendon Papers Irish 43, blames pretty well everybody. See Gray, *Famine, Land and Politics*, especially 15–16, 97–120, 213–14, 232–4, 259–61, 286–7, 305–6, for the role of providentialism.

[96] Graham to Peel, 26 September 1846, *Sir Robert Peel from his Private Papers*, ed. Parker, iii. 464; Lewis to Head, 24 November 1848, *Letters of the Right Hon. Sir George Cornewall Lewis*, ed. Lewis, 189–90.

[97] Bessborough to Russell, 3 November 1846, TNA Russell Papers PRO 30/22/5E, also 1 and 18 December 1846, ibid., PRO 30/22/5F (emphasis added).

One could not, in other words, make restorative omelettes without breaking Hibernian eggs. Nor was Clarendon, who succeeded Bessborough in May 1847, any less true a believer, arguing that 'eventually' the Famine would impose its own solution and be 'the salvation of the country ... This is a great social revolution ... conacre is no more, the middleman is no more, the squireen is becoming extinct, the system of subdividing land to make votes or raise rents is no more'—in short, 'the accumulated evils of misgovernment and mismanagement [he did not have the bad taste to identify those responsible] are coming to a crisis' and all could now be made new.[98]

Of course such anticipations of eventual famine-induced prosperity provided a kind of alibi for politicians overwhelmed by, and in some cases unsympathetic to, the sufferings of the Irish poor. For Clarendon it was, above all, the Irish themselves who were to blame for not having read the economic runes with either insight or attention, for refusing to behave as people would 'in any other country'. 'The ground', he told Russell, 'must be cleared of its present weeds, it must be trenched and fresh sown before you can hope to reap content and tranquillity.' What Ireland needed was a 'complete change of system as regards agriculture ... and that change can only be effected by the introduction of English capital, enterprise and skill'.[99]

Clarendon was preaching to the converted on both sides of the political divide. Graham, now out of office, was equally convinced that the 'regeneration of Ireland' could come about only in the wake of 'a complete revolution of property, the ruin of landed proprietors ... vast changes and vicissitudes'.[100] If, as prime minister, Russell wavered a good deal as to details, he remained steadfast on the lessons to be learned and the overall prescriptions to be applied. Cottiers, he insisted, must yield their tiny patches of ground to those 'who can afford to hire labourers', even if 'much misery will be endured in the process'.[101] Palmerston (by contemporary standards a comparatively enlightened landlord in Sligo) hoped that the ejectment of smallholders might be done 'without cruelty', but thought it 'useless to disguise the Truth [capital letter], that any great improvement in the social system of Ireland must be founded upon an extensive change in the present system of agrarian occupation ... This change necessarily implies a long continued and systematic

---

[98] Clarendon to Normanby, 2 August 1847, Bodl. Clarendon Papers Irish Letter-Book I; to Brougham, 10 August 1847 and to Russell, 10 October 1847, ibid.

[99] Clarendon to Fitzwilliam, 10 June 1848, Bodl. Clarendon Papers Irish Letter-Book II; to Russell, 18 August 1848, ibid., Letter-Book III; to Lord Mayor of London, 26 June 1849, ibid., Letter-Book IV.

[100] As reported in *Greville Memoirs*, ed. Strachey and Fulford, v. 433–4 (14 March 1847).

[101] Russell to Clarendon, 1 July 1848, Bodl. Clarendon Papers Irish 43; to Clarendon, 4 September 1849, ibid. 26. He thought the process might take 'ten or twelve years'.

ejectment of ... squatter cottiers.'[102] Palmerston's fellow absentee landlord, the Protectionist leader and future prime minister Lord Stanley (who succeeded as fourteenth Earl of Derby in 1851), told the Lords in April 1847 that the only way to stop lazy peasants from working for only six hours for 6 pence rather than twelve hours for 18 pence was to reduce the number of small occupiers and multiply 'the number of independent labourers'. Another tolerably humane landlord, the Irishman Sir William Somerville (who served as chief secretary in Russell's administration), also looked to the abandonment of conacre and the adoption of 'a better system of agriculture and the payment of money wages'; above all, he strongly objected to anything 'at variance with any system to be found in England'. And his Liberal colleague Richard More O'Ferrall was no less convinced, telling Russell in 1846 that Ireland's only salvation was to be found by its assimilating in every respect to the laws and, above all, to the institutions of the other parts of the kingdom.[103]

So much time was given by politicians of all stripes to the repeated expression of such views that even Clarendon, who of course found himself at the sharp end of the problem, was occasionally driven to reminding the cabinet that its constant concern with 'Ireland as it might be or as they wanted it to be', rather than 'as it is', too often helped generate a 'state of delusion leading to constant mistakes'.[104] And these mistakes and misunderstandings were (as had long been the case) exacerbated by misapprehensions created by the widespread usage of terms that, it was too little appreciated, often changed meaning as they crossed the Irish Sea. 'We have', as the economist Nassau Senior (a man with strong assimilationist tendencies) put it, 'transferred our English notions into Ireland. There are *there* also persons *called* landlords, farmers, and labourers, but they resemble their English types in little but name'[105]—comments that highlighted the dangers of simple-minded assimilationism, dangers that few avoided with any degree of consistency. Thus, while on 28 October 1847 Clarendon reminded Wood of the importance of Senior's distinctions by asking 'have we in England head landlords and middlemen and subtenants *ad infinitum*?', he found it perfectly possible when writing to Lansdowne on the very same day to avoid any engagement

---

[102] Memorandum by Palmerston, 31 March 1848, TNA Russell Papers PRO 30/22/7B. On Palmerston as Irish landlord, see D. Norton, 'On Lord Palmerston's Irish Estates in the 1840s', *English Historical Review*, 99 (2004), 1254–74; Hoppen, *Elections, Politics, and Society in Ireland*, 130–2.

[103] Parl. Deb. 3: xcii. 121 (29 April 1847: Stanley); Somerville to Clarendon, 27 August 1849, and to Russell, May 1850, NLI Somerville Letter-Book 1847–51 MS 46755/2; O'Ferrall to Russell, 17 March 1846, TNA Russell Papers PRO 30/22/5A.

[104] Clarendon to Bedford, 18 August 1848, Bodl. Clarendon Papers Irish 82.

[105] Senior, 'Relief of Irish Distress', *Edinburgh Review*, 89 (January 1849), 221–68, repr. in Senior, *Journals, Conversations and Essays Relating to Ireland*, i. 195–267, see especially 195, 203–7.

with the precise problems of terminology and difference acknowledged, indeed explained, in his letter to Wood.[106]

Such considerations and distinctions were generally ignored, not only by politicians, but also by those in charge of famine relief. Certainly Trevelyan, never at a loss for confident generalizations, grasped every opportunity for rolling out assimilationist plans to reform and improve Ireland's economic and social structure. The Irish must be taught to embrace Anglo-Saxon self-reliance 'instead of having recourse to the assistance of Government on every occasion'. Only then would 'spendthrift squireens' and 'bankrupt lords' go to the wall to be replaced by energetic men (among them, he hoped, many Catholics) who would help to lay 'the foundation of a more wholesome state of society'. And though he did, indeed, 'see a bright light shining in the distance', he was 'filled with melancholy when I think of the immediate prospects of the mass of the people'. Yet, how could he not but be grateful that a potential cure was being 'applied by the direct stroke of an all-wise Providence in a manner as unexpected and unthought of as it is likely to be effectual'.[107] To give Providence a helping hand, Trevelyan broadcast the fullness of his ideas in the public prints: the 'best model is that in which an educated and enlightened proprietor, the substantial farmer, and the industrious labourer on regular wages each performs his appropriate part', with louche landlords, exploitative middlemen, and ignorant cottiers swept away— a process he saw as an English 'master key to unlock the field of industry in Ireland'.[108] But, while Trevelyan certainly belonged to the strident wing of those holding such opinions, he was by no means alone, not least in Ireland itself. W. N. Hancock, a founder of the influential Dublin Statistical Society established in 1847, insisted that assimilation was demanded by no less a force than the universal laws of economics: 'The idea of having a science of exchange peculiar to Ireland, under the name of Irish Political Economy, is about as reasonable as proposing to have Irish mechanics, mathematics, or Irish astronomy.'[109] In his *Three Lectures on the Question, Should the Principles of Political Economy be disregarded in the Present Crisis* (Dublin, 1847), Hancock's answer involved not only a resounding 'No', but the same kind of references to 'the wisdom of the Almighty' that were doing the rounds in

---

[106] Clarendon to Wood and to Lansdowne, 28 October 1847, Bodl. Clarendon Papers Irish Letter-Book I.
[107] Trevelyan to Routh, 8 February and 2 October 1846, NU Trevelyan Papers CET18/5 and 18/8; to Burgoyne, 8 April 1847, ibid., CET18/13; to Monteagle, 9 October 1846, ibid., CET18/8; also to Herbert, 29 December 1847, ibid., CET18/18: 'Irish society must inevitably be recast on a new model.'
[108] 'The Irish Crisis', *Edinburgh Review*, 87 (1848), 229–319, especially 128, 243, 310, 317–18.
[109] W. N. Hancock, 'On the Economic Views of Bishop Berkeley and Mr Butt', *Journal of the Statistical and Social Inquiry Society of Ireland*, 1 (1847–9), 3. The society later changed its name to the Statistical and Social Inquiry Society of Ireland. In the mid-1860s Hancock adopted a very different (indeed a clean contrary) set of views: see Chapter 7, Section II.

political circles. The reason for the Famine's severity lay, as he noted in a report into distress in the Skibereen district commissioned by the government, in the acute backwardness of the rural economy rooted in 'feudal' conditions inimical to the development of capitalized agriculture.[110] These were views with which Statistical Society colleagues such as Mountifort Longfield and James Lawson were in full agreement, while Edward Lysaght was no less convinced that the 'wretched state of agriculture in Ireland' was more or less entirely attributable 'to the absence, rather than to the excess, of competition; to the absence of the competition of tenants possessed of capital, who can secure the rents they undertake to pay'.[111]

Those who stood outside this almost universal mid-century consensus were few in number and small in influence. Even J. S. Mill, who was showing some rather unsteady support for peasant farming, seems to have agreed with those who saw the Famine as furnishing a unique opportunity for improvement, the 'terrible calamity' having created a blank page upon which might be inscribed 'what we pleased'. Poulett Scrope, who single-handedly lectured increasingly bored MPs about the wonders of continental peasantries, was dismissed by Trevelyan as a crank bent on 'violent wholesale interference with the rights of property', while Gladstone, in what was at this stage of his career a rare intervention in Irish affairs, thought fifty years would hardly be enough time to test 'the possibility of establishing a body of small independent yeomanry in Ireland'.[112]

The increasingly severe impact of the Famine not only led to repeated demands that Irish society be reformed along English lines, but encouraged a species of linguistic inflation, which, by seeking to find words powerful enough to reflect what was happening on the ground, created an atmosphere in which only gigantic remedies could convincingly be proposed. That the purgatorial experiences of the poor demanded a great social revolution became increasingly widely accepted by ministers, politicians, and senior civil servants. Wood, the keeper of the purse strings, combined unwavering tight-fistedness with powerful visions of a brighter tomorrow 'little short of a social revolution', for which (he was quick to add) the British tax payer must not be

---

[110] T. A. Boylan and T. P. Foley, 'A Nation Perishing of Political Economy?', in C. Morash and R. Hayes (eds), *'Fearful Realities': New Perspectives on the Famine* (Dublin, 1996), 146; P. Gray, 'Irish Social Thought and the Relief of Poverty, 1847–1880', *Transactions of the Royal Historical Society*, Sixth Series, xx (2010), 143–5.

[111] E. Lysaght, 'A Consideration of the Theory, that the Backward State of Agriculture in Ireland is a Consequence of the Excessive Competition for Land', *Journal of the Statistical and Social Inquiry Society of Ireland*, 2 (1849–51), 5–6.

[112] Gray, *Famine, Land and Politics*, 12–14, 154–8; Collison Black, *Economic Thought and the Irish Question*, 30–1; B. L. Kinzer, *England's Disgrace? J. S. Mill and the Irish Question* (Toronto, 2001), 44–8, 68–70; Trevelyan to J. T. Delane, 7 February 1848, NU Trevelyan Papers CET18/20; Parl. Deb. 3: c. 979 (28 July 1848: Gladstone).

held exclusively responsible.[113] Indeed, for Wood, as for others with similar views about the operations of the divine in human affairs, the catastrophe had moved far beyond 'the failure of the cultivation of the potato' into realms of ultimate blessing and redemption, of great changes already to be discerned amid 'the transition state which I believe Ireland is now going through'. And it was, above all, the idea of 'transition' that seemed to attach some kind of 'comprehensible sense' to the Famine as an event ultimately providing a gateway to better things.[114]

That the necessary transformation would be fearful was generally accepted. Indeed, for some, fearfulness was an essential element of any ameliorative agenda, an approach brutally articulated by Macaulay, who thought it would be better in Ireland to 'extirpate a hundred thousand human beings at once, and to fill the void with a well governed population, than to misgovern millions through a long succession of generations'.[115] Trevelyan, Macaulay's brother-in-law, saw the Famine in much the same terms. For him it was fundamentally a 'natural process which is now doing all that can be desired'—a view echoed by Wood.[116] The whole crisis was nothing short of a 'wonderful social revolution', and, while 'we ought to alleviate as far as we are able through the medium of the poor law the dreadful distress with which this revolution is accompanied … I am satisfied that if we attempt to do more we shall obstruct the beneficial change and prolong the agony'. Thus nothing should be done to interfere with the determinations of an all-wise and all-necessary Providence, for these alone could ensure that 'Ireland fully participates in the social health and physical prosperity of Great Britain, which will be the true consummation of their union'.[117]

Edward Horsman, a future chief secretary, told the Commons in 1849 that 'Ireland's calamity was England's opportunity' to accelerate the 'great change' already under way: 'What human agency could not achieve, the Providence of God … stepped in to deal with … It bade the old pass away, and the finger of God pointed the British statesman to Ireland, and bade him, under happier auspices, build up the new.'[118] The prominent radical Richard Cobden

[113] Wood to Clarendon, 15 August and 23 July 1847, Bodl. Clarendon Papers Irish 31; to Bessborough, 16 September 1846, BI Hickleton Papers A4/186/1; also Clarendon to Wood, 7 September 1847, ibid., A4/57.

[114] Parl. Deb. 3: lxxxix. 1249 (12 February 1847) and 687 (1 February 1847: both Wood); Russell to Clarendon, 15 August 1847 and 20 December 1848, Bodl. Clarendon Papers Irish 43; to Bessborough, 6 November 1846, TNA Russell Papers 30/22/5E; to Clarendon, 4 September 1849, Bodl. Clarendon Papers Irish 26.

[115] C. Hall, *Macaulay and Son: Architects of Imperial Britain* (New Haven, 2012), 179.

[116] Clarendon to Lansdowne, 19 November 1848, BL 3rd Marquess of Lansdowne Papers B85 (provisional reference) reporting Trevelyan telling him this and that Wood 'is only his echo'.

[117] Trevelyan to Clarendon, 25 February 1849, NU Trevelyan Papers CET18/24: 'But I am filled with melancholy when I think of the immediate prospects of the mass of the people.'

[118] Parl. Deb. 3: cii. 815 (16 February 1849) and cvii. 846 (23 July 1849).

contemplated the Famine with similar anticipations and echoed Macaulay in acceptance—indeed rather more than acceptance—of the sufferings that others would have to endure. While agreeing that some relief must be provided, he calmly recognized that the 'transition would be a frightful process of establishing an equilibrium and of inflicting retribution for outraged rights and neglected duties'.[119] If this was brutal, the press in the shape of *The Times* was happy to sound more brutal still when contemplating the inevitability of changes made necessary, above all, by Hibernian sinfulness.

> An island, a social state, a race is to be changed. The surface of the land, its divisions, its culture, its proprietors, its occupiers, its habitations, its manners, its law, its language, and the heart of a people who for two thousand years have remained unalterable within the compass of those mighty changes which have given us European civilization, are all to be created anew.

What, above all, the backwardness of so 'primitive, rude, and barbarous [a] country' demanded was 'rulers such as ALFRED the CONQUERER', who, tougher by far than the feeble 'political martinets of this century', would ruthlessly sweep all before them and finally drag the whole 'social system' of Ireland screaming and kicking into the modern age.[120]

VI

Two measures stand out for the directness of their connection with the contemporary emphasis upon economic and agrarian transition. The first emerged out of discussions concerning the implementation of the Poor Relief (Ireland) Bill passed into law in June 1847, legislation that at last permitted boards of poor law guardians to provide relief outside workhouses, not only to the aged, infirm, and sick poor or to widows with two or more children, but even to certain able-bodied individuals for limited periods.[121] On 29 March 1847 William Gregory, Galway landowner and Peelite MP for Dublin City, introduced an amendment designed to deny relief to all those occupying more than a quarter of an acre of land and thus, even in the west, effectively excluding virtually all cottiers and conacre holders from assistance. The aim

---

[119] Cobden to Bright, 18 January 1847, *The Letters of Richard Cobden*, ed. A. Howe, 4 vols (Oxford, 2007–15), i. 466–7. J. M. Keynes's later insistence that any new state of affairs being advocated must not simply be 'better' than what had preceded it, but 'sufficiently better to make up for the evils of the transition' (R. Sidelsky, *John Maynard Keynes: The Economist as Saviour 1920–1937* (London, 1992), 62) had few votaries in the 1840s.

[120] *The Times*, 9 October 1846 and 2 April 1849.

[121] The eventual act (10 Vict., c. 31) is sometimes referred to as the Poor Law (Ireland) Amendment Act or the Poor Law (Ireland) Extension Act.

was to clear the land of its poverty-stricken occupiers, who would then be replaced by more substantial agriculturalists with significantly larger farms. This was not a new idea. During discussions preceding the introduction of the Irish Poor Law, Stanley (in 1847 leader of the opposition) had written to Russell at the Home Office suggesting that 'making the occupation of land of more than a very small extent a bar to parochial relief ... would have the double tendency of checking the periodical influx of paupers ... and ... of diminishing the inducement to hold small parcels of land'. In February 1837 he had told the Commons that 'no person renting and occupying land should be considered in such a state of destitution as to give him a right to relief'.[122] Ten years later he was still of the same opinion, and, just six weeks before Gregory proposed the quarter-acre clause, he refined his ideas further by saying that, although he did not mean 'land sufficient for a garden ... or specifying any amount', yet nothing could be 'more mischievous ... than an enactment which provides that persons with two, three, four, or five acres of land, should continue to hold that land, employing no labour, but themselves deriving assistance from the rates'.[123] In fact the Whig administration had already made efforts to enforce existing provisions by which no one with a tenement valued above £6 should be employed on public works, though the undersecretary admitted that these had been widely ignored.[124]

Gregory was, therefore, working within a context favourable to his (admittedly severe) proposals. Seventeen days before introducing his amendment he had been urged by Russell to draw up precise recommendations as to what 'ought to be the amount of land possessed in order to place a person beyond the description of destitution'.[125] In the event he settled on pretty well the smallest measure of land that could have been chosen as the cut-off point for relief, declaring airily that when a man held 'a large [*sic*] piece of land—half an acre, one, two, or three acres—he was no longer an object of pity. He did not come before the public *in forma pauperis*.' 'Many hon. members', he pointed out, 'insisted that the operation of a clause of this kind would destroy all the small farmers. If it could have such an effect, he did not see of what use such small farmers could possibly be.'[126] MPs lined up to support the proposal. Scrope, a rare exception, declared it would effect 'a perfect social revolution',

---

[122] Stanley to Russell, 18 December 1836, TNA Russell Papers PRO 30/22/2D; Parl. Deb. 3: xxxvi. 516 (13 February 1837).
[123] *Greville Memoirs*, ed. Strachey and Fulford, v. 417 (8 February 1847); Parl. Deb. 3: lxxxix. 1345 (15 February 1847).
[124] Redington to Wood, 7 May 1847, BI Hickleton Papers A4/61A.
[125] Parl. Deb. 3: xc. 1242–3 (12 March 1847).
[126] Ibid. xci. 585–7, 590 (29 March 1847). B. M. Walker, in 'Villain, Victim or Prophet? William Gregory and the Great Famine', *Irish Historical Studies*, 38 (2013), 579–99, argues that *Times* report of the debate contains linguistic differences from that in Hansard and that these ameliorate Gregory's pronouncements. While Walker makes some interesting points, these differences do not seem hugely significant.

which was, of course, precisely what its backers desired. From the government front bench Sir George Grey (the Home Secretary) praised Gregory because he himself 'had always understood these small holdings were the bane of Ireland'. What was needed was a clear-out of pauperized agriculturalists whose patches could then be amalgamated into larger and more profitable units—just as had once happened in England. Numerous Irish members declared themselves delighted, not least the Repealer M. J. O'Connell (a nephew of the Liberator), who gave Gregory 'his decided support'.[127] Indeed, Gregory's motion was accepted by the enormous majority of 117 to 7: even if one includes tellers, the only members sitting for Irish constituencies who opposed the clause were William Smith O'Brien, the member for County Limerick and soon to be the leader of the Young Ireland rising in 1848, and Alexander McCarthy, who sat for Cork City and was to lose his seat four months later. The majority included twenty-six Irish members, among them M. J. O'Connell, T. Wyse, Sir John Young, the O'Conor Don, Sir William Somerville, W. V. Stuart, and numerous Irish Tories, as well as Russell, Sir George Grey, and Disraeli, while the tellers were both Irish—Gregory himself and the self-styled 'Reformer' Richard Montesquieu Bellew, the member for County Louth.

While there were probably some differences in outlook and expectations regarding the precise effects of the Gregory clause, there can be little doubt that a cabinet majority viewed it 'as a weapon necessary for forcing the pace of transition to an Anglicised social and economic structure'.[128] Certainly both of the relevant viceroys (Bessborough and Clarendon) were fully in favour of the clause and of the assimilationist principles underlying it, though the latter worried about excessively harsh and sudden implementation.[129] The under-secretary was also hopeful that the clause would soon help to bring into being a wage-paid 'labour class as counter-distinguished from a farmer class' and thus simplify a premodern rural structure that had prevented Ireland from sharing in the rising prosperity experienced elsewhere in the United Kingdom.[130] Trevelyan scoffed at those who felt uneasy about the undoubted distress that would be caused and thought the new test for relief absolutely essential, given that 'the smallholders are totally unable to maintain themselves and their families without the potato, and the potato cannot be had'. Letting such men remain in their holdings was, he believed, merely postponing the evil day to no good purpose. *The Times*, unsurprisingly, was no less enthusiastic and hailed the increasingly 'rigorous administration of the Poor Law' for 'destroying

---

[127] The full discussion and the division are in Parl. Deb. 3: xci. 583–93 (29 March 1847).

[128] P. Gray, 'Ideology and the Famine', in C. Póirtéir (ed.), *The Great Irish Famine* (Cork, 1995), 98; idem, *Famine, Land and Politics*, 279.

[129] Bessborough to Russell, 10 April [1847], TNA Russell Papers PRO 30/22/6C; Clarendon to Russell, 8 October 1847, Bodl. Clarendon Papers Irish Letter-Book I and to ?Russell, 19 May 1848, ibid., Letter-Book II.

[130] Redington to Clarendon, 1 April 1849, TNA Russell Papers PRO 30/22/7F.

small holdings', forcing bankrupt landlords into insolvency, encouraging
emigration, and 'leaving the soil of Ireland open to industrial enterprise, and
the introduction of capital'.[131]

The precise impact of the Gregory clause is, however, difficult to pin down
with any accuracy. The fact that its enactment was almost entirely ignored in
Ireland during the general election that followed in early August 1847 suggests
that, at least among those prosperous enough to be able to vote, it raised small
interest and less opposition. Indeed, it is striking how little any aspect of the
Famine featured in the debates and campaigning that took place in the weeks
before polling.[132] The fact that the clause was not due to be enforced until
1 November 1847 may have had something to do with this, though Russell
certainly knew by early July that almost half of all those being relieved
occupied more than a quarter of an acre and would thus fall foul of the new
law.[133] However, the Poor Law Commissioners themselves proved distinctly
unkeen on adopting any rigid acreage for excluding persons from 'gratuitous
relief', thinking this should be 'dealt with according to each individual case'.
Indeed, they might almost be regarded as having torpedoed the new law when,
in May 1848, only six months after its imposition, they obtained legal advice to
the effect that relief could still be given to the wife and children of a man
occupying more than quarter of an acre, which somewhat (though of course
only somewhat) reduced the impact of the legislation passed in 1847.[134]

Russell and Sir George Grey were outraged by this and made clear to
Clarendon that they fully supported the aims that Gregory had sought to
promote.[135] And, while smallholders do, indeed, seem to have given up their
land in substantial numbers (either 'voluntarily' or in response to direct
evictions), it is not possible to attribute all, or even most, of this specifically
to Gregory, because many of the evictions were actually pursued under a Poor
Law Act of 1843, which had provided that the rates for all holdings valued at
£4 or less should henceforth become the responsibility of the landlord.[136] With
these rates now substantially increased because of the cost of relief, landlords
became increasingly keen to rid themselves of their smaller tenants. Yet none
of this undermines the argument that the whole thrust of government policy

[131] Trevelyan to Twisleton, 1 December 1847, NU Trevelyan Papers CET18/18; *The Times*, 2 April 1849.
[132] B. M. Walker, 'Politicians, Elections and Catastrophe: The General Election of 1847', *Irish Political Studies*, 22 (2007), 30–2.
[133] Prest, *Lord John Russell*, 251.
[134] *Distress (Ireland) Second Report of the Relief Commissioners*, HC 1847 [819], xvii. 79; *Copies of the Correspondence upon which the Commissioners of Poor Laws in Ireland took Legal Advice as to the Construction of the 10th Section of the Act 10 Vict. c. 31*, HC 1847–8 (442), liii. 521–3.
[135] Russell to Clarendon, 1 July 1848, Bodl. Clarendon Papers Irish 43; Grey to Clarendon, 8 June 1848, ibid. 12.
[136] Donnelly, *Great Irish Potato Famine*, 110–12; Walker, 'Villain, Victim or Prophet?', 582.

in the 1840s, both before and during the Famine, was to refashion the Irish countryside into something that would eventually come to resemble that of England: larger farms, wage-paid labourers, efficient forward-looking landlords.

And it was specifically to the last of these aspirations that the other major piece of legislation designed to bring about the new Jerusalem was devoted, the Encumbered Estates Act of 1849. The thinking behind this tapped into the long-standing British antipathy to Irish landlords, not least in those governmental circles increasingly disposed to viewing the Famine as an instrument with which to refashion the Irish countryside *and* to do this by simultaneously reshaping the character of an Irish proprietorial class that had singularly failed to do anything useful under its own steam.

The immediate aim behind the act was to provide legal means for the swift and efficient sale of heavily indebted estates, something previously difficult because the numerous mortgages with which these were invariably 'encumbered' meant that it was often impossible to identify the precise locus of ownership. Of course, some sales had always taken place, but the fact that by 1844 no less than 1,322 estates with a combined rental of £904,000 a year (possibly a tenth of the whole) were being managed by the courts indicates the extent of indebtedness and the problems associated with disposals.[137] Within a year of the potato blight's appearance, Wood, with the support of the chief secretary, was trying to persuade Russell of the importance of inaugurating a large-scale cull of bankrupt landlords by 'breaking up estates',[138] an idea that rapidly gained support across the party divide as something designed to reform and improve Irish landlordism along English lines. The hopelessly incompetent would be sent off as pensioners to Cheltenham and Bath, while new, efficient, well-funded men would take their place.

Trevelyan at the Treasury was equally keen to establish a legal framework for 'the free transfer of property from those who have not to those who have the means and disposition to improve it'.[139] Horsman, a future chief secretary, agreed, while for Bright the policy fitted in neatly with his own long-standing opposition to the law of entail by which landowners could restrict the freedom of heirs to dispose of property as they wished, a procedure that Bright regarded as clearly inimical to free-trade principles.[140] More broadly, such ideas, though generally concerned with the disposal of substantial acreages, were also in tune with proposals made in the mid-1840s by the Devon Commissioners, who had looked to the creation, not merely of stronger landlords, but also—as Wood

---

[137] Macintyre, *The Liberator*, 104; J. S. Donnelly Jr, *Landlord and Tenant in Nineteenth-Century Ireland* (Dublin, 1973), 18.

[138] Wood to Russell, 28 September 1846, TNA Russell Papers PRO 30/22/6F.

[139] Trevelyan to Burgoyne, 30 March 1847, NU Trevelyan Papers CET18/13.

[140] Parl. Deb. 3: xcv. 327 (29 November 1847: Horsman) and 984 (6 December 1847: Bright).

himself put it—of 'an independent class of yeomen ... by the sale of land in small lots'.[141]

By 1848 legislation had moved from conception to reality, helped by the famous resignation speech of June 1846 in which Peel had revealed his belief that changes in Irish tenurial arrangements deserved 'our immediate, though most cautious, support'.[142] In July 1848 Normanby wrote to Russell recalling how he had favoured policies designed to permit the sale of encumbered estates when viceroy in the 1830s and declaring that he would now be delighted if appropriate legislation was introduced to establish 'some closer connection between the money savings of the middle classes, mostly Catholics, and the interests involved in the actual possession of land'.[143] However, the Act of August 1848 was badly drafted, and it was not until the following year that effective legislation was passed. Peel had once famously wondered in connection with the Famine whether 'out of this nettle, danger, we may not pluck the flower, safety'. Now, having been consulted by ministers, he gave the Encumbered Estates Act (perceived on all sides as a key part of any such plucking) his full and enthusiastic support.[144]

Clarendon in Dublin saw the Act, if intelligently operated, as potentially inaugurating a new anglicized dawn for the Irish countryside in particular and the Irish economy in general. The 'great object' was to 'render Connaught and Munster more attractive to British capitalists', because 'no good upon a *great* scale ... can be expected until we have a pretty extensive change in the proprietary class'.[145] And soon he himself was moving from long-ingrained pessimism to something approaching restrained confidence. Ireland 'is progressing', he told Lansdowne in June 1851, and, while

> the 4 years of famine and 400 of malversation are not to be got over in a hurry, yet we shall pass through. The E. Estates Commission and the P. Law are the rough but indispensable treatment for such maladies ... Attention to business, improvement of agriculture, rigid economies and horror of squatters and subdivision are now perceptible among owners and occupiers of land.

And Tories too had begun to sing from the same hymn sheet, with the leader of the party, Lord Derby (Peel's great opponent on free trade in 1846 and

[141] Wood's Memorandum of 20 November 1846, Bodl. Clarendon Papers Irish 74; *Report from Her Majesty's [Devon] Commissioners*, HC 1845 [605], xix. 27; also *Report from the Select Committee on the Farmers' Estate Society (Ireland) Bill*, HC 1847 (505), xvii. 363–76.

[142] Parl. Deb. 3: lxxxvii. 1045 (29 June 1846).

[143] Normanby to Russell, 20 July 1848, *The Later Correspondence of Lord John Russell 1840–1878*, ed. G. P. Gooch, 2 vols (London, 1925), i. 228–9.

[144] Parl. Deb. 3: civ. 117 (30 March 1849); Maxwell, *Life and Letters of George William Frederick, Fourth Earl of Clarendon*, i. 300; *Sir Robert Peel from his Private Papers*, ed. Parker, iii. 513–16; J. B. Conacher, *The Peelites and the Party System 1846–52* (Newton Abbot, 1972), 45.

[145] Clarendon to Lansdowne, 11 December 1849, BL 3rd Marquess of Lansdowne Papers B85 (provisional reference); to Wood, 13 January 1850, BI Hickleton papers A4/57.

briefly prime minister in 1852), convinced that Ireland was now improving 'under the sharp disruption which it has undergone in the last few years'. The worst seemed to be over, and all was now set for a brighter future shaped, above all, by 'education, the poor law, the Encumbered Estates Commission, and emigration'.[146]

---

[146] Clarendon to Lansdowne, 19 June 1851, BL 3rd Marquess of Lansdowne Papers B86 (provisional reference); to Carew, 1 November 1852, T[rinity] C[ollege] D[ublin] Carew Papers MS 4021; Derby to Eglinton, 2 October 1852, Sc[ottish] R[ecord] O[ffice] Eglinton Papers GD3/5/1360.

6

Ambiguous Outcomes

I

The encumbered estates legislation seemed to embrace a policy that almost everyone felt able to welcome. From the Whig/Liberal side Russell, Clarendon, and Wood received renewed backing from Horsman and Bright, the former detecting 'the finger of God' in the business, the latter insisting that only 'free sale of land' could rescue the Irish economy from the Slough of Despond.[1] With even Stanley, the Protectionist leader and now bitter opponent of Peel, giving the Encumbered Estates Act a qualified welcome,[2] only truly brave parliamentarians dared to spit in the face of what had become the modish wisdom of the age. Step forward the second Earl of Glengall, Irish Tory activist and Tipperary landlord, who, in an authentic display of the rage felt by many old-style proprietors, denounced the Act as so much 'communism and social-ism of the deepest degree' and that 'he would recommend Her Majesty's Government to invite Louis Blanc, Considerant, and Proudhon to become the first commissioners'. Alas, not only was Glengall flogging a very dead horse, but his own standing in official circles had become so rickety that one chief secretary was driven to warn his superiors that any 'communication' from the noble earl 'must always be viewed *cum grano*'.[3]

And, indeed, at first all seemed set fair as regards the Act's putative role in the anglicization of the Irish landed class. Cornewall Lewis thought all was now 'tending in the right direction', though a 'skilled hand' would be needed 'to grasp these several tendencies and to convert them into realities'. Claren-don's successor as viceroy, Lord St Germans (who as Lord Eliot had previously served as chief secretary under Peel), also worried that Irish ruralists would, if left to their own devices, revert to the bad Hibernian habit of excessive potato

---

[1] Parl[iamentary] Deb[ates] 3: cvii. 846 (23 July 1849: Horsman) and civ. 173–4 (2 April 1849: Bright). See W. L. Burn, 'Free Trade in Land: An Aspect of the Irish Question', *Transactions of the Royal Historical Society*, Fourth Series, xxxi (1949), 61–74.

[2] Parl. Deb. 3: cxiv. 22–4 (4 February 1851).

[3] Parl. Deb. 3: cv. 1351 (11 June 1849); K. T. Hoppen, *Elections, Politics, and Society in Ireland 1832–1885* (Oxford, 1984), 292.

culture.[4] His able undersecretary, Thomas Larcom, had, however, become convinced that all would be for the best. Constantly improving educational standards were, he believed, bringing Ireland up to the 'much more advanced' economic conditions to be found in England. The Encumbered Estates Act would give 'full vent to the means of improvement brought into play' by the disasters of the Famine. Indeed, agricultural statistics were already recording a 'slow and steady increase' in crops and livestock as well as 'the diminution of the small cottier holdings—the abodes of poverty—and their consolidation into larger farms'.[5] Not only that, but substantial emigration, which many commentators (such as Nassau Senior) had seen as essential for recovery, was well under way, with some 2.1 million people leaving between 1845 and 1855.[6] And, while the census of 1841 had recorded a total population of 8,175,124, those of 1851 and 1861 reported figures of 6,552,385 and 5,798,967 respectively.[7]

Certainly visitors who came to Ireland in the early 1850s to examine post-Famine conditions tended to react with high-octane enthusiasm. In particular, their accounts reflect a conviction that, if the Famine had caused misery for millions, it had also 'created an opportunity to finally subdue, modernise, and integrate Ireland and its inhabitants' into the United Kingdom as a whole.[8] Revd J. H. Ashworth thought all would be well after a (now inevitable) influx of English capital. W. B. Webster believed Ireland had become exquisitely suited as a field for investment and even residence. Thomas Miller published a map showing the many 'residences of Scotchmen and Englishmen who have settled agriculturally in Ireland'. A writer in *Ainsworth's Magazine* for 1854 hailed 'a new era ... the Englishmen and Scotchmen have come over to farm; the yeomen, and the amateur, and the farmer find no place so cheap to farm in as the "Emerald Isle"'. Harriet Martineau, on a visit to Connemara in September 1852, reported on efficient English settlers being made 'heartily welcome' and how higher wages were weaning the people from their old belief that only the occupation of land, however minute in extent, could sustain them.[9] Sir Francis

---

[4] Lewis to Clarendon, 20 August 1849, Bodl[eian Library] Clarendon Papers C.530; St Germans to Aberdeen (the prime minister), 17 September 1853, B[ritish] L[ibrary] Aberdeen Papers Add. MS 43207.

[5] Larcom's Memorandum of January 1854 in St Germans to Aberdeen, 30 January 1854, ibid., Add. MS 43208.

[6] N. W. Senior, 'Relief of Irish Distress' (1849), in Senior, *Journals, Conversations and Essays relating to Ireland*, 2nd edn, 2 vols (London, 1868), 254–64; J. S. Donnelly Jr, *The Great Potato Famine* (Stroud, 2001), 178.

[7] *Irish Historical Statistics: Population, 1821–1971*, ed. W. E. Vaughan and A. J. Fitzpatrick (Dublin, 1978), 3.

[8] G. Hooper, *Travel Writing and Ireland 1760–1860: Culture, History, Politics* (Basingstoke, 2005), 8.

[9] Ibid. 164, 145, 163, 170; *Letters from Ireland: Harriet Martineau*, ed. G. Hooper (Dublin, 2001), 90.

Head, former lieutenant-governor of Upper Canada and commissioned by the Tory viceroy Lord Eglinton to expose the activities of the Catholic clergy in Ireland during the general election of 1852, took the opportunity in the course of an inevitably breathless *Fortnight in Ireland* to hail the social and economic wonders now being unveiled. Providence had, he wrote, overrun 'the feeble tribes' of Celtic Ireland, who had too long thought it a fine thing for men to sleep 'with their pigs and asses' and to whom 'the potato disease' had now 'very sternly' uttered 'the monosyllable "Go"'. 'This is not *my* decree, it is not the decree of the British Government, it is not the decree of the petty Irish landlord—but it is the decree of a Beneficent and Omnipotent Power whose inflexible will no man can oppose.'[10]

II

An important and related entr'acte amid all this concentration on the land question was mounted by Gladstone's budget of 1853, which for the first time extended the income tax to Ireland and, in line with the expectations created by the Famine and 'implemented' by legislation such as the Gregory clause and the Encumbered Estates Act, constituted another key aspect of the mid-century mission to assimilate.

When in 1842 Peel had reintroduced the income tax, which had lapsed after the French revolutionary wars, he had exempted Ireland on the grounds that it then possessed 'no machinery' for collection and because he was simultaneously increasing both spirits and stamp duties on property to English levels.[11] This was all undoubtedly true, though it was equally true that Peel had convinced himself that the tax was, in any case, being revived only on a strictly temporary basis. Be that as it may, there were quite a few contemporaries who thought he had made a mistake and should have extended the tax to Ireland with immediate effect.[12]

Within a few years the cost of famine relief had pushed the matter of Ireland's exemption prominently into ministerial minds. With massive relief

[10] F. B. Head, *A Fortnight in Ireland* (London, 1852), 148–50, 183. See K. T. Hoppen, 'Priests at the Hustings: Ecclesiastical Electioneering in Nineteenth-Century Ireland', in E. Posada-Carbó (ed.), *Elections before Democracy: The History of Elections in Europe and Latin America* (London, 1996), 117–38; G. Martin in *ODNB*.

[11] Parl. Deb. 3: lxi. 445–8 (11 March 1842). The policy of reducing tariffs in 1842 also had a negative effect on Ireland's agricultural economy: C. Reid, 'The "Repeal Year" in Ireland: An Economic Reassessment', *Historical Journal*, 58 (2015), 111–35.

[12] M. Daunton, *Trusting Leviathan: Taxation in Britain 1799–1914* (Cambridge, 2001), 190–1; D. Kanter, 'The Politics of Irish Taxation, 1842–53', *English Historical Review*, 127 (2012), 1123–5; J. C. Herries to Peel, 2 March 1842, *Sir Robert Peel from his Private Papers*, ed. C. S. Parker, 3 vols (London, 1891–9), ii. 523–4.

schemes being conducted by the Board of Works (during one week in March 1847 no less than 714,390 persons were being employed daily), Whig ministers such as Wood were beginning to consider extending the income tax in order to recoup at least some of the costs, while Russell reported to the viceroy that British MPs were loudly pointing out that their constituents now paid taxes that the Irish did not.[13] The relief works soon proved so inadequate and inefficient that in February 1847 the government was more or less forced to hurry through parliament the Destitute Poor (Ireland) Act, permitting widespread outdoor relief in the shape of government-sponsored soup kitchens. The quality of the food provided was basic, to say the least, but the fact that by 3 July more than three million persons were being fed daily meant that costs continued to be high. Although in theory much of this official expenditure was ultimately supposed to be refunded out of local resources, this proved more an aspiration than a reality. With the total spent on relief works from October 1846 to June 1847 amounting to £4,848,000 and on the soup kitchens to £1,725,000,[14] British politicians found it all too easy to blame the Irish as a whole for what they considered financial excess.

Throughout 1847, 1848, and 1849 MPs and ministers repeatedly reminded one another that Ireland was soaking up cash while paying, they thought, far too little in taxes. One not untypical Liberal reformer could hardly contain himself. In May 1847 he claimed that, because 'an amount of taxation of not less than £10,417,000, consisting of land and assessed taxes, income tax, window tax etc., was being paid in England, to which Ireland was not in any way subject', Irish paupers coming to Britain should be forcibly returned at Irish expense. Ten months later—indeed on St Patrick's Day—he was again in 'Heads-I-win-Tails-you-lose' mode when declaring himself 'not one of those who advocated a separate nationality; but he would say that as long as a vast burden was imposed on England, from which Ireland was altogether free, Irishmen would have no claim on the Imperial Treasury for assistance as a right'.[15]

Wood found such ideas momentarily inopportune—not now, he replied, perhaps later—though he still pushed the viceroy to reduce demands for help in the light of strongly expressed feelings about Ireland's tax exemptions.[16] Russell, for his part, had come to believe that 'nothing but participation in taxation will ever give the Irish just views on the subject of public money', though he retained (justified) doubts as to the actual amounts that extension

---

[13] Wood to Bessborough, 16 September 1846, Kanter, 'Politics of Irish Taxation', 1130; Russell to Bessborough, 4 October 1846, T[he] N[ational] A[rchives] Russell Papers PRO 30/22/5D.

[14] Donnelly, *Great Potato Famine*, 81–90.

[15] Parl. Deb. 3: xcii. 1326 (31 May 1847) and xcvii. 713 (17 March 1848: both Sir B. Hall).

[16] Ibid. xcvii. 742–6 (17 March 1848); Wood to Clarendon, 3 April 1848, Bodl. Clarendon Papers Irish 31.

would raise.[17] The opposition leader, Stanley, accused Irish landlords of dodging their financial responsibilities, and backbenchers of every hue queued up to do the same, to blame Irish proprietors for being mean and to blame the Irish in general for being tax avoiders.[18] However, in February 1849 the cabinet decided that, rather than imposing the income tax, Irish poor law unions should be obliged to levy a rate-in-aid of the most distressed unions in the south and west.[19]

Few, however, could now deceive themselves into believing that an assimilationist extension of income tax had not moved higher up the political agenda. The Whig government fell in February 1852 and was replaced by a Tory administration under the Earl of Derby (the former Stanley), which held office only until December of the same year. Derby's Chancellor of the Exchequer was Disraeli, whose ignorance of finance was equalled only by his ignorance of Ireland. Although, in truth, Disraeli's budget of December 1852 included some interesting proto-Keynesian proposals, it also—given contemporary orthodoxies—opened the door to a devastating demolition from a Gladstone determined to avenge Disraeli's earlier and vicious attacks on the now-deceased Peel and to commence the construction of his own reputation for financial brilliance and expertise.[20]

Yet it was Disraeli and not Gladstone who first put his toes into the waters of fiscal assimilation, though admittedly to a very shallow depth. The shallowness had everything to do with the Tory party's close connection with landlordism in Ireland and with Disraeli's lifelong conviction that there were few groups in society who might not somehow be encouraged to vote Conservative. Thus, while he himself had supported income-tax extension in opposition, his budget proposals were sufficiently low key at once to encourage Radicals that more might be done in the future and to mollify landowners by proposing to limit income tax in Ireland to those who fell under what were called Schedules C and E, which covered only dividends from government stock, official salaries, and pensions of certain kinds.[21]

As the government fell within days of Disraeli's efforts, it was left to Gladstone, Chancellor in the new Aberdeen coalition administration, to introduce what has (perhaps too often) been hailed as one of the great budgets of the Victorian period. Its 'greatness' certainly did not lie in the clauses

---

[17] As reported in Clarendon to Wood, 2 February 1848, B[orthwick] I[nstitute] Hickleton Papers A4/57.

[18] Parl. Deb. 3: cii. 1308 (27 February 1849: Stanley), 392–3 (7 February 1849: Christopher), 803 (16 February 1849: McGregor).

[19] Russell to Clarendon, 11 and 13 February 1849, Bodl. Clarendon Papers Irish 26. For the rate-in-aid, see Chapter 5, Section III.

[20] K. T. Hoppen, *The Mid-Victorian Generation 1846–1886* (Oxford, 1998), 150–1.

[21] Kanter, 'Politics of Irish Taxation', 1142–3; *Benjamin Disraeli Letters*, ed. J. A. Gunn et al., 10 vols to date (Toronto, 1982–), vi. 236–7.

dealing with Ireland, and indeed, shortly before drawing it up, Gladstone had admitted to Aberdeen that really he 'ought not to meddle with Irish matters of which I know so little'.[22] Sensibly he held meetings with Irish MPs. Typically he took almost no notice of their opinions, arguing that it was 'plainly absurd to say that a person with £100 per annum in Ireland, a poor country, is less able to pay the tax than a person of similar income in England' and expressing delight at being able to ensure that Irish landlords would at last have to pay their 'share'—perhaps even, he hinted, more than their share.[23] Objections about Ireland's lack of appropriate mechanisms for collecting income tax were briskly overcome by also extending to Ireland the system of so-called special commissioners hitherto rarely used in Britain because of its allegedly 'authoritarian' and centralist character.[24] In other words, for Gladstone, as indeed for others, it was perfectly acceptable to employ in Ireland means considered essentially inappropriate in England, if the expected outcome could be seen as assimilationist in the broadest sense. Ireland should have the income tax just like the rest of the United Kingdom, even if the thing could be done only by methods thought exceptional and dubious in the British 'core'.

What lay behind Gladstone's approach was not simply the idea that it was important to raise new revenue, but the notion that a crucial principle was at stake, the principle that underlay the assimilationist project as a whole. Thus Gladstone was perfectly prepared to remit the 'loans' made during the Famine, which, though (in his words) 'but a fraction, indeed, of the generous aid accorded ... to the necessities of Ireland', still amounted to 'a very heavy and enduring burden', if he could make that country pay income tax 'under precisely the same conditions ... as in England and Scotland'.[25] And he made this point of principle crystal clear to his colleagues at a meeting of the cabinet on 11 April, when he insisted 'that every step towards the equalisation of taxation had a value over and above what money it might bring'.[26]

With a handful of exceptions, the cabinet supported Gladstone's budgetary proposals concerning Ireland, with ministers outside the cabinet also expressing agreement.[27] Edward Cardwell, the President of the Board of Trade and a future chief secretary, thought it crucial that 'all parts of the United Kingdom should be viewed as one comprehensive whole', while Robert Lowe, joint Secretary at the Board of Control and Gladstone's Chancellor of the Exchequer

---

[22] Gladstone to Aberdeen, Christmas Day 1852, BL Aberdeen Papers Add. MS 43070.
[23] Gladstone to Aberdeen, 30 April 1853, ibid.   [24] Daunton, *Trusting Leviathan*, 191.
[25] Parl. Deb. 3: cxxv. 1393 (18 April 1853).
[26] Memorandum of 11 April 1853 in BL Gladstone Papers Add. MS 44778, printed in *The Prime Ministers' Papers: W. E. Gladstone*, ed. J. Brooke and M. Sorensen, 4 vols (London, 1971–81), iii. 132–6.
[27] Gladstone's Memorandum of 12 April 1853, BL Gladstone Papers Add. MS 44778, printed in *Prime Ministers' Papers: W. E. Gladstone*, ed. Brooke and Sorensen, iii. 136–8.

between 1868 and 1873, told MPs that 'they had no more right to look at Ireland as a separate part of the United Kingdom than they had a right [so] to regard Devonshire or Durham in taxation or in other matters'. Cobden, after addressing the problems thrown up by the excise duty on 'the gentleman's bottle of Lafitte' (*sic*), brusquely told Irish members to 'make up their minds to pay the same taxes as the people of England, [to] unite with us in advocating retrenchment and economy', and to spend less time fighting 'for the bauble of your lord lieutenancy and ... your Kilmainham Hospital, although it is a mere nest of jobbery'.[28] In the end, Gladstone, who showed much less concern for Irish opinion than had his 'great teacher and master in public affairs', Peel, gave what he thought a knock-out blow to Irish complaints by telling the Commons that 'the fact of a country being poor was no argument *prima facie* against the application of the tax when the tax did not attach to the class that was poor in that country'.[29]

And in this Gladstone proved rather more percipient than perhaps he realized, for, while he certainly succeeded in aligning taxes more closely throughout the United Kingdom, he failed to collect much in the way of additional revenue, himself admitting that the yield from extending the income tax to Ireland would be all of £460,000 in a full year—hardly a gigantic addition to the resources of the state or very much in comparison with Russell's estimate for *British* income tax receipts of £5.4 million in 1849.[30] Nor was the number of 'persons' in Ireland affected by Schedule D (the most significant) anything but modest: all of 16,686 in 1854 and 20,307 by 1868.[31]

What, however, Gladstone had done was to open a particularly noxious can of worms in connection with the fiscal relationship between Britain and Ireland, something that, in due course, overshadowed any assimilationist optimism created at Westminster in 1853. The extension of the income tax together with significant increases in Irish spirits duties provided ammunition for claims that (*pace* Gladstone) the poorer country was being obliged to carry a disproportionate burden. And in this respect the figures mattered less than the emotions of those who complained. Gladstone could (and did) try to explain how, despite his efforts, incomes in Ireland were actually assessed by less burdensome rules: for example, in England landlords paid tax on their full nominal rents, in Ireland only on the (lesser) poor law valuations, while Irish

---

[28] Parl. Deb. 3: cxxvi. 849 (29 April 1853: Cardwell), 936–7 (2 May 1853: Lowe), 688, 697 (28 April 1853: Cobden).

[29] Ibid. cxxvii. 532 (23 May 1853); Gladstone on Peel in *Sir Robert Peel from his Private Papers*, ed. Parker, iii. 560.

[30] Parl. Deb. 3: cxxv. 1393 (18 April 1853) and ciii. 110 (2 March 1849).

[31] *Report of the Commissioners of Inland Revenue on the Duties under their Management for the Years 1856 to 1869 Inclusive*, H[ouse of] C[ommons Paper] 1870 [C.82-I], xx. 584. 'Persons' in income tax statistics cannot be simply equated with individuals.

farmers were also assessed at lower levels.[32] But, when he then went on to declare that he could not 'assent to the general proposition that the taxation of that country [Ireland] is to be like a local shower, drawn for a while from the surface of the earth by evaporation, and then descending upon it again with fertilizing effect at the very spot from which it first arose',[33] Irish listeners of all persuasions grew irritated at the lectures they were being subjected to. Eventually Gladstone's most energetic Irish critic, the Tory MP Colonel Francis Dunne, managed to get the Commons to appoint a select committee to look into the matter, with himself chairing a group of Irish and British political luminaries such as John Pope Hennessy, The O'Conor Don, Sir Stafford Northcote, and Robert Lowe. Given its membership, Dunne cannot have been much surprised when the committee broadly rejected his views in its report of June 1865. After a lot of misty meanderings about England having 'both the heaviest and the lightest [taxation] in Europe' and how Ireland was still exempted from mighty imposts such as 'the duties on railway passengers, hackney and stage carriages, patent medicines, and racehorses', the committee concluded—in full assimilationist flight—that, should the government

> attempt to graduate the taxation which we impose upon one part of the United Kingdom so as to relieve it of some burdens on the ground of its poverty, it will be impossible to resist the argument that we ought to carry the graduation further, for the purpose of relieving individual taxpayers on the same plea. There are parts of England and Scotland which might set up a case more or less similar to that of Ireland.[34]

At bottom the whole dispute defied resolution because the statistical materials to hand were often unclear and their neutral interpretation virtually impossible. The best modern calculations suggest that what Dunne and some of the witnesses before his committee were really complaining about was that the effects of Gladstone's budgetary assimilations meant that Ireland had 'lost her relatively privileged position in the British fiscal system' and, worse still, that her growing post-famine prosperity caused the new imposts to *rise* more sharply than their equivalents in Britain. Endless arguments as to whether this was 'fair' with regard to the balance between revenue raised and expenditure distributed *in* Ireland yielded a good deal more heat than light, because relevant geographical 'locations' were often impossible to determine with any precision. Those who pointed to Ireland's 'over-taxation' were really emphasizing the tendency of United Kingdom taxation as a whole to weigh 'relatively

---

[32] Parl. Deb. 3: clxxi. 825–36 (12 June 1863); J. Morley, *The Life of William Ewart Gladstone*, 3 vols (London, 1903), i. 646–7.

[33] Parl. Deb. 3: clxxi. 827 (12 June 1863).

[34] *Report from the Select Committee on the Taxation of Ireland*, HC 1865 (330), xii. 13, 8. See P. Travers, 'The Financial Relations Question 1800–1914', in F. B. Smith (ed.), *Ireland, England and Australia: Essays in Honour of Oliver MacDonagh* (Canberra and Cork, 1990), 41–69.

heavily on the lower classes'.[35] What, however, can unequivocally be said is that Gladstone's 1853 activities rightly or wrongly injected a high degree of irritation into Irish political discourse and especially so with respect to discussions about how best to envisage the relationship between Ireland and Britain both now and in the decades to come.

III

For politicians in London the budget of 1853 inaugurated a quarter of a century or so of efforts, not only to make Ireland pay what they considered to be its fair share of taxes, but also to bear down more heavily on what had long been considered extravagance in Irish expenditure. Already in the 1840s Tory ministers had complained about the unnecessary size of the Irish administrative machine.[36] As prime minister, Peel, with a mind full of memories of his six years as chief secretary, had grown especially fierce on the point. De Grey, as viceroy, was peremptorily ordered to ask for less money, in part because, every time Ireland got more, wails went up from Scotland and England. Deluged, or so he claimed, by requests to subsidize 'Royal Canals, Grand Canals', and the like, Peel became obsessed with ludicrous micro-management, taking time off to pen an eight-page letter rejecting a minuscule grant for the Royal Dublin Society. The Royal Highland Society did not, he pointed out, get a grant, and in any case the Irish body was really only a 'club rather than a scientific society', which was indeed true, but hardly justified the attention being given to the matter. Above all, Peel complained of the endless demands from greedy Irish landowners already exempted 'from the income tax'.[37]

Peel died suddenly in July 1850 after falling from his horse. Almost immediately his closest followers (those Conservatives who had supported the repeal of the Corn Laws in 1846) began to canonize him in almost religious terms. For Aberdeen, who became prime minister in December 1852, 'a great

[35] See the excellent discussion by W. E. Vaughan in 'Ireland c.1870', in Vaughan (ed.), *A New History of Ireland V: Ireland under the Union I, 1801–70* (Oxford, 1989), 787–92. The knots into which experts could tie themselves became obvious with the reports in the 1890s of the Royal Commission on the Financial Relations between Great Britain and Ireland. See its *Final Report*, HC 1896 [C.8262 and C.8008], xxxiii. 499, which, heroically, estimated that Ireland was 'over-paying' by £5.4 million in 1859–60, £3.2 million in 1879–80, and £2 million in 1893–4. It also included an Appendix (No. XIX) giving an inconclusive account of Ireland's treatment in the budgets of 1842 and 1853.

[36] Graham to Eliot, 19 November 1841, BL Graham Papers Ir/8; to Heytesbury, 25 March 1845, ibid., Ir/21.

[37] Peel to De Grey, 13 January [1843], BL Peel Papers Add. MS 40478; to Fremantle (chief secretary), 12 June [1845], and 19 July [1845], ibid., Add. MS 40476.

light' had 'disappeared from amongst us' with 'universal grief exhibited' by all 'from the Queen to the common labourer'. For Newcastle, briefly chief secretary in 1846 and one of Gladstone's particular friends, Peel remained 'my leader still, though invisible. I never take a step in public life without reflecting, how would *he* have thought of it.'[38] But it was Gladstone who, at least with respect to the policy of economy in government, remained, throughout the whole of his public life, Peel's greatest acolyte. As Chancellor of the Exchequer (1852–5 and 1859–66) he emulated the 'leader invisible' by bearing down upon Irish expenditure at every level. Irish policeman were paid too much and the increase of 4½ pence a day proposed in January 1854 was outrageous. 'What we want is some provision which shall give the local authorities and communities [in Ireland] an interest in keeping within due limits.' His correspondent, the Peelite chief secretary Sir John Young, boasted in his reply that he himself had saved £200 on his official garden in Dublin, 'some hundreds' on convict prisons, and possibly £10,000 on the poor-law establishment, and had consistently 'discouraged, not without some rise of unpopularity ... that frequent call for public money ... characteristic of Ireland and often so pernicious to its self-exertion'.[39] Five years later Gladstone described to his wife a 'sickening' debate in the Commons during which 'all the Irish were ... most of them vying with one another in eagerness to plunder the public purse'.[40] He also moaned to his Peelite friend Edward Cardwell, then chief secretary and in the cabinet, about how 'the old business of reduction' that had 'occupied the Treasury for so many years' under Peel had—presumably between 1855 and 1858 during the outstandingly able chancellorship of Cornewall Lewis—been allowed to slacken and grow faint.[41] In reply, Cardwell, emulating Young, assured Gladstone that in Dublin the cause of cheeseparing was now receiving every official support. Indeed, he himself was pleased to be able to advise against a request from the Ulster King of Arms for a small sum to purchase for the Irish official records certain 'antiquarian papers' that no sensible English museum could possibly want to possess.[42]

All in all it would not be fanciful to identify close financial control as the leitmotiv of Gladstone's approach to Irish affairs, with Home Rule (which could also self-convincingly be turned into a 'moral' undertaking) really only a

---

[38] *Sir Robert Peel from his Private Papers*, ed. Parker, iii. 553, 559.

[39] Gladstone to Young, 5 January 1854, BL Gladstone Papers Add. MS 44237; Young to Gladstone, 1 March 1855, ibid.

[40] Gladstone to his wife, 9 April 1859, *Gladstone to his Wife*, ed. A. Tilney Bassett (London, 1936), 124.

[41] Gladstone to Cardwell, 29 September 1859, BL Gladstone Papers Add. MS 44118. For Lewis's chancellorship, see Hoppen, *Mid-Victorian Generation*, 204–6. He certainly also meant Disraeli, who was chancellor for sixteen months from February 1858.

[42] Cardwell to Gladstone, 1 October 1859, BL Gladstone Papers Add. MS 44118.

kind of subdivision within a greater economical crusade. And, while Gladstone was thinking through such notions in relation to Ireland, he was also in the late 1850s, as Lord Commissioner to the (then British) Ionian Islands off the coast of Greece, experiencing problems concerning land, nation, and faith that he was later to encounter when grappling with the 'Irish Question'.[43] For Gladstone, even more than for Peel, nothing was too small to notice when it came to Irish (or indeed Ionian) extravagance, the aim being, not simply to reduce expenditure, but to align everything to the putatively higher fiscal standards pertaining in England. Minor official posts should, therefore, be abolished in Dublin, where 'establishments are maintained ... in excess of all real wants, simply because they are Irish'. The Irish had been granted and still demanded 'public expenditure' well beyond 'the amount required for the purposes in view', forgetting that the taxes paying for such things, being 'money taken by the Government out of the pockets of the people', ought to be disbursed 'in the best, most efficient, and ... economical manner', a manner insufficiently practised in virtually all areas of Irish life.[44] And, among the Irish generally, the most undeserving supplicants for Gladstone, as for many other London politicians, continued to be the landlords, who, even after the cleansing furnaces of the Famine, were in too many cases proving resistant to modernization and reform. Among an extravagant and discontented people, it was, for Gladstone (in England and Scotland a star-struck worshipper of the 'aristocratic principle'), the landlords who complained the most and deserved the least.[45]

And, although it was admitted on all sides that the 'beneficent' effects of the Famine would probably take some time to transform Ireland's backward social and economic arrangements, their actual form and shape when they eventually appeared proved in one respect disappointing, in another a validation of the truth that one should be careful of what one asks for.

As regards the situation of Irish landlords after the Encumbered Estates Act, developments fell short of the high hopes of those who had anticipated a transformation from hopeless bankrupts into efficient rural capitalists. Admittedly, extensive sales of distressed and mortgaged properties did take place under the auspices of the Encumbered Estates (after 1858 the Landed

---

[43] B. Knox, 'British Policy on the Ionian Islands, 1847–1864: Nationalism and Imperial Administration', *English Historical Review*, 99 (1984), 503–29; H. C. G. Matthew, *Gladstone 1809–1974* (Oxford, 1986), 162–5.

[44] Gladstone to Palmerston, 22 June 1860, S[outhampton] U[niversity] Palmerston Papers GC/GL/34; to Wodehouse (viceroy), 17 December 1864, Bodl. Kimberley Papers MS 4016; to Northcote, 13 March 1865, BL Northcote Papers Add. MS 50014; Parl. Deb. 3: clxxvii. 679 (24 February 1865).

[45] Morley, *Life of William Ewart Gladstone*, ii. 582; K. T. Hoppen, 'Gladstone, Salisbury and the End of Irish Assimilationism', in M. E. Daly and Hoppen (eds), *Gladstone: Ireland and Beyond* (Dublin, 2011), 60.

Estates) Court—some 4.1 million acres with a nominal rental of £1.45 million a year in the first eight years—and undoubtedly there were those who hailed this as wondrous progress and as something that would never have happened 'if Ireland had been allowed to assert her legislative independence' and 'been left to struggle through the Slough of Despond without the advice and encouragement of Great Britain'.[46] And certainly ministers were at first delighted with their handiwork, so much so that the Irish legislation of 1849 was used as a model for the Encumbered Estates (West Indies) Act of 1854.[47] What did, however, soon become apparent was that, far from attracting floods of eager British capitalists, the machinery established in large part to achieve such an outcome was being used to allow Irish landowners who had managed to survive the Famine in tolerable shape to increase the size of their estates and also, very often, to do so on borrowed money. Out of a total of 7,489 who purchased before 31 August 1857, only 309 (4.1 per cent) came from outside Ireland.[48]

Undoubtedly this meant that the post-Famine proprietorial world was able to present (as the assimilationists had hoped) a stronger front to the world. Undoubtedly, too, landlords seem to have found it possible in the two decades after 1850 to exercise their electoral influence with tolerable and, for a time, increasing success.[49] They also, as a group, proved themselves able, again for a time, to retain a significant share of agricultural income, so that, while between 1856–8 and 1871–3 output increased by about 12.5 per cent, their tenants' incomes rose by only about 7.7 per cent.[50] On the other hand, though post-Famine owners certainly tightened up their management procedures, they were, for the most part, far from becoming the kind of capitalists the framers of the Encumbered Estates Act had hoped for. Not only were they more or less exactly—in background and outlook—the same kind of people landlords had always been, but the proportion of acreage owned by the smallest, weakest, and least effective seems to have remained fairly stable, while indebtedness levels, especially among those with modest properties, continued to be burdensome

---

[46] W. O'C. Morris, 'Social Progress in Ireland', *Edinburgh Review*, 106 (1857), 117, 108, 120.

[47] Parl. Deb. 3: cxxxiv. 488–96 (26 June 1854: Newcastle).

[48] J. S. Donnelly Jr, *The Land and the People of Nineteenth-Century Cork: The Rural Economy and the Land Question* (London, 1975), 131; Donnelly, *Great Irish Potato Famine*, 166; P. G. Lane, 'Purchasers of Land in Counties Galway and Mayo in the Encumbered Estates Court, 1849–1858', *Journal of the Galway Archaeological and Historical Society*, xliii (1991), 95–127.

[49] K. T. Hoppen, 'Landlords, Society and Electoral Politics in Mid-Nineteenth-Century Ireland', *Past & Present*, 75 (1977), 62–93; Hoppen, 'National Politics and Local Realities in Mid-Nineteenth-Century Ireland', in A. Cosgrove and D. McCartney (eds), *Studies in Irish History Presented to R. Dudley Edwards* (Dublin, 1979), 190–227.

[50] K. T. Hoppen, *Ireland since 1800: Conflict and Conformity*, 2nd edn (Harlow, 1999), 98; M. Turner, *After the Famine: Irish Agriculture 1850–1914* (Cambridge, 1996), 196–216.

and eventually ruinous.[51] Seventeen years after 1849, Earl Grey (a member of
the cabinet in that year) said that he had given up hope of ever witnessing the
nirvana once so confidently predicted. Surely by now 'we might have expected
to see ... undoubted symptoms of improvement and progress ... But, I ask, has
any man pointed out such symptoms?' Answering his own question, he
declared that 'in some respects the prospects' for Ireland 'were more gloomy
than ever'.[52] Clarendon's exhortations of 1851 that henceforth Irish 'landowners must look upon themselves as manufacturers of food and nothing
more, subject like them to active competition', seem to have been so universally ignored that he soon came to the conclusion that landlord 'misconduct'
continued to cause much of the 'hardships endured by the people'. At the same
time, other politicians, from Stanley to Gladstone, rejoiced that Irish proprietors were at last being obliged to pay more tax after years of undeserved
exemption.[53] As chief secretary in 1855, even Horsman, not famous for
sympathy with Irish tenants, went so far as to remark that one notorious
Irish landlord more or less 'deserved to be murdered'.[54] And by the mid-
1860s, when disappointments about the failure of a new landed class to emerge
had become general, all the old criticisms of Irish proprietors were once again
being given an energetic dusting-down. On becoming Palmerston's viceroy in
1864, Wodehouse lost no time in delivering a lecture to the effect that such
men maintained themselves only 'by the force of the United Kingdom' and
that ministers would refuse to furnish assistance 'in perpetuity to save landowners from measures which they have neglected to provide and which might
otherwise be forced upon them'.[55] Even a Tory chief secretary, the highly
competent Lord Naas (an Irishman and later viceroy of India), could not
contain himself when it turned out that his modest Tenant Improvement Bill
of 1867 had not 'the least chance of passing—such is the stolid ignorance and
fatuity of the Tory landlords'.[56]

The second main prong of the post-Famine assimilationist fork—the re-
adjustment of the overall structure of Irish agrarian society along English
capitalist lines—experienced a somewhat more impressive sharpening. As

---

[51] Hoppen, *Elections, Politics, and Society in Ireland*, 122, 107; L. P. Curtis Jr, 'Incumbered
Wealth: Landed Indebtedness in Post-Famine Ireland', *American Historical Review*, 85 (1980),
332–67; W. E. Vaughan, *Landlords and Tenants in Mid-Victorian Ireland* (Oxford, 1994), 130–7.
[52] *Parl. Deb.* 3: clxxxii. 364 (16 March 1866).
[53] Clarendon to Bedford, 18 May 1851, Bodl. Clarendon Papers Irish 80; to G. Grey,
2 February 1852, R[oyal] A[rchives] D21/61; *Parl. Deb.* 3: cii. 1308 (27 February 1849: Stanley);
Gladstone to Aberdeen, 30 April 1853, BL Aberdeen Papers Add. MS 43070.
[54] Chichester Fortescue's Diary (22 November 1855), So[merset] R[ecord] O[ffice] Carlingford Papers DD/SH/64/358.
[55] G. Locker Lampson, *A Consideration of the State of Ireland in the Nineteenth Century*
(London, 1907), 329.
[56] Naas to Abercorn (viceroy), 30 April 1867, P[ublic] R[ecord] O[ffice of] N[orthern]
I[reland] Abercorn Papers T2541/VR/85/18.

The Times (somewhat fantastically) put it in 1858, England itself had years ago 'given up' on the class of 'small farmers ... who went on dividing and sub-dividing ... and descending to a lower scale of cultivation' and replaced them with 'substantial yeomen, the man with 500 acres and a capital of £5,000'. And, with its own 'peasants' having 'settled into labourers' or moved into cities, it now had every right to expect the same from Ireland.[57] And where *The Times* led, the *Tyrawley Herald* (of Ballina) was pleased to follow, delighted to report in 1859 how, leaving the landlords aside, 'we are gradually ranging ourselves into two classes, the employers [tenants] who hold the land and pay the wages and the employed who hold no land and works for hire'. That, given contemporary wage levels, this was anything but a good bargain for the latter group was, however, also widely admitted.[58] Nonetheless, there is little doubt that the more substantial Irish farmers—a distinctly growing category—were now experiencing better times. It was they who led 'the general shift from tillage to pastoral agriculture ... and gained most advantage from it. No longer tied to primitive barter relationships with bound and unbound labourers, they lodged the profits of livestock sales complacently in the provincial banks that flourished during the 1850s.' But, 'if the strong farmers did well out of the Famine, the labourers were broken'.[59] In other words, what happened, at least in this respect, was pretty well exactly what British politicians and observers generally had hoped for and anticipated: the Famine, for all its horrors, had injected, or so it seemed, distinct modernities into an agrarian world very much in need of them.

What was happening was that, within a society that, unlike that of England, remained predominantly, if somewhat decreasingly, rural and agrarian, it was the farmers, together with those designated their 'assisting relatives', who now became dominant both in influence and in numbers. Whereas in 1841 they had constituted 40.3 per cent of the total occupied male 'farming' population, thereafter this figure increased steadily: to 53.4 per cent in 1861 and 60.1 per cent in 1881. Not only that, but by the late 1860s more than three-quarters of the voters in the county constituencies were farmers, whereas before the Famine the nature of the rural electorate—the crucial political class—had been determined by criteria so anomalous and bizarre that many extremely poor agriculturalists had found their way on to the rolls. In addition, the Irish Franchise Act of 1850, by radically recasting the basis upon which men could

[57] *The Times*, 15 April 1858.
[58] *Mayo Constitution*, 27 December 1859, citing *Tyrawley Herald*, in P. G. Lane, 'The General Impact of the Encumbered Estates Act of 1849 on Counties Galway and Mayo', *Journal of the Galway Archaeological and Historical Society*, 33 (1972-3), 56. For wage levels, see ibid. 57-8, and Hoppen, *Elections, Politics, and Society in Ireland*, 100.
[59] C. Ó Murchadha, *The Great Famine: Ireland's Agony 1845-1852* (London, 2011), 188-9; J. Lee, 'Women and the Church since the Famine', in M. MacCurtain and D. Ó Corráin (eds), *Women in Irish Society: The Historical Dimension* (Dublin, 1978), 37-45.

obtain the vote, further enforced an increasingly close and more 'rational' alignment between farming success and political involvement and influence.[60] But not only were traditionally subordinate groups suffering distinct numerical attrition; the countryside itself was experiencing a matching shift towards comparatively larger farming units, the Famine having had the effect of 'pulverising … the bottom strata of Irish society, their smallholdings and their mud cabins'.[61] Thus the proportion of farms more than 15 acres in extent increased substantially from 30.5 per cent of all holdings in 1845 to 50.3 per cent in 1871, while those larger than 30 acres increased more dramatically still from 7.0 per cent in 1841 to 26.9 per cent in 1871. And these changes, which accelerated during the Famine, continued in the years that followed, with the result that, over the period 1851–71, while the proportion of all farms under 15 acres fell, that of those between 15 and 50, between 50 and 100, and over 200 acres rose.[62]

All in all, therefore, the Famine, 'by crushing the traditional economy of the potato eaters, hastened the commercialisation and monetisation of economic transactions in post-famine society'.[63] And many other areas of Irish life underwent a modernization to match the changes that were taking place in farming: shops were spreading from small towns into the countryside, bank branches were increasing in number, as were newspapers. More children were going to school, and literacy rates were improving.[64] But, while such tendencies more or less reflected the hopes of politicians in London for a more vibrant and modern—a more Anglo-Saxon—state of affairs in Ireland, it simultaneously created a farming class economically stronger and eventually more politically active than before. Indeed, it was predominantly these stronger farmers who were to provide the foot soldiers for those later campaigns associated with the Land League, the National League, and their various successors. And, while it would be misleading to ignore the internal tensions within this increasingly articulate group or to exaggerate its economic firepower, there can be little doubt that the Famine, by helping to bring about a

---

[60] D. Fitzpatrick, 'The Disappearance of the Irish Agricultural Labourer, 1841–1812', *Irish Economic and Social History*, 7 (1980), 66–92; Hoppen, *Elections, Politics, and Society in Ireland*, 12–14, 102–6; Hoppen, 'Politics, the Law, and the Nature of the Irish Electorate 1832–1850', *English Historical Review*, 92 (1977), 746–76; Hoppen, 'Nationalist Mobilisation and Governmental Attitudes: Geography, Politics and Nineteenth-Century Ireland', in L. Brockliss and D. Eastwood (eds), *A Union of Multiple Identities: The British Isles, c.1750–c.1850* (Manchester, 1997), 164.

[61] L. Kennedy et al., *Mapping the Great Irish Famine: A Survey of the Famine Decades* (Dublin, 1999), 207.

[62] Turner, *After the Famine*, 66–85. Figures such as these depend upon certain assumptions concerning the basis of contemporary statistics.

[63] Kennedy et al., *Mapping the Great Irish Famine*, 163, 209.

[64] Hoppen, *Elections, Politics, and Society in Ireland*, 437–40, 456–64; M.-L. Legg, *Newspapers and Nationalism: The Irish Provincial Press 1850–1892* (Dublin, 1999).

changed state of things that happened to coincide with the assimilationist views of contemporary political society in Britain, had begun to create new and substantial problems for governments and ministers in charge of Irish affairs.[65]

Because in the 1850s and early 1860s such outcomes were neither universally nor immediately obvious, the British political classes continued for a time to think it important to go on emphasizing the necessity of encouraging, and even sometimes attempting to direct, the Irish economic and social juggernaut towards assimilationist destinations of various kinds. Thus in October 1852 the prime minister (Derby) was prepared to support legislation giving very modest rights to tenants on condition that it was designed to accelerate the adoption of 'English ideas and habits'. And, indeed, the bill in question foreshadowed later Liberal legislation in proposing to abolish 'traditional' tenures in favour of strict contract on English lines.[66]

By continuing to encourage such supposedly 'English' notions to cross the Irish Sea, it was hoped that, in due course, a situation would come about in which there would 'be no difference between the law of property in Ireland and England'.[67] Assimilation, however, implied, not only that Irish landlords should behave in a 'better' manner, but that they should be denied any special privileges and powers that their more enlightened British contemporaries did not enjoy. A future Tory Lord Chancellor of England saw no reason to 'give the Irish landlords powers ... we have denied ... to landlords in England', while a Tory MP who opposed 'the wild and democratic schemes of the Manchester School' felt quite as strongly on the matter as did Cobden, the school's living embodiment. The fear was that, if one allowed old-style Hibernian repressive practices to contaminate Britain, then, perhaps at some time in the not-so-distant future, dangerous, violent, and demotic notions of various kinds might well follow in their train.[68]

Such fears of contagion were generally fumigated by confident declarations about the certain and fixed nature of economic laws, which, as one MP put it in 1855, 'had never been violated, and never would be'.[69] And it was precisely this kind of universalism that lay behind both the ideas and the words that Palmerston employed when delivering his famous attacks on (very mild) bills

---

[65] See K. T. Hoppen, 'British Politicians and the Transformation of Rural Society in Nineteenth-Century Ireland', in S. Pašeta (ed.), *Uncertain Futures: Essays about the Irish Past for Roy Foster* (Oxford, 2016).

[66] Derby to Napier (Irish attorney-general), [29 October 1852], L[iverpool] R[ecord] O[ffice] Derby Papers 181/1; Parl. Deb. 3: cxxxi. 35 (28 February 1854: Desart). See A. Shields, *The Irish Conservative Party 1852–68: Land, Politics and Religion* (Dublin, 2007), 42, 48.

[67] Parl. Deb. 3: cxxiii. 311 (22 January 1852: Napier) and 1561 (15 December 1852: Naas).

[68] Ibid. cxxxiii. 524 (18 May 1854: St Leonards) and cxxxix. 479 (5 July 1855: Malins); Cobden to Richard, 24 June 1857, *The Letters of Richard Cobden*, ed. A. Howe, 4 vols (Oxford, 2007–15), iii. 329.

[69] Parl. Deb. 3: cxxxviii. 2233 (19 June 1855: Peacocke discussing an Irish land bill).

designed to help Irish tenants. For him it was the forces of past ages rather than any present activities on the part of Irish landowners (like himself) that were to blame for present difficulties and discontents: 'the history of the Civil War; of rebellion, of confiscation; of wholesale and violent transfers of land from class to class; of penal laws.'[70] In April 1858 he nailed his colours firmly to the mast of unrestrained contract, declaring that 'those who have mutual relations should be left to deal with each other as they please, and that any law which tends to restrict the freedom of either party in their mutual transactions is most objectionable'. Seven years later he was both prime minister and more succinct: tenant right was merely 'the equivalent to landlords' wrong ... [and] little short of confiscation'.[71]

As the politicians continued to pronounce, so the intellectuals, for the most part, happily continued to provide appropriate ideological scaffolding, though even Carlyle's flashy abuse—'Remedy for Ireland? To cease generally from following the devil: no other remedy that I know of'—was sometimes interwoven with more sympathetic insights.[72] And, while Mill's opinions on Irish land were moving in no very clear direction as he delivered himself of quasi-assimilationist observations to the effect that 'the English system of landlords, tenant farmers, and hired labourers' could no longer be considered 'impossible in Ireland as it was in the days before the Famine', Hancock and his associates in the Dublin Statistical Society were still arguing that only English notions of strict contract could provide a lasting remedy for Ireland's agrarian ills.[73]

All in all, the 1850s were years of optimism regarding the future economic and social welfare of Ireland, even if the febrile enthusiasm of travellers about the wonders of the Encumbered Estates Act soon began to wear thin. A few months after arriving in Dublin as chief secretary, the sceptical Horsman, who disliked the Irish and Irish MPs in particular (the 'shabbies' as he called them), found himself swept along by all the glorious opportunities 'so sudden, so blessed, and hopeful' now ready for the taking.[74] Gladstone's future Home Secretary, H. A. Bruce, visiting Connemara in 1855, found much to rejoice in 'a new spirit of commercial enterprise ... houses, schools, new cottages, and drained and redeemed land'—redeemed, he implied, not only physically, but

---

[70] Parl. Deb.3: cxxxviii. 168 (4 May 1855).

[71] Ibid. cxlix. 1088 (14 April 1858) and clxxvii. 823 (27 February 1865).

[72] T. Carlyle, *Reminiscences of my Irish Journey in 1849*, ed. J. A. Froude (London, 1882), 258–9. See J. Morrow, 'Thomas Carlyle, "Young Ireland" and the "Condition of Ireland Question"', *Historical Journal*, 51 (2008), 643–67; R. F. Foster, *Words Alone: Yeats and his Inheritances* (Oxford, 2011), 46–50.

[73] B. L. Kinzer, *England's Disgrace? J. S. Mill and the Irish Question* (Toronto, 2001), 106–9; P. Gray, 'The Making of Mid-Victorian Ireland? Political Economy and the Memory of the Great Famine', in Gray (ed.), *Victoria's Ireland? Irishness and Britishness, 1837–1901* (Dublin, 2004), 151–66.

[74] Parl. Deb. 3: cxxxviii. 159 (4 May 1855); Hoppen, *Elections, Politics, and Society in Ireland*, 260.

spiritually too.[75] Cornewall Lewis, now no longer merely an intellectual administrator but an innovative Chancellor of the Exchequer, pointed in 1856 to the 'small portion of the time of Parliament Ireland now occupies' as proof positive that 'the legislation of the last twenty-five years' was beginning 'to bear fruit'.[76] Even the Census Commissioners of 1851, in their concluding volume published in 1856, felt moved to report that, despite (perhaps even because of) 'famine, disease, and emigration between 1841 and 1851', their findings should be seen as, 'on the whole satisfactory, demonstrating as they do the general advancement of the country'.[77]

Such attitudes and expectations reached their legislative apotheosis in August 1860 with the Landed Property (Ireland) Improvement Act and the Landlord and Tenant Amendment Act, the former generally known as Cardwell's Act after the chief secretary, Edward Cardwell, the latter as Deasy's Act after the Irish attorney-general, Rickard Deasy. The provisions of both closely reflected assimilationist suggestions presented to Cardwell by Hancock in October 1859, chief among them an insistence that traditional tenurial 'customs' be replaced by 'written engagements'—that is, by formal contracts. Cardwell himself saw this as a direct continuation of the process begun in 1849 by the Encumbered Estates Act and hoped that the Irish countryside would thereby experience that influx of British capital that had, as yet, made disappointingly modest appearances.[78] Answering some parliamentary criticisms of his (in reality mouse-like) bill, Cardwell, never one to undervalue his own efforts, produced the extraordinary but probably sincere claim that he had now 'settled ... the land question' for years to come.[79] Deasy's matching act had a more formidable look to it, with its assertions that the relations of landlord and tenant were to be governed by the principle of strict contract and that, in effect, the tenant was henceforth to hire his land as, in the words of one legal scholar, 'he might hire a horse and cart or any other commodity'.[80] Deasy sought to do this by providing that 'the relation of landlord and tenant shall be deemed to be founded on the express or implied contract of the parties, and not upon tenure or service'—that is, not upon the various extra-legal 'customs'

---

[75] Bruce to his wife, Westport, 14 June 1855, *Letters of the Rt Hon. Henry Austin Bruce GCB Lord Aberdare of Duffryn*, 2 vols (Oxford, privately printed, 1902), i. 138–40.

[76] Lewis to Carlisle, 25 March 1856, A. Warren, 'Palmerston, the Whigs and the Government of Ireland, 1855–1866', in D. Brown and M. Taylor (eds), *Palmerston Studies I* (University of Southampton, 2007), 99.

[77] *The Census of Ireland for the year 1851. Part VI. The General Report*, HC 1856 [2134], xxvi. 58.

[78] Parl. Deb. 3: xlvii. 1553–66 (29 March 1860); Cardwell to Carlisle, 25 August 1860, C[astle] H[oward] Carlisle Papers J19/1/90.

[79] T. MacKnight, *Ulster as it Is or Twenty-Eight Years' Experience as an Irish Editor*, 2 vols (London, 1896), i. 91; Parl. Deb. 3: clix. 293–4 (11 June 1860) and clxxx. 759 (23 June 1865).

[80] J. C. Brady, 'English Law and Irish Land in the Nineteenth Century', *Northern Ireland Legal Quarterly*, 23 (1972), 35–7.

that had grown up in years past.[81] Now, this kind of thinking certainly echoed those judicial tendencies in contemporary England that upheld the validity of contracts even when entered into by palpably unequal parties, as was of course almost invariably the case with tenants and landlords. However, Irish lawyers proved less enthusiastic, with the result that interpreting the precise implications of Deasy's Act became something of a judicial football throughout the quarter-century that followed, not least because the Act's interrelated concepts of mutual agreement and free choice can hardly be said to have held firm places in 'the common currency of rural life in mid-nineteenth-century Ireland'.[82]

In practice, despite a good deal of posturing and despite the prominence of the Acts of 1860 as decorative cherries on the assimilationist cake, their impact on the ground was much less dramatic than many had expected and many others had feared. Already in 1865 W. E. Forster (a future and notably acerbic chief secretary) was convinced they had become dead letters, and, in truth, statute law had moved much less sharply towards freedom of contract than Gladstone's Irish Land Act of 1870 was to move in the contrary direction towards prescription.[83] There had, in any case, always been a few independent-minded thinkers who, even if willing to buy into promises of post-Famine agrarian assimilation, had consistently emphasized that this would take a very long time indeed, so long probably that patience on all sides would sooner or later wear exceedingly thin. Writing in 1861, Nassau Senior saw little improvement, no 'great real alteration in the habits or feelings' of a people still dependent on potatoes, still 'tools of their priests ... improvident ... enemies of every improving landlord'. When visiting Ireland in October 1862, he was told by a Catholic landowner that the best the government could do was 'to bide its time, and wait for the slow improvements which increased wealth and more diffused education will gradually produce'.[84]

IV

Such considerations and disappointments also to some extent underlay and informed certain strikingly negative and sackcloth attitudes that pervaded the British governing class's attitudes to and relations with Ireland and how it

---

[81] J. C. Brady, 'Legal Developments, 1801–79', in Vaughan (ed.), *New History of Ireland V: Ireland under the Union I*, 457–63; also Parl. Deb. 3: clviii. 1346 (15 May 1860: Deasy).

[82] P. S. Atiyah, *The Rise and Fall of Freedom of Contract* (Oxford, 1979), 387–8; Brady, 'Legal Developments, 1801–79', 463.

[83] Parl. Deb. 3: clxxviii. 586 (31 March 1865: Forster); W. E. Vaughan, *Landlords and Tenants in Ireland 1848–1904* ([Dundalk], 1984), 12. For the 1870 Land Act, see Chapter 7, Section III.

[84] N. W. Senior, *Journals, Conversations and Essays Relating to Ireland*, i. viii, and ii. 192.

should best be governed. Amid all the plans for assimilation that dominated political discourse from the 1830s onwards, amid the hopes for regeneration that the catastrophe of the Famine brought to the fore, there ran a deep vein, not simply of pessimism, but of guilt. Right through the 1830s, 1840s, 1850s, and 1860s there is no shortage of public self-blame to be found in the pages of the Parliamentary Debates, blame for deeds done long ago but also for deeds still current. And it came from pretty well every political quarter. 'For years Ireland had been misruled'; too often Irishmen have been entitled to 'consider themselves rather as victims of tyranny, than the subjects of a Government'; 'the government of Ireland has been for centuries our scandal in the eyes of Europe'; 'a tyrannical and monstrous system'; the 'original tyranny of England ... that had reduced Ireland to degradation and destitution'; the people of Ireland are 'dealt with as slaves'; Irish history is 'a disgrace'; 'nothing can be more painful to me than to refer to the history ... of Irish policy'; Ireland's true suffering has not been caused by 'demagogues, Romanism or the Celtic race [but by] ... the Government of England'.[85] But, while the frequent repetition and lacerating abasements of this kind of thing certainly suggest the fleeting presence of a species of unease, their practical impact upon policy is by no means easy to detect.

However, such pessimisms were certainly given a distinct boost in the early 1860s by the sudden and unexpected appearance of a severe agricultural depression in Ireland (and to some extent in Britain too), which cast a distinct pall over post-Famine expectations that better, assimilated, and anglicized things were either already in train or just around the corner. This downturn, which lasted from 1859 to 1864, was very severe and in some respects more severe than the famous depression of 1877–9. Drought followed by heavy rain and then drought again severely affected both the arable and livestock sectors, and it was precisely those 'strong' farmers upon whom assimilationists had pinned their hopes for economic recovery who suffered most grievously.[86] The depression's severity and duration certainly concentrated the minds of politicians and intellectuals by injecting a dose of caution into the high hopes initially raised for the Famine's potential as a dramatic force for the recasting of agrarian structures and relationships and by creating a growing realization that the much lauded remedy of assimilation might, in the end, turn out to be no more than a broken reed.

---

[85] Parl. Deb. 3: xiv. 690–1 (24 June 1832), xxvi. 361–84 (30 March 1835), lxix. 1128–36 (29 May 1843), lxxx. 542–60 (11 April 1845), lxxxix. 404–7 (25 January 1847), xcvii. 872–4 (22 March 1848), cii. 549–55 (9 February 1849), cxlvi. 1048–55 (7 July 1857), clxxvii. 720 (24 February 1865). This small selection includes comments by minister such as Russell, Peel, and, amazingly, Cecil (the future Lord Salisbury), and others not noted for their Hibernophile outlook such as Roebuck and Hume.

[86] J. S. Donnelly Jr, 'The Irish Agricultural Depression of 1859–64', *Irish Economic and Social History*, 3 (1976), 33–54.

In the mid-1860s, therefore, the whole character of the debate about how best to secure a prosperous future for Ireland was beginning to change direction in response to sudden economic shocks, to more militant forms of nationalism in Ireland itself, and to ideological shifts among those who thought most closely about how economic improvement might best be nurtured and encouraged. By 1866 even *The Times*, once so notable for its fierce and opinionated assimilationism, was beginning to regard some kind of 'halfway house' between English and traditionally Irish models of agricultural tenure as best designed to secure simultaneous efficiency and political calm.[87] Equally remarkable was the Commons debate on Ireland of February 1865 (just as the depression had come to an end), which exhibited deeply ambiguous feelings as to what should now be done. On the one hand, there were still declarations that union necessarily meant assimilation; on the other, often rather reluctantly expressed doubts were emerging about what had for three decades and more formed the overwhelming orthodoxy of political debate. Gladstone admitted that 'circumstances of a special and imperative character' might indeed 'warrant our deviating from the application of those [Union] principles'. More striking still was the intervention of Lord Robert Cecil (the future Marquess of Salisbury, prime minister, and Hammer of Hibernia), who declared that he believed the Irish when they complained of hunger and disbelieved the denials of the Dublin administration, that he rejected the chief secretary's 'caricatured' defence of Irish landlords, that the 'state of land tenure in Ireland' was by no means 'all that could be desired', that compensation for tenant improvements might well be a useful notion, that the Exchequer's (that is, Gladstone's) parsimony, though doubtless inspired by a 'patriotic desire to spare the national purse, seemed ... too hard and too theoretical for the actual condition of Ireland'. To those who blamed Ireland's failings on its Celtic people, Cecil (ironically in the light of his comments in the 1880s) reminded the Commons that France had Celtic populations 'going forward in the path of prosperity with most rapid strides'. 'Can you', he concluded in the light of such considerations, 'fairly apply to that country [Ireland] your hard maxims of political economy?'[88]

Other parliamentarians were also beginning to trim their assimilationist enthusiasms and even recently retired chief secretaries to argue that the iron law of hard facts and substantial differences demanded that Irish land law should never be forced into any kind of Anglo-Saxon straitjacket.[89] In response, true believers became very apoplectic indeed. All such ideas were, they

---

[87] *The Times*, 2 May 1866; see also the cutting from the *Irish Times* of 2 May 1866 in NLI Larcom Papers MS 7513.

[88] Parl. Deb. 3: clxxvii. 674–84 (24 February 1865: Gladstone) and 717–22 (24 February 1865: Cecil); also 807–15 (27 February 1865: Northcote).

[89] Ibid. clxxxiv. 1971 (25 July 1866: Fortescue).

asserted, so markedly 'against the law of political economy, and against the natural law which binds men by contracts they make' that 'nature' itself would inevitably 'recoil'. If ever such deviationist nostrums were actually applied, why, then Ireland would become no more than a lesser Bengal, a 'country of ryots, with nothing left but the zemindars and the tillers of the soil'. To prevent such a calamity 'our legislation should be founded on principles perfectly broad, perfectly well ascertained, perfectly defensible upon the most abstract philosophical grounds'. The increasingly talked-about alternative—'to defer to Irish opinion, and let sound principles and the elementary rules of jurisprudence cease to have their efficacy'—was a prospect too terrible and dangerous to contemplate, let alone implement.[90]

But the ideological and intellectual underpinning that had supported and sustained such arguments were now showing distinct signs of fraying at the edges or even decaying altogether. Economists such as Hancock (increasingly close to Gladstone as an advisor on Irish affairs), and the Dublin Statistical Society school in general, were losing faith in the ability of post-Famine assimilationist doctrine to connect with the present condition of Ireland and of Irish agriculture in particular. The challenge posed by Fenianism and the return of Isaac Butt to the forefront of economic and political debate (and now denouncing what he called the perennial 'transition stage' that in practice had never seemed to come to anything) proved potent solvents with regard to ideas of assimilation, as did the arguments of economists such as Mountifort Longfield and T. E. Cliffe Leslie, who were beginning to advocate policies suited to specifically Irish conditions and historical developments. As Peter Gray has percipiently pointed out, 'neither the agricultural crisis of the early 1860s nor the Fenian alarms that followed could easily be accommodated by the liberal political-economy narrative so strongly and confidently articulated in the post-famine decade'.[91] And, just as wheels had turned in the 1830s away from the view that Ireland's peculiar and *sui generis* circumstances demanded peculiar and *sui generis* treatment and towards one that sought progress and stability in aligning Irish social, economic, and political structures more and more closely to those of Britain, so now a reverse process began to gather pace. But as history, when it seems to repeat itself, does so only superficially, so the ensuing period, though notable for once again allowing, indeed emphasizing, Irish differences, for treating Ireland as a divergent entity, was never a simple mirror reflection of what had happened during the first decades after the Union. From now onwards the many policies that were to be characterized by a recognition of Irish distinctiveness were generally (though by no means always) fuelled by the same kind of desire to defuse demands for separation that had informed mid-century assimilationism rather than by the hardline

[90] Ibid. clxxxiii. 1077–87 (17 May 1866: Lowe), also cxc. 1489 (12 March 1868: Lowe).
[91] Gray, 'Making of Mid-Victorian Ireland?', 166.

coercive approach of the decades immediately after 1800. But, while the goals in view might have remained broadly the same, the use of very different means to achieve them could not fail to shape the processes adopted, and to such an extent that ultimately it was the means employed as much as, indeed rather more than, the declared aims that created contexts within which the breakdown of the Union came to be seen as possible, probable, and (by some at least) necessary, perhaps even inevitable.

Part III

Dancing to Irish Tunes, *c*.1868–*c*.1921

7

Back to the Future

I

By the end of the 1860s three developments were beginning to make it more and more difficult to sustain the general thrust of the Irish policies pursued during the previous forty years. This was not because the attitudes of the British governing classes towards Ireland and its people experienced any deep underlying change. The view that Ireland was clearly 'different', in many respects alien, remained firmly in place, as it had been both before and after 1800. But the assimilationist remedies that had dominated the mid-century decades were losing the electric charge they had formerly possessed. High hopes for the speedy effectiveness of English-style poor laws and post-Famine economic uplift were turning to dust for politicians who had once been all too enthusiastic about making the wish father of the deed. Added to a growing sense that assimilationism had not yielded many, perhaps any, of the expected benefits were, on the one hand, the shock to the Anglo-Irish political system posed by the Fenian outbreak of 1867, and, on the other, the effects of an intellectual shift away from utilitarian universalism and towards more locally focused analyses based on the history, development, and present condition of particular countries and localities. These three developments— disappointment, violence, and changes in philosophical fashion—underwent, in the late 1860s and early 1870s, a species of reciprocal fructuation in which it is not always easy to identify precise lines of influence and precedence.

Yet Ireland and its problems experienced, so far as British political circles were concerned, little in the way of perceptual alteration or adjustment. What did change was the nature of analysis and discourse as to how Ireland's perennial difficulties might best be handled from a governmental point of view. The weight of opinion was moving away from assimilationism towards what at least in certain respects constituted a kind of return to the post-Union emphasis upon special measures for special Hibernian circumstances. But, while the facts of rebellion in 1798, war with France until 1815, and extreme agrarian violence had given the Irish policies of the Tory administrations of the first three decades of the century a continuous flavour of coercion and little else, the years after 1865–8, though by no means devoid of violence or coercion, were markedly different in character—ameliorative as well as repressive—with government carrots at least as much in evidence as administrative sticks.

As with the move *towards* assimilationism in the 1830s, so in the 1860s Ireland continued to be seen as distinctly *sui generis*. However, the programmes and policies now chosen to deal with this state of affairs underwent dramatic adjustment away from remedies of a primarily Anglo-Saxon character and towards 'solutions' designed to acknowledge Irish difference, to govern Ireland (in a phrase more bandied about than explained) 'according to Irish ideas'. In an important sense this marked, among much else, a transition from unrealistic optimism to a hard-headed acceptance that the best way to keep the Irish quiet was to pander (as far as was safe and acceptable) to their own particular sense as to how social and economic relationships should be structured and arranged. Assimilation was dead. Long live pragmatic relativism.

Not the least remarkable aspect of this mutation was its speed, suddenness, and acceptance by most sections of the British establishment, for, while Tories and Liberals did indeed sustain rather different versions of the new creed, virtually everyone accepted its major predicates. But, because intellectual changes with regard to the character of and respect due to 'primitive' societies and disillusionment with mid-century failures occurred simultaneously, it is not easy to identify the crucial impetus with any certainty. Was it a case, as Keynes famously put it, of 'practical men, who believe themselves to be quite exempt from any intellectual influences ... distilling their frenzy from some academic scribbler',[1] or did the deeds precede the justifications? Probably a bit of both. Certainly the manner in which politicians seem to have marched in strict temporal step with the scribblers suggests that the worlds of pragmatism and ideas had become very closely entwined.

The agricultural depression of 1859–64 undermined the expectations of those who had hoped that the Famine would usher in an era of prosperity. In 1862 the 'Gregory Clause' of 1847 designed to encourage a more efficient and 'English' system of landholding was quietly repealed. By 1866 Earl Grey had begun to despair that the Encumbered Estates Act would ever generate the Anglo-Saxon agrarian miracles once expected of it.[2] Already by the mid-1860s increasingly loud noises were to be heard from men rapidly losing faith in the possibility of aligning Irish with British economic realities and now beginning

---

[1] J. M. Keynes, *The General Theory of Employment, Interest, and Money* (London, 1936), ch. 24.

[2] P. Gray, 'Irish Social Thought and the Relief of Poverty, 1847–1880', *Transactions of the Royal Historical Society*, Sixth Series, 20 (2010), 147–8; Parl[iamentary] Deb[ates] 3: clxxxii. 364 (16 March 1866).

to insist that assimilation should be abandoned in favour of an acceptance that Irish distinctiveness demanded specially tailored Irish remedies that—and here a solemn pause for saddened reflection generally intervened—must necessarily diverge from the more advanced procedures relevant to Britain as a whole. One of the slowest to move was Gladstone, who in 1863, 1865, and even 1866 was still firmly lashing himself to the assimilationist mast. All would be for the best, he still insisted, once Ireland had been accorded English 'rights and advantages ... the very same principles ... which are applied to the government of the rest of Her Majesty's subjects'. And he angrily denounced those who argued that 'we have one weight and one measure for this side of the Channel, and another weight and another measure for the other side'. In a curious reversal of their future roles, these remarks were immediately condemned by Lord Robert Cecil (the future Marquess of Salisbury) as 'too harsh and too theoretical' for Irish circumstances, circumstances largely created by 'the Government of England'.[3]

Although Gladstone soon became the star of the gathering *Grand Départ* from assimilationism, his initial moves were cautious, certainly when compared with those of Liberal colleagues such as Chichester Fortescue and Lord Wodehouse, who, as chief secretary and viceroy, had direct responsibility for Irish affairs. In 1866 he was still advocating extensions of the land legislation of 1860, and it was not until the end of 1867 that he publicly began to insist that Irish problems could be successfully 'grappled with' only if all those concerned would 'make a mental effort to place' themselves 'in the position of Irishmen, imbued with the natural feelings of Irishmen and under the influence of their traditions'. Privately his opinions had become evident somewhat earlier, with Fortescue eager to tell colleagues about what he called Gladstone's evolving 'doctrine that Irish interests ought to be dealt with according to Irish ideas'.[4]

Gladstone's timing on these matters is less surprising than the fact of his taking up Ireland as an issue at all. His previous involvements had been sporadic, to say the least: resignation over the Maynooth grant in 1845, a famous and uncharacteristic outburst in the same year about 'that cloud in the west, that coming storm, the minister of God's retribution upon cruel and inveterate and but half-atoned injustice', and a brief, if intense, engagement

---

[3] J. L. Hammond, *Gladstone and the Irish Nation* (London, 1938), 67; Parl. Deb. 3: clxxvii. 677 (24 February 1865); clxxxiv. 902 (16 July 1866), clxxvii. 717–26 (24 February 1865). In 1862 Gladstone had famously declared sympathy for the Confederate States of America in their attempt to free themselves from centralized union control—perhaps a foreshadowing of his imminent views on Ireland (though he later regretted having declared that the Confederate leaders had 'made a nation'): H. C. G. Matthew, *Gladstone 1809–1874* (Oxford, 1986), 133–4.
[4] Gladstone to Fortescue, 13 February 1866, So[merset] R[ecord] O[ffice] Carlingford Papers DD/SH/61/324; *The Times*, 20 December 1867; Fortescue to Wodehouse, 24 February 1866, Bodl[eian Library] Kimberley Papers MS Eng.c.4043.

with Irish taxation in 1853.[5] Was he, perhaps, as Chancellor of the Exchequer between June 1859 and June 1866, casting about for issues that might prove useful in the future or was he simply swimming with an increasingly powerful political tide? Certainly the tide was on the turn. In 1864 Wodehouse (later, as Earl of Kimberley, a stalwart of Liberal cabinets) had hardly set foot in Dublin before telling contacts in England that 'this country' could no longer 'be governed according to English principles' because, while on 'the outside' its institutions resembled those of England, on the 'inside' everything was different, strange, and complicated.[6] And such first impressions became for Wodehouse more and more convincing as the years went by. 'We must endeavour to deal with Ireland from the same point of view as the people of Ireland themselves look at it.' 'It is strange that Englishmen can never be convinced that it is worse than useless to force English ideas on Ireland.' Soon he was writing to Gladstone urging that distinctly Hibernian twists be given to any new land policy the government might have in mind.[7] Fortescue, himself Irish, was pushing the same sentiments. After some ritual genuflections to the assimilationist expedients of yesteryear, he launched into a full-blooded insistence on the 'vital difference between the circumstances of England and Scotland, on the one hand, and of Ireland, on the other', something that urgently demanded 'different legislation for Ireland to that which prevails in other parts of the kingdom'. In December 1867 he told Gladstone that 'the Irish question' was 'a question of nationality, and [that] … due consideration for Irish opinion and feeling … ought to induce the people of England to consent to many things which they would not choose to permit for themselves'.[8]

As Gladstone himself began to move towards the view that the best (probably the only) way of handling Ireland—indeed of ultimately attaching Ireland more closely to the idea of union—was by implementing bespoke legislation designed to meet Irish rather than United Kingdom priorities, so did what had once been the mere apocrypha of marginal eccentrics become almost a sacred text. Rapidly shedding earlier inhibitions, Gladstone became the increasingly vociferous prophet of the new doctrine. Irish matters were, he declared, to be placed in a particular category and treated 'with a special view to Irish objects and interests' on the grounds that it was simply wrong to make 'the opinions

[5] *Gladstone to his Wife*, ed. A. Tilney Bassett (London, 1936), 64; see Chapter 6, Section II.

[6] Wodehouse to R. Currie, 2 December 1864, J. Powell (ed.), *Liberal by Principle: The Politics of John Wodehouse, 1st Earl of Kimberley, 1843–1902* (London, 1996), 99.

[7] Parl. Deb. 3: clxxxiii. 759 (11 May 1866) and clxxxvii. 1119 (27 May 1867); to R. Currie, 15 April 1870, Powell (ed.), *Liberal by Principle: The Politics of John Wodehouse*, 121; to Gladstone, 12 February 1866, Bodl. Kimberley Papers MS Eng.c.4041.

[8] *Irish Times*, 2 May 1866 (cutting in N[ational] L[ibrary of] I[reland] Larcom Papers MS 7513); to Gladstone, 14 December 1867, B[ritish] L[ibrary] Gladstone Papers Add. MS 44121. Other ministers, he claimed, agreed with him.

of one country overrule and settle the questions' peculiar to another. Irish issues must above all be seen as 'Irish', and to a rejection of this revelation could be ascribed '700 years' of failed government, 'an intolerable disgrace, and a danger so absolutely transcending all others, that I call it the only real danger of the noble Empire of the Queen'.[9] Talking specifically of the land question, but deliberately extending the argument more generally, Gladstone insisted that 'wherever there is a peculiarity in the circumstances of Ireland it is well to adopt that peculiarity as the foundation' of any relevant legislation, 'because the Irish people will fall more easily into the regular operation of a bill which conforms to their own peculiar modes of action'[10]—a notion that men such as Melbourne, Peel, Derby, and Palmerston would have found, not merely rebarbative, but incomprehensible.

The same line of argument was soon taken up by Lord Dufferin, a member of Gladstone's first administration of 1868–74 and later viceroy of India, who supported uniquely Irish legislation because, 'though we may disapprove of adultery, it would not be proper to strangle all the illegitimate children', while Kimberley and Fortescue repeated their earlier demands for laws designed to meet Ireland's peculiar and un-English circumstances.[11] The young Earl Spencer, appointed viceroy of Ireland in December 1868 (and thereafter a regular member of Gladstone's cabinets), was soon also justifying tailor-made land legislation because of 'the exceptional condition of land tenure in Ireland'. Within weeks of his being sworn in he took time to address the Statistical and Social Inquiry Society of Ireland on the attractions of economic and social relativism—that is, the adoption of different policies for different countries and circumstances. The old idea that 'abstract theories' were capable of general application was, he declared, no longer viable. Instead, he and many others now believed that 'the principles of political economy can never be applied universally. You must consider the position of the country, the state of progress of the people before you apply its principles.'[12] In the same year Gladstone was to be found specifically denouncing the 'lazy, heedless, uninformed good intentions' that had lain behind the once sacrosanct Encumbered Estates Act, a conviction that he retained until his dying day. By 1872 he was even, with that easy romanticism that occasionally peeped through the surface

---

[9] Parl. Deb. 3: clxxxi. 271–2 (8 February 1866); to Granville, 16 January 1870, *The Political Correspondence of Mr Gladstone and Lord Granville 1868–1876*, ed. A. Ramm, 2 vols, Royal Historical Society Camden Third Series, lxxxi and lxxxii (1952), i. 87.

[10] Parl. Deb. 3: cxcix. 368 (15 February 1870); also Hammond, *Gladstone and the Irish Nation*, 80–1.

[11] Printed Cabinet Papers, 2 and 8 November and 13 December 1869, Bodl. Kimberley Papers MS Eng.c.4062.

[12] Printed Cabinet Paper, 7 December 1869, Bodl. Clarendon Papers Irish 65; *Proceedings of the Statistical and Social Inquiry Society of Ireland*, v (1868–70), 106 (address of 22 January 1869).

of rectitude and moral engagement, happy to encourage the Irish to fly the 'green flag ... for after all it is the national flag of Ireland'.[13] Soon both old-time Liberals like Russell (once the great apostle of assimilation) and future cabinet ministers like John Morley (later chief secretary) were expressing equal enthusiasm for ditching the truths of former decades and asserting that it was now 'absolutely impossible to carry on the government' of Ireland 'in conformity with the rules and maxims which were observed in England and Scotland', that, indeed, one must now treat the Irish in a fashion that paid 'implicit respect to their wishes, their deeply-rooted ideas, even their deeply-rooted prejudices'.[14]

No less striking was that at least some of Gladstone's opponents in the Tory party were moving in the same direction, a clear manifestation of the fact that, beneath bitter surface disputes and confrontational rhetoric, agreement about the new necessity of treating Ireland by means of specifically 'Irish' arrangements was never confined to any single point on the party political compass. Disraeli, unsurprisingly, had little to say, though even he was disinclined to continue applying to Ireland the supposedly universal and 'abstract' principles of political economy.[15] The Tory most keenly in favour of the new approach was Northcote, a regular cabinet member from 1866 and a future (if rather ineffective) leader of the party in the Commons. Already in 1865 he was pointing out that England and Ireland 'were like two bodies, one of which had been deprived of a limb, and which, as a consequence, ought not to be supposed to be capable of supporting as great a weight as the other'. Four years later he was plainer still in a speech to the Social Science Association that might have come straight from the mouth of Gladstone, whose private secretary he had once been. 'The facts are stubborn and cannot be bent ... the [Irish] national idea of the relations between landlord and tenant is something totally different from the national idea in England [and] ... if that is the case, you must provide accordingly'—a view he put even more strongly to Disraeli in 1870.[16] And, in words that even Gladstone would hardly yet have dared to use, he flatly told his fellow MPs in March 1868 that in matters of Irish land '*Salus populi suprema lex* [so that] ... to a certain extent

---

[13] P. Magnus, *Gladstone: A Biography*, corrected edn (London, 1960), 202; L. A. Tollemache, *Talks with Mr Gladstone* (London, 1898), 127; Gladstone to Spencer, 27 August 1872, BL Spencer Papers Add. MS 76851.

[14] Parl. Deb. 3: ccxvi. 618 (9 June 1873: Russell); J. Morley, *Ireland's Rights and England's Duties: A Lecture* (Blackburn, [1868]), 7, a view he forcibly repeated in 'Home and Foreign Affairs', *Fortnightly Review*, 23/137 (1878), 800.

[15] K. T. Hoppen, 'Tories, Catholics, and the General Election of 1859', *Historical Journal*, 13 (1970), 48–67; Parl. Deb. 3: cxcvi. 1047 (31 July 1869); also W. F. Monypenny and G. E. Buckle, *The Life of Benjamin Disraeli, Earl of Beaconsfield*, 6 vols (London, 1910–20), v. 91.

[16] *Dublin Evening Post*, 1 March 1865 (cutting in NLI Larcom Papers MS 7514); E. D. Steele, 'Ireland and the Empire in the 1860s', *Historical Journal*, 11 (1968), 77; Northcote to Disraeli, 5 March 1870, BL Northcote Papers Add. MS 50016.

the rights and private privileges of the possessors of land must cede to the wants and advantages of the people at large'.[17]

Northcote is indeed especially interesting because he was one of the few leading politicians for whom clear evidence exists of engagement with contemporary thinking about the nature and growth of primitive and advanced societies, as his attendance at the Social Science Association indicates. On the Liberal side, Spencer's appearance in 1869 at the Statistical Society in Dublin hints at similar interests on the part of an otherwise singularly unintellectual politician, while Gladstone's bouts of intense and focused reading in Irish history reveal the *modus operandi* of a political mind of unusual power characteristically seeking support for dramatic practical initiatives from conventions to which both he and others had long subscribed. While Northcote's approach—like Gladstone's—was that of an intellectual (something he was nothing like so successful in disguising as the equally cerebral Salisbury), Sir Michael Hicks Beach, not only a future Tory cabinet minister but a future chief secretary, approached the matter of Ireland from a stance of visceral distaste for Irish landowners, a distaste shared by many leading politicians of the time. Coming from such an angle, he had little hesitation in drawing clear distinctions between England and Ireland, distinctions that unambiguously implied that legislation should be closely aligned to national circumstances, an approach that Isaac Butt, the first leader of the Home Rule Party, gratefully described as involving serious 'efforts to adapt the Irish Government to the wishes of the Irish people'.[18]

II

To what extent such attitudes grew out of the dynamics of practical government or out of broad adjustments in contemporary thinking about the historical sociology of nations and states is not easy to determine. Certainly the input of economists and social thinkers is difficult to pin down beyond a realization that at least some politicians were increasingly prepared to dip into the intellectual bran tubs of the time in order to shore up arguments in favour of Anglo-Irish differentiation. And there can be little doubt that throughout the 1860s and 1870s once-dominant utilitarian and universalist modes of thought were being superseded by a broadly historicist narrative according to which cultural and economic phenomena are seen as historically determined, with every period best understood without the 'artificial' imposition of

[17] Parl. Deb. 3: cxc. 1669 (13 March 1868).
[18] Ibid. ccxxiii. 209 (22 March 1875), ccxxvii. 783 (23 February 1876), ccxxx. 744 (30 June 1876).

absolute or eternal systems of value. From this it was a short step to an insistence that societies undergo change in individually timed stages and at unequal speeds, and that such 'organic' developments meant that different laws, different values, and different approaches to social order are, at any one time, appropriate to different places and civilizations. In other words, what was suitable for England was by no means necessarily suitable for Ireland or, indeed, India. Much of this grew out of the 'great mid-Victorian reception of German scholarship' and goes back at least to the views of the Grimm brothers to the effect that, just as a language (for example, German, then the tongue of a people without a state) has its own internal form and logic, so do societies and communities, with the result that laws cannot successfully be imposed upon them from the outside. Closer to hand was the impact of Sir Henry Maine and various English practitioners of historical jurisprudence whose influence quickly spread to the world of political economy.[19] The immediate effect was to rehabilitate customary and collective norms at the expense of the contractual and individual. In the specific case of Ireland this produced a new interest in 'ancient' texts such as the Brehon Laws, which, in turn, generated a certain validation of existing peasant claims to a continuing 'ownership' of the land—claims formerly seen as at best romantic waffle, at worst revolutionary communism.

Irish intellectuals who had formerly supported universalist assimilationism now moved towards the new historicism. Although the Statistical Society in Dublin held firm to mid-century truths until the late 1860s, cracks had begun to appear before this, with its vice-president announcing in 1865 that 'our affairs' should not be 'transacted merely according to the abstract views of philosophical thinkers, even though they have had prosperous application in countries which have reached a different stage of progress'.[20] The most important Irish economist to emerge in this period, T. E. Cliffe Leslie, began to advocate policies that would have been anathema a decade earlier: legislative interference to give security to small occupiers (a recognition of Ireland's 'primitive' social and economic circumstances) and state assistance to help them purchase their holdings.[21] Earlier still J. E. Cairnes, professor of political economy in Galway and from 1866 at University College London, in decisively rejecting English agricultural models as suitable for Ireland, had insisted that 'English theories' were fundamentally at variance with 'Irish ideas', that, indeed, English doctrines of 'open competition and contract' should be closely confined to their native

---

[19] C. Dewey, 'Celtic Agrarian Legislation and the Celtic Revival: Historicist Implications of Gladstone's Irish and Scottish Land Acts 1870–1886', *Past & Present*, 64 (1974), 30–70, at 36. I owe much to this brilliant article.

[20] M. E. Daly, *The Spirit of Earnest Inquiry: The Statistical and Social Inquiry Society of Ireland 1847–1997* (Dublin, 1997), 2, 32–4; *Journal of the Statistical and Social Inquiry Society of Ireland*, 4 (1864–8), 235.

[21] See Cliffe Leslie, 'The State of Ireland, 1867' in Leslie, *Land Systems and Industrial Economy* (London, 1870), 5–33.

heath. Instead he demanded that the state should intervene actively in matters of Irish land and thus exercise 'large supervision and control'.[22]

The Irish Comtean Henry Dix Hutton shared an increasing enthusiasm for economic relativism with his fellow members of the Statistical Society when arguing that a single template of laissez-faire notions should never be applied willy-nilly to societies of widely different circumstances: 'English land tenure ... does not furnish a universal standard ... There is no country to which English tenure ... is less applicable than Ireland.'[23] Most remarkable of all in this respect was W. N. Hancock (joint editor of the Brehon Tracts), who, having been a passionate critic of tenant right (that is, Hibernian notions of tenure) before 1865, became an equally passionate advocate of the custom thereafter. The remarkableness lay not simply in his shift in opinion but in the fact that he is known to have influenced Gladstone both in this respect and with regard to other Irish policies such as those relating to agrarian violence.[24]

Although much attention has been given to the role of John Stuart Mill in these matters, his actual influence on political decision-making was never remarkable, despite his membership of the House of Commons between 1865 and 1868. Indeed, his crablike progress as to suitable remedies for Irish discontents confused fellow intellectuals and men of affairs more or less equally. While in parliament he made one striking speech on 17 May 1866, the impact of which was almost certainly blunted by widespread distaste for his windy and preachy tones.[25] Attacking the question in reverse, Mill insisted that 'Irish circumstances and Irish ideas as to social and agricultural economy are the general ideas and circumstances of the human race; it is English circumstances and English ideas that are peculiar'. 'Ireland', he concluded, 'is in the main stream of human existence and human feeling and opinion; it is England that is in one of the lateral channels.'[26]

However, Mill's practical recommendations in the 1865 edition of *Principles of Political Economy*—land reclamation assisted by emigration—were put forward so hesitantly as to be virtually invisible.[27] When, therefore, his

[22] T. A. Boylan and T. P. Foley, *Political Economy and Colonial Ireland: The Propagation and Ideological Function of Economic Discourse in the Nineteenth Century* (London, 1992), 156–7.

[23] R. D. Collison Black, *Economic Thought and the Irish Question 1817–1870* (Cambridge, 1960), 57; also H. D. Hutton, 'Tenures and Land Legislation in British India', *Journal of the Statistical and Social Inquiry Society of Ireland*, 5 (1869–70), 152, 158.

[24] Dewey, 'Celtic Agrarian Legislation', 45; K. T. Hoppen, *Elections, Politics, and Society in Ireland 1832–1885* (Oxford, 1984), 375–6.

[25] B. L. Kinzer, *England's Disgrace? J. S. Mill and the Irish Question* (Toronto, 2001), 166–7; A. Lang, *Life, Letters, and Diaries of Sir Stafford Northcote, First Earl of Iddesleigh*, new edn (Edinburgh, 1891), 143: 'His speech ... was very ineffective both in manner and matter ... [he] has acquired the nickname of the Windmill.'

[26] Parl. Deb. 3: clxxxiii. 1088 (17 May 1866).

[27] Kinzer, *England's Disgrace?*, 171. See also Mill to Cairnes, 8 November 1864, *Collected Works of John Stuart Mill*, ed. F. E. Mineka and Others, 33 vols (Toronto, 1963–1991), xv. 965.

dramatic pamphlet *England and Ireland* appeared in 1868 with its demands that Ireland be treated on its own terms, the violence of the language (and the reactions to it) made the measures proposed seem more extreme than they actually were.[28]

Indeed, without much benefit from Mill's pamphlet, Gladstone was already in early 1868 convincing himself that delay on Irish reforms was impossible and that, with regard to land, matters had pushed well beyond 'the stage of compensation for improvement into the very dangerous ... one of fixity of tenure in some form or other'.[29] Others too had become no less convinced that significant changes with regard to governing Ireland were demanding urgent attention. In August 1866 one of the members for Nottingham ('a considerable employer of labour' in Ireland) had attacked those who thought that institutions operating in England 'ought also to be fitted for a people different altogether in race, in condition, and in religion'. Eighteen months later another English MP, the son of the Duke of Newcastle, argued that the only way to preserve the Union was to ensure that the affairs of each of 'the three kingdoms ... were managed according to their own wishes', while the former chief secretary, Edward Horsman, denounced those who simply wanted to force Ireland into 'conformity with English laws and customs, and feelings, and even prejudices and requirements'.[30]

III

When Gladstone became prime minister for the first time in December 1868, two Irish issues stood at the forefront of his agenda: disestablishing the Anglican Church of Ireland and land reform. Disestablishment was tackled first because it was the easier project, a matter of pragmatic *Realpolitik*, with the added bonus that it was the only major issue capable of uniting virtually all sections of the Liberal Party.[31] More generally, it also possessed those qualities politicians crave: symbolic importance and practical insignificance. While still in opposition Gladstone had confidently taken up the issue in the early months of 1868, in effect projecting himself as already somehow in overall control of official business. While the final legislation possessed the great advantage in the prime minister's eyes of not costing money—indeed some

[28] E. D. Steele, 'J. S. Mill and the Irish Question', *Historical Journal*, 13 (1970), 216–36, 419–50.

[29] Gladstone to Clarendon, 17 February 1868, Bodl. Clarendon Papers c.523.

[30] Parl. Deb. 3: clxxxiv. 1957 and 1961 (2 August 1866: Osborne), cxc. 1332 (10 March 1868: Clinton) and 1472 (12 March 1868: Horsman).

[31] Gladstone to Bishop Hinds, 31 December 1868, J. Morley, *The Life of William Ewart Gladstone*, 3 vols (London, 1903), ii. 259.

money was actually saved—the Church (whose adherents constituted only a tenth of Ireland's population) obtained rather better terms than its feeble claims merited: some £16 million was taken away and some £10 million given back, the difference (in a distinctly revolutionary move) being made available for 'non-religious' purposes such as the relief of poverty, agricultural improvement, higher education, and the like.[32]

Gladstone did not hide the fact that his disestablishment legislation marked a clear shift in the approach to be adopted when dealing with Irish affairs. Not only did he support it on the grounds that no small minority should possess 'the national endowments of the country', but because there was, in his opinion, absolutely no prospect that anything similar would ever cross the sea to England. 'We must', as he put it, 'deal with this Irish question as an Irish question' and not constantly feel that Irish precedents might provide comfort for those hoping that similar policies would eventually be applied in England or Scotland. For W. E. Forster (a future chief secretary), disestablishment showed, above all, how important it was that the legislation for 'each country should be in accordance with the feelings and the interests of the country affected'.[33] And other Liberal leaders agreed. Kimberley thought a continuation of church establishment in Ireland 'contrary both to justice and [to] policy', while the emollient Granville (rather than the nervously exhausted Gladstone) actually undertook the negotiations for a final settlement.[34]

Although, unsurprisingly, there were some Tory diehards with regard to disestablishment, notably Gathorne Hardy, who fulminated about ruling 'on Irish principles' and putting 'Ireland on a different footing from England', few Tories, from Disraeli downwards, made urgent efforts to defend the Church of Ireland, and certainly there was widespread agreement that no pledges should be given for 'maintaining absolutely unchanged' the original 'state of ecclesiastical affairs'.[35] As one Conservative backbencher noted, the bill marked 'an entirely new mode of dealing with the Irish question', a mode that had been summarized in the formula 'We must legislate for Ireland according to Irish ideas'. Or, as Gladstone, the eternal optimist, put it, while the bill might indeed play to Irish ideas, 'its general purpose and substance' were designed to give to the Union 'those roots which unfortunately it has never yet adequately struck

---

[32] K. T. Hoppen, *The Mid-Victorian Generation 1846–1886* (Oxford, 1998), 594–5.

[33] *The Times*, 20 December 1867; Parl. Deb. 3: cxcii. 806 and 784 (22 May 1868: Gladstone and Forster).

[34] Kimberley to Gladstone, 12 February 1866, Bodl. Kimberley Papers MS Eng.c.4041; Matthew, *Gladstone 1809–1874*, 194.

[35] Parl. Deb. 3: cxciv. 2071 (23 March 1869: Hardy); Disraeli to Derby, 4 March 1868, L[iverpool] R[ecord] O[ffice] Derby Papers 146/4; R. Shannon, *The Age of Disraeli, 1868–1881: The Rise of Tory Democracy* (London, 1992), 39; *Disraeli, Derby and the Conservative Party: Journals and Memoirs of Edward Henry, Lord Stanley 1849–1869*, ed. J. Vincent (Hassocks, 1978), 331.

in the hearts and affections of the people'.[36] This hope—that deliberately separate and tailor-made legislation would somehow, by mechanisms rarely specified, create closer and more amicable feelings—remained henceforth as central to Gladstone's policies as it recurrently proved incapable of yielding the expected results.

The other major Irish issue of the time—land reform—possessed 'little of the mandate which it was hard to deny the electorate had conferred upon Irish disestablishment'.[37] It also alarmed many Whigs, was complicated, and required far more in the way of research and enquiry, though these last were always something the prime minister enjoyed. Indeed, it is not entirely fanciful to suggest that it was precisely the need for rapid and suitably angled historical and legal investigation that proved not the least attractive aspect of the matter for Gladstone, a politician for whom dramatic shifts of policy often disguised a good deal of hidden quasi-academic cogitation. Not only that, but—for all the attacks made upon the new land legislation—there can be no doubt that its author always remained something of a devotee of aristocratic and landed society and a believer in the ultimately conservative and preservative nature of his radical reforms (a disposition he shared with contemporaries, most notably Parnell). While still merely contemplating legislation, he had told a Liberal who was soon to be invited into the cabinet of his keen conviction that it was, above all, 'vital not to worry the question, but to do enough to settle it ... [though] it would be an unpardonable error to divest the landlord of his character as a landlord, for with his rights would go the last hope of his performing his duties'. Nor was a later comment that he himself had always been 'a firm believer in the aristocratic principle ... I am an out-and-out *inequalitarian*' ever untrue or, indeed, ever inflexible either.[38]

Always a great bookman, Gladstone now began to read voraciously about Ireland, with (as he put it) the advantage of ignorance and a lack, or so he claimed, of preconceptions.[39] To a substantial degree, his sources were 'historical', such as the writings of W. N. Hancock, who had himself, of course, recently turned a mighty somersault to become a keen supporter of special 'Celtic' legislation with respect to land. It was important, Gladstone now declared, that all his ministerial colleagues should take the same 'large dose of Irish history ... which I have partially drunk myself'. He began to talk of 'old customs', of 'tribal property', of 'historical and traditional rights', not least because such tropes had the effect of hiding potentially radical reforms beneath a reassuringly conservative disguise. And, when eventually introducing the bill

[36] Parl. Deb. 3: cxcvi. 1037–8 (31 May 1869: Butler-Johnstone) and cxciv. 416 (1 March 1869: Gladstone).

[37] Matthew, *Gladstone 1809–1874*, 194.

[38] Gladstone to Halifax, 1 October 1869, B[orthwick] I[institute] Hickleton Papers A/4/88; Morley, *Life of William Ewart Gladstone*, ii. 582.

[39] Collison Black, *Economic Thought and the Irish Question*, 62–3.

in February 1870, he defended its provisions in large part on the grounds that they chimed in with 'old Irish ideas and customs' that had never been 'supplanted except by the rude hand of violence'.[40]

It was an approach to which Gladstone turned again and again in future years, notably when cogitating about the possibility of Home Rule and in late 1885 ordering even colleagues whose political antennae were strikingly different from his own to 'inform' themselves 'on certain historical cases' in order to follow his own example and acquire 'a historical and therefore a comprehensive view of the Irish question'.[41] His other main line of attack involved the deployment of comparative analogies. When thinking about Home Rule, he drew the cabinet's attention to 'the prolonged experience of Norway (I might perhaps mention Finland) and the altogether new experience of Austro-Hungary'. In 1869–70 he mounted an extensive official inquiry from British diplomats abroad 'concerning the tenure of land in Europe', a project that took so long that it probably had little effect on anything but the bolstering of his own preconceptions on the matter.[42]

The crucial outside influence on the legislation of 1870 turned out to be a short book by George Campbell (an Indian administrator and judge just returned from a visit to Ireland) entitled *The Irish Land*, first encountered by the prime minister on 11 August 1869. Its straightforward sentences helped to concentrate a mind prepared, but perhaps still somewhat confused, by the writings of more sophisticated intellectuals. Above all, it appealed because of Campbell's forceful advocacy of a policy that, unlike some alternatives, had absolutely no implications for the situation in other parts of the United Kingdom. Thus, while any simple change in the law of contract possessed clear 'imperial' resonances, Campbell's solution of extending the existing tradition of Ulster tenant-right (that is, the sale of the right of occupancy) as a means of recognizing customary rather than contractual land relationships in Ireland fitted splendidly into Gladstone's by now firmly anti-assimilationist mentality. 'The English system of annual tenancy with landlords' improvements', Gladstone now concluded, was 'so remote from Irish ideas and practice ... that it can make no special demands on us'.[43]

[40] Gladstone to Argyll, 8 January 1870, BL Gladstone Papers Add. MS 44101; Parl. Deb. 3: cxcix. 340 (15 February 1870).

[41] BL Gladstone Papers Add. MSS 44770–1 (1885–7) show evidence of extensive reading about the Union and the Irish Parliament; to Hartington, 11 September 1885, Ch[atsworth] H[ouse] Devonshire Papers 340.1808.

[42] Gladstone to Hartington, 8 September 1885, ibid. 340.1804 and Hartington's reply, 10 September 1885, BL Gladstone Papers Add. MS 44148; *Part I: Reports from Her Majesty's Representatives respecting the Tenure of Land in the Several Countries of Europe: 1869*; also *Part II: 1869–70*, H[ouse of] C[ommons Paper] 1870 (C.66 and C.75), lxvii. 1–930; E. D. Steele, *Irish Land and British Politics: Tenant-Right and Nationality 1865–1870* (Cambridge, 1974), 102–4.

[43] Matthew, *Gladstone 1809–1874*, 195; Gladstone to Argyll, 24 January 1870, BL Gladstone Add. MS 44101.

While, therefore, the Disestablishment Act had constituted the first shot in the campaign, the Land Act marked the real beginning of the process of Irish differentiation that was to dominate the next fifty years. Under the eyes of eternity, its actual provisions were modest enough, but the rights it conferred upon tenants were to lead to greater things: compensation for improvements made without the landlord's consent, restrictions on the power to evict, statutory endorsement of the right of tenants to sell 'interests' in their holdings, rent controls, and much more besides.

Given the Act's comparative mildness, especially with respect to the exclusion from its provisions of tenants evicted for arrears of rent, it is unsurprising that Irish agriculturalists soon began to demand more. Especially notable was how, within a very few years, farmers of all kinds started to rally to the cause of Home Rule candidates in both rural and urban constituencies.[44] At the same time, the increasingly political tone adopted by the various Farmers' Clubs throughout the country helped to lead the rural tenantry into a new agrarian agitation. Societies and clubs for farmers had, of course, a long history, but until the late 1860s they had been little more than social organizations concerned with conviviality and improvements in agricultural practice. The 1870s, however, witnessed a notable increase in both their number and politicization with the result that demands for further land reform grew and prepared the ground for the more dramatic politico-agrarian alliance of Davitt and Parnell.[45]

In the light of these later developments, it is unsurprising that British politicians subsequently regarded the 1870 Act as furnishing the thin end of a wedge that was eventually to prise open the concessions and innovations that were to follow. Of course, even at the time it generated a certain amount of both practical and ideological opposition.[46] Remarkable, however, is how rapidly this subsided. Robert Lowe quickly accepted that the Act trod 'exclusively on Irish ground' and harboured no implications for wider initiatives. And, while some MPs bemoaned the loss of what had once been universal verities, nearly all recognized that the old-style science of political economy had simply 'broken down', at least as far as the world of practical affairs was concerned.[47] The only significant figure never to accept the new departure was the eighth Duke of Argyll, who, having joined Gladstone's first and second

---

[44] *Galway County Election Petition*, HC 1872 (241-I), xlviii, 627–32, 815; J. Elland to I. Butt, 7 January 1874, NLI Butt Papers MS 8696; Hoppen, *Elections, Politics, and Society in Ireland*, 327, 468–9.

[45] S. Clark, *Social Origins of the Irish Land War* (Princeton, 1979), 214–21; *Nation*, 30 January 1875.

[46] Parl. Deb. 3: cc. 1984–5 (28 April 1870: Montagu) and ccii. 56 (14 June 1870: Lifford).

[47] Ibid. cc. 1200–1 (4 April 1870); 'The Parliamentary Diaries of Sir John Trelawny, 1868–73', ed. T. A. Jenkins, Royal Historical Society *Camden Miscellany* Fifth Series, iii (1994), 389 (5 April 1870).

cabinets, resigned in 1881 over the issue of Irish land and thereafter developed increasingly extreme views about Celtic history, efficient farming, and giving in to agrarian radicalism.[48] Salisbury in 1873—his leadership of the Tory Party and prime ministership still in the future—was no less furious but adopted a very different and more effective line. What was done was done. It now remained to find the best and most truly conservative means by which to live with and perhaps even defuse Gladstone's revolutionary Act.[49]

As time went on it rapidly became accepted wisdom that the Land Act of 1870 at once reflected and helped to create an important change in the Anglo-Irish political weather, its operative mildness overshadowed by widespread perceptions of portentousness. Already in 1876 the fifteenth Earl of Derby (whose restless changes of allegiance found him at various times in cabinets led by his father, by Disraeli, and by Gladstone before ultimately becoming Liberal Unionist leader in the Lords) was denominating it 'the one really revolutionary measure which parliament in my time has passed'. Spencer, a very different man, regarded 1870 as marking the watershed between an English-oriented approach to Irish legislation and one in which policies were increasingly based—'and there has been a necessity for it—on the customs and laws which prevailed in Ireland'.[50] And it was a point of view adopted, propagated, and insisted upon by men who agreed on little else. By 1907 the Marquess of Crewe, a former viceroy, was even disinterring ancient arguments and reminding colleagues how in the 1830s the then dominant policy of assimilation had unthinkingly dismissed the percipient and Hiberno-centric conclusions of the Whately Commission on poverty in Ireland.[51] Indeed, the usages deployed by Gladstone in 1870 eventually came to constitute a kind of Hibernian source kitty from which items could be plucked when needed to bulk out arguments in favour of land reform or Home Rule itself. Not that Gladstone's approach, whether in 1870, 1881, or 1886, was ever an exclusively historicist one, his 'naturally syncretic mind' resembling nothing so much as 'a palimpsest on which the development of Victorian thought was fruitfully engraved'.[52] Yet, not only had he hit upon novel and powerful ways of engaging with Irish problems; he infected a wider political world with an outlook it might otherwise have taken longer to adopt. Already in 1881 the

[48] Argyll to Gladstone, 4 and 7 January 1870, BL Gladstone Papers Add. MS 44101, 26 December 1880, ibid., Add. MS 56446; to Cowper, 15 July 1880, K. C. Cowper, *Earl Cowper KG: A Memoir* (privately printed, 1913), 379.

[49] Salisbury, 'The Emergence of the Radicals', *Quarterly Review*, 135/270 (1873), 564; also Parl. Deb. 4: li. 864 (23 July 1897).

[50] *A Selection from the Diaries of Edward Henry Stanley, 15th Earl of Derby (1826–93) between September 1869 and March 1878*, ed. J. Vincent, Royal Historical Society Camden Fifth Series, iv (1994), 316 (4 August 1876); Parl. Deb. 4: xxviii. 654–5 (13 August 1894).

[51] Parl. Deb. 4: clxxviii. 1117 (22 July 1907).

[52] Dewey, 'Celtic Agrarian Legislation', 59.

Bessborough Commission examining the 'workings of the Landlord and Tenant (Ireland) Act of 1870' fell smoothly into line when concluding that 'a living tradition of possessory right, such as belonged, in more primitive ages of society, to the status of men who toiled the soil', still vigorously coloured the Irish agrarian mind.[53] By then Gladstone seems to have succeeded in more or less corralling his leading acolytes—as well as some Tories—into seeing things in much the same way: that policy must be based on restoring 'ancient rights' flowing from 'native' Irish sources, because this would render any resulting legislation supportive of traditional values, of landlords, of a stable social order, and (so he and others fondly hoped) of the Union itself.[54]

IV

If the 1860s and 1870s saw an unambiguous abandonment of certain mid-century ways of dealing with Ireland, in some other respects the views of ministers and politicians changed hardly at all. Thus, while the identification and selection of 'remedies' were no longer based on the assumption that what was good for one part of the United Kingdom must automatically be good for the others, the age-old conviction that Ireland was totally unlike England—distinct, different, idiosyncratic, abnormal, at times incomprehensible—remained almost entirely intact. What had changed was not, in London eyes, the nature of the Irish disease, but how best it might be treated, perhaps even cured. Difference, once something to be eradicated, now became something to acknowledge, work with, and utilize for the good of all—on both sides of the Irish Sea.

Whereas, in the 1840s and 1850s, laws had received support because they were designed to bring an end to Irish particularism, in the half-century from 1870 the very opposite applied. Politicians fell over themselves to emphasize that Irish problems demanded Irish solutions, almost as if that was in itself a complete and overarching policy capable of rendering all kinds of special treatment effective and universally acceptable. But exactly how far should differentiation be acknowledged, even encouraged? Was this perhaps a road with no ending, a road that might lead towards and even into a landscape

---

[53] *Report of Her Majesty's Commissioners of Inquiry into the Working of the Landlord and Tenant (Ireland) Act, 1870*, HC 1881 [C.2779], xviii. 6–8.

[54] K. T. Hoppen, 'Gladstone, Salisbury and the End of Irish Assimilationism', in M. E. Daly and Hoppen (eds), *Gladstone: Ireland and Beyond* (Dublin, 2011), 53; Gladstone, 'Further Notes and Queries on the Irish Demand', *Contemporary Review*, 53 (1881), 321, and *The Irish Question ... with an Addendum* (London, [1886]), 24–5; Parl. Deb. 3: cciv. 1080 (8 April 1886); Gladstone to Hartington, 11 September 1885, Hammond, *Gladstone and the Irish Nation*, 406.

where distinctiveness might become inexorably transformed into something more extreme, something destructive of the Union itself and of the United Kingdom polity that had come into being because of it?

In the short and medium term there can be no doubt that the acknowledgement of Irish difference was now made to stand at the centre of law-making and government generally. At times it came to seem as if many in London no longer gave much sustained attention to Ireland at all beyond uttering mantras about the importance of governing according to Irish ideas. By 1887 Gladstone was even (seriously) repeating what Peel had put forward as a joke in the very different context of 1826—namely, the insight 'that the mass of Irishmen are so intensely Irish', a kind of summation—in part amusing, in part contemptuous—of how Ireland was perceived throughout the Union period as a whole.[55]

Those lining up to add their voices to the growing chorus in favour of Gladstone's initiative in actively acknowledging the Irish difference included men of all political persuasions: Tories as different as Iddesleigh (formerly Northcote), Carnarvon, Walter Long (up to a point), Arthur and Gerald Balfour, Wyndham, Dudley, Hicks Beach;[56] Liberal Unionists such as Goschen, Joseph Chamberlain, and Lansdowne;[57] Liberals such as Cowper, Harcourt, Denman, Ripon, Crewe, and Haldane,[58] in addition to those already mentioned such as Spencer, Kimberley, Fortescue, and indeed many others. Even exotics took up the cry, men such as the second Baron Ashbourne (aka Liam Mac Giolla Bhride) when appearing kilted in the House of Lords and addressing peers in Irish, his words dutifully recorded (though without the appropriate

---

[55] 'Notes and Queries on the Irish Demand', *Nineteenth-Century*, 21 (1887), 171; Peel to Goulburn, 29 September 1826, S[urrey] H[istory] C[entre] Goulburn Papers 304/37.

[56] Iddesleigh to Carnarvon, 7 September 1885, A. Hardinge, *The Life and Letters of Howard Molyneux Herbert, Fourth Earl of Carnarvon*, 3 vols (London, 1925), iii. 191; Carnarvon to Ponsonby, 17 October 1885, T[he] N[ational] A[rchives] Carnarvon Papers PRO 30/6/53; Long to A. Chamberlain, 29 September 1906, B[irmingham] U[niversity] A. Chamberlain Papers AC7/4/9; Parl. Deb. 3: cccxxv. 503 and ccclii. 761 (25 April 1888 and 16 April 1891: A. J. Balfour); *The Times*, 8 April 1897 (G. Balfour); Wyndham to A. Chamberlain, 4 January 1903 [*recte* 1904], BU A. Chamberlain Papers AC16/3/35, and Wyndham to Frewen, 14 October 1903, *Letters of George Wyndham 1877–1913*, ed. G. Wyndham, 2 vols (privately printed: Edinburgh, 1915), ii. 84; Redmond to Dudley, 29 May 1905, NLI Redmond Papers MS 15186, and Dudley to W. Churchill, 1 November 1905, C[hurchill] C[ollege] C[ambridge] Churchill Papers CHAR2/23/36–7; Hicks Beach to Salisbury, 28 July 1886 G[loucestershire] R[ecord] O[ffice] St Aldwyn Papers D2455/PCC/31.

[57] Parl. Deb. 3: ccciv. 1462–4 (13 April 1886: Goschen); *Mr Chamberlain's Speeches*, ed. W. Boyd, 2 vols (London, 1914), i. 238 (25 October 1881, given while still a Liberal); Lansdowne to A. Chamberlain, BU A. Chamberlain Papers AC11/1/56.

[58] Cowper to Spencer, 8 March 1881, Cowper, *Earl Cowper*, 480; Harcourt to Morley, 13 December 1886, Bodl. Harcourt Papers 15; Parl. Deb. 5 (Lords): i. 47 (17 February 1909: Denman); Parl. Deb. 4: clxxxiii. 38 (29 January 1908: Ripon); Parl. Deb. 5 (Lords): xiii. 423–4 (27 January 1913: Crewe); Parl. Deb. 4: liii. 791 (16 February 1898: Haldane).

superscripts) by Hansard's stenographers.[59] Indeed, so pervasive had this kind of thinking—this way of 'solving' the Irish question—become by the first decades of the twentieth century that few remained immune to its charms. By 1907 even the King's Speech at the opening of parliament included a phrase (penned, it seems, by Redmond himself) to the effect that London would now always 'govern according to Irish ideas'. As Augustine Birrell, the chief secretary, insouciantly put it in 1911, any fool could tell that Ireland was in all respects 'different': 'When you land in Kingstown, you know it—you know it in two minutes.' His successor, the Tory Henry Duke, almost fell over himself to tell parliament that Ireland 'must have separate and Irish treatment ... that principle ... will be absolutely recognized'.[60]

In September 1887 a future leader of the Southern Irish Unionists, owner of large estates in Surrey and Cork, and at the time Financial Secretary at the War Office, produced a memorandum in which he noted that, while full Anglo-Irish assimilation might have worked immediately after the Union, its subsequent implementation had always been doomed to fail, with the result that 'of late especially the tendency has been to legislate for Ireland according to Irish ideas, with the effect of making the contrast between English and Irish institutions more striking than ever'.[61] When looking at Ireland, noted Lord Carlingford (the former Chichester Fortescue) at much the same time, one should 'forget England and Scotland and ... think, if a comparison is to be made, of ... India'.[62] In similar vein the Gladstonian MP and eminent scientist Sir Lyon Playfair pointed to the failures that had flown from the policy of trying to govern Ireland according to English ideas: 'we have tried to anglicize the country, and now her suppressed nationality is the main spring of our troubles.'[63] A quarter-century later the former viceroy Lord Crewe catalogued the harvest of moving from English to Irish 'ideas': 'a different marriage law, a different system of education, a totally different system of police and of the administration of justice, an altogether different land system, [an increasingly] different Poor Law, a totally different licensing system, and different enactments on such subjects as lunacy, industrial schools, fisheries, and I know not how many more'.[64]

---

[59] Parl. Deb. 5 (Lords): xxx. 481 (27 June 1918). The translation would be: 'We have Irish in Ireland ... I would prefer to speak no other language but I fear the majority [a nice touch!] of you would not understand me. If you did understand I would continue to plead this story all night.' I am grateful to Nicholas Canny for help in this matter.
[60] L. Ó Broin, *The Chief Secretary: Augustine Birrell in Ireland* (London, 1969), 18; Parl. Deb. 5 (Commons): xxi. 1167 (15 February 1911) and civ. 278 (12 March 1918).
[61] Memorandum by W. St J. Brodrick (later Lord Midleton), 30 September 1887, BU J. Chamberlain Papers JC8/4/3/22.
[62] Parl. Deb. 3: cclxxxix. 380 (16 June 1884). See S. B. Cook, *Imperial Affinities: Nineteenth-Century Analogies and Exchanges between India and Ireland* (New Delhi, 1993).
[63] Parl. Deb. 3: cccv. 1366 (18 May 1886) and cccxiii. 916 (14 April 1887).
[64] Parl. Deb. 5 (Lords): xiii. 423–4 (27 January 1913).

V

From the mid-1830s to the mid-1860s—that is, during the high enthusiasm for assimilation—coercive legislation for Ireland was (with the exception of the—in truth tolerably mild—reaction to Smith O'Brien's Rising of 1848), if not entirely abandoned, notably less frequent, less widespread, and less severe than it had been in the decades immediately after the Union. However, from the late 1860s things begin to go into reverse.[65] With the Fenian Rising of 1867, with bombing campaigns in Britain, with intense (if uneven) agrarian violence from the 1870s onwards, the nature and severity of the measures adopted by governments after 1868, while obviously driven by short-term events, were not unconnected with the abandonment of assimilation and its related imperative of maintaining broadly similar systems of law and order throughout the United Kingdom as a whole.

The execution in November 1867 of three Fenians—the 'Manchester Martyrs'—marked the implementation of a very different penal policy from that deployed after 1848, one as readily adopted by Liberal as by Conservative administrations. Two years later, Fortescue as chief secretary was telling Gladstone that 'Fenianism and Ribbonism' (the latter a long-standing form of violent protest) could not be checked by 'a constitution which is framed for Yorkshire and the Lothians' and should be met with 'stern measures of repression accompanying strong measures of redress',[66] words that might well have become the motto of virtually every administration that was to govern Ireland over the next fifty years. From the opposition benches, Salisbury, having displayed some surprisingly beneficent attitudes towards Ireland in the 1860s, was now beginning the process of disguising what was in truth a remarkably similar approach with respect to (at least certain) 'Irish ideas' behind a stance of graceless—but in party terms rewarding—nonchalance typified by his remarks at a Royal Academy exhibition to the effect that Lady Butler's painting *An Eviction in Ireland* was a thing of such 'breezy beauty' as almost to make 'him wish he could take part in an eviction himself'.[67] Already by the early 1870s (if not before) Salisbury had come to the conclusion that the Irish were violent primitives best tamed by a judicious mixture of coercive sticks and occasional reformist carrots carefully calibrated to meet specifically Irish needs. 'You are dealing', he told his fellow peers, 'with a population of a lower civilization in many points than your own ... In this country you are content ... only to guide; in Ireland it is essential that you should govern.' Not only was this so, but it was also important to remember

---

[65] V. Crossman, *Politics, Law and Order in Nineteenth-Century Ireland* (Dublin, 1996), 202–30; R. B. O'Brien, *Dublin Castle and the Irish People*, 2nd edn (London, 1912), 59–61.

[66] Fortescue to Gladstone, 30 November 1869, BL Gladstone Papers Add. MS 44122.

[67] [Lady] E. Butler, *An Autobiography* (London, 1922), 199.

that the British 'system of judicature' was 'framed for the Teutonic stock, and fit for a civilized nation' and thus anything but suitable for 'a Celtic nation, part of which is in the very depths of barbarism ... Trial by jury has failed in Ireland, let us see if India or the Colonies can provide an alternative.'[68]

At first Disraeli's Tory administration of 1874–80 (in which Salisbury served as Indian and Foreign Secretary) had a fairly easy time with respect to Irish unrest. By 1879, however, the Land War in Ireland was in full swing and prominent Liberals were beginning to convince themselves that, should the election due in 1880 produce the expected Liberal majority, Irish coercion must be among the first legislative priorities.[69] Within months of the Liberal victory Spencer, speaking with the authority of a former lord lieutenant and now a member of the cabinet, visited Dublin, found that the new viceroy (Lord Cowper) did not 'inspire confidence', decided that coercion of some kind was necessary, and, on his return, was surprised that Gladstone himself was much 'less vehement against strong measures for Ireland than I expected'.[70] W. E. Forster, the new chief secretary, was even hotter for a forceful and un-English approach and keen to allow 'the Irish Executive to shut up any person they consider dangerous'.[71]

Hartington, who had served as chief secretary between 1871 and 1874 and was now in the cabinet, where he disguised strong views behind a laconic exterior, wanted immediate coercion and railed against colleagues who sustained 'sentimental and illogical objections to the use of force'. For a time Gladstone agonized, intertwining phrases like 'when the time comes' with talk of 'defending proprietary rights without mawkish susceptibility' against the agrarian unrest now taking hold of Ireland, and notably so in the West not hitherto prominent in that respect.[72] However, after a brief and characteristic interval of hand-wringing, he soon came round, as Morley reported to Chamberlain after a dinner with the prime minister, who had taken him aside 'to a corner and revealed his coercion, much as a man might say (in confidence) that he found himself under the painful necessity of slaying his mother. It was downright piteous—his wrung features, his strained gesture, all the other signs of mental perturbation in an intense nature.'[73]

The hand-wringing over, ministers embarked on a bout of coercion enforced with zeal and very effectively combined with the concessions offered in

---

[68] Parl. Deb. 3: cc. 825 (29 March 1870) and ccvi. 32–3 (2 May 1871).

[69] Kimberley to Ponsonby, 30 September 1879, Powell (ed.), *Liberal by Principle: The Politics of John Wodehouse*, 145–8; also to Gladstone, 4 October 1880, ibid. 151.

[70] Spencer to Hartington, 21 and 26 October 1880, ChH Devonshire Papers 340.1027–8; also to Gladstone, 22 November 1880, BL Gladstone Papers Add. MS 44308.

[71] Forster to Gladstone, 25 October 1880, ibid., Add. MS 44157.

[72] Hartington to Gladstone, 15 November and 19 December 1880, ibid., Add. MS 44145; Gladstone to Cowper, 24 November 1880, ibid., Add. MS 56449.

[73] Morley to J. Chamberlain, 31 December 1880, BU J. Chamberlain Papers JC5/54/368.

the Land Act of 1881 (for which, see Chapter 8, Section II). Indeed, Gladstone proved to be 'as ruthless a wielder of power as any contemporary when he saw a necessity or a benefit', his combination of coercion and concession in 1881–2 seriously undermining the impact of the Land League, which was proclaimed illegal in October 1881.[74] The eventual release from jail of its leader, Charles Stewart Parnell, and the so-called Kilmainham Treaty of May 1882, though they forced the arch-coercionist, Forster, to resign, were followed, less than a week later, by the Phoenix Park murders, when a group calling itself the Invincibles killed both the new chief secretary, Lord Frederick Cavendish (who was married to Mrs Gladstone's niece), and Thomas Burke, the under-secretary, near their official residences just outside Dublin. This inevitably led to renewed coercion, now in the increasingly successful hands of Spencer, appointed viceroy for the second time on 3 May and for the next three years the senior figure in Ireland's governing duumvirate, his two chief secretaries, the troubled and ineffective G. O. Trevelyan and the calm and useful Henry Campbell-Bannerman, playing the—now unusual—role of second fiddles to the lord lieutenant.[75] And Spencer—impressively bearded, suspicious of 'ideas', at once ponderous and determined—proved the *beau ideal* of the Irish coercer, though it would be wrong to suppose that his attitude to Irish affairs was determined by little else. Undoubtedly, however, the Prevention of Crime (Ireland) Act, which came into force in July 1882, introduced extremely stringent powers—so stringent, in fact, that not all of them were ever actually employed.[76]

VI

If ever there was a decade that dramatically highlights the policy of treating Ireland differently it was the 1880s, even if the approach adopted was not simply a literal rebirth of repression in the immediately post-Union mode. But, while amelioration was now also on the menu, the coercion employed— whether by Liberal or Conservative governments—left little to the imagination. At Spencer's urging and with Gladstone's approval, a new post of assistant undersecretary for police and crime was established to coordinate and supervise the security organizations in Ireland, a completely new initiative

---

[74] H. C. G. Matthew, *Gladstone 1875–1898* (Oxford, 1995), 198.
[75] J. H. Murphy, *Ireland's Czar: Gladstonian Government and the Lord Lieutenancy of the Red Earl Spencer 1868–86* (Dublin, 2014), 201–8, 237–41, 336–8.
[76] C. Townshend, *Violence in Ireland: Government and Resistance since 1848* (Oxford, 1983), 166, 172–3.

in almost every respect.[77] Spencer briskly admonished cabinet colleagues who expressed doubts about so radical a departure from British norms. For his part, Gladstone almost gloried in the severity of it all, especially when reporting on Irish affairs to the queen, who was told that even the prime minister's 'appetite' for 'coercion' was 'decidedly less' than that of many backbench Liberals.[78] The Liberal cabinet minister most given to verbal rage about Ireland, Sir William Harcourt (who, as Home Secretary, exercised a certain supervision over Irish affairs), seized the opportunity to demand 'the most resolute and sternest determination to enforce the law ... [and] put the iron heel of government on the head of these foul conspiracies'. But Harcourt's bark was always fiercer than his bite, so that, despite later rants to the effect that Cromwell's 'only mistake ... was when he offered [the Irish] the alternative of Connaught', he always calmed down into a sort of sullen acceptance that coercion might prove most effective when matched by concessions to Irish opinion, especially with regard to land.[79] Less carnivorous Liberals, like the future chief secretary, James Bryce, nervously pointed to the fact that 'strong measures were tried in Ireland during the first thirty years of this century; but at the end of the time the condition of Ireland was as bad as before'. Joseph Chamberlain (now in the cabinet) saw the truth of this but percipiently pointed out that, whereas the immediate post-Union period had experienced coercion *tout court*, the 1880s were marked by an attempt, not only to be tough on crime, but also to be tough on its causes, lest England create 'a Poland within four hours of our shores'.[80]

The Conservatives (in power from June 1885 to January 1886 and then from July 1886 to August 1892 and from June 1895 to December 1905), though of course taking a different line with regard to certain (though only certain) Irish matters, differed hardly at all when it came to security issues, with the result that Spencer's role as coercer in chief was smoothly taken over by Arthur Balfour on becoming chief secretary in March 1887.[81] But even for Balfour severe measures with deliberately non-British provisions were almost never

---

[77] *The Red Earl: The Papers of the Fifth Earl Spencer 1835–1910*, ed. P. Gordon, 2 vols, Publications of the Northamptonshire Record Society, xxxi and xxxiv (Northampton, 1981–6), i. 24–5; R. Hawkins, 'Government versus Secret Societies: The Parnell Era', in T. D. Williams (ed.), *Secret Societies in Ireland* (Dublin, 1973), 100–12; Murphy, *Ireland's Czar*, 159–60.

[78] Spencer to Chamberlain, 25 May 1882, BU J. Chamberlain Papers JC8/9/3/10, in reply to Chamberlain's letter of 24 May 1882, ibid., JC8/9/3/9; Gladstone to the Queen, 10 May 1882, TNA CAB 41/16/24; Gladstone to Chamberlain, 8 June 1882, Bodl. Harcourt Papers 8.

[79] Harcourt to Gladstone, 9 July 1882, Bodl. Harcourt Papers 8; to Spencer, 2 January 1883, ibid. 41; Lewis Harcourt's Journal for 14 January 1886, ibid. 376; Parl. Deb. 3: cclxix. 463 (11 May 1882); also Trevelyan to Hartington, 21 January 1883, ChH Devonshire Papers 340.1312; Hartington to Granville, 25 January 1883, ibid. 340.1315.

[80] Parl. Deb. 3: cclxix. 977–8 (18 May 1882: Bryce) and cclxxvi. 803 (23 February 1883: Chamberlain).

[81] C. B. Shannon, *Arthur J. Balfour and Ireland 1874–1922* (Washington, 1988), 33–44; L. P. Curtis Jr, *Coercion and Conciliation in Ireland 1880–1892* (Princeton, 1963), 174–215.

(as they often had been in the early nineteenth century) merely worthwhile on their own account, but necessary to secure conditions in which it might prove possible 'to settle the land question' and other matters besides.[82] Even so, the Criminal Law and Procedure (Ireland) Act of 1887 was certainly a very drastic piece of legislation, marking as it did the abandonment of the long-standing convention by which coercive laws were always 'temporary' and required regular parliamentary renewal. The 1887 act incorporated a clause whereby all or any of its (potentially very severe) provisions could be brought into force simply by the lord lieutenant declaring any district or districts 'disturbed'—a mechanism invoked with particular frequency after 1917. But, while this was certainly dramatic, novel, and un-British, in many other respects Balfour's approach was almost identical to that adopted by the Liberals between 1880 and 1885. His chief success lay in putting some (not very lasting) backbone into the landlord class and in 'allowing his own party and their allies to feel justified in rejecting Nationalist demands as emanating from a small group of self-serving and power-hungry individuals prepared to use any means to gain their objectives'.[83]

What the actions of Spencer and Balfour mainly achieved was to inject into the establishment mind—and not least that of Dublin Castle—the belief that severe coercion was both an acceptable and a potentially successful way of dealing with Irish discontents. Although Balfour undoubtedly contained and even temporarily defeated the land agitation of the late-1880s, renewed outbreaks during the 1890s, the activities of the United Irish League founded in 1898, and the so-called Ranch War of 1906–9 (aimed at large graziers rather than at traditional landlords) vividly demonstrate the limits of the 'approach repressive'.[84] And, while clearly the effects of the First World War, the rising of 1916, and the collapse of the Parliamentary Party after the general election of 1918 produced enormous changes in the political life of Ireland—shifts in the economy, a sharpening of nationalist demands all round, a revival of the physical force movement, increased anxieties among (especially southern) Irish Unionists—none of this seems to have undermined the convictions of those British politicians who, looking back to the 1880s, resolutely upheld the view that firmness, inflexibility, and coercion remained a singularly effective policy in the face of Sinn Féin and the growing unrest of the times.

---

[82] Parl. Deb. 3: cccxxvii. 1389, 1393 (26 June 1888).

[83] C. Campbell, *Emergency Law in Ireland, 1918–1925* (Oxford, 1994), 8, 16–17, 54–8; Crossman, *Politics, Law and Order in Nineteenth-Century Ireland*, 154, 179; Hammond, *Gladstone and the Irish Nation*, 572–3.

[84] K. T. Hoppen, *Ireland since 1800: Conflict and Conformity*, 2nd edn (London, 1999), 104–5, 114, 140; P. Bew, *Conflict and Conciliation in Ireland 1890–1910: Parnellites and Radical Agrarians* (Oxford, 1987), 35–166; P. Bull, *Land, Politics and Nationalism: A Study of the Irish Land Question* (Dublin, 1996), 109–40, 172–9.

VII

If such certainties had numerous devotees, four subsequently emblematic figures stand out as symbols, in this respect at least, of the initial though eventually moth-eaten attractions of clinging to the past: Walter Long, who in May 1918 began to act on the cabinet's behalf 'with regard to Irish affairs in general',[85] Lord French, viceroy from April 1918 to April 1921, Sir Harmar Greenwood, chief secretary from April 1920 onwards, and David Lloyd George, prime minister from December 1916 to October 1922. That the first two knew something of Ireland and the latter two almost nothing seems in no way to have differentiated them in the matter of taking a hard line, for all four adhered equally—and, as it turned out, unhelpfully—to the philosophy of 'one more push', which, though effective in the 1880s, had, in the very different circumstances in which they found themselves, lost whatever leverage on events it had once possessed. Long, briefly chief secretary in 1905 and for a time leader of the Irish Unionists, clung limpet-like to the view that unrest could be put down only by the strongest of means. While this had always been his opinion, it became more stridently expressed as British rule began to fall apart.[86] French, a distinctly less able character, combined bluster with consistent ineffectiveness. Given to believe that he would be the 'sole Governor of Ireland', the 'actual and not merely the nominal Head' of a 'quasi-military administration', he was admitted to the cabinet in October 1919, together (unprecedentedly) with the various chief secretaries with whom he served and with whom, after initial cordiality, he invariably fell out.[87] By the summer of 1920 he had become an irrelevance, a development that in no degree halted the stream of his endless advice, as typified by a comment of April 1919 that 'of course we have to rule with a rod of iron' and by later rants about throwing barbed-wire entanglements around rebellious towns, setting up 'large concentration camps', and adopting a policy of widespread internment.[88] If French was noted for ineffective vehemence, Greenwood became notorious for a remorseless and unjustified optimism in the face of disaster. For him the

---

[85] Cabinet Minutes TNA CAB 23/6 (10 May 1918).

[86] See, e.g., Long to Lloyd George, 30 August 1918, P[arliamentary] A[rchives] Lloyd George Papers F/33/1/18; to French, 27 June 1918, W[iltshire and Swindon] R[ecord] O[ffice] Long Papers 947/9/229; to A. Chamberlain, 20 September 1918, ibid. 947/9/180; Long's memoranda 'Ireland' of 1 June 1918 for the war cabinet TNA CAB 24/53 GT 4728 and 'Situation in Ireland' of 24 September 1919, TNA CAB 24/89 GT 8215.

[87] K. T. Hoppen, 'A Question None Could Answer: What was the Lord Lieutenancy for? 1800–1921', in P. Gray and O. Purdue (eds), *The Irish Lord Lieutenancy c.1541–1922* (Dublin, 2012), 148.

[88] French to Long, 17 April 1919, WRO Long Papers 947/9/230; 'Lord Oranmore's Journal, 1913–27', ed. J. Butler, *Irish Historical Studies*, 29 (1995), 584; Memorandum of 17 December 1919 in French to Londonderry, 3 January 1920, I[mperial] W[ar] M[useum] French Papers JDPF/8/1D; to Churchill, 30 January 1920, ibid.

application of strong measures was for ever the prelude to better times in the future, a future that invariably failed to appear.[89] More acute observers either found him ridiculous from the start or wasted little time in coming to that conclusion. Maurice Hankey, the cabinet secretary, thought he 'talked awful tosh about shooting Sinn Féiners at sight, and without evidence, and [about] frightfulness generally', all before he had even set foot in Ireland. Very different men, including the senior civil servant Warren Fisher and the right-wing Tory MP Lord Hugh Cecil, rapidly lost patience with Greenwood's promises that better times were just around the corner, for, as Fisher put it, 'unintelligent and undirected brute force is no substitute for scientific well-planned operations involving leadership and discipline'.[90]

It was, however, Lloyd George who, as prime minister, probably had the greatest impact on the unpredictable shifts of British policy in these years, not least by blowing hot and cold in ways that for too long substituted bouts of bad temper for periods of sustained analysis (though flashes of insight were never absent). He spent a good deal of time talking tough à la Greenwood, insisting that any kind of truce with rebels 'would be an admission that we were beaten' and might well 'lead to our having to give up Ireland'. Indeed, as Lord Midleton recorded at the time, Lloyd George had been 'strongly in favour of severe measures' as far back as April 1918 and 'wished to teach Ireland a lesson', a view that, significantly, he himself did not seem fully to share. Indeed, it was by no means the case that Tory leaders invariably proved less flexible in their attitudes towards evolving Irish realities than their Liberal counterparts.[91] By December 1920 Lloyd George was advocating martial law (a concept neither he nor most politicians really understood), having a few weeks earlier declared that the government now 'had murder by the throat'. Although, of course, the prime minister eventually changed his tune, he took longer to do so than colleagues like Winston Churchill, who had also once been a fully paid-up member of the 'baying for blood' school of thought.[92] All in all, government policy in the period 1918–21 was marked by loud affirmations that the iron fist, which had succeeded in the past, would succeed again, punctuated by doubts, worries, and fitful failures of nerve. Not only that, but up to the spring of 1920 remarkably little sustained attention of any kind was

---

[89] See, e.g., Greenwood to Bonar Law, 25 and 28 September 1921, PA Bonar Law Papers 103/3/24 and 27; to Long, 24 September 1920, BL Long Papers Add. MS 62425.

[90] S. Roskill, *Hankey: Man of Secrets*, 3 vols (London, 1970–74), i. 153 (8 May 1920); Parl. Deb. 5 (Commons): cxxxviii. 671 and 682 (21 February 1921: Cecil and Barnes); Fisher to Bonar Law, 11 February 1921, PA Bonar Law Papers 103/1.

[91] Lloyd George to Bonar Law, 10 May 1920, PA Bonar Law Papers 103/4/2; Cabinet Minutes, 30 April 1920, TNA CAB 23/21; Midleton's memorandum of 30 April [1918], TNA Midleton Papers PRO 30/17/38; Parl. Deb. 5 (Lords): xlii. 515 (24 November 1920: Grey).

[92] Parl. Deb. 5 (Commons): cxxxv. 2610 (10 December 1920); *The Times*, 10 November 1920; R. S. Churchill and M. Gilbert, *Winston S. Churchill*, 8 vols (London, 1966–88), iv. 452, 664–5.

given to Irish affairs by the cabinet in general and the prime minister in particular. Lloyd George, who allowed all sorts of second-rate performers to occupy the Irish stage, himself pursued contradictory policies well past the eleventh hour.[93] And in this sense, if no other, the successes of Spencer and Balfour some thirty years before cast a long shadow by encouraging politicians to believe that the one truly effective way of treating Ireland as a special case— the imposition of coercive force—having 'worked' in the years immediately after the Union and in the 1880s, would, by historical inference, furnish a sovereign remedy should Ireland again display symptoms of sustained rebellion and unrest.

VIII

What the turn towards treating Ireland 'according to Irish ideas' had certainly not changed was the widespread perception in British political circles of Anglo-Saxon superiority, a perception equally capable of underpinning assimilationist tendencies, on the one hand, and, on the other, the very different remedies for Irish ills that dominated the period from the late 1860s onwards.

A year after being appointed viceroy in November 1864, Kimberley—a man by no means hostile to reformist legislation—concluded a (rather patronizing) salute to Irish male courage and female chastity with insights about 'genial' Hibernian manners too often disguising 'violence and boastfulness ... unsupported by corresponding vigour and steadiness in action'.[94] A year later Disraeli marvelled that the chief secretary (Lord Naas) possessed cool judgement, 'a quality rare, in any degree, in an Irishman'.[95] Seamlessly the view of the Irish as generous, impulsive, unreliable, shallow, violent, primitive, unthinkingly brave, and almost certainly corrupt, retained its grip upon the British imagination, as powerful after the 1860s as before. The Irish character was made up of 'proverbial [a key term] lawlessness and vindictiveness', noted a report sent to Disraeli in 1867. Naas's successor, an Englishman, found the corruption 'exceeded all that he had expected, or could have believed'.[96] The Earl of Derby told Disraeli in 1874 that the only thing upon which all in

[93] *The Last Days of Dublin Castle: The Mark Sturgis Diaries*, ed. M. Hopkinson (Dublin, 1999), 7; M. Hopkinson, 'Negotiation: The Anglo-Irish War and Revolution', in J. Augusteijn (ed.), *The Irish Revolution 1913–1923* (Basingstoke, 2002), 126–8; R. Fanning, *Fatal Path: British Government and Irish Revolution 1910–1922* (London, 2013), 188–276.
[94] 'A Journal of Events during the Gladstone Ministry 1868–1874', ed. E. Drus, Royal Historical Society *Camden Miscellany* Third Series, xxi (1958), 9–10 (14 December 1865).
[95] Disraeli to Derby, 27 September 1866, LRO Derby Papers 146/2.
[96] Reports in Bodl. Disraeli Papers 38/1 (7 June 1867); *Disraeli, Derby and the Conservative Party*, ed. Vincent, 340 (17 February 1869).

Ireland were at one was 'the duty of spending more English money on Irish soil', while Spencer and Forster were in (unusual) agreement in believing the Irish to lack 'moral courage' in large part because of uncontrolled impulsiveness, Spencer adding that he would never have an Irishman as his private secretary.[97] And so, behind all the discussions of land reform and land purchase, of Home Rule, of more democratic local government, of helping Ireland's poorer districts, this underlying sense of patronizing distrust and distaste continued its relentless grip upon both public discourse and the mentalities of those in charge of the state.

While Salisbury's comparing of the Irish to Hottentots in 1886 (as, less notoriously, Thackeray had already done in 1842) is well known,[98] Liberals were no less active (if rather less publicly so) in the deployment of unlimited abuse. The Irish lacked any kind of business sense, having been 'demoralized by the teachings of persons who urge them to repudiate their just liabilities'; they knew nothing of 'the high, pure public spirit' that reigned in England; they constituted 'a mongrel race' whose only saving grace was that it was leavened by 'no small proportion of Teutons'.[99] Even John Morley, chief secretary 1886 and 1892–5 and a devoted supporter of Gladstone's land and Home Rule policies, could not prevent certain deep-seated negativities from occasionally rising to the surface. Writing from Dublin to Rosebery in 1892, he noted—in words that could have flown (indeed had flown) from the pen of Robert Peel when holding the same office—how 'an oily cove gave me a real treat the other day. He began with a noble exordium about the blessedness of my mission in Ireland, and then slowly unfolded the truth that the true way of healing the woes of centuries and reconciling two kindred peoples, was to make his brother an RM [Resident Magistrate].' 'Say what you will,' Morley recorded in his diary, 'Irishmen are not a gracious race. They have grace on the surface, but scratch the surface and underneath you find the hard core, brittle, cold and in a small way sinister, in short infernal'[100]—a comment that leads to the clichéd conclusion that, with friends like that, enemies become almost redundant.

---

[97] Derby to Disraeli, 15 September 1874, Bodl. Disraeli Papers 58/2; Spencer to Hartington, [c.16 January 1871], ChH Devonshire Papers 340.8; Forster to Gladstone, 27 October 1872, ibid. 340.505.

[98] *The Times*, 17 May 1886; D. Kanter, *The Making of British Unionism, 1740–1848: Politics, Government and the Anglo-Irish Relationship* (Dublin, 2009), 168. Irish children knew all about Hottentots through the *Fourth Reading Book* (1861 edn) published by the Irish Commissioners of National Education: 'They are short, stunted, ugly, with yellow skins and woolly hair' (J. Coolahan, 'The Irish and Others in Irish Nineteenth-Century Textbooks', in J. A. Mangan (ed.), *The Imperial Curriculum: Racial Images and Education in the British Colonial Experience* (London, 1993), 61.

[99] R. G. C. Hamilton, 17 July 1885, GRO St Aldwyn Papers PCC/54; Trevelyan to Spencer, 7 September 1883, BL Spencer Papers Add. MS 76958; Parl. Deb. 3: ccciv. 1236 (9 April 1886: Sir John Lubbock).

[100] Morley to Rosebery, 5 September 1892, N[ational] L[ibrary of] S[cotland] Rosebery Papers MS 10046; Morley's Diary for 17 June 1893, Bodl. Morley Papers MS Eng.d.3455. See

What Morley said privately, other MPs were more than willing to say out loud, with one in 1893 boldly declaring the Irish as a whole ignorant and often illiterate, proof of which could, he noted, be found in the fact that the electors in Liverpool who regularly returned an Irish Nationalist member (T. P. O'Connor) were fifteen times more likely to be unable to read and write than other voters in the town. Another ascribed all of Ireland's troubles to its high levels of lunacy, something that could only increase if unrest was not forcibly suppressed.[101] Nor did such confident formulations diminish as time went on; quite the reverse. Lord French was never at a loss for instant national psychoanalysis, something not without an impact upon his style of government: the Irish were (as many agreed, not least Walter Long) 'peculiarly liable to be influenced by their immediate environment. Place them in suitable surroundings and they are just as easily aroused to imperial enthusiasm as, in the contrary sense, they are filled with hatred and anger by a few crafty sedition-mongers and young priestly fanatics.'[102] The Irish, noted a Tory minister who had resigned from the cabinet in 1916 in protest over alleged dalliance with Redmond, were 'a wholly irrational incomprehensible and contemptible race' who might well, for all he knew, end up 'slobbering the king with loyalty before twelve months are passed'.[103]

No less characteristic was a kind of anthropological assessment and representation of those inimical to the continuation of British rule, as when one participant in the Irish Convention of 1917 phonetically recorded a conversation with a Home Rule delegate. 'Oi have often read about ye, but Oi have never met ye and Oi have never hurrd you before; and to tell you the Truth, now Oi have met ye and now Oi have hurrd ye, Oi loike ye a great deal better than Oi expected.'[104] Others, notably Augustine Birrell, the longest serving of all post-Union chief secretaries (January 1907 to May 1916), combined good intentions with a kind of amused weariness typified by the comment that 'no Irishman hated another Irishman nearly as much as all Irishmen hated Englishmen'.[105] And Birrell's notably disengaged superior, the prime minister Herbert Asquith, operated (if that is quite the right word) along similar lines. After the breakdown of the so-called Buckingham Palace negotiations of July

also Derby to Eglinton, 3 December 1858, Sc[ottish] R[ecord] O[ffice] Eglinton Papers GD3/5/1388.

[101] Parl. Deb. 4: xi. 256 (13 April 1893: Kenyon-Slaney) and 404 (14 April 1893: Field).

[102] French's memorandum for the war cabinet, 8 October 1918, WRO Long Papers 947/9/230; also his memorandum, 17 December 1919, in letter to Londonderry, 3 January 1920, IWM French Papers JDPF/8/1D.

[103] Selborne to Salisbury, 29 July 1921, *The Crisis of British Unionism: Lord Selborne's Domestic Political Papers, 1885–1922*, ed. G. Boyce (London, 1987), 231–2.

[104] Parl. Deb. 5 (Lords): xlii. 470–1 (13 November 1920: Lord Oranmore and Browne).

[105] Parl. Deb. 5 (Commons): xxxix. 1558 (18 June 1912).

1914 attended by Irish Unionists such as Carson and Craig and Nationalists such as Dillon and Redmond, he noted:

> Redmond assured us that when he said good-bye to Carson the latter was in tears, and that Captain Craig who has never spoken to Dillon in his life came up to him & said: 'Mr Dillon will you shake my hand? I shall be glad to think that I have been able to give as many years to Ulster as you have to the service of Ireland.' Aren't they a remarkable people? And the folly of thinking that we can ever understand, let alone govern them![106]

Within two years an impossibility of understanding had been transmuted into something close to an impossibility of action. Asquith was in Downing Street when the first news of the Easter Rising of 1916 arrived just after midnight. The civil servant who was with him in the room recorded the prime minister's words: 'Well, that's really something'—after which he went to bed.[107]

Whatever, therefore, were the implications of the 1860s swing away from assimilationism and towards an open and almost universal acceptance that henceforth it would be best to work with, rather than against, the grain of Ireland's distinctiveness, they did not necessarily imply or lead to greater administrative or political effectiveness or even to more sustained engagement. And while, of course, much of the motivation that lay behind this 'new' way of treating Ireland was bound up with hopes that it would generate increased attachment to the Union, a consistent, even remorseless, application of different laws and policies almost inevitably widened rather than diminished the already substantial gulf between the two islands. Save in unusual cases (such as the Scottish Land Act of 1886) the sauce now more and more considered appropriate for the British goose was no longer thought suitable for the Irish gander. And, if changes in the intellectual weather had something to do with this, so also perhaps did the arrival of a new generation of prime ministers. Between 1828 and 1868 governments of all stripes had predominantly been led by men with substantial knowledge of Ireland, as chief secretaries, as landlords, as frequent visitors. Wellington, Melbourne, Russell, Peel, Derby, and Palmerston all fall into this category. However, when Disraeli and Gladstone reached the top of the greasy pole in 1868, this ceased to be the case. The former never visited Ireland at all, while one of the latter's two trips lasted less than a month, the other less than twenty-four hours. Salisbury, Rosebery, Asquith, and Lloyd George had little personal knowledge of Ireland, while Balfour, who had some, never ceased to see the place as a wild and alien land deserving wild and alien remedies.[108]

---

[106] Asquith to Venetia Stanley, 24 July 1914, *H. H. Asquith: Letters to Venetia Stanley*, ed. M. and E. Brock (Oxford, 1982), 122.

[107] Roskill, *Hankey: Man of Secrets*, i, 265.

[108] K. McKenna, 'From Private Visit to Public Opportunity: Gladstone's 1877 Trip to Ireland', in Daly and Hoppen (eds), *Gladstone: Ireland and Beyond*, 77–89. Campbell-Bannerman was, of course, an exception.

However that might be, there can be little doubt that the increasingly dramatic changes in the rationale informing the Irish policies of successive governments marked a no less significant departure regarding the relationship between Britain and Ireland than the better-known 'new departures' of the 1870s did with respect to a coalescence between the forces of violent and constitutional nationalism within Ireland itself.

8

Doing it on the Cheap: Liberals

I

In the half-century before 1921 there was rarely much dispute between the main political parties in Britain regarding the importance of abandoning mid-century attempts to assimilate Ireland into the social, economic, and political norms of Britain in general and England in particular. Indeed, apart from obvious disagreements over constitutional arrangements—disagreements in which sound and fury sometimes counted for more than substance—the deepest lines of division had more to do with the precise implementation, rather than the overall necessity, of treating Ireland according to its own distinct requirements, an approach that both Liberals and Conservatives persuaded themselves would best help to keep Ireland within the kingdom established by the Act of Union of 1800. What this meant was that the real gulf between the parties so far as Ireland was concerned had now come to lie between, on the one hand, Liberals determined above all to save money in pursuit of Gladstone's ideal of the minimal state and, on the other, Conservatives with a more pragmatic (Gladstone would have said irresponsible) disposition to address Irish problems by the deployment of substantial, sometimes very substantial, amounts of cash—cash supplied, as their opponents pointed out, in large part by taxpayers outside Ireland.[1] For most Liberals, perhaps for almost all, the major attraction of Home Rule was that it would save a great deal of money. For Conservatives large-scale expenditure seemed a small price to pay to keep the various competing forces within Ireland relatively quiet and relatively satisfied.

Already in the early days of the move away from assimilation Liberals lost little time in emphasizing the importance of cutting an extravagant Ireland down to financial size. As Chancellor of the Exchequer, Gladstone agonized over every Hibernian penny, convinced that Irish demands had more to do

---

[1] H. C. G. Matthew, *Gladstone 1809–1874* (Oxford, 1986), 109–28, 217–27; Matthew, *Gladstone 1875–1898* (Oxford, 1995), 162–8; K. T. Hoppen, *The Mid-Victorian Generation 1846–1886* (Oxford, 1998), 48–9, 119–23, 148–51, 205, 211–15, 605–6, 648–9; see also Chapter 9.

with extracting 'a certain sum of public money' than with the 'discharge of duty ... upon the scale which it may require'.[2] Excessive expenditure was, he felt, bad for pretty well every citizen but especially bad for the Irish, so long prone to the tactics of the begging bowl. 'I deprecate', he announced in 1866, 'all Irish policy founded on a mere system of money grants. You cannot raise a country, you cannot liberate a country, you cannot ennoble a country, you cannot descend into and purge the sources of discontent, by a policy such as this.' Contrasting himself with the Conservatives, he declared that he would never lend himself to any 'endeavour to bribe Ireland into union with this country by the mere vulgar expedient of doses of public money'. Not even his Peelite colleague Edward Cardwell (chief secretary 1859–61 and 'a most capable man') had, he complained, been able to 'effect a reform' and cut Ireland's endless demands down to an even vaguely tolerable size.[3] Never one to shrink from publicly dispensing high-minded medicine, Gladstone had no hesitation in proclaiming his economic message hot and strong during a brief visit to Ireland in 1877. But, while making no attempt to disguise his contempt for 'dealing out large doses of public money', he tried to sugar the pill by implying that any extravagance had been the result of excessive centralization and the 'abridging [of] local institutions'.[4] Already then the Liberal message that was to achieve dramatic expression in the 1880s—that devolution and retrenchment were inseparable twins—was in no way being disguised.

It was, above all, the agricultural depression of the late 1870s, the consequent unrest in Ireland, and the increasing demands that land policy be taken in a more radical direction that persuaded the Liberal leadership that further concessions to Irish tenants must be accompanied by serious economic adjustments. Thus, in the minds of Gladstone and many of his colleagues, further Irish reforms, whether to do with land or with devolved government, were not alternatives to the saving of money, but quite the reverse. Concessions, in other words, would have to be paid for by those who most loudly demanded them and paid for not simply by changes in outlook but by responses of a distinctly monetary kind.

As Liberal administrators grappled with the growing complexity of Irish politics in the early and mid-1880s and in particular with increasingly strident demands for agrarian reform and Home Rule, so an insistence on economy became a central concern for those in charge of government. Within months of Liberal victory at the general election of April 1880, Gladstone and his chief

---

[2] Gladstone to Kimberley, 13 November 1865, Bodl[eian Library] Kimberley Papers MS Eng. c.4036.

[3] Parl[iamentary] Deb[ates] 3: clxxxiv. 1941 (2 August 1866); *The Times*, 20 December 1867; Spencer's memorandum of a conversation with Gladstone, 14 October 1871, B[ritish] L[ibrary] Spencer Papers Add. MS 76850.

[4] *The Times*, 8 November 1877.

lieutenants launched a full-frontal attack on what they saw as Ireland's endless and excessive demands upon the public purse—demands that they felt the previous Tory administration had done little to resist. As early as 8 May Gladstone briefed his new chief secretary, W. E. Forster, in words that leap from the page. 'I do not recollect', he wrote, 'ever during nearly 10 years for which I have been Finance Minister, to have received from a Secretary for Ireland ... a *single suggestion* for the reduction of any expenditure whatever.' Forster should gird his loins and take a scythe to Hibernian profligacy. It was a matter of 'real importance', because Ireland had 'been illegitimately paid for unjust inequalities by an unjust preference in much lavish public expenditure'. So cross was Gladstone that he even aimed a retrospective kick at his great hero, Sir Robert Peel, who had, he declared, made the egregious mistake of placing the cost of the Irish Constabulary on the consolidated fund, with the result that, as the Irish population declined, police numbers nonetheless continued to rise at, it seemed, unstoppable expense.[5]

On coming into government, Gladstone and his ministers were immediately faced with virtually irresistible demands for a dramatic extension to the changes introduced by the Land Act of 1870. But, while they were not unwilling to make further concessions, all were agreed that, whatever their precise nature, these could not involve any significant additional expenditure on the part of the state. However alarming the outlook in Ireland, it would never be proper 'to charge the English [*sic*] Exchequer in whatever disguise, with a very large, perhaps a huge, liability as the price of a land act founded on a set of principles altogether new to our general legislation'. And such financial restraint must necessarily apply, said the prime minister, to payments and subsidies of all kinds, whether to tenants or—and here he was even more insistent—to landlords.[6] Especially notable was Liberal unwillingness to do much to help tenants to buy their farms, for, while a few Radicals like John Bright were keen on the idea, its potential expense greatly limited the provisions for purchase included in the Land Acts of 1870 and 1881. Spencer, Carlingford, and Kimberley all now expressed a strong distaste for any proposals based on the expenditure of large sums of public money or, as Gladstone himself noted: 'It is very desirable for us to be chary about contracting largely the relations of creditor and debtor between the British Treasury, on the one hand, and the Irish tenant—especially the Irish small tenant—on the other.'[7]

[5] Gladstone to Forster, 8 May and 25 October 1880, BL Gladstone Papers Add. MSS 44544 and 44157.
[6] Gladstone to Forster, 7 December 1880, ibid., Add. MS 44158.
[7] J. L. Hammond, *Gladstone and the Irish Nation* (London, 1938; repr. London, 1964), 222; Parl. Deb. 3: cclxix. 1271 (22 May 1882).

Both land and constitutional reform were, therefore, in Liberal eyes, above all designed to keep costs in check. Indeed, Gladstone's earliest thoughts about constitutional devolution for Ireland were powered, above all, by the belief that responsibility for local government would automatically oblige the hitherto profligate Irish to cease regarding London as a bottomless source of extraneous cash. As Spencer told Hartington in 1882: 'Mr G, chiefly I think to get public expenditure thrown on local rates, and to make a beginning that way, is very anxious we should develop a local government bill for Ireland.' Nor were Spencer as viceroy or his chief secretary Trevelyan any less convinced of the absolute necessity of getting the Irish to manage at least certain 'of their own affairs' on the urgent grounds that 'some means' had to be found of creating 'machinery which may in some degree protect the Treasury from local and provincial demands of money'.[8] Spencer moaned about his inability to cut costs in Ireland without the establishment of 'local bodies' that might protect the 'imperial government' from importunate demands and force the Irish to administer public works with greater efficiency and less expense.[9]

Liberal leaders quite deliberately set out to present a public contrast between their own parsimony and the tendency of the Tory opposition to demand that money be thrown at every Irish problem, especially when landlords might be the recipients. After a Commons debate in June 1883 during which a 34-year-old Tory backbencher (Arthur Balfour) condemned the Liberals' 'narrow view' of finance and insisted that state-aided land purchase alone could turn 'the very class which would otherwise be ranged against law and order' into 'its foremost upholders', Trevelyan exploded with rage against Tory profligacy. 'There were' present, he told Spencer, 'about 100 Irish landlords and Parnellites, united to bleed the Treasury to the tune of 300 millions; and nobody for the public except Mr G. Lefevre, and myself'.[10] 'To place the state and the Treasury', as, according to Gladstone, the Tories' potentially 'enormous transaction' would do, into a 'position of creditorship' was 'like putting a bastard premium on every attempt to disturb the relations between England and Ireland'. Already, indeed, Gladstone had come to the view that the only way to reduce government spending in Ireland was to set up 'local institutions' in that country, which, once faced directly with the problem of balancing revenue against expenditure, would reduce the latter to match the former.[11]

[8] Spencer to Hartington, 10 December 1882, Ch[atsworth] H[ouse] Devonshire Papers 340.1287; Trevelyan to Gladstone, 23 December 1882, BL Gladstone Papers Add. MS 44335.
[9] Spencer to Gladstone, 25 October 1882, BL Gladstone Papers Add. MS 44309 and 25 May 1883, Add. MS 44310.
[10] Parl. Deb. 3: cclxxx. 412–68, at 423 (12 June 1883: Balfour); Trevelyan to Spencer, 13 June 1883, BL Spencer Papers Add. MS 76957; also Morley in *The Times*, 30 September 1885.
[11] Parl. Deb. 3: cclxxx. 453 (12 June 1883); Gladstone to Granville, 22 January 1883, *The Political Correspondence of Mr Gladstone and Lord Granville 1876–1886*, ed. A. Ramm, 2 vols (Oxford, 1962), ii. 10.

Gladstone's views resonated widely across the Liberal Party and especially so among its more advanced elements, with Joseph Chamberlain's so-called Radical Programme of 1885 advocating limited devolution on the grounds that 'the constant claims which are now made on the English [sic] Exchequer would be avoided; Irishmen would be called upon to pay for what they wanted, and to guarantee on Irish credit the loans which they may think it desirable to raise in order to carry out their experiments'.[12] While, in the end, Chamberlain did not believe that Home Rule was a price worth paying for even so desirable a state of things, Gladstone did, and it was precisely during the months when his mind was moving in that direction that he—as it turned out rather optimistically—concluded that the Irish 'Chapter of grievance properly so called, is pretty well closed' and that, even more pertinently, 'the Chapter of material aid, eleemosynary aid, cannot close too soon'.[13] The two were inexorably linked, as were both to his fructifying ideas about Home Rule.

And, although the Liberal Home Rule Bill of 1886 was shot down in the Commons, the party's adherence to the precepts of economical government survived unscathed so far as Ireland was concerned. Indeed, perhaps the most surprising thing about Gladstone's Commons speech of 8 April 1886 in favour of the bill was that he presented his plans as, above all, morally inspired and designed to bring 'justice' to Ireland, rather than (scattered references notwithstanding) 'a big budget proposal to discipline Ireland financially', something that at least some of the future Liberal Unionists might well have been willing to accept.[14] The reason may have lain in the fact that running alongside the Home Rule Bill was a land purchase measure of staggeringly un-Gladstonian extravagance (for which, see Section II), an aberration so far as the Liberal Party was concerned and something that made it temporarily difficult for the prime minister to put on any kind of shining armour with respect to economical restraint. However, the simultaneous sinking of both measures meant that Liberal cheeseparing could be resumed after the very briefest of intervals almost as if nothing untoward had happened at all.

Addressing the Midlothian voters immediately after the defeat of Home Rule, Gladstone demanded a 'stoppage of a heavy, constant, and demoralising waste of public' money in Ireland. By August 1886 he was, with oblivious disregard of his own proposals a few weeks earlier, condemning the land purchase plans of the Tory government that had now come to power as 'radically bad ... an act of rapine on the Treasury of the country'. Worse still, 'a new chapter of excess' was being opened with lavish expenditure on public

[12] J. Chamberlain et al., *The Radical Programme* (London, 1885), 259; T. W. Heyck, *The Dimensions of British Radicalism: The Case of Ireland 1874–95* (Urbana, IL, 1974), 91–2.

[13] Gladstone to Knowles, 5 August 1885, Hammond, *Gladstone and the Irish Nation*, 410.

[14] See the important essay by Martin Maguire, 'Gladstone and the Irish Civil Service', in D. G. Boyce and A. O'Day (eds), *Gladstone and Ireland: Politics, Religion and Nationality in the Victorian Age* (Basingstoke, 2010), 208–32, especially 209–11.

works, all in an 'attempt to divert the Irish nation by pecuniary inducement from its honourable aim of national self-government'.[15] And so it went on—and, indeed, on and on. The Irish nation had always, both before and after the Union, been guilty of 'extravagance in the expenditure of money'. 'Civil expenditure' in 1887 was 16 shillings per person in Ireland (twice the British level) at a public cost of £2 million. In 1887 and 1888 Sir William Harcourt (a future Liberal Chancellor of the Exchequer) denounced Tory fiscal recklessness with respect to land purchase and military and police costs in Ireland, puzzled, or so he claimed, by opponents who threw 'millions after millions to people' they simultaneously denounced 'as robbers and villains'.[16] With equal enthusiasm Liberal backbenchers condemned Tory policy in Ireland as 'doses of coercion followed by draughts of money' as 'carrying a stick in one hand and a money bag in the other'.[17] And, while still in opposition in 1891, John Morley (a past and future chief secretary) angrily denounced the Salisbury administration's establishment of the Congested Districts Board designed to improve conditions in the West of Ireland as no more and no less than a gigantic waste of taxpayers' money,[18] a classic case of allowing the absence of governmental responsibility to shape the nature of political opinion.

With the Liberals back in power from August 1892 to June 1895, demands for and efforts towards economy gathered renewed force. This was especially evident in the case of the second Home Rule Bill of 1893, which contained important divergences from that of 1886 designed to 'reduce the ability of the Irish executive to draw on the British Treasury'. Gladstone was now even fiercer about bearing down on costs in Ireland, which he told MPs had become 'incredibly, almost immeasurably, wasteful'.[19] Home Rule would, he believed, enable the Exchequer to slash spending in Ireland and return to stricter standards of economy, an expectation that persuaded him to favour substantial administrative autonomy in the hope that this would relieve the London government of many irksome responsibilities.[20] Any sums that were to be granted to help establish devolved ministries under the bill were to be repaid as soon as possible. Indeed, because London would, under Home Rule, no longer be able to accept any prevaricating nonsense from the Irish, it might well prove

[15] A. O'Day, *Parnell and the First Home Rule Episode 1874–87* (Dublin, 1986), 204; W. E. Gladstone, *The Irish Question ... with an 'Addendum'* (London, [1886]), 28.

[16] Parl. Deb. 3: cccxxv. 490 (25 April 1888: Gladstone); Gladstone, 'Notes and Queries on the Irish Demand', 184; A. G. Gardiner, *The Life of Sir William Harcourt*, 2 vols (London, 1923), ii. 48, 65.

[17] Parl. Deb. 3: cccxxxi. 561 (29 November 1888: Lawson) and cccxxxviii. 988 (19 July 1889: Cossham).

[18] C. Breathnach, *The Congested Districts Board of Ireland, 1891–1923: Poverty and Development in the West of Ireland* (Dublin, 2005), 30.

[19] Maguire, 'Gladstone and the Irish Civil Service', 211; Parl. Deb. 4: x. 1604–5 (6 April 1893).

[20] D. Brooks, 'Gladstone's Fourth Administration 1892–1894', in D. Bebbington and R. Swift (eds), *Gladstone Centenary Essays* (Liverpool, 2000), 230.

necessary to 'present to them not quite but something like an ultimatum' on the matter.[21]

The new Liberal viceroy, Lord Houghton, was in full agreement and pointed to 'the almost universal expectation [in Ireland] of government aid for local wants', something the Tories had encouraged and which should now be brought to a complete and immediate stop. Alas, he also admitted that this would probably never happen, because few in Ireland expected the Home Rule Bill to pass and even fewer saw Home Rule itself 'as a complete substitute for other legislation or for expenditure of money'.[22] At the Exchequer, Harcourt had taken on Gladstone's mantle as cheeseparer in chief, harassing the Irish Office for economies of every kind. As chief secretary, Morley agreed in theory—'this corruption of Irish civil self-respect by doles and sups is nauseous and revolting'—but blamed the Tories for raising expectations and *force majeure* for the fact that certain cuts were simply impossible. 'It is not a question of choice with me. There has never been a more parsimonious minister in any office than I am here ... At every turn I have shown myself to be, and am fiercely blackguarded for being, the "greatest screw" that ever sat in this office.'[23] It was, indeed, this sense of helplessness that pushed many Liberals to support Home Rule in the hope that it alone could compel the Irish to live in the land of hard knocks rather than in a British-protected Never-Never Land of economic subsidies and doles. Hence their criticisms of some of the provisions of Tory local government legislation for Ireland in 1898, which men as different as Lloyd George and Reginald McKenna (as well as various backbenchers) denounced as excessively generous to Ireland in general and to Irish landlords in particular.[24]

As Lloyd George, then a 32-year-old Liberal backbencher, put it in January 1895:

> The Tory policy towards Ireland was the policy of giving them millions of money to buy land, make harbours, build railways, and even to supply them with potatoes. They would give them everything except freedom ... The Liberal policy was, no more subsidies, no more grants, but that of power to the people to work out their own salvation.[25]

---

[21] Gladstone to Harcourt, 16 January 1893, Bodl. Harcourt Papers MS 13.

[22] Houghton (later Crewe) to Queen Victoria, 10 and 14 January 1893, C[ambridge] U[niversity] L[ibrary] Crewe Papers c.57 and c.36.

[23] Harcourt to Morley, 10 January 1895, Bodl. Harcourt Papers MS 27; Morley Diary for 30 November 1894, Bodl. Morley Papers MS Eng.d.3461; Morley to Harcourt, 11 January 1895, Bodl. Harcourt Papers MS 27.

[24] Parl. Deb. 4: xxxvi. 186 (16 August 1895), lv. 459–76 (21 March 1898), lxii. 538–9 (21 July 1898).

[25] *South Wales Daily News*, 18 January 1895, addressing the National Liberal Federation at Cardiff. As Lloyd George spoke, 'Mr Tom Ellis, who was seated on the platform, lost control of himself, and shouted out repeatedly in pure Cymraeg, "Da iawn, fy machgen i, da iawn" ["Very good, my boy, very good"]'. I am grateful to Howell Lloyd for help in this matter.

And it was a contention Liberals continued to formulate for the next decade and more. In 1899 Sir Charles Dilke denounced the Tories, not for trying to 'kill Home Rule by kindness', but for killing it 'by jobbery'. Morley in 1902 was still expressing doubts about the policy of state-aided land purchase and initially declared the Wyndham Land Act of 1903 wildly and dangerously improvident.[26] Even some Tories had occasional qualms about the approach their party had adopted, not least Gerald Balfour, chief secretary from July 1895 to November 1900, who found it difficult to overcome a distaste for 'the almost universal recklessness about money in Ireland' and was especially irritated when Irish Unionists reverted—as they too often did—to type as Hibernian mendicants. When Edward Carson, recently arrived in the Commons, demanded increased pay for Irish schoolteachers, Balfour wearily announced that 'the conclusion I am drawn to is that *all* the Irish members will invariably come down to the House and press for money when they think it can be squeezed out of the Treasury'.[27]

While for many Liberals (such as James Bryce when chief secretary in 1906) some form of devolution had always remained attractive on the Gladstonian grounds that it might eventually prove to be a device for saving money,[28] the party's long-standing attachment to Irish economy was dramatically undermined by a development that had little or nothing to do with Ireland at all but that also, in a rather roundabout manner, strengthened the hands of those who thought Home Rule deserved support, if only to exclude Ireland from a new, dramatic, and very un-Gladstonian bout of pan-United Kingdom extravagance. The extravagance was provided by Lloyd George's decision as Chancellor of the Exchequer to inaugurate, as from 1 January 1909, the payment of pensions to (most of) those aged 70 and over with incomes of less than £31 10s. a year. The rate was at first 5 shillings a week for those earning less than £22 and lower sums on a sliding scale for those between this and the maximum income permissible. For old-style Gladstonians, this was an abandonment of the sacred principle of the minimal state. For Ireland it provided a financial bonanza, not only for pensioners but for the country at large. An especially substantial proportion of those aged 70 and above obtained pensions in Ireland, partly on grounds of poverty and partly because, civil registration of births not having been introduced in Ireland until 1864 (twenty-six years later than in England and Wales), it was easier to pull the wool over official eyes in Dublin than in London.

---

[26] Parl. Deb. 4: lxxiii. 1516 (5 July 1899: Dilke), ci. 895 (24 January 1902: Morley), cxxii. 118 (7 July 1903: Morley).

[27] G. W. Balfour to his wife, [late 1890s], T[he] N[ational] A[rchives] Balfour Papers PRO 30/60/14; E. Marjoribanks and I. Colvin, *The Life of Lord Carson*, 3 vols (London, 1932–4), i. 274–5 (emphasis added).

[28] Parl. Deb. 4: clii. 417 (21 February 1906) and clviii. 109–12 (28 May 1906); M. Fraser, *John Bull's Other Homes: State Housing and British Policy in Ireland 1883–1922* (Liverpool, 1995), 41–2, 61–74.

Statistics (which are admittedly not always consistent) provided by the chief secretary in 1913 suggest that, while 89.3 per cent of those of appropriate age were in receipt of pensions in England and Wales, the Irish figure was 101.6 per cent! Official data suggest that by March 1912 the cost of old-age pensions in Ireland had reached about £3 million a year, much of it provided by taxpayers in other parts of the United Kingdom.[29] The so-called Primrose Committee on Irish Finance, which reported in 1912, estimated that in 1910–11 total Irish expenditure (a third going on old-age pensions) exceeded revenue by at least £1 million and that 'the excess of Irish expenditure over Irish revenue will *with a continuance of the existing conditions of partnership with Great Britain* show a further substantial increase in the immediate future'. The Committee pointed out that, had Home Rule preceded the introduction of pensions, 'it is very doubtful indeed if an Irish Parliament would have in that regard followed the example of Great Britain'.[30]

And this conclusion was, indeed, quite correct, because the diminishing band of true Gladstonians in matters of finance included the leaders of the Irish Parliamentary Party, much exercised by the danger that their followers might be 'demoralized by British doles', a devotion to economy later seamlessly adopted by the Sinn Féiners in charge of the Irish Free State, whose enthusiasm for slashing welfare spending would have delighted Gladstone's heart.[31] For British politicians too, and especially Liberals, a key reason for supporting some form of devolved administration in Ireland always had a good deal to do with hopes that this would lead to savings and cost-cutting all round. Introducing the third Home Rule Bill in 1912, the prime minister (Asquith) took the occasion to denounce the Unionist opposition's long and distinguished history of facilitating a 'freer and more copious outflow to Ireland of imperial doles' and to glory in the fact that, once the bill had become law, the Irish themselves would become responsible for their own wastefulness. Such sentiments delighted many of his listeners (and not least the chairman of the Labour Party in the Commons), all of whom looked forward to the happy day when government in Ireland would be carried on at 'much less cost to the British taxpayer'.[32] And, when, in September 1914, Sir Matthew Nathan (who always travelled third class) arrived in Dublin to take

---

[29] See the figures provided by the chief secretary (Birrell) to 31 March 1913 in Parl. Deb. 5 (Commons): lii. 1671 (5 May 1913) adjusted by data in *Old Age Pensions (Ireland)*, H[ouse of] C[ommons Paper] 1913 (3), xli. 247–50.

[30] *Report by the Committee on Irish Finance*, HC 1912–13 [Cd 6153], xxxiv. 10–11.

[31] P. Jalland, 'Irish Home Rule Finance: A Neglected Dimension of the Irish Question, 1910–14', *Irish Historical Studies*, 23 (1983), 233–53; G. Dangerfield, *The Damnable Question: A Study in Anglo-Irish Relations* (Boston, 1976), 63–4; J. J. Lee, *Ireland 1912–1985: Politics and Society* (Cambridge, 1989), 125; K. T. Hoppen, *Ireland since 1800: Conflict and Conformity*, 2nd edn (London, 1999), 191.

[32] Parl. Deb. 5 (Commons): xxxvi. 1417, 1426 (11 April 1912: Asquith) and xxxvii. 1789 (30 April 1912: Parker).

up the post of undersecretary, he too was delighted to find Redmond, Dillon, and their financial expert J. J. Clancy in no way opposed to his plans for saving money by cutting the Irish civil service down to size—the 'suspicion that Nathan's advice may have been shaped by British rather than Irish interests' never, it seems, having crossed their minds.[33]

II

The hopes of mid-nineteenth-century assimilationists that the Famine would, for all its horrors, bring about substantial improvements by more closely aligning Irish rural society to the tripartite Anglo-Saxon model of landlords, tenants, and wage-paid labourers and that landlordism, energized by the Encumbered Estates Act, would become stronger and more capitalistically inclined were, in some respects at least, tolerably fulfilled. It had, after all, been the pre-Famine economically complex assemblage of cottiers, conacre holders, and other 'labourers' who had suffered the greatest attrition during the terrible years after 1845, falling as a proportion of the total occupied male farming population from about 60 per cent in 1841 to 40 per cent in 1881, while the proportion of farmers and their 'assisting relatives' moved in the countervailing direction.[34] At the same time, and despite important regional differences, those farmers with (for Ireland) tolerably substantial holdings were assuming a higher social and political prominence. By 1881 almost a third of holdings above 1 acre were larger than 30 acres and almost a quarter were between 30 and 100 acres in size—a very different state of things from that which had existed during and before the early 1840s.[35] At the same time, the Famine, by weeding out the most distressed landlords, had enabled the more successful men to buy additional land through the Encumbered Estates Court, thereby— for a time at least—consolidating their position and increasing their share of agrarian income as a whole. In other words, despite a good deal of ingenuity in adapting to market forces, notably by moving from tillage to pasture, Irish farmers' profits fell behind the rise in output and rent during that part of the quarter-century after the Famine (1856–8 to 1871–3) that can most reliably be determined by opening and closing groups of years tolerably free from unusual disturbances likely to affect underlying trends. The resulting mixture of a declining labourer element, an increase in the proportion of more

[33] M. Maguire, *The Civil Service and the Revolution in Ireland, 1912–38: 'Shaking the Blood-Stained Hand of Mr Collins'* (Manchester, 2008), 25–7.

[34] K. T. Hoppen, *Elections, Politics, and Society in Ireland 1832–1885* (Oxford, 1984), 105.

[35] Hoppen, *Elections, Politics, and Society in Ireland*, 91; M. Turner, *After the Famine: Irish Agriculture, 1850–1914* (Cambridge, 1996), 65–94.

substantial farmers (now also given a clearer electoral voice by provisions in the Irish Franchise Act of 1850), and an immediate, though temporary, growth of landlord income and influence—all of them items desired by the assimilationists—soon proved a very toxic combination indeed, a classic example of the truth that one should be careful of what one prays for.[36]

In the event, instead of producing the kind of anglicized nirvana that so many in Britain had expected, these interwoven 'outcomes' of the Famine generated, in all but the shortest terms, discontent, instability, and demands for further and very un-British changes and reforms. Farmers now had more political power. They were more and more angered by the economic resurgence of landlords when their own incomes were diminished by the agricultural depression of 1859–64. They were far from satisfied by the modest concessions delivered by Gladstone's Land Act of 1870. Under the impact of a serious global downturn in the late 1870s, they began to organize, to act under the umbrella of overtly political organizations, led, first by Isaac Butt and then—much more aggressively—by Charles Stewart Parnell. In short, their increasingly lively agitation (though far from lacking internal tensions of its own) faced the incoming Liberal administration of 1880 with an unstable situation in which it soon became apparent that the 1870 Act could no longer be regarded as having provided any kind of 'solution' to the problems of Irish land.[37] Indeed, it was not long before a Liberal chief secretary had come to the conclusion that the most menacing political group in Ireland consisted of 'the class of farmers who have quite an inordinate and dangerous influence on the parliamentary action' of Irish MPs and whose power could best be reduced by opening the electoral floodgates to men at the lowest ends of the social scale—a curious reversal of those views of influence and hierarchy that had dominated the mid-century years.[38]

However, on once again becoming prime minister in April 1880, Gladstone at first proved one of the least 'advanced' members of the cabinet with regard to Irish land reform. But, while he himself was notably reluctant to accept the fact that his earlier legislative handiwork had, because of its modest ineffectiveness, stoked resentment and agitation in Ireland, the new chief secretary, W. E. Forster, quickly realized that the 1870 Act had raised expectations it had

---

[36] Hoppen, *Ireland since 1800*, 97–8; Turner, *After the Famine*, 196–216; Hoppen, *Elections, Politics, and Society in Ireland*, 17–18.

[37] J. S. Donnelly Jr, *The Land and the People of Nineteenth-Century Cork: The Rural Economy and the Land Question* (London, 1975), 132–72, 251–376; P. Bew, *Land and the National Question in Ireland 1858–82* (Dublin, 1978), *passim*; S. Clark, *Social Origins of the Irish Land War* (Princeton, 1979), 246–304; W. L. Feingold, *The Revolt of the Tenantry: The Transformation of Local Government in Ireland, 1872–1886* (Boston, 1984), 50–90; D. Jordan, 'Merchants, "Strong Farmers" and Fenians: The Post-Famine Political Elite and the Irish Land War', in C. H. E. Philpin (ed.), *Nationalism and Popular Protest in Ireland* (Cambridge, 1987), 320–48.

[38] Trevelyan to Gladstone, 26 October 1883, BL Gladstone Papers Add. MS 44335.

singularly failed to fulfil and that more now needed to be done. But Spencer, who had just visited Ireland, at first remained unhappy about radical change, while Gladstone's own views continued to be informed by a deep (if not always effective) desire to make sure that landlords were not completely deprived of a central place in Irish rural society.[39] In a cabinet paper of December 1880 and in correspondence with the queen, he declared himself equally opposed to 'fundamental changes in the nature of [Irish] property' and to 'all attempts to reconstruct society by more ambitious plans'.[40] Yet he also saw that the distress of the times required a new approach and that this could be successful only if based on legal and economic principles of a distinctly non-British character. In Ireland, he believed, tenants lived from 'hand to mouth' and should not therefore suffer ejectment 'for not paying' what they were simply unable to pay—a notion that Gladstone (with that sporadic mental elasticity that never deserted him) convinced himself was 'less in disparagement of the ordinary rules of property than what we had done in the Land Act' of 1870. Given the extent of Irish distress, it was therefore 'impossible to apply, without qualification of any kind', such 'ordinary rules'. For the moment at least, though not for very long, such deviant admissions could be disguised beneath large helpings of Gladstonian opacity: 'At the same time, and in perfect consonance with this view of the matter, I view without jealousy, indeed with sympathy, whatever tends to tie up and inclose as it were this intervention so as to fasten it upon the peculiar and exceptional circumstances of the case.'[41]

Twin assumptions kept the whole enterprise afloat as far as Liberal ministers were concerned: first, that something peculiarly 'Irish' and unexportable to Britain was involved, and, secondly, that the whole business would, in a manner rarely analysed in any detail, help landlords to retain some kind of significant place in Irish society.[42] The Duke of Argyll, who had joined the cabinet in April 1880 only to resign twelve months later, thought such views at once dangerous and fantastical, creating, as he claimed, 'a life that was death to ownership of land in Ireland—as ownership is enjoyed and understood in

---

[39] A. Warren, 'Gladstone, Land and Social Reconstruction in Ireland 1881–1887', *Parliamentary History*, ii (1983), 155–6. Gladstone, according to his private secretary, hoped that in 1870 he had 'touched the question once and for all' (*The Diary of Sir Edward Walter Hamilton 1880–1885*, ed. D. W. R. Bahlman, 2 vols (Oxford, 1972), i. 83 (30 November 1880)); Parl. Deb. 3: ccliv. 798 (19 July 1880: Forster); ibid. ccliv. 1367 (26 July 1880: Forster); Spencer to Hartington, 26 October 1880, ChH Devonshire Papers 340.1028.

[40] TNA CAB 37/4/81; to Queen Victoria, 31 December 1880, TNA CAB 41/14/36.

[41] Gladstone to Argyll, 14 and 15 June 1880, BL Gladstone Papers Add. MS 44104.

[42] Argyll to Gladstone, 13 July 1880 and 16 December 1883, BL Gladstone Papers Add. MSS 44104 and 56446; to Dufferin, 12 December 1880, A. Lyall, *The Life of the Marquis of Dufferin and Ava*, 2 vols (London, 1905), i. 191; *Diary of Sir Edward Walter Hamilton 1880–1885*, ed. Bahlman, i. 99, 108 (10 January and 14 February 1881); Gladstone to Argyll, 14 April 1881, BL Gladstone Papers Add. MS 44105.

every civilized country'.[43] Gladstone, however, was convinced that the simple act of adopting 'separate [that is, separate from Britain] principles for land legislation in Ireland' was enough to make everything safe and prevent any merely Hibernian novelties from crossing the Irish Sea. Hartington, to whom such prime-ministerial bromides were addressed, remained profoundly sceptical and began a gradual move towards the Tory policy of purchase, regarding, as he did, any placing of a 'heavy charge on the English [*sic*] Exchequer' a lesser evil than what, in his view, Gladstone was about to embark upon—namely, a wholesale 'confiscation of the rights of property'.[44]

The first attempt at Irish land legislation by Gladstone's second ministry—the Compensation for Disturbance Bill providing limited redress for certain tenants evicted for not paying their rents—was defeated in the House of Lords in August 1880, having already led to the resignation of Lord Lansdowne, a junior minister and a low-key herald for Argyll's departure from the cabinet in April 1881. This failure, together with reports from two royal commissions on the land question and the necessity, as Gladstone saw it, of balancing coercion (of which he was to prove something of a votary) with agrarian reform, led eventually to the Land Act of 1881. Though falling short of the demands being made by the Land League in Ireland, this went considerably further than the Act of 1870, something Gladstone always felt rather nervous about. Basically the Act granted the famous 3 F's—fixity of tenure, fair rent, free sale—though the prime minister tried to disguise this by inserting a good deal of needlessly equivocal language into the bill and by skirting around the glaring contradiction between its support for the survival of smallholdings and the economic case for larger farms by simply refusing 'to enter into the economical part of the subject at all'.[45] Indeed, at one point he was driven to insisting mysteriously that 'The "3 F's" I have always seen printed have been three capital F's; but the "three F's" in this Bill, if they are in it at all, are three little f's'.[46]

However, leaving aside such bizarre equivocations, the bill's most important clauses provided for the setting-up of a Land Court empowered to control rents according to criteria favourable to the tenants, with the result that, over the next twenty years, the rents of about 60 per cent of all occupiers (working almost two-thirds of cultivated land) were reduced by an average of 22 per cent.[47]

---

[43] Argyll to Gladstone, 5 April 1881, BL Gladstone Papers Add. MS 44105.

[44] Hartington to Gladstone, 9 and 19 December 1880, BL Gladstone Papers Add. MS 44145; Gladstone to Hartington, 12 December 1880, ibid.

[45] Parl. Deb. 3: cclx. 918 (7 April 1881) and cclxiii. 1419 (20 July 1881). Lord Carlingford (soon to succeed Argyll as Privy Seal) thought that, after a two-hour conversation, Gladstone's views remained 'very hard to understand' (Carlingford's Diary for 25 March 1881, BL Add. MS 63689).

[46] Parl. Deb. 3: cclxiii. 1419 (20 July 1881).

[47] M. Turner, 'Rural Economies in Post-Famine Ireland *c.* 1850–1914', in B. J. Graham and L. J. Proudfoot (eds), *An Historical Geography of Ireland* (London, 1993), 329.

Gladstone regarded all this as designed to 'save the principle of property from shipwreck'—a rather unconvincing genuflection to his long-held admiration for social hierarchy—but even more was it designed to place the cost of the operation firmly (indeed exclusively) upon landlord rather than government shoulders.[48] The powers of Irish landowners were now severely circumscribed. They lost income that they might otherwise have retained, and they could not rent to whomever they pleased, nor at market rates, with the result that the land market collapsed.

The main purpose of the 1881 Act was to make Irish proprietors pay for the economic ravages of the time. But, if it therefore gave a victory to the farmer community, it did so only in a manner that exacerbated the tensions that had long existed *within* that community as a whole. In particular, little or nothing was done to meet the demands of small western tenants for more land. And, while the Act's provisions certainly helped (together with severe coercion) to dampen agrarian agitation, their character and partiality undermined any success they might otherwise have possessed in defusing agrarian discontent in general. Some ministers, like Kimberley, were relieved that little or no state subsidies were involved, that, as he put it, no 'eleemosynary gifts of public money' were to be made to 'Irishmen' who would only have reacted by demanding more, though he agreed that it was now hopeless 'to apply to Ireland the same principles we applied in England'.[49] Others, like Forster, convinced themselves that no great concession had been made, because true 'freedom of contract' had never really existed in Ireland at all, and that, therefore, it trod on no ideological toes to admit that a system of 'dual ownership' (with both landlord and tenant subjected to legal restrictions and controls) was peculiarly suited to Irish circumstances.[50]

What Gladstone had done was to keep almost all of his senior colleagues and his party united behind a policy of Irish differentiation tempered by extreme financial caution and by a good deal of hot air designed to disguise the 1881 Act as less radical than it turned out to be. A few Liberals even began to trip down Gladstone's own memory lane by again talking about the sanctity of old Celtic customs, organic development, and the wondrous roles of chieftains and tribes.[51] And it was such things that most clearly revealed

---

[48] W. E. Gladstone, 'Mr Forster and Ireland', *Nineteenth Century*, 24 (1888), 454. The insignificant purchase provisions of the 1881 Act—under which a mere 731 holdings were bought, even fewer than under the 1870 legislation—fully reflected the ministry's reluctance to spend taxpayers' cash.

[49] Kimberley to Gladstone, 11 June 1881, BL Gladstone Papers Add. MS 44226; Parl. Deb. 3: ccliv. 1932 (2 August 1880).

[50] Forster to Gladstone, 7 December 1880, BL Gladstone Papers Add. MS 44158; Parl. Deb. 3: cclx. 1155–6 (25 April 1881).

[51] Parl. Deb. 3: cclvii. 609 (12 January 1881: Lefevre) and cclxi. 81 (9 May 1881: Summers); Ripon to Forster, 26 May 1881, BL Ripon Papers Add. MS 43537: The scheme was 'conservative in the truest sense' (Parl. Deb. 3: cclxiv. 236–7 (1 August 1881: Carlingford), cclxiv. 355

how Gladstone's particular political genius had made it at least temporarily possible to portray the 1881 Act as at once conservative and radical by—as his private secretary noted—seeming to be able 'to confine within the *narrower* bounds the operation of *exceptional* expediencies called for by the *peculiar* state of Ireland'.[52]

Above all, Liberal land policy in the period 1880–5 implied that state-aided purchase should be avoided if at all possible. Thus, while bowing to 'Irish ideas' and to the very different circumstances that prevailed in Ireland had, for Liberals, become acceptable, indeed admirable, it remained equally important that the United Kingdom Treasury should be protected against the substantial costs that might flow from purchase on any but the smallest scale. But, if the feeble purchase provisions in the legislation of 1870 and 1881 made this plain enough, the preservation of rigid fiscal austerities became more and more difficult as the years went by and circumstances changed and evolved.

In 1869 Gladstone had been fierce on the point that it was simply wrong on all sorts of grounds to 'force a peasant proprietorship into existence' in Ireland. 'I do not', he had told Fortescue, 'like to bring the Government into the land market as a buyer.'[53] Hence his dislike even of the modest purchase clauses added to the 1870 Act at the insistence of John Bright, which he feared might open the way to 'making the State a great Land Jobber'.[54] Nor did the Irish Land War of the late 1870s and early 1880s immediately change the Liberal position. When the Bessborough Commission proposed a more decisive move towards purchase in January 1881, Gladstone and other Liberals were horrified, tossing about words like 'wild' and insisting that the British taxpayer should be protected against schemes that might cost as much as £5 million a year.[55] Four years later one well-informed observer claimed that Charles

---

(1 August 1881: Spencer), cclxiv. 517 (2 August 1881: Selborne), cclxix. 1449–50 (23 May 1882: Cowan)).

[52] *Diary of Sir Edward Walter Hamilton 1880–1885*, ed. Bahlman, 108 (14 February 1881); Parl. Deb. 3: cclxi. 601 (16 May 1881: Gladstone); Gladstone to Spencer, 4 December 1881, BL Spencer Papers Add. MS 76853.

[53] Gladstone to Fortescue, 15 September 1869, So[merset] R[ecord] O[ffice] Carlingford Papers DD/SH/61/324. He did not regard the 6,057 sales under the Disestablishment Act of that year as effecting any economic or social reform but simply as a means of 'breaking up properties' (H. Shearman, 'State-Aided Land Purchase under the Disestablishment Act of 1869', *Irish Historical Studies*, 4 (1944), 61).

[54] Gladstone to Granville, 24 May 1869, *The Political Correspondence of Mr Gladstone and Lord Granville 1868–1876*, ed. A. Ramm, Royal Historical Society Camden Third Series, lxxxi and lxxxii (1952), i. 22; Gladstone to Bright, 22 May 1869, J. Morley, *The Life of William Ewart Gladstone*, 3 vols (London, 1903), ii. 282–3; to Queen Victoria, 26 January 1870, *The Letters of Queen Victoria*, Second Series, ed. G. E. Buckle, 3 vols (London, 1926–8), ii. 6.

[55] *Report of Her Majesty's Commissioners into the Working of the Landlord and Tenant (Ireland) Act, 1870*, HC 1881 [C.2779], xviii. 35–56; *Diary of Sir Edward Walter Hamilton 1880–1885*, ed. Bahlman, i. 91 (19 December 1880); also *The Diaries of Edward Henry Stanley, 15th Earl of Derby (1826–93) between 1878 and 1893: A Selection*, ed. J. Vincent (Oxford, 2003), 281 (15 November 1880); Gladstone to Forster, 7 December 1880, BL Gladstone Papers Add. MS

Russell (then a Liberal MP and later Lord Chief Justice of England) had in 1881 moved an amendment in favour of more generous terms only to find Gladstone leaving his seat on the Treasury Bench, coming over and sitting 'down beside him' and strongly urging that he desist, saying 'I have made the tenure clauses of the bill so attractive that I shall by them wean the Irish peasant from the idea of purchasing his holding'.[56]

But, while Gladstone and other Liberals remained, to say the least, extremely cautious about purchase, already by 1880 one can detect stirrings of an idea that seemed to offer a way out of the dilemma posed by the party's long-standing adherence to fiscal rectitude. Writing to Forster in December 1880, Gladstone, after excoriating 'state purchase, state-landlordism, state creditorship', suddenly admitted that he would entirely change his mind 'if we can combine this ... with ... the establishment of local self government in the Irish counties. The matter would then have in it a healthy principle of life and the impulse of public opinion would measure its operations.'[57] Sixteen months later this idea—that purchase *tout court* was a mark of the devil, but, if combined with some device for making the Irish directly responsible for the loans involved, could be sprinkled with redemptive angel dust—was beginning to assume a more concrete shape. In April 1882 Gladstone, though remaining as staunch as ever against Tory notions of establishing 'the Irish tenant under a scheme of vast width as the debtor of the British Exchequer', had become happy to consider plans being drawn up by a cabinet colleague, Hugh Childers (soon to become Chancellor of the Exchequer), to set up county boards in Ireland that 'were to be the authorities' to carry out and supervise any system of purchase, a scheme that 'I think offers a way of escape from a plan in which the last state would be worse than the first'.[58]

Soon other Liberal ministers were adopting a similar approach and seeing the establishment of Irish local bodies responsible for the debts involved in purchase as providing the best 'way of escape' from the dangers of financial irresponsibility.[59] Even so, an overall disposition *against* purchase continued to dominate the Liberal mind, with Gladstone in particular unable to rid himself of a visceral distaste for anything the Tories might do in that direction.

44158; Kimberley to Gladstone, 11 June 1881, ibid., Add. MS 44226; Carlingford's Diary for 12 April 1882, BL Add. MS 63690.

[56] *Dublin Castle and the First Home Rule Crisis; The Political Journal of Sir George Fottrell, 1884-1887*, ed. S. Ball, Royal Historical Society Camden Fifth Series, xxxiii (2008), 106.

[57] Gladstone to Forster, 15 December 1880, Hammond, *Gladstone and the Irish Nation*, 187.

[58] Gladstone to Forster, 30 April 1882, BL Gladstone Papers Add. MS 44160; Hammond, *Gladstone and the Irish Nation*, 186.

[59] Spencer to Gladstone, 28 February 1884, BL Gladstone Papers Add. MS 44311; to Trevelyan, 5 March 1884, BL Spencer Papers Add. MS 76961; Kimberley's Memorandum, 13 May 1884, BL Gladstone Papers Add. MS 44228; Carlingford's Memorandum, 14 May 1884, ibid., Add. MS 44123.

Indeed, a kind of Gladstonian split personality seems to have developed over the whole matter. As late as June 1883, the prime minister was still publicly denouncing opposition policies that might involve the state in an 'almost incredible guarantee'. Yet in the spring of the previous year he had given permission for Treasury officials to collaborate with a leading Tory, W. H. Smith, in drawing up a possible cross-party scheme for the state-aided purchase of Irish land.[60] However, when it came to substantive legislation, the Liberal government continued to incline against anything of a dramatic or expensive nature. Trevelyan introduced a feeble bill in May 1884, and another was announced in May 1885. Both sank without trace. And Gladstone, to the annoyance of his then chief secretary, Campbell-Bannerman, maintained a generally 'evasive' attitude to the matter right up to the last days of the ministry in June 1885.[61]

It was the short-lived Tory administration under Salisbury that held office for the next seven months that finally implemented state-assisted purchase on a significant scale by means of the so-called Ashbourne Act of August 1885. Although this was introduced by Ashbourne (now Lord Chancellor of Ireland and a member of the cabinet) in language designed to appeal predominantly to landlords, and although only £5 million was provided initially, the Act marked a massive ideological departure from Gladstone's feeble efforts of 1870 and 1881, the entire money being advanced at annual repayments lower than existing rents—a kind of 'something for nothing' bargain that few tolerably solvent farmers could resist. The number of holdings sold under the Act and its amending legislation had, by 1888, reached 25,367 as compared to the 1,608 sold under the legislation of 1870 and 1881 *combined*, while almost £10 million had been advanced.[62]

Most Liberals were highly critical of such lavishness, many reacting with a kind of appalled fascination at the fiscal heresies involved. Gladstone denounced the plan to lend money at cheap rates over forty-nine years as, among other things, a regrettable and 'real subsidy to the Irish landlords'.[63] Spencer was also unimpressed, wanting to proceed much more gradually so as to ensure (something he thought the Tories were not doing) that only what might reasonably be regarded as an 'intelligent, independent, and enlightened

[60] Parl. Deb. 3: cclxxx. 446-7 (12 June 1883); Hammond, *Gladstone and the Irish Nation*, 257–8; Matthew, *Gladstone 1875–1898*, 200–1.

[61] J. E. Pomfret, *The Struggle for Land in Ireland 1800–1923* (Princeton, 1930), 226–8; *Diary of Sir Edward Walter Hamilton 1880–1885*, ed. Bahlman, ii. 866 (18 May 1885); Parl. Deb. 3: ccxcviii. 971–2 (20 May 1885: Gladstone); J. A. Spender, *The Life of the Right Hon. Sir Henry Campbell-Bannerman, GCB*, 2 vols (London, [1923]), i. 80–3; *Lord Carlingford's Journal: Reflections of a Cabinet Minister 1885*, ed. A. B. Cooke and J. R. Vincent (Oxford, 1971), 103 (15 May 1885).

[62] Pomfret, *Struggle for Land in Ireland*, 307.

[63] Gladstone to J. Chamberlain, 1 August 1885, B[irmingham] U[niversity] J. Chamberlain Papers JC5/34/37.

class of small proprietors' would eventually emerge. He thought the terms too generous, as did colleagues like Shaw Lefevre, who saw the whole thing as little more than a system of relief for improvident Irish landlords. Nearly all Liberals agreed that the Act was 'fraught with novelty', would cost far too much, and amounted to little more than 'an immediate and most valuable present' to all those in Ireland who had long been expert in the arts of the mendicant.[64] While, therefore, Liberal opposition was fairly general, its terms differed from one man to another. Gladstone obtained his firmest support from Radicals, who, as the editor of the *Fortnightly Review* noted, thought it 'intolerable that the Irish peasant should always be allowed priority in the deliberations of the Government over the labouring classes of England'.[65]

And then came the bombshell. For various complex reasons involving equal doses of long-term thinking and immediate pragmatism, Gladstone had begun to turn 'Home Rule' for Ireland 'into a legislative proposal in the autumn of 1885', something he was able to inject into the world of practical decision-making when he returned as prime minister in February 1886. By thought processes that, despite much subsequent analysis, remain largely mysterious, the prime minister convinced himself that constitutional devolution both required and could be made to underwrite a significant land purchase scheme. 'There were', as the best interpreter of the issue has written, probably two things that lay behind this: 'the strategic argument that an orderly Ireland now could not be so without a considerable degree of peasant proprietary, and the tactical argument that without the opportunity for escape which land purchase gave to the landlord class, a Home Rule bill would have no chance of passing'.[66] And, indeed, this may well have been the case, but it had equally been the case made by the Tory government of 1885–6, whose proposals Gladstone had been the first to denounce. The only new element was the importance given by Gladstone to the fact that any new parliament and administration in Dublin resulting from Home Rule would now become 'responsible' for the debts incurred by tenants purchasing their holdings.[67] And, while this was undoubtedly a neat idea and might certainly be seen as a

---

[64] Parl. Deb. 3: ccxcix. 1343–4 (21 July 1885: Spencer), ccc. 1086–93 (4 August 1885: Shaw Lefevre) and 1623–9 (10 August 1885: Davey); Sir George Campbell (Gladstone's guru on land reform in 1869–70) condemned the wild excess of the legislation; the initial £5 million would, he declared, become more than £200 million in no time at all: Parl. Deb. 3: ccc. 1634.

[65] Heyck, *Dimensions of British Radicalism*, 91–2, 195–6.

[66] Matthew, *Gladstone 1875–1898*, 216, 244.

[67] See Gladstone to Queen Victoria, 23 May 1885, TNA CAB 41/19/38, where he was already arguing that any purchase scheme would only be 'safe when guarantees were given to the Treasury by a local Irish authority or when such an authority was substituted for the Treasury', something that had not been the case with the scheme 'promulgated in recent years under auspices called Conservative'; also Gladstone to Queen Victoria, 13 March 1886, TNA CAB 41/20/10.

'necessary' precondition for large-scale purchase, it could hardly be regarded as a fully 'sufficient' one.

Puzzlement over Gladstone's reasoning is increased by the modest force of his arguments, the massive scale of his proposals, and his very rapid reversion to type once the Tories had returned to office after the defeat of Home Rule in the summer of 1886. And the proposed expenditure was undoubtedly enormous and would, had it ever been called upon, have made Gladstone's bill of 1886 much the most expensive land purchase scheme in the whole of the nineteenth century. Nor were matters helped by vagueness as to the precise amounts that might be involved, itself hardly a notable advertisement for the prime minister's much-vaunted economic and financial expertise. First there was talk of £120 million, then of £60 million, then of £50 million, reductions that Gladstone admitted were made for largely presentational reasons and could always be abandoned once the bill had become law. Whatever else this was, it was certainly treating Ireland very differently from Britain and doing so with a vengeance. But Gladstone had now convinced himself (a process usually tortuous but also usually definitive) that 'only by exerting *to the uttermost* our financial strength' could there be any hope of sustaining 'the burden of an adequate land measure'.[68]

But it was the enormous amounts bound up in Gladstone's proposals that, quite apart from all other considerations, fatally undermined his bill. 'Vivid pictures', Morley later recalled, 'were drawn of a train of railway trucks two miles long, loaded with millions of bright sovereigns, all travelling from the pocket of the British son of toil to the pocket of the idle Irish landlord.'[69] And, the more Gladstone defended himself with talk of a responsible Irish 'authority' standing between the 'British Treasury' and 'the individual occupier and farmer in Ireland' and of how restitution of some kind was ethically required because 'the deeds of the Irish landlords are to a great extent our deeds, we are *participes criminis*', the more critics mocked his tearful moralism or, as W. H. Smith pointed out, recalled how the prime minister had blocked all previous plans of any substance on the grounds that these had emanated from politicians of whom he disapproved.[70]

---

[68] Gladstone to Harcourt, 12 February 1886, Bodl. Harcourt Papers MS 10, where Gladstone talks of a scheme 'calculated on a scale which will *exceed* that of any former transaction of this country' and argues that 'without an adequate land measure we cannot either establish order or face the question of Irish Government ... The case appears to be one altogether exceptional.'

[69] Morley, *Life of William Ewart Gladstone*, iii. 325.

[70] Parl. Deb. 3: ccciv. 1786–7 (16 April 1886: Gladstone) and 1825 (Smith). Gladstone seamlessly combined comments about being '*participes criminis*' with hopes that most Irish landlords would remain in post and not sell out and that 'even the Irish Nationalists' might 'desire that those marked out by leisure, wealth, and station for attention to public duties' would eventually 'become, in no small degree, the natural, and effective, and safe leaders of the people' (Parl. Deb. 3: ccciv. 1794).

When the Home Rule Bill was defeated in the Commons on 8 June 1886, the purchase bill, which, because of its complexity, had actually taken priority as regards preparation, sank with the overall wreckage. Salisbury returned as prime minister, and the Tories held office until December 1905, with only a brief Liberal interval between August 1892 and June 1895. With respect to Irish land, the real significance of all this lay in the speed and enthusiasm with which Liberals of all kinds dropped the idea of state-aided purchase. Gladstone, who was determined to give Home Rule another outing if at all possible, behaved as if his massive plans of 1886 had been no more than a bad dream. On 27 July, two days after Salisbury had succeeded as prime minister, he sent a memorandum to senior colleagues announcing that they could 'no longer maintain the inseparability' of the Home Rule and purchase bills. While Spencer thought this merely meant that the 'twinship' of the two measures had been broken, Harcourt more realistically proclaimed 'that any land purchase scheme for Ireland was [now] impossible' as far as the Liberal Party was concerned.[71] For his part, Gladstone simply seems to have lost interest in spending money on Irish land when tenurial legislation (as in 1870 and 1881) could be introduced at virtually no cost at all, at least so far as the Exchequer was concerned. When in 1887 the so-called Round Table discussions about a possible reunion between Gladstonian Liberals and those (like Chamberlain and Hartington) who had departed over Home Rule took place, Gladstone made no effort to raise land purchase as a possible topic for discussion.[72]

What seems to have happened was that Gladstone, increasingly obsessed with the importance of Home Rule, had simply reverted to earlier and fiercely parsimonious attitudes. It was not that rejection of purchase had become a primary passion—he remained relaxed about the handful of (mostly younger) Liberals such as Haldane, Grey, and (less consistently) Morley who still supported the idea[73]—so much so that it had somehow fallen off Gladstone's radar and become lost amid the nether regions of fiscal propriety. In 1888 Gladstone strongly opposed Tory plans to extend the provisions of the Ashbourne Act, but still found it possible to tell those Liberals who took a different view that dissent 'of this kind does not in any way shock or shake me.

---

[71] Gladstone's Memorandum of 27 July 1886, BL Gladstone Papers Add. MS 44772; Spencer to Harcourt, 31 August 1886, Bodl. Harcourt Papers MS 45.

[72] J. Chamberlain, *A Political Memoir 1880–1892*, ed. C. H. D. Howard (London, 1953), 243 (4 January 1887).

[73] See H. C. G. Matthew, *The Liberal Imperialists: The Ideas and Politics of a Post-Gladstonian Elite* (Oxford, 1973), 266; Parl. Deb. 3: cccxx. 1668 (20 November 1888: Grey); Grey to Haldane, 8 November 1890, N[ational] L[ibrary of] S[cotland] Haldane Papers MS 5903; Morley to Gladstone, 1 August 1887, BL Gladstone Papers Add. MS 44255, though Morley also displayed bouts of Gladstonian irritation about Tory extravagance, e.g. Parl. Deb. 3: ccix. 1142–3 (21 September 1886) and cccx. 910–11 (8 February 1887).

I have a comfort in referring them very much to the nature of the Liberal Party, and the laws under which it exists, laws on the whole healthful and beneficial and free.'[74] Whatever this characteristically obscure comment actually meant, it certainly did not mean that expenditure on the purchase of Irish land had, or was likely ever to, become a pressing priority for the Liberal Party.

And, indeed, within the party as a whole, it was undoubtedly Gladstone rather than Haldane and Grey who represented majority opinion. Harcourt became ever stronger in his denunciations of Tory extravagance, of buying 'up at a capital sum, at the expense of the British taxpayer, land upon a rental which it is impossible the land could ever obtain'. Labouchere thought the same, while backbench Liberals denounced Tory lavishness as primarily designed to prop up undeserving Irish landlords, a tawdry policy of 'kicks and ha'pence', as wrong in the second particular as in the first.[75] As the Radical Sir Wilfrid Lawson put it in 1890: 'You might as well buy up all the post-horses because the posting business has gone wrong', adding (in words that would have shocked his leader): 'What use are landlords? I am a landlord myself. I never found out what use I was.'[76]

In July 1891 Spencer recorded Gladstone's belief that 'he and other Liberals in the H. of Commons' now considered themselves 'pledged not to use the Imperial credit for the purpose of Irish Land Purchase'. And during the general election campaign of 1892 Liberal placards were posted around English constituencies denouncing Tory profligacy especially as regards the £35 million that it was (inaccurately) claimed Salisbury's government had spent on state-assisted land purchase in Ireland. Indeed, six months before the election Gladstone had talked to a confidant of the Tories' 'reckless expenditure in Ireland', their purchase scheme being nothing more than 'a precedent for rankest socialism'.[77] Small wonder, therefore, that the Home Rule Bill of 1893 was not accompanied, as had been the case seven years earlier, by any scheme for purchase, something that Liberal Unionists like Devonshire (the former

---

[74] Gladstone to Haldane, 21 November 1888, NLS Haldane Papers MS 5903; also R. B. Haldane, *An Autobiography* (London, 1912), 111–12 (based on NLS Haldane Papers MS 5921).

[75] Parl. Deb. 3: cccviii. 196–7 (20 August 1886: Harcourt) and 325 (23 August 1886: Illingworth), cccxxx. 1762–3 (21 November 1888: Labouchere), 1705–7 (20 November 1888: Neville), cccxliii. 1654 (29 April 1890: Labouchere).

[76] Parl. Deb. 3: cccxlix. 153 (27 November 1890: Lawson); also cccx. 1179 (10 February 1887: Fowler), cccxiii. 1567 (22 April 1887: Kimberley), cccxiv. 29 (26 April 1887: Reid), cccxvii. 569 (12 July 1887: Lefevre), cccxlix. 387 (2 December 1890: Reid), ccclii. 247–8 (10 April 1891: Labouchere).

[77] Spencer's Memorandum of a conversation with Gladstone, 28 July 1891, *The Red Earl: The Papers of the Fifth Earl Spencer 1835–1910*, ed. P. Gordon, 2 vols (Northampton, 1981–6: Publications of the Northamptonshire Record Society, xxxi and xxxiv), ii. 171–3; Parl. Deb. 4: vii. 344 (11 August 1892: Sir E. Clarke); Brooks, 'Gladstone's Fourth Administration', 230.

Hartington) took delight in pointing out, not least because Spencer and others had so strongly stressed the inseparability of the two policies in 1886.[78]

After once again entering opposition in 1895, the Liberals, now no longer led by Gladstone, largely lost interest in land purchase. When the matter occasionally reached the surface of consciousness, it was quickly put back in its box by posing the crucial question 'How can we ask the B[ritish] Taxpayer to lend his credit at present to so huge an extent?' and by puzzlement as to how any scheme could be devised sufficiently generous to make it possible for quasi-bankrupt Irish landlords to emerge with money in the bank.[79] The Gordian knot was finally cut by the Tories in 1903 by means of the hyper-expensive Wyndham Act of that year (for which see Chapter 9, Section III). In 1907 a Liberal chief secretary (Birrell) still shuddered over the cost. 'We have started upon a path which if it is pursued involves *millions*. Yet how can we stop & say "Not a yard further"?'[80] But only two years later the Liberals themselves threw in the towel. Wyndham's Act, as Birrell noted, had simply made it impossible to remain standing on good old Gladstonian ground. Even so, Birrell's own Act of 1909, though generous by Liberal standards, was more restrictive and notably less expensive than its mighty Tory predecessor, a sort of final genuflection to the Gladstonian ghosts of yesteryear. As it turned out, these lingering mini-meannesses, while not pleasing many farmers, certainly pleased the leaders of the Irish Parliamentary Party, who (John Dillon chief among them) distrusted land purchase as designed to take the Irish public's eye off the Home Rule ball. For them, as Alvin Jackson has observed, 'a penny-pinching Liberal purchase measure was in some ways ideal', indicating as it did 'the productivity of the Liberal alliance without offering any permanent land settlement in advance of Home Rule, and without offering enough ... to lure Irish nationalists into the British embrace'.[81]

But, while Tories and Liberals differed fundamentally on purchase and Home Rule, they remained in close agreement that Ireland could now most effectively be ruled by policies and laws that neither of them would have supported in Britain. What distinguished the parties was how best this Hibernicized agenda could be configured and implemented rather than anything to do with the intellectual or pragmatic analysis upon which a now common adoption of Anglo-Irish differentiation about the fundamentals of Irish government had increasingly come to be based.

---

[78] J. H. Murphy, *Ireland's Czar: Gladstonian Government and the Lord Lieutenancies of the Red Earl Spencer 1868–86* (Dublin, 2014), 387.

[79] Campbell-Bannerman to Spencer, 5 January 1901, BL Spencer Papers Add. MS 76873; Spencer to Campbell-Bannerman, 9 January 1901, ibid.

[80] P. Jalland, 'A Liberal Chief Secretary and the Irish Question: Augustine Birrell, 1907–1914', *Historical Journal*, 19 (1976), 433.

[81] A. Jackson, *Ireland 1798–1998: Politics and War* (Oxford, 1999), 161.

III

Not only did the Irish policy of the Liberal Party now depend upon the idea that Irish problems were most effectively addressed by following essentially Hibernian rather than Anglo-Saxon predicates (something now almost a cross-party truism), but the thread connecting the particular programmes carried out by successive Liberal administrations had come to be spun largely from the principles of fiscal prudence, an idea that had, quite clearly, *not* become a cross-party postulate. Thus Home Rule in 1886 and 1893 was attractive to Gladstone and his followers, not only for the emotional and 'moral' reasons so eloquently put forward in the prime minister's speech of 8 June 1886, but because it could so easily (if not always convincingly) be portrayed as, above all, a cheap policy capable of protecting British taxpayers from the ravages of ever-accelerating Celtic extravagance. What, therefore, united Liberal land reform and Liberal Home Rule was not simply a joint adherence to the notion of dealing with Ireland according to 'Irish ideas', but the fact that both were consciously designed to save money and prevent taxes from ballooning out of control.

When money was not directly involved, then relics of the old assimilationism might, in certain limited circumstances, still be tolerated. This was most obviously the case with regard to the franchise and constituency changes introduced by the so-called Third Reform Act(s) of 1884–5.[82] Thinking about reform in these areas had been evident among ministers for some time, and the precise details were hammered out by means of cross-party negotiations led by Gladstone, on the one side, and Salisbury, on the other. As early as 1883 views were being expressed by members of the cabinet as to how Ireland might be affected by legislation that would, for the first time, deal with the United Kingdom as a single entity. Hitherto Ireland (and Scotland) had been subject to individual franchise legislation and, indeed, the Irish franchise (left virtually intact by the Second Reform Acts of 1867–8) had remained almost unchanged since 1850.

Ministers were worried that any sudden increase in electoral 'democracy' in Ireland would greatly assist the increasing power of Parnell's Home Rule Party, that, in other words, assimilation in this respect would be a thoroughly bad thing from London's point of view. However, not only did they persuade themselves that uniformity of electoral provision throughout the United Kingdom had become unavoidable and that any refusal would add to Irish grievances and agitation, but they also argued themselves into the rather optimistic conclusion

---

[82] More precisely, the Representation of the People Act of 1884 and the Redistribution of Seats Act of 1885, which followed the important Corrupt Practices Act of 1883. See K. T. Hoppen, 'The Franchise and Electoral Politics in England and Ireland 1832–1885', *History*, 70 (1985), 202–17.

that a decisive extension of voting rights in Ireland, by enfranchising smaller farmers and landless labourers, would undermine Parnell's power base, which they believed depended heavily upon support from larger agriculturalists. It might, as one chief secretary pointed out, 'do good ... by bringing in a counterpoise to the class of farmers who have quite an inordinate and dangerous influence on the parliamentary action of the representatives and ... by affecting the classes at present excluded with some sense of political responsibility'.[83]

Gladstone clung to the belief that giving agricultural labourers the vote in Ireland might well restrain rather than encourage Parnell. 'I think', he wrote in October 1883, 'it should not be assumed that the more limited franchise is the more conservative. I even would say, with plausibility if not more, that in so far as the Irish franchise is to be considered, its badness is such that it could not be aggravated.'[84] Having come to a view, Gladstone went all the way, telling followers that excessive caution was now both politically impractical and almost certainly counterproductive. Spencer, more wary in these matters, had come to the same conclusion, seeing no harm in 'bringing the Irish labourers into the constituencies because they do not pull now with the farmers. They might moderate each other.'[85] Harcourt characteristically (and rightly) thought the Liberal game in Ireland long lost, for, even if a more limited franchise was possible (which it was not), few if any seats would actually be saved from the fast-moving Parnellite juggernaut. Others persuaded themselves that uniformity of franchise throughout the Kingdom actually involved an acceptance of the 'temperaments and requirements' of the Irish people and could therefore rather mysteriously be seen as constituting a kind of acknowledgement of Ireland's right to have 'ideas' of its own.[86]

Three points need to be made about the relationship between the electoral reforms of 1884–5 and the Irish policies of the party leaders. In the first place, the expectations of Gladstone and others that giving Irish labourers the vote might hinder rather than assist Parnell were (though in the end wrong) neither fanciful nor absurd. For many years agricultural labourers in Ireland had been notably exploited by farmers of various kinds, and it was, therefore, by no means unrealistic to imagine that this might generate deep electoral

---

[83] Trevelyan to Gladstone, 26 October 1883, BL Gladstone Papers Add. MS 44335; W. A. Hayes, *The Background and Passage of the Third Reform Act* (New York, 1982), 83–4, 87; Carlingford's Diary for 25 October 1883, BL Add. MS 63691. For the government's dilemma on the matter, see P. H. Bagenal to W. H. Smith, [1884], R[eading] U[niversity], Smith (Hambleton) Papers PS8/135.

[84] Gladstone to Hartington, 23 October 1883, BL Gladstone Papers Add. MS 44546; to Trevelyan, 23 October 1883, ibid.

[85] Gladstone to Hartington, 3 December 1883 and 1 March 1884, Spencer to Hartington, 21 October 1883, all ChH Devonshire Papers, Secret Service Box.

[86] Harcourt to Spencer, 29 December 1883, Bodl. Harcourt Papers MS 42; Spencer to Harcourt, 30 December 1883, ibid.; Herbert Gladstone's speech at Leeds: *The Times*, 13 February 1883.

differences between the two groups. However, while labourers, as a proportion of the rural population, had substantially declined after—and because of—the Famine (something British politicians had of course predicted and welcomed), Parnell's party proved surprisingly effective in appealing to a pan-class alliance in the non-landlord sector as a whole. By 1880–1 the Land League, as part of the delicate and shifting acrobatics it was then performing between the various interests it sought to mobilize, had ceased to ignore the labourer question, and not without result and response, something observers in London and Dublin Castle signally failed to take on board.[87] In the second place, fears that the franchise reforms of 1884–5 would unleash the Parnellite hound missed the point, for that animal had long been on the loose. Not only had Parnell's National League increased its branch network from 818 to 1,261 in the six months leading up to the elections of November and December 1885, but Home Rulers had won no less than twenty-one of the twenty-three by-elections they had contested outside Ulster since the general election of 1880.[88] Indeed, Parnell himself had become convinced that he would win possibly eighty seats in 1885 even without further franchise extension (he actually won eighty-five), while Gladstone and Spencer had always been rightly sceptical about the effect an altered franchise would have 'in augmenting the power of Parnellism'.[89] In the third place, Ireland was in fact treated very differently from England and Scotland in the important matter of the redistribution of seats. While in 1801 and 1832 Ireland had, on population grounds, been substantially under-represented at Westminster, the effects of the Famine had begun to reverse this. Carlingford had pointed out in 1883 that a falling Irish population (falling even more dramatically when measured against rising numbers in Britain) should logically lead to fewer MPs.[90] But Gladstone thought differently. Cutting the number of MPs below its existing level of 103 would, he believed, have too many negative consequences for other parts of the United Kingdom. And, in any case—and here the prime minister adopted his grandest and airiest style—it was foolish to waste time on the 'paltry difference between 70 members or 80 members or 90 members' for Ireland. He rejoiced that, even after 1884–5, national franchises would not be 'absolutely identical' and was clearly happy to continue with the well-established system of having quite separate boundary

---

[87] Hoppen, *Elections, Politics, and Society in Ireland*, 90, 94–104, 179–80, 343–53, 473–9.

[88] Ibid. 276–7; B. M. Walker (ed.), *Parliamentary Election Results in Ireland, 1801–1922* (Dublin, 1978), 127–9. They also won a seat in Ulster and failed to contest two very small and corrupt southern boroughs. The Dublin University constituency has been excluded.

[89] F. S. L. Lyons, *Charles Stewart Parnell* (London, 1977), 265; Gladstone to Hartington, 29 December 1883, BL Gladstone Papers Add. MS 44146; for Spencer, see Gladstone's Memorandum about the relevant cabinet meeting, *The Prime Ministers' Papers: W. E. Gladstone*, ed. J. Brooke and M. Sorensen, 4 vols (London, 1971–81), i. 103–4 (written years later).

[90] Carlingford to Spencer, 12 November 1883, BL Spencer Papers Add. MS 76910.

commissions and registration processes for England, Scotland, and Ireland.[91] All in all, such franchise equality as was introduced in 1884–5 was the result, not so much of conviction at Westminster, as of demands from Irish nationalists for 'equal treatment', demands that could be, and not infrequently were, withdrawn as circumstances required: equality as to voting rights, clear differentiation (that is, inequality) when it came to land legislation, expenditure, Home Rule, or, in this case, Ireland's allocation of MPs.

IV

While meeting Irish demands on the matter of franchise was a tolerably big thing, moving towards various versions of devolution was a very much bigger thing. It was certainly so for Gladstone, who, always a self-analyser, identified four occasions in his long political life when Providence had endowed him 'with anything which can be called a striking gift ... What may be termed appreciation of the general situation and its result.' Two (perhaps two-and-a-quarter) of these concerned Ireland, most prominently the 'proposal for religious equality ... in 1868' (that is, disestablishment) and that for 'Home Rule ... in 1886'—land reform, something Gladstone had never felt entirely at ease with, being notable for its absence from the list.[92] Home Rule, entirely predictably, is included because its acceptance by Gladstone and the majority of the Liberal Party was one of the most significant changes of gear in Victorian political life as well as perhaps the prime example of treating Ireland differently or, in the contemporary phrase, 'according to Irish ideas'. And, while it is, of course, dangerous to read retrospective inevitability into Gladstone's journey, it is no less (perhaps even more) misleading to dismiss all the early intimations of what was to come as unimportant, irrelevant, mere short-term expedients.[93] In old age, Gladstone himself rightly insisted that he had only once—in September 1871 at Aberdeen—spoken publicly against Home Rule 'soon after the movement was set on foot', rather misleadingly going on to detect support for devolution in his speech on the Address of 9 February 1882, a speech actually shot through with qualifications and doubts as to the

---

[91] Parl. Deb. 3: cclxxxvii. 1089 (1 May 1884), also cclxxxv. 116 (28 February 1884); D. Nicholls, *The Lost Prime Minister: A Life of Sir Charles Dilke* (London, 1995), 151–4.

[92] *Prime Minister's Papers: W. E. Gladstone*, ed. Brooke and Sorensen, i. 136. The 'quarter' was 'the renewal of the income tax in 1853'.

[93] As is largely the argument of the otherwise deeply interesting A. B. Cooke and J. Vincent, *The Governing Passion: Cabinet Government and Party Politics in Britain 1885–86* (Brighton, 1974), especially 48–54.

practicality of making clear distinctions between purely 'Irish' and essentially 'Imperial' affairs.[94]

Faulty and self-justifying recollections should not, however, obscure the fact that, even during his first administration and notwithstanding the Aberdeen speech, Gladstone exhibited anxiety about the over-centralization of government in Ireland, together with matching signs of a conviction that some remedy for this was urgently required. It would, therefore, be misleading to regard denunciations by Liberal leaders in the 1870s of Home Rule (then a very nebulous concept) as evidence of blanket opposition to more acceptable forms of constitutional and legislative devolution. Spencer, who in October 1871 thought (as did Kimberley) that 'nothing would justify giving Home Rule', nonetheless told Irish interlocutors 'that the difficulties were not for all time'.[95] Indeed, less than three weeks after the Aberdeen speech, he met Gladstone at Hawarden and was—as viceroy—given a lecture about the importance of decentralizing the administration of Ireland. He raised worries about Irish jobbery, to which Gladstone replied: 'Oh Yes I do not say that it should be done wholesale but that opportunity should be seized ... when it could safely be done.'[96] Nine months later the prime minister was still much exercised by the importance of reviving and extending 'local self-government in Ireland' as a kind of protective homeopathic remedy that might eventually provide the basis for medicines of altogether greater potency. At more or less the same time the now-retired Earl Russell publicly argued in favour of 'provincial councils for legislative purposes' in Ireland, a proposal that Gladstone hailed as admirable in every way, not least because of its distinctly 'conservative' character.[97]

On going to the country in early 1874, Gladstone issued an address welcoming 'every improvement in the organisation of local and subordinate authority, which, under the unquestioned control of Parliament, would tend to lighten its labours and expedite the public business'. Spencer at once wrote from Dublin, pointing out that many Home Rulers could adopt this as an accurate 'definition' of their own principles and as an admission that 'the

---

[94] Parl. Deb. 4: xvi. 1489 (30 August 1893); R. B. O'Brien, *The Life of Charles Stewart Parnell* (London, [1910]), 561–2 (interview with Gladstone on 28 January 1897); *The Times*, 27 September 1871; Parl. Deb. 3: cclxvi. 260–6 (9 February 1882).

[95] Spencer to Hartington, 22 October 1871, ChH Devonshire Papers 354.79; Kimberley's Memorandum of 28 June 1871, BL Gladstone Papers Add. MS 44224; Kimberley to Dodson, 27 September 1871, *Liberal by Principle: The Politics of John Wodehouse, 1st Earl of Kimberley, 1843–1902*, ed. J. Powell (London, 1996), 130.

[96] Spencer's Memorandum of 14 October 1871, BL Spencer Papers Add. MS 76850. At the same meeting Gladstone 'admitted with some humorous shame that he had never been to Ireland, and said that he always kept that dark'.

[97] Gladstone to Spencer, 26 July 1872, BL Gladstone Papers Add. MS 44307; Hartington (then chief secretary) to Granville, 6 June 1873, ChH Devonshire Papers 340.535; Gladstone to Hartington, 3 February 1883, ibid. 340.1320.

Government winked at Home Rule'. Gladstone's put-down response came two days later: 'The paragraphs in my Address to which you find that objection is taken by some rather week-kneed brethren was read to and unanimously approved by the cabinet.'[98]

Having been defeated at the general election of February 1874, Gladstone not only retired from the party leadership but, with one important exception, remained silent on Irish matters. The exception was his three-week visit to Ireland in the autumn of 1877. During this he spoke again of the wonders of local government in all the 'shapes in which it is known to our history or agreeable to the spirit of our arrangements' and how these might be further developed in full accordance with 'the greatness of the country and the safety of its institutions'. He also, in a notable nod to the importance of acknow-ledging Irish distinctiveness, declared that 'dead and slavish uniformity is one of the greatest enemies of national excellence'. In the words of a recent analysis of the visit, he 'doffed his cap to Irish nationalism and O'Connell in particular … and visited the Bank of Ireland, the former home of the Irish parliament'. It can hardly, then, have been a surprise that there were those who saw all this as implying 'a compromise with Home Rule', and it was, indeed, remarkable how closely and publicly Gladstone associated himself with O'Connellism at more or less the precise moment that Parnell was coming to the fore in Irish political life.[99] Small wonder that the very day after Gladstone's return to England Hartington felt the urgent need to persuade Granville (and perhaps himself) that his leader had actually gone no further on the issue 'than I should like to go, or the average Liberal would like to go', only to find Gladstone casually claiming that, while in public his 'lips' had 'been closed' on the matter of 'local government' in Ireland, he actually went very much further than the 'average Liberal'—a remark simultaneously misleading regarding his recent remarks in Dublin and portentous for the future in general and the future of the Liberal Party in particular. Indeed, already in 1872 Hartington had—despite the Aberdeen speech—begun to worry that Gladstone's 'views on Home Rule are much too liberal' and that if the Home Rule Party would 'only propose to maintain the supremacy of the Imperial Parliament he does not much mind what they go in for'.[100]

[98] *The Times*, 24 January 1874; Spencer to Gladstone, 30 January 1874, and Gladstone to Spencer, 1 February 1874, *The Red Earl*, ed. Gordon, i. 116–17.

[99] K. McKenna, 'From Private Visit to Public Opportunity: Gladstone's 1877 Visit to Ireland', in M. E. Daly and K. T. Hoppen (eds), *Gladstone: Ireland and Beyond* (Dublin, 2011), 77–89; Lyons, *Charles Stewart Parnell*, 55–69.

[100] Hartington to Granville, 13 November 1877, TNA Granville Papers PRO 30/29/22A; Gladstone to Granville, 20 November 1877, *Political Correspondence of Mr Gladstone and Lord Granville 1876–1886*, ed. Ramm, i. 58; Hartington to Spencer, 11 May 1872, BL Spencer Papers Add. MS 76892.

The events of autumn 1877 did nothing to calm Hartington's fears or the fears of those with similar views, many of them returned to power after the Liberal victory at the general election of April 1880. Within months Gladstone had become more or less equally convinced about the importance of unleashing coercion to deal with the increasing agrarian violence in Ireland and of introducing remedial measures to address current discontents. As in 1868–70, he was reading intensively among historical sources, in particular the speeches and debates of the union period, which engendered surprise 'at the narrowness of the case upon which the [Irish] Parliament was condemned'. While assuring his new chief secretary that he nourished no dreams of actually 'reviving the Irish Parliament', he did not disguise a belief that 'greater facilities' must now be given for 'the transaction of sectional, and therefore for Irish subjects', and lost no time in preparing a memorandum to that effect. Although the same kind of reading about the Union was repeated in October 1885 just as the final leap towards full Home Rule was taking place, already the memorandum sent to Forster in October 1880 (and later printed for cabinet use) provides evidence of the prime minister's characteristic 'now-you-see-it, now-you-don't' way of analysing 'devolution' as a means of 'satisfying … the call for what is styled (*in bonam partem*) "local government", and (*in malem*) "Home Rule"'.[101] For a man so aware that politics was not only the art of the ideal but also the art of the practical, this was a significant admission of movement as far as Irish matters were concerned.

By September 1881 Gladstone was happy to tell the voters of Leeds 'that Home Rule has for one of its senses Local Government, an excellent thing to which I should affix no limits except the supremacy of the Imperial Parliament' and to insist that such views—as Hartington had noted nine years earlier—were nothing new as far as he was concerned.[102] For Joseph Chamberlain, now in the cabinet for the first time, this was very shocking indeed. While, like his leader, prepared for significant Hibernocentric reforms on the land question, he entirely refused to contemplate any tampering with what he dismissively called Ireland's 'sentimental grievance—the Union'. As no concessions could therefore be made on this, Chamberlain's only alternative was 'war to the knife', a conclusion that the prime minister, though in many ways prepared for severe doses of temporary coercion, consistently failed to reach.[103]

---

[101] Gladstone to Forster, 25 October 1880, BL Gladstone Papers Add. MS 44157; *Diaries of Edward Henry Stanley, 15th Earl of Derby … between 1878 and 1893*, ed. Vincent, 815–16 (about a visit to Hawarden on 1 October 1885); Hammond, *Gladstone and the Irish Nation*, 200.

[102] Gladstone to Granville, 16 September 1881, *The Political Correspondence of Mr Gladstone and Lord Granville 1876–1886*, ed. Ramm, i. 293.

[103] P. T. Marsh, *Joseph Chamberlain: Entrepreneur in Politics* (New Haven, 1994), 149; Chamberlain to Morley, 18 October and 18 December 1881, BU J. Chamberlain Papers JC5/54/381 and 421.

What drove Gladstone and some of his senior colleagues into a crablike shuffle towards constitutional adjustment was a growing belief in the healing (indeed unifying) power of administrative and legislative devolution linked to the age-old Liberal hankering after cheap government. In Ireland the two responsible ministers, Trevelyan and Spencer, supported some kind of self-government because this alone could, they believed, 'protect the Treasury from local and provincial demands for money', Spencer in particular agreeing with Gladstone about the importance of getting 'public expenditure thrown on local rates' despite acute worries as to how this would work in a country where 'all parties combine to fleece the Treasury'.[104]

Already by April 1882 Gladstone was drawing up plans for a bill creating four 'provincial councils' in Ireland to deal with education and certain other matters and with modest powers to enter into the land market by being allowed to 'capitalize' their annual grant incomes. He was, indeed, moving with increasing speed, having convinced himself that 'the least danger is going forward at once. It is liberty alone which fits men for liberty.'[105] While this was, of course, a recipe for virtually unlimited activity, Gladstone did not find it easy to solve the inherent contradiction between a continuing dislike of 'any sort of assembly (for Ireland) in Dublin'—a question 'not in the nearer future'—and the overwhelming importance of 'creating local bodies in Ireland who can deal with us in an Irish sense'.[106]

Quite rapidly, therefore, by January 1883 the proposed provincial councils were being envisaged as something much grander than at first conceived, with Gladstone excitedly noting that

> peasant proprietary—the winter's distress—the state of the labourers—the loans to farmers—the promotion of public works—the encouragement of fisheries—the promotion of emigration—each and every one of these questions has a sting, and the sting can only be taken out of it by our treating it in correspondence with a popular and responsible *Irish* body.

Best of all, not only would such a plan stop government as a whole from seeming 'to the common Irishman ... an exotic, a foreign thing', but it would be economical in the very best sense by reducing the burden on taxpayers and simultaneously underpinning the deeper values of tradition and hierarchy, 'for, regarding the scheme as conservative, I incline to consider this form of it

---

[104] Spencer to Hartington, 10 December 1882 and 13 January 1883, ChH Devonshire Papers 340.1287 and 1310.

[105] Carlingford's Diary for 12 April 1882, BL Add. MS 63690; Trevelyan to Spencer, 3 January 1882 [*recte* 1883], BL Spencer Papers Add. MS 76952; Gladstone to Forster, 12 April 1882, BL Gladstone Papers Add. MS 44545.

[106] Gladstone to Granville, 30 November, 11 and 13 April 1882, *The Political Correspondence of Mr Gladstone and Lord Granville 1876–1886*, ed. Ramm, i. 461, 358, 359–60.

the most conservative'.[107] What, therefore, Gladstone was seeking was fiscal
prudence through the establishment of increasingly powerful authorities in
Ireland, a consolidation of the values generated by traditional social forces,
and a real and distinct salute to Irish distinctiveness, all of them designed to
strengthen the Union, which, in his opinion, had been so necessarily but
insensitively enacted in 1800. Some of his colleagues, notably Spencer and
Granville, eventually went along with much of this. Others, notably Hartington and Chamberlain, did not.[108] Spencer, who had initially been a very
reluctant devolutionist, became more and more convinced that repression
was of limited value. 'We have begun with the Land Act,' he noted in
September 1884, 'we go on with the Franchise, we must carry a large and
wide measure of Local Government ... I think it very probable that we shall
come to what is very like the Home Rule called for by the best Nationalists.'[109]

The logjam broke in 1885. A crisis in May had exposed differences with
regard to Ireland within a Liberal cabinet rapidly falling into irritation and
exhaustion. Eventually three members—Chamberlain, Dilke, and Shaw
Lefevre—offered their resignations, which were neither accepted nor withdrawn.[110] Then on 8 June the government was defeated in the Commons on
an amendment to the budget. After a few weeks of haggling, Salisbury took
over at the head of a minority Tory administration, with (and this turned
many Liberal stomachs) a certain amount of, in the event, rather wavering
Parnellite support. The Tories, with a distinct eye on the main chance of
parliamentary survival, failed to renew coercion, while Gladstone, clearing out
his official room, 'had a moment to fall down and give thanks for the labours
done & the strength vouchsafed me there: and to pray for the Christlike
mind'.[111]

A few days before the crucial Commons vote of June 1885, Gladstone
had indicated that he now wanted to go beyond Chamberlain's devolution
proposals (the so-called Central Board scheme), for, as he put it, the good of
the 'Empire'. He had found it impossible to 'avoid ... the pretentions of some
body or other to speak for Ireland', something inherently 'much more formidable than the antics of a Central Board essentially municipal and not

---

[107] Gladstone to Trevelyan, 30 December 1882, BL Gladstone Papers Add. MS 44546; *Diary of
Sir Edward Walter Hamilton 1880–1885*, ed. Bahlman, ii. 392 (24 January 1883); Gladstone to
Hartington, 3 February 1883, ChH Devonshire Papers 340.1320.
[108] Granville to Gladstone, 15 April 1882, *The Political Correspondence of Mr Gladstone and
Lord Granville 1876–1886*, ed. Ramm, i. 361; Spencer to Gladstone, 22 February and 25 May
1883, BL Gladstone Papers Add. MS 44310; Hartington to Granville, 16 April 1882, TNA
Granville Papers PRO 30/29/22A; Gladstone to Queen Victoria, 23 May 1885, TNA CAB 41/
19/38.
[109] Spencer to E. G. Jenkinson, 18 September 1884, *The Red Earl*, ed. Gordon, i. 31.
[110] See Spencer's Memoranda of 19 May and 22 June 1885, *The Red Earl*, ed. Gordon, i.
300–5, also 285–6.
[111] Lyons, *Charles Stewart Parnell*, 279–81; Matthew, *Gladstone 1875–1898*, 181–2.

parliamentary'. He told the queen that the crucial point was to make 'the Government in Ireland Irish', an aim once again put forward as 'in the highest sense conservative' because 'even good laws are not likely to be loved when the administration of them is not in native hands'.[112] During the late summer and early autumn opinion continued to shift. Hartington thought Gladstone's 'state of mind about Ireland' at once 'alarming' and 'uncommonly unintelligible' and more or less told him so. On the very same day (8 August) Spencer found his leader self-absorbed but determined on some significant *démarche*. On his worrying that one concession would inevitably lead to another, Gladstone replied: '"Yes but that is the case with all reform," to which I said that may be, but [we should] not … give power to a very dangerous set of men. He said the dangerous character of the men did not affect him, for there they were in the House of Commons & they must be dealt with.' But Spencer too was coming to the conclusion that something fairly dramatic would soon have to be unveiled, perhaps even an experiment involving a 'form of federal government with Home Rule … We must try new lines of policy.' What, above all, was convincing him that Gladstone was moving in the right direction was an increasing bitterness about Salisbury's self-interested and, he thought, immoral behaviour in pandering to the Parnellites by dropping coercion on coming into office in June. 'Our old methods of redressing every grievance and maintaining law and order by coercive measures' had become hopeless 'after the Tory surrender last July. No stability of policy in that direction is [now] possible.' It had, therefore, become absolutely necessary to try something new, however dangerous and radical that might at first seem.[113]

Gladstone reached the Acceptance-of-Home-Rule finishing post ahead, but not all that far ahead, of his consentient colleagues. On 10 September he had written to one then sympathetic but later to repudiate his legacy to emphasize the importance of seeing Ireland in a new way. 'What I do think of is the Irish nation, and the fame, duty, & peace of my country. Some of you, to speak freely—and without this why speak at all—seem to me not to have taken any just measure of the probable position of a serious dispute with the Irish nation.'[114] And then, on 17 December, Gladstone's own and decisive conversion to Home Rule was made public by his son by means of a press leak soon known as the 'Hawarden Kite' (after Gladstone's Flintshire residence). Quite apart from

---

[112] Gladstone to Hartington, 30 May 1885, BL Gladstone Papers Add. MS 44148; to Spencer, 6 June 1885, BL Spencer Papers Add. MS 76862; to Queen Victoria, 23 May 1885, TNA CAB 41/19/38.
[113] Hartington to Granville, 8 August 1885, TNA Granville Papers PRO 30/29/22A; to Gladstone, 12 September and 17 December 1885, BL Gladstone Papers Add. MS 44148; Spencer to Granville, 8 August 1885, TNA Granville Papers PRO 30/29/22A; to Lansdowne, 16 August 1885 and 2 February 1886, BL 5th Marquess of Lansdowne Papers, 'Further Correspondence M' (provisional reference).
[114] Gladstone to Rosebery, 10 September 1885, NLS Rosebery Papers MS 10023.

the implications of this for immediate political circumstances, it marked Gladstone's final recognition that Ireland was indeed that very grand and notable thing—a 'nation'. Long an admirer of Italian unification on national grounds, Gladstone had felt less confident about the Irish case. Now there could be no doubts. Ireland was not only an entity in every important sense distinct from England and Scotland; it was also something that could properly be called a nation, and one that Gladstone (always a keen student of the nuances of usage) could now honour with the occasional use of a capital letter 'N'. Nationhood did not, of course, necessarily imply independence—and Gladstone always hoped that his policies would cement the Union—but it certainly implied a very great deal both in practical and, no less important, in emotional terms.

During the parliamentary debates that followed in 1886 Gladstone's use of the words 'nation' and 'nationality' became, in the Irish context, frequent, grinding, and passionate. 'Irish nationality vents itself in the demand for ... separate and complete self-government, in Irish, not in imperial, affairs' (the rider was important). 'Can anything', he asked in almost Parnellian language, 'stop a nation's demand?' And, though Scottish virtues were ever admired by Gladstone the arch-Caledonian, the admission that notions of 'patriotism' were 'stronger in Ireland even than in Scotland' was a mighty admission indeed.[115]

A few weeks after the kite Gladstone told a colleague that 'every Irishman worth a farthing' had opposed the Union in 1799–1800 and that if he had 'been an Irishman he should have done so to the utmost. He believed in Nationality as a principle—whether Italian, Greek, Slav, or Irish.'[116] And this was, of course, the crux of the matter and the ultimate basis for abandoning assimilation in favour of Home Rule or, as some feared, in favour of something even more extreme. The easiest response was simply to deny that the Irish were a nation 'in any true sense ... as the Portuguese, the Dutch, or the Danes were each a nation, having separate and distinct languages, laws, customs, blood, and appearance ... Pure Celtic blood was a thing unknown, and Ireland had no right to call herself a separate nation.'[117]

Gladstone nonchalantly declared the Hawarden Kite a damp squib, because it had contained 'little that I have not more or less conveyed in public declarations, in principle nothing'. This was, however, a minority opinion.

---

[115] Parl. Deb. 3: ccciv. 1081–2 (8 April 1886) and 1542 (13 April 1886), cccvi. 1237 (7 [*recte* 8] June 1886). On 21 January 1885 Parnell had declared in Cork that 'No man has a right to fix the boundary of the march of a nation. No man has the right to say, "Thus far shalt thou go, and no further"' (O'Brien, *Life of Charles Stewart Parnell*, 318).

[116] *Diaries of Henry Edward Stanley, 15th Earl of Derby ... between 1878 and 1893*, ed. Vincent, 826 (13 January 1886). The following day Lewis Harcourt recorded that 'Mr Gladstone declaimed against the Union this evening & said that all the misfortunes of Ireland have occurred since and in consequence of it' (Lewis Harcourt's Journal, Bodl. Harcourt Papers MS 376 (14 January 1886)).

[117] Parl. Deb. 3: cccv. 1206 (17 May 1886: Hobhouse); Parl. Deb. 4: viii. 377 (3 February 1893: Kilmorey).

Some percipient observers had undoubtedly seen how the Gladstonian wind was blowing and had read between the lines of predictions about the imminent appearance of 'a mighty heave in the body politic'. Yet, in the short term at least, the whole business, both for the political classes and for the general public, came as a very considerable shock.[118]

It did, however, come too late to affect the outcome of the general election called once the franchise reforms of 1884–5 had been fully implemented. The results pleased almost no one, at least not immediately. Parnell obtained his expected success and now led a parliamentary force of 86. With the Liberals returning 334 and the Conservatives 250 members, Salisbury had failed to escape from his minority chains. On the Liberal side, Chamberlain was the chief loser and now saw himself in imminent danger of disappearing down the ravine that had opened up between his expectations and the fact that, among Radical MPs, his own following still constituted a minority, a possibility that aggravated his visceral response to the Hawarden Kite as 'death and damnation that we must try and stop'.[119] It also required no deep insight for Gladstone to realize, first, that he could not now lead a government relying exclusively on Liberal MPs, and, second, that the possibility of a calm interval for 'educating' his party about Home Rule had vanished. Nonetheless, some at least of his chief lieutenants, notably Spencer and, more surprisingly, Harcourt (a man who could never spot a problem without wanting to kick someone in the ankles), swung more or less immediately behind the new policy, Harcourt percipiently noting that 'resistance is more likely to resemble our old failure in the War of Independence of 1776 than the success of the North in the American Civil War'.[120]

Although by now Gladstone had become a full-blooded Home Ruler, he first tried to persuade the Conservatives to take up the policy themselves. Whether this was based upon any real hope that the Tories would mix high-mindedness with self-interest (getting rid of Irish MPs from Westminster, and so on) or simply a procedure for clarifying his own mind and forcing Salisbury to make a decisive move is unclear: probably both considerations were in play, though at different levels of consciousness. In the event, Salisbury merely laughed. 'Gladstone', he told Lord Randolph Churchill, 'has written to Arthur [Balfour] a marvellous letter saying that he thinks "it will be a public calamity if this great subject should fall into the lines of party conflict"—& saying he

---

[118] Gladstone to Hartington, 17 December 1885, BL Dilke Papers Add. MS 43891; also to Hartington, 10 and 18 November 1885, ChH Devonshire Papers 340.1827 and 1833; Gladstone to Rosebery, 13 November 1885, NLS Rosebery Papers MS 10023.

[119] Chamberlain to Dilke, 17 December 1885, BL Dilke Papers Add. MS 43887.

[120] Harcourt to Hartington, 24 December 1885, Bodl. Harcourt Papers (Additional) MS 28; to Chamberlain, 25 December 1885, ibid.; Spencer to Granville, 29 December 1885, TNA Granville Papers PRO 30/29/22A; to A. J. Mundella, 31 December 1885, Sh[effield] U[niversity] Mundella Papers MS 11A.

desires the question should be settled by the present Government. His hypocrisy makes me sick.'[121]

As a result, Gladstone returned to office on 1 February 1886 with Parnellite support. Although in doing so he had played his cards with skill, the obstacles that lay ahead remained formidable: the House of Lords, Ulster, the kaleidoscopic Liberal Party itself. By now he was, publicly and privately, a convinced Home Ruler, though the precise contours of what this involved remained to be established. Once back in Downing Street he started filling slips of paper with details as to the precise 'system of autonomy' that was to 'be granted to Ireland'.[122] Long-standing beliefs rose again to the surface. The Irish, he told a bemused Queen Victoria, were anything but radical, and Home Rule would result in the election of Irishmen 'to a great extent conservative'. It was not enough that laws should be 'good laws'; it was important that they be seen to 'proceed from a congenial native source'. Home Rule would protect taxpayers from all the 'waste of public treasure which is involved in the present system of government'. It would provide the only adequate protection for the large-scale scheme he was now (uniquely) preparing for land purchase in Ireland. 'Tightening the tie is frequently', he told the Commons, 'the means of making it burst, while relaxing the tie is very frequently the way to provide for its durability.'[123]

The powers Gladstone's bill proposed to give to an Irish 'legislative body', though considerably greater than those possessed by the provincial assemblies in Canada, were, however, rather less than those of the Canadian dominion parliament. Matters of defence, foreign policy, and international trade were the chief items over which London was to retain control. Provisions were included to protect minorities. Irish MPs were (after much wavering) to remain at Westminster. Only on the question of finance did serious differences arise between Gladstone and Parnell. Here much posturing and bidding went on, not because of any deep economic analysis, but because both men thought it important to be seen to strike a good bargain. Initially Gladstone suggested that Ireland should bear one-thirteenth of imperial costs. He then agreed to one-fifteenth and remained deaf to further demands. Curiously, in the bill itself the proposition was expressed in fixed-money terms unalterable for thirty years, a provision that, in the light of subsequent inflation, would have

---

[121] Salisbury to Churchill, 24 December 1885, P. [T.] Marsh, *The Discipline of Popular Government; Lord Salisbury's Domestic Statecraft, 1881–1902* (Hassocks, 1978), 85; Gladstone to Mundella, 16 December 1885, ShU Mundella Papers MS 18.

[122] Memorandum of 3 November 1910 by Edwin Montagu (then undersecretary for India) of a conversation with John Morley, T[rinity] C[ollege] C[ambridge] Montagu Papers AS1/6/21.

[123] Gladstone to Queen Victoria, 23 March 1886, *The Letters of Queen Victoria*, Third Series, ed. G. E. Buckle, 3 vols (London, 1930–32), i. 89; Parl. Deb. 3: ccciv. 1080–1, 1084 (8 April 1886) and cccvi. 1224–5 (7 [*recte* 8] June 1886); Gladstone, *The Irish Question ... with an 'Addendum'*, 24–5.

represented an amazing bargain for the Irish and would not have come up for renegotiation until—of all years—1916.[124]

In the early hours of Tuesday, 8 June, the Commons debate on the second reading came to an end with the kind of majestic exhortation that Gladstone could do so well.

> Go into the length and breadth of the world, ransack the literature of all countries, find, if you can, a single voice, a single book ... in which the conduct of England towards Ireland is anywhere treated except with profound and bitter condemnation ... Think, I beseech you, think well, think wisely, think, not for the moment, but for the years that are to come, before you reject this bill.[125]

These were just the sentiments to make Salisbury once again feel sick, and they were not enough. When, shortly afterwards, MPs voted 341 to 311 against the government, it was found that no less than ninety-four Liberals had gone against Gladstone and another half-dozen had abstained.[126]

V

Naturally the government fell and was replaced by a Tory administration, which, apart from a short interval, remained in office until December 1905. Gladstone now led a Liberal Party purged of his most pertinacious critics, many of whom went on to form the Liberal Unionist Party in alliance with the Conservatives, who, in turn, now rechristened themselves Unionists in honour of their opposition to Home Rule. What this meant was that, although Irish issues were by no means always uppermost in the minds of British politicians after 1886, all of the parties to which they belonged had effectively nailed themselves to an Irish cross, with the result that Ireland had now unambiguously become the hinge upon which their differences turned. The newly named Unionists had, in effect, been transformed into political vampires, dependent for life-giving doses of cohesion upon Home Rule—the very issue they despised—remaining the great question of the day. And the Liberals (save between December 1905 and January 1910) were to find it impossible to form a government without the support of those Irish MPs whose presence at Westminster so many of them wished either to erase or at least to reduce.

The man who emerged from the wreckage of 1886 with almost undiminished bounce was the 76-year-old Gladstone, still confident that the best way

---

[124] Matthew, *Gladstone 1875–1898*, 249–53; J. Loughlin, *Gladstone, Home Rule and the Ulster Question 1882–93* (Dublin, 1986), 69–76.

[125] Parl. Deb. 3: cccvi. 1239–40 (7 [*recte* 8] June 1886).

[126] W. C. Lubenow, 'Irish Home Rule and the Social Basis of the Great Separation in the Liberal Party in 1886', *Historical Journal*, 28 (1985), 128.

of recognizing Ireland as a different and distinct country or 'Nation' was to continue the quest for Home Rule. Indeed, he seems almost to have revelled in what he now perceived to be a personal ability to read the runes of the future. It was, he claimed, only his own Home Rule proposals that had succeeded in emasculating potentially far more serious Irish agitation for a total repeal of the Union, though he warned that excessive delay might well, 'as in former cases', reignite 'the extension of the demand'.[127] He clung to beliefs that Home Rule would save British taxpayers vast sums of money, that it was in every sense a 'profoundly conservative' concept that would rescue Irish landlords from ruin and secure United Kingdom cohesion and prosperity. He contrasted this with the intransigence and extravagance of Salisbury's party, arguing that 'in Ireland each refusal of self-government will have to be gilded with a new coating of public money', a prediction as self-justificatory as it turned out to be accurate.[128] And, although Gladstone played an active part in the Round Table negotiations of early 1887 aimed at Liberal reunion, it is difficult to characterize his attitude as one seriously and earnestly looking for compromise with those who had left the party the previous year, some of whom (like Trevelyan) were, in any case, beginning to return.[129] On the whole, those who had remained loyal continued to be so, though not always for the same reasons. Common, however, was a feeling that Home Rule would simultaneously acknowledge the reality of Irish distinctiveness and open the delicious prospect of having to spend less time at Westminster and in Whitehall upon the endless and unappealing minutiae of Hibernian complaints, something about which Liberals felt at least as strongly as many Unionists. Men such as Spencer and Kimberley tended to take the high-minded road; men like Harcourt (though there were, in truth, few men quite like him) wanted above all to free themselves from the Irish incubus that had been (and was), they believed, distorting their party's values and electability.[130]

The result was that, when the general election of July 1892 produced a majority of about forty for a Liberal–Nationalist combination, Gladstone was determined to mount another bid for Home Rule. To those who had suggested some lesser concession—perhaps giving Dublin powers like those of the recently created (by the Unionists) London County Council—he forcefully

---

[127] Gladstone to Bryce, 17 July 1886, Bodl. Bryce Papers MS 10.

[128] Gladstone, 'Notes and Queries on the Irish Demand', 185; Parl. Deb. 3: cccxvii. 100 (7 July 1887); *The Diary of Sir Edward Walter Hamilton 1885–1906*, ed. D. W. R. Bahlman (Hull, 1993), 64 (26 August 1887); Gladstone to Queen Victoria, 28 October 1892, *The Gladstone Diaries*, ed. M. R. D. Foot and H. C. G. Matthew, 14 vols (Oxford, 1968–94), xiii. 126.

[129] M. Hurst, *Joseph Chamberlain and Liberal Reunion: The Round Table Conference of 1887* (London, 1967), *passim*.

[130] Spencer to Lansdowne, 9 July 1886, BL 5th Marquess of Lansdowne Papers 'Further Correspondence M' (provisional reference); *Liberal by Principle: The Politics of John Wodehouse, 1st Earl of Kimberley*, ed. Powell, 371 (29 September 1886); Harcourt to Spencer, 25 October 1889, Bodl. Harcourt Papers MS 45.

replied 'Never—never—Nothing shall induce me to have part or lot in such a frustration of Irish hopes and the justice of the Irish demand.' By now his mind was 'so fixed on Ireland, that all else escapes him'. Not only did he regard himself as 'chained to the oar', but he was determined that all who followed him must row with equal enthusiasm, something not made easier by the catastrophic split in the Irish Parliamentary Party brought about by the Parnell divorce case of 1890.[131]

Gladstone's Home Rule Bill of 1893 'reflected all the strengths and weaknesses of the 1886 bill and, unlike the 1886 bill, it stood alone. The Land Bill, central and integral in the 1886 plan, was not repeated.' The new bill was, therefore, a 'straightforward proposal for constitutional amendment'. It sought to establish an Irish legislature with a British-style executive dependent upon it. 'Ireland would enter gradually into her full powers, with legislation on land, the judiciary, the police, and finance only permitted after a variety of intervals.' At first there was uncertainty as to whether Irish MPs would continue to sit at Westminster; eventually it was agreed that they would. A good deal of confusion surrounded the bill's financial provisions, which, in the event, proved less generous than had been the case in 1886.[132]

Although Gladstone knew that, even if the bill passed the Commons, it would be thrown out by the Lords, he calculated that the Lords could not continue in such negativity for all time and that eventually the blockage would be overcome. The Unionists opposed every clause. The committee stage alone took sixty-three days. Gladstone bore far the greatest burden, held up, he believed, by some external force, by 'a strength not my own'. On 1 September the bill passed the Commons by 301 to 267, a majority of thirty-four—far too small to intimidate the Lords, who brusquely turned it down by 419 to 41.

When Gladstone resigned as prime minister six months later, the cause of Home Rule as a (if not *the*) major Liberal issue was effectively put into cold storage. As Colin Matthew has written, the 'cause' was not dead but it now 'lacked the vitality and the urgency to take on and defeat Unionism'. Already in November 1892, while the bill was being drawn up in cabinet, Morley (then chief secretary) had felt depressed: 'It was an odious, an undignified, a discouraging scene. I dare say the barons were no better when framing Magna Carta.'[133] Those who had never been very keen or indeed very knowledgeable were more than happy to abandon what they had begun to regard as an old man's obsession. Harcourt, noted Morley, 'knows and cares as much

---

[131] Morley's Diary for 3 July 1891, Bodl. Morley Papers MS Eng.d.3449 and for 4 March and 23 June 1892, MS Eng.d.3450; Gladstone to Ripon, 23 July 1892, BL Ripon Papers Add. MS 43515: 'I am bound to Ireland as Ulysses was to his mast.' Parnell died on 6 October 1891, leaving a much divided party. Gladstone, despite his piety, proved strikingly non-judgemental regarding Parnell's private life.

[132] Matthew, *Gladstone 1875–1898*, 335–40.

[133] Ibid. 340; Morley's Diary for 11 November 1892, Bodl. Morley Papers MS Eng.d.3452.

about Ireland as he does for the North Pole'.[134] A mere week after becoming Liberal prime minister, Lord Rosebery (once Gladstone's blue-eyed boy) was putting the boot into his predecessor's legacy with a parliamentary aside that could hardly have been more deliberate. 'Before Irish Home Rule is conceded,' he told his fellow peers, 'England, as the predominant member of the partnership of the three kingdoms, will have to be convinced of its justice and equity.'[135] Given that England had returned a large Unionist majority (262 to 194) at the election of 1892, this implied a very long postponement indeed.

While the Unionist return to government in 1895 rendered such comments external to the world of decision-making, they nonetheless played to an increasingly significant group within the Liberal Party, the so-called Liberal Imperialists, who, initially at least, looked to Rosebery as their chief. Prominent here were Haldane, Grey, and Asquith, rising stars of the post-Gladstone party, all of them keen to attract the Liberal Unionists back to the fold and to encourage 'the politics of the centre which they favoured'. However, the group lacked cohesion, and it was not long before splits appeared between an increasingly disenchanted Rosebery, who thought Home Rule simply wrong, and the others who thought it merely inexpedient. Already as early as 1896 the more pragmatic tendency was gaining the upper hand, with the adoption of Haldane's famous 'step-by-step' approach, the view that Home Rule could be introduced only in instalments rather than, as Gladstone had proposed, all at once.[136] Asquith, speaking at Dewsbury in 1897, wanted the 'Irish people' to be able 'to govern themselves upon their own soil, by their own citizens, in accordance with their own ideas, and to meet their own social requirements', sentiments in full accord with Gladstone's notions of Irish differentiation and effectively preparing the way for the more famous Ladybank speech of September 1901. In this Asquith admitted that, whatever the difficulties associated with Home Rule, the Irish problem would not go away and would not, as the Unionists hoped, be 'extinguished ... by land purchase'. Given this, he admitted that Liberals could not simply throw over Gladstone's legacy and that 'imperialists' like himself were obliged to concede that, as far as Ireland was concerned, the best policy must be that of 'giving as large and as liberal a devolution of local powers and local responsibilities as statesmanship can from time to time devise'.[137]

While, therefore, Gladstone's departure unsurprisingly led to a reappraisal of his methods and policies, not least with regard to Ireland, by the first years

---

[134] Morley to Spencer, 19 August 1896, D. A. Hamer, *John Morley: Liberal Intellectual in Politics* (Oxford, 1968), 318.

[135] Parl. Deb. 4: xxii. 32 (12 March 1894).

[136] Matthew, *The Liberal Imperialists*, 265–78; H. W. McCready, 'Home Rule and the Liberal Party, 1899–1906', *Irish Historical Studies*, 13 (1963), 316–48.

[137] *The Times*, 9 January 1897 and 30 September 1901. Grey reintroduced the phrase 'step-by-step' in his Newcastle speech the following month: ibid. 12 October 1901.

of the twentieth century even those Liberals most committed to such re-examinations were, with one exception, coming to the view that the Irish issue could not be ignored for ever, that some form of devolution would have to be granted, but that, if one kept one's fingers crossed, the next Liberal majority might be so large that the Irish Party's influence would be correspondingly small. The exception was Rosebery, now departing into some exotic political gallery in which he proved to be the sole exhibit. While he denounced others for sitting with 'fly-blown phylacteries' bound round obsolete policies, in reality it was he who was being left behind.[138] More than a year earlier Haldane had told the electors of East Lothian that, though full Home Rule might require 'special authority from the constituencies', significant progress could not be long delayed.[139] And much the same message was being broadcast by the Liberal leadership throughout the years of opposition between 1895 and 1905. Ireland should cease to be the single priority, but it should remain within the party's armoury ready to be deployed with fuller force when the occasion demanded. Even when trying to play down Gladstone's moral rhetoric and portray the issue as pragmatic rather then ideological, old tropes about the impossibility of seeking 'to govern Ireland according to British ideas and not according to the ideas of Ireland' were regularly brushed up in front of audiences in various parts of the kingdom with, however, little real awareness of the fact that 'Irish ideas' were themselves things of almost infinite elasticity.[140]

It was curiously the Unionists who allowed their opponents to push the Home Rule question into the background, and especially so in 1903. This unintentionally helpful act took two main forms. In the first place, Unionist divisions over tariff reform (whether the United Kingdom should abandon the policy of free trade) so divided the party that, for the first time since 1886, Liberals could plausibly point to something other than Home Rule as the main dividing line in British politics. In the second, the enormously ambitious Irish Land Purchase Act introduced in 1903 shifted attention away from Home Rule and towards agrarian matters, over which Liberals were prepared (indeed delighted) to be able to take something of a back seat. As, however, the prospect of another general election came closer—one was eventually held in January 1906—intense Liberal jockeying for position on the Irish question inevitably took place. On the one hand, it seemed important not to make too much of the issue. On the other, it seemed no less important to keep channels of communication open to the leaders of the (now reunited) Irish

---

[138] *The Times*, 17 December 1901 for Rosebery's Chesterfield speech.
[139] Election Address of September 1900 in NLS Haldane Papers MS 5905.
[140] See, e.g., Asquith's Newbury speech of January 1897 and Haldane's Dunblane speech of December 1901: *The Times*, 9 January 1897, and Matthew, *The Liberal Imperialists*, 275–6, where it is percipiently noted that 'the difficulty that "Irish ideas", as expressed by Nationalist MPs, now included a demand for an "independent Parliament" … was not resolved'.

Parliamentary Party and its eighty or so MPs.[141] And, while Asquith felt it important in October 1905 to warn that Home Rule in the Gladstonian sense would not 'be part of the policy of the next Liberal Government ... step by step should be the aim', the actual leader of the party, Sir Henry Campbell-Bannerman (a former chief secretary), gave what were in fact rather similar views a more positive spin by saying that 'the opportunity of making a great advance on this question of Irish government will not be long delayed'.[142]

The general election of 1906 gave the Liberals an overall majority (some 398 out of a House of 670 MPs), so that they no longer depended on the votes of the Irish nationalists. With no Gladstone to stir things up, it was inevitable that step-by-step would be the policy adopted under the prime ministership of the sympathetic Campbell-Bannerman and then, from May 1908, under that of the less sympathetic Asquith. Yet, however much some Liberals hoped that the Irish ogre would now cease to hover over proceedings at Westminster, only those altogether lacking in political insight could have been unaware that this was not the last general election that would ever be held, that it was very likely (even perhaps inevitable) that the support of Home Rule MPs would again be required, and that it was not a good idea, therefore, to antagonize such men into outright rebellion and distrust.

That this was, indeed, the 'normal' state of things highlights the fact that the behaviour of governments in London with regard to Ireland was always the result of an interplay between considerations of an essentially British character (often indeed the predominant element) and reactions to the sometimes contradictory demands of groups in Ireland itself. And the impact of such groups naturally depended upon their success in being able to make life difficult for the powers that be and to generate a sense of moral guilt for the 'wrongs' done in the past and perhaps still being done in the present. Inevitably, therefore, London's willingness to turn a sympathetic ear was closely connected with and related to Ireland's ability to annoy and disturb. Yet outcomes and processes were always unpredictable. Thus O'Connell's massive popular campaign for repeal of the Union in the 1830s and 1840s had entirely failed to achieve its ends, while the shift in 1868–70 towards disestablishment and land reform had had little or nothing to do with the comparatively feeble Irish protestations of the time (the Fenians not excepted) and more or less everything to do with ideological mutations among those in charge of the state.

---

[141] See the memorandum of 14 November 1905 by Redmond (the party's leader) in N[ational] L[ibrary of] I[reland] Redmond Papers MS 15171(1) about having breakfast with the Liberal leader, Campbell-Bannerman, who declared himself 'stronger than ever for Home Rule. It was only a question of how far they could go in the next Parliament'; also Redmond's notes of a conversation with Morley on 9 April 1905, ibid., MS 15233(2); also Bryce (a few days after being appointed chief secretary) to Redmond, 14 December 1905, ibid., MS 15174(1).

[142] Matthew, *The Liberal Imperialists*, 282–4.

While, therefore, it proved transcendently important for Liberal governments after 1905 to ensure that their followers in England, Scotland, and Wales had their demands attended to and that social reforms of a general kind should take precedence for the time being, it also became more and more evident as time went on that in the longer run considerations of this kind did not seriously modify 'the means by which the Liberals tackled the reform of Irish government', quite the reverse.[143] The Snow White of Irish self-government might well have been put to sleep for the time being, but (almost) every Liberal knew that the imminent arrival of a handsome electoral prince offering the seductive kiss of Home Rule remained a very distinct possibility indeed.

---

[143] Matthew, *The Liberal Imperialists*, 286.

9

Throwing Money About: Conservatives

I

The most substantial disagreement between Liberals and Conservatives regarding Ireland from the 1870s onwards was not over whether that country should be treated differently from Britain with respect to economic, social, and political affairs—all were more or less agreed that it should be so treated—but over the precise manner in which its universally acknowledged differences might best be made manifest in terms of policy and administration. In particular, the parties adopted distinct approaches to the crucial issues of land and constitutional change. Regarding land, British politicians faced a virtually united island, with farmers in all four provinces unanimous as to what they most desired: tenurial reform combined with subsidies from government to help them buy their holdings. On the constitution, Ireland was far from united, with Ulster in particular and Protestants in general opposed to any espousal of Home Rule.

While Gladstone's first administration exhibited distinct signs of movement away from the assimilationism of the mid-century period, Disraeli's government of 1874–80 was notable for a 'policy' of more or less pretending that Ireland did not exist, a myopia adopted in the hope that ignorance would prove to be bliss and that averting one's gaze might make problems disappear. And in this analysis Disraeli proved, for a time, tolerably correct—perhaps lucky might be a better term.[1] Some of his ministers, however, worried that persistent neglect would store up trouble for the party. Others agreed with their leader, if only because they found Ireland and its problems tedious and unappetizing. 'I spent a long afternoon in the House [of Commons] listening to Irish rubbish,' recorded one member of the cabinet, who, when later elevated to the Lords, found even that chamber awash with 'Irish jobbery'.[2]

---

[1] Disraeli to Richmond, 5 March [1874], W[est] S[ussex] R[ecord] O[ffice] Richmond Papers 865: 'Our policy is to keep Ireland in the background.'
[2] *The Diary of Gathorne Hardy, Later Lord Cranbrook 1866–1892*, ed. N. Johnson (Oxford, 1981), 234, 661.

Sir Michael Hicks Beach, chief secretary from 1874 to 1878, though raised to the cabinet in August 1876, thought himself otherwise so ignored that he complained to a colleague that there 'was only too much truth in the statement in Parnell's letter that, for these 4 sessions, hardly one day can be named in which Irish Government business ... has been brought on "when useful discussion can be obtained", i.e. at an early hour in the evening'.[3] While Disraeli eventually woke up to the fact that severe distress in Ireland was generating equally severe violence and unrest, it was by then—notwithstanding vapid talk in his Address before the general election of April 1880 about the government's devotion to 'the improvement of Ireland and the content of our fellow-countrymen in that island'—far too late.[4]

During the Liberal administration that followed, Tory leaders did little to sharpen either their swords or their minds with respect to Ireland. By the time they briefly returned to office in June 1885, they were neither united nor well informed, prone to making 'public utterances' without, as one admitted, much in the way of 'prudence' or 'harmony'.[5] The new prime minister, Salisbury (once—but no longer—open-minded about Ireland), at first opposed any 'bold move', to the despair of his chief secretary, who found 'the same hopeless indifference and ignorance [about Ireland] in every quarter, plus an amount of prejudice which would drive John Bright wild with envy'. The 'mental condition of the party as regards Ireland' was, he told the viceroy, 'one of Cimmerian darkness. They know and understand nothing—hate the subject—but hate still more a proposal to make a change.'[6] Indeed, at this time the only member of the cabinet who had anything useful to say about Ireland was Salisbury's chief rival, that worthy and dull man of insight Stafford Northcote, newly created Earl of Iddesleigh. Long open to creative thinking about Ireland, he stood out for a willingness to treat '"Irish ideas" with great tenderness, so long as we are firm against separation ... Such phrases as "Home Rule" are capable of any interpretation' and should, he insisted, be thought about rather than simply dismissed.[7]

---

[3] Hicks Beach to Northcote, 1 June 1877, B[ritish] L[ibrary] Northcote Papers Add. MS 50021; to Disraeli, 20 July 1876, Bodl[eian Library] Disraeli Papers 118/1 and G[loucestershire] R[ecord] O[ffice] St Aldwyn Papers PCC13.

[4] Disraeli (now Beaconsfield) to Marlborough, 8 March 1880, C[ambridge] U[niversity] L[ibrary] Marlborough Papers Add. MS 9271/4; W. E. Monypenny and G. E. Buckle, *The Life of Benjamin Disraeli, Earl of Beaconsfield*, 6 vols (London, 1910–20), vi. 514–16.

[5] Carnarvon to Salisbury, [18 September 1885], P[arliamentary] A[rchives] Ashbourne Papers B/25/15, *The Ashbourne Papers 1869–1913*, ed. A. B. Cooke and A. P. W. Malcomson (Belfast, 1974), 95–6.

[6] Sir W. Hart Dyke to Carnarvon, 6 November 1885, BL Carnarvon Papers Add. MS 60825; Carnarvon's Diary for 21 November 1885, ibid., Add MS 60925, recording a conversation with Hart Dyke. For Salisbury's views as a young MP, see Parl[iamentary] Deb[ates] 3: clxxvii. 719–20 (24 February 1865).

[7] Iddesleigh to Carnarvon, 7 September 1885, T[he] N[ational] A[rchives] Carnarvon Papers PRO 30/6/55; also to Gibson (later Ashbourne), 17 October 1880, PA Ashbourne Papers B/71/7. He died in January 1887.

Gladstone's adoption of Home Rule and its parliamentary defeat in June 1886 brought the previously inchoate (even non-existent) views of the Tory leadership into a clear coalescence around Salisbury's policy of immobility on the constitutional issue interlaced with dexterous flexibility on agrarian reform when clothed in the garb of state-assisted land purchase. Already Salisbury's minority government of 1885–6, desperate for parliamentary support from any quarter, had passed the first significant purchase measure in the shape of the so-called Ashbourne Land Act of August 1885, which advanced the entire purchase money repayable by annuities lower than rents. Gladstone, amnesiac with respect to his own lavish bill of 1886, later attacked what he denounced as a Tory policy 'in the highest degree wasteful', involving as it did the spraying-about of 'large sums of public money' upon a country notorious for reckless financial inefficiencies.[8] While this may well have constituted the immediate grounds for Gladstone's dismay, other Liberals were no less distressed by the manner in which Irish politicians now began to contrast Tory generosity with their own fiscal stinginess. The Tory government's response, especially as presented by Salisbury's nephew, Arthur Balfour (chief secretary 1887–91), consisted of little more than languid references to 'our old friends "bribery and coercion" … and all that sort of thing. I do not know why I should bore the House and bore myself by repeating what I have said on former occasions.'[9] In the face of Liberal anger over a 'policy of kicks and coax, of cane and candy, of stroking the cat with the hair on one side and against the hair on the other', Salisbury gloried in what he called his defence of the rights of property as the one bulwark against chaos and confiscation.[10] His stance was soon translated into a kind of Tory mantra. 'What the country wants now is rest and calm, steady, quiet, but firm administration, wholesome food and drink', so much better an approach than the lurching uncertainties of Liberal administrations. And, remarkably, some Liberals almost came to agree. As late as February 1916, the long-serving chief secretary, Augustine Birrell, when hailing with his characteristic mixture of perception and innocence the imminent arrival of a 'new Ireland' full of promise and prosperity, gave the main credit to those land and local government reforms for which his political opponents had been largely responsible.[11]

---

[8] W. E. Gladstone, *The Irish Question … with an 'Addendum'* (London, [1886]), 28; Gladstone, 'Notes and Queries on the Irish Demand', *Nineteenth Century*, 21 (1887), 185.

[9] Morley to Campbell-Bannerman, May 1895, Bodl. Morley Papers MS Eng.c.7068; Parl. Deb. 3: cccxxxviii. 904 (17 July 1889: Balfour).

[10] Parl. Deb. 3: cccxliii. 1043 (21 April 1890: Wallace) and cccxlii. 1368–9 (21 March 1890: Salisbury).

[11] W. Long to J. S. Sandars, 15 March 1905, BL Balfour Papers Add. MS 49776; to A. J. Balfour, 5 December 1907, ibid.; Birrell to Midleton, 25 February 1916, TNA Midleton Papers PRO 30/67/31.

II

The background and context to the Conservative/Unionist land purchase legislation of the period 1885–1903 was based on anything but enthusiastic support for the Irish landowning community, even if tribal loyalty was not entirely absent. Indeed, of the chief political actors of the years after 1870, it was Gladstone who—whatever his deeds—most frequently appeared in the verbal garb of a devotee of traditional landed society. Men such as Balfour and Salisbury were altogether more hard-headed and less romantic as to what they were about, with the result that long-established British critiques of Irish landed proprietors experienced no significant mitigation in this later period.[12]

Indeed, if one were looking for private (even public) antipathy towards Irish landlords, the correspondence of Conservative politicians would provide a larger haul than that of their opponents, not least because of the visceral distaste created by having to defend the so obviously indefensible. The fact that both Disraeli and Salisbury appointed Hicks Beach chief secretary does not suggest any tenderness to landed feelings. Hicks Beach, a future Chancellor of the Exchequer, made few attempts to hide a deep contempt for Irish landed society. Ashbourne, the Irish Lord Chancellor and a member of the cabinet, emerges as something of a master of understatement in his assessment: 'I don't think he liked the Irish gentry, I think he *disliked* them, and his manners were ungracious and unsympathetic.' And at both the beginning and the end of his career fellow Conservatives were struck by the strength of his steady contempt for Irish landlords.[13] Lord Randolph Churchill, no slouch when it came to colourful abuse, thought Hicks Beach's denunciations of what were, *au fond*, our 'natural friends' went further perhaps than it was altogether proper to go.[14] In fact, Hicks Beach rather delighted in sly public affirmations of his views, as when he told the Commons in April 1893 that he had 'never been a bigoted defender of the Irish landlords', something few in his audience could have regarded as anything other than an amusing and self-deprecating joke.[15]

---

[12] See Gladstone to Halifax, 1 October 1869, B[orthwick] I[nstitute] Hickleton (Halifax) Papers A4/88; Parl. Deb. 3: ccciv. 1794, 1803 (16 April 1886); Gladstone to Bryce, 1 October 1892, Bodl. Bryce Papers 10; Ashbourne to Salisbury, 16 December 1886, H[atfield] H[ouse] Salisbury Papers 3M/E.

[13] Ashbourne's 'Diary' for October 1898. PA Ashbourne Papers A/1/1; Lowther to Marlborough, 7 November 1879, CUL Marlborough Papers Add. MS 9271/4; Wyndham to A. J. Balfour, 30 April 1903, BL Balfour Papers Add. MS 49804.

[14] Churchill to Salisbury, 22 August 1886, CUL Lord Randolph Churchill Papers MS 9248/14/1691A—a letter that found its way into Hicks Beach's own papers: GRO St Aldwyn Papers PCC/82.

[15] Parl. Deb. 4: x. 1627 (6 April 1893).

The joke could so easily be made because so many British Tories agreed. Disraeli (now Earl of Beaconsfield) fell in with the common perception of Irish landlords as, above all, cowards 'apparently inclined to put their tails between their legs' when faced with opposition from tenants and Irish nationalists. 'If honesty', he declared, 'is the best policy, cowardice is certainly the worst.' Northcote thought much the same and in 1881 pointed to the importance of making it clear that opposition to Gladstone's second Land Bill—in his view 'a measure of general advantage'—should not stem merely from the fact that 'it would be inconvenient to a small body of landowners'.[16] From a different perspective, Lord Cranbrook, who heartily disliked Gladstone's legislation, was appalled to find that some Irish landlords—hoodwinked, he thought, by Liberal blandishments—were rolling over and accepting the bill despite its, in his eyes, manifold defects.[17]

Salisbury's maverick Irish viceroy of 1885–6, Lord Carnarvon, was no less distressed by the behaviour of Irish proprietors, but for rather different reasons. To him such men were always takers of favours and never givers of anything in return, seeming to 'think that the government is to do everything for them'. Indeed, he thought that English landlords like himself had suffered far more from the economic downturn of the times, while in Ireland it was the tenants who had experienced the greatest distress.[18] Hartington, once he had abandoned Gladstone and become a Liberal Unionist, did not allow the change of allegiance to make him any less critical of the landlords of Ireland (where his own father owned no less than 60,000 acres in Waterford and Cork). 'They have', he told Lord Randolph Churchill, 'very few friends and if they are encouraged to claim their rights and if disorder could justifiably be put down to their account, they would have still fewer.'[19] When the Salisbury government appointed Major-General Sir Redvers Buller as a 'Special Commissioner' to deal with unrest in Kerry and Clare in the summer of 1886, though Parnellites were enraged, ministers can hardly have been much surprised to find that Buller soon persuaded himself that it was the proprietors who were most to blame. For 120 years, he told the chief secretary, 'British bayonets have backed landlords in extracting excessive rents and have supported them in grossly neglecting their tenants'. As landlords in England were

---

[16] Beaconsfield to Cairns (himself Irish), 7 December 1880, TNA Cairns Papers PRO 30/51/1; Northcote to Cairns, 16 April 1881, ibid., PRO 30/51/5. See also J. E. Gorst to W. H. Smith, 14 July 1881, R[eading] U[niversity] Smith (Hambledon) Papers PS7/58.

[17] *Diary of Gathorne Hardy*, ed. Johnson, 478 (6 July 1881).

[18] Carnarvon to Queen Victoria, 22 August 1885, TNA Carnarvon Papers PRO 30/6/53; to Hicks Beach, 23 and 25 September 1885, ibid., PRO 30/6/53 and GRO St Aldwyn Papers PCC/78; Carnarvon's Diary for 30 October 1885, BL Carnarvon Papers Add. MS 60925.

[19] Hartington to Churchill, 14 September 1886, Ch[atsworth] H[ouse] Devonshire Papers 340.2050; G. H. De Burgh, *The Landowners of Ireland: An Alphabetical List of the Owners of Estates of 500 acres Valuation and Upwards in Ireland* (Dublin, [1878]), 126–7.

making voluntary rent reductions in the face of distress, so it was 'both fit and righteous to give some help to the Kerry peasants'.[20]

When Arthur Balfour became chief secretary in March 1887 and soon surprised his critics (especially those in the Home Rule Party) by consistent and steely effectiveness, his success in putting backbone into the proprietorial cause disguised bitter private condemnations of Irish landlords' lack of resolve, selfishness, and reliance upon England's guiding hand. Within a few months he was driven 'to despair' by the pathetic response of landowners to the nationalist 'Plan of Campaign'. Unwilling to combine energetically 'for any other purpose than that to abuse the government', they behaved like frightened rabbits rendered immobile by the glare of Parnell's agrarian headlights.[21] And this was, indeed, as far as Balfour was concerned, virtually a song without end and one he continued to deliver over the years that followed: 'What fools the Irish landlords are'; 'It is utterly useless to help the Irish landlords', who are 'totally without discipline, wholly ignorant ... and much more successful in embarrassing their friends than in beating their foes'; 'They have never known when to resist, or when to yield, and we cannot expect them to learn wisdom at a moment's notice'.[22] It was a feeling too strong to be confined to private communications and spilled out into parliamentary debates with such force that one Irish landlord wailed in the House of Lords about Unionist land legislation containing 'a bias against the landlord ... in every page'. Another rather more central figure in the Irish proprietorial universe frankly told Balfour in 1894 that 'nobody in England' of any party 'cares a rap about the Irish landlords'.[23] Indeed, forcefully made denunciations of Irish landlords by prominent Unionists such as Balfour's brother Gerald (chief secretary 1895–1900), Lord Cadogan (viceroy 1895–1902), and even the fifth Marquess of Lansdowne (himself owner of vast Irish estates) gave considerable credence to such complaints about being abandoned by those ostensibly most committed to the proprietorial cause.[24]

---

[20] Buller to Hicks Beach, 15 November 1886, GRO St Aldwyn Papers PCC/45; L. P. Curtis Jr, *Coercion and Conciliation in Ireland 1880–1892: A Study in Conservative Unionism* (Princeton, 1963), 154–6.

[21] Balfour to King-Harman (undersecretary), November 1887, B. E. C. Dugdale, *Arthur James Balfour: First Earl of Balfour*, 2 vols (London, 1936), i. 150. The Plan of Campaign, initiated in late 1886, involved tenants offering landlords no more than a 'fair' rent and being 'protected' when evicted as a result.

[22] Balfour to Salisbury, 2 November 1889, Curtis, *Coercion and Conciliation in Ireland*, 217; to Salisbury, 29 February 1888, ibid. 239; Cabinet Paper of May 1889, TNA CAB 37/25/31; Balfour to Cranborne, 11 August 1896, Bodl. Sandars Papers MS Eng.hist.c.729: J. S. Sandars was Balfour's private secretary 1892–1915.

[23] Parl. Deb. 4: xliv. 1230 (31 July 1896: Clonbrock); Brodrick (later Midleton) to Balfour, 26 October 1894, BL Balfour Papers Add. MS 49720.

[24] R. B. O'Brien, *Dublin Castle and the Irish People*, 2nd edn (London, 1912), 9; Cadogan to Salisbury, 25 January 1899, PA Cadogan Papers 1475; Lansdowne to Long, 19 December 1907, BL Long Papers Add. MS 62403.

What for long kept Irish landlords afloat in the new Unionist universe of 1886–1905 was a feeling that there was, from the British party's point of view, simply no alternative to backing even such feeble devotees against the massed hordes of Home Rule nationalism. But even this might have faltered had it not been for the kind of man Salisbury (prime minister for almost fifteen of the seventeen years between 1885 and 1902) turned out to be. Salisbury, who could move between high political sophistication and know-nothing doggedness with the smoothness of a snake-oil salesman, tended to apply the latter mode of analysis and operation to Ireland (which, as a country, he plainly disliked) and towards Irish landlords in particular, whose cause he defended with dour rearguard resistance for reasons that went well beyond Ireland itself. Not that this implied any positive love of Irish landlords, quite the reverse, for Salisbury was as irritated by their behaviour as were most Unionists. In particular, their lily-livered failure to support him in his opposition to Gladstone's Arrears Bill of 1882 rankled very deep indeed.[25] In 1896 he was still complaining that what he—accurately enough—called 'our clients in Ireland' were behaving neither 'generously or fairly', not least in their failure to realize how beneficial it would be if all Irish MPs were removed from Westminster, thereby significantly decreasing the Unionist disadvantage in the House of Commons.[26]

Salisbury's Irish policy had, therefore, nothing much to do with his persistent dislike of 'our clients' and everything to do with his declaration of 1872 that 'Ireland must be kept, like India, at all hazards: by persuasion if possible; if not, by force'. As a result, he swallowed his feelings and, while always publicly 'scathing of individual miscreants and enraged by occasional collective lapses', remained 'a determined patron of Irish landlords' for want of better alternatives.[27] Much the lesser aspect of this patronage concerned appointments, titles, and honours—always critical for recipients but tedious for ministers. More important were the two core aspects of Irish policy during the period of Unionist hegemony after 1885—namely, coercion and land purchase. Both were specifically and distinctly *Irish* policies involving procedures that no government of the time would ever have consistently followed in the rest of the United Kingdom. But, while both were peculiarly Hibernian, coercion had been around for as long as anyone could remember as a kind of plaster for Irish discontents. Land purchase, however (Gladstone's baby steps of 1869–70 and 1881 aside), was something new. Not only that, but it also spoke forcefully to the condition of landlords, many of whom were becoming increasingly

[25] Salisbury to Northcote, 10 August 1882, Curtis, *Coercion and Conciliation in Ireland*, 33; A. Roberts, *Salisbury: Victorian Titan* (London, 1999), 267–71; to Northcote, 21 December 1884, BL Northcote Papers Add. MS 50020.

[26] Salisbury to Cadogan, 22 December 1896, PA Cadogan Papers 971.

[27] [Salisbury], 'Hansard's Reports, 1871, 1872', *Quarterly Review*, 133/266 (1872), 572; A. Jackson, *The Ulster Party: Irish Unionists in the House of Commons, 1884–1911* (Oxford, 1989), 154.

despondent about their own economic and social futures. More important still—and often overlooked at the time—it constituted the beginnings of a long-fused British disengagement from direct responsibility for crucial aspects of Irish affairs and their tedious complexities. Whether consciously so developed or not, purchase could ultimately free London governments from any *direct* involvement in Irish agrarian relationships and, by extension, from many other Irish matters as well. If Home Rule amounted to a kind of uncoupling as far as London was concerned, state-assisted purchase involved resonances and intimations of a very similar kind.

Although Tory inclinations towards purchase really took to the air in the early 1880s, they had been taxiing down the runway as far back as 1870, when Gladstone had done as little as he possibly could to meet John Bright's enthusiasm for providing loans to help Irish tenants buy their holdings. With Gladstone doing his best to resist calls for purchase, Salisbury was doing the opposite, arguing in favour of peasant ownership on the grounds that 'there would be more security in Ireland if the base of property were widened', a policy he thought altogether sounder than the Liberal propensity for tinkering with the details of tenurial law.[28] Other peers saw this—as they saw Gladstone's very different approach—as fully in line with the view that Ireland was to be treated in ways especially tailored to its peculiar needs, with Salisbury's colleague Lord Cairns unsentimentally laying out the alternatives as far as the Tory Party was concerned: 'You must either satisfy the Irish tenants by giving them a slice of the property of the landlords, or you must satisfy the landlords with English money.'[29]

Disraeli's 1874–80 administration began to think about Ireland only in its last months, when violence fuelled by agrarian distress was making it impossible to ignore the country. Although Northcote at the Exchequer maintained a tight grip on expenditure, the heads of a purchase bill were drawn up only months before the government was defeated at the general election of April 1880. This defeat came as something of a shock for some leading Conservatives, though, as regards Ireland, they rapidly found it restorative to coalesce around support for state-assisted land purchase, not least because this provided them, not only with a policy of Irish differentiation, but with a clear (though potentially very expensive) alternative to Gladstone's 1881 Irish Land Act, with its emphasis on adjustments in tenure rather than provisions for purchase.[30]

---

[28] Parl. Deb. 3: ccii. 75–6 (14 June 1870).
[29] Ibid. 202 (Cairns), 215 (Halifax), 374 (Hatherley)—all 16 June 1870. The distinguished historian W. H. Lecky (a future Liberal Unionist MP) felt much the same at the time: 'I think a number of peasant proprietors would be one of the most useful and, in the best sense of the word, conservative elements in Irish life' ([Elizabeth Lecky], *A Memoir of the Right Hon. William Hartpole Lecky* (London, 1909), 69, also 140).
[30] A. Warren, 'Disraeli, the Conservatives and the Government of Ireland: Part 2, 1868–1881', *Parliamentary History*, 18 (1999), 160–1; F. Thompson, 'Attitudes to Reform: Political Parties in Ulster and the Irish Land Bill of 1881', *Irish Historical Studies*, 24 (1985), 338.

Soon Northcote too was coming to the view that 'peasant proprietorship' might not be without its advantages and that, while the Irish should be told that no 'amount of crying' would turn 'two and two' into 'five', purchase facilities should be made more readily available, even to the extent of taking 'compulsory powers' to acquire land for resale to 'small holders'.[31] What Northcote was now advocating with positive enthusiasm, others were taking on board as the least bad alternative to Gladstone's policies. One vociferous Tory MP even claimed as early as November 1880 that both Disraeli and Salisbury had become passionate advocates of purchase, a claim at the time more mischievous than pellucidly accurate.[32]

But Tory ministers *were* slowly turning towards purchase as the best policy for dealing with Ireland's agrarian problems and discontents, though some were taken aback by the enthusiasm shown by Irish landlords for Gladstone's bill of 1881, an enthusiasm that did not, on the whole, increase admiration for their landed allies in Ireland.[33] Worries about expense and about the stead-fastness of Irish landlords were quickly overcome by the conviction that only purchase could provide a permanent and complete solution to what was rapidly becoming a very pressing difficulty indeed. Even the Neanderthal Tory Duke of Richmond, who had headed a Royal Commission inquiring into the land question, was attracted by some of Gladstone's ideas, because agriculture in Ireland was 'so very different from what we are accustomed to in England or Scotland that the same rules could not apply' with respect to either tenure, the consolidation of holdings, or ownership in general.[34] All in all the Tory Party as a whole, though by no means keen on certain aspects of the 1881 bill, had little hesitation in accepting those parts of it that required the expenditure of money, an earnest of the party's future lavishness with respect to Irish land and to Irish social and economic affairs as a whole.[35]

Expense alone, Northcote began to insist, could not be allowed to torpedo the absolute necessity of embarking upon the creation of 'peasant proprietary classes'.[36] In this, his chief ally was to be one of the party's rising stars, the wholesale news tycoon W. H. Smith, whose social background rendered him something of a necessary man in a party consisting so generally of owners of broad agricultural acres. Although Lord Randolph Churchill wittily referred to

---

[31] Northcote to Gibson (Ashbourne), 18 December 1880, PA Ashbourne Papers B71/9; to Cairns, 18 December 1880, TNA Cairns Papers PRO 30/51/5.
[32] J. E. Gorst to Lord Randolph Churchill, 9 November 1880, CUL Lord Randolph Churchill Papers MS 9248/1/23.
[33] Cairns to Beaconsfield, 3 December 1880, Bodl. Disraeli Papers 91/4; Salisbury to Beaconsfield, 20 December 1880, Thompson, 'Attitudes to Reform', 339.
[34] Richmond to Beaconsfield, 9 December 1880, WSRO Richmond Papers 865; to Cairns, 11 July 1880, TNA Cairns Papers PRO 30/51/4.
[35] [K. C. Cowper], *Earl Cowper, KG A Memoir* (privately printed, 1913), 495.
[36] Northcote to Cranbrook, 16 December 1880, 24 November 1881, 23 January 1882, Su[ffolk] R[ecord] O[ffice] Cranbrook Papers HA43/T501/271.

Northcote (whose Devon estates were on the small side) and Smith as 'Mar-shall and Snelgrove' after the Oxford Street department store, it was they who were to prove mainly responsible for establishing purchase as the party's core policy so far as Ireland was concerned and for ensuring its acceptance on the grounds that Irish circumstances required an approach that could never prove suitable for—and would therefore never be applied to—the rest of the United Kingdom. Smith had attacked Gladstone's second Land Act precisely because of its feeble purchase provisions and because its rent reduction clauses actually lessened the attractions of purchase in general.[37] In the spring of 1882 he visited Ireland (his firm had a large branch in Dublin) to examine the whole question and was much influenced by a paper sent him by the now elderly Mountifort Longfield (a former economics professor at Trinity College Dublin and judge of the Landed Estates Court) arguing for the importance of creating peasant proprietors 'on the side of law and order' and pointing out that only by setting loan repayments below existing rents could any scheme succeed.[38] Gladstone, most unusually, allowed the Treasury to assist Smith in drawing up a bill and permitted two Liberal colleagues to do the same. However, in the event, this proved to be little more than window dressing on the part of a prime minister never enthusiastic about purchase and soon actively under-mining Smith's ideas by 'raising questions about the difficulties' of integrating any scheme into 'the political process, and the need for its proponents to accompany it with Irish local government' reforms.[39]

Gladstone's obvious reluctance about purchase provided strong reasons for Conservative enthusiasm. The first resignation from the Liberal government took place as early as August 1880, when the fifth Marquess of Lansdowne (a junior minister at the India Office) departed because of anxieties over the land question in Ireland. In particular he disliked Gladstone's ideas about tenurial reform, his own distinct preference being for purchase, a disposition that helped to push him into Liberal Unionist arms after 1885.[40] Of more importance was Salisbury's support for purchase as a counterweight, indeed as an alternative, to the changes in tenure proposed by Gladstone, which would, he thought, reduce the landlord to little more than 'a sort of mortgagee upon the estate' and produce a system of dual ownership in which he would hardly

---

[37] Parl. Deb. 3: cclx. 1585 (2 May 1881).

[38] H. E. Maxwell, *Life and Times of the Right Honourable William Henry Smith MP*, 2 vols (London, 1893), ii. 57, 61, 347–53; see also A. J. Hamilton Smyth of Athlone to Smith, 30 April 1882, R[eading] U[niversity] Smith (Hambledon) Papers PS8/30, strongly supporting the scheme 'ascribed to you, for purchasing the landlords' interests and re-selling them to the tenants on re-payment by instalments spread over a number of years. Such a scheme appears to be supported by both classes in the country.'

[39] H. C. G. Matthew, *Gladstone 1875–1898* (Oxford, 1995), 201.

[40] Parl. Deb. 3: cclxiv. 278–9 (1 August 1881); Lansdowne to Bessborough, 27 February 1882, WSRO Bessborough Papers 166.

be entitled 'to be called a landlord' at all. Far better to cut the Gordian knot, provide state money for purchasers, create a peasant proprietary, and allow landlords the decency of a dignified exit.[41]

Once the 1881 bill had become law, Salisbury at once moved into a characteristically 'realist' mode, his final conversion emerging in April 1882 in the shape of two dramatic interventions. The first and most public consisted of a widely reported speech made in Liverpool, where he declared himself 'not one of those who believed that after a revolutionary step [the 1881 act] you can go back ... If you wish to establish peace and content in Ireland you must do your best to bring the ownership of land [again] into single hands'. Only thus, he declared, could one negate the Liberals' 'social revolution and ... restore the conservative instincts of society in Ireland', something that of course Gladstone claimed to be precisely the aim of his own policies.[42] Edward Hamilton, soon to become Gladstone's principal private secretary, saw Salisbury's pronouncements as entirely opportunistic. Purchase, far from being the Tory's 'only child', had long, he argued, been simply a 'foundling' rejected by all until necessity suggested otherwise, a comment not entirely, but substantially, a case of the sourest of sour grapes as far as Liberals were concerned.[43] Salisbury's other crucial and almost simultaneous departure on purchase took the form of his signature to the *First Report from the Select Committee of the House of Lords on Land Law (Ireland)* dated 28 April 1882. The committee, with its distinct Tory bias (it also included Cairns, Marlborough, and Abercorn), came down decisively against the feeble purchase clauses of the 1881 Act and in favour of more extensive state assistance and of the view that, unless tenant repayments were pitched well below existing (and now officially controlled) rents, success would continue to prove elusive.[44] The shift in Conservative thinking towards purchase on terms generous to both landlords and tenants was now well under way and virtually unstoppable. By 1883 Arthur Balfour was announcing that any return to the happy days of 'large proprietors and competitive rents' was now impossible and that it had become vital to destroy the 'artificial [Liberal] system of dual ownership' by establishing in its place a 'rational system ... of small holdings in fee simple', which, being translated into plain text, meant that purchase had now become the only 'sensible' (that is, Tory) policy available.[45]

---

[41] Parl. Deb. 3: ccliv. 256–7, 267 (1 August 1881).

[42] *The Times*, 3 April 1882. Northcote spoke next and expressed full approval. See *Florence Arnold-Foster's Irish Journal*, ed. T. W. Moody and R. Hawkins (Oxford, 1988), 447 (13 April 1882); also Carnarvon to Salisbury, [5] February 1885, HH Salisbury Papers 3M/E.

[43] *The Diary of Sir Edward Walter Hamilton 1880–1885*, ed. D. W. R. Bahlman, 2 vols (Oxford, 1972), i. 251 (13 April 1882).

[44] *First Report from the Select Committee of the House of Lords on Land Law (Ireland)* H[ouse of] C[ommons Paper] 1882 (249), xi. 3–9.

[45] Parl. Deb. 3: cclxvi. 1771 (27 February 1882: Balfour) and 1983 (2 March 1882: Hicks Beach), cclxvii. 550 (9 March 1882: Northcote), cclxxx. 423–5 (12 June 1883: Balfour).

III

When in June 1885 Salisbury became prime minister at the head of a minority government dependent to some extent on Irish support, it was, therefore, no surprise that purchase (and an abandonment of coercion) constituted the main planks of policy with regard to Ireland, the whole business propped up by rickety underpinning from the new viceroy Lord Carnarvon's highly personal support for some kind of constitutional federalism. Where Carnarvon *was* in tune with party feeling was in the conviction that, because Ireland, as he told the queen, 'is so little like any other place', some species of identifiably Hibernian approach to government was both necessary and inevitable.[46] And what all this actually meant was soon unveiled in the shape of the first really significant land purchase measure ever enacted, the Ashbourne Act of August 1885 introduced to parliament within twenty-four days of the ministry's coming into office. Although a comparative minnow compared with subsequent legislation, its unambiguous confirmation of Tory commitment represented something distinctly new and distinctly (and exclusively) Irish. The Treasury was to provide an initial £5 million to enable tenants to borrow the whole purchase price at 4 per cent over forty-nine years and at an annuity that would not exceed their original rents. Salisbury stoutly defended the bill and declared himself convinced that it would be the first of many, while Parnell hailed it as a step in the right direction and confirmation that the land question might well be settled 'permanently upon the basis of an occupying ownership'.[47]

From the Tory perspective, matters hung fire when Gladstone returned to office in February 1886 pledged to the introduction of Home Rule. But, when that programme went down to defeat in June and Salisbury came back, purchase was quickly restored as the chief heraldic device on his party's now unambiguously Unionist escutcheon. Already in the last days of Salisbury's first administration rumours had circulated—especially in connection with W. H. Smith and his former tormentor Lord Randolph Churchill—that the Tories were about to extend the Ashbourne Act by providing additional funds—rumours that some Liberals saw as confirmation of an imminent unlocking of taxpayers' money ('soft words and hard cash') and others jealously identified as a potentially successful plan for creating 'a peasant proprietary which will install into the minds of the masses a sense of property and a sense of respect for property'.[48]

---

[46] Carnarvon to Queen Victoria, 3 August 1885, TNA Carnarvon Papers PRO 30/6/53.
[47] Curtis, *Coercion and Conciliation in Ireland*, 44–5.
[48] Lewis Harcourt's Diary for 24 January 1886, Bodl. Harcourt Papers MS 377; *The Times*, 30 September 1885 (speech by Morley); Parl. Deb. 3: cccii. 618 (8 February 1886: Hamilton); *The Diary of Sir Edward Walter Hamilton 1885–1906*, ed. D. W. R. Bahlman (Hull, 1993), 30 (12 March 1886).

Salisbury, never one to miss an opportunity of temporarily suppressing a favoured policy if, by doing so, his opponents might suffer embarrassment, unhesitatingly attacked Gladstone's Home Rule related purchase proposals of April 1886 in a speech at St James's Hall in London. Yet, underneath the bluster, his words, with their emphasis on the amounts rather than the principles involved, were carefully chosen to allow a rapid return to Tory normality once Gladstone had been levered out of Downing Street. Gladstone's scheme, he announced, was so 'fantastic' that nothing of the kind had ever before been 'attempted ... in the experience of the human race'. But, while this was all great stuff—not least the final flourish about how much better it would be to spend the sums proposed to help 'emigrate another million of the Irish people'—it was in truth, as the history of his own subsequent administrations amply proved, no more than hot air.[49] And, within weeks of Salisbury's return, his new Chancellor of the Exchequer (in the unlikely shape of Lord Randolph Churchill) was busily reiterating the established Tory approach: no more rent revisions à la 1881 because 'we are rather bound to the other solution ... single ownership', a policy that, he mischievously pointed out, had been (if very briefly) adopted by Gladstone himself a few months earlier.[50] Churchill, always keen to spot disagreements potentially useful to himself, drew rather unconvincing distinctions between Salisbury's devotion to 'the high ground of the rights of property' and Hicks Beach's greater ideological flexibility, though these were in reality differences without much traction so far as Tory land policy was concerned. In fact, virtually all Unionists saw purchase as the only way of extinguishing the hated 'Liberal' dual ownership system and of providing landowners with a settlement 'containing some at least of the elements of finality'.[51] Though Gladstone was given to making the fairly obvious point that it was becoming clear that 'the enemies of Home Rule' were now 'the keenest promoters of land purchase in the interest of the Irish landlords', his analysis hid the undoubted truth that, while the Tory approach was certainly designed to help their landed clients in Ireland, it was equally firmly based on the notion that purchase alone could 'solve' the whole question of Irish agrarianism in ways that went well beyond the narrow concerns of the proprietorial community itself.[52]

---

[49] *The Times*, 17 May 1886. Labouchere later pointed to its evident insincerity: Parl. Deb. 3: ccclii. 248 (10 April 1891).

[50] Parl. Deb. 3: cccviii. 129–30 (19 August 1886). Churchill was already convinced that the Ashbourne Act was but a small token of a mighty future wave of Tory purchase legislation: to J. Chamberlain, 4 October 1886, B[irmingham] U[niversity] J. Chamberlain Papers JC5/14/25.

[51] Churchill to Hartington, 13 September 1886, GRO St Aldwyn Papers PCC/82; Lansdowne to Hartington, 9 September 1886, ChH Devonshire Papers 340.2044.

[52] See Gladstone, *The Irish Question ... with an 'Addendum'*, 23 (22 August 1886), where he again defended his own purchase proposals because they had been protected by 'security' in the shape of his proposed 'responsible' authority in Ireland, while the Tories had fatally established 'direct relations between the Treasury and the individual occupant of the soil in Ireland'.

Throughout Salisbury's second administration (July 1886 to August 1892) purchase became more and more firmly embedded as the Unionist policy of choice, with disagreements confined to matters of detail. In other words, Unionists, quite as much as Gladstone though travelling by a different route, were basing their approach to Ireland upon fundamental notions of divergence from United Kingdom norms, something that men like Grey, Melbourne, Russell, Wellington, and Peel would have considered at once ineffective and simply wrong. As a result, Unionist support for state-assisted land purchase never flagged. Joseph Chamberlain from a radical perspective might initially have thought that landlords were being treated with excessive generosity, but he too soon came round to seeing things in a more positive and distinctly Hibernian light.[53] Lansdowne, a very different Liberal Unionist, put forward the proposition now gaining increasing leverage across party lines to the effect that the creation of a property-owning farmer class would not only reconstruct 'Irish society' on essentially conservative lines but would put 'Irish agriculture on its legs again'. Hicks Beach regarded purchase more pragmatically, but no less enthusiastically, as offering the only route by which a troublesome island could be kept quiet and some unlovely landlords saved from financial ruin.[54] What was, above all, remarkable was how relaxed senior Unionists had become about finding the cash to support purchase and their other Irish policies. As chief secretary, Arthur Balfour told Goschen (who, in a remarkable coup, had replaced Churchill as Chancellor) that there could be no question of cutting back expenditure in Ireland if 'friction' was to be avoided, that, 'in whatever language it may be clothed, the proposal of the Government is to make the Imperial Exchequer responsible for the payment of interest on that [Government Land] Stock' employed in raising funds to make purchase possible.[55] Indeed, so speedily successful had Ashbourne's Act become that the money allocated was soon used up and ministers were obliged to scratch around for additional funds.[56] It is, however, very revealing of party differences that, when W. H. Smith approached Gladstone in July 1888 for cross-party agreement on the grounds that it 'would be a serious misfortune if a break were allowed in the progress of the land purchase scheme', Gladstone, convinced that it was all becoming no more than 'a subsidy to the Irish

---

[53] J. Chamberlain to A. J. Balfour, 30 and 31 March 1887, BU J. Chamberlain papers JC5/5/42 and 43; Hartington to Chamberlain, 18 December 1890, ibid., JC5/22/50; Chamberlain to Lansdowne, 30 September 1888, BL 5th Marquess of Lansdowne Papers 'Chamberlain I' (provisional reference).

[54] Lansdowne to Salisbury, 8 December 1887, BL 5th Marquess of Lansdowne Papers 'Early Career 15' (provisional reference); Parl. Deb. 3: cccx. 1339 (11 February 1887).

[55] Balfour to Goschen, 13 October 1887, 22 October 1890, and 31 October 1891, Bodl. Goschen Papers Dep.c.183.

[56] Morley to Harcourt, 29 October 1888, Bodl. Morley Papers MS Eng.d.3574.

landlords', flatly refused to modify what he now claimed had long been economic 'principles of the utmost consequence'.[57]

Arthur Balfour's rapidly growing enthusiasm for purchase proved important, not only in increasing his uncle's support, but because he himself was to succeed Salisbury as prime minister in 1902. In a paper for the cabinet in February 1889 he even claimed (with what seriousness it is impossible to recover) that the creation of a new class of owner-occupiers would ensure that 'hostility to England [would] soon be etherealized into a mere poetic shadow'. For his part, Salisbury announced that purchase would 'create a moral and political force which will frustrate the efforts of future agitators to raise occupiers against owners'.[58] Wanting to have the best of all possible worlds, he saw Unionist land policy as helping to keep many landlords in place, while seeding, as it were, the countryside with enough purchasing farmers 'so that the present uniformity of condition and feeling which enabled agitators to turn the whole political and social force of the occupiers against the landlords will be arrested and broken'.[59] Of course there were some Unionists who thought that such optimism outran good sense, that, indeed, 'when Irish landlords are wanderers on the face of the earth, they will be able to turn round on their English compatriots[!] and say "Hodie mihi, cras tibi"'.[60] The Liberal Lord Kimberley interpreted the policy to mean something no less worrying to Unionists in general—namely, that purchase was anything but a conservative force in the usually touted meaning of the word, but would, as he put it in March 1890, inevitably increase the likelihood of Home Rule.[61] By then, however, Salisbury had shed earlier doubts. Farmers who owned their land were indubitably 'a class in the highest sense conservative', and, more important still, he denied the Duke of Argyll's (now outdated) insistence that 'the relation of landlord and tenant was ... universal throughout the world'. Could anyone, he asked, deny that the Irish case was totally different from that of the rest of the United Kingdom, and that, being different, it could only be improved by remedies of a targeted and uniquely Irish character?[62]

The short-lived Liberal administration of August 1892 to June 1895 was devoid of initiatives regarding purchase. Gladstone was now engaged with Home Rule to the virtual exclusion of everything else and showed no

[57] Smith to Gladstone, 12 July 1888, Bodl. Harcourt Papers Add. MS 10; Gladstone to Smith, 13 July 1888, ibid.; Gladstone to J. Chamberlain, 1 August 1885, BU J. Chamberlain Papers JC5/34/37.

[58] TNA CAB 37/23/5 (20 February 1889); Parl. Deb. 3: cccxlix. 29 (25 November 1890).

[59] Salisbury to T. Waring, 2 May 1890, Curtis, *Coercion and Conciliation in Ireland*, 351; also Parl. Deb. 3: cccxxx. 1721–2 (20 November 1888: Sinclair) and cccxli. 132 (12 February 1890: Brooke).

[60] Parl. Deb. 3: cccxliii. 1337 (21 April 1890: Bruce): 'Me today, you tomorrow'.

[61] Ibid. cccxlii. 1426–7 (21 March 1890).

[62] Ibid. cccliv. 1573–4 (26 June 1891).

inclination to adopt the twin-track policy of 1886. Rosebery, who succeeded him as prime minister in March 1894, had no interest in Ireland and certainly not in Home Rule or land purchase, reacting to a letter from his viceroy by rapidly forwarding it elsewhere with the nonchalant comment: 'It is not a subject which interests me, or with which I am thankful to say that I have anything to do.'[63]

By contrast, even in opposition the Unionists continued to worship at the shrine of purchase. Arthur Balfour told the Commons in August 1893 that it was the only way of dealing with the 'Irish Question', while Irish Unionists insisted that existing schemes should be expanded, that more money was needed, that even compulsion might be required to persuade reluctant land-lords to sell, and that, if these things were not done, Protestant farmers in Ulster and elsewhere might be tempted to desert the cause by promises of better legislation from the nationalist side.[64] At the general election of July 1895 (which the Unionists won handsomely) Balfour told the voters of his constituency of Manchester East that purchase was 'the key of the land question in Ireland, and if the land question ... were settled there would be no other Irish question at all'—a view echoed by his brother Gerald (the new chief secretary) when telling the voters of Leeds that any 'ultimate solution' must lie, not in the principles enshrined in the Liberal Act of 1881, but 'in promoting the more rapid and effective working of the Land Purchase acts passed by Unionist governments in 1885 and 1891'.[65]

Gerald, therefore, introduced another purchase bill the following year in order to speed up a process that was, he claimed, already turning its benefi-ciaries into 'thriftier and better citizens', while Arthur (now the virtual co-leader of the government) took the opportunity to attack those many Irish landlords who resisted his policies, gave the party little active support, and had swallowed Gladstone's nostrums of 1881—a clear indication that purchase was not universally regarded by British Unionists as merely or even primarily a device for bailing out their landed 'friends' across the Irish Sea.[66] Indeed, Arthur grew incandescent with rage over what he regarded as the selfish follies of Irish landlords 'who have never known when to resist, or when to yield', who were spreading falsehoods among their English sympathizers

---

[63] Rosebery to Morley, 20 November 1894, N[ational] L[ibrary of] S[cotland] Rosebery Papers MS 10130.

[64] Parl. Deb. 4: xvi. 184 (14 August 1893); Memorandum by J. Atkinson (a former solicitor-general and future attorney-general for Ireland) enclosed in S. McDonnell to A. J. Balfour, 2 November 1893, Bodl. Sandars Papers MS Eng.hist.c.725. Schomberg McDonnell was Salisbury's private secretary.

[65] *The Times*, 11 July 1895; ibid. 6 July 1895; C. B. Shannon, *Arthur J. Balfour and Ireland 1874–1922* (Washington, 1988), 83. The brothers frequently discussed Irish matters.

[66] Parl. Deb. 4: xxxix. 781 (13 April 1896: G. W. Balfour) and xliii. 964–5 (29 July 1896: A. J. Balfour).

and behaving 'with incredible folly throughout'.[67] While, therefore, Unionist purchase schemes were undoubtedly designed to provide financial sustenance to the landowners of Ireland, to fulfil, as it were, a debt of honour to men who shared many of the ideological and social characteristics of landowners in general, their main significance for Unionist leaders lay in their hoped-for capacity to *solve* the Irish land question once and for all. The Treasury might be far from ecstatic about purchase, but the business went ahead all the same, with powerful support from both Arthur Balfour and from the government's most prominent Liberal Unionist, Joseph Chamberlain.[68]

The result was that, by the time Salisbury left office to be replaced by Arthur Balfour, the Unionist commitment to land purchase could already be measured out in impressive amounts of government cash. Under Gladstone's Acts of 1870 and 1881 £753,337 was advanced to 1,608 purchasers. Under a series of Unionist measures between 1885 and 1896 the equivalent numbers were £23,139,428 and 72,201 respectively—a ratio in cash terms of 1 to 30, in terms of buyers of almost 1 to 45.[69] Of course, the various purchase programmes did not follow precisely similar or equal trajectories, but the shifts of gear generated by individual acts—1885, 1887, 1888, 1889, 1891, 1896—were predominantly related to changes in the value of the stock increasingly used to facilitate proceedings, to general economic circumstances, and to the effects of external shocks such as those produced by the Boer War. By 1896 Gerald Balfour as chief secretary overbore (with his brother's support) all hesitation by pointing out that it was rather 'late in the day' for Unionists to be teaching the Irish the 'sacredness of contracts', that forward movement was essential to discourage prospective buyers from delaying potential transactions, that relaxing the terms of repayment would, if anything, make it easier to recoup loans, that, at bottom, a policy of spraying money at Irish problems was the best policy as also by now a—perhaps the—distinctively Unionist policy.[70]

However, the best was yet to come when the apotheosis of Unionist prodigality towards Ireland became manifest under Gerald Balfour's successor as chief secretary, George Wyndham, who held the office from November 1900 to March 1905 and joined the cabinet in August 1902. An extraordinary

---

[67] A. J. Balfour to Cranborne (Salisbury's eldest son), 11 August 1896, Bodl. Sandars Papers MS Eng.hist.c.729. For strong objections from a Tory peer, see Richmond to Cranbrook, 4 August 1896, SuRO Cranbrook Papers HA43/T501/257.

[68] A. Gailey, *Ireland and the Death of Kindness: The Experience of Constructive Unionism 1890–1905* (Cork, 1987), 84. See Chamberlain to Londonderry, 25 February [1898], P[ublic] R[ecord] O[ffice of] N[orthern] I[reland] Londonderry Papers D2846/3/10/9: 'Even if these schemes cost money I believe they will prove a good investment in the long run.'

[69] J. Pim, 'The Present Position of the Irish Land Question', in J. H. Morgan (ed.), *A New Irish Constitution: An Exposition and Some Arguments* (London, [1912]), 197–8; J. E. Pomfret, *The Struggle for Land in Ireland 1800–1923* (Princeton, 1930), 307.

[70] Shannon, *Arthur J. Balfour and Ireland*, 89–90; Pomfret, *Struggle for Land in Ireland*, 229–30, 262, 271–5.

figure—sentimentally romantic about Ireland, given to dramatic outbursts, the kind of handsome man who looks at himself in the mirror each morning with considerable approval—Wyndham transported himself (and for a time others) into colourful realms of extravagance by means of an ameliorative condescension that was all his own. Days after being appointed he told Arthur Balfour that the only disagreement to be found among parties in Ireland related, not to the principle, but only to the details of purchase. The viceroy, Cadogan, he declared was an ignorant fool, with whom communications resembled 'speaking through a megaphone with a pudding in its orifice'. With nine-tenths of the people hanging back from agitation, now was the time for a truly 'constructive policy'.[71] Even Salisbury, now in the last months of his premiership, got carried away. The cabinet, he told the new King Edward VII, had persuaded itself to relax Treasury controls and boost purchase loans in order to prevent any slowing-down of sales.[72] Arthur Balfour, who succeeded him in July 1902, was more enthusiastic still, both with regard to the whole idea of purchase and to the amounts the government should make available. In February 1902 he urged the Chancellor of the Exchequer to provide more money at cheaper rates, not least to keep the Protestant farmers of Ulster from abandoning the Unionist cause. A few weeks later Wyndham was telling the Commons that generosity was easily the best policy.[73] By September 1902 he had started dropping unsubtle public hints that he would soon take the Treasury by the scruff of the neck, that, indeed, 'British credit was unlimited' with regard to the purchase of Irish land.[74] He and the new prime minister agreed that 'purchase as against court-fixed rents' had long been 'the policy of the Unionist Party'. They also, however, agreed, that the existing terms must be 'modified ... by making a more liberal use of British credit and by extending the term of repayment', something they (disingenuously) claimed did not involve 'giving' substantial amounts of additional cash to either tenants or landlords. Balfour, who may well in private have remained unconvinced by this last and distinctly meretricious claim, described to the king how—in a phrase of astonishing insouciance—he had persuaded the cabinet 'that in the interests of a great policy minor difficulties must be ignored'.[75]

	Although Wyndham's Land Bill of 1902 failed to make progress, it mollified opinion in Ireland and paved the way for the more dramatic measure enacted in

---

[71] Wyndham to A. J. Balfour, 26 November 1900, 20 September, and 2 November 1901, BL Balfour Papers Add. MS 49803.

[72] Salisbury to Edward VII, 25 November 1901, TNA CAB 41/26/26.

[73] A. J. Balfour to Hicks Beach, 15 February 1902, GRO St Aldwyn Papers PCC/88; Parl. Deb. 4: cv. 1032 (25 March 1902).

[74] P. Bull, 'The Significance of the Nationalist Response to the Irish Land Act of 1903', *Irish Historical Studies*, 28 (1993), 285–6.

[75] Balfour to Edward VII, 26 November 1902 and 10 March 1903, TNA CAB 41/27/35 and 41/28/5.

August 1903. On introducing this second bill, Wyndham insisted that substantial 'cash aid is necessary' because Ireland's present and historical economic circumstances were so very unlike those of England. He wanted up to £150 million in the hope that every single relevant acre would be sold by November 1918.[76] The prime minister saw Wyndham's proposals as offering so 'unique [a] chance ... of really settling the Irish Land controversy' that all opposition must be ignored.[77] Wyndham was exultant when the bill became law and saw its passage opening up the prospect of improving the efficiency of the chief secretary's administrative apparatus in Ireland now more and more closely involved in the measure's successful implementation. 'Ireland', he told Balfour, 'is in a plastic state. We can mould her almost at our will. Ireland is at the moment more friendly than ever before ... If I stay [as chief secretary] the Land Act is a success. If I go—this sounds outrageously conceited, but it is true—a failure. They will resent my leaving them and by "they" I mean both sides.'[78] And, if Wyndham's fantasies about having turned himself into Ireland's universal nanny proved far from the truth, the 1903 Act was nonetheless a very mighty Act indeed, not least because it contained highly attractive bribes: to landlords prepared to sell entire 'estates' (a very elastic term) a *cash* bonus of 12 per cent not subject to family or other charges, and to tenants annuities fixed well below (sometimes as much as two-fifths below) the rents they actually paid.[79]

While, as Edward Carson pointed out at the time, the Act was in itself no 'permanent solution' to all of Ireland's ills and while sales proved slower than had been anticipated so that Wyndham's hopes for 'completion' by 1918 were not achieved until after the implementation of the Free State's legislation of 1923, its importance cannot be overestimated with respect both to practical results (which included the creation of divisions within the Home Rule Party) and to psychological effects.[80] After 1903 no one could doubt the direction the land policy of successive British governments was taking and would inevitably continue to take. So clear was this that in 1909 the Liberal administration under Asquith felt obliged to continue the process with broadly similar legislation of its own, though—true to its Gladstonian roots—this involved some pruning of the

---

[76] A. Jackson, *The Ulster Party: Irish Unionists in the House of Commons, 1884–1911* (Oxford, 1989), 160–1; Parl. Deb. 4: cxx. 182–3 (25 March 1903).

[77] Balfour to Devonshire, 4 June 1903, Bodl. Sandars Papers MS Eng.hist.c.739.

[78] Wyndham to A. Chamberlain, 14 October 1903, BU A. Chamberlain Papers AC16/3/6; Wyndham's Memorandum of 16 October 1903, ibid., AC16/3/8A; Wyndham to Balfour, 4 November and 23 September 1903, BL Balfour Papers Add. MS 49804 and Bodl. Sandars Papers MS Eng.hist c.742.

[79] D. Meleady, *John Redmond: The National Leader* (Sallins, Co. Kildare, 2014), 37; P. Cosgrove, 'Irish Landlords and the Wyndham Act, 1903', in T. Dooley and C. Ridgway (eds), *The Irish Country House: Its Past, Present and Future* (Dublin, 2011), 90–109.

[80] E. Marjoribanks and I. Colvin, *The Life of Lord Carson*, 3 vols (London, 1932–4), i. 342–3; F. Campbell, *Land and Revolution: Nationalist Politics in the West of Ireland 1891–1921* (Oxford, 2005), 90–2.

lavishness shown by Unionists six years before. Up to 1902 £26,056,379 had been advanced to 79,842 tenants—the great bulk by Unionist administrations. Between 1903 and March 1912 the equivalent figures were £506,165,548 and 150,333 individuals. By 1920 almost two-thirds of agricultural land had been 'purchased', with many more transactions in the pipeline.[81]

Although Liberals were eventually obliged to follow the Unionist example, they did so without enthusiasm, for, as Lord Crewe (a former viceroy) put it, Wyndham's Act amounted to obliging British taxpayers to provide protection money for the sake of 'peace … one of the most persistent and successful blackmailers that exist'. A Liberal backbench MP was shocked by Wyndham's willingness to satisfy Irish landlords' 'hereditary itching palm', the 12 per cent bonus little more than a rather grand way of telling them 'You may keep the change'.[82] While some Liberals wrote off their opponents as irredeemable spendthrifts when it came to Ireland (an opinion not entirely absent even in Unionist circles),[83] more gleeful colleagues pointed out that purchase on this scale would inevitably lead to some form of Home Rule, the very destination Unionists were so keen to avoid. As James Bryce argued ten months before becoming Liberal chief secretary in December 1905, the whole thrust of Unionist policies over the previous decade had in actual fact contrived to bring Home Rule 'nearer in two ways—They give more power to the masses and they lessen the dangers feared in 1886 and 1893. The process of nature seems to me to be working for Home Rule; and it will come about under one English party, just as much as under another.'[84] Nor was he the only Liberal who thought like this. Kimberley, for example, had long come to the same conclusion.[85] And even some Tories feared that this was exactly what their own approach was doing, while Campbell-Bannerman, the Liberal leader in 1903, was convinced that Unionist extravagance must sooner or later lead to the appointment of something like Gladstone's 'intermediate' authority to prevent the costs of purchase from running entirely out of control, with the result that eventually 'the old policy, the Liberal policy of 1886 and 1893, will, in the words of its great author, "hold the field"'.[86] Whatever the element of wish-fulfilment in such declarations, they were by no means fanciful. Struggle

---

[81] Pim, 'The Present Position of the Land Question', 197–8; Pomfret, *Struggle for Land in Ireland*, 275, 307; Campbell, *Land and Revolution*, 91; also Parl. Deb. 5 (Commons): lv. 1723–4 (21 July 1913: Birrell); TNA CAB 37/120/86 (14 July 1914).

[82] Parl. Deb. 4: cxxvi. 1173–4 (3 August 1903: Crewe) and cxxii. 39 (7 May 1903: Atherley-Jones).

[83] Parl. Deb. 4: cxviii. 305 (8 December 1908: Cox); H. Robinson, *Memories: Wise and Otherwise* (London, 1914), 166–7.

[84] Bryce to Dicey, 3 February 1905, N[ational] L[ibrary of] I[reland] Bryce Papers MS 11011.

[85] Parl. Deb. 3: cccxlii. 1426–7 (21 March 1890): 'The more you can put the land into the hands of the tenants in Ireland the stronger will the Home Rule Party become.'

[86] Parl. Deb. 4: cxxi. 1228 (4 May 1903: Coghill); J. A. Spender, *The Life of Sir Henry Campbell-Bannerman*, 2 vols (London, [1923]), ii. 89 (19 March 1903).

as they might, both British parties, now increasingly enmeshed in convictions about Irish differentiation, were putting forward policies that contained clear implications for the future, implications that might well, in certain circumstances, help to weaken the closeness of the administrative and political links created in 1800 and might perhaps even undermine the whole basis of the Union itself.

IV

Nor was land purchase the only field in which Unionist governments proved themselves ardent advocates of treating Ireland differently and doing so in ways designed to mollify the majority in that country. Thus, although Liberals and Unionists differed considerably, indeed often violently, over education policy in England, they moved more or less in tandem so far as Ireland was concerned. For the Unionists this was no great problem, because their Irish policies did little or no violence to the denominationalism that they favoured. But, for those Liberals who still supported the idea of mixed, even of exclusively 'secular', education, the acceptance of Irish difference was a very big thing indeed.

As early as 1873 Gladstone had tried to grapple with Irish university education (where Catholics experienced notably inferior conditions) by proposing to set up an institution that would, he over-optimistically hoped, satisfy everyone by being nominally 'secular' but acceptable to Catholics because of various restrictions placed upon the teaching of certain 'delicate' disciplines. The bishops, however, rejected Gladstone's bill, which was defeated in the Commons by a majority of three.[87] This had a number of consequences. It brought about the more or less total collapse of the Irish Liberal Party. It consolidated the idea that Irish educational matters (like Ireland generally) demanded 'special' treatment. And it established the broad ground plan for the Liberal legislation of 1908 that was finally to lay the whole question of Catholic university education in Ireland to rest.

Education was, indeed, one of the very few areas of Irish concern that Disraeli's government of 1874–80 addressed with even minimalist interest. As chief secretary, Hicks Beach obtained cabinet approval for initiating discussions about intermediate education with the Irish Catholic bishops in December 1876. Relevant legislation followed in 1878, as did some mild university reforms favourable to Catholics in 1879. Though both fell very far

---

[87] Parl. Deb. 3: ccxiv. 406–7, 416 (13 February 1873: Gladstone); H. C. G. Matthew, *Gladstone 1809–1874* (Oxford, 1986), 197–200; J. Morley, *The Life of William Ewart Gladstone*, 3 vols (London, 1903), ii. 434–45.

short of clerical aspirations, they together constituted an attempt to address Irish problems in a distinctively Irish (in this case denominational) manner. That the Tory viceroy, the Duke of Marlborough, would have liked to go further—as would his son, the young Lord Randolph Churchill, who acted as his father's unofficial private secretary in Dublin—suggests that future party leaders might well continue to prove sympathetic to Catholic demands.[88] What made this particular aspect of Irish differentiation especially remarkable was that it also attracted support from prominent Liberals, among them unlikely figures such as James Stansfeld and W. E. Forster, respectively a strong and a pragmatic opponent of denominational education in England. And this was the case precisely because both men were convinced that what was appropriate for England was by no means automatically appropriate for Ireland, that politicians in London must 'pay deference to Irish ideas', that 'the wishes of the Irish people, expressed through the majority of their representation', ought to be given substantial weight, and that any suggestion that Irish questions be treated 'purely in accordance with English opinion' would lead to disasters as damaging as they were inevitable.[89] That even such radicals were prepared to accept denominationalism in Ireland is dramatic evidence of how far the thrust of differentiation had already gone.

Again, in August 1885, Spencer, recently Gladstone's viceroy in Ireland, was prepared to make concessions to the demands of the Catholic hierarchy on university matters, though his free-thinking colleague John Morley showed rather less enthusiasm and suspected the Tories of being altogether too keen on keeping the bishops happy, something they revealingly defended on the grounds that Ireland was not England and required treatment suitable to its own peculiar needs.[90] As chief secretary, Wyndham had no difficulty in rebutting claims that Irish educational requirements were being neglected by providing the Commons with a long list of special arrangements made by Unionist governments to meet the 'peculiarities and even ... the prejudices of the people it was intended to benefit'.[91] If, under the judgement of eternity, some of these arrangements were hardly remarkable, successive chief secretaries proved consistently proud of their modest recognitions that in parts of Ireland schoolteachers might be allowed, even encouraged, to conduct their

---

[88] C. B. Shannon, 'Lord Randolph Churchill's Irish Apprenticeship and its Aftermath, 1877–85', in R. McNamara (ed.), *The Churchills in Ireland: Connections and Controversies* (Dublin, 2012), 70, 73, 82; R. V. Comerford, 'Isaac Butt and the Home Rule Party, 1870–77', in W. E. Vaughan (eds), *A New History of Ireland VI: Ireland under the Union, II, 1870–1921* (Oxford, 1996), 27; D. H. Akenson, 'Pre-University Education, 1870–1921', ibid. 523–38.

[89] Parl. Deb. 3: ccxli. 1516 (15 July 1878: Stansfeld) and ccxlvii. 653–4 (25 June 1879: Forster).

[90] Spencer to Lansdowne, 16 August 1885, BL 5th Marquess of Lansdowne Papers 'Further Correspondence M' (provisional reference); Morley to Gladstone, 30 August 1889, Bodl. Morley Papers MS Eng.d.3571; Parl. Deb. 4: i. 970 (22 February 1892: Jackson); Balfour to Goschen, 31 October 1891, Bodl. Goschen Papers Dep.c.183.

[91] Parl. Deb. 4: cxxxiii. 429–39 (18 April 1904).

classes through the medium of the Irish language (in Wyndham's words 'an heirloom of the Irish'), it being 'an article of the Unionist creed that within the ambit of the Empire there shall be room for the co-operation of races, maintaining each a memory of its own past'.[92]

However, despite the consistently greater Unionist sympathy for Catholic demands that education follow denominational lines, it was the Liberals who in 1908 finally settled long-standing grievances about the inferior university education offered in Ireland to those Catholics who, like their bishops, found the overtly Anglican Trinity College Dublin and the 'secular' Queen's Colleges in Galway, Cork, and Belfast not to their taste. That, indeed, it was the Liberals who, in the person of the chief secretary Augustine Birrell, managed to enact the relevant and complex legislation is a clear sign of how deeply Irish differentiation had come to inform the imagination and the actions of the parties at Westminster.[93] Birrell's Act provided that, under the outward disguise of a nominally secular university, there would lurk a distinctly denominational body—the National University of Ireland—with colleges in Dublin, Cork, and Galway, with Belfast hived off into a separate Queen's University acceptable to Presbyterians. Legislative and more general protection was provided 'against interference in religious [i.e. Catholic] beliefs, and by the *de facto* if not *de jure* presence of large numbers of Catholics among the staff and students and by the opportunity for' the Catholic seminary at Maynooth to transform a version of itself into a 'recognised college' of the new 'national' institution. Not only that, but the deliberately 'amorphous nature' of the legislation allowed for the possibility of further shifts in both a Catholic and a nationalist direction. Birrell, later much criticized for his hyper-relaxed approach to Irish government, had achieved a great success by a sleight of hand at once effective and impressively opaque. Everyone had received a prize, with only some Ulster Unionists and a few British Nonconformists annoyed at what they saw as a palpable success for traditional Catholicism.[94] The leader of the Irish Parliamentary Party, John Redmond, made no effort to hide the fact that in practice the National University would be a Catholic university, just as Oxford and Cambridge were still essentially

---

[92] Parl. Deb. 4: xciv. 878 (21 May 1901: Wyndham); also Bryce to MacDonnell, 13 August 1906, Bodl. MacDonnell Papers MS Eng.hist.c.350: 'You have done wisely to appease [Douglas] Hyde over Gaelic teaching'; Aberdeen to Bryce, 15 February 1905 [*recte* 1906], NLI Bryce Papers MS 11011; D. H. Akenson, *The Irish Education Experiment: The National System of Education in the Nineteenth Century* (London, 1970), 382; F. S. L. Lyons, *Ireland since the Famine* (London, 1971), 76–7.

[93] For earlier Unionist declarations in favour of the kind of university reforms achieved in 1908, see Arthur Balfour's Cabinet Paper of 12 November 1898, TNA CAB 37/48/82, and Parl. Deb. 4: liii. 826 (16 February 1898).

[94] S. M. Parkes, 'Higher Education, 1793–1908', in Vaughan (ed.), *A New History of Ireland VI: Ireland under the Union, II 1870–1921*, 566–9; S. Pašeta, *Before the Revolution: Nationalism, Social Change and Ireland's Catholic Élite, 1879–1922* (Cork, 1999), 21.

Protestant and the new University of Khartoum (in British-controlled Sudan) essentially Muslim.[95] Warm support came from Arthur Balfour, who saw the act as an Irish solution to an Irish problem despite the obvious inability of its institutional manifestations to provide 'the independent and the mutual education of young men brought together, absolutely free to say what they like and think what they like', which he and his kind fondly thought they themselves had experienced at England's ancient universities.[96]

On this particular issue, not only had the policy of Irish differentiation led to unashamedly Hibernian treatment; it had even produced overall agreement in London as to the specific manner in which that treatment was to be put together and applied. The Irish had, in effect, been consulted. And what they wanted was separate development for the denominational communities in their country, an approach that the Irish school system had long come to terms with and that the new university arrangements fully recognized. No attempt was made in London 'to change the character of the demands'. Birrell, and pretty well everyone else, had 'decided to accept those realities, and Ireland was well pleased'.[97]

V

If land purchase and (intermittently) coercion constituted the most substantial Hibernian dishes on the menu of the Salisbury and Balfour administrations, they were regularly garnished with further examples of the Unionist disposition to prop up Irish policy upon cushions of government cash. Irish railways, for example, unlike those in Britain, received considerable help by way of loans from official sources, being regarded as a form of public works such as fisheries, harbours, and land reclamation. Expansion after the 1880s under predominantly Unionist auspices was partly subsidized by the state. Under various acts (chiefly those of 1889 and 1896) some 309 miles of so-called light railway track were built in the remoter western regions at a cost of £1.85 million, no less than 84 per cent of it provided by the government.[98] Such opposition as there was to this kind of largesse came—predictably—from the Liberal side, one MP telling the Commons in 1889 that the whole business was

[95] Birrell to Campbell-Bannerman, 30 October 1907, BL Campbell-Bannerman Papers Add. MS 41240; Parl. Deb. 4: clxxviii. 784–91 (11 May 1908).

[96] Parl. Deb. 4: cxciii. 636 (25 July 1908).

[97] D. W. Miller, *Church, State and Nation in Ireland 1898–1921* (Dublin, 1973), 204.

[98] H. D. Gribbon, 'Economic and Social History, 1850–1921', in Vaughan (ed.), *A New History of Ireland VI: Ireland under the Union, II 1870–1921*, 309–14; Cadogan to Salisbury, 30 September 1895, HH Salisbury Papers 3M/E.

no more than the classic Unionist policy of 'carrying a stick in one hand and a money bag in the other'.[99]

An even more dramatic departure from British norms was the establishment in 1891 of the Congested Districts Board, a state-sponsored body designed to improve the economic and social conditions of those areas in the west considered unable to support their existing populations. From the start, Liberals like Morley condemned the Unionists for coming up with yet another expensive and wasteful means for involving the government in affairs that were none of its business. Although initially most of its operating funds came from balances remaining in the so-called Church Surplus Fund set up after the disestablishment of the Church of Ireland, it soon acquired additional resources from sympathetic ministers (and distinctly unsympathetic Treasury officials), allowing it to embark on 'improvements' and further transfers of land from owners to tenants in the designated areas. Under its auspices, some two million acres were acquired at a cost of £9 million with another £2.25 million spent on improving the farms thus created.[100] Already in September 1895 Gerald Balfour found himself on a tour of Connacht being greeted with considerable, if self-interested, enthusiasm 'due in part to gratitude for past favours, in part to gratitude for favours to come'. 'What do you think', he asked the viceroy, 'of a chief secretary being received with bonfires in Swinford, right in the heart of Dillon's constituency?'[101] Some thirteen years later even a Liberal chief secretary felt inclined to hail the Board as 'a real national [i.e. Irish] institution' full of promise for still greater things to come.[102] Yet one issue the Board had not then succeeded in addressing with any success was the reluctance of landowners to sell their untenanted grazing land for redistribution, because more could be gained by renting it to highly commercial cattle graziers on the so-called eleven-months system, a failure that generated the last major agrarian disturbance of pre-independence Ireland, the Ranch War of 1906–9, when meetings were held of those 'who wished to smash and finish ranching and land monopoly' and cattle were illegally removed from graziers'

---

[99] Parl. Deb. 3: cccxxxviii. 988 (19 July 1889: Cossham).

[100] C. Breathnach, *The Congested Districts Board of Ireland, 1891–1923: Poverty and Development in the West of Ireland* (Dublin, 2005), 30; Gribbon, 'Economic and Social History, 1850–1921', 286; W.L. Micks, *An Account of the Constitution, Administration and Dissolution of the Congested Districts Board for Ireland from 1891 to 1923* (Dublin, 1925), 115–16, 124, 150, 152–3.

[101] G.W. Balfour to Cadogan, 23 September 1895, PA Cadogan Papers 729; to Salisbury, 23 September 1895, HH Salisbury Papers 3M/E. After 1905 Gerald Balfour abandoned politics for higher things as one of the main actors in a spiritualist/eugenics 'Plan' to save humanity from chaos, his role being that of impregnator of the suffragist Winifred Coombe-Tennant who then gave birth to the unsuspecting Henry (putative Saviour of the World) who went to Eton, Trinity College Cambridge, the army, MI6 (where he worked with Kim Philby), ending up as a Benedictine monk and entirely failing to enact the part assigned him in the spiritualist 'scripts' that had originally underpinned the 'Plan': J. Gray, *The Immortalization Commission* (London, 2011), 80–6.

[102] Birrell in TNA CAB 37/93/71 (2 June 1908).

land at night and brought to secret markets or left to wander along country roads, an activity that soon became known as 'cattle driving'.[103]

The Congested Districts Board was, however, by no means the only, or even the main, institutional manifestation of Unionist willingness to 'solve' Irish problems with the help of the British taxpayer. Eight years after its foundation, another uniquely Irish body was created in the shape of the Department of Agriculture and Technical Instruction under the leadership of the progressive Unionist busybody Horace (later Sir Horace) Plunkett. This had been under discussion for some time and had, from the start, been seen as something quite different from the kind of agricultural management applicable to the rest of the United Kingdom. Indeed, some observers thought it little short of a Unionist 'measure of Home Rule to Ireland in agriculture', while others saw it as a logical extension of the activities devolved to the Congested Districts Board in 1891.[104]

Thus, by the beginning of the twentieth century, successive Unionist governments had set up a number of pioneering agencies responsible for the development of Ireland's major economic sector: Plunkett's Department of Agriculture and Technical Instruction, the Congested Districts Board, and a Land Commission to implement Unionist purchase acts from 1885 onwards. None had counterparts in Britain. All were deliberately and distinctly Irish as to character and mode of operation. All were the work of a party whose very title derived from opposition to devolution, a party that was, however, now beginning to dance to some very Irish tunes indeed.

And, even in an important aspect of directly *political* life, where superficially it might look as if Salisbury's government had, for once, determined on a policy of assimilation—namely, local government—close reading reveals a much more nuanced and complex state of affairs. Briefly put, the eventual, partial, and delayed granting of local-government reform to Ireland in 1898 was arrived at only with the greatest reluctance, and had nothing to do with any overt policy of assimilation and almost everything (as had been the case with the franchise in 1884–5) with the lack of viable and convincing alternatives.

In 1888 a Local Government Act introduced a new system of local administration for England and Wales, with fifty county councils for the former and twelve for the latter—in effect a complete overhaul of the structures laid down by the Municipal Reform Act of 1835, Scotland being accorded similar provisions in 1889. Ireland, however, still functioned under its feeble

---

[103] D. S. Jones, 'The Cleavage between Graziers and Peasants in the Land Struggle, 1890-1910', in S. Clark and J. S. Donnelly Jr (eds), *Irish Peasants: Violence and Political Unrest 1780-1914* (Madison, WI, 1983), 375–417.

[104] Parl. Deb. 4: xlv. 12 (19 January 1897: Kenyon) and xlviii. 1033–4 (12 April 1897: G. W. Balfour); R. B. McDowell, *The Irish Administration 1801–1914* (London, 1964), 223–9; M. Digby, *Horace Plunkett: An Anglo-American Irishman* (Oxford, 1949), 84–116.

Municipal Reform Act of 1840 and, more importantly, under the highly undemocratic system established by the Irish Poor Law Act of 1838. Although everyone had long known that changes were likely with respect to England and Wales, both Liberal and Unionist ministers proved distinctly reluctant to modernize the system in Ireland, one of the few exceptions being Joseph Chamberlain, who saw progress in the matter as a possible and (to him) attractive alternative to Home Rule.[105] In 1886 the Unionist viceroy, Lord Carnarvon, warned against assimilation. 'The conditions of things are different in the two countries; and an identity of local institutions in Ireland ... may not only be useless, but ... very harmful.' And a few months later the cabinet decided to leave Ireland alone.[106]

In 1888 itself, as the bill for England and Wales was being discussed in government and parliament, Unionist ministers made it clear that Ireland would be ignored. As Arthur Balfour put it: 'What is equality? Equality of treatment implies similarity of conditions ... [and] that necessary similarity ... does not at this moment, at all events, exist.' It was a view supported, not only by Unionist intellectuals like A. V. Dicey—who thought the idea that 'an arrangement that succeeds in Birmingham will succeed in, say, Limerick ... in itself absurd'—but, more importantly, by the prime minister, Balfour's uncle Lord Salisbury.[107]

Unsurprisingly, therefore, when the Unionists eventually came round to framing a local government bill for Ireland, its provisions were, as Arthur Balfour told the cabinet in November 1891, so complicated and modest that little danger was to be expected to the party's allies in that country. Indeed, the whole business was so obviously seen as no more than an irritating necessity—'going through the motions' might be a good description—that one authority has convincingly wondered whether the bill introduced in 1892 was 'ever meant to pass' at all.[108] The bill was announced as differing completely from that passed for England and Wales, as a measure deliberately designed 'for a condition of Irish society which has little or no parallel out of Ireland'. Both government and opposition MPs spent time discussing the many ways in which it diverged from British precedents.[109] No one can have been amazed

[105] Trevelyan to J. Chamberlain, 7 January 1883, BU J. Chamberlain Papers JC5/70/4; Chamberlain to W. H. Duignan, 17 December 1884, ibid., JC5/3/1/24.
[106] Parl. Deb. 3: cccviii. 54 (19 August 1886); Curtis, *Coercion and Conciliation in Ireland*, 153; also Memorandum of 30 September 1887 by W. St J. Brodrick (later Lord Midleton), BU J. Chamberlain Papers JC8/4/3/22.
[107] Parl. Deb. 3: cccxxv. 503 (25 April 1888); Dicey to Balfour, 29 April 1890, BL Balfour Papers Add. MS 49792; Salisbury to Balfour, 16 January 1889, ibid., Add. MS 49689; also Hartington to J. Chamberlain, 18 February 1890, BU J. Chamberlain Papers JC5/22/50.
[108] Balfour's Cabinet Paper of 2 November 1891, TNA CAB 37/30/28; A. Gailey, 'Unionist Rhetoric and Irish Local Government Reform, 1895–9', *Irish Historical Studies*, 24 (1984), 54.
[109] Parl. Deb. 4: i. 712 (18 February 1892: A. J. Balfour), iv. 1385 (19 May 1892: Wyndham), 1395–6 (19 May 1892: H. Gladstone) and 1692 (24 May 1892: W. E. Gladstone); C. B. Shannon,

when the bill failed to make progress, least of all those who had drawn it up. And when, three years later and at the fag end of Gladstone's last administration, the Irish Parliamentary Party put forward a bill of its own, it too collapsed under assault from hostile MPs repeatedly making the point that Ireland was not England, that provisions suitable for one would be poison for the other, and that, alas, Ireland completely lacked England's long local-government experience 'based on a body of law and custom dating back as far as the Norman Conquest, and, as regarded ecclesiastical provisions, as far back as the Anglo-Saxon period'.[110]

The bill that eventually became the Irish Local Government Act of 1898 might, therefore, seem an unlikely outcome of what had gone before, given that it yielded at least some significant ground to those who wanted Ireland to be treated as England had been ten years earlier. In fact, the bill was drawn up at the last minute with comparatively little preparation or thought and with the intention of solving problems that had nothing to do with local government at all. In the Commons, Gerald Balfour did his best to highlight its Irish peculiarities—and these did exist—while the Liberal opposition enjoyed itself in pointing to delusory Unionist hopes that local-government reform would somehow undermine the case for Home Rule. As a former liberal viceroy pointed out, if Irish 'Jacobins and revolutionaries are to be once and for all contented by being given the control of their lunatic asylums, their technical instruction committees, and ... ancient monuments, they cannot be such dangerous revolutionaries after all'.[111]

What had happened was that the government had been taken by surprise a few months earlier by an outburst of agitation about the matter of Ireland's 'over-taxation'. As a result, local-government reform, as Arthur Balfour openly admitted in May 1897, was now seen by ministers primarily as a pragmatic device for breaking a parliamentary impasse created by all parties in Ireland combining to demand compensation for the tax burdens now officially 'revealed'. Not only did Balfour bend to this increasingly irritating Irish wind, but he sought to defuse matters by deploying one of the classic Tory remedies for threatening Irish discontents: large poultices of cash. In a drastic departure from English practice, the whole incidence of local taxation in Ireland was to be changed, with the Treasury henceforth paying half the poor rates (which delighted landlords) and half the county cess (which delighted farmers). So, for all their Anglo-Saxon trappings, the local-government reforms of 1898 were

'The Ulster Liberal Unionists and Local Government Reform, 1885–98', *Irish Historical Studies*, 18 (1973), 417–18.

[110] Parl. Deb. 4: xxxiv. 550–1 (29 May 1895: Arnold-Forster), 547 (Smith-Barry), and 556 (Byles).

[111] Parl. Deb. 4: liii. 1228 (21 February 1898: G. W. Balfour), lxii. 144 (18 July 1898: Lloyd George) and 568 (21 July 1898: Crewe), lv. 507–9 (21 March 1898: Morley); also Robinson, *Memories: Wise and Otherwise*, 126–7.

in fact designed as instruments of bribery.[112] Far, therefore, from representing any kind of return to assimilationism, the 1898 Act—essentially a short-term solution to a pressing Irish problem—was so garnished with rewards for everyone that few could resist the generosity of its Unionist charms.

And, indeed, the whole 'financial relations' issue, from which the Act had been designed to provide a distraction, furnished instead yet another platform upon which Unionists could display their credentials as upholders of Irish distinctiveness. Unlike Gladstone, who, in the 1850s, had taken pains to draw Ireland into a convergent United Kingdom embrace on fiscal matters, Unionists now followed a very different line, even though the possibility of this had in fact been opened up by Gladstone himself, when, after the failure of the Home Rule Bill of 1893, he had set up a royal commission to examine the financial relations between Britain and Ireland, the report from which eventually appeared in September 1896.[113] This contained two explosive conclusions, neither of them unambiguously convincing but both appealing to Irish political gladiators of almost every stripe. The first was the striking recommendation—supported by the commission's technical experts from the Treasury and the world of banking—that Ireland should be treated as a distinct and separate entity when it came to matters of revenue and expenditure, 'striking' for the simple reason that in a unitary state (as the United Kingdom supposedly was) it was usually individuals or corporations that constituted taxable entities and not geographical areas. Any injustice done to Ireland arose simply because indirect taxes bore more heavily on the poor and Ireland contained more poor people. Indeed, as the economist Nassau Senior had pointed out many years before, 'Ireland is overtaxed because she is poor rather than poor because she is overtaxed'.[114] Having, nonetheless, fixed upon areas rather than individuals, the commissioners then concluded that Ireland was undoubtedly overtaxed and had been overtaxed (though in diminishing degrees) since the 1850s.[115] These two conclusions, in themselves politically

---

[112] Parl. Deb. 4: xlix. 1042–3 (21 May 1897: A. J. Balfour): the bill is, in important respects, 'a wide departure from the course which we have pursued in England and Scotland [Irish Cheers]'; V. Crossman, *Local Government in Nineteenth-Century Ireland* (Belfast, 1994), 92–3; Shannon, 'The Ulster Liberal Unionists and Local Government Reform', 420–1; B. O Donoghue, *Activities Wise and Otherwise: The Career of Sir Henry Augustus Robinson 1898–1922* (Sallins, Co. Kildare, 2015), 31–2.

[113] The financial provisions of the 1893 bill initially contained serious errors of calculation that had to be drastically and hastily amended in committee: P. Travers, 'The Financial Relations Question 1800–1914', in F. B. Smith (ed.), *Ireland, England and Australia: Essays in Honour of Oliver MacDonagh* (Canberra and Cork, 1990), 46–7.

[114] L. Kennedy and D. S. Johnson, 'The Union of Ireland and Britain, 1801–1921', in D. G. Boyce and A. O'Day (eds), *The Making of Modern Irish History: Revisionism and the Revisionist Controversy* (London, 1996), 44–5.

[115] *Final Report by Her Majesty's Commissioners Appointed to Inquire into the Financial Relations between Great Britain and Ireland*, HC 1896 [C.8262], xxxiii. 63–4, 112–14; Gribbon, 'Economic and Social History, 1850–1921', 327–31.

challenging, were, in combination, potentially explosive. Ministers were taken aback by the cross-party Irish campaign for 'compensation' that ensued. Salisbury complained how 'our [Unionist] clients in Ireland' were proving no less eager wavers of the begging bowl than their nationalist opponents.[116] Gerald Balfour thought that, while few in Ireland had actually read the report, 'every party, condition, and creed are ... convinced that Ireland is being robbed by the present system to the tune of $2^1/_4$ millions'. He saw no way out of accepting that Ireland was, indeed, a separate and distinct 'financial entity' for the purposes of both revenue and expenditure. As the viceroy sadly told Salisbury, no other course was now possible, what with landlords 'smarting under the reduction of rents' and sitting 'on the same platforms with Catholics, Home Rulers, and all those whom they formerly shunned'.[117]

As it happened, the commission's very terms of reference had, more or less ineluctably, led to the conclusions presented in its final report (something that neither politicians nor Treasury officials could overcome), while the evidence given by financial experts had been at once highly complicated and highly contradictory.[118] The chief witness from the Treasury, Edward Hamilton (formerly Gladstone's private secretary), wrung his hands, prepared lengthy memoranda, and assured the chief secretary that, while he did not 'underestimate the difficulties and objections attaching to the treatment of Ireland as a separate entity', it was 'the least evil ... [because] the moment you give it up, the set-off of expenditure falls to the ground'.[119] 'History and facts', he concluded, 'force one to treat Ireland' separately, a necessity he tried to render palatable to his political masters by hinting that further and more rigorous analysis might well reveal that Ireland was beginning to get more than its fair share of the kingdom's riches.[120]

Whatever the reason, those in power showed little reluctance in revealing themselves as enthusiastic adopters of this comparatively recent manifestation of the doctrine of Irish differentiation. Arthur Balfour had no doubts at all, telling the Commons in July 1898 that he had 'never taken the line ... that to treat Ireland as a fiscal entity which may for some purposes deserve special consideration is inconsistent with Unionist principles'.[121] Joseph Chamberlain was no less emphatic. History, precedent, and present policy might all give

---

[116] Salisbury to Cadogan, 12 December 1896, PA Cadogan Papers 971.

[117] G. W. Balfour to Cadogan, 8 November 1896, ibid. 939; Cadogan to Salisbury, 8 and 17 December 1896, HH Salisbury Papers 3M/E.

[118] Travers, 'The Financial Relations Question 1800–1914', 46–50.

[119] Hamilton to G. W. Balfour, 21 October 1896, TNA Balfour Papers PRO 30/60/18; also Hamilton's 63pp. memorandum of 30 September 1896, TNA CAB 37/42/37, in which, though he says he would like to ignore the commission's report, he admits that Ireland cannot simply be treated as 'a group of counties'.

[120] *Diary of Sir Edward Walter Hamilton 1885–1906*, ed. Bahlman, 333–5 (22 December 1896, 12 and 20 January 1897).

[121] Parl. Deb. 4: lx. 1228 (5 July 1898).

them pause, but it was impossible to circumvent the undoubted fact of Ireland's constituting, not only 'a separate financial entity', but a separate entity in all sorts of other respects such as local taxation, education, ecclesiastical affairs, and the land question.[122] Less than six years later others were pushing this line further still. Winston Churchill, days before moving from the Unionist to the Liberal Party, insisted, in a speech on the Finance Bill of 1904, that, because Ireland was 'a separate taxable area' and unquestionably more than a 'mere group of English counties', consideration should be given to providing it with its own 'separate Exchequer' and with 'autonomous power to regulate the expenditure of money', thereby embracing rather than ignoring 'all the differences of race, of religion, of interest, of occupation, and of history'.[123] It was an opinion with which the Irish Liberal Unionist scholar-politician, W. H. Lecky, was in full agreement. While himself an MP (1895–1903), he denounced those who continued to view Ireland as possessing 'a kind of intermittent and fluctuating personality something like Mr Hyde and Dr Jekyll' in the face of clear and growing evidence of individuality and difference. Indeed, 'there was hardly any single subject of legislation in which Ireland was not legislated for separately. They had separate legislation about Church Establishments, about land, police, local government, education, and even, in some respects, about marriage'. While for Lecky this seemed no more than an acceptance of reality, for Unionists it was a dangerous argument all the same as the (almost certainly nationalist) 'Hear Hears' that followed his remarks undoubtedly indicate.[124]

Despite, therefore, the well-known desert so far as Home Rule was concerned that marked the period between 1893 and 1910, this acceptance of Ireland's separate financial status certainly strengthened its grip on the political mind. A mere fortnight after entering the cabinet as chief secretary, Wyndham was telling C. T. Ritchie, soon to become Chancellor of the Exchequer, that, regardless of any small print in the Act of Union, regardless of 'academic argument over Financial Relations', regardless of 'arithmetical calculations' by supposed experts, Ireland constituted a separate and special economic phenomenon requiring, above all, large injections of cash 'because she lacks private initiative and capital'.[125] When once again demanding more money in October 1903, Wyndham drove the Treasury (which had so impotently submitted to the Royal Commission in 1896) into paroxysms of ineffective indignation. Irish exceptionalism was out of control; alone among the 'three countries' it was always wanting to eat its cake and have it. Indeed, 'the

---

[122] Chamberlain's Cabinet Paper of 17 December 1896, TNA CAB 37/43/56 and BU J. Chamberlain Papers JC8/3/3/2; also Hamilton's Memorandum JC8/3/3/3.
[123] Parl. Deb. 4: cxxxv. 229 (18 May 1904).
[124] Ibid. xlviii. 201 (31 March 1897).
[125] Wyndham to Ritchie, 25 August 1902, BL 5th Marquess of Lansdowne Papers 'Papers as Foreign Secretary III' (provisional reference).

manner in which Ireland has been financed in the past has been in the highest degree reckless and wasteful. Mr Wyndham's principles would not only stereotype but aggravate all the errors of the last 50 or 60 years'. In practice, however, this amounted to little more than the rage of Lear in the face of tempests and storms, with Ritchie's successor as Chancellor, Austen Chamberlain, reduced to making a note to remind himself 'Timeo Wyndham et dona ferentes'.[126]

A year later in October 1904 the most senior Treasury civil servant, who was married to the daughter of an Ulster businessman, told Churchill that Ireland's peculiar financial status involved huge privileges not accorded to the other parts of the United Kingdom. Ireland's so-called imperial contribution was exiguous to say the least. She was able to borrow at undeservedly low rates of interest and 'if she had treated her other creditors as she has treated us she would probably have been warned off all the stock exchanges of Europe'.[127] Officials worried about Irish profligacy and about what would happen if Home Rule ever involved the complete collapse of 'financial control' by 'the United Kingdom'.[128] While nationalist politicians in Ireland pointed to the Royal Commission of the 1890s to insist that Ireland be separately treated, those in London increasingly (and with much justice) pointed out that, whatever had been the case in the past, by the twentieth century Ireland was, by any standards, receiving a very good financial deal indeed, something that became even more dramatically true with the introduction of old-age pensions in 1908/9.[129] As a result, few could now doubt that Ireland was receiving very considerable benefits in the balance of public income and expenditure, with the unsurprising result that the Treasury began to develop an increasingly benevolent view of Home Rule and of the savings it would almost certainly yield as far as the British taxpayer was concerned, a view strengthened by the findings of a Committee on Irish Finance under Sir Henry Primrose (another of Gladstone's former secretaries and subsequently Chairman of the Inland Revenue Board), which reported in October 1911.[130]

---

[126] Wyndham's Memorandum of 16 October 1903, BU A. Chamberlain Papers AC16/3/8A with attached comments by Treasury officials; Chamberlain's marginal comment on a letter from Wyndham of 31 October 1903, ibid., AC16/3/10, based on the *Aeneid* (II. 49) 'Timeo Danaos et dona ferentes' ('I fear Greeks even those bearing gifts').

[127] Sir G. Murray to Churchill, 8 October 1904, C[hurchill] C[ollege] C[ambridge] Churchill Papers CHAR2/18/30.

[128] Memorandum by Sir A. MacDonnell (undersecretary), 8 February 1905, Bodl. MacDonnell Papers MS Eng.hist.c.370; also Cabinet Papers from the Treasury, 2 and 25 July 1906, ibid., c.369.

[129] See the Cabinet Paper by Reginald McKenna (recently Financial Secretary at the Treasury and a future Chancellor) of 20 March 1907, TNA CAB 37/87/42, insisting that 'the return made to Ireland is vastly in excess of the estimated amount of her overtaxation'.

[130] Travers, 'The Financial Relations Question 1800–1914', 68; *Report of the Committee on Irish Finance*, HC 1912–13 (Cd 6153), xxxiv. 7–40; P. Jalland, 'Irish Home Rule Finance: A Neglected Dimension of the Irish Question, 1910–14', *Irish Historical Studies*, 23 (1983), 233–53.

The Great War changed everything, including the Anglo-Irish fiscal relationship. From having become by 1914 something of a liability, the economic consequences of armed conflict and especially the huge increase in agricultural prices, turned Ireland—now the food basket of the war effort—from an undoubted debtor into an even more undoubted creditor within the United Kingdom as a whole. Indeed, Ireland's imperial contribution entered positive territory so swiftly that between 1915 and 1921 'she contributed the enormous sum, by nineteenth-century standards, of £83 million', an 'imbalance' that led Michael Collins to devote some time when negotiating the Anglo-Irish treaty of 1921 to demanding—with absolutely no success—large sums in compensation.[131]

This important wartime change of gear in the economic relationship between Ireland and Britain does not, however, seem to have affected London's attachment to the idea that Ireland had become and should remain a distinct fiscal entity. In February 1916 Edwin Montagu (then in the cabinet as Financial Secretary to the Treasury and some months later to turn down the office of chief secretary) lectured his most senior civil servant about the importance of treating Ireland as in no way 'analogous to a series of English counties or even Scotland',[132] though, during the crucial years that followed, the default mode of both ministers and officials seems gradually to have become one of doing little more than seeking refuge in a kind of despairing obfuscation with regard to Ireland's financial realities. For all the (often damaging) certainties in other areas of government, it had apparently become quite impossible 'to ascertain what the Irish revenue really was'. Eminent academics were earnestly consulted, to no effect. Cabinet committees and the Treasury produced statistics while simultaneously noting that 'the subjoined figures are all estimates and ... very conjectural'.[133] Clinging to a view of Irish fiscal distinctiveness seems, indeed, to have provided one of the few certainties amidst turbulent seas. All in all, Arthur Balfour concluded in February 1919 that a middle path would be best, that while no devolved administration should be treated with excessive parsimony 'nor would I overpay them on the principle which induces a man to give a larger sum to an organ-grinder in order to induce him to play his too familiar tunes in somebody else's street'.[134]

---

[131] W. E. Vaughan, 'Ireland c. 1870', in Vaughan (ed.), *A New History of Ireland V: Ireland under the Union I 1801–70* (Oxford, 1989), 792; Gribbon, 'Economic and Social History, 1850–1921', 342–54; Kennedy and Johnson, 'The Union of Ireland and Britain, 1801–1921', 43.

[132] Montagu to Sir T. Heath, 7 February 1916, T[rinity] C[ollege] C[ambridge] Montagu Papers AS1/8/18.

[133] Memorandum 'Taxable Capacity of Ireland', November 1919, Bodl. Worthington-Evans Papers MS Eng.hist.c.905, and TNA CAB 24/93 C.P. 189, with comments by Austen Chamberlain, TNA CAB 24/94 C.P. 201.

[134] Balfour to Lloyd George, 10 February 1919, TNA CAB 24/98 C.P. 681.

VI

Whatever conclusions on financial affairs senior Unionists like Balfour had come to by 1919, the one matter upon which they, unlike their Liberal opponents, were broadly agreed was that, however much the Irish protested and claimed the contrary, Ireland was not in any real sense a 'nation' with or without Gladstone's erstwhile initial capitalization. And, given that politics often, sometimes mostly, revolves around the use of words, the whole question of 'Ireland a nation' had of course an especially powerful charge in connection with Gladstone's initial conversion to Home Rule in 1885. Before then the deployment of national nomenclature had been, at least among those actually in charge of Irish affairs, not especially portentous with regard to decision-making on the ground. Thus Chichester Fortescue's reminder to Gladstone in 1867 that the Irish question involved matters of 'nationality' should best be narrowly interpreted as constituting a signal that the assimilationism of the previous thirty or forty years was no longer fit for purpose.[135] But, with the advent of an unambiguous Home Rule policy in the mid-1880s, the linguistic turn became more urgent, more important, and politically more significant.

Where Gladstone and his followers differed from their Unionist opponents was not simply over the nature of Irish government and administration but over fundamental beliefs as to how and why changes in such government and administration might or might not be justified. It was not that ideology generated practice, or indeed the reverse, but that the two were and remained so inextricably linked that it is almost impossible to unravel any primacy of influence. Not long before Gladstone announced his conversion, Joseph Chamberlain was already making it clear that he could 'never consent to regard Ireland as a separate people with the inherent rights of an absolutely independent community. I should not do this in the case of Scotland, or of Wales ... Ireland, by its geographical position, and by its history, is part of the United Kingdom'—a manifesto that broadly laid down the lines of debate that were to be pursued over the next thirty and more years.[136] Already by then, however, some Irish Tories were beginning to grasp that the ceaseless denunciations of 'Irish' political and agrarian infantilism that their British counterparts found so appealing were now worryingly (if also perhaps flatteringly) suggesting that they too were no longer perceived as 'Irish' but merely as some kind of outlying extensions of the British motherland, extensions that might, if push came to shove, find themselves ground down between more powerful 'national' groups with less ambivalent positions in the ethnic universe of the time.

---

[135] Fortescue to Gladstone, 14 December 1867, BL Gladstone Papers Add. MS 44121.
[136] Chamberlain to W. H. Duignan, 17 December 1884, BU J. Chamberlain Papers JC5/3/1/24.

As Gladstone became more and more committed to Home Rule—'my politics are now summed up in the word "Ireland"'[137]—so he began more and more to turn to terms derived from or connected with the word 'nation'. Already in September 1885 he was worrying that colleagues were insufficiently aware of the dangers flowing from any 'serious dispute with the Irish nation'. 'What I do think about', he insisted, was both 'the Irish nation and the fame, duty, and peace of my country'. 'Have Hon. Gentlemen', he asked the Commons, 'considered that they are coming into conflict with a nation?'[138] It was not enough that the Irish be given 'good' laws; they must have laws that 'proceed from a congenial and native source [because] ... we find ourselves face to face with Irish nationality'.[139] As, under Gladstone's tutelage, there developed a Liberal conjuncture between the words 'Ireland' and 'nation', so Unionists moved decisively in the opposite direction. By the time of the second Home Rule Bill in 1893, Liberals as different as Haldane, Campbell-Bannerman, and Stansfeld (all past or future cabinet ministers) were regularly talking about Irish 'national sentiment', about 'Ireland as a nation', about— and here Gladstone's ventriloquist voice can be heard from the mouths of others—how 'there was no principle or sentiment implanted in the human heart of a truer and higher conservative character than the principle or sentiment of nationality' in general and of Irish nationality in particular.[140]

While such convictions temporarily lost their ardour in some Liberal breasts after 1893[141]—only to revive when in January 1910 electoral arithmetic once again plucked Home Rule from the political chorus line to feature centre stage—Unionists of all kinds began to place increasing reliance on the belief that, though nationality as a concept might be applicable to Britain or to the United Kingdom, it had nothing much to say (indeed it was dangerous) when placed into any close relationship with the smaller island to the west. Joseph Chamberlain was especially fierce. There was no such thing as a 'distinct nationality' in Ireland. 'I will never recognize a separate political nationality in Ireland', a country whose history displayed little more than 'the petty squabbles of a number of hostile tribes only pacified by the British settlement'.[142] An English Catholic Unionist MP (a Westminster exotic not least as

---

[137] Matthew, *Gladstone 1875-1898*, 296 (12 October 1886).

[138] Gladstone to Rosebery, 10 September 1885, NLS Rosebery Papers MS 10023; Parl. Deb. 3: cccvi. 1237 (7 [*recte* 8] June 1886).

[139] Gladstone's Paper on 'Irish Nationality', BL Gladstone Papers Add. MS 44772.

[140] Parl. Deb. 3: cccv. 941 (13 May 1886: Campbell-Bannerman); Parl. Deb 4: x. 1773 (7 April 1893: Haldane) and 1735-7 (7 April 1893: Stansfeld).

[141] See Chapter 8, Section V; also Sir Edward Grey's distinctly cagey declaration that, 'while Ireland will never be a separate country, she will always be a separate community' (Parl. Deb. 4: cxviii. 850 (25 February 1903)).

[142] *Mr Chamberlain's Speeches*, ed. C. W. Boyd, 2 vols (London, 1914), i. 295 (12 October 1887) and i. 310 (28 May 1888); P. T. Marsh, *Joseph Chamberlain: Entrepreneur in Politics* (New Haven, 1994), 313 (14 February 1889).

a graduate of the 'Universities of Münster, Westphalia, and Innsbruck') 'denied that the Irish had ever been a separate nation in the strict sense of the word', to which a Scottish MP later mockingly responded by pointing to the Salisbury government's deep-seated anglocentricism as personified by the Secretary for War's description of 'the Scottish Borderers' as 'English' troops— a species of topographical triumphalism with which Irish politicians were all too familiar.[143] Gladstone's second Home Rule Bill drew forth a stream of particularly strong Unionist assertions that, whatever else Ireland might be, it was not a 'nation'. When a Liberal peer asked his fellows whether Ireland was a nation, Salisbury simply shouted 'No', while Hartington declared the Catholic Irish to be little more than 'uninstructed peasants' who could in no way be recognized as constituting a 'nation'.[144] Arthur Balfour, deploying historical tropes pioneered by Chamberlain, put it all down to the vagaries of the distant past. 'The fact is that before the English power went to Ireland, Ireland was a collection of tribes waging constant and internecine warfare, without law, without civilization,' something that meant that any independent parliament in Dublin would find itself all too inevitably drinking 'from the bitter, narrow and polluted streams of purely Irish history'.[145]

As time went on it became more and more necessary for the Unionist case to combine a willingness to treat Ireland as a distinct entity—certainly in administrative matters but also more widely—with an equivalent and fervent disposition to reject any of its claims to nationhood beyond what Chamberlain once dismissively referred to as matters of 'sentimental nationality'.[146] That there were contradictions in such an approach was something that seems to have passed more or less rippleless over the surface of Unionist mentalities. A not unrepresentative upholder of such ideas was the extreme (as well as extremely idiosyncratic) Lord Hugh Cecil, later hailed as leader of a parliamentary ginger group known as the 'Hughligans'. One of Salisbury's younger sons, Cecil, solved the question of Irish nationality by denying anything of the kind to Scotland, England, and Wales, while hinting that perhaps only the United Kingdom deserved to be seen in the full light of nationhood. Better still, it was the empire as a whole that demanded so unrestrained an allegiance. In a complicated mixture of modernity and old-style patriotism, he denounced Home Rule as 'a sort of atavism' on the grounds that 'nationalism, applying to these smaller nationalities, is a danger and a hindrance to the future progress of the [significant word] race'. Yet, unlike some of his party colleagues, he eventually came to realize that 'Irish nationality', though 'unhistorical' and

---

[143] Parl. Deb. 3: cccxxii. 608 (16 February 1888: de Lisle) and cccxxxv. 69 (9 April 1889: Clark).

[144] Parl. Deb. 4: xvii. 424 (7 September 1893); *The Times*, 17 April 1893.

[145] Parl. Deb. 4: xi. 972–3, 991 (21 April 1893), also xii. 393 (8 May 1893: Gibbs), 509 (9 May 1893: Ambrose), and 1177 (17 May 1893: Smith).

[146] Marsh, *Joseph Chamberlain*, 313.

'absurd', had become so unambiguously a 'fact' that it demanded some kind of recognition on the part of those in charge of the state.[147]

In this, Cecil, however eccentric, managed to adopt the politics of reality somewhat earlier than those many colleagues who seem to have believed that simple denial was enough to defuse and circumvent the new situation created in 1910 by the dependence of a Liberal government upon the parliamentary votes of the Irish Party. Arthur Balfour denounced Redmond's acceptance of a form of Home Rule as the thin end of a wedge designed to give national status to an entity that, historically, had never been a nation except—he noted—in the overexcited minds of certain eighteenth-century Irish Protestants like Grattan and Flood.[148] Austen Chamberlain saw things in much the same light. 'My root objection to Home Rule was the idea of "Ireland a nation" ... that was separation and must issue in separation.'[149] For the fourth Marquess of Salisbury (eldest son of the late prime minister) the real sticking point was 'the recognition of Irish nationality', while for his Liberal Unionist colleague, the fifth Marquess of Lansdowne, even Ulster exclusion would not remove objections to treating Ireland 'as a separate nation'.[150] In April 1912 the fiercely imperialist Leopold Amery insisted that the real 'nation' could only be the United Kingdom as a whole, 'one on the ground plan of the universe, more compact than the island nation of Japan or the sea-girt nation of Italy'.[151] Earl Stanhope referred to Ireland as no more than a 'geographical expression' devoid of all the essential attributes of nationhood, 'common stock ... religion ... the same outlook'.[152]

Against all this, Liberals resorted to straightforward assertions that Ireland was indeed a nation in the full meaning of the term. When a Unionist asked Asquith, then introducing the third Home Rule or Government of Ireland Bill in 1912, what 'nation' was most closely involved in the legislation, he replied 'the Irish nation' without expansion or elaboration.[153] But, as strong rhetoric and threats of violence mounted after 1911–12 and though some Unionists, notably Balfour, continued to unroll strains of denial regarding Irish nationhood[154]—

---

[147] Parl. Deb. 4: cxli. 673–4 (20 February 1905); Parl. Deb 5 (Commons): xxi. 1093–4 (15 February 1911); Cecil to W. Ormsby Gore, 23 October 1918, PA Lloyd George Papers F/67/1/47.

[148] Balfour to J. L. Garvin, 22 October 1910, Bodl. Sandars Papers MS Eng.hist.c.761.

[149] Chamberlain's Memorandum of 27 November 1913, BU A. Chamberlain Papers AC11/1/21; to Bonar Law, 2 December [1913], PA Bonar Law Papers 31/1/3.

[150] Salisbury to Lansdowne, 11 September 1913, BL 5th Marquess of Lansdowne Papers 'Ireland V' (provisional reference); Lansdowne to Bonar Law, 16 October 1913, ibid.

[151] Parl. Deb. 5 (Commons): xxxvii. 1786–7 (30 April 1912) and lviii. 241 (11 February 1914).

[152] Parl. Deb. 5 (Lords): xv. 117–18 (11 February 1914).

[153] Parl. Deb. 5 (Commons): xxxvi. 1401 (11 April 1912).

[154] War Cabinet Minutes for 21 February 1918, Bodl. Duke Papers MS Dep.c.917; Balfour to Lloyd George, 2 November 1921, PA Lloyd George Papers F/3/5/17. Lloyd George had his doubts too, but, ever the pragmatist, persuaded himself that they should be overcome: Parl. Deb. 5 (Commons): cxviii. 1052–4 (21 July 1919) and cxxiii. 1171 (22 December 1919).

reiterations that qualified him for exclusion from Lloyd George's team negotiating the Anglo-Irish Treaty of 1921—others were beginning to prepare themselves for forms of compromise associated with the possibility that, if 'nationhood' could be confined to only a part (even if the larger part) of Ireland, then its full and final implementation could still somehow be seen as having been withheld, evidence that it was not only the Irish side that agonized over matters of political symbol and nomenclature.

Not that the collapse of the Irish Parliamentary Party after the general election of 1918 or the armed conflict that followed in 1919 and led to the increasing prominence of Sinn Féin under the leadership of Eamon de Valera in any way obscured the truth that in such matters the devil invariably takes up residence in the detail. De Valera's quasi-theological presentation of the Irish case in the months leading up to the talks of autumn and winter 1921[155] doubtless irritated British ministers while reminding them of the arguments with which they would be obliged to deal. By then, however, a new element had gradually wormed its way into the equation, an element that was, in the end, simultaneously capable of being deployed as a card to trump long-standing Unionist denials that Ireland could ever be recognized as a nation and of releasing from the bondage of such a view the other equally long-standing Unionist belief that, whatever about nationhood, Ireland was undoubtedly a distinctly different place, a place that could in no way be usefully compared to the other parts of the United Kingdom. This element was, of course, the idea of 'partition', an idea that ultimately made it possible—even for Unionists—to free the angel so long imprisoned in the marble of the Union of 1800, an angel whose more and more clearly Hibernian form had started to take recognizable shape once the rejection of the mid-nineteenth-century assimilationist and integrationist programme had begun to take hold.

---

[155] See *Correspondence relating to the Proposals of His Majesty's Government for an Irish Settlement*, HC 1921 (Cmd 1502), xxix. 407–14.

10

Partition or Squaring (Some) Circles

I

The long-held view in British political circles—especially, but not exclusively, among Conservatives—that Ireland's being an island was not itself sufficient proof that its inhabitants constituted a 'nation' was met by Irish nationalists, not with finely honed arguments to the contrary, but, for the most part, with a simple almost automatic negative. Ireland was an island, therefore it was a country, therefore it was inhabited by a nation. And, because this was for nationalists no more and no less than a truth universally acknowledged, further insights were seen as unnecessary with regard to the denominational, political, social, economic, or regional differences that were, and always had been, a notable feature of Irish life.

And this stance of almost self-willed blindness was as common to O'Connell and Parnell as to Redmond and de Valera, for all of whom nationalism could be articulated only as universal, as gathering all those living on the island into a single embrace permitting no self-exclusion. However, as time went on, this kind of view was more and more obliged to overlook the growing fissures that were developing between the Protestant majority in the North of Ireland and the Catholic majority elsewhere. In an almost proto-Marxian manner, nationalists saw the Protestants of Ulster as suffering from a species of 'false consciousness', a state of things so obvious as to require neither analysis nor explanation. This led not merely to ignorance but to consistent lack of attention, it being much easier to turn a blind eye than to enter into any kind of engagement with the doubtless—from a nationalist point of view—rebarbative views of many, indeed the majority, of Ulster's inhabitants. What this meant was that, for the most part, the great nationalist leaders of the Union period, while endlessly *asserting* national unity, actually *practised* a version of politics based on an implicit acceptance of separate communities. Ignoring Ulster made it much easier to sustain the image of a single coherent Irish entity.[1] Equally, many observers in

---

[1] For characteristic instances for the years after 1890, see R. F. Foster, *Vivid Faces: The Revolutionary Generation in Ireland 1890–1923* (London, 2014), 198–200, 272–3, 324.

Britain, without finding it necessary to acquire minute knowledge, saw in Ulster proof that Ireland was anything but a coherent unit demanding uniform understanding or uniform control.

O'Connell's 'almost instinctive feeling for the country as an entity', together with his close 'identification of the Irish nation with Irish Catholicism', left little room for subtleties beyond repeated claims that 'the nation' meant no more and no less than 'all the inhabitants' of the island.[2] He not only knew little of Ulster; he knew virtually nothing at all. His movement's efforts to expand northwards—the so-called invasion of Ulster mounted by his erratic associate John Lawless—descended into farce. He himself was once subjected to a painful grilling in front of a parliamentary committee during which he admitted that his knowledge of Ulster was 'necessarily[?] somewhat rude and indistinct', because 'I have never been in the North, except when going specially to Monaghan'.[3]

Parnell displayed no greater acquaintance, though his party's 'invasion of Ulster' in 1883 proved rather less bungled than O'Connell's. His own rhetoric simply swept aside all differences and tensions between northern Protestants and southern Catholics, while his notorious weakness with statistics proved useful in helping to dismiss important economic distinctions between North and South. At 'no point in his career did he define what he thought the Irish nation to be, a dereliction in which he was by no means alone'.[4] Speaking in July 1886 at an election meeting in England, he held up a political map of Ireland and pointed derisively to the Ulster Unionist constituencies coloured in yellow: 'This little yellow patch covered by my forefinger represents Protestant Ulster … and they say now they want a separate parliament for this little yellow patch up in the North-East', a place, he seemed to imply, that might well be found somewhere near the North Pole.[5]

Where O'Connell and Parnell led, others followed, not least the inheritor of Parnell's mantle, John Redmond. 'The argument about Ulster', Redmond insisted during a Commons debate on the second Home Rule Bill of 1893, 'is false and misleading.' And why? Well, because 'there is no Ulster question', a truth determined by the fact that (nine-county) Ulster actually contained 'a fair majority of Catholics' (which it did not). And, as the resistance of Ulster's

---

[2] A. Macintyre, *The Liberator: Daniel O'Connell and the Irish Party 1830–1847* (London, 1965), 127; O. MacDonagh, *The Emancipist: Daniel O'Connell 1830–47* (London, 1989), 29.

[3] F. O'Ferrall, *Catholic Emancipation: Daniel O'Connell and the Birth of Irish Democracy 1820–30* (Dublin, 1985), 211–13; *Report from the Select Committee on the State of Ireland*, H[ouse of] C[ommons Paper] 1825 (129), viii. 82–3.

[4] J. Magee, 'The Monaghan Election of 1883 and the "Invasion of Ulster"', *Clogher Record*, 8 (1974), 147–66; A. Claydon, 'The Political Thought of Charles Stewart Parnell', in D. G. Boyce and A. O'Day (eds), *Parnell in Perspective* (London, 1991), 164; F. S. L. Lyons, *Charles Stewart Parnell* (London, 1977), 349–51.

[5] J. Loughlin, *Gladstone and the Ulster Question 1882–93* (Dublin, 1986), 145–6, 126.

Unionists to Home Rule increased, so the argument shifted to claims that *their* views were grossly exaggerated and might safely be ignored because Ulster's endless complaints and talk of war reminded John Dillon 'of nothing more than the drunken man who calls out "Will none of you come and hold me before I go and kill the fellow across the street"'.[6]

As the whole question of Home Rule once again entered the world of practical politics after the general election of January 1910, so the majority of nationalist leaders—there were a few exceptions[7]—clung to the view that, if only one pretended that Ulster Unionism was in the final analysis a toothless tiger, all would be well. As early as 1911 Redmond publicly mocked talk of an Ulster provisional government, denied the existence of anything that might be called an 'Ulster Question', and denounced Carson's resort to 'a sordid appeal to religious prejudice and religious fear'.[8] But, while it might be convenient for Redmond to insist that 'Irish Catholics and Irish Protestants alike are children of Ireland', that 'the two nations theory is to us an abomination and a blasphemy', or that 'the idea of our agreeing to the partition of our nation is unthinkable', events in the real world were increasingly undermining his words. When Carson argued in February 1914 that Home Rulers had 'never tried to win over Ulster. You have never tried to understand her politics,'[9] he might more accurately have accused his opponents of simple ignorance than of anything approaching deliberate misunderstanding.

Somnambulism about Ulster was by no means confined to Redmond, with T. P. O'Connor (despite—perhaps because of—close personal contacts with Lloyd George) long maintaining a remarkably complacent stance with regard to the difficulties created by Ulster Unionism's rejection of Home Rule.[10] But, if the bulk of the Irish Parliamentary Party continued to work on the assumption that keeping one's fingers crossed remained a viable policy, then Dillon at least seems to have concluded in early 1914 that it was no longer possible to 'coerce' Ulster into a united Home Rule Ireland, though the Republicans who came to prominence in the years after the Easter Rising of 1916 and the game-changing election of December 1918 seem to have lacked any kind of 'northern policy' beyond 'minimum demands' that Unionists had no 'right' to secede from the 'Irish nation' as a whole. Indeed, among many nationalists, even the

---

[6] D. Gwynn, *The Life of John Redmond* (London, 1936), 80; F. S. L. Lyons, *John Dillon: A Biography* (London, 1968), 346, 333.

[7] Such as William O'Brien of the All-for-Ireland League and later Father Michael O'Flanagan of Sinn Féin: see P. Bew, 'Moderate Nationalism and the Irish Revolution, 1916–1923', *Historical Journal*, 43 (1999), 733–4, and T. Hennessy, *Dividing Ireland: World War I and Partition* (London, 1998), 146–7.

[8] D. Meleady, *John Redmond: The National Leader* (Sallins, Co. Kildare, 2014), 204–5.

[9] J. P. Finnan, *John Redmond and Irish Unity, 1912–1918* (Syracuse, NY, 2004), 61–2; Parl[iamentary] Deb[ates] 5 (Commons): lviii. 177 (11 February 1914).

[10] E. S. Doherty, '"Ulster will not Fight": T. P. O'Connor and the Third Home Rule Bill Crisis, 1912–14', in G. Doherty (ed.), *The Home Rule Crisis 1912–14* (Cork, 2014), 102–17.

most tentative suggestion that Ulster might require individually tailored treatment became, after 1916, virtually taboo.[11] Even those who, like de Valera, occasionally (and mostly in private) expressed a certain flexibility on the matter, were never able to stop themselves from appealing to their intransigent supporters with counter-productive denunciations of Ulster Unionists as a 'foreign garrison' and 'not Irish' at all. But all that this achieved was to delay those eventual and more hard-headed realizations—shared by pretty well all those directly involved in the Treaty negotiations of 1921—that, in the final analysis, all-Irish unity must remain a secondary consideration in the face of the necessity of securing an outcome compatible with minimum republican demands as to constitutional arrangements.[12]

II

While nineteenth- and even early twentieth-century Irish nationalism tended to operate as if Ulster was, at heart, no more than a slightly eccentric version of Leinster, politicians in London were inclined to adopt one of two rather different—but not unrelated—positions. The first was emphasized by Gladstone's conversion to the idea of 'Ireland a nation'. The other consistently held Ireland to be so deeply divided as to render its claim to unitary nationhood fanciful, even immoral. And, once the assimilationism of the 1830–70 period had begun to fade, it becomes easy to find both views contained within the capacious British trope kitty about Irish differentiation. For one group, Ireland was *sui generis*, therefore it should have Home Rule. For the other, Ireland was *sui generis*, therefore it should be accorded all sorts of special treatment short of Home Rule. And, while Conservatives and Unionists became more and more eager to emphasize the deep differences *within* Ireland between Ulster and the other three provinces, Liberals tended, either to do much the same, or (like Gladstone) to adopt the nationalist stance of simply writing Ulster out of the script altogether.[13] The similarities between the parties on Ireland were, therefore, no less obvious than the differences.

---

[11] T. M. Healy, *Letters and Leaders of my Day*, 2 vols (London, [1928]), ii. 538; C. Townshend, *The Republic: The Fight for Irish Independence* (London, 2013), 171–2; indeed, some talked of Ulster as 'hostile territory' or the six 'Carsonian counties' (ibid. 281); Meleady, *John Redmond: The National Leader*, 8.

[12] J. Bowman, *De Valera and the Ulster Question 1917–1973* (Oxford, 1982), 32–8, 54–6, 60.

[13] N. C. Fleming, 'Gladstone and the Ulster Question', in D. G. Boyce and A. O'Day (eds), *Gladstone and Ireland: Politics, Religion and Nationality in the Victorian Age* (Basingstoke, 2010), 140–1; Gladstone to Hartington, 3 December 1883, Ch[atsworth] H[ouse] Devonshire Papers 'Secret Irish Box'.

Although British references to Ireland's strong regional distinctiveness can be found well before the 1880s—indeed for ministers like Peel and viceroys such as Wellesley, Clarendon, and Eglinton Irish regionalism had been an accepted fact inducing many snide comparisons with the English heptarchy of the Anglo-Saxon period[14]—it was the first Home Rule episode that concentrated attention on the matter in new and intense ways. Gladstone, in line with his developing views of Ireland, found it convenient to follow nationalists in avoiding close engagement with the fact that Ulster stood apart, not just economically and religiously, but politically as well. When approached on the question of Ulster, he generally sought refuge in a vague insistence that it was not for him to take initiatives. What this amounted to was the possibility of minor concessions to northern Protestants but nothing approaching what Gladstone himself described as 'separate treatment'.[15] Fellow Liberals like Spencer agreed that it was up to Ulster Unionists, a group he viewed with distinct suspicion, to put forward proposals of their own, though (unlike Gladstone) he feared that 'excluding a particular part of Ireland' from Home Rule might eventually become an issue that could not easily be avoided. One of the few Gladstonian Liberals to take the Ulster Question seriously was James Bryce, a future chief secretary and himself a native of Belfast, who sent a memorandum to Gladstone in March 1886 arguing that Ulster resistance to Home Rule should not be dismissed as the sole preserve of a narrow Orange clique.[16]

Unsurprisingly, it was the Conservatives and future Liberal Unionists who in 1886 most strenuously put forward the argument that Ulster distinctiveness was a good reason for rejecting Home Rule as a whole. Joseph Chamberlain made the obvious point that, if Catholic Ireland deserved Home Rule, then Protestant Ulster was no less entitled to particular consideration. Ireland, for

[14] Peel to Heytesbury, 17 October [1844], B[ritish] L[ibrary] Peel Papers Add. MS 40479; Wellesley to Grey, 1 February 1834, D[urham] U[niversity] Grey Papers GRE/B58/173; Clarendon to Russell, 23 December 1848, Bodl[eian Library] Clarendon Papers Irish Letter-Book III; Eglinton to Derby, 10 September 1852, L[iverpool] R[ecord] O[ffice] Derby Papers 148/2/; also Parl. Deb. 3: xv. 259 (6 February 1833: Macaulay); Sir F. Heygate MP to Lord Mayo, 8 January 1868, N[ational] L[ibrary of] I[reland] Mayo Papers MS 11167: 'You do not make allowance for the wonderful difference between the political and religious atmosphere of the North and South of Ireland. They are different countries and when the Republic comes it [Ulster] cannot … [be included] with the South and West.'

[15] T. Macknight, *Ulster as it Is or Twenty-Eight Years' Experience as an Irish Editor*, 2 vols (London, 1896), ii. 189; Parl. Deb. 3: ccciv. 1053–4 (8 April 1886), but see *The Times*, 30 July 1887; also Gladstone to Queen Victoria, 29 March 1886, T[he] N[ational] A[rchives] CAB 41/20/12. G. M. Young (*Today and Yesterday: Collected Essays and Addresses* (London, 1948), 29) claimed, without providing evidence, that in Gladstone's 'collected writings on Ireland (a book of 370 pages) Ulster receives two passing mentions—one a quotation from Castlereagh'.

[16] Loughlin, *Gladstone and the Ulster Question*, 132–40; Spencer's Memorandum, 19 March 1886, BL Gladstone Papers Add. MS 44313; Bryce's Memorandum, 12 March 1886, ibid., Add. MS 56447.

Chamberlain, consisted of 'two nations ... separated by religion, by race, by politics, by social conditions', with the Protestants notable for 'honest praiseworthy industry' and for 'almost all the cultivated intelligence of the country'.[17] Other future Liberal Unionists, notably Derby and Hartington, felt much the same, pointing to the 'fact' that Ireland was 'not a unanimous country' and worrying how a loyal Ulster would be treated under any possible Dublin government.[18] Even more did Tories in these years see Ulster distinctiveness—something they repeatedly stressed—furnishing a barrier to Home Rule in general, a conviction held as strongly by mavericks like Lord Randolph Churchill and weighty men of sense like W. H. Smith, both of whom knew more about Ireland than did most of their senior party colleagues.[19] What, however, few if any of these London gladiators realized was that, by mobilizing Ulster distinctiveness in order to stop Home Rule in its tracks, they were from the start playing a dangerous game, because already the first stirrings were taking place aimed at ensuring that, should Home Rule prove unstoppable, a fallback position of exclusion from any Dublin administration was something that needed to be kept very firmly in mind, a development that logically implied that Home Rule might be allowed to go through so long as Ulster had no part in it.[20]

This was a significant shift in position by opponents of Home Rule and went beyond the mere acceptance of general Irish distinctiveness (a feature of Unionist governments from at least 1886 onwards) and towards an emphasis upon Ulster's regional distinctiveness *within* Ireland, an emphasis that was to become the universal mode of Hibernian analysis among British Unionists (and even among some Liberals) and especially so at those times when it looked as if Home Rule might once again achieve some purchase upon the politics of the day. While, therefore, rumblings can already be detected in the years immediately following Gladstone's failure of 1886,[21] a major efflorescence of such views occurred in connection with the second Home Rule Bill of 1893.

[17] *Mr Chamberlain's Speeches*, ed. C. W. Boyd, 2 vols (London, 1914), i. 266 (21 April 1886) and i. 282 (11 October 1887); Chamberlain to Dilke, 26 December 1885, B[irmingham] U[niversity] J. Chamberlain Papers JC5/24/457; Harcourt to Gladstone, 13 January 1887, Bodl[eian Library] Harcourt Papers 11. Simple anti-Catholicism often lay behind such remarks.
[18] Derby to Hartington, 18 December 1885, ChH Devonshire Papers 340.1855; P. Jackson, *The Last of the Whigs: A Political Biography of Lord Hartington, later Eighth Duke of Devonshire (1833–1908)* (Cranbury, NJ, 1994), 203.
[19] For Churchill, see *The Times*, 15 February 1886, and Parl. Deb. 3: ccciv. 1333 (12 April 1886); for Smith, his election address of 17 June 1886, R[eading] U[niversity] Smith (Hambledon) Papers PS9/150.
[20] Macknight, *Ulster as it Is*, ii. 383; D. C. Savage, 'The Origins of the Ulster Unionist Party, 1885–6', *Irish Historical Studies*, 12 (1961), 207–8.
[21] *The Times*, 9 June 1887, where Bright insists that Ulster constituted a distinct 'nationality'; E. F. Biagini, *British Democracy and Irish Nationalism 1876–1906* (Cambridge, 2007), 259–60; *Mr Chamberlain's Speeches*, ed. Boyd, i. 287 (12 October 1887), P. T. Marsh, *Joseph Chamberlain: Entrepreneur in Politics* (New Haven, 1994), 265.

By then, however, Gladstone must have known what to expect, as Unionist leaders in Britain were gradually dropping their earlier patronizing, even critical, views of Ulster's peculiarities in favour of a (to them) more useful emphasis upon the wondrous loyalism of Ireland's North-East. Thus, while in the mid-1880s men as different as Carnarvon and Salisbury had made no bones about their contempt for the whinings of Orangemen—Carnarvon thought them simply 'demented', Salisbury 'troublesome and unreliable ... Their loyalty to the party is not a very fierce passion'[22]—by the early 1890s the anti-Home Rule usefulness of Orangeism had come into clearer focus and was now being embraced by party leaders with what was designed to look like a warmer cordiality. Not long before his defeat at the general election of 1892, Salisbury (with Arthur Balfour's full approval) began to talk much about Ulster and the splendid characteristics of its Protestant inhabitants. He knew of nothing 'more important' than their 'dread of being put under the despotism of ... [Catholic] foes'. Kings and parliaments had, he declared, no right to 'sell' the 'people of Ulster ... into slavery', any more than James II had had in 1690. 'These things', he told a large meeting of the Primrose League, were not, in any case, to be decided 'by ethical considerations ... They were usually decided by the consideration whether the resistance is likely to succeed. That is the consideration which has its interest for us too.'[23] With these brutally frank words, Salisbury established the 'rules' for all future Unionist deployments of the Ulster card, whether (as at first) played to try to block Home Rule altogether or (as later) to finesse Ulster exclusion as a device for granting it. His speech, which ended with talk of 'civil war', was, indeed, the authentic exposition of a new approach and foreshadowed the more famous lucubrations of a later Unionist leader, Andrew Bonar Law, at Blenheim Palace in July 1912.[24]

Salisbury's words opened the floodgates, and his lieutenants rushed towards rhetorical bolsterings of Ulster in the face of Gladstone's renewed demand for Home Rule. Salisbury himself visited Belfast in May 1893 to spread a favourite message: that 'the tendency throughout the world is not towards separatism, but to consolidation'. And the fact that a copy of this speech is to be found in Bonar Law's papers renders the latter's almost word-for-word replication uttered—also in Belfast—in April 1912 less original than it has sometimes been made to seem.[25] Balfour echoed his uncle and talked of the huge

---

[22] Carnarvon to Cranbrook, 2 September 1885, Su[ffolk] R[ecord] O[ffice] Cranbrook Papers HA43/T501/262; Salisbury to Lord R. Churchill, 16 November 1885, C[ambridge] U[niversity] L[ibrary] Lord Randolph Churchill Papers MS 9248/9/1066a.

[23] *The Times*, 7 May 1892; also Parl. Deb. 4: iv.1712 (24 May 1892: Balfour).

[24] That he could 'imagine no length of resistance to which Ulster can go, in which I shall not be prepared to support them' (R. Blake, *The Unknown Prime Minister: The Life and Times of Andrew Bonar Law 1858–1923* (London, 1955), 130).

[25] Typescript in P[arliamentary] A[rchives] Bonar Law Papers 40/4/84 (where are also to be found speeches by Lord R. Churchill and Arthur Balfour, as if Bonar Law was taking a private

differences between the North and South of Ireland and how it was 'madness to suppose that in Ireland you find a single nation with one single set of aspirations'. What had, he insisted, now become obvious was that, even according to 'every rule' laid down by Gladstone himself, 'Ulster deserves exceptional treatment' with regard to any proposal for Home Rule.[26] And, where Unionist leaders led, Unionist followers followed.[27] But, as they had done in 1885–6, so the Unionists of Ulster, not fully trusting their British associates, began once again to look more closely to their own resources. A Convention League was established, constituency associations revived, local groups set up (some of them affiliated to an Ulster Clubs Council), and Ulster Unionist MPs solidified themselves into an increasingly coherent group under the leadership of Colonel Edward Saunderson. Some years later, in 1905, the foundation of the Ulster Unionist Council marked, not only a further step in provincial organization, but confirmation that the priorities of Ulster Unionists were diverging more and more from those of their counterparts in the South of Ireland. No less significant was the fact that already in 1893 a number of Unionist MPs (including Edward Carson) had considered putting forward an amendment to Gladstone's bill designed to exclude Ulster from its provisions and had only desisted when it became apparent that the House of Lords could torpedo the bill without their help.[28]

Although all of this demonstrated the vigour of Ulster's resistance to Home Rule, it also signalled a degree of independence from British leaders, whose priorities naturally ranged far beyond matters Hibernian. But, while Salisbury found Ulster Unionists almost as troublesome as southern nationalists, the British party became increasingly ardent in its insistence that Ireland was a deeply splintered society, that Home Rule merely sought to paper over such divisions, and that 'the Irish claim, if it is to be admitted at all, is a claim not to one parliament but to two'.[29] Even some Liberals were keen to assert that

correspondence course on how to handle Ulster). His own speech of April 1912 is in ibid. 44/P/3: 'The whole history of the modern world is the history of a movement towards union ... Ireland is not, and has never been, a nation.' See note 14, and Edward Cooke's (anonymous) *Arguments for and against an Union*, 8th edn (Dublin, 1798), 8–10, and Parl. Deb. 3: i. 97 (2 November 1830: Peel).

[26] *The Times*, 5 April 1893 (Balfour); Parl. Deb. 4: viii. 23 (31 January 1893: Salisbury) and 1404 (14 February 1893: Balfour).

[27] Parl. Deb. 4: viii. 1665 (16 February 1893: Waring), x. 1889 (10 April 1893: Smith), xi. 143 (12 April 1893: Loder), xvii. 573 (8 September 1893: Cranbrook), xi. 361 (14 April 1893: Hamilton); Lord [G. R.] Askwith, *Lord James of Hereford* (London, 1930), 222; W. S. Churchill, *Lord Randolph Churchill*, new edn (London, [1951]), 813.

[28] A. Jackson, *The Ulster Party: Irish Unionists in the House of Commons, 1884–1911* (Oxford, 1989), 44–50, 235–40, and *Sir Edward Carson* (Dundalk, 1993), 30; P. Buckland, *Irish Unionism: Two: Ulster Unionists and the Origins of Northern Ireland 1886–1922* (Dublin, 1973), 16–21.

[29] Salisbury to Cadogan, 25 February 1896, PA Cadogan Papers 840; Parl. Deb. 4: cxli. 674 (20 February 1905: Cecil) and clxxxvii. 144 (30 March 1908: Percy); also St L. Strachey to Bonar Law, 17 November 1911, PA Bonar Law Papers 24/3/50.

Ulster was very 'different' from the rest of Ireland and to wonder what, if anything, might be the implications of this increasingly accepted fact.[30]

III

As is well known, the enormous Liberal victory at the general election of January 1906—a victory that allowed the party to govern without the support of the Irish Parliamentary Party—did nothing to bring Liberal interest in Home Rule up to Gladstonian levels. Of no less significance, however, is the fact that by 1906 those elements within the party least enamoured of Home Rule had either, as in the case of Rosebery, departed the field, or, especially under the steady leadership of Campbell-Bannerman (prime minister from December 1905 until April 1908), become reconciled to some movement on matters Irish on the understanding that initially at least such movement should not be dramatic. But, though none of this pleased men such as Redmond and Dillon, it marked progress of a kind, even if progress that tended to follow lines that Unionists had rather begun to make their own. However, in a departure from Unionist practice, Redmond, Dillon, and their chief lieutenants were now regularly consulted about matters of legislative detail, patronage, and the small change of Irish politics in general.[31]

It is easy to minimize the Irish actions of the Liberal government of 1905–10, not least because Asquith (who became prime minister in 1908) did little to disguise his boredom with pretty well everything to do with the smaller island.[32] But it is—and indeed was—quite possible to read the runes in more 'positive' ways. In the first place, the Liberals, whatever their initial feebleness on Home Rule itself, passed a number of important measures consolidating Unionist legislation and reflecting a shared assumption of Irish difference. Especially notable were the University Bill of 1908—a typically Irish solution to an Irish problem—and a first decisive advance into the hitherto Unionist territory of land purchase in 1909. Secondly, whatever Irish nationalists may have thought, there was a widespread and growing feeling among British Liberals that their modest reforms would—indeed must— inexorably lead to more dramatic legislation along Home Rule lines. As

---

[30] Harcourt to Gladstone, 13 January 1887, Bodl. Harcourt Papers 10; Haldane to his Mother, 9 October 1894, N[ational] L[ibrary of] S[cotland] Haldane Papers MS 5952.

[31] F. S. L. Lyons, *The Irish Parliamentary Party 1890–1910* (London, 1951), 109–29, 218–54; A. O'Day, *Irish Home Rule 1867–1921* (Manchester, 1998), 207–39; L. Ó Broin, *The Chief Secretary: Augustine Birrell in Ireland* (London, 1969), *passim*. See the long and cosy correspondence Redmond maintained with Bryce and Birrell in NLI Redmond Papers MSS 15174 and 15169.

[32] See Asquith to Birrell, 6 November 1907, Bodl. Birrell Papers 23.

early as 1899 Haldane (later a member of Campbell-Bannerman's and Asquith's cabinets) had predicted that 'a time will come when parties [in the Commons] are more evenly balanced' and the logjam delaying Home Rule would be removed, as had Herbert Gladstone (another future cabinet minister), himself no less convinced that 'sooner or later the Nationalists will have the balance of power in the House of Commons'.[33] While of course such forecasts amounted to little more than intelligent guesswork, the temporary disappearance of Home Rule as a viable issue after 1893 has tended to disguise their predictive accuracy and eventual realization.

It is, in any case, misleading to exaggerate Edwardian Liberalism's want of interest in Ireland. Certainly Asquith lacked Gladstone's and even Campbell-Bannerman's commitment to Home Rule, but, as Alvin Jackson has pointed out, he was never 'distinguished by political passions of any type'. The problem for Redmond was not that Asquith was hostile to Home Rule, 'but that he needed to be convinced of its utility'.[34] And that this would eventually come about was something that many Liberal observers were—just as Haldane and Herbert Gladstone had been in 1899—becoming more and more persuaded of as time went on. In particular, Wyndham's dramatic Land Act of 1903 was seen, not as something that might staunch the demand for Home Rule, but as the very opposite.[35] Although even some Unionists suspected that this might well prove to be the case, Arthur Balfour, grandly dismissing such fears, thought it important to 'abstract' the 'mind altogether from these considerations in dealing with the matter'.[36] But, as one Liberal MP pointed out to his newly converted colleague, Winston Churchill, in 1904, all that was required was for the 'Irish' to 'hold the balance of power', and Home Rule would speedily rise to the top of the party's agenda.[37] In any case, as another Liberal argued in 1905, Irish matters always tended to move well beyond their initial starting points. Indeed, 'every pledge' previously given that the limits of concession had been reached—whether by Gladstone or Salisbury or Joseph

[33] Parl. Deb. 4: lxvi. 1199 (16 February 1899: Haldane); Gladstone to Campbell-Bannerman, 8 December 1899, BL Campbell-Bannerman Papers Add. MS 41215; also Campbell-Bannerman to Gladstone, 26 October 1905, BL Herbert Gladstone Papers Add. MS 45988. See Haldane's Address at the general election of 1906, NLS Haldane Papers MS 5907.

[34] A. Jackson, *Home Rule: An Irish History, 1800–2000* (London, 2003), 106.

[35] Parl. Deb. 4: cxxii. 43 (7 May 1903: Atherley-Jones), 95 (7 May 1903: Rickett), 127 (7 May 1903: Morley), cxxv. 1336 (21 July 1903: Campbell-Bannerman), cxliv. 1506 (12 April 1905: Campbell-Bannerman), xli. 828 (21 February 1905: Harwood).

[36] Parl. Deb. 4: cxxv. 1338 (21 July 1903), also cxxi. 1228–9 (4 May 1903: Coghill) and cxxvi. 1218 (3 August 1903: Arran).

[37] C. P. Trevelyan to Churchill, 17 October 1904, C[hurchill] C[ollege] C[ambridge] Churchill Papers CHAR2/18/48–50; also Churchill to Redmond, 7 April 1908, R. S. Churchill, *Winston S. Churchill*, II, Companion Part 2 (London, 1969), 764–5.

Chamberlain—had invariably 'been broken', with the result that forward 'progress' had come to acquire an unstoppable and remorseless inevitability.[38]

By 1907 ministers were queuing up to declare that Home Rule was the ultimate goal of the plans and proposals they had in mind. While, of course, such affirmations were designed to please their Irish allies, they also undoubtedly reflected the belief that, as Crewe (the Lord President of the Council and a former viceroy) put it: 'You cannot get over the probability that you might find yourself advancing, step by step, in the direction of Home Rule.' Or, as his colleague the Lord Chancellor (of England) admitted: 'You cannot touch Irish Government without taking a step towards Home Rule ... Whatever you do you inexorably head up to that ... [and it will come] as tomorrow's sun is to rise.'[39]

Clearly the Irish Parliamentary Party wanted more than words, even words like this. And Redmond was making it ever more evident that—as a new general election approached—his support depended upon unambiguous guarantees. And his support might, indeed, well matter because Asquith's government had locked itself into a bitter struggle with the Unionists and the House of Lords over Lloyd George's budget of April 1909 (which also contained provisions repugnant to Redmond's staunch and powerful supporters in the Irish drinks trade). In October 1909 Haldane was telling the king that the Irish nationalists would probably prove critical in any post-election parliament, just as Redmond, in unusually forceful mode, was demanding greater clarity about the Liberal commitment to Home Rule.[40]

Asquith gave the requisite public pledge at a large meeting in the Albert Hall on 10 December 1909, and the general election the following month did, indeed, present Redmond's party with the balance of power, a result confirmed by another election in December. In 1911 the Parliament Act deprived the House of Lords of its power to delay money bills, restricted its power over other bills to a suspensory veto of two years, and reduced the maximum duration of a parliament from seven to five years. And then the third Home Rule Bill was introduced by Asquith in April 1912.

Behind all this lay intense inter-party conversations in late 1910 largely initiated by Lloyd George and taken seriously by at least some Unionists as part of wider talks about the possibility of coalition. Although these had clearly run into the sands by November of that year, the very fact that they had taken place at all suggests greater flexibility beneath the surface of public events than

---

[38] Parl. Deb. 4: cxlv. 1422 (9 May 1905: Lough). The undersecretary Antony MacDonnell (author of the feeble Council Bill of 1907) seems to have believed much the same: MacDonnell to Birrell, [September 1907], Bodl. MacDonnell Papers MS Eng.hist.c.354.

[39] Parl. Deb. 4: clxxi. 796–7 (20 March 1907: Crewe) and 806–7 (20 March 1907: Loreburn), also clxix. 200 (13 February 1907: Birrell).

[40] Haldane's Memorandum of 6 October 1909 about conversations at Balmoral, NLS Haldane Papers MS 5908; Redmond to Morley, 27 January 1909, Bodl. Morley Papers MS Eng.d.3581.

was apparent at first sight, something about which, already in October 1910, Carson—as leader of the Irish (effectively Ulster) Unionist MPs—had begun to express serious anxieties.[41] Initially Balfour had assumed that Lloyd George's main aim was to rid politics altogether of their Irish importunities. In fact it was to pawn off the Irish with a modest measure of devolution in the hope that the presentation of a united British front would force them to accept.[42] However, speeches from Asquith in December 1910 indicated that the Liberals would now definitely go for Home Rule as long as it was not 'inconsistent with our imperial interests', while other Liberals like Sir Edward Grey rejoiced that Home Rule would give parliament time to deal with matters intrinsically more important than the little local difficulties that constituted the tedious fare of Irish complaints.[43]

Not only, however, did these inconclusive cross-party conversations form an important backdrop to Asquith's introduction of the Home Rule Bill in 1912, but so did two other developments of more than equal significance. The first was the growing militancy of Ulster Unionism. In February 1910 Carson had been elected leader of the Irish Unionists as a whole. In September 1911 he addressed a large body of Orangemen and other Unionists outside Belfast just as their opposition to Home Rule was becoming ever stronger, their preferred ways of aborting it ever more forceful, and their independent organizations ever better established. Whereas under Saunderson resistance had been largely confined to parliamentary combat, Carson was more and more obviously presiding 'over the preparations for civil war'.[44]

The second development was the replacement of Balfour as Unionist leader by Andrew Bonar Law in November 1911, although this proved a less straightforward matter than many at first thought, for, while Balfour had generally found Ulster Unionists unpalatable[45] and Bonar Law had acquired a public character for immovable firmness on Ulster, these reputations (especially in Bonar Law's case) were neither altogether nor consistently deserved. While the intellectual Balfour actually tended to mean what he said, Bonar Law—the public sea-green intransigent—proved himself the nimbler pragmatist of the two, a fact he brilliantly disguised by high-octane rhetoric suggesting the

---

[41] R. Fanning, *Fatal Path: British Government and Irish Revolution 1910–1922* (London, 2013), 44–5. See A. Chamberlain to Balfour, 25 October 1910, Bodl. Sandars Papers MS Eng. hist.c.761: we must be careful not to adopt 'a simple *non possumus* attitude … for opinion has changed and is changing still now in England as well as in Ireland'; also Carson to Lady Londonderry, [*c.*27 October 1910], P[ublic] R[ecord] O[ffice of] N[orthern] I[reland] Londonderry Papers D2846/1/1/55.

[42] See Balfour's Memorandum of October 1910, Bodl. Sandars Papers MS Eng.hist.c.761.

[43] Typed extracts of speeches by Asquith at St Andrews and Bury St Edmunds on 7 and 12 December and by Grey at Berwick on 2 December 1910 in Bodl. Sandars Papers MS Eng.hist. c.762.

[44] Jackson, *The Ulster Party*, 320–1.

[45] See, e.g., Parl. Deb. 4: cxlv. 1449 (9 May 1905).

contrary. What always informed Balfour's views were, first, Ireland's lack of national unity and, secondly, the absolute and overriding necessity for entities like the United Kingdom to avoid disintegration because—just as his uncle had argued—'the whole tendency of modern times is the creation of great states and communities'. Any move to the contrary would, he believed, lead to decline and collapse in a world of international conflict in which only the fittest would survive.[46] Such sub-Darwinian views meant that Balfour was to prove himself an extremist in Irish matters: certainly Tom Jones (Lloyd George's confidant in the cabinet secretariat) saw him in 1912 as the most 'irreconcilable' of British ministers.[47] More generally it meant that, when hard facts knocked on the door, Balfour was unsentimental about looking them in the face. Thus in November 1919 he was ready enough to ditch the 'disloyal' South of Ireland (its 'loyal' element notwithstanding) so long as the Six Counties could remain within the United Kingdom, because Ireland had 'never in all the centuries, been a single, organised, independent State'.[48]

Bonar Law, for all his forceful words, was a very different politician, above all, a determined manipulator of any means to hand that might further the ultimate cause. And the ultimate cause was not the defeat of Home Rule, but the defeat of the Liberal government and its replacement by one led by himself.[49] His displacement of Balfour looked dramatic because the latter had long troubled his colleagues by a species of nuanced discrimination that played badly with more red-necked followers, especially when, just weeks before his dethronement, he had announced that Home Rule should be opposed 'so long as we are entitled to assume it is Gladstonian Home Rule'. Walter Long (a former chief secretary and Carson's predecessor as leader of the Irish Unionists) had unsurprisingly denounced this for implying that 'there was some form of Home Rule' to which Balfour 'would not offer relentless opposition'.[50] But, when it actually came to a choice of Balfour's successor, the most obviously anti-Home Rule candidate (Long) was rejected in favour of Bonar Law, whose credentials as an Ulster sympathizer were still unclear, who had made his reputation as an opponent of tariff reform rather than Home Rule, and whose leanings towards Lloyd George's coalition ideas in 1910 hardly reflected the views or actions of 'an unreconstructed loyalist'.[51]

---

[46] Parl. Deb. 4: viii. 197 (31 January 1893), xxxii. 558–9 (29 March 1895), clxxxvii. 216 (30 March 1908); Parl. Deb. 5 (Commons): xxxvii. 53 (14 April 1912).

[47] *Tom Jones: Whitehall Diary*, ed. K. Middlemas, 3 vols (London, 1965–71), iii. 85.

[48] TNA CAB 24/93 CP 193 (25 November 1919).

[49] J. Smith, *The Tories and Ireland 1910–1914: Conservative Party Politics and the Home Rule Crisis* (Dublin, 2000), 4–5, 46–9, 106–8.

[50] Long to Balfour, 29 September 1911, Bodl. Sandars Papers MS Eng.hist.c.764, and BL Long Papers Add. MS 62403.

[51] Jackson, *Home Rule*, 116–17; A. Chamberlain, *Politics from the Inside: An Epistolary Chronicle 1906–1914* (London, 1936), 193.

IV

What became more and more evident during the months after Asquith's introduction of the third Home Rule Bill was that the attitudes of British politicians in general and ministers in particular had, over the previous decades, become thoroughly embedded in a context of Anglo-Irish differentiation. Not only that, but the acceptance of, indeed emphasis on, the existence of a deep gulf between North and South *within* Ireland imposed restraining considerations upon thinking about how Ireland might best be governed or, if it came to that, set adrift. What this meant was that, while initially all concerned convinced themselves that they were talking the language of Home Rule and the Union, they soon discovered that they were in fact expressing themselves through an increasingly fluent version of 'partition speak' and that it was this that was above all to furnish the political grammar without which serious constitutional adjustments would prove impossible. Of course, there were those who, from the beginning, realized that this was a dangerous development. Carson, himself a Dubliner, was obliged to adopt what amounted to a split personality on the matter. One minute he was telling Ulster audiences (as in September 1911) that, should Home Rule come to pass, they—or, as he put it, 'we'—would have to 'become responsible for the government of the Protestant Province of Ulster'.[52] And then, only days later, he was in Dublin desperately trying to calm Southern Unionists fearful that Ulster was preparing, perhaps even delighted, to leave them in the lurch. Proceedings in Ulster were, he told them, no more than a fail-safe device for stopping Liberal plans once and for all, because 'Home Rule is impossible for Ireland without Belfast', an assertion of rapidly diminishing persuasiveness.[53]

To say that Carson was aware of the dilemma he faced on becoming Irish Unionist leader in February 1910 is an understatement. When in November 1911 Bonar Law showed him a letter from a prominent Unionist journalist to the effect that Ireland clearly consisted of two quite separate 'national units', he responded nervously. The question was, he said, 'one of delicacy', for, while Ulster Unionists 'have always declared they would not desert the South and West, Unionists outside Ulster are prone to be very jealous and suspicious that they will be deserted'. Indeed, separate treatment might well prove inevitable, though he rather hoped that that day had not yet come. And, while one historian sees this as clear evidence that Carson was already thinking about

---

[52] Just as the Ulster Unionist Council was deciding that 'the time has now come when we consider it our imperative duty to make arrangements for the provincial government of Ulster'. See H. M. Hyde, *Carson: The Life of Sir Edward Carson, Lord Carson of Duncairn* (London, 1953), 291; R. McNeill, *Ulster's Stand for Union* (London, 1922), 52.

[53] E. Marjoribanks and I. Colvin, *The Life of Lord Carson*, 3 vols (London, 1932–6), ii. 104. On Carson's tergiversations, see N. Mansergh, *The Unresolved Question: The Anglo-Irish Settlement and its Undoing 1912–72* (New Haven, 1991), 46.

partition, another takes a different view.[54] Whatever the truth of the matter, Carson's private sentiments in November 1911 do not suggest that the delineations of an everlastingly united Ireland were ineradicably inscribed upon his heart. In any case, certain leading British Unionists of the fiercer variety were also beginning to wonder whether Ulster exclusion from Home Rule might not prove to be the solution to all their problems, especially in the event of a violent confrontation between Ulster resistance and extreme nationalist demands.[55]

Such developments were the almost inevitable outcome of the passing of the Parliament Act in 1911, which, however much Unionists might complain, implied that Southern Ireland would, sooner rather than later, be lost to the nationalists, but that Ulster would be 'saved'. After 1911–12, therefore, Unionism in Britain revolved largely around securing the exclusion of Ulster from the provisions of Asquith's bill, a change in orientation that was very much the achievement of Bonar Law, who found it consistently useful to emphasize the now accepted wisdom of Ulster exceptionalism and the existence within Ireland of two distinct nations 'separated from each other far more acutely than either is separated from the people of Great Britain'. Indeed, Bonar Law's greatest political talent lay precisely 'in his ability to make a virtue out of necessity'.[56]

Two developments in 1912 ensured that Bonar Law's exclusionist project— based as it was upon decades of assumptions about Irish differentiation as well as upon more immediate contingencies—would provide the lever that would make the settlement of December 1921 possible. The more striking was the Solemn League and Covenant of September, when, amid demonstrations of theatrical melodrama, large numbers signed their names to a declaration that —echoing the language of seventeenth-century documents—declared that amid the present turmoils they would 'stand by one another in defending for ourselves and our children our cherished position of equal citizenship in the United Kingdom, and in using all means which may be found necessary to defeat the present conspiracy to set up a Home Rule Parliament in Ireland'. While this was all very dramatic, it changed little as regards Home Rule's parliamentary progress, though its strikingly modern propaganda-style accompaniments—threats of violence and importations of weapons—were all factors of undeniable resonance and effect.[57] Of greater parliamentary

---

[54] St L. Strachey to Bonar Law, 17 November 1911, PA Bonar Law Papers 24/3/50; notes by Carson on this letter, [18 November 1911], ibid. 24/3/57, G. Lewis, *Carson: The Man who Divided Ireland* (London, 2005), 81, versus Meleady, *John Redmond: The National Leader*, 218.

[55] Lord Selborne's Memorandum of 4 September 1911, BU A. Chamberlain Papers AC9/3/58; Selborne to Lord Willoughby de Broke, 12 September 1911, PA Willoughby de Broke Papers 3/69; Salisbury to Selborne, 12 September1911, Bodl. Selborne Papers 6/116.

[56] S. Evans, 'The Conservatives and the Redefinition of Unionism, 1912–21', *20th Century British History*, 9 (1998), 10–14.

[57] Hyde, *Carson*, 317–22; Jackson, *Home Rule*, 118–19.

significance was the amendment to the Home Rule Bill proposed in June by Thomas Agar-Robartes, the independently minded Liberal MP for St Austell. Amendments at this stage of the bill's progress mattered a good deal, because, under the procedures laid down by the Parliament Act, once a bill had gone through all its stages in the Commons, the Lords could delay it for two years only *provided* that no further changes of any kind were introduced. Agar-Robartes proposed that the four most Protestant counties in Ulster—Antrim, Armagh, Down, and Derry—should be excluded, because, with Ireland so obviously consisting of 'two nations different in sentiment, character, history, and religion ... we have it on the best authority that Orange bitters will ... never .... mix with Irish whisky [*recte* whiskey]'.[58] Though the amendment was defeated by 320 votes to 251, the discussions it elicited more forcefully bring to mind the cliché of 'setting the cat among the pigeons' than that of creating 'storms in teacups'.

Until only a few months before Agar-Robartes's intervention almost everyone in the Liberal cabinet had simply ignored the Ulster question. The only exceptions were Lloyd George, Churchill, and Birrell, the last of whom was a more acute interpreter of Irish realities than is often assumed, even if lack of action often tended to belie his intelligence.[59] Indeed, most Liberals, convinced that they had long possessed a viable policy of Irish differentiation (Home Rule) that could when needed be smoothly moved on to the high road of political necessity, proved slower than their opponents in recognizing that some serious mechanical adjustments might soon require implementation. Unionists, by contrast, could hardly avoid noticing that *their* version of differentiation—the Union tempered by mountains of money—was, under the impress of agitation from Ulster, beginning to look distinctly in need of some very dramatic modifications indeed.

In February 1912 the cabinet at last awoke from its slumbers to realize that something might well have to be done about the North of Ireland, and that this might have to involve some form of partition, preferably temporary. Two months later Churchill was telling the Commons that 'the perfectly genuine apprehensions of the majority of the people of North-East Ulster' could not and should not be ignored.[60] In the meantime, leading Unionists continued to emphasize that Ireland consisted of two nations, while—two weeks before Churchill's Commons speech—Bonar Law was giving private hints that Home Rule might well be possible if individual Ulster counties were given the right to 'remain outside the Irish Parliament', a clear indication that he was by no

[58] Parl. Deb. 5 (Commons): xxxix. 771–4 (11 June 1912).
[59] P. Jalland, *The Liberals and Ireland: The Ulster Question in British Politics to 1914* (Brighton, 1980), 57–9.
[60] Asquith to Edward VII, 7 February 1912, TNA CAB 41/33/35; Parl. Deb. 5 (Commons): xxxvii. 1718 (30 April 1912).

means opposed to applying an Irish (or Ulster) solution to the distinctly Irish problem of Home Rule.[61]

Agar-Robartes's amendment, however, presented Unionists with considerable problems. Should they support it and thus, by implication at least, accept Home Rule if accompanied by partition or should they reject it and go for broke in the hope of keeping the United Kingdom intact? What followed exposed not only the implications of such a choice but how, at the end of the day, the key Unionist players opted for the realism of odds on rather than the hazards of odds against. It was now that the more irreconcilable Robespierres of Unionism emerged, the men who—some to the bitter end, some less permanently—attached themselves to the cause of 'No Change under Any Circumstances'. Men like Lord Selborne belonged to the resolutes; men like Walter Long 'as one connected by the closest ties with the Provinces of Leinster and Munster' eventually caved in.[62] But the bulk of the party took a much more realistic and less intransigent line while disguising their manœuvres by hot words and bold phrases. Logically (if that is quite the right word) almost all MPs should have voted against Agar-Robartes: Unionists because they allegedly opposed Home Rule root and branch, Liberals because they supported it. In the event, most Unionist MPs voted in the minority. In other words, the bulk of Unionist MPs now supported the very policy (Ulster exclusion) that rendered Home Rule for the rest of Ireland a gatheringly distinct probability. Of course, this inconvenient fact had to be disguised, especially from British irreconcilables and the increasingly (and rightly) worried Irish Unionists (or 'loyalists') outside the North-East. While Balfour, a master of sophisticated brutality, made little effort to disguise the *Realpolitik* of what was happening, Bonar Law tried to pretend that Unionists could both have and eat their cake all at the same time. He and others would, he declared, vote for the motion, though this would 'not for a moment ... take away my opposition to Home Rule'. Indeed not. 'But while we oppose this Bill root-and-branch, yet we ... will support any amendment which, bad as the Bill seems to us to be, would make it less bad than it was before the Amendment was introduced'[63]—sentiments worthy of Jesuit casuists of the very first rank.

Lloyd George, himself sympathetic to the Ulster cause, had little trouble seeing through such sophistries. Unionists, he declared, had always been reluctant to propose exclusion because they realized that this would open

---

[61] R. J. Q. Adams, *Bonar Law* (London, 1999), 111; speech in Belfast of 9 April 1912, typescript in PA Bonar Law Papers 44/P/3; also Parl. Deb. 5 (Commons): xxxvi. 1465 (11 April 1912: Castlereagh), xxxvii. 1890 (1 May 1912: Finlay), 1786–7 (30 April 1912: Amery), xxxviii. 98 (6 May 1912: Butcher), 688–9 (8 May 1912: Bonar Law).

[62] Selborne to Bonar Law, 5 July 1912, PA Bonar Law Papers 26/5/10; Long to Bonar Law, 4 June 1912, ibid. 26/4/7; also T. Comyn Platt to Selborne, [*c.* September 1912], Bodl. Selborne Papers 77/14.

[63] Parl. Deb. 5 (Commons): xxxix. 810–11 (11 June 1912: Balfour) and 778–81 (Bonar Law).

the door to Home Rule. They had now themselves not only opened the door but taken away the key.[64] Nor were Lloyd George and Liberal realists such as Churchill and Grey at all displeased. Just like Bonar Law and Balfour, they too were already looking to exclusion as the way out of the Irish difficulty. The fact that none of them voted against Agar-Robartes made that clear enough. Indeed, within months Churchill was providing public proof of his support for special treatment for Ulster while trying to persuade Redmond that Home Rule was in the bag if only all concerned were prepared to buy off the last remaining obstacle—namely, 'the opposition of three or four Ulster counties'.[65] Agar-Robartes had blown up the dam. Bonar Law had moved, as had Balfour. And so too did Carson, who, like his colleagues, was, in effect and despite his denials, now preferring pragmatic safety to principled uncertainty. His most significant intervention in the debate had not been to denounce the idea of exclusion but to insist that Tyrone and Fermanagh be added to the four counties Agar-Robartes had named, an intervention that delineated the six-county area established in 1921 and was already waving goodbye to Cavan, Monaghan, and Donegal.[66]

As early as June 1912, therefore—before the Solemn League and Covenant, before Bonar Law's Blenheim Palace speech—partition had begun (especially among certain Unionist and Liberal leaders) to assume an air of something approaching inevitability. What this also meant, as observers were not slow to point out, was that some form of Home Rule was becoming equally inevitable, and that, as Ulster Unionism triumphed, other elements would suffer a matching and corresponding collapse, most obviously 'loyalists' outside and nationalists within the excluded area.[67] Partition, in other words, was becoming an integral part of any possible 'outcome'. Indeed, during the Agar-Robartes debate, only four of the twenty-five Unionist speeches had adopted the tactical approach of supporting the amendment merely as a wrecking device designed to derail Home Rule as a whole,[68] and even minority self-delusions of this kind were—for all save a devout handful—soon blown away amid strengthening winds of change, a process that took all of six months. Some years later a leading Ulster Unionist, shedding crocodile tears, recalled how, as the bill made progress in 1912, it had became more and more obvious

---

[64] Parl. Deb. 5 (Commons) xxxix. 1119–28 (13 June 1912).

[65] Jalland, *The Liberals and Ireland*, 104–5; Churchill to Redmond, 31 August 1912, NLI Redmond Papers MS 15175.

[66] Parl. Deb. 5 (Commons): xxxix. 1068 (13 June 1912).

[67] Parl. Deb. 5 (Commons): xxxix. 822 (11 June 1912: Simon); A. Jackson, 'Irish Unionism, 1905–21', in P. Collins (ed.), *Nationalism and Unionism: Conflict in Ireland, 1885–1921* (Belfast, 1994), 35–46, 189–90.

[68] Jalland, *The Liberals and Ireland*, 94.

to those with any kind of insight that a move was under way to ensure that Home Rule would go through in return for partition. By December, Carson too—how reluctantly is uncertain—was lining up in favour of exclusion and putting forward the convenient belief that, by some mysterious and hermetic means, 'the interests of Unionists in the three other provinces' would thus 'be best conserved'.[69] And then, on New Year's Day 1913, he himself proposed an amendment to the bill to exclude all nine Ulster counties, thus giving implicit consent to Home Rule for the rest of Ireland. Again, there were promises that it was really all a charade to abort the bill as a whole. But few now believed anything of the kind. Even Asquith's continuing rejection of the idea seems to have been based as much upon a characteristic reluctance to spend time thinking up anything new as upon careful or sustained analysis.[70]

To say that the next two years were taken up by no more than an exercise in crossing 't's and dotting 'i's would be an exaggeration, but not a very egregious one. Of course, much remained to be settled. What should be the precise area excluded? Would exclusion be permanent? How far could Redmond and his party be bullied? How completely could Southern Unionists be abandoned to their fate? But it was such 'details' that largely took up the time of politicians in the months before the outbreak of the First World War—itself, of course, an unexpected and mightily complicating element as far as the Irish question was concerned. Even so, it is clear that over the period 1912–14 the leaders of both Unionists and Liberals simultaneously lighted upon matching and interrelated programmes that were pragmatic and realistic and in full accord with the parallel, if distinct, tendencies towards Irish differentiation that had characterized British party politics for forty years and more.

Indeed, the Irish question had come to assume a very distinct shape that, when responding to impacts on one side (such as Home Rule), seems automatically to have generated a matching and countervailing effect on the opposite side (partition), with the result that disputes had come to assume the character of what more recently has become known as a 'zero-sum game'. What could not, however, be totally or permanently concealed was that any likely solution would create losers as well as victors—itself, of course, another kind of 'matching'. But, while Ulster nationalists seem to have had virtually no friends, Southern Unionists, with their social and political connections in Britain, proved just about able to mount a final forlorn act of defiance before it became blindingly obvious that their defences consisted of no more than Potemkin village fortifications of the flimsiest kind.

---

[69] McNeill, *Ulster's Stand for Union*, 132–3.
[70] Jalland, *The Liberals and Ireland*, 108–11; M. Laffan, *The Partition of Ireland 1911–1925* (Dundalk, 1983), 33–4.

V

As the Home Rule bill meandered through parliament, so, in secret and then more brazenly, Unionist leaders began to make it clear that omelettes (partition) could not be made without breaking eggs (the Union). Once that genie was well and truly out of the bottle, it moved forward at considerable speed, with only a derelict rearguard pointing out the dangers of precipitation.[71] Already in July 1913 Bonar Law's Commons speech on the bill revealed fairly explicit recognition of nationalist Ireland's right to self-government so long as appropriate safeguards were provided.[72] By autumn the process was gaining momentum as matters moved from the realms of possibility into those of the distinctest of distinct probabilities. Already in September it had become unambiguously clear that key Unionists were prepared to grant Home Rule in return for partition. At first they baulked at the precise degree of devolution that might be given to Southern Ireland, but soon serious reservations on even that point were more or less abandoned.

By the early summer of 1914 the only major roadblock on the Unionist side was manned by an unstable combination of Willoughby de Broke diehards and Southern Irish Unionists supported by senior figures with Irish connections such as Lansdowne and Long. Two of the ostensibly 'extreme' Unionists, Bonar Law and F. E. Smith, proved to be among the most flexible, because both believed that, once Ulster had been 'saved', little else mattered, certainly not the Southern Unionists, who struck many British observers, including Balfour, as a pretty effete and feeble lot.[73] Bonar Law negotiated semi-secretly with Asquith in October and November 1913. He made ritualistic obeisances to the claims of Southern Unionists before telling the prime minister that, in the final analysis, he would be quite prepared to throw them 'to the wolves'. Partition was, indeed, quite rapidly being transformed for many Unionists from a wrecking to a facilitating device that, far from making Home Rule impossible, was helping to make it entirely and almost unavoidably probable.[74]

Especially notable is the manner in which Carson bent with the prevailing Unionist wind, his being yet another case of rhetoric attempting to disguise

---

[71] Parl. Deb. 5 (Lords): xiv. 926 (14 July 1913: Willoughby de Broke); Willoughby de Broke to Halsbury, 5 July 1914, BL Halsbury Papers Add. MS 56375; Amery to Bonar Law, 27 December 1913, PA Bonar Law Papers 31/1/57; Memorandum by 5th Marquess of Lansdowne, 26 October 1913, BL Cecil of Chelwood Papers Add. MS 51085.

[72] Parl. Deb. 5 (Commons): lv. 74 (7 July 1913).

[73] Bonar Law to Balfour, 16 September 1913, BL Balfour Papers Add. MS 49693; Smith to Lloyd George, 26 September and 6 October 1913, PA Lloyd George Papers C/3/7/1 and 2; Bonar Law to Lansdowne, 4 October 1913, PA Bonar Law Papers 33/5/67; Lansdowne to Bonar Law, 10 October 1913, ibid. 30/3/16; [2nd] Earl of Birkenhead, *F. E. Smith, First Earl of Birkenhead* (London, 1959), 225; J. Campbell, *F. E. Smith, First Earl of Birkenhead* (London, 1983), 325–6.

[74] Jalland, *The Liberals and Ireland*, 154. See J. Smith, *The Tories and Ireland*, 4–7, 34–6, 97–117, for a different reading of these developments.

reality. As early as September 1913 he was telling Bonar Law that 'on the whole things are shaping towards a desire to settle on the terms of leaving "Ulster" out' and implying that the only major decision still to be made concerned the eventual size of the excluded area. A few days later Bonar Law reported this happy news to the king's secretary. Carson, he wrote, does not find impossible 'the idea of having some form of Home Rule provided Ulster was excluded'.[75] Indeed, even Carson was beginning to think his Southern Unionist colleagues gutless compared with their Northern counterparts and not 'prepared to run any risks', only to be reminded that, while this was doubtless true, they might still be in a position to cause trouble before inevitably sinking beneath the waves.[76]

In December 1913 Carson told Asquith that he would accept an immediate Irish settlement as part of an overall scheme of devolution on condition that Ulster would maintain a separate existence until the imperial parliament had finally pronounced.[77] In truth, Carson's need to speak to several audiences at once had begun to render his position so contradictory that it could be 'saved' only by means of arguments that depended upon his listeners being prepared to believe six impossible things before breakfast. His famous outburst in the Commons of March 1914 that the temporary exclusion of Ulster then being offered amounted to no more than 'a stay of execution for six years' was instantly undermined by his allowance that, as the Liberals had now admitted 'the principle of exclusion', the whole business could 'be worked out by negotiation'. If ever there was a case of the subtext demolishing the text, this was it, as Carson's tortuous efforts four weeks later to explain what he had said clearly show.[78]

Unionism's loud attachment to Ireland's constitutional integration made Bonar Law more cautious in public than in private, though countervailing pressure was created by the electorate's disenchantment with the whole long-winded business in general. 'They are', he told a supporter in October 1913, 'so sick of the whole Irish question that they would vote in favour of trying an experiment so long as the Ulster difficulty was solved.'[79] Many years later Lord Crewe (who had been Irish viceroy in the 1890s) recalled telling Lord

---

[75] Carson to Bonar Law, 20 September 1913, PA Bonar Law Papers 30/2/15; Bonar Law to Lord Stamfordham, 1 October 1913, ibid. 33/5/64.

[76] Carson to Lansdowne, 9 October 1913, PA Bonar Law Papers 30/3/23; Lansdowne to Carson, 11 October 1913, ibid.

[77] A. J. Ward, 'Frewen's Anglo-American Campaign for Federalism, 1910–21', *Irish Historical Studies*, 15 (1967), 272.

[78] Parl. Deb. 5 (Commons): lix: 933–6 (9 March 1914) and lx. 1677 (6 April 1914).

[79] Bonar Law to J. P. Croal, 18 October 1913, PA Bonar Law Papers 33/6/84; D. G. Boyce, *Englishmen and Irish Troubles: British Public Opinion and the Making of Irish Policy 1918–22* (London, 1972), 108. What popular feeling there was in Britain was more on behalf of Ulster than of Irish Unionism in general: D. M. Jackson, *Popular Opposition to Irish Home Rule in Edwardian Britain* (Liverpool, 2009), *passim*.

Randolph Churchill that getting too closely tied up with Ulster would turn British politicians into servants rather than masters. Churchill had replied that they could then ' "tell Ulster to go to the devil" ' and I said "That is exactly what you will never be able to do" '.[80]

Of course the policies of governments had always, sometimes closely sometimes casually, reacted to events in Ireland itself. In these years this was unusually important, as feelings on all sides in Ireland grew ever more violent and extreme. Four months after the mass signing of the Solemn League and Covenant in September 1913 an Ulster Volunteer Force came into being. Carson announced that a provincial Ulster government would be set up if Home Rule came into effect and the standing committee of the Ulster Unionist Council constituted itself the 'Central Authority for the Provisional Government'. In November 1913 the Irish Volunteers were formed in Dublin as a nationalist response. And, if such developments gave forth a distinctly quasi-legal air, then the refusal in March 1914 of army officers to enforce Home Rule if required to do so—the so-called Curragh Mutiny—was an even more dubious episode in that regard, though it certainly achieved its objective of pushing any plans for the forcible coercion of Ulster Unionism entirely off the agenda—a crucial development so far as all the relevant parties were concerned. Indeed, only five weeks after the 'mutiny', guns were being brought into various Northern ports for the Ulster Volunteers, while in July 1914 far smaller numbers were imported by the Irish Volunteers at Howth in County Dublin.

In the meantime, Unionist leaders in Britain found themselves more and more in the situation Crewe had outlined in 1893. Balfour for one now realized that a growing number of Liberal ministers had become ready to settle on exclusion, though he worried that Ulster's tactics would 'find Nationalist imitators in Munster and Connaught', while Austen Chamberlain, though still having doubts, was delivering himself of mysterious statements to the effect that 'the Union to me is sacred ... but the Act of Union is not quite the same thing'.

'If Asquith', he noted in November 1913, 'chose (and he may choose) simply to exclude Ulster, we should be done' and 'a great body of English and Scottish opinion would turn against us'.[81] What the majority of Unionist leaders in Britain had come to realize was that, one way or another, exclusion meant Home Rule. Even men like Curzon, a proponent of strong resistance, had become convinced that the imminence of 'civil war in Ireland' rendered exclusion the only practical solution available.[82]

---

[80] Boyce, *Englishmen and Irish Troubles*, 167.

[81] Balfour to Bonar Law, 23 September 1913, PA Bonar Law Papers 30/2/20; A. Chamberlain to Willoughby de Broke, 23 November 1913, PA Willoughby de Broke Papers 6/9.

[82] Parl. Deb. 5 (Lords): xv. 204 (12 February 1914) and xvi. 748 (6 July 1914: both Curzon); Parl. Deb. 5 (Commons): lviii. 151 (10 February 1914: Chamberlain), 274 (11 February 1914: Bonar Law), lx. 1387 (2 April 1914: Balfour); *The Times*, 19 February 1914 (Balfour).

Apart from the complete irreconcilables, a few somewhat less extreme figures such as Lansdowne and Long still held out for a settlement short of Home Rule, in part because they had not yet accepted that the necessity of exclusion could no longer be ignored. Both men were particularly concerned that exclusion would inevitably mean that Unionists outside the North-East would (as Bonar Law had privately admitted) be thrown to the wolves and both were still in a position to cause trouble within the party as a whole.[83]

One chimera that had been, and to some extent continued to be, seen by some Unionists as offering an acceptable way out of their dilemma was federalism, the idea that Irish devolution could somehow be configured within a larger constitutional system for the United Kingdom as a whole. But, while this had obvious attractions, its manifest implausibility rendered it no more than fanciful to all those who could see that theoretical perfections could never straighten the crooked realities with which they were faced. As Lansdowne put it in 1913, to talk 'glibly' and in the 'abstract' about 'the adoption of the federal principle' was one thing, to make it practical or acceptable was something else altogether.[84] In the end, all that 'federalism' actually achieved was to delay the acceptance of any kind of Home Rule by those like Long whose attachment to Southern Unionism was especially strong.

And, just as Unionists were edging ever closer to Home Rule plus exclusion, so too were Liberals, though typically Asquith proved both ill informed and ill disposed to decisiveness.[85] Unionist leaders had, however, become convinced by late 1913 that the prime minister was moving in the same direction as themselves and that other Liberals such as Churchill, Lloyd George, and Grey were leading the way.[86] At a cabinet meeting in November 1913 ministers discussed various ideas and came to the view that at least some kind of temporary exclusion for (an unspecified) Ulster—perhaps for five or six years—would be a plan worth pursuing with both the Irish Parliamentary Party and the Unionist opposition. This, as Ronan Fanning, has rightly said, 'marked an irreversible step towards partition'.[87]

---

[83] Parl. Deb. 5 (Lords), xv. 70 (11 February 1914), xvi. 391 (23 June 1914), xvi. 538 (1 July 1914: all Lansdowne); Long to Lord R. Cecil, 6 February 1914, BL Cecil of Chelwood Papers Add. MS 51072; Parl. Deb. 5 (Commons): lx. 1043 (31 March 1914: Long).

[84] Lansdowne to Chamberlain, 31 October 1913, BU A. Chamberlain Papers AC11/1/47. See J. Kendle, *Ireland and the Federal Solution: The Debate over the United Kingdom Constitution, 1870–1912* (Kingston and Montreal, 1989).

[85] He thought that Fermanagh and Tyrone had Protestant majorities, whereas their Catholic proportions were (in 1911) 56.2% and 55.4% respectively: Laffan, *The Partition of Ireland*, 36–7.

[86] Balfour to Bonar Law, 23 September 1913, PA Bonar Law Papers 30/2/20; Smith to Lloyd George, 26 September 1913, PA Lloyd George Papers C/3/7/1; Memorandum by Salisbury, 26 October 1913, BL Cecil of Chelwood Papers Add. MS 51085; Chamberlain to Bonar Law, 2 December [1913], PA Bonar Law Papers 31/1/3; B. B. Gilbert, *David Lloyd George: A Political Life*, 2 vols (London, 1987–92), ii. 96; Fanning, *Fatal Path*, 84.

[87] Asquith to George V, 14 and 26 November 1913, TNA CAB 41/34/34 and 36; Fanning, *Fatal Path*, 90.

It also marked the beginning of that long calvary of compromise that Redmond, still blindly minimizing the force of opposition to Home Rule in Protestant Ulster, seems unable to have prevented himself from walking in the months and years to come.[88] Indeed, developments in late February and early March 1914 illustrate 'with a brutal clarity the comparative insignificance of the Irish [Parliamentary Party] as an influence over what was ostensibly their own Home Rule measure'. Within a few days Redmond conceded, first, exclusion (to be voted on by individual counties) for three years, then for five years, and then (on 6 March) for six years.[89] Whatever else this gave the impression of, it was not consistency or impressive musculature on the part of constitutional nationalism. Few doubted that in due course the word 'temporary' would disappear, a development that was left to hang in the air when Home Rule was eventually enacted in September 1914 and then suspended for the duration of the war.

VI

Both the war and the outbreak in 1916 of the Easter Rising constituted unexpected and complicating factors regarding British government in and of Ireland. The first forced greater global matters on ministerial attention and thus postponed an Irish settlement. The second aborted the arrangements put together in 1914, and, though eventually producing a state of things that greatly extended the constitutional concessions offered by London, did not affect the *direction* of travel that had been pursued, admittedly with fluctuating enthusiasm, since 1910, since 1893, since 1886, perhaps even since 1870. It also did not fundamentally alter or replace the device by which Home Rule/ Independence was rendered possible—namely, partition. In other words, the ultimate effects of 1916 and the subsequent Anglo-Irish conflict of 1919–21 were confined to shaping the precise character of the constitutional settlement. They had little effect upon the general principle of disengagement or, as it turned out, upon matters geographical.

The First World War also allowed the prime minster to do what he liked best—both about Ireland and more generally—and this was to do as little as

---

[88] Redmond to Asquith, 24 November 1913, NLI Redmond Papers MS 15165; J. McConnel, *The Irish Parliamentary Party and the Third Home Rule Crisis* (Dublin, 2013), 276. Later Redmond was to dismiss Sinn Féin's importance just as he had dismissed Ulster's: *Inside Asquith's Cabinet: From the Diaries of Charles Hobhouse*, ed. E. David (London, 1977), 220. D. Meleady (in *John Redmond: The National Leader*, 202–95) takes a different view, arguing— and not without effect—that Redmond was in fact trying to play a comparatively skilful hand until overwhelmed by the slow and inexorable realization that partition was becoming inevitable.

[89] A. Jackson, *Ireland 1798–1998: Politics and War* (Oxford, 1999), 166; Fanning, *Fatal Path*, 102–4.

possible. At the same time it increased rather than reduced the fissures within Irish society as a whole, something Redmond's dramatic support for the allied cause did little to temper or diminish. The voluntary organizations that sprang up in Ireland in response to the war were, from the first, entirely divided along politico-denominational lines, with a deep sense of separation permeating bodies such as the largely Unionist Ulster Gift Fund, on the one side, and the Irish Women's Association, on the other. Thus, while the forces supporting the war were effectively partitioned, those opposing it were, in their more extreme versions of nationalism, broadly united. And, while Ireland had in many ways been 'partitioned' for a century or more, the psychological effect of this pre-existing state of things was greatly exacerbated by the impact of and the reactions to the unfolding military and civil events of 1914–18.[90]

While Redmond had been effectively—indeed brutally—sidelined in 1914, normal party political service continued almost as if consulting the leaders of the Irish Party about unimportant matters could somehow compensate for more substantial humiliations.[91] Although official reactions to the Rising that broke out on 24 April 1916 reveal a distinct sense of surprise, Birrell had actually been 'watching affairs' and receiving regular reports on possible unrest in the months before, while a cabinet minister touring Ireland in February and taken aback by obvious discontents had concluded 'that we are not only wrong but on dangerous lines in treating Ireland as analogous to a series of English counties or even Scotland'.[92]

In the short term the most striking result of the Rising and the execution of some of its leaders was not the increasingly sympathetic reaction among Irish nationalists (however important that was eventually to prove) but the manner in which it galvanized the government—and even the lethargic Asquith—into mounting a speedy attempt to bring the settlement of 1914 back to life. Asquith himself came to Ireland, denounced its local administration as 'practically derelict' and a 'costly and futile anachronism', saw to it that the chief secretary (Birrell), the undersecretary (Nathan), and the viceroy (Wimborne) all resigned, and then, within a matter of weeks, characteristically allowed the utterly useless Wimborne to slide back into his post.[93]

---

[90] S. Pašeta, 'Women and War in Ireland, 1914–18', *History Ireland*, 22/4 (2014), 24–7, which gives other examples; Hennessy, *Dividing Ireland*, 235–6.

[91] Wimborne to Redmond, 9 January 1915, NLI Redmond Papers MS 15232; Memorandum by Matthew Nathan (undersecretary) for Birrell, 24 March 1915, Nathan to Birrell, 16 June 1915 and 24 October [1915], all Bodl. Birrell Papers Dep.c.299.

[92] Birrell to Midleton, 25 February 1916, TNA Midleton Papers PRO 30/67/31; E. Montagu to Sir T. Heath, 7 February 1916, T[rinity] C[ollege] C[ambridge] Montagu Papers AS1/8/18.

[93] Confidential Prints of 19 and 21 May 1916, PA Bonar Law Papers 63/C/5; *Royal Commission on the Rebellion in Ireland, Report of Commission*, HC 1916 [Cd 8279], xi. 174. For perceptive comments on Wimborne as 'the Emperor of the Asses', see Lady Cynthia Asquith, *Diaries 1915–1918* (London, 1968), 126, 128, 163, 223. Sensible women never remained alone with him.

The most sharp-witted thing that Asquith did was to appoint Lloyd George to negotiate with the various Irish parties in the hope that some mutually acceptable settlement might yet be agreed. Lloyd George, in a dazzling display of verbal conjuring, almost succeeded. Redmond moved further towards accepting six-county exclusion and obtained reluctant endorsement for this from Northern nationalists. The issue of exclusion's time frame was fudged by Lloyd George, something that might well have brought renewed stalemate later had negotiations not foundered on the bitter opposition of Southern Unionist sympathizers within a cabinet that had been reconstituted in May 1915 as a coalition administration consisting of Unionist and Labour members as well as Liberals. Long, who had bayed for blood immediately after the Rising, denounced Lloyd George's plan from the start, but—in a spirit of simultaneously wishing for two contradictory things (something all too prevalent at the time)—claimed also to have accepted that the status quo had become unsustainable.[94] He rightly suspected that both Balfour and Bonar Law were 'soft' on Home Rule: 'the former has long ago forgotten all his experiences in Ireland and of recent years has not kept in touch with Irish affairs, and the latter has no actual knowledge of the country'.[95]

Given that Lloyd George's scheme was, indeed, backed both by Liberal ministers and by Unionists such as Balfour, Bonar Law, and Worthington-Evans, as well as by Carson and his Ulster lieutenant James Craig,[96] the whole business seemed cut and dried until the as-yet undead corpse of Southern Unionism, like the legs of some deceased frog agitated by galvanic electricity, jerked into such effective action that everything came to a sudden halt. Three cabinet ministers—Selborne, Lansdowne, and Long—threatened to resign. Others lined up behind them.[97] In the event only Selborne resigned. But it was Lansdowne's intransigent speech to the House of Lords painting the proposal in the worst possible light that finally persuaded Redmond that his own initial assent must be withdrawn.[98] Even in the short term Lansdowne's intervention proved a classic case of shooting oneself in the foot. It soon

---

[94] Long to Asquith, 27 April and 24 May 1916, W[iltshire and Swindon] R[ecord] O[ffice] Long Papers 947/9/144; Long's Memorandum for cabinet, 15 June 1916, Bodl. Selborne Papers 80/185; Long to G. Stewart, 30 July 1916, WRO Long Papers 947/9/362.

[95] Long to Lansdowne, 3 June 1916, WRO Long Papers 947/9/268.

[96] 'The Irish Settlement Meeting of the Unionist Party, 7 July 1916', ed. D. McMahon, Irish Manuscripts Commission: *Analecta Hibernica*, 41 (2009) 201–70.

[97] See, e.g., Lansdowne's Memorandum of 2 June 1916, BL 5th Marquess of Lansdowne Papers 'Ireland X' (provisional reference); Parl. Deb. 5 (Lords): xii. 387–9 (16 June 1916: Selborne); Selborne's Memorandum of 30 June 1916, Bodl. Selborne Papers 80/226; Lord R. Cecil's Memoranda of 30 June and 15 July 1916, WRO Long Papers 947/9/179; Memorandum by Salisbury of 13 June 1916, BU A. Chamberlain Papers AC14/5/15; Lloyd George to Carson, 3 June 1916, PRONI Carson Papers D1507/A/17/7.

[98] Parl. Deb. 5 (Lords): xxii. 645–52 (11 July 1916). See D. W. Savage, 'The Attempted Home Rule Settlement of 1916', *Éire-Ireland*, 2 (1967), 132–45.

became clear that it was not the unambiguously 'Irish' Southern Unionists who had found the strength to derail Lloyd George's plan, but their British or (like Lansdowne) Anglo-Irish allies. They themselves emerged, even more clearly than before, as distinctly toothless characters dependent upon supporters whose constancy—as later became clear—was anything but reliable. Lloyd George and Carson joined Redmond in extreme disgruntlement over Asquith's feebleness and the ability of the Southern Unionists to mount this last and self-defeating Hurrah.[99] Lloyd George thought his failure would stoke up 'incalculable' trouble in the long run and wondered at the foolishness of men like Long—'with such pretensions of being an English gentleman'— actively working to undermine Carson's influence in Ulster.[100]

The only positive thing that emerged from the debacle was precisely the thing that both Southern Unionists and the Parliamentary Party most feared— namely, the entrenchment of partition as the key to almost everything.[101] By the end of 1916 Lloyd George was prime minister and faced with immediate military problems so great that little time was left for grappling with Irish issues. In May 1917 he offered a quick bill for the immediate application of the Home Rule Act with temporary exclusion for Ulster. When this predictably failed to satisfy everyone, he set up a 'Convention of Irishmen of all parties for the purpose of producing a scheme of Irish self-government', which then met from 25 July 1917 to 5 April 1918 and counted, from his point of view, as a useful tool for kicking the whole troublesome business into the long grass. The most powerful and united group in the Convention, the Ulster Unionists, proved stonily intransigent in their attachment to partition; the least powerful, the Southern Unionists (now left by their British allies to their own feeble resources), proved amenable just as such an approach was no longer useful currency. The delegates from Redmond's party could not agree even among themselves and split in January 1918, while Sinn Féin boycotted an enterprise that, despite or perhaps because of its long-winded wordiness, never really succeeded in moving much beyond the land of posturing make-believe.[102]

---

[99] C. Addison [then a Liberal junior minister and later in the cabinet], *Four and a Half Years; A Personal Diary from June 1914 to January 1919*, 2 vols (London, 1934), i. 212 (22 May 1916) and i. 234 (23 July 1916); J. D. Fair, *British Interparty Conferences: A Study of the Procedure of Conciliation in British Politics, 1867–1921* (Oxford, 1980), 133–4.

[100] Lloyd George to Dillon, 10 and 20 June 1916, PA Lloyd George Papers D/14/2/24 and D/14/3/22; to Asquith, 10 June 1916, ibid., D/14/2/22: 'Sinn Feinism is for the moment right on top.'

[101] 'The Irish Settlement Meeting of the Unionist Party', ed. McMahon, 208–9; Mansergh, *The Unresolved Question*, 95.

[102] Parl. Deb. 5 (Commons): xciii. 1995–6 (21 May 1917: Lloyd George); Londonderry to his Mother, 23 September 1917, Du[rham] R[ecord] O[ffice] Londonderry Papers D/Lo/C682; T. West, *Horace Plunkett: Co-Operation and Politics: An Irish Biography* (Gerrards Cross, 1986), 161–4, 174; Memorandum by H. E. Duke (chief secretary), 27 September 1917, TNA CAB 24/27 GT 2137; Lloyd George to H. Barrie (a delegate), 21 February 1918, PA Bonar Law Papers 85/B/11; and generally R. B. McDowell, *The Irish Convention, 1917–18* (London, 1970).

With the effective collapse of the Convention, Lloyd George, never one to stick to failing tactics when in pursuit of long-term strategies, realized that it would be sensible to get men like Long (who was by now beginning to see how the partitionist wind was blowing[103]) on his side, with the result that from April 1918 Long headed a succession of committees given the task of producing the outlines of a viable Anglo-Irish settlement. These committees included a variety of other ministers such as Curzon, Barnes, Addison, Fisher, Duke, Balfour, and Chamberlain, and, in their final incarnation, were instrumental in drawing up the Government of Ireland Bill passed into law in December 1920. With the committees labouring away in a context of dramatic political and military developments in Ireland itself, their deliberations took on an air of nitpicking unreality. Redmond had died in March 1918, and the general election held at the end of that year had reduced his party to a rump of six MPs. Sinn Féin returned seventy-three (who refused to take their seats at Westminster) and Unionists of various kinds the rest. A month later the ambush at Soloheadbeg in County Tipperary marked what is usually regarded as the opening of the increasingly violent Anglo-Irish War that lasted until the truce of July 1921. Long's committees, though clearly aware of all this, proved slow to adapt to such dramatically changing circumstances, not least because of the views of Long himself, ever keen to examine impractical plans before eventually realizing that a new and to him unappealing world was in process of being born. Already before Soloheadbeg repeated calls had been issued that, before all else, the Irish administration 'should restore respect for government, enforce the law, and above all, put down with a stern hand the Irish–German conspiracy which appears to be widespread in Ireland'. Long, in full Panglossian mode, told the prime minister that in six months he himself could see to it that Ireland would become 'quiet' and thirsty for whatever measure of self-government Britain felt inclined to concede.[104]

What is, however, most significant about the deliberations of Long's committees (effectively Lloyd George's subcontractors for Irish affairs) is how, after considering almost every alternative—federalism, ideas for an overarching 'council' that would somehow staple together a country that seemed to be falling apart, something amounting to British withdrawal from Ireland's domestic affairs so that 'all Irishmen' could see themselves as 'self-governing'—the only plan that survived involved a recognition that some kind of Home Rule facilitated by some kind of partition was now unavoidable.[105] If certain committee members still hoped to postpone the evil day of

[103] R. Murphy, 'Walter Long and the Making of the Government of Ireland Act, 1919–20', *Irish Historical Studies*, 25 (1986), 82–96.

[104] Memorandum of 9 May 1918, PA Bonar Law Papers 83/3/21; Long to Lloyd George, 9 March 1918, PA Lloyd George Papers F/32/5/10.

[105] Long to Lloyd George, 18 April 1918, PA Lloyd George Papers F/36/5/23; D. G. Boyce and J. O. Stubbs, 'F. S. Oliver, Lord Selborne and Federalism', *Journal of Imperial and Commonwealth*

partition for as long as possible, others, notably Balfour, hoped for the opposite on the old grounds that Ireland had never been a single political entity in the first place.[106] And, while some had initially distrusted their chairman's seriousness about finding a viable solution, Long's increasing annoyance at the way in which Southern Unionists kept 'crying for the moon, and appealing to us here to protect them' persuaded even him that partition had become the only realistic game in town.[107]

VII

As violence increased in Ireland throughout 1919, 1920, and early 1921 with the government oscillating uncertainly amid plans for harsh measures, martial law (which no one really understood), and deliberate reprisals,[108] and with the whole matter of partition assuming more and more prominence in official circles, the thinking of the new Sinn Féin militants continued to linger in that oblivion of unknowing that notions of a divided Ireland had long occupied among nationalists of all colours from O'Connell onwards. Because for them Ireland simply *was* a nation, there was no more to be said or analysed or kept in the forefront of political consciousness. As, on the one hand, reality began to dawn even upon those British minds hitherto happy to switch off the here-and-now—Salisbury's and Selborne's are good examples—so, on the other, de Valera and his lieutenants seem to have been prepared, even willing, to park the possibility of Ulster exclusion into some distant and unregarded mental area labelled 'Independence will Make all Problems Disappear', where it could rest without disturbing the purity of republican certainties.[109]

The idea of partition and its centrality to any possible settlement had, however, by now not only entered the soul of British politics; it had also

History, 5 (1976), 72; J. Kendle, *Walter Long, Ireland, and the Union, 1905–1920* (Dublin, 1992), 132–71; Long Committee Report, 4 November 1919, Bodl. Worthington-Evans Papers MS Eng. hist.c.901; Cabinet Minutes, 3 December 1919, TNA CAB 23/18.

[106] Balfour, 'The Irish Question', 25 November 1919, TNA CAB 24/93; also R. Fanning, 'Britain, Ireland and the End of the Union', in *Ireland after the Union: Proceedings of the Second Joint Meeting of the Royal Irish Academy and the British Academy*, introduced by Lord Blake (Oxford, 1989), 105–20; C. B. Shannon, *Arthur J. Balfour and Ireland 1874–1922* (Washington, 1988), 246–8, 251.

[107] Addison, *Four and a Half Years*, ii. 536, 541; Long to French, 8 January 1920, I[mperial] W[ar] M[useum] French Papers JDPF8/3.

[108] C. Townshend, *The British Campaign in Ireland 1919–1921: The Development of Political and Military Policies* (Oxford, 1975), *passim*.

[109] Salisbury to Selborne, 1 March 1920, Bodl. Selborne Papers 7/86; also Parl. Deb. 5 (Lords): xxv. 226–33 (21 May 1917: Lansdowne); Parl. Deb. 5 (Commons): lxvii. 500 (6 July 1919: Cecil); Bowman, *De Valera and the Ulster Question*, 12, 29–75.

become increasingly fashionable internationally. The peace arrangements after the First World War sliced continental Europe into new units along new lines with the precise delineation of boundaries occasionally the product of plebiscites, as happened notably in the mixed German–Polish areas of Allerstein and Marienweder in East Prussia and in Silesia, though German claims (as in the Sudetenland and South Tyrol) were often ignored.[110] And, while long-standing British denials that Ireland was inhabited by a single 'nation' clearly rendered partition available as a potentially useful device for bringing conflict to an end, the unspoken nationalist avoidance of the issue rendered it more useful still.

This is not the place to enter into a detailed account of the Anglo-Irish war of 1919–21, the truce of July 1921, the Treaty of December 1921, and the establishment of two Irish states. But what is clear is that by the time of the truce both the IRA and the British had effectively fought themselves to a standstill. The leaders of the former realized that they could never achieve total success, those of the latter (and Lloyd George and Churchill proved both the fiercest and the least consistent among them) that the investments of money and men required for victory could no longer be generated in the new post-war world. As is well known, even those in Ireland who most strongly opposed the Treaty concentrated, not upon the fact that partition was one of its key provisions, but upon the, to them, inadequate extent to which Irish nation-hood had been recognized. Ulster was, in its new six-county redoubt, more or less ignored during the angry debates that took place in the Dáil once the Treaty had been signed, and the 'concession' made by Lloyd George that there would be a Boundary Commission to propose modifications was seized upon by all sides 'because it offered a way of seeming to do something about partition without actually having to do anything' at all.[111]

While it goes without saying that the importance of the armed conflict of 1919–21 is an undoubted fact, its result was acceleration rather than any change of direction. From 1870 at least both of the main political parties in Britain had rejected the earlier policy of attempting to 'solve' Irish questions by gradually integrating the social, economic, and political characteristics of the smaller island into those of the larger. The fact that for Liberals this came to mean some version of devolution while for Conservatives it meant adopting economic and social policies specifically (and regardless of expense) tailored to Ireland's perceived needs was a difference that only some powerful solvent could fully eradicate. It was partition, with its solidification of the notion that

---

[110] T. G. Fraser, *Partition in Ireland, India and Palestine: Theory and Practice* (London, 1984), 32–3.

[111] T. Bartlett, *Ireland: A History* (Cambridge, 2010), 409. It has been remarked that de Valera's chief objection to the Treaty was that, in its final form, it was 'not *his* compromise' (R. Fanning, *Éamon de Valera: A Will to Power* (London, 2015), 126–7).

Ireland had always been fractured, that eventually provided the solvent required. Of course, there was nothing 'inevitable' about any of this. The actual outcome of 1921–2 was not a *necessary* result of what had gone before. It was, however, both a *logical* and an entirely relevant one.

Though Sinn Féin representatives grew angry and hot during the Dáil debates that led to the Treaty's approval by 64 votes to 57—an outcome that led to a bitter civil war—on the British side (Unionist as well as Liberal) all was relief, with only one voice spoiling the universal sense of demob satisfaction. That was the voice of Carson, who, however much he had been forced to bend to Ulster's intransigence, had never abandoned a belief in the importance of maintaining some strong bond between Britain and Ireland *as a whole*. He now poured out his bitterness in the House of Lords in December 1921.

> All of a sudden they [British Unionists] say that Home Rule is not good enough; you must have the real thing; the country must abandon Ireland at the very heart of the Empire to independence, with an army, with a navy, with separate customs, with ministers at foreign courts, and delegates to the League of Nations ... I was in earnest. What a fool I was. I was only a puppet ... in the political game that was to get the Conservative Party into power.[112]

This outburst was prompted, above all, by Carson's realization of his own failure. 'His beloved Ireland had degenerated into two provincial, illiberal statelets—a process which in truth had been in progress since at least the 1890s and which his rhetoric had served to disguise, especially from himself.'[113]

That it should have been F. E. Smith, now Lord Chancellor of England and once one of Carson's most public (though not always private) supporters, who yielded nothing to good taste in announcing that 'as a constructive effort of statecraft' Carson's speech 'would have been immature upon the lips of a hysterical school-girl' shows how mightily the weather had changed.[114] It was also Smith (now Lord Birkenhead) who, in another speech in the same month, demonstrated how partition had enabled the two main British parties to push their long-maturing coalescence regarding Irish differentiation into something like unanimity. Not only did his sentiments eerily echo those of Gladstone's Commons speech on Home Rule of June 1886, but so closely did his actual words that one might almost think that he had read it. In 1886 the Liberal prime minister had spoken of those 'golden moments of our history—one of those opportunities which may come and may go, but which rarely return, or, if they return, return at long intervals, and under circumstances which no man can forecast'.[115] Birkenhead, one of the signatories of the Treaty and only

---

[112] Parl. Deb. 5 (Lords): xlviii. 39, 44 (14 December 1921).
[113] A. Gailey, 'King Carson: An Essay on the Invention of Leadership', *Irish Historical Studies*, 30 (1996), 84.
[114] Parl. Deb. 5 (Lords): xlviii. 204 (16 December 1921).
[115] Parl. Deb. 3: cccvi. 1237 (7 [*recte* 8] June 1886). See Chapter 8, Section IV.

hours after its signing delivered himself (at a meeting in Birmingham) of much the same convictions—a clear and unvarnished indication of party unity over Ireland and also, more tellingly still, a sign that the long-revolving circle set in motion by the Union of 1800 was now being, if only for a time, successfully squared.

> I believe there has come to us in our day and in our generation one of those supreme opportunities which come once and once only ... Do not believe that ever again can things be quite the same ... Never tell me that the old Irish difficulty, as our ancestors and our grandparents knew it, can be the same ... In the days that lie in front of us, we have made up our minds to the policy, and we intend at all hazards to play the hand out.[116]

If throughout Ireland similar hands continued to be played with restless vigour, for those in Britain whose forerunners had been charged in 1800 with governing Hibernia the playing, in anything like the old style, had come to a halt—only to start once again for politicians with no relevant experience in very different circumstances half a century or so later.

[116] *The Times*, 7 December 1921.

List of Manuscript Sources

Abbot Papers: Papers of Charles Abbot, 1st Baron Colchester: The National Archives, Kew

Abercorn Papers: Papers of James Hamilton, 1st Duke of Abercorn: Public Record Office of Northern Ireland, Belfast

Aberdeen Papers: Papers of George Hamilton-Gordon, 4th Earl of Aberdeen: British Library, London

Addington, Henry, 1st Viscount Sidmouth: see *Sidmouth Papers*

Anglesey Papers: Papers of Henry William Paget, 1st Marquess of Anglesey: Public Record Office of Northern Ireland, Belfast

Ashbourne Papers: Papers of Edward Gibson, 1st Baron Ashbourne: Parliamentary Archives, Westminster

Auckland, William Eden, 1st Baron: see *Sneyd Papers*

Balfour Papers: 1. Papers of Arthur James Balfour, 1st Earl of Balfour, British Library, London; 2. Papers of Arthur James Balfour and Gerald William Balfour, 2nd Earl of Balfour: The National Archives, Kew

Bedford Papers: Papers of John Russell, 6th Duke of Bedford: Woburn Abbey, Bedfordshire

Bessborough Papers: Papers of John William Ponsonby, 4th Earl of Bessborough *and* Frederick George Brabazon Ponsonby, 6th Earl of Bessborough: via West Sussex Record Office, Chichester

Birrell Papers: Papers of Augustine Birrell: Bodleian Library, Oxford

Bonar Law, Andrew: see *Law, Bonar Papers*

Broughton Papers: Papers of John Cam Hobhouse, 1st Baron Broughton: British Library, London

Bryce Papers: Papers of James Bryce, 1st Viscount Bryce: Bodleian Library, Oxford *and* National Library of Ireland, Dublin

Butt Papers: Papers of Isaac Butt: National Library of Ireland, Dublin

Cabinet Papers: CAB 23: Cabinet Minutes 1916–39; CAB 24 Cabinet Memoranda 1916–39; CAB 37 Papers printed for Cabinet 1880–1916; CAB 41 Letters from Prime Ministers to Monarchs: The National Archives, Kew

Cadogan Papers: Papers of George Henry Cadogan, 5th Earl Cadogan: Parliamentary Archives, Westminster

Cairns Papers: Papers of Hugh McCalmont Cairns, 1st Earl Cairns: The National Archives, Kew

Camden Papers: Papers of John Jeffreys Pratt, 2nd Earl Camden: Centre for Kentish Studies, Maidstone *and* Trinity College Dublin

Campbell-Bannerman Papers: Papers of Sir Henry Campbell-Bannerman: British Library, London

Canning Papers: Papers of George Canning: British Library, London

Carew Papers: Papers of Robert Shapland Carew, 1st Baron Carew: Trinity College Dublin

Carlingford Diaries: Diaries of Chichester Samuel Fortescue, 1st Baron Carlingford: British Library, London

Carlingford Papers: Papers of Chichester Samuel Fortescue, 1st Baron Carlingford: Somerset Record Office, Taunton

Carlisle Papers: Papers of George William Frederick Howard, 7th Earl of Carlisle: Castle Howard, Yorkshire

Carnarvon Papers: Papers of Henry Howard Molyneux Herbert, 4th Earl of Carnarvon: The National Archives, Kew *and* British Library, London

Carson Papers: Papers of Sir Edward Henry Carson, Baron Carson: Public Record Office of Northern Ireland, Belfast

Castlereagh Papers: Papers of Robert Stewart, Viscount Castlereagh (and 2nd Marquess of Londonderry): Public Record Office of Northern Ireland, Belfast

Cecil of Chelwood Papers: Papers of Edgar Algernon Robert Gascoyne-Cecil, 1st Viscount Cecil of Chelwood: British Library, London

A[usten] Chamberlain Papers: Papers of Austen Chamberlain: Birmingham University (Cadbury Research Library)

J[oseph] Chamberlain Papers: Papers of Joseph Chamberlain: Birmingham University (Cadbury Research Library)

Churchill (Lord Randolph) Papers: Papers of Lord Randolph Churchill: Cambridge University Library

Churchill Papers: Papers of Sir Winston Leonard Spencer-Churchill: Churchill College Cambridge

Clarendon Papers: Papers of George William Frederick Villiers, 4th Earl of Clarendon: Bodleian Library, Oxford

Cranbrook Papers: Papers of Gathorne Gathorne-Hardy, 1st Viscount Cranbrook: Suffolk Record Office, Ipswich

Crewe Papers: Papers of Robert Offley Ashburton Crewe-Milnes, 1st Marquess of Crewe: Cambridge University Library

Derby Papers: Papers of Edward George Geoffrey Stanley, 14th Earl of Derby: Liverpool Record Office

Devonshire Papers: Papers of Spencer Compton Cavendish, Lord Hartington (and 8th Duke of Devonshire): Chatsworth House, Derbyshire

Dilke Papers: Papers of Sir Charles Wentworth Dilke: British Library, London

Disraeli Papers: Papers of Benjamin Disraeli, Earl of Beaconsfield: Bodleian Library, Oxford

Downshire Papers: Papers of Arthur Blundell Sandys Trumbull Hill, 3rd Marquess of Downshire: Public Record Office of Northern Ireland, Belfast

Duke Papers: Papers of Henry Edward Duke, 1st Baron Merivale: Bodleian Library, Oxford

Eglinton Papers: Papers of Archibald William Montgomerie, 13th Earl of Eglinton: Scottish Record Office, Edinburgh

Elliot of Wells Papers: Papers of William Elliot: National Library of Scotland, Edinburgh

Fortescue Papers: Papers of Hugh Fortescue, 2nd Earl Fortescue: Devon Record Office, Exeter

Foster Papers: Papers of John Leslie Foster: Royal Irish Academy, Dublin

French Papers: Papers of John Denton Pinkstone French, 1st Earl of Ypres: Imperial War Museum, London

George, Lloyd Papers: Papers of David Lloyd George, 1st Earl Lloyd George of Dwyfor: Parliamentary Archives, Westminster

Gladstone Papers: Papers of William Ewart Gladstone: British Library, London

Gladstone (Herbert) Papers: Papers of Herbert Gladstone, 1st Viscount Gladstone: British Library, London

Goschen Papers: Papers of George Joachim Goschen, 1st Viscount Goschen: Bodleian Library, Oxford

Goulburn Papers: Papers of Henry Goulburn: Surrey History Centre, Woking

Graham Papers: Papers of Sir James Graham: British Library, London. These are widely available on microfilm produced when at the Cumbria Record Office. References are as on the films, not least because some items have since been lost.

Granville Papers: Papers of Granville George Leveson-Gower, 2nd Earl Granville: The National Archives, Kew

Grey Papers: Papers of Charles Grey, 2nd Earl Grey: Durham University

Haldane Papers: Papers of Richard Burdon Haldane, 1st Viscout Haldane: National Library of Scotland, Edinburgh

Halifax, Charles Wood, 1st Viscount: see *Hickleton Papers*

Halsbury Papers: Papers of Hardinge Stanley Giffard, 1st Earl of Halsbury: British Library, London

Harcourt Papers: Papers of Sir William George Granville Venables Vernon Harcourt: Bodleian Library, Oxford

Hardinge Papers: Papers of Henry Hardinge, 1st Viscount Hardinge: McGill University, Montreal

Hardwicke Papers: Papers of Philip Yorke, 3rd Earl of Hardwicke: British Library, London

Hartington, Spencer Compton Cavendish, Lord: see *Devonshire Papers*

Hatherton Papers: Papers of Edward John Littleton, 1st Baron Hatherton: Staffordshire Record Office, Stafford

Hickleton Papers: Papers of Charles Wood, 1st Viscount Halifax: Borthwick Institute, York

Home Office Papers: Irish Series HO 100: The National Archives, Kew

Howick Letters: Letters of Henry George Grey, Viscount Howick and 3rd Earl Grey: National Library of Ireland, Dublin

Kimberley Papers: Papers of John Wodehouse, 1st Earl of Kimberley: Bodleian Library, Oxford

Lansdowne Papers (3rd Marquess): Papers of Henry Petty-Fitzmaurice, 3rd Marquess of Lansdowne: British Library, London

Lansdowne Papers (5th Marquess): Papers of Henry Charles Keith Petty-Fitzmaurice, 5th Marquess of Lansdowne: British Library, London

Larcom Papers: Papers of Sir Thomas Larcom: National Library of Ireland, Dublin

Law, Bonar Papers: Papers of Andrew Bonar Law: Parliamentary Archives, Westminster

Leveson-Gower Letter Books: Letter Books of Lord Francis Leveson-Gower, 1st Earl of Ellesmere: National Archives of Ireland, Dublin

Liverpool Papers: Papers of Robert Banks Jenkinson, 2nd Earl of Liverpool: British Library, London

Lloyd George, David, 1st Earl Lloyd George of Dwyfor: see *George, Lloyd Papers*

Londonderry Papers: Papers of Charles Stewart Vane-Tempest-Stewart, 6th Marquess of Londonderry: Public Record Office of Northern Ireland, Belfast *and* Durham Record Office, Durham

Long Papers: Papers of Walter Hume Long, 1st Viscount Long: Wiltshire and Swindon Record Office, Chippenham *and* British Library, London

MacDonnell Papers: Papers of Sir Antony Patrick MacDonnell: Bodleian Library, Oxford

Marlborough Papers: Papers of John Winston Spencer-Churchill, 7th Duke of Marlborough: Cambridge University Library

Mayo Papers: Papers of Richard Southwell Bourke, 6th Earl of Mayo: National Library of Ireland, Dublin

Melbourne Papers: Papers of William Lamb, 2nd Viscount Melbourne: Royal Archives, Windsor (widely available on microfilm) *and* Southampton University

Midleton Papers: Papers of William St John Fremantle Brodrick, 1st Earl of Midleton: The National Archives, Kew

Mitford Papers: Papers of John Mitford, 1st Baron Redesdale: Gloucestershire Record Office, Gloucester

Montagu Papers: Papers of Edwin Samuel Montagu: Trinity College Cambridge

Monteagle Papers: Papers of Thomas Spring Rice, 1st Baron Monteagle: National Library of Ireland, Dublin

Morley Papers: Papers of John Morley, Viscount Morley of Blackburn: Bodleian Library, Oxford

Mulgrave Papers: Papers of Constantine Henry Phipps, 1st Marquess of Normanby: Mulgrave Castle, Yorkshire

Mundella Papers: Papers of Anthony John Mundella: Sheffield University

Normanby, Constantine Henry Phipps, 1st Marquess of: see *Mulgrave Papers*

Northcote Papers: Papers of Stafford Henry Northcote, 1st Earl of Iddesleigh: British Library, London

Northumberland Papers: Papers of Hugh Percy, 3rd Duke of Northumberland: Alnwick Castle, Northumberland

Palmerston Papers: Papers of Henry John Temple, 3rd Viscount Palmerston: Southampton University *and* British Library, London

Peel Papers: Papers of Sir Robert Peel: British Library, London

Pelham Papers: Papers of Thomas Pelham, 2nd Earl of Chichester: British Library, London

Perceval Papers: Papers of Spencer Perceval: British Library, London

Pitt Papers: Papers of William Pitt: The National Archives, Kew

Pitt (Pretyman) Papers: Papers of William Pitt collected by his secretary, G. Pretyman Tomline: Cambridge University Library

Redesdale, John Mitford, 1st Baron: see *Mitford Papers*

Redmond Papers: Papers of John Redmond: National Library of Ireland, Dublin

Richmond Papers (4th Duke): Papers of Charles Lennox, 4th Duke of Richmond: National Library of Ireland, Dublin

Richmond Papers (6th Duke): Papers of Charles Henry Gordon-Lennox, 6th Duke of Richmond: West Sussex Record Office, Chichester

Ripon Papers: Papers of George Frederick Samuel Robinson, 1st Marquess of Ripon: British Library, London

Rosebery Papers: Papers of Archibald Philip Primrose, 5th Earl of Rosebery: National Library of Scotland, Edinburgh

Russell Papers: Papers of Lord John Russell, 1st Earl Russell: The National Archives, Kew

St Aldwyn Papers: Papers of Sir Michael Edward Hicks Beach, 1st Earl St Aldwyn: Gloucestershire Record Office, Gloucester

Salisbury Papers: Papers of Robert Arthur Talbot Gascoyne-Cecil, 3rd Marquess of Salisbury: Hatfield House, Hertfordshire

Sandars Papers: Papers of John Satterfield Sandars (A. J. Balfour's private secretary 1891–1915): Bodleian Library, Oxford

Selborne Papers: Papers of William Waldegrave Palmer, 2nd Earl of Selborne: Bodleian Library, Oxford

Sidmouth Papers: Papers of Henry Addington, 1st Viscount Sidmouth: Devon Record Office, Exeter

Smith (Hambledon) Papers: Papers of William Henry Smith: Reading University

Sneyd Papers: Papers of William Eden, 1st Baron Auckland: Public Record Office of Northern Ireland, Belfast (copies)

Somerville Letter-Book: Letter-Book of Sir William Meredyth Somerville, 1st Baron Meredyth: National Library of Ireland, Dublin

Spencer Papers: Papers of John Poyntz Spencer, 5th Earl Spencer: British Library, London

Talbot Papers: Papers of Charles Chetwynd Talbot, 2nd Earl Talbot: Public Record Office of Northern Ireland, Belfast *and* Staffordshire Record Office, Stafford

Trevelyan Papers: Papers of Sir Charles Edward Trevelyan: Newcastle University

Vansittart Papers: Papers of Nicholas Vansittart: British Library, London

Victoria, Queen, Correspondence: Royal Archives, Windsor

Wellesley Papers: Papers of Richard Wellesley, Marquess Wellesley: British Library, London *and* National Library of Ireland, Dublin

Wellington Papers: Papers of Arthur Wellesley, 1st Duke of Wellington: Southampton University

Westmorland Papers: Papers of John Fane, 10th Earl of Westmorland: National Archives of Ireland, Dublin

Whitworth Papers: Papers of Charles Whitworth, 1st Earl Whitworth: Centre for Kentish Studies, Maidstone

Wickham Papers: Papers of William Wickham: Hampshire Record Office, Winchester

Willoughby de Broke Papers: Papers of Richard Greville, 19th Baron Willoughby de Broke: Parliamentary Archives, Westminster

Wodehouse, John (Lord Wodehouse): see *Kimberley Papers*

Wood, Sir Charles, 1st Viscount Halifax: see *Hickleton Papers*

Worthington-Evans Papers: Papers of Sir Laming Worthington-Evans: Bodleian Library, Oxford

Permission to consult the Papers of Thomas Hamilton, 9th Earl of Haddington (Viceroy of Ireland December 1834 to April 1835), at Mellerstain, Berwickshire, was refused by the 13th Earl.

Index